The Maximalist

THE RISE AND FALL OF TONY O'REILLY

The Maximalist

THE RISE AND FALL OF TONY O'REILLY

Matt Cooper

Gill & Macmillan

Gill & Macmillan
Hume Avenue, Park West, Dublin 12
www.gillmacmillanbooks.ie

978 07171 6721 0

Designed by Carole Lynch
Edited by Rachel Pierce at Verba Editing House
Index compiled by Eileen O'Neill
Printed and bound by CPI Group (UK) Ltd, Croydon, CRO 4YY

This book is typeset in Linotype Minion and
Neue Helvetica.

The paper used in this book comes from the
wood pulp of managed forests. For every tree
felled, at least one tree is planted, thereby
renewing natural resources.

A CIP catalogue record for this book is available
from the British Library.

5 4 3 2

To my family, Aileen and the children,
Andie, Aimee, Millie, Zach and Harry.

ACKNOWLEDGEMENTS

There are many people who were patient with me and forgiving of me over the last year as I researched and wrote this book and I would like to thank them greatly for that. There's my family, of course: my children Andie, Aimee, Millie, Zach and Harry, and their mother and my wife, Aileen, who put up with my locking myself into my study on a very regular basis and did not complain about my absences. I suspect they thought it was better that I was there than in North Korea, where I had travelled for my previous project.

There was also my production team at *The Last Word* on Today FM, Patrick Haughey, Mary O'Hagan, Mary Carroll, Diarmuid Doyle and Juleigh Ni Gháibhain, to whom I'm indebted on a daily basis, and a host of other freelance replacements, and of course Killian Murray who moved job at the start of the year, as well as Peter McPartlin, our chief executive. Thank you also to my *Irish Daily Mail* editor Sebastian Hamilton for accepting my deadline-encroaching weekly column with such interest and enthusiasm. I also have to apologise to my business partner at Playmaker Media, Ciaran O'hEadhra, for my absences from programme-making over the last year. There'll be more time for brainstorming and pitching documentary ideas for television now that this book is done.

As for the content of the book, as distinct from helping me to make the time to do it, there are countless people who gave interviews, both on and off the record, and who helped me flesh out the detail that I had gathered. To them I owe deep and sincere thanks. Many of them asked that their identities be protected, largely out of concern that anything they say might be misconstrued or misinterpreted, particularly by the subject of this book. They did not want to say anything that might lead to further upset to somebody who they respect and did not want to hurt, especially when that was not their intention. That was understood and appreciated. For that reason I'm not thanking other sources publicly, as not all of them are quoted, lest those who helped off-the-record are identifiable by a process of elimination. To all of the people who helped with quotes, or who offered documents such as speeches and letters to assist in my work, I offer my sincere thanks.

I hope I have managed to be fair to Tony O'Reilly as the subject of the book, and accurate in the recounting of his remarkable life story, but also to all of those who were and are close to him. I was also conscious that things happened during the course of the writing of this book – such as the death of his first wife, Susan – that required sensitivity and I hope I have achieved that.

I was able to draw upon a wide and diverse range of previously published material, which was particularly important for the first section of the book, where many of the people involved in O'Reilly's early life have died or were too ill to give interviews. I made various attributions in the course of the text to this material, but I want to acknowledge again the usefulness of, in particular, books by Ivan Fallon, Ivor Kenny and Harry Walsh in this regard.

Tony O'Reilly was never shy about giving interviews, despite his stated regard for his privacy, and that provided an enormous amount of material contemporary to the events which are described. I was fortunate that I had a few of my own formal interviews with O'Reilly upon which to draw too, as well as many other conversations that took place during the decade in which I worked for him as editor of *The Sunday Tribune*.

Conor Nagle, in particular, and Catherine Gough have been more than accommodating, understanding and encouraging in their roles at Gill & Macmillan, and I thank them for the confidence in me and, again, their patience. Special thanks are reserved for my editor, Rachel Pierce, who had wonderful ideas as to how to structure and sharpen the text, as well as a forensic eye for detail and accuracy. It was an absolute pleasure to work with her. I must also mention my agent Faith O'Grady and, importantly because he kept me on track to complete my work load, my fitness trainer and friend Paul Byrne. Thanks too to Kieran Kelly for the sympathetic legal read.

Tony O'Reilly's life has been remarkable, one of the most extraordinary about which I could have chosen to write. It is a life full of many great achievements but also its faults and disappointments. I hope I have done justice to cataloguing, explaining and interpreting his public life. I hope you have enjoyed the story.

CONTENTS

SECTION 1
1906–1989: From humble beginnings

SECTION 2
1987–1999: Legend and branding

SECTION 3
2001–2006: A man for a new century

SECTION 4
2006–2009: A threat to all he'd built

SECTION 5
2009–2015: 'If you can meet with Triumph and Disaster and treat those two impostors just the same . . .'

THE MAN WHO HAD EVERYTHING

Tony O'Reilly strode into the twenty-first century, an Irishman apart. He seemingly had all that any man could have wanted and, not only that, more of those things than anyone else possessed. He had more money than any other living Irish-born person, making him a billionaire. He had more power than any other unelected citizen, as owner of the lion's share of Ireland's non-State-controlled media. He had been a sports star and was still lauded for his star turn over 40 years earlier as a youthful international Rugby Union player, whose individual try-scoring records as a member of the British & Irish Lions team remain unbroken. He'd had a serious health scare in the mid-1990s, but he'd recovered from it and showed few signs of slowing down the exhausting pace at which he lived. His charisma was enormous, his access to the rich and famous ready, his circle of friends and acquaintances stretched across the globe. He was feted for his public-speaking abilities, his ability to engage, enthral and entertain. He was a captivating private conversationalist, full of amusing stories when it suited, well able to dominate discourse with the power and range of his intellect if that was more appropriate; there seemed to be little about which he did not know or could not offer an informed opinion. He had the ability to make people in his presence feel like they were the most important thing in the world at that moment, if he chose to confer his benediction. His accurate recall of events was astounding and of literature was learned.

While he may not have retained the striking good looks of his youth, women still swooned in his presence. He was happily married, for a second time, to Chryss Goulandris, a Greek shipping heiress and Fifth Avenue, New York native who, reportedly, was even richer than he was. He had six adult children, three of whom worked with him in family-controlled businesses although, in an apparently rare setback, one was on the point of leaving. He had a cordial relationship with his ex-wife, Susan, an Australian who now lived in London, so much so that she and Chryss would occasionally meet at family and social functions and he would jokingly introduce them to others as 'my wives'. Neither visibly demurred at the description. He owned many trophy properties: there was a 750-acre stud and mansion called Castlemartin and luxury homes in Dublin city centre, west Cork, the Bahamas and Deauville, in France. He stayed in the most expensive suites at the St Regis Hotel in New York, at the Berkeley in London or at Le Bristol in Paris whenever he visited those cities. He had full use of a corporate jet to take him around the world.

He was an iconic figure to some, a hero who had achieved in business what no Irish person had achieved before, who had been a trailblazer for what now seemed more commonplace. He was lauded for his charitable endeavours and generosity to people in need. Damn it, he could even play the piano to performance standard and sing and have people ask to hear more because they genuinely liked it, not because they were ingratiating themselves with him. He did indulge a lot of kowtowing, but this was hardly surprising: a man who played such a big game naturally had an ego to match.

It wasn't enough. It was so much, and yet it wasn't enough. If O'Reilly was probably the most significant non-political figure in Ireland in the second half of the twentieth century – if you leave out the artists whose work he often championed and bought or quoted – he was determined that during the twenty-first century he would build on that reputation, would copper-fasten his legacy in Ireland's history books. His need, what some would call his greed, and not just for money but for regular approbation, was naked and unabashed. In a 1999 interview with *Businessweek* magazine he admitted freely that he was 'a maximalist ... I want more of everything'.

Not everybody loved or admired or respected him, however. His self-confidence was interpreted by some as overbearing arrogance, a sense of entitlement, and sometimes a crude use of coercion to get his way.

Some actively despised him, not just for how he behaved but for what they perceived him to be, for what he believed and for what he symbolised, and his greatest critics were often his fellow Irish citizens. His critics, often in hushed tones, sometimes more strident, accused him of abusing his power, particularly with regard to his media interests. They muttered that he cut corners to accumulate and maintain his wealth and deceived the gullible along the way, being mindful of the laws of libel to which he might resort. They found him, despite everything, shallow. They wondered if he was a chimera, lacking substance, especially when they perceived that in championing brands, O'Reilly was really hyping his own, creating an illusion from which only he would truly benefit. His critics saw him as vain, some regarded him as a narcissist.

This angered O'Reilly greatly. He wanted to be loved, just as he wanted to be rich, respected and feted. He was a self-made man, after all: he had not inherited material wealth from his parents, enjoying their love and their willingness to pay for a good education to allow him fulfil his talents and ambitions, but no inheritance to match those ambitions. He had enjoyed some outrageous good fortune along the way, even if he put his success down to his willingness to work as hard as he could and his cleverness in decision-making and pursuing personal connections. Why couldn't people set aside their envy and jealousy, give him the credit he had rightfully earned? He was a tall poppy, yes, but why did others want to cut him down?

Sometimes he brought his critics to Castlemartin, for one of his legendary parties, in an effort to seduce and convince; others he punished by exclusion. The parties held at his mansion – which was far removed from the relatively modest circumstances in which he had been brought up on the northside of Dublin, less than 50 miles away – were a proud display of prosperity, patronage and place. This was where he commanded, like a modern Irish chieftain, a High King of culture and ostentatious wealth, as he presided over his mansion, stud farm and 750 acres of land. Before his time, this place had been the seat of Anglo-Irish aristocracy. Now, O'Reilly, a common Catholic, had fashioned an aristocracy all of his own making.

The prosperity was clearly his; guests were there to acknowledge and admire the very aura of his material successes – the artworks, the architecture and the antique furniture. He dispensed the patronage; visitors accepted his invitation if they were family, friend, employee or third party and they were expected to appreciate their status in being granted this form of approval. Their place was something invitees were expected to understand; while they were regarded as being of some value or accomplishment, they were reminded none-too-implicitly that they were in the presence of the main man, in his manor, on his terms.

O'Reilly had always loved a big party, especially one where he was the centre of attention, something he'd been used to from an early age. The invitation to a 'dinner dance' or 'supper', requesting the pleasure of your company and that of a 'plus one' (usually already nominated by him), typically came in the post on an embossed card that bore the Castlemartin crest. An invitation by telephone suggested that you might be a late addition, but that was not an insult; no doubt you were not the only one. In the early years of his ownership of Castlemartin, bought in 1972 when he was just 38 years old, the year before he took control of Independent Newspapers (IN), invitations were in the names of Tony and his wife, Susan; after they divorced, the invites to the resumed parties held from 1991 onwards came from Dr AJF O'Reilly and his new wife, Chryss; from 2001 onwards they were from Sir Anthony and Lady Chryss O'Reilly, as befitted their newly acquired status. The reply went to the public relations (PR) company Murray Consultants, which oversaw the staging of each event on O'Reilly's behalf.

There were a number of parties most years, but the biggest was usually that held on a Saturday evening in August to coincide with a sponsored horse race, The Heinz 57, which would take place at the Phoenix Park track the following day or, after it closed, at Leopardstown in County Dublin. Up to 300 people would be hosted in an enormous, specially erected marquee attached to the side of the 28-room manor, which, although it often catered for dinner parties for up to 80 people, could not cope with these expanded numbers without the extension. The guest list was designed to impress, to make attendees feel as if they belonged among an elite. It comprised politicians, businessmen in O'Reilly's employment and not, sports stars old and new, poets and other writers, and some of his personal friends gathered and kept over the years. There were regulars, occasionals and one-off invitees, the men all dressed in lounge suits and the women in stylish cocktail dresses, apart from the rare occasions when black-tie was required. Otherwise, O'Reilly would almost certainly wear his favoured uniform of a dark navy-blue pinstriped power suit, a powder blue shirt with white collar and cuffs, a subtle yellow or green elephant-print tie with matching silk handkerchief in his breast-pocket, and always black leather shoes, all impeccably tailored to demand, clothes that clearly cost thousands of dollars or euro.

The guest lists were a 'who's who' of Irish life and beyond. It would not be unusual to see the Taoiseach of the day and the leader of the opposition at the same party, rivalries cast aside for one evening. All of the taoisigh, from Jack Lynch to Bertie Ahern, had attended a number of times, with the notable exception of Charles Haughey, an old friend O'Reilly fell out with because of their greatly different approaches to political dispute and terrorist activity in Northern Ireland. A minister for finance of the day was also likely to make the cut, local TD Charlie McCreevy being a particular favourite during his term of office (1997–2004), as well as a smattering of other ministers who might be in favour and others of whom a favour might be needed, if not now then possibly in the future. Foreign political leaders also visited, although sometimes at other times of the year for the smaller, more intimate dinners of just dozens of people. Nelson Mandela, Bill Clinton, Ted Kennedy, Peter Mandelson and Henry Kissinger were among those who came to dine and stay, as well as other worthies from Britain, Australia, Canada and the USA. When Gordon Brown, Chancellor of the Exchequer in Britain at the time, before he became Prime Minister, came to Dublin, it was on the corporate jet that Independent News & Media (INM) and Waterford Wedgwood shared and that was largely maintained for O'Reilly's use. A phone call was made to the Taoiseach's office and Ahern's staff organised that a police escort whisk Brown through the busy traffic to his Kildare destination, even though he was not fulfilling any public engagements.

Then there were the celebrities: Hollywood actors like Paul Newman, Gregory Peck and Sean Connery. Many rugby internationals made the cut, largely because of O'Reilly's previous fame as one of the game's most successful players during its amateur era. These guests were mainly Irish, but from different generations: from the 1948 Grand Slam-winning captain Karl Mullen to 1970s stalwarts like Ray McLoughlin and Fergus Slattery, to 1980s heroes like Hugo McNeill and Willie Duggan, some of whom O'Reilly had played with, although many not. His best friend, the former rugby international Jim McCarthy, was always present: he had become one of his key business associates, too. There were many cultural figures: the poet Seamus Heaney, whose work O'Reilly loved to recite publicly, perfectly mimicking Heaney's northern accent, was among those who attended regularly, his support for the Ireland Funds (the charitable organisation O'Reilly founded with American businessman Dan Rooney) and its aims gratefully acknowledged.

The events were stuffed with businesspeople, most of whom were in the employ of one of O'Reilly's many companies: INM, Waterford Wedgwood, Atlantic Resources (and when it was gone, its off-shoots, Arcon and Providence Resources), Fitzwilton and, of course, the American food giant Heinz, where he made the bulk of the money that was reinvested in his Irish interests. The Americans saw how successful and lionised the boss was in his homeland. Key executives in his various companies knew whether or not they were in favour by virtue of invitation or exclusion. There were many journalists, too, the editors of his newspaper titles, business-page editors and some respected writers, such as Robert Fisk of *The Independent*, and Eamon Dunphy, even after he had left the *Sunday Independent* in high dudgeon over his perception of low standards in the paper, and other admired scribes from non-INM titles, such as Kevin Myers of *The Irish Times*, before he crossed the River Liffey to the *Irish Independent*.

Every guest was met at the door by the smiling face and cheery comments of the man who seemed to know everybody who was coming, no matter how seemingly insignificant by comparison to him. He rarely forgot a face or name and often had an anecdote ready to flatter the guest before he effortlessly moved on to greeting the next. He commanded the room, and not just because of his 6 ft 2 in. height. Some people were delighted to be there, thrilled to be part of his court, delighted to stay as late as 4.00am or 5.00am when the sing-song was in full flight at the baby grand piano in the front lobby of the main house. Good wine – a Le Montrachet white or a Château Lynch-Bages red – compensated for food that was usually quite ordinary, hotel-type fare: standard chicken or salmon dishes with some vegetables on the side. It was expected that you would have fun; it didn't matter if you got a little drunk as long as you didn't let yourself down by falling down. O'Reilly would be up himself until the small hours, but he would never be drunk. He would sometimes take to the piano himself and sing, and he could do it better than most.

Some guests were somewhat less deferential or impressed, although rarely to his face, feeling compelled to be there by the needs of their job or position, bored by what quickly became to them the sameness of each occasion. Even the music was entirely predictable: jazz pianist Jim Doherty led a trio of musicians who played old standards from an earlier era and either Anne Bushnell or Sonny Knowles did the crooning. One year O'Reilly's sons, Gavin and Tony jnr, arranged for more contemporary music to be performed as a replacement; their father saw to it that their mistake was not repeated again.

If the guest list was partly designed to demonstrate his standing in Irish society, then the setting gave him the opportunity to showcase his vast wealth, the material expression of his rising in the world. Castlemartin was the lavish bricks-and-mortar declaration of his own improvement, that he now had his own seat, accompanied by a stud farm: the symbolic possessions of a new Irish gentry to replace the old English landlords. 'There was a day not long ago when people named O'Reilly stood outside a house like this, their noses pressed to the panes,' he told a *Wall Street Journal* reporter in the 1970s who was invited to tour the estate.

The house had been purchased from Lord Gowrie in the early 1970s when it was 'in a condition of stately decline' due to a combination of being vacant for a number of years and from the depredations of previous tenants, the great rock band of the era, The Rolling Stones, or the singer Donovan. 'We keep expecting to find blond groupies bricked up in the fireplace,' O'Reilly liked to joke about the restoration process.

The renovations took years and 'it cost a fortune, but I think the result was worth the time and money'. The house, originally built in 1713 on two floors, has 28 rooms and is 26,000 sq ft. Architectural aficionados enjoyed features such as the elegant cut-stone front door-case with bolection mouldings surmounted by a swan-necked pediment, surrounding a teal-blue front door. They noted how the front hall was panelled in plaster and ornamented with Corinthian pilasters. An inner hall was tiled, with a marble fireplace, and was dominated by a cantilevered dual staircase, under which there was a Bechstein baby grand piano and an Irish harp, and two doors to the downstairs toilets. There was a Picasso to admire and a giant canvas of O'Reilly, painted by Derek Hill.

The staircase brought the visitor up to the 10 spacious en-suite bedrooms, two of which were in the attic. Back downstairs, the house had six reception rooms, all overlooking the River Liffey. The drawing room had an Adam fireplace and the dining room retained all of its original plasterwork, with the walls covered in fabric and floor-to-ceiling shimmering gold silk curtains, all bathed in the glow of an enormous Waterford Crystal chandelier. O'Reilly kept a formal and luxurious study on this floor, dark green and lined with shelves of books – mainly historical and particularly involving warfare – where he did his reading, either for work or leisure, to the sound of the music he loved, either at the partner's desk or on the more comfortable sofa seating. There was a long breakfast room, with a glass wall and a panoramic river view, and an Aga in the kitchen. The bulk of the furniture was clearly antique and expensive and the house was carpeted with many luxuriously soft rugs. It was an expensive building to maintain and heat: there are more than 100 solid teak windows throughout the house. The Coach House – where the likes of Mandela had stayed – had been converted to provide five bedrooms, and there was a large swimming pool surrounded by guest apartments. There was also a vast solarium and cavernous salons. There was a simple log cabin down at the riverbank, which held a hot tub that was given to O'Reilly by his second wife as a birthday gift. The main feature of the boardroom, which was located near the Coach House, was a table that seated 28 and a lectern for making presentations; many of his Irish executives made their presentations there over the years.

There were photographs, pictures and paintings of O'Reilly all through the house, many from his rugby-playing days, of him with his family and with various business and political associates, all of them portraying landmark occasions in O'Reilly's life. There was one of him playing tennis at the White House with the elder, first former President George Bush, signed: 'Tony, greetings from the White House Field of Combat – George Bush.' There was a photo of him in casual attire showing Kissinger the expanse of the Castlemartin domain. A photo of Paul Newman had the caption: 'Okay, it's settled, you'll replace Redford in *Butch Cassidy II*.' There was a giant painting of him in a pinstripe suit with a bottle of Heinz ketchup. There was a framed *Irish Independent* page from 1973, announcing that Tony O'Reilly had won control of the group for £1,100,000.

O'Reilly loved showing off Castlemartin: guests wandered reasonably freely, to admire the architecture and décor and to gape at the paintings. Sometimes he, or one of his assistants, would conduct a tour before everyone sat to eat. His art collection was one of Ireland's most expensive, with the highlight from 2000 being a work by Claude Monet. The collection featured work by Walter Osborne, William Ashford, William Sadler, Sir William Orpen, Camille Souter, Seán Keating and William Mulready. One of his former editors, Andrew Marr of *The Independent* in London, recounted once sitting down for an important meeting with O'Reilly and remarking that a painting hanging on the wall over his shoulder looked like a Turner; O'Reilly replied smilingly, 'It is a Turner.' He was one of the first of the modern generation of Irishmen to collect paintings by Jack B. Yeats, all of which were displayed prominently.

There were horses everywhere too, as Castlemartin was a substantial stud farm, and was so even before O'Reilly met Chryss, for whom this was her main interest. It had expanded over the years by acquisition of neighbouring farms and was now 750 acres in size, three times what he had purchased originally. It was limestone land, 20 acres of which had been devoted to amenity and shelter belts, divided into 53 paddocks fenced with stud rail.

Before the guests arrived at the house they passed through a magnificent set of wrought-iron entrance gates that dated from the eighteenth century but that were updated to allow for electronic opening and closing, controlled from a security room in the main house over a mile away. The guests then drove along a road with lush green paddocks on either side, some sheltered by the large number of giant oaks and chestnut trees. There were cattle on display, a distinctive herd of expensive Belted Galloway and what he described as the best collection of Charolais in Ireland, which he boasted that people came from all over the country to see.

It hasn't always been like this. In the 1970s Lanning Roper, an acclaimed American landscape architect and garden designer, was given the task of creating a garden and of altering the contours of the parkland to admit a better view of the Liffey as the river makes a dramatic sweep towards the house, and then turns to flow away from it. Roper planted a beech hedge 'forecourt' at the entrance to the house, open on the side of a magnificent formal lime avenue, which was planted on axis to the front door 200 or more years ago.

And yet for all the tours and talk and pride, O'Reilly was rarely there to enjoy it all. He was a visitor to his own home. He had admitted this to his friend and long-standing INM director Ivor Kenny, in a 1986 interview for Kenny's book *In Good Company*. 'Business is tyrannical,' O'Reilly had lamented. 'One achieves economic independence, but not the freedom that should go with it. I have been in this home [Castlemartin] one day since August. It's a great home and it means a lot to me. It says a lot about me, about my drives and ambitions, about my pride in Ireland and about my pride in being Irish: waging war on the international front and coming home to my fortress, so to speak. Yet I don't get time to enjoy it.'

He would enjoy use of the house for almost another 30 years, but in late 2014 it, along with most of his other material possessions, and the things he held dear, would be gone from him, taken in the most undignified of circumstances. He would blame others, malign fate and, occasionally, himself, but the circumstances of that loss beggar belief and add to the fascination generated by this man. Friends and foes watched in astonishment as he made mistakes a man of his capabilities should not have made, and others took advantage of that. He was chased by banks to repay his debts, his money apparently entirely gone. He disappeared into near-seclusion as his legendary self-confidence evaporated and he no longer wanted to see anybody. It was a long way from north Dublin to Castlemartin, and it has been a long way from Castlemartin to where he is today: a man of means with no means to resolve his financial difficulties. This is the story of how and why.

A SPECTACULAR PAST, AN EVEN MORE SPECTACULAR FUTURE

The turn of the century was heralded by a party that O'Reilly did not attend personally, but that he still enjoyed enormously because of his corporate involvement in it. O'Reilly's attention – like an estimated billion other television viewers worldwide – was arrested by the celebrations at Times Square in New York, where a 'time ball' was lowered from the roof of One Times Square to mark the Millennium. The piece was called the 'Star of Hope', and it was made at O'Reilly's Waterford Crystal plant in Kilbarry, County Waterford.

The time ball creation was loaded with symbolism, befitting the occasion: it consisted of a central circle and a seven-pointed star, the former representing the Earth and the latter the seven continents. It weighed 1,070 lb and was 6 ft in diameter, adorned with 504 triangle-shaped crystal panels, each side 4–5 in. long, 96 strobe lights and spinning, pyramid-shaped mirrors. More than 40 Waterford crafts-men and designers contributed to its design and construction, and when it was shipped from Ireland in November 1999, it was accompanied on its journey to Times Square by the Mayor of the city.

The ball was lowered, starting at one minute to midnight, by 141 ft down a pole, to complete its journey at the stroke of the new century. A proud O'Reilly, who watched it with his wife and mother-in-law and other family members in the Bahamas, saw it not only as a

wonderful marketing opportunity for Waterford Crystal – with somewhat typical hyperbole he called it, in publicity released in advance of
the event, 'the zenith of public awareness' for the brand – but as an
event that was, despite its populism, an opportunity for an appropriate
display of great craftsmanship and style. As a keen history buff,
O'Reilly also enjoyed knowing that in 1907 Adolph Ochs, then owner
of *The New York Times*, had commissioned the first ever ball dropped
to mark the New Year celebrations in New York.

At the start of the new century, O'Reilly was nearing completion of
an almost 30-year career with the giant American food company
Heinz, where he had risen to the top positions within just a few years
of arriving from Ireland, and now owned just short of 2% of all the
company's shares. He would announce in the coming weeks that after
27 years as part-time chairman of INM he would take the role on a
full-time basis, while simultaneously remaining as part-time chairman
of Waterford Wedgwood. He was also about to embark on an
acquisition spree, personally and corporately. He knew that the time
left to him was finite, but he had certainly not lost his sense of
ambition nor his determination to be at the centre of things, for as
long as that centre would hold.

Eight months on from that night of worldwide celebration in which
Waterford Crystal played such an important part, I travelled to
O'Reilly's château in Deauville, France, in August to interview him for
The Sunday Tribune. Our meeting was just a little more than a fort-
night before O'Reilly was due to chair his last annual general meeting
(AGM) as chairman of HJ Heinz. That wasn't the only hook for the
interview, however. O'Reilly had turned 64 that year, as had two other
titans of the Irish business scene, Tony Ryan and Michael Smurfit. I
decided to interview all three men to find out their views on the big
issues of the day, but also to discover what continued to motivate
them as their pensionable years loomed, and why none of them
seemed likely to retire.

They took some persuading to participate: a certain degree of
scepticism was expressed by all three at the outset about the premise
of our engagement. They all seemed somewhat insulted by the idea
that they might consider retiring, that my interest might be in their
past rather than their future, or that their careers were no longer as
dynamic as they had been.

They shared many characteristics, such as an obsessive work schedule, an almost unbelievable amount of air travel, fractures in marital relationships caused by long absences from home (wherever home actually was, because they all owned many properties) and an apparent need not just to have money but to be seen to be spending it, particularly on charitable donations and on houses and art that demonstrated the elevated and enhanced positions they had reached. They were competitive and, according to legend, could be ruthless, albeit to different degrees. They angered differently: when riled, O'Reilly spoke slowly, with an icy calm; Ryan was volcanic; Smurfit was spiteful.

Appearances were very important to all three men. They all spoke and behaved in a manner that emphasised their perceived stature, with accents that had changed as they aged, in O'Reilly's case to include a mid-Atlantic twang. They were almost always immaculately turned out, dressed in the most expensive of suits and ties, of the type worn by City of London types and other obviously wealthy men. Occasionally, they would be seen wearing expensive cashmere jumpers and slacks as leisurewear; Smurfit often wore golf clothes, the only one of the trio to have a love for the game. Each strived to convey polish, to emphasise achievement.

O'Reilly might have had some extra reasons for sensitivity about the timing of the interview. He had not enjoyed a particularly good press in some parts of the media in previous years. Controversy dogged his final years as chief executive (CEO) at Heinz; allegations were rife of excessive pay for him and of his board of directors being packed with indulgent cronies to facilitate that. His reputation for probity in Ireland had been questioned too, as had his exercise of power in Ireland via his media interests. He had been linked to payments made to a corrupt former minister and a blazing row with a former Taoiseach had been revealed. O'Reilly had been linked, wrongly, to a tax evasion scandal that had engulfed many businessmen and politicians of his vintage and he had threatened to sue *The Irish Times* to protect his reputation. He had lost in the bidding process to run a mobile phone licence in competition to the incumbent State operator, beaten by a consortium led by Denis O'Brien, a brash and upcoming businessman who was more than 20 years his junior and who was to become one of the most significant figures in O'Reilly's later years.

At Deauville, O'Reilly delighted in telling me about the provenance of the Normandy house. It was located on the same site where William the Conqueror had kept his eleventh-century castle. 'There is something piquant about an Irishman living next to the former home of a Frenchman who subjugated the English,' he said, laughing. But that wasn't the reason O'Reilly had chosen it. He had asked the estate agent which house had provided the living accommodation for the Nazi commanders in the area during the Second World War. From his extensive reading of the history of the period, he knew they had always requisitioned the best living-quarters in an area during occupation. This was the house he now wanted and was prepared to buy, price undisclosed.

As O'Reilly warmed up over a light lunch of salad on the patio in the bright sun – he explained that he now dieted very carefully as part of his life-long battle against weight gain – he spoke about the efficacy and prurience of the tribunals investigating allegations of corporately funded political corruption; the effect of their revelations on the reputation of former Taoiseach Charles Haughey; the 'incorruptibility' of the Irish civil service, judiciary and An Garda Síochána (the Irish police force); the change of Ireland from a political to a 'consumerist' society; the 'casino-like' nature of Wall Street; the chances that Britain would eventually join the euro to help provide larger markets for its manufacturing output; his perception of reduced respect in Ireland for academic achievement; and the waning influence of the Catholic Church in Irish society. He was well versed and authoritative on all subjects. This was, after all, the character Henry Kissinger had dubbed Ireland's 'renaissance man'.

On 12 September 2000 he would attend his last AGM as chairman of the American food giant Heinz, which he had joined in 1971. 'It will be sentimental to a degree, but I expect that it will be very enjoyable,' he mused. He reeled off the facts as had appeared in the already published annual report. In 1979, when he had become CEO, the company had sales of $2.5 billion, profits of $110 million and a stock market value of $900 million. Now it had sales of $9.4 billion, profits of $925 million and a market capitalisation of $23 billion. His shares and options in Heinz were worth $270 (€355) million at his retirement. He was not in the least shy about repeating any of this.

'Happily, because of the system we use at Heinz of high-risk, high-reward, many of the people have been greatly enriched. There were

107 millionaires in the company at one stage and at least 30 people have left with over $26 million of option gains. It was a tremendous success for the company to provide that wealth for shareholders and employees. It was very satisfying for me professionally and worthwhile for my friends … A friend once said to me, "always back self-interest because it's working for you 24 hours a day". The food industry is not necessarily the most exciting and to get the best out of people it is necessary to incentivise them.'

But he insisted that it wasn't all about the money. 'There was also a great human aspect, as the degree of amity, friendship and collegiality that we developed proved that you don't have to be mean and tough, or mean anyway, to succeed.'

As part-time chairman of Heinz for the previous three years, O'Reilly's work pattern had altered. 'The rhythm of my life has changed. When you have worked for a large company like Heinz with 100,000 people depending on your appearance at regular times in their lives and you have to concentrate on budgets, sales figures, businesses to acquire and dispose of, a certain structure evolves around the formal things that you have to do. Now I read more, non-stop almost. I spend most of my day reading, not deciding, not talking to people but reading. I have never had more to read because we're at a point in technical innovation where we have to try and understand what is happening to us so we won't get whacked.'

But he wasn't slowing down, despite previous musings – some disclosed in interviews going back as far as 1986 – about a desire to take a break from business once his time at Heinz ended. 'The thoughts of a sabbatical have been overtaken by the Internet and new technology and a sense of being underwhelmingly (sic) aware of what's happening in the world. A sabbatical is not something that I have the luxury of at this stage … But the one thing I do have because of my Irish middle-class background is a firm sense of danger and anyone in business today who does not have a firm sense of danger doesn't know what is happening.'

It wasn't just a year for corporate accumulation. O'Reilly was in the business of collecting personal baubles, too. The most spectacular was his acquisition, in May 2000, of a painting by the French impressionist Claude Monet, *Le Portail (Soleil)*, which cost him €24 million. In 1892 and 1893, Monet had painted 27 views of the façade of Rouen cathedral in north-western France. He did so at different times of the day and in different weather conditions. There's one in the early morning sun, one in bright sunlight, another on a grey day, one at sunset, yet another on a hazy morning. One hangs in the Louvre in Paris, another in the city's Musée d'Orsay, and another in the National Gallery of Art in Washington D.C. O'Reilly hung his at his Castlemartin estate, a *Le Portail (Soleil)*, a view in midday sunlight.

As a 15-year-old boy in 1951, O'Reilly had travelled with a friend, Frank Turvey, on a cattle-boat from Drogheda to Dieppe and begun a cycle to Paris, taking in as much as they could of the destruction caused by the Second World War. They stopped en route in Rouen and when sitting in a café opposite the cathedral, drinking glasses of Normandy cider, a Frenchman explained the effect the changing light had on the cathedral's façade and described how Monet had painted more than 20 versions of it. 'He told us impressionism was about the reality of a building being so, but perceptions of it being quite different,' O'Reilly told his RTÉ radio interviewer Pat Kenny in May 2000. The more cider he drank, the more impressionist Rouen cathedral became to him. 'It opened a whole new world to both of us; Monet and his circle created new horizons of wonderment and excitement as they altered the course of viewing the world through art forever more.'

He said his art collection was inspired by such life experiences, and put together on the basis of choice rather than fashion or value. 'Art is the ultimate democracy,' he said. 'It's about what delights your eye and your senses.'

During our conversation in Deauville, he briefly mentioned the influence of Peadar O'Donnell. Previously he had credited O'Donnell with 'igniting in me a life-long interest in art, its interpretations, its secret messages and its different meanings'. He said that O'Donnell 'decoded the paintings of Yeats as he explained to me patiently, then as a 10-year-old, the meaning of a painting called *The New Road*.'

O'Donnell was an extraordinary character to have mentored O'Reilly as a child and for the businessman to continue to cite at many junctures of his life: he stood for so much that O'Reilly came not just to reject but to despise, and yet O'Reilly's respect and affection for O'Donnell's memory remained obvious.

O'Donnell was a staunch republican and Marxist, a leading organiser for the Irish Transport and General Workers' Union (ITGWU) and an active member of the Irish Republican Army (IRA) during the War of Independence (1919–21). He led many IRA raids on targets in counties Derry and Donegal and rose to the rank of commander of the IRA's Donegal Brigade. In 1922 he was elected as a representative on the anti-Treaty IRA's army executive, and in April that year was among the anti-Treaty IRA men who took over and destroyed part of the Four Courts building in Dublin, an action that helped to spark the civil war as well as destroying many valuable records of national importance. Although O'Donnell escaped from the Four Courts, he was later caught by the Free State Army and imprisoned at Mountjoy. He went on hunger strike for 41 days and in 1923, while still in prison, was elected as TD (*Teachta Dála*, member of parliament) for Donegal. On his release from internment in 1924 he became a member of the executive and army council of the anti-Treaty IRA and editor of *An Phoblacht*, the republican newspaper.

O'Donnell later split with the IRA because he believed it had not done enough to support land redistribution and workers' rights. He founded the Republican Congress in 1934 – two years before O'Reilly was born – claiming its overriding aim was the maintenance of a united front against fascism. Its influence was minimal and short-lived. He continued to write and agitate, albeit on the periphery, aided by the use of a large inheritance obtained by his wife, Lile. He was, according to one contemporary, a 'professional agitator'.

O'Reilly came to know him through O'Donnell's nephew, with whom he went to school. Peadar Joe O'Donnell lived on the Upper Drumcondra Road on the northside of Dublin, not far from the Griffith Avenue home where O'Reilly grew up. Peadar Joe had been born in New York, but when he was just five years old his father had been killed in an accident. His uncle Peadar and Lile, who were childless, brought him to Dublin and raised him as their own.

In November 1982, the Abbey Theatre hosted a special celebration of O'Donnell's work. The commentator Fintan O'Toole said O'Donnell was 'notable as much as anything for being the last surviving member of the executive of the old Irish Republican Army'. Equally as notable was O'Reilly's speech at the event, lionising his old mentor for the five summers that O'Reilly had spent as a child and teenager in O'Donnell's second house in Dungloe, County Donegal.

'He almost reared me,' O'Reilly said proudly. 'Peadar was uncle

Peadar to me and his wife was Auntie Lil ... I learnt how to fish there, how to row and how to drink altar wine.' These were 'sunlit days, and both glittering and glamorous as well,' O'Reilly continued. 'I remember Peadar's glittering conversation and the notion that we were both interested in Marx ... he in Karl, I in Groucho.'

O'Donnell died in May 1986 and there is no recorded detail of how he felt about his young protégé's eager embrace of capitalism. But whatever about his accumulation of wealth, it is not hard to imagine that O'Donnell would have been astonished, appalled even, by O'Reilly's acceptance in late 2000 of an offer of a knighthood from Queen Elizabeth of the United Kingdom of Great Britain and Northern Ireland, and his subsequent request that he be addressed and known as Sir Anthony O'Reilly.

O'Reilly had boasted of his nationality, indeed even traded on it at times. He had founded the Ireland Funds to promote such ideals. 'I don't think there was any doubt what the theme in his life is,' said Kingsley Aikins, who ran the Ireland Funds for him for nearly 20 years. 'He sees the Irish as one of the great tribes of the world and he's a leader of it.' His Irish identity was an element of his personal brand and its marketing; the idea of him as a Knight of the Realm was contradictory, at the very least.

As an independent State and a republic since 1948, Ireland did not merely disapprove of its citizens accepting or using titles from other sovereign states but actively forbade it, with a caveat. Article 40.2.2 of Bunreacht na hÉireann (Constitution of Ireland) states: 'No title of nobility or honour may be accepted by any citizen except with the prior approval of the government.' This meant O'Reilly could exploit a loophole if he wished, but only if he was permitted to do so.

The first approach on behalf of O'Reilly was made to government in November 2000. Taoiseach Bertie Ahern was told by his secretary, Dermot McCarthy, that O'Reilly was being offered the title as a reward for his 'long and distinguished service' to Northern Ireland. The Ireland Funds had raised hundreds of millions of euro in charitable donations for the island, most of which had been spent north of the border: the fund-raisers had acted as a considerable block to the fund-raising efforts of the IRA in the USA and, in retrospect, could be the actions that most firmly secure O'Reilly's place in Irish history. However, a considerable block of opinion, especially in nationalist circles, suggested that some of O'Reilly's newspaper titles – the *Sunday Independent*, in particular – had not been helpful during the peace process that culminated in the signing, by Ahern, British Prime Minister Tony Blair and various Northern Irish politicians, of the Good Friday Agreement in 1998, which enforced a new political settlement that largely ended terrorism by both nationalists and loyalists.

O'Reilly was in a tricky legal situation. He knew of the constitutional position, but he had an argument ready. This son of a deceased senior Irish civil servant claimed that he had always maintained dual citizenship because he had been born in Ireland prior to its leaving the British Commonwealth in 1949. This meant, he maintained, that he was technically entitled to accept without Irish government approval. However, the regularity with which he, and representatives from the British government, contacted the Taoiseach's department to seek official permission in the coming weeks suggested that O'Reilly was not quite certain of his legal position and was worried about the public interpretation of the situation were he not to get the required permission and instead act unilaterally.

He had in mind the cautionary tale of what had happened to a rival in the British newspaper market, Conrad Black, at that time proprietor of the *Daily Telegraph* group of newspapers. Just two years earlier the Canadian Prime Minister Jean Chrétien had publicly rebuked his British counterpart, Tony Blair, for approving honours for two British-Canadian citizens, including Black. A major row ensued, in which Black's Canadian newspapers championed the cause of their master, but Chrétien would not back down. Black renounced his Canadian citizenship.

O'Reilly did not want to face anything like that. Publicly relinquishing his Irish citizenship to accept a British knighthood could have created a public backlash large enough to affect his personal reputation and deliver negative consequences for his business interests. His aim was to have his cake and to eat it: revelling in his Irish citizenship, while holding a British title – just as he boasted of the Irish credentials of most of his businesses while personally remaining non-resident for tax purposes.

To O'Reilly's frustration, however, Ahern reverted to type when faced with having to make a decision he didn't want to make. Ahern dithered about doing anything at all. He has never spoken publicly about this dilemma, but there was a combination of personal and political to it. While Ahern had developed close relationships with members of the British government and had shown great pragmatism in dealing with Ulster unionism, he remained a nationalist at heart. The idea of an Irishman taking a British knighthood was anathema. Politically, he was worried about a backlash should the public perceive him as indulging a rich man's whim, but he was far more fearful of the potential threat, however real, that O'Reilly's newspaper titles might turn on him should he deny the man what he wanted. On the other hand, he could see the potential for having O'Reilly 'owe him one' should he acquiesce: there could be long-term benefits in editorial coverage in INM titles.

Ahern waited until the last moment possible. On the last working day before Christmas, Ahern brought about 20 members of his office staff for drinks at Doheny & Nesbitt's pub near Government Buildings. McCarthy arrived soon after, seeking a word in private: O'Reilly's people had been in touch again, demanding a definitive answer. There was now an additional problem: various ministers had gone home for Christmas and would not return for a Cabinet meeting to deal with such a minor matter. McCarthy suggested something remarkable, something done only in the most extreme and important of circumstances: an incorporeal Cabinet meeting, conducted by telephone. Various ministers were called and asked for their approval. Most were surprised, but agreed when told it had been sanctioned by Ahern. O'Reilly was able to happily inform the British that he could accept the title – but he was now in Ahern's debt.

The news, when it was announced on New Year's Eve 2000, came as a considerable surprise to many people, not least among his family and friends, particularly when it became clear to them subsequently that he intended to use the title and wanted to be addressed as Sir Anthony. Some Irish businessmen and celebrities before and since have accepted honours from the British government: Bob Geldof, Peter Sutherland, Bono and Niall FitzGerald are among those who have been offered and accepted knighthoods. But they have tended to do so quietly … and they did not insist on being addressed as 'Sir'. Nobody challenged O'Reilly on it, however, not even closest friends, for fear of the reaction they might get to such impertinence. 'We were really worried that it would affect the perception of him in Ireland, that it would overshadow all that he achieved,' said one family member. But they reckoned that he had a need for acceptance and approval among the British, going back to his days as a rugby star and then as a businessman, and that he would not be dissuaded. 'He did have a thing with how the British treated him, as an Irishman, as they did with all Irishmen,' the same family member remarked. 'He found it all a bit condescending, this "isn't he very charming, very amusing?" stuff but still not taking him entirely seriously. Well they had to when he was Sir Anthony, when he owned one of their most important newspapers.'

While to other Irish people the idea of kneeling to the Queen of England, of wanting to get the taps on the shoulders, would be construed as a sell-out of one's identity, to O'Reilly it was an important arrival and a confirmation of his elevated status. That was important to O'Reilly because he had been shocked to the core to discover, when a teenager, that his parents were not married, as he had assumed, and that his legal status in Ireland was that of a bastard. He'd long felt that he had overcome this handicap, but now he had proof – a title was not just confirmation that he had arrived but was a departure point for a new journey, in which he would seek out and amass even more.

A NOTE ON SHARES

Ownership of a company depends on how many shares a person or entity has in it. The percentage of the shares owned is the key point, not the absolute number. There is no requirement on a company to have merely 100 shares. Indeed, if a company wants to issue new shares to raise money, it can do so; of course, that reduces or dilutes the existing shareholders, unless they buy an equivalent number of the newly issued shares to maintain their percentage shareholding. In publicly quoted companies, the type that O'Reilly favoured, the shares can be freely bought and sold without restrictions being imposed by existing shareholders as to who else can have shares. There are some limited rules on ownership and control – and trading in the shares – imposed by the Stock Exchange and there are also laws applying under the Companies Acts. To have absolute control of a company it is necessary to have more than 50% of the shares, but in practice it is possible to control a company with between 20% and 30% if the other investors do not band together to take control themselves. That is easier for a dominant shareholder if the other shareholders are financial institutions, such as insurance companies, who buy and sell shares for investment purposes and do not want any involvement in the management of the company.

SECTION 1

1906–1989: From humble beginnings

CHAPTER ONE

SECRETS AND LIES

Tony O'Reilly's father was a remarkable man, who found himself in situations that were rare and controversial for the time into which he was born and whose behaviour, in putting himself into those positions, was most unconventional.

His father was born John Patrick Reilly in Drogheda, County Louth, on 14 March 1906, the fifth of six children and the third of four sons. He grew up on Mayoralty Street, in the centre of the town, and his family were relatively prosperous by the standards of the time – his father being one of the very first in the town to buy a car and to operate a taxi service.

Reilly joined the civil service in 1925, shortly after the creation of the Free State, as a member of the Customs and Excise service (now Revenue Commissioners). He qualified by passing a tough exam for which he had studied diligently, despite not having the initial educational qualifications required. He also did so under a false name. He was too young to join the service, so he applied for the position under the name of his older brother, Patrick Joseph Reilly, who had been born in 1903 and therefore did meet the age requirements. To further confuse matters, he began describing himself under a variation of his original name, as John Patrick O'Reilly, or Jack O'Reilly. No explanation has been offered as to how and why he adopted the prefix O'.

He was posted initially to Dublin, but in 1926 was moved to Bailieboro, County Cavan, and then to Clones, County Monaghan, to deal with cross-border smuggling. A year later he was transferred to Wicklow. There he became captivated by a striking young woman, nearly three years his junior, called Judith Agnes Clarke. Her father was well-off: he was a third-generation builder who was responsible for many of the churches, schools, convents and cathedrals in the area. Now in his sixties and one of the most respectable men in the area, Judith's father had recently used his accumulated riches to buy a large house in the Wicklow Hills, called Mount Carmel, for his retirement. He and his wife were not too impressed by the attentions young John Patrick O'Reilly was showing towards their daughter, one of the youngest of their six children.

Judith's parents were not present when their daughter married Jack, as he now called himself, at the Church of the Assumption on Dublin's Howth Road on 2 February 1928, far from her home town. The young woman, now 20 years old, was six months pregnant. To have become pregnant outside of marriage was highly unusual at the time and would have been considered a matter of great scandal – although such things happened more often than was acknowledged. Judith's uncle, Fr Patrick O'Byrne, carried out the ceremony and her elder brother and sister acted as witnesses. No one would ever suggest afterwards that the young couple had been anything other than happy to marry; they did not appear to have been forced to marry against their will.

Somehow, Jack financed lodgings in an apartment at Anglesea Road in Ballsbridge, in Dublin. There, their first child, Judith May, who became known later as Juliette, was born on 17 May 1928. There would be more children in quick succession. A second girl, Margaret Mary Constance, later known as Ria, was born 13 months later. Their third child, and only boy, Julian Patrick, was born on 15 December 1930.

The family moved many times around Dublin during this period. Jack furthered his studies, qualifying as a barrister at the King's Inns law school while continuing in his day job at the Customs and Excise service. To give him space to study, and as he apparently struggled to cope with three small children in a confined space, Judith often brought the children back to Mount Carmel, where she was helped by her mother; her father died in 1929 at the age of 62. Jack wrote to her regularly, professing how much he loved and missed her. However, he began fresh legal studies at Trinity College Dublin and there, again most unusually according to the mores of the time, he began an affair with another young woman, a student called Petite O'Hagan; at around that time, Judith became pregnant with their fourth child.

Jack's relationship with O'Hagan did not last long, although whether this was a result of Judith confronting the woman is not known.

O'Hagan informed Judith that she was entering a convent; sadly, within a year of doing so she developed a brain tumour and died. Meanwhile, Jack and Judith's fourth child, a girl called Eveleen, was born on 12 May 1932.

Judith remained in hospital for a year after the birth of her fourth child, apparently requiring lengthy treatment as the result of a perforated appendix. Judith's aunts and mother, much older women, took on the burden of raising the four very small children in Wicklow. Jack subsequently sent the two older girls, aged just five and four, to a boarding school at a French-run convent called Le Bon Sauveur in Holyhead, North Wales. The destination was convenient in that it was at the end of a direct ferry route from Dublin, but the decision had all the appearances of Jack hiding his little daughters away.

Jack needed somewhere else to live. The story told many, many years later to Tony O'Reilly was that his father took up lodgings in a house in Dublin run by a retired policeman from Ballyforan, County Roscommon, by the name of O'Connor. He had 10 children, but the one who caught Jack's eye was a beautiful young woman called Aileen who, at 22 years old, was eight years younger than him. Like Judith, Aileen was tall, auburn-haired and attractive, but she was warm and outgoing where Judith was regarded as quiet and reserved. Jack and Aileen fell in love. It is not clear at what stage he told her that he was married and had four children whom he had, in effect, abandoned. Whatever the timing of it, in 1935 Aileen and he decided to leave her father's house together, as if they were husband and wife, but without the status and legal protection afforded by marriage to their relationship.

His behaviour and circumstances – in a new State whose laws, regulations and mores were becoming very much dictated by the Catholic Church, where sex outside of marriage was widely condemned, divorce was unavailable and co-habitation almost unheard of – was extraordinary. That his career, in the service of the State, continued to prosper in these circumstances, either because he hid it or it was tolerated, was remarkable.

Things were to become even more complicated. By 1936, when the couple were living at 100 Pembroke Road, Ballsbridge, Aileen was pregnant. On 7 May 1936 she gave birth to a boy at the National Maternity Hospital at nearby Holles Street, in Dublin. The boy was named Anthony Joseph Francis O'Reilly, to be called Tony, after Aileen's favourite brother. His parents were declared on the legal documents as Mr and Mrs John Patrick O'Reilly, as if they were married. His father entered the word 'traveller' for his profession, ignoring his role in the Customs service and his qualification as a barrister.

When he was an infant the new family moved to 349 Griffith Avenue, on the north side of Dublin, near Glasnevin, and O'Reilly remembered his childhood there very fondly. It was a good sized semi-detached house on a wide, tree-lined road, with traffic passing only occasionally. It was a safe environment in which he and the many other young boys in the area could play. While Jack may have been somewhat more aloof – partly due to his character, partly to his circumstances – he still went along with the open-door policy Aileen operated with neighbours. Those who sang or played an instrument or told stories were most welcome in the house and Jack could be persuaded to sing at times. There was no television in those days, but there was never a shortage of entertainment in the house and O'Reilly quickly developed his own piano skills to a high level, allowing him to participate fully.

It was a relatively comfortable childhood by the standards of the time, even though his father struggled to provide for two families on a civil service salary, particularly when school fees were added. His two little daughters had returned from Wales at the start of the Second World War and although Jack contributed, it did not cover much of Judith's costs. Jack largely cut himself off from his first family when Tony was born, although he would see more of his children as the years progressed. Judith would allow him to take them on day-trips in his car with a chaperone, as long as Tony, oblivious to the existence of his half-brother and three half-sisters, was not present.

His parents brought him up as part of a Catholic family, going to Mass each Sunday together as Mr and Mrs O'Reilly with their son. He would get a Catholic education, too, but it would be a private one, of the kind available only to an elite in Irish society. O'Reilly was six years old when he was first sent to Belvedere College, the school that was to play such an influential and positive role in his life. Belvedere was run by a Catholic order of priests called the Jesuits. It was a school designed to produce professionals: doctors, dentists, lawyers, civil servants and more priests, although its most famous past pupil was the novelist James Joyce, a man whose work was controversial in Ireland at that time. The fees were IR£17 per year, sizeable in those days. The school was located in an elegant Dublin townhouse once owned by Lord Belvedere in Great Denmark Street, not far from O'Connell Street and many of the tenements of Dublin's north-inner city.

O'Reilly first went to Belvedere in 1942 and was the only boy in his class who had not yet received the sacrament of Holy Communion. Quite a fuss was made of him when, as a seven-year-old, he received his First Communion. The school rector, Fr Gubbins, gave him the present of an orange to mark the occasion, telling Tony that it was very valuable and 'the peel is too'. Neither O'Reilly nor any of the boys had ever seen what he subsequently called 'this extraordinary invention', but it gave O'Reilly a story to tell in later years. O'Reilly ate the orange, but afterwards told the story of how he had torn up the peel and sold it for a penny a piece, 'thereby showing a propensity for commercial deception which has not left me since'.

He was required to play rugby from the start, even though what the young boys of that age played was only a vague resemblance of what they would play later. One day his mother, watching proudly, the only mother there, asked the priest overseeing the play, and who apparently had no idea who she was, how the boys were getting on. The story goes that the priest looked around and then replied, 'the red fellow's the best'. It was a story that mother and son would share with amusement for years to come, last told as she was dying.

O'Reilly was 10 years old when he started playing rugby in earnest. He was reported as being 'worthy of mention' in the annual review of the school rugby team. A year later he was under-11 captain and *The Belvederian*, a school publication, noted that he was 'invaluable in the back line'. He played originally at out-half, to get him close to the action.

He was not tall or bulky in his early years, but he was very fast and strong, with good hands and a natural flair for the game. He was picked for the Junior Cup team three years in a row and was captain in 1951, his third year. *The Belvederian* noted that his 'defence as well as attack was excellent and his quick start combined with real pace made him a marked man in every sense of the word. He has one admirable virtue: he is quite unselfish and never hesitated to give his man a run in which to make sure of a try which he has made. We are quite sure he is a player of class in the making.' However, the school annual also noted that 'Tony O'Reilly, achieving more bruises than glory, spoiled his play at out half and centre by being too individual'. Fr Tom O'Callaghan – or The Bull, as he was known – worried about the 14-year-old's attempts 'to force the openings'. O'Reilly remembered that he was 'a little better, not much, but a little better than the others'.

O'Reilly enjoyed remarkable freedom as a teenager, encouraged by his parents. The trip to France – which later in life prompted the Monet purchase – was an unheard-of adventure for someone that young without parental supervision, even then in an era when boys were expected to grow up and look after themselves at an earlier age. His father had given him a new bicycle of the type rarely seen in Ireland in those days: a racing bike with drop handlebars and light-weight wheels with thin tyres, common nowadays but exotic back then. O'Reilly constructed a plan to cycle through France, Belgium and Denmark, into Sweden. An uncle in Drogheda heard of a Dutch cattle-boat that would take passengers to Dieppe, France, on a three-day journey for a very small fee and O'Reilly persuaded Frank Turvey, his best friend, to join him. They were 15 years old and Tony had £22 and Turvey had £17. It was not a salubrious crossing. Turvey com-plained that 'their nostrils suffered the accumulated smell of cow dung and French tobacco, smoked by the sailors'.

Two days into their trip a wheel on O'Reilly's bike punctured and could not be repaired. The tube could not be replaced either; the model of bike was so new, nobody could find a replacement tube that would fit. The boys travelled to Paris by train instead and took two weeks to spend their money before returning home.

Back at school in September 1951, O'Reilly was brought onto the school's Senior Cup team, although aged only 15 years and four months. He was also picked with Leinster schools team and a clear trait was emerging: he played better with better players; when playing with lesser players, he tried to do too much himself.

Already O'Reilly showed an ability to multi-task. He would ride to school in the morning to attend 7.30am mass, then cycle home again for breakfast, grab his schoolbags and return to school for 9.30am when lessons began. After classes there was nearly always some sport to play, or there would be a school play in which to act, or a school choir session in which to sing. He was a member of the Belvedere Newsboys' Club, which helped children from more deprived circum-stances in the local area. The subsequently prominent car salesman

Bill Cullen, who celebrated his rise from the slums in his auto-biography, claimed that the older O'Reilly taught him how to box. The Jesuits imposed a tight discipline, which he absorbed and learned from, but to which he never objected.

In his first, second and third years of secondary school he had played a female role in school stage musicals, including the *Pirates of Penzance, Ruddigore* and *Iolanthe*. One year he appeared in the lead role in the Gilbert and Sullivan opera *The Mikado*, during the Christmas break. The school annual reported that 'A. O'Reilly was equipped with every natural gift to play the Mikado, a fine presence, very good voice, natural ease and confidence; he did more than justice to the part but scarcely full justice to himself. We mean that while the thing was well done and would do credit to any school acting, it was less than his best. There was a somewhat casual air, and approach, as if he was doing this kind of thing every day of his life, and becoming a little tired of knowing he does it so well.'

He was not a particularly gifted academic scholar at this stage, other than at English, by far his favourite subject. His hectic sports career and an early tendency to spend long hours socialising – singing and playing the piano at parties, and delivering jokes as a mimic – may have inhibited his natural intellectual abilities.

'He was a boy of great confidence without being bumptious,' said Fr Reidy, who taught him mathematics and English. 'There are some boys who can talk to a master without in any way giving offence and Tony had that gift. Even as a teacher you could relate to him. A number of boys have that, but Tony had it to an extra degree.'

He was rarely in trouble, was usually surrounded by a group of friends who were often older than him, and took part in everything going on in school, from chess to drama to debating. Kevin McGoran, his lifelong friend, recalled how O'Reilly went out of his way to know everyone. When McGoran joined the school he had a reputation as an excellent tennis player, so O'Reilly went out of his way to invite him for a game. He also recalled O'Reilly casually playing the piano in the school hall – 'Smoke Gets in Your Eyes' – when the other boys were frantically doing last-minute cramming before the Intermediate Certificate exams.

Rugby was his main interest. On his first season on the Senior Cup team, Belvedere had lost the semi-final unexpectedly to Terenure, and in his second season, the year he was doing his Leaving Certificate, the final State secondary school exam, Belvedere was beaten by the same school again at an early stage of the competition. It seemed as if O'Reilly's dream of a Senior Cup medal would not come true.

But Tony was young, just turned 17, and was entitled to re-sit the Leaving Certificate. The Jesuits wanted him to stay for another year, and his parents agreed: the idea of him roaming the streets as a young third-level student was a little worrying, given his obvious love of a party. His parents had indulged him with a seventeenth birthday party – they had hired a local club hall specially for the occasion and brought in caterers, which was almost unheard of at the time – but they wanted to keep some element of control and thought that another year with the Jesuits would afford them that. The school also wanted to win the Cup and Tony, a year older, would give it the best chance of winning.

Now standing 6 ft 2 in. in height, 14 stone in weight and able to break 10 seconds for the 100 yards in full rugby kit, Tony enjoyed a wonderful repeat year in school, scoring 42 tries in 21 games, which was a new schools record. Before one match that year, Jack presented Tony with a copy of Kipling's poem 'If', drawing special attention to certain words that O'Reilly would always cherish: 'If you can meet with Triumph and Disaster And treat those two impostors just the same … Yours is the Earth and everything that's in it, And – which is more – you'll be a Man, my son.' O'Reilly said later: 'My father had always impressed on me that it's easy to win, but it's hard to lose.'

Losing didn't seem to be on Tony's agenda, however. Belvedere got to the Cup final, played at Lansdowne Road on St Patrick's Day, as was the tradition. Another tradition is that the mothers of the captains of both teams are present and ready, if their son's team has won, to present the Cup to her son. Aileen bought a new hat for the occasion, in the hope that she would be presenting to her son.

Instead, everything went awry. Blackrock were leading near the end of the game when Belvedere attacked, and one simple pass would have put Tony into a gap from which he most probably would have scored the winning try. Instead his opposite number, Tom Cleary, gambled on an intercept, held the ball and sprinted nearly the length of the pitch to win the game for Blackrock. 'So I wait until they've disentangled themselves, and remembering that poem and what my father said, I go over and shake hands with him. Then I go back behind the posts, they take the kick, they win the Cup. Mrs Brophy presents the prize and my mother's new hat doesn't get to present the prize.'

O'Reilly left Belvedere happy that he had received what he later called 'a diverse and thorough education that prepared me for what I was to do'. He liked to joke that the Jesuits were 'top in humility', but they had also played another very significant, and for a long time unknown, role in his upbringing.

In his 1994 biography of O'Reilly, author Ivan Fallon – who soon after the publication of the book was appointed to a senior executive position at Independent Newspapers (IN) – wrote that something of a myth had grown up about O'Reilly's beginnings being modest. In assessing O'Reilly's education, Fallon noted that it was 'difficult to imagine a better grounding for a future industrialist, lawyer, writer or any other successful man. His parents may not have been wealthy, but they were intelligent, devoted and motivated. Their son never lacked for anything, and never missed out on whatever he wanted to do. If anything, they may have erred on the side of spoiling him, but fortunately never had the money for that. They provided a stable, loving and totally supportive background which gave him huge self-confidence and gregariousness in later life – something very much rarer in wealthier households.'

What Fallon also revealed in the book was a secret that O'Reilly had kept from most people for many years – although there were also many people who knew the truth of it. There had been one major incident at Belvedere that was to leave a lasting impression on him. In the year that he moved onto the Senior Cup squad, a couple of the Jesuit priests called him to a study for a private chat. They delivered news that was utterly unexpected to O'Reilly and deeply shocking. They told him that there was something he had to know about himself, something they believed he had not been told by his parents: they told the 15-year-old Tony that his parents, Aileen and Jack, were not married, as he believed, and worse, that his father was already married with four children, a half-brother and three half-sisters of whom young O'Reilly had no knowledge.

According to the mores of the time, his parents were living in a condition of mortal sin and should not even be taking communion on their visits to Sunday mass. They behaved as if they were a married couple, but it was a charade. It went further than that, however, and with potentially serious consequences for their son. The Irish State made it explicit in law that illegitimate children were second-class citizens. The Legitimacy Act of 1931, passed five years before O'Reilly was born, allowed that a child born out of wedlock might inherit its mother's property if she died without making a will, but it refused to grant any such rights of succession to the estate of a child's natural father, even though the latter was much more likely to have assets and money.

That the unmarried O'Reillys had been allowed to send their son to a privileged school in the circumstances of mid-twentieth-century Ireland – a deeply conservative and Catholic country – was in itself remarkable. That O'Reilly affected to Fallon that the revelation had not thrown him and that he hadn't bothered to bring up the issue with his parents on the day it was revealed to him, or at any other stage for more than 20 years afterwards, seems even more remarkable. It seems an impossible secret for a 15-year-old to harbour silently, and then for so many years. One can only imagine the jumble of emotions he must have experienced as he cycled home to his parents that evening. He explained it to Fallon as thinking: 'Well, I wonder will I mention it?' He judged by their demeanour that they clearly had no idea the priests had told him. He decided not to say anything.

Many years after the publication of Fallon's book, O'Reilly was asked about this incident by an American interviewer. He said that he had felt no shame and had eventually been able to discuss it with his parents. 'It was a sniff of gunpowder about your past,' he said, the interviewer remarking how he was 'flashing his jaunty smile'. O'Reilly explained that Ireland in 1936 'was a very old-fashioned, rigid society. My mother had this boy under unusual circumstances. I was her little boy, and she was determined that the best would happen to me.' Generously, he also declared: 'I have four brothers and sisters, and they were the ones who were short-changed because they lost out on their father.'

He may have come to terms with the story by the time he approached old age, but the story was very nearly not included in Fallon's biography, *The Player*. Fallon saw it as central to the book, but he and O'Reilly debated strongly its inclusion, although O'Reilly denied that subsequently. O'Reilly still feared the repercussions to his image from disclosure; Fallon knew it would be dishonest of him as a biographer to exclude it, so important was it to a better understanding of O'Reilly's motivations.

In assessing what he called 'the forces which drove him almost demonically at times', Fallon had attributed to O'Reilly's first wife, Susan, the belief that knowledge of his illegitimacy meant that 'he had to prove to the world that he was better than anyone else'. Remarkably, O'Reilly only told Susan the truth of his situation many years into their marriage, long after their own children had been born. The first clue, had she recognised it, came at a dance in Wicklow when a man told her that he knew O'Reilly's brother. Susan replied that her husband did not have a brother, and the man apologised and left. Somewhat mystified, Susan asked Tony about it only to be told that there were always people telling stories about him and not to take any notice of it. Susan, along with other friends, came to believe that the shock of the revelation became a motivation for him to strive harder, to prove himself, to achieve more than anyone else. He wanted people to know him for his abilities rather than his perceived shame.

It was not something that O'Reilly spoke about, most certainly not at home – either in his parents' house or in the home he created with Susan. Although having said that, during the 1970s when young men and women began turning up as guests at his Pittsburgh home in America who turned out to be O'Reilly's nephews and nieces, this fact was not hidden from his own children. 'It didn't seem to bother him,' said his own son, Tony jnr. 'It may have been a contributing factor to his drive, but not in a negative way.'

Nonetheless, O'Reilly had kept it quiet on occasions when he could have addressed it. In late December 1986, for example, he gave an extraordinarily frank interview to Ivor Kenny, later published in the book *In Good Company*, in which he referred to himself as an only child. 'I had a particular attachment to both my father and my mother, enjoying the shelter of their love for me, and was very close to them … I think I get my sense of humour from my mother and my sense of appreciation from John, my father. It was not a strict upbringing.' His reticence to address the issue may have been understandable: his mother was still alive but in ill-health, and she might not have wanted something so sensitive and private to be disclosed by him.

There was relatively little comment in Ireland about the revelation when it came to light in 1994, other than expressions of surprise. In late twentieth-century Ireland, far fewer cared than might have been the case in previous generations. It changed few attitudes about him, although some claimed they could now understand him a bit better. O'Reilly was not happy about an essay that appeared in the British publication *Granta* in 1996, however, penned by journalist Fintan O'Toole, which assessed O'Reilly's personal revelation with more bluntness than was apparent in Fallon's biography. O'Toole pointed out to his international audience that it was not until 1987 that the legal concept of illegitimacy was removed in Ireland:

> Well past the age of fifty, O'Reilly, as well as being the richest man in Ireland, was also, secretly, a second-class Irishman.
>
> O'Reilly's position was in one sense less shameful than that of the child of an ordinary unmarried mother: he was cherished and recognised by both his natural parents. But in another sense it was more darkly secretive. For most illegitimate children, the sin was acknowledged and open, the shame explicit. There was, at least, little else to be revealed. But for him, his public identity was a subterfuge. His parents pretended to be married and concealed the existence of a whole other family. His cupboard contained not a skeleton, but several living reminders of what was being hidden: his half-siblings. Not only was the existence of his father's other family a secret, but so was the fact that he himself knew about it.
>
> One can never know how much one's inner life is shaped by social circumstances, and no one else can ever guess. But it is hard to avoid the belief that something of his anomalous origins must be present in what Tony O'Reilly has become. It may be there in his obsessive, driven hunger for success … and it must have been there in the overwhelming desire to control news, to have power over image and information.

O'Toole was also of the belief that 'if at any time in his youth, his family background had been revealed, it would have caused not just personal hurt but probably fatal damage to his public career'. That would not have been a reflection of O'Reilly but of the Ireland of his youth and early adulthood. He may have downplayed it subsequently, but any amateur psychologist would suggest that it drove his ambition to succeed and his need to be acknowledged for whatever successes he achieved.

CHAPTER TWO

THE FLYING IRISHMAN

O'Reilly graduated from Belvedere in the summer of 1954, interested in becoming a barrister, believing his ability to speak publicly and eloquently, which he had been honing in debates at Belvedere, would fit him well for this part. His father dissuaded him. Barristers were, and are, sole traders, who have no income when they are not working – a factor that wouldn't suit somebody who had ambitions to play rugby at a higher level. His father argued that there would be more stability in a career as a solicitor, so father and son agreed on his going to University College Dublin (UCD) to study law. They also organised, with help from the priests at Belvedere, that he would be apprenticed simultaneously to a past pupil, Gerry Quinn, who was one of the leading figures at Old Belvedere Rugby Club. That's why O'Reilly played his adult rugby with that club, instead of following the custom of the time of playing senior rugby for his university.

The parting verdict of the *Belvederian* on his rugby prospects was that 'he had almost everything a footballer needs – size, weight, pace, mobility – but perhaps he needs a little cooler judgement to make for perfection'. It was perhaps not surprising, then, that Old Belvedere started him in the thirds. He was not particularly committed to rugby initially, enjoying the freedom of college life, especially now that his father, indulging him again, had given him the gift of a second-hand Fiat 500, a small car for a man of his size. He became something of a party animal – although never drinking alcohol because of the car – staying out until near dawn, cutting the engine of the car near home and coasting the rest of the way so the noise wouldn't wake his parents. He particularly enjoyed female company, and it was reciprocated, much to the envy of the other young men. It wasn't just his looks that attracted women but his gregariousness and ready smile and his ability to compliment. He was fun to be with.

O'Reilly made his debut for the Old Belvedere firsts in November 1954, after half of the first team were dropped for having missed an away game against Galwegians the previous week because they got waylaid in a pub in Athlone, halfway along the road to Galway. He was picked to play in the centre. In the first minute of the game his opposite number, Captain Billy Ringrose (a famous name in show-jumping), tackled him so hard that O'Reilly lost a front tooth. Holding his tooth in one hand for the rest of the match, he still scored the only try of the day.

He played against the Cork side Dolphin the following week and received rapturous write-ups in the sporting press for his performance. A week later he was selected to play against Queens University, Belfast, who had Cecil Pedlow – already an international and later to become one of O'Reilly's closest friends – as his opposite number. Jack Kyle, already a legend of Irish rugby and another to become a future close friend, played for Queens at out-half. O'Reilly scored two tries and was picked to play for Leinster against Ulster at Ravenhill the follow-ing week. Debates raged in the sports pages as to whether he was being rushed along too fast – 'some rough handling and crash tackling could have the effect of knocking the edge off his present keenness and ability' – or whether his ability demanded he be moved onto the international team at the first opportunity.

O'Reilly was suddenly aware that the latter was possible for him, as long as he did not suffer a disaster in the forecasted heavy rain at Ravenhill, which was eminently possible given the reputation of its two hard-man centres: Noel Henderson and Dick Chambers. He feigned injury, didn't play the game and instead went to Wicklow with his friend, Frank 'Porky' O'Rourke.

'I went climbing the Sugar Loaf, a peak in nearby Wicklow instead,' said O'Reilly, 'and I learnt a great deal about Irish rugby by doing so. A reporter at the match decided the centres had not done too well that day and proclaimed that by comparison I must be the best centre in the country. By not playing I did my prospects no harm and after one more club game, was named in the final trial.'

Three days before Christmas he was selected for that trial, played alongside Henderson and scored one try, for which he ran the entire length of the pitch, and he set up two more. A few days later an official letter arrived from the Irish Rugby Football Union (IRFU) to his parents' home in Santry, informing A. O'Reilly Esq. that he had been selected to represent Ireland against France at Lansdowne Road on 22 January 1955. He was told to respond with his acceptance immediately. His jersey would be supplied, but it would have to be returned immediately after the game or he would have to pay 40 shillings for it. He was told to bring his own clean white shorts for the game, and training gear, his own towel and soap and have his boots in 'good, playable condition'. O'Reilly spent the evening celebrating and when he got up the following day was photographed at home for the *Evening Press*. 'I am delighted, and, of course, very much surprised,' he said. 'It was most unexpected.'

The team met only on the morning of the match at the Shelbourne Hotel, in time for lunch and a team-talk, which was delivered by the man who would become O'Reilly's lifelong best friend, the Dolphin wing-forward Jim McCarthy. He was warned how difficult he would find international rugby, especially against a team that had beaten Scotland comprehensively in its previous game. Ireland had won only one game the previous season – one of the reasons why O'Reilly had been promoted.

The speed of the game came as a shock to O'Reilly and one mis-judgement in defence allowed France the opportunity to score what would prove to be the only, and match-winning, try. 'The youngster showed admirable temperament in not allowing himself to be worried by a defensive error which led to the French try and his handling and passing were most expert,' *The Irish Times* reported. It was a tough introduction and it suddenly had people talking about a perceived weakness instead of all his strengths.

He kept his place for the next game, against England, but it happened to him again: his opposing number, the highly rated Jeff Butterfield, made a break and O'Reilly was left floundering as the Englishman raced over the try line. O'Reilly redeemed himself with his first try in international rugby and Ireland salvaged a 6-6 draw (in those days, a try was worth just three points, as against four subsequently and then five), but there was now much chatter about his defensive abilities. There were many who felt he would, and should, be dropped. He wasn't, but he now carried an unwanted reputation that he would find hard to shake off. Scotland won the next game against Ireland 12-3, and O'Reilly, again at centre, did little of note.

O'Reilly's ambitions were not restricted to staying in the Irish team. He was now focused on gaining selection for the British & Irish Lions tour to South Africa that summer. A 23-3 defeat to Wales in the final game of the Five Nations ought to have put paid to that ambition, but O'Reilly was the best of the Irish players in defeat. 'I decided there was no point in being conservative about this game, so I'd run all afternoon. All my Christmases came true, and although we were well beaten, I was able to show a lot of skill and a lot of pace.' He was selected – a remarkable achievement for a young man just out of school, who had been playing third team rugby only the previous October.

Going on a four-month tour with the British & Irish Lions would cause him to miss his first year exams at UCD and he would have to repeat them the following year. His father actually wanted him to turn down the Lions in favour of his exams, but O'Reilly was determined to go; he knew he might never get another chance.

The modern-day British & Irish Lions rugby tour is vastly different from the two in which O'Reilly participated in the 1950s. The modern tour is completed in a period of six to seven weeks, and is televised live. It is a highly commercialised enterprise for which the players are rewarded handsomely, although much is still made of the honour of selection. The old style tours of O'Reilly's era would run for over four months, had many more games and news of the matches appeared in the following day's newspapers, perhaps to be accompanied afterwards by some newsreel footage shown in cinemas. The players were not paid but received £2 and 10 shillings pocket money each week, as long as they provided receipts for their expenses.

The teams in which O'Reilly played – in South Africa in 1955 and subsequently in Australia and New Zealand in 1959 – were led by Irishmen, Robin Thompson and Ronnie Dawson respectively, but the interest generated for the Irish sporting public was limited by comparison to the saturation coverage afforded to the teams led by Brian O'Driscoll in 2005 and Paul O'Connell in 2009. Rugby union in Ireland in the 1950s was played by a relatively small number of people, despite the large crowds that would go to Lansdowne Road for international games. It laboured too, and with some justification, under the burden of being regarded as mainly a game for an elite, wealthier class, many of whom had no love for traditional Gaelic games. That rugby was played on a 32-county basis and accommodated all religious traditions equally was applauded by many, but disdained by others.

The team travelled without great expectation as the last Lions team to win a test series in South Africa had been in 1896. Since 1906 the South Africans had won every international match they had played in Britain, Ireland and France. Nonetheless, despite the low expectations the tour was also the first to be accompanied by a full press contingent, boosting interest in the sport in Britain and Ireland greatly.

The first time that O'Reilly stepped onto an airplane was on 11 June 1955. He discovered that he was a nervous flier, something that never left him, which is incredible given the amount of time he was to spend on aircraft subsequently. The team arrived at Jan Smuts Airport to a big crowd of fans and photographers. The Welsh out-half Cliff Morgan, who was to become one of O'Reilly's close friends, also acted as choirmaster and had prepared the players to sing a repertoire of hymns and arias. They began on the tarmac with the Welsh rugby song 'Sospan Fach' and progressed into the difficult Transvaal anthem 'Sarie Marais'. The South Africans loved it.

They were to be enormously generous hosts, motivated perhaps by the isolation visited upon them by other sports and countries that were appalled by the apartheid regime imposed upon black and people of other non-white origin in the country. It was to the shame of rugby in that era, and for a good 30 years-plus afterwards, that the sport tried to ignore the politics of the country, to say that sport remained separate from politics, when in fact the exclusion of non-white players from South African teams was a simple example of discrimination. O'Reilly and the tour party were silent on such matters and it fell to players in later generations to publicly express their revulsion at the regime. This group enjoyed themselves too much to notice.

The South Africans accommodated them in style: fleets of cars with drivers were put at their disposal; they were housed in luxury hotels when available; and access to cinemas and clubs were all available to them for free. On the first visit to Pretoria they were stopped by police who grouped their cars into a convoy and then, with motorbike out-riders, escorted them into the city with all the pomp of a visiting head of state. There were visits to Kruger National Park and the diamond mines at Kimberley and some wonderful beaches that were a far remove from those where O'Reilly had learnt to swim.

O'Reilly loved it, moving easily in the company of senior business-men, politicians, farmers or just rugby fans, developing a taste for high living that would never leave him. A constant stream of former Springbok players came to meet the visitors, giving O'Reilly an early indication of the value of networking. Much to the consternation of Thompson and tour manager Jack Siggins, two rather austere men from Belfast, O'Reilly's self-confidence developed quickly, shaking off any initial shyness about his age and experience to become the life and soul of the party, taking responsibility alongside Morgan to organise sing-songs and play practical jokes. The management could not believe, or approve of, how little sleep O'Reilly sought or seemed to need, or how much partying he believed was appropriate. His saving grace was that he would not drink alcohol.

He was fortunate that Cecil Pedlow was also on the tour and they became a double act. 'He stood out wherever he went,' recalled Pedlow. 'Tony and I would be lent a car and we'd cruise around the best areas of Johannesburg on a Saturday night after a match. When we saw lots of cars, we'd stop, knock on the door and ask them if that was where the party was. If it wasn't a party, then it was once the people had seen Tony standing at the front door.'

This was where O'Reilly first fully understood the attraction he held for women – and how being on a rugby tour allowed him to exploit that as many young women flocked to the parties attended by the players. 'Tony O'Reilly was a young god, very handsome,' said tour member Douglas Baker, 'and the girls swooned over him, so he enjoyed himself thoroughly'. The players were not jealous: O'Reilly would make introductions to a large number of women and even if he almost invariably connected with the most striking women, there were plenty of others for the players to meet.

'He always drew attention to himself, not because he was trying to but because he had such a winning way and a quick turn of phrase,' said Pedlow. 'Others on the team, and people whom we met, found what I always found with him: he makes you feel the better for seeing him. He makes you feel as if it's you who's being funny. And he could go up or down at any level, even when he was nineteen.'

Phil Davies, the English centre, remembered O'Reilly as 'the tour character'. He said he was a '19-year-old with a very bright mind and tremendous speed and elusiveness on the wing, allied to an Irish sense of humour. Over the years he has so eloquently teased and properly caricatured my forthright approach and last second off-loads in the centre, with accompanying public school speech. But it was the wings that scored the tries, as they continued to do in New Zealand in 1959, so I've always felt that he could say what he liked.'

None of O'Reilly's off-field successes would have been possible, or indeed tolerated by the rest of the touring party and management, if he had not established himself as a star player in the first place.

O'Reilly was in the best physical condition of his life. A tall man, he now weighed 13 stone, 10 lb, about a half a stone lighter than he had been with Ireland during the season. He had trained hard in Dublin before travelling, but he now benefited from two hard sessions every day at the team's base at altitude, at 5,000 ft above sea level at Vereeniging. He would also find the hard grounds of South Africa suited his running game.

The nature of Lions tours was to allow the squad a long build-up with games against local clubs and provinces before the 'test' games against the host international side. Those teams were highly motivated to beat the Lions and some of the games were ferocious, with con-siderable risk to limb if not life. The matches also required the team to travel vast distances by bus and train, from altitude to sea level and back again. Combined with the active social life, it was exceptionally demanding physically and, in time, mentally on the players.

Those games made O'Reilly a star. The local fans loved his ability not just to score tries but how he did it, often through long, strong runs with opponents finding it so difficult to tackle him to the ground. That he was only 19 and had such striking looks, particularly his red hair, only added to the strong impression he made on all who saw him in action. The Lions were also playing an extraordinarily attractive running, rather than kicking, style of rugby, scoring 60 tries in the first 12 non-international games. O'Reilly scored 11 of those so when the management decided to carry this style of rugby into the test matches, O'Reilly's selection became inevitable. By this stage, O'Reilly, who was selected for the tour as a centre, had moved to the left-wing, such was the effectiveness of the combination of Butterfield and Davies in the centre, particularly in their ability to get the ball to the wings.

The first test was played at Ellis Park in Johannesburg in front of over 90,000, the biggest crowd ever to attend an international rugby match. It has gone down in rugby history as one of the great games, as the Lions established a 23-11 lead, scoring five tries in the process. O'Reilly had run in the fifth. However, the high altitude got to the Lions and, exhausted, they conceded two tries in injury time at the end of the second half. All the South African kicker van der Schyff had to do to win the game for the Boks with the very last action of the game was to the kick the conversion of the second try. The occasion unnerved him and he shanked the ball wide. O'Reilly later described the victory as one of the most euphoric moments of his life.

O'Reilly had a poor game in the second test, however. It was lost by 25-6 and many of the criticisms about O'Reilly's defence returned as his direct opponent, van Vollenhoven, scored three of the home team's tries. O'Reilly was switched to the right wing for the third test, which the Lions won by 9-6.

The final test was played in Port Elizabeth in mid-September. O'Reilly was picked this time in the centre, in the hope of better utilising his powerful running. It was a controversial decision among the Welsh – somewhat akin to the decision 58 years later to exclude Brian O'Driscoll from the final test of the Lions tour to Australia to make way for a Welsh player – because it meant that Davies was dropped. O'Reilly had possibly his best game of the tour – even though South Africa won easily, outscoring the Lions by five tries to two and by 22 points to 8 overall – and he scored another fine try, in the corner, in the last minute. He was injured badly, though, by a tackle that came in after he had grounded the ball, dislocating his exposed right shoulder. He howled with the pain and manager Jack Siggins came onto the pitch to wrench the shoulder back into place. O'Reilly was taken away with his arm in a makeshift sling and in his absence – no substitutes were allowed in those days – South Africa scored another try. The series was drawn two games apiece and it wouldn't be until 1974, and then again 1997, that Lions teams would win the series in South Africa.

It was a triumph for O'Reilly personally. He had scored 16 tries in 15 games, equalling the existing individual record on a tour.

The authors of *Behind the Lions* (2013) said that 'in many ways, this was the ultimate Lions tour. It was not so much in the results that the significance springs, even though by coming away with a drawn series in an epic quartet of matches, the Lions avoided defeat for the first time in decades of touring; it was not even the class shown by both sides in the matches or the sheer style of open rugby played by the Lions, and it was more than the enormous crowds at the four stadiums. It was the sheer glamour, and from the moment that the party hopped their way down from London as the first Lions to fly, South Africa welcomed them with a reverence, entertaining them at every turn and treating them like film stars.' It described O'Reilly as 'the extraordinary 19 year old Irish prodigy' and as a 'strapping presence' on the wing to score the tries.

'Perhaps the most glorious sight in rugby was to see O'Reilly in full flight,' said Morgan. 'Like the rest of Tony's life, not one of his tries he scored was ordinary. Everything was slightly spectacular. He was only 19, but he had the wit and wisdom of someone 20 years older. He gave the tour a touch of class. It made you feel slightly inadequate that you weren't in the same mental bracket. He towered over you in every sense.'

'It was a heady experience over a period of 18 months,' O'Reilly said 30 years later. 'I had to learn to live with myself. I had to understand the ephemeral nature of fame: how to come from being the darling of the crowd, as I came up, to where the crowd turned against me and displayed a degree of antagonism at my appearance which surprised me: I thought I was the same player I was six months earlier. Suddenly I realised the fickle nature of fame, and particularly, I realised how, in Ireland, achievement often becomes an object of envy or derision. I had to learn to wrestle with all those contradictions. It was exciting and it was hardening.'

He arrived back in Dublin on 1 October, arm in sling, to be met on the airport tarmac by his anxious mother. He indulged himself fully in a party life by night and met with various girls in coffee shops by day, neglecting both studies at UCD and work in Quinn's office. He was developing expensive habits, too. He had a college friend who worked in the bar at the Gresham Hotel and who used to slip him and whatever girl he had with him drinks for free. He and his female companion of the evening would also dine for free at a restaurant called Alfredo's, where he played the piano and sang for a while in return; he always ensured that the proprietor never gave the game away that it was effectively a job, pretending to his companion that he just happened to be there by chance, but that while he was, he might as well play and sing.

He was heading for major problems with both his college degree and his solicitors' exams, which had to be taken if he was to qualify. He didn't neglect his rugby training though, sometimes working out twice a day. He was in fine shape for his first big game back in Lansdowne Road on 31 December 1955. To mark the opening of a new stand, a selection of players from Ireland and Scotland played an England and Wales combination. The home team lost but O'Reilly stood out, scoring two fine tries.

The 1956 international season did not go well, however. Ireland lost by 20-0 at Twickenham against England. As he walked off the field, O'Reilly remarked to fellow Lion Tom Reid that the result was dreadful. 'Well, sure aren't we lucky to get the nil,' Reid replied. In the crowd that day was the Irish actor Noel Purcell, a Hollywood favourite, and Al Corfino, the casting director at MGM, the movie studio that was casting for a new action movie called *Ben Hur*. Purcell was trying to persuade Corfino that O'Reilly was perfect for the title role. O'Reilly wasn't interested and didn't even turn up at the party to which he had been invited to meet Corfino, much to Purcell's chagrin. Charlton Heston got the part and, in truth, O'Reilly might only have been given an audition at best, but he was able to use the story that he was in the running for the part to add to his legend and in time it became reported, inaccurately, that he had turned it down. He still had his rugby to concentrate on, scoring a try away to France and another in Scotland and assisting in the defeat of Wales.

That season Ireland got a new scrum-half, another man who was to become one of O'Reilly's great friends, Andy Mulligan. He was even more of the *bon viveur*, acting the dandy as he chased girls, success-fully. He didn't see much of O'Reilly during the summer, however, as for the summer of 1956 O'Reilly gave up everything except study:

> The management of time is a critical element in success and it required a certain absolute discipline, because, having analysed my own particular facilities, I realised I was not, as a student athlete, capable of leading a balanced life. I was not capable of absorbing the strain and commitment of playing international rugby and

studying at the same time. I couldn't do both. So I divided the year into seven months and five months. For seven months I played football and tended nominally to my studies. I then stopped: cut myself off completely, refused to read a newspaper, did not listen to the radio, talk to my friends or take telephone calls. I went into monk-like seclusion for five months. I took only one weekend off during that period. From May to October each year I was in total seclusion. As a result I did reasonably well academically, getting fifth place in the BCL at University College (Dublin), first place in part one of the solicitors' final and third place in part two.

Each September, however, he would go to Wales and play rugby as a 'guest', claiming expenses with the somewhat looser arrangements over the payment of money that were in place there. This money would keep going through until Christmas and in the New Year he would concentrate on international rugby.

He took his finals in the autumn of 1958. 'Having regard to your feats in the rugby field at this time these were no mean academic achievements,' the secretary of the Law Society wrote to him. He was enrolled as a solicitor that November, but he never practised. Instead, he left for England.

He got a job in Leicester as a trainee management consultant with Weston-Evans, a company that made glazed piping, and he played for the city's famous club. It was desperately dull work, but over the next two years he learnt about basic accounting, production techniques and standard unit costings, things that would stand him in excellent stead later on. He spent much of his time on the factory floor, watching how things were done and working out how to do them better. He lived in Ashby-de-la-Zouch and bought himself a white TR3 sports car, which he often drove to London at weekends where he'd meet up with Mulligan.

He was on the cover of *World Sports* magazine in February 1959, and the feature writer Vivian Jenkins compared him to some of the great 'characters' in world sport at the time: cricket's Denis Compton, football's Stanley Matthews, snooker's Joe Davis and golf's Henry Cotton. 'It wasn't only that they were great players,' wrote Jenkins. 'They had something else – personality, glamour, call it what you will – that raised them out of the common rut. People wanted to know more about them, they hit the headlines and, once there, they stayed there. Such a man in rugby, already, is the fabulous young Irish three-quarter Tony O'Reilly.'

Playing for Ireland in that era did not provide many opportunities to display all of those qualities. The 1959 home international against England ended in a 3-0 defeat, with the Irish backs, including O'Reilly, Pedlow, Mulligan, Henderson and Brophy, getting the blame from the papers, with many contrasting O'Reilly's performance for Ireland with those for the Lions. The answers were obvious, and not just because Mick English at out-half kicked so much; Ireland simply weren't good enough. He was moved to the wing for the game in Wales and scored a try in the 8-6 defeat. It was not a good season, however, at least not in an Irish jersey. O'Reilly's exploits on the previous tour meant that his selection on the 1959 British & Irish Lions tour was always probable, but the performances of the Irish team of which he had been a member for the previous four years meant it was by no means certain. As it happened, he was to be among only six players out of 30 to be retained from that tour.

His selection came at a good time personally. He had found the season difficult, trying to combine his new job with training and playing for Leicester. He had put on weight – he was now 14 stone 7 lb, which was 11 lb more than he had been on the South African tour – and he would need to train hard to regain the shape, strength and speed he had enjoyed four years earlier. The paucity of the challenge offered by the Irish team in the Five Nations meant that he needed the step-up in level that playing New Zealand would require, both mentally and physically.

He also knew that the trip had the potential to be great fun, especially with female company. Friends like Pedlow were not selected, but new ones were and Ronnie Dawson was captain – the first Irish Catholic to get the job, which raised questions as to whether he would stand for 'God Save the Queen' when played as an anthem before the tests. Niall Brophy, his old schoolboy rival from Blackrock College, was also picked as a wing. 'I would like to think that there were a lot of stars in that side but because of his record, Tony shone brighter than the rest,' Dawson said, many years later.

The series in Australia was won by two tests to nil. He scored a try in the first test, won 17-6, and in the second game, which the Lions won again, 24-3, O'Reilly scored a try described as one of the best of his career, carrying three tacklers over the line with him as he ran at full pelt. The Australian matches were a warm-up effectively for what was to come, but there were to be significant off-field events that would be central to the remainder of O'Reilly's life.

They arrived in New Zealand to a procession of cars led by a band, with thousands cheering them on. There were receptions, dinners, speeches and visits to local beauty spots on the way. 'After his record-breaking success of the 1955 tour there was an air of expectancy in the Antipodes for the arrival of the Golden Boy,' wrote rugby journalist J. B. G. Thomas. 'For them he was the wing extraordinaire – big, strong, fast and handsome.'

As in South Africa four years previously, there was a long build-up to the test games with the host country, with the local provincial sides particularly brutal in how they put it up to the Lions. O'Reilly had more than the opposition to contend with; his star status was under assault from the English wing, Peter Jackson, a much smaller, lighter player who scored try after try with his elusive jinking and swerving running style and ability to find gaps by cutting back inside. Jenkins wrote that 'he brings the crowd to its feet with anticipation every time he gets the ball'.

Rugby is a team game – and the ethic of the game very much demands that – but O'Reilly did not like being upstaged by Jackson. Something of a personal duel developed between the two, which could have been damaging to the team but in fact may have brought out the best of both – even if it led to some allegations of O'Reilly being selfish on the pitch at times when he should have passed. He was also criticised as being 'apt to go up too early for diagonal kicks-ahead and be given offside'. Both he and Jackson were targets for the opposing defences and there was controversy over the use by the home teams of shoulder-pads inside their jerseys, to give extra heft to their tackles.

The first test against the All-Blacks, as New Zealand's test team was known, in mid-July in Dunedin was a highly controversial game, which led indirectly to a change in the scoring system to give greater reward to tries. New Zealand won 18-17, courtesy of six penalties by full-back Don Clarke. The Lions scored four tries, O'Reilly and Jackson each getting one, and converted two and still lost. The game was full of refereeing decisions in favour of the home team and one decision in particular, near the very end as the Lions were poised to score another try, caused particular anger.

That evening, at the formal post-test dinner, New Zealand officials talked about winning 'within the framework of the rules' for which, said the president of the host rugby union Gordon Brown in his after-dinner speech, 'no apologies need to be offered'. O'Reilly and Mulligan, who had joined the tour as a replacement for another injured player, seized upon this phrase and wove into the cabaret act they now put on for the other players on every occasion they could, such as on buses moving between host cities. They called it Two-Y-Front and modelled it on the popular British radio programme of the time, *The Goon Show*, which starred Peter Sellers and Spike Milligan. 'Andy had a guitar and he'd entertain us on trains, planes and on the bus,' said Noel Murphy, a wing-forward from Cork who later managed a Lions tour to South Africa in 1980. 'They were a double act. If they went into the opera house in Auckland, they'd have filled the place.' On one occasion a recording of their performance found its way to New Zealand national radio where it was aired, leading to requests for further performances.

The Lions went into the second test short of players because of a combination of injuries and 'flu. They competed well in the first half and remained with a good chance of winning the game. O'Reilly was the victim of the most controversial incident in the second half. He had followed a kick-ahead and gathered the ball and was powering for the line with only Clarke in front of him. He swerved inside, drawing Clarke with him and then chipped the ball over Clarke's head and went after it. Clarke didn't go after the ball, but instead dropped his shoulder and ran into O'Reilly. In the modern era, a referee would automatically give a penalty try and at least a yellow card for 10 minutes in the sin-bin, if not a red to remove the offending player from the game. Instead, this referee merely awarded a penalty to the Lions, which they scored to take them into an 8-6 lead, but it was Clarke who scored the match-winning try and conversion four minutes from the end. The legend had it that O'Reilly, who never blamed Clarke publicly for his actions, was heard to say as he crashed to ground, 'sure I'd have done the same thing myself'.

Four days later he was the subject of an assault in a game against a combined King Country-The Counties side, having a chunk of hair ripped from his scalp while simultaneously another player punched him in the ribs, just above the heart. He passed out, leading one local paper to accuse him of a 'theatrical fainting fit' when he was in fact genuinely injured – and angry when he woke up. He scored three tries in response.

The third test, at the end of August, was lost by 22-8 and O'Reilly was blamed for getting ahead of his centre, David Hewitt, and losing a try-scoring position at a crucial juncture of the game; others blamed Hewitt for trying to beat Clarke himself instead of passing. The series was now lost 3-0, with one test to play. There were four more non-international games to play, too, which was difficult for some of the players who now wanted to go home. But O'Reilly was determined to have fun and he had the personal challenge of wanting to beat Jackson for the unofficial prize of top try scorer on the team. O'Reilly scored two remarkable long-distance tries in the first of those four games, causing Jenkins to comment: 'Though he had done very well on this tour and scored his full quota of tries, the flying Irishman had never quite produced the kind of runs that had brought him such fame in South Africa in 1955. Now at last he showed he could still do it.' He went into the final test with a total of 16 tries on tour – one more than Jackson.

He scored one of the three unconverted tries in the 9-6 victory in the final test, courtesy of opportunism on the part of Mulligan at scrum-half, who put him in. It was regarded as one of the best games of his career. Jackson scored too, but he was beaten by one try by O'Reilly. His record of 17 tries in New Zealand is one that almost certainly will never be beaten. 'It was a very exciting experience trying to beat Ken Jones's try-scoring record,' O'Reilly recalled 45 years later. 'I equalled him four matches from the end and then had to try to find a way to beat his record. I finally got the try to do it in about the last minute of the final test, which was the great game of the tour for me. First of all we beat them fair and square and we beat them in Auckland, which was really their home ground, and I got that vital seventeenth try that I had been trying to get for the previous four matches. I can still feel the heavy ball and the mud on my face as I went through the last tackle of Don Clarke.'

He was one of only five players who had played in all six test matches in Australia and New Zealand and his popularity with the group was such that his fellow Lions carried him shoulder-high from the field. 'Our outstanding players were Tony O'Reilly and Peter Jackson,' said fellow Lion Alan Ashcroft, 'who could score tries and create total havoc among the opposition'.

In his book *Kings of Rugby*, Terry Maclean subsequently described O'Reilly as a relatively straight runner, relying on his speed, weight and a ferocious hand-off either to out-run the opposition or to crash his way through. 'For a man of 23, he was astonishingly mature of mind,' wrote Maclean. He noted that his experiences at an early age 'had given him immense self-confidence … At a long range guess, one felt reasonably sure that he would in time become president or premier of the republic.' Interestingly, he added: 'one can only hope that the remarkable possibilities of this young man as student and thinker would not be harmed by too great an affection for witty display and by a strange regard, almost amounting to envy, for those fortunate folk who move through the world with a lordly calm based upon a secure place in the world.'

Others saw the serious side to him at work on the trip, too. 'We were at a reception and the prime minister of New Zealand was there and they'd just announced the Budget,' said Syd Millar from Ballymena, who later became one of the game's most important administrators, 'so O'Reilly had him in the corner and after a while we saw the PM nodding. O'Reilly was telling him where he'd gone wrong in the Budget.' It was a sign of where his interests were moving.

The tour was to be the highest point of his rugby career, and all achieved by the age of 23. O'Reilly only played another nine times for Ireland as he started to give priority to his career and to socialising. He didn't have time for the training required to get his weight down, even after he moved back to Ireland and a new job in Cork, and a lack of fitness made him more prone to injury. His real interest was only in the internationals, and even then perhaps not as much as it should have been. He played only once for Ireland in the 1960 season, injuring his shoulder in the 8-5 defeat to England at Twickenham, making him unavailable for all the season's other games, all of which Ireland lost. The following season he again only managed one game, a victory over England at Lansdowne Road, before another shoulder injury kept him out of all the other games. But he decided to go on Ireland's short summer tour to South Africa in 1961. He came up with an idea that he and Mulligan would form a company called Ireland International, which would market Irish goods on the tour. O'Reilly and Mulligan contacted various South African importers and secured orders for products they would bring with them, such as Irish whiskey cake, tweed clothes and knitted woollen sweaters made in Donegal. They brought their own business suits and in each city they took a hotel suite in which they laid out samples and displays and invited locals to a reception. The rest of the squad were not happy that they seemed more interested in these activities than in training, but the two entrepreneurs came back with £1,000 in cash and even some orders for the Irish manufacturers. With an eye to the future, O'Reilly decided to spend his share on his bank manager in Cork, Tom Casey of the Munster and Leinster Bank. Casey and his wife were brought to London, put up in a five-star hotel, given a gourmet dinner and taken to a rugby match.

He didn't play on the national team in 1962 because of injury. In January 1963 he played against France and scored only his second try for Ireland at Lansdowne Road, with a run from 30 yards that included a hand-off of his French opponent winger and three tacklers hanging off his back as he crossed the line to ground the ball. But Ireland lost 24-5 and the following day the selectors announced that he was being dropped for the next game. 'Seldom can the slings and arrows of outrageous fortune have affected anyone in rugby as severely as O'Reilly,' wrote Paul McWeeney in *The Irish Times*. 'In the 21st minute of Saturday's match he was the hero of his native land and received a tremendous ovation as he ran back after scoring his try – less than 24 hours later, he is cast into outer darkness.'

There was considerable debate as to whether it was the correct call, but everyone agreed that O'Reilly had never played anywhere near as well for Ireland as he did on tour for the Lions. In 26 internationals so far, O'Reilly had scored only five tries, one on the tour to South Africa in 1961. In 10 test matches for the Lions against Australia, South Africa and New Zealand, he had scored six tries. 'The only time we touch the ball for Ireland is when we autograph it afterwards,' he said. The rules in that era allowed direct kicking to touch from any part of the field and Ireland never played a running game. O'Reilly would have thrived in the modern game, where his power and pace might be compared to wingers like the Irishman Tommy Bowe or the Welshman George North, both Lions too. He actually returned to the Irish team for the subsequent Scottish and Welsh matches because Niall Brophy was injured, but the Welsh game was his last for Ireland – before a dramatic recall in somewhat bizarre circumstances seven years later.

CHAPTER THREE

THE STARTING POINT

There were strict standards of behaviour for young men and women in the 1950s and early 1960s in Ireland, when the mores of the Catholic Church – and its unimpeachable command that nobody engage in sex outside of marriage – were still dominant. Legend had it that one of the reasons Tony O'Reilly enjoyed his rugby trips to other countries so much was the opportunity it provided to him to meet with women, of his own age and sometimes quite a few years older. He had a strong charismatic presence anyway, which always had an effect on women, but add to that his striking looks and the fame that he carried and it was a winning combination that made him very attractive to all the women who met him. 'It was quite a vivid time in my life,' he said in an interview for *The Player*, utilising quite a degree of understatement. Ivan Fallon wrote that O'Reilly 'was not by nature monogamous'.

One woman did catch his attention in Dublin more than others, however. He met Dorothy Connolly on the night of the Schools Cup final in 1954. They got on very well for the most part, but she was a strong personality and they clashed many times, although given O'Reilly's behaviour that was not perhaps surprising. Many people were surprised when he proposed to her in early 1959, before he headed off on the Lions tour, and that she accepted. They were due to be married in 1960.

That didn't stop O'Reilly from planning to meet with other women when he was away with the Lions. He was aware that members of the English cricket team, who had toured Australia a year earlier, had the phone numbers of some of the women they had met. O'Reilly contacted the English opening batsman John Edrich and secured his 'little black book'. His tactic was to phone the women listed and say he was a friend of Edrich's and ask for a date. One of those O'Reilly contacted was June Finlayson, a local beauty queen, who introduced him to the various parties in Melbourne. When the Lions were moving on from there O'Reilly asked her for the addresses of a few friends in Sydney, the tour's next port of call. She recommended a friend called Susan Cameron but then had second thoughts, saying that Susan had a boyfriend and would probably soon be engaged.

At a party in Sydney, O'Reilly met a young woman called Helen Hayes who he learned was a friend of Susan's. 'You'd be the luckiest man in the world to get a date with her,' she told him. That piqued O'Reilly's interest and having discovered that Susan worked as a receptionist for a doctor in Sydney, he got the required phone number. 'The top of the morning to you, Susan,' he boomed down the phone when he rang her. 'You don't know me but I'm a friend of June Finlayson, and I'm one of the British Lions touring team.' She had no idea what he was on about and refused to meet him, having the legitimate excuse of being bridesmaid at a wedding that week.

Still sight unseen, he bombarded her with phone calls, possibly encouraged by reports that her father, Keith Cameron, was a mining executive with extensive land and livestock interests and was quite wealthy. Susan had been born in Bendigo, a town 70 km from Melbourne, but she had attended one of Australia's premier boarding schools. She was used to an elegant lifestyle. He persisted, and finally she agreed to meet him at Usher's Hotel in the heart of Sydney, where a reception for the team was taking place. 'I had never had a blind date in my life,' she said, 'and I had to meet him in this hotel where I was likely to see some of my friends, and here came this creature towards me in the tightest trousers you have ever seen and a blazer with a great big emblem on it, and this red, red hair. I thought he looked a bit of a teddy boy, and I was just hoping, all the time we were having a drink, that I wouldn't see anyone I knew.'

O'Reilly still persisted. He rang her the next day, having secured two tickets for that evening's performance of Tchaikovsky's *Romeo and Juliet* at the Sydney Concert Hall. 'Ever been there?' he asked grandly. 'Yes,' she replied. 'I played there last week.'

They met a few more times during his spell in Sydney. 'He left swearing undying love, and after that I got two letters and then there was dead silence, and I just got on with my life,' said Susan later. Not surprisingly, he had made no mention to her of Dorothy or his engagement.

On moving from Leicester to live in Cork after the tour, to take up his position with Suttons, O'Reilly was his usual popular presence in his new city. He decided to break the engagement with Dorothy, although they were to remain on good terms. In August 1960 Andy Mulligan rang him from London to say that Susan had arrived three weeks earlier, but had no interest in contacting him. O'Reilly instructed Mulligan to get Susan's phone number. He was going to Cornwall with the Irish Wolfhounds rugby team in September, travelling via London. He rang her and suggested that she travel down to Cornwall for that weekend. She quickly dismissed the idea as inappropriate. He got her address anyway and at the end of August 1960 he took a taxi to her new flat to begin the process of wooing her. When he got there, he had no money to pay the fare. Brazenly, he asked Susan for a loan of £3, which she refused to give him; one of her flatmates had to stump up the cash instead. O'Reilly persisted, even if he was not receiving much encouragement. The difficulty of the chase seemed only to motivate him, and that she was also beautiful – something of a Grace Kelly lookalike – and rich undoubtedly helped.

He persuaded Susan to come to Ireland after Christmas to see him play rugby against England at Lansdowne Road. She stayed with his parents and enjoyed an excellent welcome from Aileen, in particular, something that she appreciated greatly. A few weeks later Susan travelled to Cork and O'Reilly drove her along the coast to Kinsale, Glandore and Castletownshend and then on into Kerry and the Ring, with stops in Sneem and Waterville. He brought her to Derrynane House, home of Daniel O'Connell, and told her the history of the Catholic Emancipation Movement. His charm offensive was working.

In the summer of 1961 he and Susan began discussing marriage, but O'Reilly was reluctant. She was firm: he made the commitment or she returned to Australia. They were engaged on 31 August 1961, a year to the day after he had arrived in his taxi at her London flat. Jack was somewhat suspicious of Susan at first and remained aloof, but Aileen's relationship with Susan deepened. 'She just embraced me, which was amazing, because this golden light was her son, and here was this girl from overseas come to marry him.' Susan described Tony's relationship with his mother as 'touching and warm, and he really admired her'. Susan quit her job in London and moved to Dublin to live with Tony's parents, while he continued to live and work in Cork and commute to Dublin at weekends. Susan's father flew in from Australia to meet his future son-in-law and he too stayed with the O'Reillys in Santry, immediately forming a good relationship with Jack.

A wedding date was set for 5 May 1962. O'Reilly had started a new job in Dublin five weeks earlier, as general manager of An Bord Bainne (The Milk Board). They were married at University Church on St Stephen's Green by Professor Patrick Dempsey, a priest with whom O'Reilly had become friendly at University College Cork (UCC) when he was lecturing part-time there on finance. There were 350 people in attendance, the men in full morning dress, and outside the church were hundreds of UCD students who had been on their way to a march protesting against a bus strike but who, when they saw what was going on, decided to stay and watch the spectacle instead. Jim McCarthy was his best man, with Ronnie Dawson and Andy Mulligan his grooms-men. The *Irish Evening Mail* described the event as being 'like something from a film production'.

The newly-weds went for a three-week honeymoon in Portugal, at Lisbon and Estoril, and nine months and five days later their first child was born, Susan, on 10 February 1963. There would be five more children over the next three years: Cameron was born on 29 April 1964; Justine on 25 November 1965; and the triplets, Caroline, Gavin and St. John Anthony (to be known as Tony jnr), arrived on 17 December 1966.

Before the children came along, O'Reilly had enjoyed his time in Cork working for Suttons, a distributor of agricultural inputs, such as fertiliser and seed, that had expanded into things like the provision of domestic coal supplies. He was an assistant to the chairman, Jack Sutton. The salary, at IR£2,000 per year, was excellent – more, indeed, than his father was receiving as one of the most senior people in the Revenue Commissioners.

Cork was also home to the man who was becoming his closest friend – despite a gap in ages of over a decade: Jim McCarthy. O'Reilly stayed regularly with his family, even though he had arranged his own flat. 'When Tony first arrived he would always refer to "your house, Jim, and your wife and your children", but he soon switched from yours to ours. I didn't mind him saying "our house" and "our kids" and "our dog", but when he started saying "our wife" I was glad Susan turned up,' recalled McCarthy.

O'Reilly's landlady was so taken with the young man who had rented the top floor of the large house she shared with her daughter after her husband's death that she would give him back part of his weekly rent to help cover the cost of the party lifestyle he continued to enjoy. He also played a bit of rugby with the local Dolphin club – McCarthy's – but injury meant that he did not turn out too often for the team at Musgrave Park or elsewhere.

The Suttons job was not entirely taxing – his boss was more amused by O'Reilly's ideas for expansion and change than anything else – but it was extremely useful to O'Reilly's career development. He dealt with co-op managers and individual farmers. His rugby fame was not necessarily an advantage with people who were steeped largely, although not exclusively, in Gaelic games. He was very much an urban sophisticate, but he learnt to understand them and their attitudes and it helped hone his skills as a salesman and as a persuader. He came to regard this period as 'the beginning of the beginning'.

In Suttons he was also to meet one of the most important people in his life: Olive Deasy. She worked as an assistant to Sutton but 'did for' all of the senior managers, organising their appointments, taking phone calls and writing up dictation. Somewhat stern, she became fond of O'Reilly, and the appreciation was mutual. She was to spend the rest of her career working for him, moving from job to job, devoting considerable hours to his organisation. She was like many older women who fell for his charms: she indulged him but also disciplined him, loving him like a son. She was also to become helpful to Susan over the years with the children.

Jack Sutton was killed tragically in a car accident in late 1961, but the English head office felt O'Reilly was too young to be promoted to replace him as chairman. O'Reilly looked for a new challenge. Bord Bainne was set up that year to try to find some way to get better value out of Ireland's dairy industry. The challenge that was set for it was to find a way to provide a consistent supply of dairy product for export as well as enough food for domestic consumption. A year on from its foundation, Bord Bainne was still without a CEO. In early 1962, O'Reilly was approached to become its 'chief officer'.

O'Reilly had been recommended to Paddy Power of Ballyclough Co-op, the chairman of Bord Bainne. O'Reilly drove to Mallow where Power briefed him by writing in pencil on a napkin, expressing his ideas for getting away from butter production and moving into cheese, dried milk and chocolate crumb. He told O'Reilly that he would be interviewed by the board, but that he was not to reveal that they had met privately in advance.

The formal interview took place at Leeson Street in Dublin soon afterwards, but with other co-op representatives and some government nominees present, as well as Power. O'Reilly had prepared well and it proceeded nicely until near the end, when Power asked O'Reilly about the import price of one of his most important products at Suttons: Polish coal. O'Reilly smiled politely and laughed. 'Mr Power, if this interview turns out to be unsuccessful from either of our points of view, next Monday I'm going to be trying to sell you Polish coal. I'm not going to tell you the margins on Polish coal to get this job or any other.' Within days O'Reilly was told the job was his, at £3,200 per annum salary plus company car, a black Mercedes. He was allowed to bring his secretary, Olive Deasy, also to be employed by the company.

Bord Bainne was essentially an intervention agency, which subsidised farmers and guaranteed them both a price and a market for their products. The farmer wanted to sell at the highest price and the manufacturer wanted to buy at the lowest price, so the government, through Bord Bainne, paid for two-thirds of the difference between the two. Hundreds of thousands of families depended on this system for their livelihood. It also gave O'Reilly – as the man signing the cheques, IR£1 million worth of them in a year – great power, if he knew how to use it properly.

O'Reilly needed more people around to help him as he sought to get to grips with what needed to be done. In an older man called Joe McGough – a former army officer and lawyer who had retired from the armed forces in his mid-40s but who needed a new challenge – he found a very capable company secretary and, more importantly, an experienced sounding-board. McGough was also a character, who loved the social scene and who became the latest partner in an O'Reilly double act.

Despite the ideas Power had written on his napkin, O'Reilly remained more interested in the traditional product of butter, particularly as it used more milk than the other products Power had suggested. Britain imported vast quantities of butter, but of the 412,000 tonnes it imported each year, only 12,000 tonnes came from Ireland. Consumption was rising in Britain and that country didn't have the required dairy herd to become self-sufficient, importing mainly from Denmark and New Zealand.

'I approached the position with a sense of interest and curiosity. I was fascinated by the concept of the job, but I had essentially an urban background,' O'Reilly admitted. 'I started on 1 April 1962 and announced to the board in July the plan to launch a new consumer pack for butter on the British market.'

Armed with research from the Economist Intelligence Unit (EIU), a research group run by *The Economist* newspaper in London, and in league with its economist Garret FitzGerald, later Fine Gael leader and Taoiseach and a key consultant to him, O'Reilly had the idea to create a brand for Irish butter, one that would allow Irish exporters to attract a higher price and therefore a higher profit margin.

Now he had to convince civil servants of the merits of innovation and of marketing. 'I told a story that illustrates this point in September 1962 at the Agricultural Science Convention in Dublin,' he said. 'Two shoe salesmen visit Nigeria many years ago. Both review the characteristics of the market. Both cable home their responses, as follows. The first salesman's cable read: "The people in Nigeria don't wear shoes. No opportunities for sales. Returning home immediately." The second salesman's cable read: "The people in Nigeria don't wear shoes. Therefore, opportunities for sales virtually unlimited. Double my allocation immediately".'

O'Reilly needed guaranteed supply. He asked agriculture minister Paddy Smyth if the government would allow the import of foreign butter for the domestic market in the unlikely event that Bord Bainne ran short of butter for export. Smyth agreed, reluctantly.

The new product had to be hygienic and capable of a good shelf-life. It had to look so attractive that customers would pay more for it than the New Zealand equivalent. A parchment wrapper was selected as the covering, so the customer could see the butter. It was decided not to put the word *Irish* into the title, because there was still some kick-back in Britain, 20 years on, about the decision of the State to remain neutral during the Second World War. Nonetheless, the name still had to suggest Irish green pastures, the beauty of the Irish country-side and quality. It was called 'Kerrygold Irish Creamery Butter', to be sold in half-pound packets with a green and yellow wrapping, despite scoffing in Ireland that Kerry was a rugged county where little dairy farming took place. 'I explained to the board that it was a very strong name; it had a strong K, it was very well recognised and had an obvious Irish background,' O'Reilly recalled. One of the directors, Martin Mullally, pointed out that there were 'no cows in Kerry at all', but O'Reilly insisted that was not the point and once again he prevailed.

The marketing slogan chosen was: *Discover The Secret of Kerrygold, it's Pure Village Churned*. O'Reilly recalled one particular presentation to the board where famous broadcaster Terry Wogan's future wife, Helen Joyce, and the Rose of Tralee winner Josie Ruane wore short green skirts and tight white blouses, acting as milk-maids. 'You could feel the temperature in the room rising, and after it was over Paddy Power turned to me and said: "If that's marketing, I'm all for it",' said O'Reilly.

Plenty of people were willing to tell O'Reilly that he would fail and it rankled with him that he thought some people desired that, even though it would not be in the national interest. O'Reilly knew he had one chance of success and he decided to launch in the last quarter of 1962.

He had to educate his board, made up of co-op and government representatives, on the difference between marketing and selling without condescending to them. 'Marketing was a concept not known even to our board. Ireland was selling surpluses on a staccato basis. A dry summer and the creameries were out of stock and out of the market,' he said. To secure distribution in the UK, he allowed a British company to pack the butter in its own blending plants. There was a commercial logic to this, as the scale would allow for efficiencies, whereas each Irish co-op doing its own thing was wasteful and would lead to variations in standard. It also gave him a dedicated sales force, which he couldn't afford to put together. He assured the co-ops that they would be compensated from the greater profits that would be made.

There was opposition, particularly from a Department of Agriculture official on the board called Tony Hennerty. 'Young man,' he told O'Reilly, 'you are proposing to bring the Irish farmer face-to-face with the British housewife and they are patently unsuited to each other.' The board did not want to abandon the traditional 28 lb boxes of butter and adopt flashy consumer packs, yet it relented and gave him an advertising budget of £75,000 – a third of what New Zealand spent promoting its butter sales in England. It wasn't just the board he had to convince, but also the members of the multitude of co-ops throughout the country. Many farmers were suspicious of the young Dublin man, with the fast car and faster talk, swinging into meetings and telling them what they needed to do. Power, rapidly becoming a mentor, took a frustrated O'Reilly aside one day and putting an arm around his shoulders said in a slow, deliberate voice: 'Tony, let me tell you one thing about the Irish co-operative movement – you'll get fuck-all co-operation from it.' His situation was made more difficult by the negative and distrustful attitude of the government nominees on his board. The *Irish Farmers Journal* lampooned him in a cartoon that showed him emerging from a rugby scrum made up of New Zealanders, Australians and Danes (who are not known for playing rugby), looking like Superman but with a baby's soother in his mouth. He worked the co-ops like a politician, going to all of the creamery dinner dances, making speeches and going out onto farmers' lands to talk to men in their cowsheds.

Television and newspaper advertisements were readied and a decision was taken to hire five special 'dairymaids' to promote the brand in retail outlets, including Olive White, the Miss Ireland of the time, and Joyce again. It might not be considered acceptable in the twenty-first century world of business, but in the swinging sixties a company could launch a product by using beautiful young women in short skirts and tight tops. As it happened, the Kerrygold women turned out to be astute analysts of the potential of various shops, and their information was crucial in deciding where the concentration of supplies should be made. There were prizes for customers who completed the slogan *I have just tried Kerrygold Irish Creamery Butter and I think it is excellent because...* and sent it back on part of the wrapping they had torn off their finished packet. Little linen leprechaun dolls became highly popular prizes and extra staff in Ireland, who normally dealt with the crossword entries to the *Irish Press*, had to be brought in to clear the backlog of entries.

In its first four weeks Kerrygold managed a 18.5% market share, almost double its target, but the problem now was supply. Even so, O'Reilly decided to sell Kerrygold into Malta, Gibraltar, Cyprus, the Middle East and the USA. By 1964 this had expanded into 25 countries, including Italy, Trinidad and Lebanon. O'Reilly's ambitions grew and he got the export rights for cheese, cream, condensed milk, milk powder, butteroil and chocolate crumb, giving Bord Bainne a monopoly of all Irish dairy products. He exported all of the country's available dairy products, and in three years he grew Bord Bainne's sales to IR£20 million, which was nearly 10% of all Irish exports at the time. In 1962 Bord Bainne sold 8,300 tonnes in Britain, which had grown to 13,400 tonnes by 1966 and to 24,400 tonnes by 1970.

He may have had some luck, but he also made his own luck. With Kerrygold, O'Reilly showed what could be done with the right concept and a quality product securing a premium price. He helped focus the Irish dairy industry as an efficient producer and marketer of milk products around the world. Without the success of Bord Bainne, it is arguable as to whether Irish agribusiness powerhouses such as Kerry Group and Glanbia, which are among the biggest food ingredient companies in the world, would have followed the successful path that they did subsequently. He also served as an inspiration to other Irish exporters of all hues, giving them self-confidence, but also helping to change foreign perceptions of the pleasant but essentially feckless Irish.

There was an incident that could have derailed his achievements and further ambitions, had things turned out differently. In 1963 O'Reilly, when driving, was involved in a collision with a cyclist. It was getting dark as he drove his black Mercedes between Urlingford and Johnstown one Sunday afternoon. His story was that he was driving at around 80 miles per hour when he was dazzled by the lights of an oncoming car. Suddenly, he heard a loud thump and a scream and felt a blast of cold air on his face. He braked and stopped the car about 100 yards up the road and suddenly realised the top half of the car had been largely removed. He looked back and saw a body in the middle of the road and another man tending to it. 'That was the moment when I realised the cowardice in all of us, because my first instinct was to drive off, to hit and run.'

He was in shock, knowing that he had to go back but unable to bring himself to do so. Eventually he returned down the road to where a crowd was gathering and shouting to fetch a priest, a sign that they felt the man was going to die, or had. 'I remember seeing this bloke lying there in the road, blood pumping out of him and my whole life passing in front of me.' O'Reilly shouted that it was a doctor they needed, not a priest, although it was the latter who arrived first.

A passer-by, Jack McDonnell, recognised O'Reilly and invited him to sit with his family in his car while they waited. A garda sergeant arrived, recognised O'Reilly and sympathised with him, as did other locals who claimed the victim, James Neary, had a bit of a reputation for cycling in the middle of the road with no lights on his bike. O'Reilly got back to Dublin at midnight and went to his parents' house. Jack questioned him about the circumstances of the accident, particularly whether he had consumed alcohol, which he hadn't. Dr Dick Power, who had been at UCD with O'Reilly, was contacted at the Kilkenny hospital where Neary had been taken and reassured Tony that the victim was alive, 'but he's got a four-inch hole in the back of his head which is so big, we can see him thinking'.

A week later the *Kilkenny Journal* reported in a single paragraph that Neary had been involved in a 'collision with a motorcar', his second in a year, but did not name O'Reilly. It said Neary had no lights or reflector and was on the wrong side of the road when it happened, and he had received serious head injuries and was unconscious for a time. However, O'Reilly was formally charged with driving with undue care and attention and a few months later appeared in court. The case was heard over three days in the High Court on 7, 8 and 12 July 1965. O'Reilly defended the case in front of Mr Justice Murnaghan, but was fined £4 and his insurance company met the damages of £2,841. The case never made the newspapers; by a happy coincidence there was a national strike, starting that day. O'Reilly's brush with the law never became a talking point or an issue for him, and he was free to continue in his role at Kerrygold and put that unfortunate incident behind him.

Kerrygold remains a considerable Irish business story in itself and O'Reilly regards it as one of the greatest successes of his life, not just because of the product it became (and still is) but also because of what he learnt on the job at Bord Bainne. He realised that enthusiasm and single-mindedness were useful attributes but only if used in combination with the skills of other people, brought together in a team with common purpose. 'It was the most enjoyable job I ever had, a real voyage of discovery with a wonderful group of people,' said O'Reilly, as recently as 2011. It was a very auspicious start to his career and foreshadowed the level of success still to come.

CHAPTER FOUR

THE WORST TURNS OUT FOR THE BEST

The Bord Bainne success attracted some notice internationally. It was inextricably linked to O'Reilly's name, helped in no small part by his fame from his rugby exploits – rugby being the favoured sport of so many business owners and executives. In 1965 he was approached by the chairman of Fisons, a large British fertiliser and chemical company, to see if he might be interested in taking charge of its African interests, to be based in South Africa on an enormous salary of £25,000. O'Reilly canvassed opinion as to his options, including that of the Minister for Finance Jack Lynch, to whom he had become close. Lynch advised him to stay in Ireland, increased his salary at Bord Bainne and topped it up by putting him on the boards of the Irish Agricultural Finance Corporation and Nítrigen Éireann. O'Reilly was now on an annual income of over £4,000 per year with expenses and a car.

O'Reilly was able to live a very comfortable life on his Bord Bainne salary. He celebrated his thirtieth birthday with a big party at the new family home in Mount Merrion in Dublin, which already boasted paintings by Jack B. Yeats. He and Susan now had three children and she was pregnant with triplets. Meanwhile, his Bord Bainne office was in a Georgian building on Merrion Square and was an exceptionally large and grand room, befitting a successful man, complete with a Paul Henry painting over the carved mantelpiece. He could have said that he had it made, if that was the limit of his ambitions. It wasn't.

Lynch was central to the next big move in O'Reilly's life. He wanted him to deal with a crisis at Erin Foods, a subsidiary of the Irish Sugar Board. It had been run for years by General Michael Costello, but he had resigned after Lynch had received reports that suggested the decorated War of Independence veteran was an incompetent business executive who was costing the State a small fortune.

Costello had been in charge of the company for just over 20 years. He had forcibly broken the tradition of strikes among Irish Sugar workers. He oversaw the creation of Erin Foods in 1959, as a partnership with the co-op movement, when scientists at the company's Carlow research facilities patented a method of freeze-drying vegetables, so they could be reconstituted simply by pouring boiling water onto them. Ireland did not have a history of vegetable growing in any large scale, but Costello reckoned that could be changed, just as a sugar-growing business had been developed. Costello invested heavily in plants to freeze-dry the new supplies of peas, carrots, cabbage and potatoes and then advertised the products heavily to consumers for household and catering uses. There was initial considerable sales success in Ireland in those days before home freezers, and the products seemed to have a big future.

Costello decided that if O'Reilly had been able to sell large quantities of butter to Britain, he could do the same with freeze-dried vegetables. He would build his own sales force, however, and design his own packaging. O'Reilly later came to believe that Costello fell in love with the process by which he got his product, which was irrelevant to how customers enjoyed eating it. 'What matters is the presentation, the recipe, the taste, the capacity to engage the customer's excitement and imagination, and to deliver consistent, high-quality good taste,' said O'Reilly. 'His products didn't deliver.'

Costello had covered Erin's losses with profits from the sugar business. He didn't grow enough sugar in Ireland because it wasn't economic, so he blended the Irish output with cheap imported Caribbean cane and sold that to the various chocolate companies that had established themselves in Ireland, such as Cadbury and Rowntree. But when world sugar prices soared, his costs went up accordingly and he made heavy losses on the contracted fixed-price sales of sugar to the chocolate companies. The Irish Sugar Company plunged into heavy losses and could no longer cover the losses at Erin. Costello went to the Department of Agriculture to look for money but the minister, Charles Haughey, refused and instead hired consultants to examine the books. Losses of £4 million were identified and a need for a further £15 million investment – enormous sums in that era. Costello's prized AFD (air freeze-dried) process was already going out of fashion as frozen foods became popular, and the growing of vegetables in parts of Ireland was simply uneconomic.

O'Reilly had no real interest in the Erin Foods job – and was due to bring his pregnant wife and three children to Spain on holidays the next day – but Lynch insisted that a civil servant deliver six management consultant reports on Erin Foods, compiled by the firm of Arthur D. Little, to O'Reilly. These outlined how this business had lost £3 million on sales of £2 million the previous year in Britain. O'Reilly heard a damning critique of Costello's performance as boss of Irish Sugar and an offer of that job to O'Reilly, on behalf of the government, including its Erin Foods subsidiary. O'Reilly remained unenthusiastic, but reluctantly accepted. He said later that he went from 'the best job I ever had to the worst'.

O'Reilly demanded that he be paid whatever Costello had been paid, having heard rumours that he had an excellent contract. It was better than he could believe: he was to be paid £12,500 per year, which was more than three times his pay at Bord Bainne. He was given a chauffeured Mercedes and a driver called Arthur Whelan – or 'Wheels' as the O'Reilly children were to rechristen him – who was to remain O'Reilly's driver for decades. Olive Deasy moved with him, too.

Even before he had taken up the job the Sugar Company's finance director, Vincent Ferguson, arrived at O'Reilly's Bord Bainne office and spelt out a financial disaster worse than the one in the reports O'Reilly had received. It was to be the start of an extensive and lengthy business relationship and friendship with Ferguson, but it also convinced O'Reilly almost immediately that there might be no point in putting more money into Erin in its existing form. In the UK, Bob Norman, the local manager, told him that the company was experiencing 'negative sales': the company was having more products returned to it by retailers than it was selling in a week. Sales administration and distribution costs were 120% of the product price. There was a culture of excess in the sales force Costello had established, including a fleet of cars and generous expense accounts. Norman advised him to sell, or to partner with another food company.

O'Reilly kept quiet on the extent of the problems, leading to unreal expectations in Ireland as to what he might achieve. *Business & Finance* magazine suggested that O'Reilly 'should provide the necessary marketing expertise to help Erin Foods achieve its ambitious targets'. A week later it declared that 'Mr O'Reilly's appointment is being hailed in trade circles in Britain and Ireland as the start of a determined bid by the government to expand the entire marketing range of Irish processed food products in export markets'.

The magazine was highly influential in business circles at the time, decades before business coverage was extended in various newspapers. O'Reilly couldn't let this sit. Two of the magazine's key personnel were to become essential parts of his life from here on: the editor Nicholas Leonard would later become a key partner in various companies; and reporter Jim Milton would become his main PR consultant in Ireland, always intercepting questions for O'Reilly from the media and contacting journalists to let them know what O'Reilly was up to and why. But that was for the future.

Within three weeks of its original comments the magazine's attitude towards the future of Erin Foods – and the problems it faced – had changed dramatically and its position was now remarkably sympathetic to the way O'Reilly was thinking privately. It reported that 'The government has decided to postpone for a year the crucial decision on whether Erin Foods is to go all out for expansion at an estimated capital cost of £15 million, or whether it should be content with lesser objectives. This postponement is understandable with the resignation of Lieut. Gen. Costello and the appointment of Mr O'Reilly. Reappraisal at senior management level has inevitably been delayed.'

O'Reilly took up the job formally in December 1966 and began a tour of potential partners for the Erin Foods business. Seventeen of the target companies he approached showed no interest. Norman had worked with Heinz previously and he arranged for O'Reilly to meet Tony Beresford, the company's UK boss. By the end of their meeting Beresford was interested in Erin Foods as a source of raw vegetables and meat for his factories in Britain. They agreed to further talks in the New Year.

O'Reilly had domestic issues to which he had to attend: the birth of the triplets on 17 December. He planned a holiday in the Canary Islands with Susan and flew out on 12 January. There he was joined by

Charles Haughey. Ferguson was left in Dublin to run the numbers with Heinz and O'Reilly was worried about being out of their depth in negotiations with a big multinational company. The idea that he and Ferguson had developed, with Haughey approving, was for the establishment of a joint venture: Heinz-Erin.

Once he returned to Ireland, O'Reilly brought the Heinz executives to see the Erin factories in Mallow, Thurles and Carlow, all of which had been built adjacent to the sugar plants. Remarkably, given his known attention to detail, as he waited for Beresford in Cork Airport O'Reilly realised that he was going to be showing off plants he had not seen himself. He had to run ahead of Beresford at each location to tell the local plant managers to pretend that O'Reilly was a regular visitor. He got away with it. Costello had not skimped on laboratories and production facilities and Beresford was sufficiently impressed to decide that he wanted to go ahead with a deal. Beresford wanted a R&D capability that he felt Heinz lacked. Erin Foods had invested heavily in horticultural development and it was the one investment made by Costello that paid off. Beresford only got approval for the investment from head office in Pittsburgh after Heinz insisted that two of its American executives be included on the new Heinz-Erin board.

O'Reilly and Haughey worked hard together on the presentation of the deal to the public. Haughey announced it in the Dáil as being 'clearly in the national interest', but there were many loud complaints about a giveaway. Costello led the charge and continued it for years to come, partly defending his own legacy but also motivated by a genuine sense that the national interest was not being served and that he was right notwithstanding what evidence was offered to the contrary. His condemnation of the deal was based more on nationalistic rhetoric than commercial logic. He described the deal as a betrayal and sell-out, a cave-in to 'foreigners' and to the British, in particular, even though Heinz was ultimately American-owned. 'The widespread goodwill for Erin Foods is being used to promote a foreign owned brand name,' he said. He criticised the 'servile role' played by the Erin Foods sales force in Ireland, the promotion of 'the sales of products made in foreign factories, produced in foreign countries, at prices higher than those paid to Irish farmers.' He said it 'was like other foreign firms, looking for something for nothing or something for little, anyway. In fact, they got something for nothing. Nobody had anything to gain in this country, but naturally enough the people who delivered to Heinz had a lot to gain.'

O'Reilly obviously thought the opposite; he felt lucky to have done a deal and felt that, in the circumstances, 'I'd done a damn good job'. There was agreement in the pages of *The Irish Times*, where it was described as 'a better solution for the farmers' predicament than anyone could have foreseen' and had got the government 'off an unpleasant hook'. O'Reilly had proved himself a 'formidable negotiator in bringing such a complicated arrangement to a successful conclusion within three months of the first round of talks'. Haughey was also praised: 'he has made his decision and given approval with record swiftness'.

O'Reilly was dismissive of Costello and his arguments. 'The fact that his views and mine don't always coincide is a matter of his judge-ment and mine as to how economics operate,' he said. 'Costello was a patriot, but he was also a bully. His patriotism blinded him to the commercial realities of the marketplace. Costello had an enormous social experiment that he was conducting covertly under his great cover profit gleaned through cheap sugar cane prices, and he had put plants into improbable places which were hostile to growing vegetables. You just can't grow vegetables competitively on the hillsides of Donegal.' O'Reilly felt, correctly, that the real future for Irish agriculture lay in beef and dairying and not in horticulture.

Erin Foods and Irish Sugar never provided O'Reilly with the excite-ment of Bord Bainne. It was a more negative environment, involving cutting and repairing, instead of the ambitious growth he had sought and achieved at Bord Bainne. It had its compensations, mostly financial. O'Reilly's enhanced salary allowed him to move his much bigger family to a far bigger home. He purchased a Georgian house called Columbia, at Delgany in Wicklow. It had acres of grounds and woods at the edge of the sea, views as far as Greystones and the Wicklow coast and its own gate lodge and a long, tree-lined driveway. It was just an hour's drive from Dublin. He added a tennis court and a swimming pool and converted two acres into glasshouses where he grew tomatoes commercially. He hired Jim Kelly as farm manager, who again stayed with him until retirement. Susan loved the new house, but it curtailed her involvement with Tony at the many dinners he attended in Dublin. He was around more at the weekends when he insisted on large lunches and dinners for many guests, with his parents regularly in attendance.

O'Reilly developed his relationship with Heinz further. By 1969 the sale of Erin Foods products, packaged soups and catering packs was put in the control of the Heinz sales force as the relationship between the companies deepened. He visited Pittsburgh, his first time in the USA, soon after the creation of Heinz-Erin had been completed. He travelled on the last voyage of the *Queen Mary*, leaving Southampton on 31 October 1967, then met with Burt Gookin, CEO of Heinz. He played tennis, attended meetings and saw the local sights, but most importantly, he formed a good impression of the company – as it did of him.

CHAPTER FIVE

THE MODERN FACE
OF HEINZ

When he visited Pittsburgh for the first time, O'Reilly made a big impression on Heinz CEO Burt Gookin. This only became apparent to him several years later, when he pulled his own personnel file upon his arrival to Heinz in a senior position. Gookin had so liked O'Reilly's charm that he had earmarked O'Reilly not just for a senior role with Heinz in the UK – which is what he got initially – but in Pittsburgh, too. Gookin had spoken to Jack Heinz about the young Irish executive and between them they secretly hatched a plan to phase in O'Reilly via the UK subsidiary.

Gookin first approached Beresford in late 1968, to ask if he would approve of O'Reilly as his replacement now that he was approaching his sixtieth birthday. Beresford was asked to remain as vice-chairman, to guide O'Reilly given his lack of experience in UK business, but O'Reilly also had to be persuaded. Gookin decided to pitch the job while on a golfing trip to Ireland that took in visits to the Irish Heinz-Erin plants. He offered a salary of US$75,000 plus share options and other sweeteners that made the entire package worth more than US$100,000 annually. O'Reilly was already exceptionally well paid by Irish standards, but this would give him three times as much, and hints were dropped as to further progress if he did well managing the 12,000 Heinz employees in Britain. He was thrilled, but did not accept immediately.

O'Reilly rang Jack Lynch. The Taoiseach, on his way to an official function, swung by the car park of the Sugar Company and O'Reilly jumped into the State car for a chat, during which he explained his position. He told Lynch that he was torn between his personal opportunity and his ambition to serve the State. Friends of O'Reilly claimed subsequently that Lynch offered him the position of Minister for Agriculture if he stayed, promising to accommodate him by making him a Senator, where a vacancy was due to arise.

That claim has gone into folklore and has been treated as fact for many years, but some remain sceptical, and indeed disbelieving, that Lynch would have done such a thing. The former government press secretary Frank Dunlop said: 'It is true that the two men knew and liked each other – both had been sporting heroes and Jack certainly admired O'Reilly's management skills – but to offer a high-profile Cabinet job to somebody not even remotely involved in party politics would have been completely at odds with the political culture of the time and caused considerable ill-feeling amongst TDs, to say nothing of serving ministers.'

That would have been especially true in Haughey's case, because he saw himself as Lynch's successor sooner rather than later and did not want a rival emerging, most especially not one getting preferential treatment.

'When I asked Jack Lynch about the story I got neither a denial nor a confirmation,' said Dunlop. 'O'Reilly had a holiday home in west Cork at which Jack was sometimes a dinner guest. I was left with the impression that at some stage when he was Taoiseach in the late sixties, he had asked O'Reilly for advice about something or other and, having received some words of wisdom, said something to the effect that he wished he had him in his Cabinet as Minister for Agriculture. I can imagine him making such a remark. I can also imagine him doing so in the hope that it might do O'Reilly no harm.'

It wasn't enough for O'Reilly to have received a brilliant job offer, which would attract great attention and praise, he also had to have it be known that he had passed up on great opportunities in taking it.

Surprisingly, given his known closeness to Fianna Fáil, Fine Gael also courted O'Reilly at the time. Its approach to stand for the party in the 1969 general election was made to him on Liam Cosgrave's behalf by Garret FitzGerald. 'I had the authority of the party to talk to him,' FitzGerald said later. 'I wasn't authorised, so far as I can recall, to say to him that he would be a minister, but he obviously would have had a good prospect of ministerial office given his abilities. But then he got the offer of the Heinz job in England. And he said to me: "Garret, if I get the Heinz job I can make a hundred thousand pounds clear in five years and come back and enter full-time into politics".

Nonetheless, O'Reilly spoke afterwards of agonising over the decision and of being influenced by Susan, who was prepared to put up with a lot but who would not be in favour at all of him engaging in a political career. 'It's not that I am not interested in politics and the political process,' he said later. 'Having been with Bord Bainne and the Irish Sugar Company, I was aware of the enormous impact of politics at local and national levels and the Minister for Agriculture was a supreme figure. But I did not want to become a party politician.'

He accepted a five-year contract with Heinz UK. He told Gookin and Beresford that he would join Heinz but that he also wanted to retain close contact with Ireland, where his 'emotional and intellectual involvement' lay. He wanted the right to have separate commercial interests, as long as he could show that they did not interfere with Heinz. Instead of playing golf at weekends he would be playing 'Celtic Monopoly'. He further insisted on bringing Olive as secretary and Arthur as driver and said he wasn't available to start until May 1969. The demands constituted an enormous show of chutzpah on his part, but Heinz agreed to it all.

When O'Reilly arrived, Heinz UK had the dominant market share in products like baby food, and very large shares in ketchup, canned soups, pickles, baked beans, salad cream and spreads. He invested heavily in television advertising and got the reward of significantly increased sales and market shares. He had inherited a US$30 million investment in plant and facilities and increased the sum committed. He found that he was able to achieve his goals without too much difficulty.

He decided to move the family to a large house in Farnham Common, a half-hour from Heinz's Middlesex office, instead of leaving them in Delgany. He had Arthur, now living with the family, drive him each day. He went to regular meetings in the City. In a comment to Fallon that may explain why he later accepted the knighthood, Susan said: 'You could see it pleased him very much to be asked up to the City for a lunch, and he always felt they were just slightly condescending because he was Irish, and he would come back feeling wonderful because he had run rings around them all intellectually. So it was a very challenging time for him personally there, but it was a personal challenge of proving that he was superior to most of the people he was mixing with.'

Susan had not been concerned about moving to England with him; her big commitment had been not returning to Australia. It was hard for her with so many small children and her husband's habit of either being out socialising or bringing people to his home. Olive came to live with them, too, helping with the child-minding, as did Arthur. Susan said that she 'realised, very early in our marriage, that we were not going to have many intimate dinners alone together. There were always going to be hundreds of people around'. On other occasions she said, somewhat poignantly, that to eat with Tony alone they would have to go out from their own home, and that even then, as they would always meet somebody, she could hardly remember ever having a romantic meal alone. It was very different from the time when he was seeking her hand.

He also began travelling more extensively for work, joining international Heinz management conferences for which he prepared assiduously. Don Wiley, later to become the main legal counsel at Heinz, described O'Reilly's arrival at a resort called The Cloisters, at Sea Island in Georgia, soon after he took over in the UK: 'That was the first time Tony came, and he was delightful. Everyone took to him immediately. But I don't recall any of us thinking he was designated in any formal way as Gookin's successor. He was obviously headed for higher things, sure, but Gookin didn't tell any of us what he had in mind. When Burt appointed him, I had thought – as most others I talked to did – that it was a gutsy move on his part, hiring a young Irish Catholic out of Dublin to go and run that bastion of British industry, the Heinz UK company. But they really needed someone like Tony over there.'

O'Reilly networked extensively and effectively. He played tennis with the others, ran and swam, and performed Gilbert and Sullivan and Irish songs on the piano. After his trips to Pittsburgh – and the rounds of dinners at various houses of the directors – he remarked that the well-educated, rich American was far more of an archetypal old-style gentleman than anything he had seen in Ireland or England. He was impressed, and he wanted more of it.

In October 1969 he decided to play rugby again, this time with London Irish, as if he didn't have enough to do, especially with six young children at home. His interest in rugby had been occasional since he had finished with the Irish international team in 1963 because of his business commitments. He had taken the captaincy of the Old Belvedere club team for the 1963/64 season, even though his commitments with Bord Bainne were many. He would arrive in his Mercedes shortly before the game was due to start or travel in a separate carriage on the train, dictating to his secretary Olive Deasy, who came with him, initially to the astonishment of the other players. There were stories of the kick-offs being delayed until he arrived. The season was unsuccessful. He was ready to play the 1964/65 season but got injured, and then in 1965 he tore his Achilles' tendon and lost the next three seasons as a result. Now aged 33, he played his first game in first-class rugby for five years against Bath and had one try disallowed. He played in seven of the team's next 14 games, but made relatively little impact.

In mid-February 1970 he was partying in Annabel's nightclub in Berkeley Square when he got a phone call from Ronnie Dawson, his old Lions captain who was now the Irish team coach. He was needed at the grounds of the Honourable Artillery Company in the City the following morning for a training session. The winger, Billy Brown, had injured his ankle and might not be fit to play at Twickenham against England on Saturday. O'Reilly returned home at 3.00am and tried to get some sleep, not least because he also had a Heinz UK board meeting that morning.

He left that meeting early and was chauffeured by Arthur to the training session, where the media was waiting. Whelan opened the car door for his boss with a salute, giving the following day's newspapers another angle to the story. The Irish captain, Willie John McBride, took a look at O'Reilly in the dressing-room and smiled: 'Well Tony, in my view your best attacking move tomorrow might be to shake your jowls at them.'

Brown failed the fitness test on a snow-covered ground and O'Reilly was in. 'To say this is the most bizarre situation in international rugby for many years is to make an understatement,' wrote Paul McWeeney in *The Irish Times*. 'This is a gambler's throw and there must be many who are apprehensive as to its value.' Back in Ireland, many rugby fans said it was unfair on a young player called Frank O'Driscoll, who should have been given his chance. Frank never got to play for Ireland, but his son Brian would later make up for that.

As they ran onto the pitch one of the English team commented to O'Reilly: 'Tony, we'll never be able to get past you, there just isn't room on the pitch'. He hardly saw the ball during the game, not receiving a single pass. Even his line-out throwing, the job of the winger in those days, was criticised, as he struggled to throw the ball straight, as required. England won 9-3, courtesy of three Richard Hiller penalties, but at least O'Reilly got another story out of the day for his after-dinner speeches – and this was one that needed little embellishment: 'At the very last minute I was suddenly reduced to bravery. A long English rush was terminated when – completely out of character – I dived at the feet of the English pack. As I emerged from momentary unconsciousness, I heard a loud and, I must confess, Irish voice, shouting from the crowded terrace: "And while you're at it, why don't ya kick his fuckin' chauffeur too?"' Tom Kiernan, the Lions captain in 1962 and full-back on the Irish team that day, subsequently called it O'Reilly's 'guest appearance' and said that 'It was the most unusual thing I experienced at Twickenham. That was saying something: O'Reilly had written the programme notes for the game in his guise as a former international.

It was the end of O'Reilly's rugby career, although not of his love of the game. He would be inducted into Rugby Union's Hall of Fame in 2007, an acknowledgement that his career, while quite short, was quite brilliant. He only played 12 times for Leinster, captaining the team twice. He played 13 games for Ireland in the centre and 16 on the wing. He played 22 consecutive games from 1955 to February 1960, earned six more caps between 1961 and 1963 and received his last cap in 1970. He scored five tries, and should have been credited with a sixth in a game against Scotland. He played 10 test matches for the British & Irish Lions, nine on the wing and one in the centre, scoring six tries. He did not participate in any Triple Crown (beating England, Wales and Scotland in a single season) or Grand Slam (adding in France as well) winning team, to his great regret. His career came at a price: he dislocated both shoulders numerous times, broke his leg and nose, lost many teeth and, most significantly in later life, suffered a number of back injuries.

He had a profile and an image for many Irish people, and the wider rugby community, that can be compared to what Brian O'Driscoll enjoyed in the twenty-first century. O'Reilly's profile could not be exploited commercially because of the strict amateur status of the game at the time, but he used the contacts developed through sport in his career. The game taught him how to win and lose, the euphoria of success, the disappointment of defeat. It instructed him in how to be part of a team, but also how to stand out as part of one.

O'Reilly always acknowledged his debt to the game in the many interviews he conducted during his business career. 'Good health and energy which gave me the ability to shine as a sportsman,' he subsequently told *People* magazine in 1974. 'Rugby taught me training, pace and instinct. Confidence. Academic achievement. Hard work. A keen sense of danger – the ability to know when something's going to go wrong.'

'Where rugby did help was in sharpening one's sense of combat,' he told Jeffrey Robinson for the book *The Risk Takers* in 1990. 'In drawing a clear correlation between reward and effort, there's nothing as obvious as a fellow who hasn't trained in the heat of battle. You have to learn to roll with the punches. Effort brings its own reward. From the point of view of training in a discipline, football, or indeed any sport is damn good, but football, be it soccer or rugby, has the added dimension that in the final analysis your excellence as a player is terribly dependent on other people … Particularly if you played where I did on the right wing or the left wing where you're at the end of a long chain of consequence. If the ball doesn't reach you in the right mode, you can end up in the local hospital.'

O'Reilly was two years into his UK Heinz contract when Gookin told him he wanted to move him to Pittsburgh. He was offered a seat on the main board of Heinz, with the title of 'senior vice president – north America and Pacific'. Most significantly, John Connell, the man regarded as most likely to succeed Gookin, was transferred to Britain. O'Reilly, the youngest member on the board, was now one of 10 people in the corporate headquarters who controlled everything. But again, before agreeing to the move, he insisted that he be allowed to continue develop his personal Irish business interests. Again Heinz acquiesced. 'I talked to my first boss at Heinz', recalled O'Reilly, 'and said, "I have a business in Ireland that I might go back to one day, do you mind?" And he said, "Tony, let me tell you about America. If the price of Heinz stock goes up, you've got a job. If it goes down, you'll be back in Ireland picking potatoes again".'

Like so many Irish of previous generations the O'Reilly family decamped for the USA on a ship, but this journey was to be entirely different. This family, accompanied by a nanny and grandparents Jack and Aileen, and the two family dogs, travelled on the QE2, in the lap of luxury. The six children were aged between four and seven years old and came to dine with their parents each evening. 'You could see the couples seated at tables for two gaping at this, thinking: "Jesus, they must have another potato famine in Ireland, they're coming at us in waves", chortled O'Reilly. On arrival in New York the family was whisked off to stay at the Berkeley Hotel and then enjoyed a week seeing the sights. Eventually they boarded the private Heinz jet, which brought them the rest of the way to Pittsburgh.

Their new home, in Fox Chapel, was a 15-room, Tudor-style house overlooking a golf course. On the manicured 14-acre grounds there was a greenhouse, a Scottish rose garden, a Japanese garden with arched wooden footbridge, a swimming pool, tennis courts and a front lawn as big as a rugby pitch. It had its own chapel, the previous occupant being so devout that the local bishop often called to say Mass for her. That wasn't the most important reason for O'Reilly to want it: although Pittsburgh is a hilly city, the back garden was flat and indeed big enough to cater for a rugby or American football pitch, which he installed. He bought the property for US$250,000.

Pittsburgh was an industrial city, originally based on the steel industry. There were still 120,000 steelworkers employed in the city when O'Reilly arrived, but the number declined to just one-tenth within a decade, making the financial health and presence of Heinz even more important economically, and indeed psychologically. It was a city of powerful families, such as the Mellons – of Irish stock, who controlled Gulf Oil, Koppers and Alcoa, as well as Mellon Bank, all headquartered in the city – the Carnegies, Fricks and Westinghouses. It had a large Irish contingent, but also large Greek, Russian, Italian and German communities. O'Reilly liked to call it 'the most international village in America'.

O'Reilly went to work, finding out how the systems operated at Heinz headquarters, where the power resided. Gookin was what O'Reilly regarded as a 'dry accountant', but the more he got to know him, the more he liked him. Gookin had brought Heinz from a near bankrupt state to a much more efficient, stable company: he had laid the foundations upon which O'Reilly would build. The pair worked closely for an hour each morning at around 7.30am in Gookin's office, discussing issues and personnel.

Some of his new colleagues admitted subsequently to being awe-struck by O'Reilly's range of abilities and his charisma. 'He had this huge personality, and quick wit, and was the best speech-maker I had ever heard in my life. He could sing and play piano, tell jokes, quote Oscar Wilde or Churchill – and he knew more about your business than you did,' said Dick Beattie, one of the Heinz executives. Not everybody liked him, at least initially. 'Before I met Tony,' admitted Ray Good, 'I hated him. I just couldn't believe the fantastic build-up he was getting.' Good was later promoted to be head of Heinz US and became an O'Reilly fan. But others were not converted. 'He was charmingly demanding or demandingly charming,' said Charles Berger, an executive who left.

O'Reilly went out of his way to win over people with his sociability. The Fox Chapel home regularly hosted weekend parties, at least when he wasn't going back to Ireland. With Heinz, he started a tradition of an annual game of touch American football between management from 'world headquarters' and 'Heinz USA'. It was an idea copied from the Kennedys and became a major Heinz event, known as the 'Souperbowl'. It placed O'Reilly right at the heart of the company, with families involved, but with business conducted as much as pleasure obtained. The sport all became very serious, as O'Reilly liked to show off his running ability, albeit in a different game.

O'Reilly found the patrician chairman Jack Heinz, who had handed over the chief executive role to Gookin, somewhat harder work to win over. This Heinz was a remarkable character, too, but of almost aristocratic demeanour or, as O'Reilly described him, as of 'stratospheric elegance'. Three times married, friends of British royalty and of the richest and most famous, highly educated, successful as an adventurer, incredibly curious (having toured the Soviet Union 22 times, including during the height of the Cold War), Heinz was not easily impressed by rising stars in an organisation he had run since 1941 after his father died suddenly. He was energetic and autocratic and demanded the respect of being called Mister Heinz whereas everyone else was on first-name terms. He was interested in advertising and PR, and in the nutrition of the foods, but O'Reilly came to realise that his chairman had a weakness when it came to the financials. He was not a professional manager. Under Jack's watch, Heinz had experienced crisis in 1963, as its profits in the USA disappeared and it maintained its market strength merely in ketchup and vinegar. Jack was not persuaded until 1966 that he had to take a part-time role as chairman, for the company's good; he resented Gookin for that.

O'Reilly, reckoning that the family lineage meant Jack was going nowhere, decided he had to get onside with the older man. To do so, he had to discover the traditions of the company within the city – and when he did that, he understood what a legacy it was with which he hoped to be entrusted. Heinz was a pioneer in the American food industry, from bottling horseradish at the time of the American civil war, revolutionising production methods and deeply influencing kitchen habits. The first Heinz also had a flair for marketing, putting his product in clear glass bottles, enabling buyers to know that his products were of the highest quality and not adulterated by fillers. Even in the 1970s the company was boasting that quality was its first priority.

O'Reilly's confidence was such that in 1972, just nine months after arriving, he requested that Gookin make him responsible for all operations worldwide. In October 1972, the Irishman was made executive vice-president and chief operating officer (COO), raising him above all other vice-presidents and making him the second highest ranked executive at Heinz, on a salary, before perks, of $250,000. The likes of John Crossen, moved to be head of Heinz in Europe and South America, resented the promotion, attributing it to the excellence of O'Reilly's self-promotion more than his ability at the job. 'His ambition was so patently obvious,' said Crossen later, 'but you had to admire his skill. He was a very charming guy – in the Irish way.'

O'Reilly quickly tightened his grip, introducing an annual week-long management session at which each executive had to present a paper on the past year, immediate plans and budget for the next year. It was nerve-wrecking for many of those making presentations, particularly because of O'Reilly's remarkable recall, without the aid of written notes, of discussions that took place months or even years previously.

As his reputation soared, Heinz began to fear that he might return to Ireland to tend to his investments there – and O'Reilly encouraged the speculation. He sought the position of company president. Gookin agreed; having identified O'Reilly as his likely successor many years earlier, he didn't want to go looking for a new one now. When the chairman announced his promotion, he lauded his choice as 'a unique guy. He has the disciplined mind of a lawyer. He's a highly creative marketing man, and a natural Irish humanist'.

The *Financial Times* in 1973 focused on the amount of time O'Reilly was spending on his interests outside of Heinz. Challenged as to how he managed his time, O'Reilly quipped, 'I don't play golf'. That was fine, but only to a point, because nobody at Heinz had expected him to develop quite as many outside interests as he had. 'Put at its simplest, no-one in, around or associated with Heinz can accuse the executive vice-president of not putting in the hours on their behalf,' observed the *Financial Times*. 'But they can, and indeed they do, say along the Heinz cocktail party circuit out in Pittsburgh that he does not neglect his own interests in the process.'

O'Reilly was aware of the high-wire act in which he was engaged. In August 1973 *Forbes* magazine noted that it wasn't just that he was a foreigner that raised eyebrows upon his promotion – as that hadn't stopped other large US companies doing likewise – or that he had been with the company only six years: 'What seemed strange was that O'Reilly had, and will keep, extensive business interests outside Heinz.'

O'Reilly replied that in Ireland he remained 'merely an investor strategically employing my capital. I am not at all involved in management, and investment decisions don't require as much time as management.' Pressed further he replied, 'Perhaps I have a schizoid personality. I love challenges and the one at Heinz is important to me. It means I have competed successfully against some of the best managerial talent in the world.'

The results at Heinz kept improving, earning O'Reilly protection and praise. He also continued the habit of giving regular interviews to newspapers and magazines, believing that he could charm any interviewer into writing favourably about him. It satisfied his ego, but it also created an impression of him from which he could profit. It was like the saying: 'give a man a reputation for getting up early in the morning and he can stay in bed until midday'.

The issue would not go away, however. In November 1974 *People* wrote of his 'double life' as Heinz chief and Irish tycoon. 'I guess I play the corporate game the same way I played rugby,' he told the magazine. 'I used to stand around on the field for long periods, then I'd move. Masterly inactivity, you might call it. I felt if there was only going to be one of two chances to make a long run that would lead to points on the scoreboard, I had to conserve my energy for them.' At Heinz, 'I play my cards as close as I can to my chest, then do something so dramatically different that the defense is all running the wrong way.'

In his 1976 chairman's report Jack Heinz noted that it had taken the group more than a century to reach sales of $1 billion, but 'now, only four years later we are well on our way to the second billion'. Profits were touching $100 million – a 135% increase since O'Reilly joined – and the renewal of the American business, which Gookin had started but O'Reilly had driven, was getting praised on Wall Street.

O'Reilly was visible and his personality and drive were given credit for improving the direction and philosophy of the company. He dominated strategy discussions. Now the shareholder statement at the front of the annual report was signed by Jack Heinz, Gookin and O'Reilly. He was given credit for tightening stock controls, improved marketing efforts, the removal of low-volume and low-margin products and the seeking out of new replacements. He spent considerable time working on tomato ketchup, trying to improve production, benefiting particularly from the irrigation of the Californian desert, where ketchup tomatoes (as distinct from salad tomatoes) were then grown in volume. Surprisingly, Heinz ketchup had been losing money and market share. O'Reilly was to benefit from a technological breakthrough made before his arrival: instead of making ketchup from fresh tomatoes, the company's scientists developed a process of making tomato paste, which could be transported in bulk, stored and turned into ketchup throughout the year. The supply was no longer tied to the year's harvest. O'Reilly joined at a time of a further breakthrough: a new strain of firmer, crack-resistant, disease-free tomato, with a thicker skin, higher pectin and better colour, as hard as an orange. Now the production of ketchup could be done in a much smaller number of plants.

O'Reilly wanted to abandon the concentration on sales volume and to focus on profit margins. 'Heinz made a god of volume, as a lot of American companies do, so we shot the god of volume and we elevated a new god called mix.' All waste and unprofitable lines were to be eliminated. The process led to the closure of 14 factories and the removal of 8,000 jobs. Even though Heinz was founded on pickles, O'Reilly decided to reduce the company's involvement in the business, to some internal dismay given that the company was as associated with pickles as with tomato ketchup.

'A cradle-to-grave mentality and a way of life was over,' wrote Eleanor Foa Dienstag in her history of Heinz. 'For some it was the beginning of the end. For others it was the day the sleeping giant, Heinz USA, at last awoke.'

O'Reilly was a powerful presence at the presentations to stockbroker analysts. He could explain his company's charts flawlessly and was able to command the relevant information to almost every question that was asked of him. He remembered the name of every analyst and was usually able to quote back at them any research about Heinz, or its competitors, that they had produced, or make reference to questions they had asked the year before. It was flattering to them, but it was also a powerful tool for him to use.

O'Reilly strengthened his position at times by letting it be known that he had been courted by other American companies, such as Seagrams, the alcoholic drinks company, and CBS, the television broadcaster. In March 1977 the board decided that O'Reilly would become CEO in July 1979 on Gookin's retirement, and would also retain the title of president. O'Reilly was to be only the fifth CEO in Heinz's history.

Before he took on the position he made a rare acquisition of another major business, one that came to be synonymous with him. The purchase of WeightWatchers, the famous diet business, came about almost by accident. A meeting had come about because of another acquisition Heinz was making of a company with which WeightWatchers had a connection. The main shareholder in WeightWatchers was an elderly American called Al Lippert. He and O'Reilly took to each other immediately at this meeting. 'It was, I would say, love at first sight, or fascination at first sight,' Lippert said later. 'I was so impressed with his vitality and his knowledge and his personality that basically we spent two hours just swopping stories, telling each other jokes and talking about incidents which had occurred in our lives.'

Lippert had suffered three heart attacks and wanted to sell the business, but couldn't find a buyer he believed to be suitable. He believed fully in his concept of re-educating people's eating habits. He had dropped 53 lb in weight by using the method; his wife had shed 50 lb. 'There are no gimmicks, no secrets, no pills – it's just an honest effort to teach people what we ourselves have learnt,' he said. WeightWatchers wasn't really a food company. Its core business was a classroom system aimed at women aged between 25 and 55 years who wanted to lose weight. It was a self-help support system, almost a food version of Alcoholics Anonymous. Lippert expanded it using a franchise system and probably his more inspired business decision was to register the WeightWatchers trademark throughout the world.

O'Reilly wanted to manufacture the food that these women were being encouraged to eat, but he also saw an opportunity for diversification – a business connected to food but with retail possibilities in a growing market, not just in the USA but worldwide. He met Lippert again and he was so impressed by his innovative flair, he decided that not only did he want to buy the company but bring him onto the Heinz board, too. A deal was done at Castlemartin, valuing WeightWatchers at $72 million. It brought Heinz into a service business that Heinz, until then solely a food manufacturer, knew nothing about. It was a rare innovative move at Heinz on O'Reilly's part, where management rather than entrepreneurship was the watchword. Gambles were something he kept for his Irish interests.

CHAPTER SIX

BECOMING INDEPENDENT

A s often as 20 times a year O'Reilly would leave the Heinz HQ in Pittsburgh late on Friday afternoon, head for the airport and catch a flight to New York. At JFK Airport he would board the overnight flight to Dublin. He would spend the weekend attending to his Irish businesses, and partying into the small hours of Sunday morning. He would then fly back on Sunday evening, usually via London because there wasn't a suitably timed Dublin outbound flight, unless he had a reason to fly somewhere else on Heinz business. He would always be in Gookin's office before him on Monday morning, asking him how the weekend golf had been, as if that had been his occupation too. He was fortunate enough to be delayed only occasionally by bad weather or missed flights. It was a somewhat insane schedule, both physically and mentally, and one that few people would have attempted, but his acolytes insisted that he undertook it with exceptional good humour and that tiredness did not affect his judgement.

He had good reason to push himself like this: there was a lot of money at stake. The Irish commercial interests that O'Reilly purchased and extended in parallel with his Heinz career were substantial, to say the least. Over the period of the first six years in which he worked at Heinz, O'Reilly looked as if he had created great wealth in Ireland out of near nothing, which added to the growing legend; he soon found himself standing on the edge of a financial precipice, however, with a great load of debt pushing him from behind, due to a combination of circumstances beyond his control and his own poor judgement and ill-considered ambition. A situation developed at his Irish businesses that would have taxed the confidence and character of most, that would have been a full-time obsession as the stakes rose, yet O'Reilly carried it at a time when he was climbing near the top of the corporate ladder at one of America's most famous companies. On top of this, the fact that he would, and could, endure the physical challenge of crossing the Atlantic at weekends created plenty of speculation as to what was going on in O'Reilly's head. It was no surprise that his business colleagues, investors, the media and indeed some of the general public asked questions about the appropriateness and sustainability of his double life. It was a question that was repeated often until he retired from an executive role in Heinz in 1997 and, in the latter years, with vehemence in some quarters.

It seemed that while Heinz was a solid career, it was too much like 'dry accounting' to O'Reilly, who couldn't resist the wild call of the speculative side of business. While others would have salted away their growing wealth and enjoyed their leisure time, O'Reilly sought out more business challenges, apparently needing to be visible on an Irish stage, desiring both money and affirmation from the public, as well as the self-satisfaction of achievement. He leaped at Vincent Ferguson's suggestion that they set up a company that itself would buy other companies, in full or in part, and that would do so quickly to create a group of companies of considerable scale. As they had little money, Ferguson's idea was that they should buy a small company – known in the jargon as a 'shell' – and then issue further shares in it as payment for any companies they bought, instead of cash – as was becoming an increasingly common and controversial practice in the USA and Britain. While the issue of new shares would dilute the holding of original shareholdings – for example, where there might have been 1,000 shares in issue there would be 2,000 now, meaning that if O'Reilly had once held 50% of the holding company he would now have just 25% – the idea was that the value of the company would increase and the smaller percentage shareholding of the bigger entity would be worth more than a big share of a small company. Once they reached a certain scale, they could then borrow even more money to buy even more businesses. It wouldn't necessarily matter what type of companies they were – or if they had any relationship to each other –

as long they thought they could increase the profits at those companies through better management. The optimal situation would be to take over ailing or underperforming, but potentially profitable companies, and then turn them around by getting rid of existing management and substituting their own instead. Nicholas Leonard, the former *Business & Finance* editor, who now worked with Allied Irish Investment Bank (AIIB) and with Ferguson, was the third promoter of the idea.

Ferguson and Leonard secretly worked out the plans and structures for their new company while working with AIIB. O'Reilly used his contacts in Britain to interest National Westminster Bank, banker to Heinz, in becoming an investor. It agreed that its Irish subsidiary, Ulster Bank, would buy 25% of the capital of this new company and put in another £400,000 in loans. O'Reilly had 30% of the shares and Ferguson and Leonard 22.5% each. It now had £500,000 to spend; all it had to do was find something to buy.

The first purchase was a company called Crowe Wilson, a wholesale draper and warehouse business that made modest profits and kept a low profile. Its main asset was its stock market listing and its ability to issue shares quickly and relatively cheaply. They offered £446,250 for a one-third share of Crowe Wilson, and it was accepted. Once the deal was completed the new company, which was to be named Fitzwilliam Securities, took two rented rooms at 5 Lower Merrion Street. The name was taken from the city's elite tennis club, to create an impression of age and stature for something that was brand new and out of nothing. Frank Lemass, brother of the former Taoiseach Seán Lemass, was brought in as deputy chairman.

The deal was completed on the day that O'Reilly announced he was moving to Heinz in the USA. Other investors bought the shares in the hope and expectation of being part of something very valuable: Crowe Wilson shares quickly doubled in price because of hype, not because anything had been done. That was only the start of it: Crowe Wilson, boosted by plenty of favourable press and some acquisitions, increased its stock exchange value ten-fold in the following 12 months.

O'Reilly's aspirations for the company were set out in a letter he wrote to Dr Alan Mooney, the Crowe Wilson chairman, in February 1972. He acknowledged criticisms that he was engaged in a form of pyramid selling to the public, that people buying the shares were betting, not investing. 'I emphasise, however, that there is no substitute for good management,' he wrote. 'All the pyramiding in the world will turn to nothing if the underlying management skills, attention to detail and constructive business building processes are not handled with care and attention. It is dull, it is demanding, but it is essential. I am placing particular pressure on Vincent and Nicholas at this juncture, to ensure that these management processes receive detailed attention from them and that they provide Bob Dalzell, Jim McCarthy, Ronald Crampton, John Moore and to a lesser extent Sean McKone, with constructive support, critical examination and an enlightened approach to their financial problems.'

All of the names that O'Reilly had listed had become involved as executives with Crowe Wilson as it engaged in a process of rapid growth by acquisition. 'If this is not done, our businesses will not develop with that cohesion which is precedent to sustained profit,' he said. He wrote again to Mooney later that month confirming that he, Ferguson and Leonard 'have had nothing other than paper benefit in direct financial terms since the original investment. They, or indeed I should say we, are still some way away from being in a position to actually realise cash from the paper wealth which has been created'.

The first big acquisition was the wholesale and retail hardware specialists Thomas Dockrell and Co., one of the main suppliers to the building trade in Dublin. It was old, established, under-capitalised and had strong asset backing, with largely uninvolved shareholders and a far from dynamic board of directors. It was chaired by Fine Gael TD Maurice Dockrell, who was seduced by the potential of a tie-up with O'Reilly's ambitions. Its shares were rated cheaply by comparison with Crowe Wilson's. It was also going to be the opportunity for O'Reilly to introduce his best friend, Jim McCarthy, to his business orbit. In October 1971 Dockrell's announced that it had purchased JS McCarthy, a painting and decorating company McCarthy had inherited from his father that specialised in large contracts, such as churches and local authority housing, in Cork and Dublin. Jim McCarthy had been co-opted to the Dockrell's board and made managing director, before engaging in a spate of acquisitions of similar businesses on both sides of the border.

Sean McKone, an old school friend of O'Reilly's, sold him over 30% of the shares in his house-building company. Crowe bought a distribution company, Chemist Holdings of London, for £2 million. In buying John Daly & Co. Ltd. of Cork, where Ferguson had been on the board, O'Reilly secured the franchise for Coca-Cola, Fanta and 7-Up in Ireland and made it a 32-county venture by adding a 75% share in Coca-Cola Bottling (Ulster) equivalent. On 1 November 1972 Fitzwilliam announced that it had purchased 16.14% of the equity in New Ireland Assurance. Between April 1971 and early August 1972 the shares in Crowe Wilson increased from 14p each to 158p. It made Crowe Wilson the third most valuable industrial company on the Dublin stock market, with a value of more than £20 million.

Ken Whitaker, the Central Bank governor and the most respected economic strategist in the country, was so worried that he made a rare public statement at an investment conference: 'Within the last two years we have witnessed an astonishing wave of mergers and take-overs in these islands,' he said. He warned that it was paper money that was being produced, not goods. 'It surely cannot be desirable socially or economically that financial transactions should yield bigger gains than production.' He was told sharply from the floor that, 'It seems a little untimely for Dr. Whitaker to dampen enthusiasm for enterprise'.

Business & Finance observed in March 1972 that 'Crowe Wilson fires ahead on all cylinders. There is of course the obvious danger that it will drift into the problems that have been the death knell of many conglomerates. If an empire over-sprawls it can be impossible to effect any worthwhile rationalisation measures even at administrative level. A lack of relevant management skills in all areas also takes its toll on profits. So far these dangers have been admirably countered. Leonard and Ferguson have concentrated on common problems such as tighter financial control and speeding management information flow. The pay-off here has been reduced costs for many of the companies within the group.'

O'Reilly still needed something very big, to give far more heft to Crowe Wilson than it had managed to attain so far. He wanted a stand-out acquisition with such prestige and standing that it would drive up the value of the whole Crowe group. His eye fell on an Irish firm that was both efficient and at the same time a soft target, and that he also thought would benefit greatly from the boost to agriculture that was coming from Ireland's imminent entry to the European Economic Community (EEC): he settled on Goulding's.

One of the oldest firms in Ireland, Goulding's had been manufacturing fertilisers in Cork since 1855. By the 1960s it dominated the
Irish fertiliser market, specialising in compounds and blends of
nitrogen, phosphates, potash and potassium, all of which are critical
to the production of beef on good grassland. Fertiliser in the 1960s
was used on only about a third of Irish grassland. The use of fertilisers
in Ireland was projected to grow by almost 300% in the 1970s.

Goulding's had used its cash-flow to diversify into plastics, jewellery,
system building and property development, but it was the potential of
the fertiliser business that really interested O'Reilly. The company had
two plants, one in Dublin and one in Cork, and the latter was regarded
as having a strong R&D unit. Goulding's, which was 20% owned by the
giant British Imperial Chemical Industries (ICI), had embarked on a
joint plan with Richardson's, which was itself half owned by ICI, to
construct a £9 million efficient fertiliser plant in Belfast. The company
was also building a state-of-the-art new manufacturing facility at East
Wall in Dublin, featuring all the best in expensive new technology.

In the summer of 1971 the company chairman, Sir Basil Goulding,
had carried out a detailed study of Goulding's shareholders. He discovered that 56% did not know the company's annual turnover. They
were equally ignorant of its return on capital, the state of health of
other companies in the Goulding group, and the relationship with ICI.
Only one in three shareholders read the annual report.

O'Reilly had read the reports diligently for years. This company had
the type of balance sheet he craved; it would catapult him into the big
time. Part of the attraction of the business too, although it had to be
left unspoken, was that it was a relic of the Irish Protestant ascendancy
that would be falling into Catholic hands. O'Reilly wanted to engineer
a reverse takeover, whereby Goulding's would buy his company but
the Fitzwilliam management would take control of operations.

To his shock, however, O'Reilly was slower in making his pitch and
lost out on a deal when Con Smith, an old college rival who had made
his fortune as a car salesman, struck a similar deal with Goulding
instead. The news was delivered to O'Reilly in America by his father
over the phone and while his father reassured him that there would be
other opportunities, the competitive animal in O'Reilly was seething
at the loss. The following day his father rang again with far more
shocking news. Con Smith and a group of 11 other well-known Irish

businessmen had been killed in a plane crash shortly after take-off from Heathrow Airport in the UK; they had been en route to Brussels for a meeting about Ireland's entry to the EEC. It was a tragedy, but business carried on and two days later Goulding rang O'Reilly offering him the deal that had been intended for Smith. The following Saturday, O'Reilly was sitting in Basil Goulding's Delgany mansion. He and Basil charmed each other. 'Old Basil had a wonderful engaging manner and he was tremendously witty, a true, gentle, Irish eccentric. He and I fell madly in love with each other,' O'Reilly said afterwards.

It was agreed that Crowe Wilson would buy Goulding's, but that the combined entity would then trade under a new name. Basil suggested Fitzwilton, the name he had given to a prestige office-block near the Grand Canal in Dublin that would be part of the deal, and where O'Reilly would subsequently take up residence. It sounded enough like Fitzwilliam to satisfy O'Reilly's ego. When the deal was done, Goulding had 70% of the new entity and Fitzwilliam the other 30%, with an option for the latter to increase the percentage over time. This structure meant that O'Reilly personally would have three times as many shares in the new entity as Basil. Fitzwilton would have sales of over £50 million, employ 4,400 people and produce profits initially of £2.5 million. O'Reilly became deputy chairman to Basil, but the rumours flew about that O'Reilly was about to ditch his job at Heinz to come home. Many wondered why Goulding would want to sell his business, valued at £10 million, to O'Reilly and his friends in exchange for shares in their much smaller entity. Richard Keating, the financial editor of *The Irish Times*, wrote that 'Goulding's shareholders needed an injection of new management and of course they welcomed the speculative interest that increased Fitzwilton's share price'. In the first four weeks after the acquisition, Fitzwilton's share price doubled.

Business & Finance interviewed O'Reilly, Leonard and Ferguson in August 1972, 15 months into their venture, the initial £500,000 investment now seemingly worth £6.3 million – all achieved apparently without producing any new goods, buying new machinery or hiring extra workers. 'All it took was a clear view of the economy, deep research into the key growth sectors, an ability to seek the right companies, a willingness to pay a generous price, confidence, flair and the courage of their convictions,' the magazine gushed. 'And the trio took a fundamental decision to reject the asset stripping idea so earnestly pursued by Jim Slater in the UK.'

That was a reference to the controversial practice of buying under-performing companies with undervalued assets, stripping out the costs, often by firing workers, and breaking up the companies by selling the assets piecemeal to rival firms, usually at great profit. 'In general terms,' said O'Reilly, 'we're pragmatic against a fairly clear background of what we wanted to do and how it should be done. We are a mixture of enlightened merchant bankers and friendly cross-examiners while at the same time retaining fire-fighting control in case of an emergency. By buying into independently successful companies it has also eased the management problems. The Fitzwilton team has joined the board in all cases, has applied stricter financial controls and where necessary has strengthened the existing managements.'

O'Reilly was named 'Man of the Year' by *Business & Finance* in January 1973. Reporter Jim Milton wrote in the weekly magazine that 'meeting the three together, one can feel the unity of the team, the awareness that each has something to contribute to the other which, when woven together, makes a formidable and irresistible whole'.

As if all of that was not enough, O'Reilly was making other invest-ments, this time without Ferguson and Leonard in tow. Ollie Waldron, a former Irish rugby international from Cork, persuaded him to invest in Tara Exploration and Mining, a Canadian-backed company that was seeking to develop a large lead and zinc mine at Navan in County Meath. He told O'Reilly that shares in Tara – trading at $16 at the time – would be worth $60 once the Irish government issued enhanced mining licences.

O'Reilly set up another company, called Fitzwilliam Resources. In April 1972 it raised $7.2 million to buy 6% of the equity in Tara. O'Reilly's new family investment vehicle, Columbia Investments, had 37.5% of this new venture and McCarthy and old school friend Sam Stephenson had other large shareholdings. Another investor was Des Traynor, MD of Guinness Mahon bank, which provided all of the borrowed money. (Traynor was revealed years later, after his death in 1994, to have been Charles Haughey's 'bagman' for the accumulation of cash and the operator of a secret illegal bank that facilitated widespread tax evasion by an elite in Irish society.)

O'Reilly joined the board of Tara and was not impressed by what he found. He attended his very first meeting immediately after he had disembarked from a flight from the USA, where he had just attended a very formal and well chaired meeting of the Heinz board. What he saw was the stuff of Celtic cliché, although there was probably the usual element of embellishment in O'Reilly's subsequent retelling of the tale. He said there were two men he didn't recognise sitting at the table – one who hadn't removed his peaked cap and another wearing a Hawaiian shirt, open to the chest. He asked the company secretary who they were. One, he was told laughingly, was 'Pat's uncle', a reference to the CEO Pat Hughes, 'and he's going to sing at the coffee break'. It was not an auspicious start to something that would almost turn into a ruinous investment.

———

O'Reilly may never have won a trophy during his rugby career, but contacts made within the game helped him to win control, in 1973, of one of his greatest corporate prizes: Independent Newspapers (IN). Few had him marked as a likely owner of newspapers. The company, publisher of the *Irish Independent, Sunday Independent, Evening Herald* and *The Kerryman*, had been in the Murphy family for generations, established by William Martin Murphy, another product of Belvedere College. Murphy is best remembered for his role in the infamous 1913 Lockout, when he broke the attempts by the trade union movement to secure better wages and working conditions. He was celebrated in verse by W.B. Yeats 'as fumbling in the greasy till' and 'adding the halfpence to the pence'. Murphy responded that making money was as respectable an occupation as writing poetry.

Murphy also deserved to be remembered as a brilliant and innovative businessman who did much for Dublin and Ireland. Born in Bantry, County Cork, in 1844, he was one of the beneficiaries of O'Connell's Catholic Emancipation. He was one of the original great Irish builders, constructing schools, churches, railways and bridges, but then also winning contracts to lay train tracks in Britain, Argentina and the west of Africa. He used the money to buy the Imperial Hotel in Dublin and the city's first great department store, Clery's, both on O'Connell Street. He started his own newspaper in 1896, the *Daily Nation*, and merged it with the *Irish Independent* when he bought the latter out of bankruptcy. He was said to lose £100,000 each year on producing the paper but when asked why replied, 'some men have as their pastimes hunting, gambling or some other form of frivolity, but the *Independent* gives me the necessary relief from the hard and prosaic world I have to face as a man of business'.

Further generations of the Murphy lineage did not have his drive or intellect, which is not an insult because few would have had, nor interest in maintaining control of the papers, especially when the shares were spread among many relatives. Independent Newspapers had a complicated share structure, although it was of a type reasonably common in high-profile, family-owned media companies at the time, both in Ireland and abroad. It had two classes of shares: A shares, which exercised control of the company; and B shares, whose owners received dividends but had no input into the control of the enterprise.

The controlling A shares were held in the main by T.V. Murphy, known to all as Tommy, and other members of his family, along with some members of the Chance family who were related by marriage. Few of them had a direct involvement in the management of the company or received much income from the shares. Oliver Chance had been the most senior member of the latter family, but when he died in August 1972 debate broke out among the family members as to whether it was worth keeping the shares, as those A shares represented only 4% of the overall number of shares in the company. Their only perceived value was in selling them, as the annual income from them was so limited.

Speculation spread in late 1972 and early 1973 that members of the extended family were open to selling, especially in advance of the rumoured introduction of a capital gains tax (CGT) in 1973 for those selling assets. Michael Smurfit was spoken about as a possible buyer, given his knowledge of the printing industry, as was the controversial Australian newspaper baron Rupert Murdoch, who was generating opprobrium because of the standards of his stewardship of *The Sun*, *The News of the World*, *The Times* and *Sunday Times*, allegedly breaking agreement after agreement with the unions and politicians and doing as he wanted. Rumours that Murdoch was looking to Ireland prompted the Minister for Industry and Commerce, Paddy Lalor, to declare that 'a situation in which ownership or control of Irish newspapers passed into non-Irish hands would be unacceptable' to the government.

Few people considered that O'Reilly, not just busy with Heinz but with his plethora of other Irish investments, would be interested, but he had started secret manoeuvres that he hoped would lead to an agreed takeover. O'Reilly invited Tommy's son, Rodney, to whom he was introduced by his rugby contacts, to visit him in Pittsburgh and O'Reilly suggested that he would be happy to make the younger man chairman of IN if he supported O'Reilly's plan for investment.

O'Reilly had to move quickly, however, as all of the speculation about other bidders had driven the price of the B shares up in value by almost a third, to the point where the whole company was now valued at about £4.8 million. On 4 March 1973, the company announced a 120% increase in profits for the previous year to £770,000. O'Reilly also engaged in initial negotiations with T.V. Murphy's personal financial adviser, the accountant Russell Murphy, famous later for stealing money from his best-known client, the RTÉ broadcaster Gay Byrne. O'Reilly found Murphy to be a somewhat eccentric character to deal with, particularly his habit of getting up from his desk and walking around behind the back of the person with whom he was in conversation while continuing to talk. Nonetheless, negotiations progressed to the point where T.V. Murphy was prepared to host O'Reilly at his Carrickmines home on a Sunday morning, the day after a rugby international at Lansdowne Road that O'Reilly had flown in to attend.

O'Reilly found the 71-year-old T.V. Murphy in a state of high agitation that morning as he confessed that he had done the unthinkable: he had skipped mass, such was the crisis provoked by that morning's *Sunday Independent*. It had published an exposé by the famed investigative journalist Joe MacAnthony into the controversial operations of the Irish Hospitals' Sweepstakes, a raffle that raised enormous sums from the diaspora in the USA but that had also made its organisers very wealthy indeed. Many of those who featured in the article were friends and acquaintances of Murphy's and in the case of the main man, Paddy McGrath, near neighbours. Murphy did not want to have to face them about this and O'Reilly thought he would be doing Murphy a favour by relieving him of the burden of ownership.

A deal was concluded on Friday, 16 March 1973. O'Reilly purchased all the A shares for £10.95 each, or £1.1 million in total, which in truth was a massive premium on their true value but which was necessary to take management control from the Murphy and Chance families. There was to be an unwanted twist for him, however. The Stock Exchange decided that anyone who acquired effective control of the company (which O'Reilly had done) would then be required to make a bid to buy the remainder of the shares, in this case the B shares. O'Reilly had not anticipated this and could not afford the full cost of it. He was furious. There were 10 days of rows between his advisers and the stock market authorities and the latter would not yield. He had effectively paid £1.1 million to buy 4% of a company that was worth less than £5 million.

One of his advisers in AIIB, Jerry Casey, came up with a formula to offer to the B shareholders, at a cost of about £4.5 million if O'Reilly had to buy all of the shares himself. However, O'Reilly put together a consortium that included Fitzwilton and friends in a personal capacity to support him, and it made an offer for all of the B shares. Fortunately for O'Reilly, only about 47% of the existing shareholders opted to sell under the terms O'Reilly offered; about 53% of the shares stayed in their original hands. As part of the offer, Casey came up with an idea that O'Reilly should be allowed to increase his shareholding in the company, through the issue of new shares, if it met a series of financial targets over the coming years, so as to eventually give O'Reilly just under 30% of all the shares, smoothing the overall cost of the purchase to him. There was uproar when the terms of the deal were announced, with one firm of stockbrokers, Dudgeon & Sons, publicly commenting that they were 'far too generous to Mr O'Reilly' and *Hibernia* magazine calling it 'so outlandish as to be scarcely credible'. One major financial institution, also a large shareholder in Fitzwilton, indicated that it would oppose the deal. Eventually O'Reilly persuaded it to abstain and in September shareholders approved the deal for him to take control of IN.

O'Reilly honoured his promise to make Rodney Murphy chairman and brought another member of the Chance family, Tom, onto the board in May 1973. O'Reilly took the position of deputy chairman. Bartle Pitcher and Liam Healy, two men who were to become pivotal to O'Reilly's subsequent running of the company, were already there. O'Reilly soon added Leonard and Freddy Boland, a former diplomat. A board resolution on 21 September 1973 increased the maximum number of directors, from seven to 15. O'Reilly liked large boards, something that would come to be regarded as a weakness many years hence.

This deal was different from all of the others O'Reilly had completed because of the nature of the company he had purchased and memories of his often speculated about political ambitions. The left-of-centre magazine *Hibernia* asked if O'Reilly was going to be 'an Irish Beaverbrook', a reference to the controversial deceased owner of the *Express* newspapers in the UK when it was a major entity, and a war-time political ally of O'Reilly's hero, Winston Churchill. 'Ownership and control of Independent Newspapers offers not only a near monopoly investment in a near impregnable area of Irish industry, it also bestows a unique power base in Irish society,' it suggested. It may not have been necessarily true at that time, but it was to become the case in the future. *Hibernia* also highlighted dealings in IN shares by Leonard prior to the announcement of O'Reilly's purchase and on which Leonard made a very large profit.

O'Reilly's arrival was also a matter of great concern to journalists, worried about their jobs, terms and conditions. The Abbey Street National Union of Journalists, (NUJ) chapel (branch) had been in dispute with the outgoing owners about the future of the company. They reckoned that they had a powerful bargaining position on O'Reilly's arrival because he would not want his era to start with a strike and a loss of much needed cash-flow and that he could therefore be persuaded to make concessions.

O'Reilly decided to deal with the NUJ personally and did so on the Friday evening after the announcement of the acquisition. He restored to the payroll those journalists who had been fired by the previous regime for striking and promised there would be no further changes to work practices or any redundancies. He declared that the company and its subsidiaries would 'recognise the rights of editorial freedom' and that the newspapers 'would maintain their character'. He committed that ongoing negotiations about pay and conditions would be concluded 'within a reasonable time'. However, he refused a request for journalistic representation on the board.

O'Reilly gave a radio interview in which he stated that the reason for the takeover was 'primarily commercial'. He said he wanted IN to 'continue its aggressive commercial standards and for reasonable commercial expansion, either in Ireland or abroad.' He said that the concerns of journalists were 'legitimate' and that he had given them 'specific assurances in relation to editorial freedom (and) quality of employment'. He said that he would be a hands-off proprietor and that he drew 'a specific distinction between ownership and management'. Asked about how much power ownership of newspapers might give one person, O'Reilly replied: 'That concern is legitimate. Each man in his own way has to show that he means what he says in terms of the commercial and editorial freedom of his papers. If he abuses that decision, the concern expressed will be shown to be legitimate.'

He went further by giving an interview to another financial reporter at the *Irish Independent,* Colm Rapple, who would later become a thorn in his side before moving across to the *Irish Press* group of newspapers. O'Reilly spoke of his belief in the power of market research techniques to shape editorial content and expressed optimism that advertising revenues for the papers would increase as Ireland became an increasingly consumerist society. He said the newspapers should use market research 'to find out the drift, trend and inclination of the population [as] part of a broad dialogue with the public'. O'Reilly emphasised that any evolution would take place along consultative, rather than autocratic, lines.

'I am a great believer in putting facts on the table and talking about them,' he said. 'I would certainly talk about these with the editors and the other members of the board. If I thought that there was a major shift in the lifestyle of the community, and which ought to be reflected, and that there were facts to prove that this was the case, and that the papers were ignoring them, I would certainly bring it to the attention of the board and I would expect to get a reasonable refutation as to why we shouldn't change. I mean – I'm not saying that the paper is polarised for all time along its present path, and that I won't make an impact. It's hard to say that you won't make an impact.'

He promised that he was 'not going to change the editorial direction of the paper in a two-party country away from its present level to create an uncertainty in the minds of loyal supporters of the paper. That is the greatest guarantee of all, the fact that the editorial policy of this paper has won the benediction of such a wide audience.'

But as important in mollifying employees was the fact that O'Reilly quickly agreed a major pay rise for IN staff, believing it was justified by the high circulation of the newspapers and the anticipated additional advertising revenue. It proved to be not the wisest decision. Looming external events would prove to be near-disastrous for finances at IN, as at his other interests, and this was not something he could afford.

In August 1973 O'Reilly wrote to shareholders and said that he wanted to expand into advertising, publicity and commercial radio and television and not just in Ireland. He wanted IN to become 'an international communications group'. It would be a long time before O'Reilly had the opportunity to begin chasing that dream. Instead of scaling more heights and setting about achieving the recognition and status he craved, O'Reilly was about to face the first major financial crisis of his life.

CHAPTER SEVEN

CRISIS MANAGEMENT AND DAMAGE LIMITATION

I f 1973 was supposed to be a year of economic and social liberation for Ireland as a result of entry to the EEC – and in time that would prove to be the case – it didn't feel that way in the initial years of membership. The anticipated boom, upon which O'Reilly and many other businessmen had made their projections, did not materialise. Instead, external events caused crisis in Ireland, leading to sky-high interest rates on borrowings, rampant inflation, soaring unemployment and depressed consumer spending. O'Reilly's companies were not strong enough to withstand the earthquake caused by a sudden surge in oil prices imposed by the Organisation of Petroleum Exporting Countries (OPEC) or the subsequent aftershocks. Nor was O'Reilly's personal financial position strong enough: he was way too highly borrowed, despite his income from Heinz.

The biggest problem for Fitzwilton came at the supposed jewel of its crown, Goulding's. It was hit by a double-whammy: demand for its products fell dramatically, just as the costs of its raw materials soared. The former was caused by high interest rates. Farmers had invested heavily in expanding their stock to take advantage of bigger EEC markets. They had borrowed to do so and were now squeezed by the higher cost of servicing those loans just as demand for beef fell and the prices they could command. The loss of a major live cattle export contract to Libya that year was devastating for the State. Farmers cut their costs drastically and one of the first inputs to go was fertiliser, particularly as they planned not to replenish stock in the following year. But it got worse as the cost of rock phosphate – the basic raw material for fertiliser – increased fivefold, an extraordinary and unsustainable rise. The plants were entirely dependent on securing supplies from Morocco, and the Africans, watching how the OPEC nations were increasing the price of oil, decided to impose their own price rises. Goulding's tried to impose higher prices, which was impossible. Stocks of unsold fertiliser piled up; Goulding's sales and profits slumped, before turning into heavy losses; production had to be curtailed through many temporary plant closures. Lenders to Fitzwilliam became extremely worried, as did those to O'Reilly personally.

If 1973 had ended badly, then 1974 promptly made things even worse for everyone in Ireland – and for exiles with significant investments, like O'Reilly. As interest rates soared, the cost of servicing O'Reilly's debts could not be met out of his enormous $350,000 Heinz income. He could potentially go bust, and after the January 1974 government Budget he feared that greatly.

Relevant to all of his interests was a declaration that interest on borrowings as a tax-deductible expense for investors in a company was no longer allowed. Capital gains tax on the profits from the sale of shares was introduced for the first time, and interest rates – at the time under the control of the minister, who could direct the Central Bank – were raised to an eye-watering 18%. His investment in Tara Mines was the main immediate problem, as export tax relief for mining products was abolished. Even before that, the investment in Tara had become something of a millstone because, despite Waldron's optimism, the government had decided not to issue the required licences and environmental rows broke out about the structure of the mine, delaying production. The shares had fallen to $12 instead of rising to $60.

According to the tale that went around Dublin subsequently, O'Reilly, who was in Puerto Rico with McCarthy for a holiday that January, went into a rare fury when he heard news of the Budget. His friend, somewhat in a state of shock himself given that his own resources were rather less than O'Reilly's, asked, 'what does this mean for us, Tony?' O'Reilly looked at him and stated coldly and slowly, 'It means, Macker, that we're fucked.'

O'Reilly was not prepared to go down without a fight, however, and somehow he turned the situation to his advantage. He and McCarthy flew back to Ireland immediately to work out some deal to save them from financial ruin. Quickly, O'Reilly decided he had to sell the Tara shares. It was time for the super salesman to go to work again and to use his old rugby contacts. He phoned friends in the mining business in South Africa and somehow persuaded Cominco, a subsidiary of the giant Anglo-American company, to bid to buy Tara, starting the bidding process at the inflated price of $25 per share. This somehow persuaded another company called Noranda, which was already an investor in Tara, that it should take control, which it did, after winning a takeover battle. This allowed the O'Reilly consortium to sell its holding for $11.25 million, producing a big profit of over $4 million from a situation where it seemed that O'Reilly might lose all. In February 1974 *Business & Finance* revealed that 'Fitzwilliam Resources clears £2.2 million in sale of its Tara shares'. It estimated that O'Reilly made a £820,000 profit, Fitzwilton £380,000, McCarthy £360,000, Stephenson £280,000, Traynor £225,000 and Guinness & Mahon £137,000. 'The most interesting thing about this capital gain is that when the royalty income to the exchequer from the mining company profits since 1965 is compared with it, Fitzwilliam Resources is seen to have fared much better in eight months than the State has done over a nine-year period.'

More important than the satisfaction of having averted doom and of making a big profit was the use of the money that accrued to O'Reilly. It was to provide enough money to pay the interest on all of his other loans over the next three years.

It didn't mean that his crisis was over, however. He had to stop Goulding's from bringing everything else in the Fitzwilton group down with it. Fitzwilton shares peaked at 150p in September 1972. By the end of 1973 they were down at 80p and by September 1974 they were down to 36p. All of O'Reilly's capital gains at Fitzwilton – his original £37,500 investment had at one stage shown a return of 3,400% – evaporated, to the horror of his lenders. O'Reilly's ability to cope with stress was being tested, to put it mildly. 'I was full of piss and vinegar,' he said later about that time. 'You don't know till afterwards how near the edge you'd gone.'

The falling share price put more than O'Reilly under pressure. There was utter shock, and not a little anger, in the investment community when *The Irish Times* revealed that Leonard had sold about half of his Fitzwilton shares early in 1975, raising £175,000, and his IN shares for £265,000, and that Ferguson had sold some Fitzwilton shares too. They had not acted illegally, but if these men had lost confidence in the recovery of the company, then what hope was there for other investors?

Meanwhile, at IN, advertising revenues slumped, as companies did what they always do in a recession: view marketing as the first cost to be easily cut. Independent Newspapers still managed a 15% rise in net profit before taxation to £885,000 in the 1973 financial year, but then advertising revenues began to reduce at increasing speed, just as inflation, averaging over 20% annually, took hold of costs.

Independent Newspapers was constrained in its response by the law. Government controls over pricing meant that IN could not recoup its additional costs easily through price hikes on the papers, having to make applications for increases that might or might not be granted. The increase in wages granted previously by O'Reilly to solve an industrial relations crisis was now a major burden. In short, 1974 was a financial disaster. Despite an almost 22% increase in turnover, largely as a result of inflation, pre-tax profits slumped by three-quarters to £208,910. Newsprint costs soared by 140% and a week-long dispute with newsagents affected distribution and revenues.

Casey's big plan to give O'Reilly more control of IN, through the deferred convertible shares, was in trouble. The conversion of the 'deferred' shares into dividend-bearing ordinary shares could not take place until certain specified levels of profit and earnings per share had been achieved and O'Reilly was far off them. He needed IN to have profits in 1974 of no less than £950,000, but instead the newspapers achieved only £450,000 and the company had to deposit the deeds to the newspaper titles with AIIB as security against £450,000 of its debts. His following year's profit target had been set at £1.2 million, but instead the company made just £203,000 in profit, and that was after cost-cutting that removed 105 jobs.

O'Reilly had to find another income flow to pay the bills on the money he had borrowed to buy IN. The company could not afford to pay other than token dividends – £4,000 in total – but O'Reilly's interest bill on his IN borrowings in those early years amounted to £130,000 or £140,000 per annum, depending on the rates of interest charged by the banks in any year. That was why the money from Tara was so important to him.

Over at Fitzwilton the pressure was intensifying, and the Tara deal did not solve any of its problems. Its debts had climbed to £40 million and plans for further expansion had to be ditched. There were now 64 companies within the group and these had a combined turnover in excess of £60 million. The trading profit was over £5 million, but this was not enough to cover interest repayments on the debts.

The crisis reached its tipping point in the summer of 1975 when Henry Schroeder Wagg, a firm of London bankers, stopped a £1 million credit line. Then the Irish banks panicked and insisted that their own nominees would have to be put into the board of Fitzwilton, to oversee an orderly sale of assets to pay down debts.

O'Reilly was humiliated and angry, although it could have been worse: a receiver could have been appointed and he and fellow investors would have lost control of the company immediately, along with any chance to recover some of their own investments. However, Sir Basil was 'retired' at the insistence of the banks and replaced by Michael Dargan, a man with an excellent reputation in Irish business for his achievements in the semi-State sector with Aer Lingus. Tom Hardiman, later to be director-general at RTÉ, was also sent in, as was Lord Killanin, best known as the head of the Olympic International Committee but also a member of many corporate boards in Ireland. O'Reilly threatened to quit the board if Dargan did not accept the appointment of Jim McCarthy as CEO; it may have been an empty threat, but Dargan agreed. It was a move that was to put McCarthy in a very difficult position in the coming years. He had a fiduciary responsibility to act as the board wanted and in the best interests of all shareholders in the company, but he was to find that his best friend made many demands of him that ran contrary to what the chairman and other directors wanted.

Dargan's job was to get money back for the banks as quickly as possible, even if the prices to be achieved from asset sales were not the optimal. This immediately put him at loggerheads with O'Reilly, who wanted more time to achieve better prices. O'Reilly did not share the confidence of the banks that Dargan would achieve the best prices possible, especially after the first asset, the property that served as company HQ in Dublin, was sold to a British pension fund – representing coal-miners – at what many said, probably correctly, was an absurdly low price of £3 million. But that was the nature of fire sales, and it was only one of many that would infuriate O'Reilly.

Sale after sale was made. The shares in New Ireland Assurance were sold to PMPA (Private Motorists Protection Association) and two fertiliser companies in Northern Ireland were sold. The Victoria Hotel in Cork and a prime development site on Burlington Road in Dublin went too. Particularly sore was the loss of Chemical Holdings of Britain, a pharmaceutical distributor of potentially considerably more value than the sales price suggested. The conglomerate's plastics division was sold to Smurfit, textile company Crampton's went back to its original family owners and the Goulding's property division was sold too.

Some old supporters were displaying some jaw-dropping levels of hindsight as they observed these disposals. *Business & Finance*, probably the company's biggest cheerleader on its way up, noted that 'the failure to foresee trends or the reluctance to take precautionary steps has blighted the management image'. By the end of 1975 the borrowings had been reduced to £23 million. However, Goulding's continued to haemorrhage cash and the losses continued to mount. Over 200 workers were laid off as a temporary measure, as the plant in Dublin was closed for five months and in Cork for three months.

O'Reilly took personal responsibility for finding a solution to the Goulding's impasse. He brought his family on holidays to Florida for Thanksgiving in late 1975, but while the children played by the pool he took to the phone and spent two days making what he estimated was close to 200 phone calls, contacting every superphosphate manager he could find in the USA, seeking a deal for a new supplier to replace the Moroccans. He secured nine interviews. Of those only one, a company called Williams of Tulsa, Oklahoma, was interested; one was enough. It agreed to ship its own rock phosphate from its American mines to Ireland, which would be a profitable enterprise for it, even if the eventual sales of fertiliser might not be. It bought a half share in Goulding's for $10 million, agreed to supply raw materials at world commodity prices and guaranteed a further $2 million loan, but it cut the deal at a price: the Dublin plant would have to be shut, costing 360 jobs, meaning production would be limited to Cork.

'Of all the deals I've ever done, that was perhaps the most critical,' O'Reilly said later. He believed that it was the deal that saved

Fitzwilton from collapse, but it may well have saved him financially. At the subsequent Fitzwilton AGM, O'Reilly expressed sympathy with all those made redundant and pointed out that Fitzwilton 'have paid out twice the statutory amount' in compensation to them.

Many were not impressed and there was plenty of criticism in the mainstream press. Of particular significance, in hindsight, was a pamphlet entitled 'Tony O'Reilly's greatest game', published by Sinn Féin, The Workers Party (SFWP), excoriating his performance for allowing a native capitalist firm to be destroyed and taken over by a foreign multinational. It alleged that 'The brightest star in the team of Irish capitalism had shown that he and his club were morally and physically bankrupt'. It claimed that 'on its own, with the strength it had back in 1971, Goulding's could have ridden out the fertiliser recession. But O'Reilly had drawn off so much of its life blood to boost Fitzwilton that, by 1975, it was too weak to carry on without the funds they normally had in the past.'

It was a contentious argument, and one delivered from a particular political perspective, but it served as a counterbalance to the subsequent efforts by O'Reilly to portray Fitzwilton's efforts at Goulding's as crucial to the latter's survival. O'Reilly told *Irish Business* that Goulding's might never have survived but for Fitzwilton putting cash into the company during the recession, enabling it to avoid liquidation. The author of the SFWP pamphlet was not disclosed, but those involved in the party at the time remember it as the work of its most brilliant polemicist, Eoghan Harris, who would later become one of O'Reilly's staunchest supporters during subsequent crises.

Other assets still had to be sold, again at prices that O'Reilly came subsequently to regret bitterly: the Coca-Cola bottling business was sold for £3.1 million to a Greek company and, within two decades, this business had expanded so much that it was reckoned to be worth over £100 million. But one particular acquisition was to be sold at a massive profit, clearing the balance of Fitzwilton's debts. In 1972 O'Reilly had organised a $9 million loan from Mellon Bank to help buy 27% of the shares in National Mine Service in the USA. In September 1976, O'Reilly persuaded Chessie Systems to pay $18.7 million for the stake. The exchange rate between the dollar and the Irish pound had moved dramatically in Fitzwilton's favour during that period, increasing the profit.

All told, Fitzwilton had sold assets valued on its books at £43 million for £42 million and had not just cleared all its debts but had shareholders' funds and cash in the bank of about £12 million. That was an achievement of sorts, but for most the experience would have been deeply chastening and humbling. O'Reilly was not most men. He was angry with the banks for forcing him into decisions he hadn't liked and was particularly resentful of Dargan as their representative. The salvation of Fitzwilton, O'Reilly told Dargan, was all the work of the original promoters: 'we did it, we sweated through it, with our good names involved in it, we told you there was value in the company and now you're telling us that we should go back in and borrow again to become an investment company – well, not with you as shareholders.'

He ignored the fact that the same people O'Reilly praised had been responsible for creating many of their own problems and were only cleaning up their own mess, with significant help from the bank representatives he so reviled. After a major row Dargan agreed to resign as Fitzwilton chairman and Lord Killanin replaced him.

Fitzwilton's remaining assets included a 24% share in IN, 50% of Goulding's, which was barely breaking even, and Dockrell's, which was losing money, and some minor textiles interests. Liquidation was an option. O'Reilly's shares, which had cost him £30,000, were now worth about £400,000, even at the reduced share price.

His reputation had taken a battering, his time had been consumed at the expense of other things he could have been doing and he had been on the verge of financial disaster. A man as self-aware as he was would surely learn from the experience and develop a more considered approach towards the making of acquisitions and the financing of them. He would have to ask himself if he had devoted sufficient time to the job at Fitzwilton: at the key times he had chaired the executive committee of five men, but how often had he really been there when he was needed? Was being on the end of a phone, once his day job at Heinz was done, really good enough? Had he spread himself too thinly? The option was open to him to concentrate on his day job at Heinz and have IN as a potentially lucrative and most definitely interesting side-line, if he really needed another hobby. He could even spend more time with his wife and family.

A few years earlier, when he was promoting the early days of Fitzwilton, O'Reilly had given an interview to veteran *Sunday Press* reporter John Kelly, who had supplied O'Reilly with a list – ego, power, glory, money, patriotism – and asked him to pick from it to describe his motivation. 'It's a cocktail,' he replied. 'It's a combination of commitment, family, people, ego, institutions, country and to some degree money – although I don't think that's the primary catalyst.' In his 1994 biography, *The Player*, Ivan Fallon would argue that 'Fitzwilton was as much about creating a reputation as it was about making money'. Whatever it was, he would not let it go now.

At IN there were crises too, if not on the scale of the Fitzwilton debacle. It wasn't until 1976 that there was real improvement in profits and an opportunity for O'Reilly to convert some of his deferred shareholding. The only consolation to O'Reilly was that people continued to buy and read the newspapers in considerable numbers. More than four-fifths of the adult population of Ireland read one or more of the group's publications every week; more than half read the *Sunday Independent* regularly; a third read the *Irish Independent* daily; and more than a fifth read the *Evening Herald*. The fiscal year 1977 was, according to chairman Rodney Murphy's report, 'perhaps the most important year in the history of Independent Newspapers'.

O'Reilly had purchased a newspaper that had long been associated with support for Fine Gael and the assumption was that he would continue that for fear of losing readers, notwithstanding his close friendship with Fianna Fáil leader Jack Lynch. Support for Fianna Fáil was the *Irish Press*'s territory. However, the paper's support for the 1973–77 Fine Gael/Labour coalition government was judged by many to have waned, not because of its performance in relation to Northern Ireland but because of the January 1976 Budget introduced by Minister for Finance Richie Ryan. The following day's front page contained a three-word headline that could have passed for editorial comment, or tabloid headline, given the inclusion of an exclamation mark: 'No Way, Richie!' The editorial inside attacked a Budget that it claimed represented merely the 'sad culmination of the budget policy pursued over the past few years'. It charged that the government could not escape responsibility 'for pursuing its liberal spending policies on the current side to a point of crisis'. Observers wondered if Fine Gael might lose its main newspaper support and wondered what, if anything, O'Reilly had to do with this editorial movement, although coverage in subsequent weeks was more favourable to the government, especially when it enforced what was known as a 'pay pause' for all companies in an effort to fight inflation.

O'Reilly made one major acquisition for IN during the 1970s: a new tabloid newspaper called the *Sunday World*. It had been launched on 25 March 1973, a tabloid modelled on the style of such British Sunday newspapers but with an Irish agenda and approach to issues. While O'Reilly had spoken of using market research techniques to guide the titles he was acquiring at IN, the promoters of the *Sunday World* had put all of that into action already, creating a title that was the product of market research and targeted marketing, somewhat to the consternation of newspaper traditionalists. Its marketing slogans were risqué for the time: it suggested that a million Irish women weren't being satisfied every week – by their Sunday papers. The massive advertising campaign used slogans like 'We Go All The Way' and 'Are You Getting It Every Sunday?' One of its owners, Gerry McGuinness, boasted that it was irreverent, anti-Establishment, and talked about sex in a way not heard before in Ireland. Irish people lapped up the classic tabloid banner headlines, short paragraphs of easily understood text, celebrity columnists and a pugnacious anti-Establishment attitude that saw government, and many powerful individuals, as fair targets.

The new paper sold well in rural areas, although some people hid it inside their other newspapers or simply would not bring it home, reading it in the pub after Mass and dumping it before arriving home. It sold well in the west of Ireland on a Monday morning; men who hadn't been allowed to bring it home on a Sunday bought it to bring to work instead. Some years later, when O'Reilly was exploring the possibility of purchasing it, one of his senior executives told him his elderly grandmother – who lived in a fairly remote and rural part of the country – bought it because 'everybody does be talking about it'.

In May 1978 a deal was completed for IN to buy 58% of the *Sunday World* and 23% of Newspread, a distribution company that delivered the paper into the shops, effectively buying out McGuinness's partner Hugh McLoughlin and a number of other small investors, at a cost of just over £2.6 million in cash and shares. McGuinness retained his 42% interest and his position as CEO. The IN titles were not strong at the time: the evening paper was losing out consistently to the *Evening Press,* and the *Sunday World* had eaten into the *Sunday Independent*'s market share. There was a growing feeling that O'Reilly restricted investment in what he had, preferring instead to try to buy what was working elsewhere and to do so at prices whereby he could make profit more from financial engineering than from genuine product development. Anything he did with what he already had was usually more defensive. Where was all of the marketing-led innovation and development that had been promised?

Joe Hayes, from North Kerry, had been a salesman at the tobacco group Gallaher's for over a decade before he joined the Middle Abbey Street titles as head of marketing in 1978. Hayes was full of ideas. Just over two years later he would be promoted to be MD of the Irish operations, even though he would show little respect for or patience with much of the ceremony with which O'Reilly would increasingly conduct himself. Personality differences aside, the important thing was that O'Reilly was seemingly ambitious enough to put three people with strong marketing backgrounds into the key positions at IN: Hayes in Abbey Street; McGuinness at the *Sunday World*; and O'Reilly himself at the overall helm. Having overcome near financial Armageddon, the question now was just how ambitious O'Reilly would be for his fledgling newspaper empire.

CHAPTER EIGHT

LIKE FATHER, LIKE SON

While O'Reilly was hell-bent on achieving professional success and status, he wasn't in any way as focused on his personal life and the fact and impact of this seemed to be dawning on him. Family matters, his place in Ireland and the strain under which he was putting himself seemed to weigh on his mind as he became more successful and busy. In January 1973 he told *Business & Finance* that he travelled around the world four times in the previous year. 'And I don't like flying. I'm a devout coward in that respect. It does compound the strain. The thing I resent most is that I've put myself into a lifestyle that is really grinding. While there may be an aura of romance, success, all that nonsense, the realities of it are grinding hours, lack of sleep, detailed analysis of financial reports, business planning cycles, absence from home …'

He didn't have to do it all, of course; he had chosen to bring it all upon himself and that drive was not convincingly explained, at least not by the information in the public domain at the time. Some of his answers to questions stretched credulity a little. Asked how he felt about being wealthy, he laughed: 'I don't think money, per se, matters much. Once I'd crossed that crucial divide money has never really had any compelling interest for me.' But clearly money did matter to him. The more telling, unanswered question was why it mattered so much, why he sought it at the expense of other things in his life.

'My children are almost a memory at this stage,' he said. 'That to me is a minor tragedy that could escalate to a major tragedy. I don't believe I can keep up the pace I am working at the moment for the rest of my life.' In another interview he spoke of 'the absence from home occasioned by a heavy 150,000 mile a year travel schedule. It would be my view that this is not unduly stressful to the children in their early years, but I have some doubts that it might become more stressful now that they have reached ten years on and their early teens.'

It was an interesting contrast to the support he had received from his parents as an only child. He spoke many times of his parents in interviews over the years, with obvious affection and respect. In one interview he described his father as 'methodical' and his mother as having a 'gay and effervescent personality'. In another, after his father had died in 1976, he admitted to his father developing a degree of pomposity as he grew older – something with which the son would become afflicted in time. 'I think I get my sense of humour from my mother and my sense of appreciation from John, my father. It was not a strict upbringing.' He spoke of regular phone contact with his father when in the USA, that he 'would rarely make any serious decision without talking it over with him first. I didn't necessarily need his agreement, but I would like to distil it with him first'. Jack travelled to Pittsburgh when he could, relishing the opportunity to meet with all of Tony's friends at the dinner table. Aileen did not travel as often, with O'Reilly later surmising that it may have been because of embarrass-ment about the status on her passport, which said 'Unmarried'. Jack loved having the grandchildren at his home in Sutton, too, 'driving around on his lawnmower in the garden, trying not to drive over us as we played', as one of them remembers him to this day.

Surprisingly, little mention was made of Susan in most of those interviews, other than admiration for the time she spent with the children. His lifestyle was hard on her. It didn't just leave her to spend lots of time with the children – she enjoyed it greatly and she had help and she did it in a way that her children, as adults, admired and loved her for – but it was hard nonetheless because it meant she spent very little time with her husband, which was not conducive to the quality of the marriage. Again, O'Reilly was showing personality traits remarkably similar to his father's. He did not attend to his marriage properly. It is not surprising, then, that Susan did not learn of her husband's illegitimacy until the Christmas of 1973, more than 12 years after they had been married. Just like his parents held their secret from him, Tony kept the same secret from his wife.

Although she did not see much of her husband, Susan was still very much involved in his projects and plans. She took on the responsibility for that year's trophy purchase: Castlemartin, bought for £200,000, or £800 an acre. The children also took to the project of contributing to its refurbishment during the summer of 1973 with some gusto. Modern health and safety rules would never allow it, but as the workmen gutted and rebuilt the enormous house, the six children ran riot on-site. They were allowed to create huge pictures on the walls, which Susan photographed before they were replastered. As one of her sons later said appreciatively, 'my mother overcompensated in a positive way for my father not being there, but it seemed to work'. With the energetic input of Susan and the children, Castlemartin was recreated as a stately family home.

There was an accident that year that had a major impact on their lives. Jack had a new car, an Audi that Tony had bought for him, and he loved bringing Aileen and one or more of the children on trips in it. Jack decided they would head for the west of Ireland by a circuitous route, going via Cavan where he had served as a customs officer many years before, with just O'Reilly's eldest, young Susan, in tow. He lost control of the car on a sharp bend on a narrow road, the car hit a wall, turned over and righted itself again. Jack was uninjured but his main concern was for his grand-daughter, who had bumped her head badly. It was not as serious as the knock Aileen had taken, however: she was unconscious and had suffered cuts to her face that would require 65 stitches and leave a scar.

She was taken to Cavan Hospital, where she awoke, but within hours she suffered a major stroke, most likely brought on by the accident. O'Reilly was in Pittsburgh when he heard the news and he ordered that Aileen should be moved to a hospital in Dublin, while he rushed back across the Atlantic. Things did not seem too bad initially – as her speech was unaffected and the paralysis only slight, the doctors were confident that she would recover. However, she fell in the hospital a few weeks later and had another stroke. It would be the start of a long, slow, punishing decline in her health. She blamed Jack for the crash – saying that he had been going too fast – whereas he blamed some unknown fault in the car and, according to Fallon, 'the accident seemed to bring out a smouldering resentment between her and Jack which was to affect the last years of their lives together'.

The realisation of the proximity of death seems to have stirred Jack to try to resolve his marital situation. Jack became convinced that he might be able to get an annulment of his marriage to Judith from the Catholic Church, which would leave him free to marry Aileen. He sought the counsel of his nephew, Fr John Geary, a son of his eldest sister Mary, who had not spoken to him since he had abandoned Judith. Geary had taken it upon himself to try to mend bridges, prompted mainly by an experience with his, and Tony's, aunt Cathleen, another of Jack's sisters. She had come home from India, where she had served as a nun for 45 years, for a brief visit and she too had refused to meet with Jack. However, just before she left Ireland again, she asked Geary to deliver some gifts to her brother. It had a powerful impact on the aging Jack and he insisted that Geary must meet Tony. They did once in Ireland, but when Geary moved to Toronto to become president of the Holy Ghost Fathers, he began regular trips south of the border to meet Tony and Susan and the family for Thanksgiving or Easter, staying a week at a time.

Geary and Jack had discussed the issue of marriage many times, but Geary advised that there was no way an annulment could be granted, especially as the existence of four children was proof of consummation. Still, Jack contacted Judith and started discussing the idea of annulment with her, much to her horror. Much of this had happened in advance of Aileen's strokes, but now the circumstances of her ill-health added impetus to Jack's campaign. He arranged for Geary to meet with his eldest son, Julian, when both were in Dublin and during the conversation Geary asked how Judith would react to the idea of divorce and if Julian could raise it with her. It was a strange request on many levels, not least that divorce was not legal in Ireland. Judith was furious, not surprisingly, when he broached it with her.

Judith's life without Jack had not been easy, for a multitude of reasons, some of them financial. O'Reilly's half-brother and half-sisters had endured difficulties throughout their lives, some but not all as a result of their father's abandonment of them. Julian emigrated and became a successful businessman, first in Canada and the USA, and then in the Bahamas. Juliette, a domestic science teacher, had a bad car accident with her six-month-old daughter and Judith had to take over the rearing of the child for a while. Ria was very bright academically, but she was paralysed from the waist down by polio at the age of 17: she was forced to abandon a planned career in medicine because in those days there was no wheelchair access in universities.

She married and moved to New Zealand, but died at the age of 39 without having ever met her famous half-brother. Eveleen had moved to London and Jack's big idea was that Judith should go to live with her so as to gain residency and therefore obtain a 'foreign divorce' that would have some standing in Ireland. Eveleen would have nothing to do with the idea either and resented the distressing impact on her mother of her father's manipulative schemes.

It may have been the strain of all that had happened during 1973 – his parents' car accident, his mother's strokes, the realisation that all of his Irish commercial activities were going to be more difficult to manage financially than had been anticipated – but at Christmas, O'Reilly brought up the issue with his house guest, Geary, in front of a stunned Susan. He asked if his father ever spoke of his 'rather unusual background'. Geary replied that 'he talks of little else'. O'Reilly wanted to know if his father still thought that he didn't know. Geary told him that Jack was convinced his son didn't know and prayed every night that he wouldn't find out, for fear that his son would cut him off.

O'Reilly asked Geary to fly to Dublin the next day, to tell Jack that he knew and that 'it's not of the slightest significance to me'. He said that he would fly over to visit his parents the following Saturday. Fallon reported in *The Player* that Geary would later wonder about O'Reilly's assertion that his parents' situation didn't matter to him. Geary pondered on the pace that O'Reilly set himself and his competitive drive. 'I wondered whether there was some compensation mechanism at work here,' he said. Geary discussed it with other close friends of O'Reilly and apparently they thought much the same – that far from being of no importance, it was one of the driving forces of his whole life.

As promised, O'Reilly went to Dublin and his parents' house in Santry. They embraced, cried and never mentioned it again.

It was an enormous relief to Jack, particularly, that his son had not rejected him, and he went to tell Judith of it. It seemed to strengthen his resolve about legalising his position. Amazingly, while visiting Eveleen in London, Judith decided to give her husband what he wanted. Julian flew from the Bahamas to help her with the divorce and brought her back to Wicklow. They began the necessary legal process, but suddenly Judith's health gave out. She took to her bed and was dead within 10 days. Her last words, spoken to her housekeeper, apparently were: 'isn't it strange how easy you could be taken?' Jack attended her wake and his presence was tolerated by his children and the extended Clarke family.

A week later Jack and Aileen married. They did so at the Jesuit chapel at Belvedere, with Jim McCarthy acting as best man. They did not invite Tony or any other family members, not even Fr Geary. O'Reilly subsequently told Fallon that 'it was a minor course correction, not an event they wanted to share'. O'Reilly said he happened to be in Dublin the same day and rang the Stephen's Green Club to book a table for dinner for himself and Susan. He reported the manager as saying to him, 'Oh, Mr O'Reilly, you must be coming to your father's party tonight. Oh my God, they're having a party the likes of which you've never seen. We've got bottles of wine out of the cellar that haven't seen the light of day since the British were here. It's going to be fantastic ...' O'Reilly said that he wouldn't be there and instead he and Susan went to the Soup Bowl in nearby Molesworth Street and toasted his parents at midnight.

Jack died two years later, in April 1976. He had an operation for a gallbladder problem but suffered a stroke during it. Tony and Susan rushed back from the USA to be at his bedside. He never regained consciousness and died four weeks later. None of his four children from his original marriage had been to his bedside, because they didn't want to meet Tony or Aileen. Eveleen said, 'All I could think about was, he never said he was sorry.'

CHAPTER NINE

A LASTING LEGACY: THE IRELAND FUNDS

O'Reilly left Ireland for Pittsburgh not long after the violent sectarian conflict in Northern Ireland had escalated. 'I've seen Ireland riven as I wouldn't have expected when I left 10 years ago,' he told *The New York Times* in an interview published in 1981. 'People like myself have a responsibility to accelerate dialogue,' he said, referring to political efforts to find a peaceful settlement and his active engagement in behind-the-scenes or extra-curricular efforts to affect a political resolution that would bring about peace. 'I think all of us are prisoners of our childhood,' he said. 'Ireland has a very strong intellectual pull.'

O'Reilly had grown up more interested than many of his generation in Northern Ireland and the circumstances of its creation. Many southern Irish, once the Civil War had passed, tried to get on with establishing the Republic as an independent sovereign State. Despite rhetoric about desiring reunification of the island and a heavy emphasis on imposing nationalist rule, surprisingly few actually paid much attention to the institutionalised injustices that had been entrenched quickly to the disadvantage of Catholics.

O'Reilly was deeply conscious of having been brought up in a Catholic school but the Jesuits did not focus on the politics of nationalism in the way that, for example, Christian Brothers-controlled schools did. Instead, the Jesuits brought up these children to rule the society in which they found themselves and to focus on change, albeit limited, from the top, down. O'Reilly was schooled in politics elsewhere: at home, through his father; as a senior civil servant of the new State; by his mother's brother, Tony O'Connor; and on his trips to Donegal with Peadar O'Donnell.

O'Connor was another member of O'Reilly's family with a secret, one that he revealed, almost fully, as late as 1975, a year before the Ireland Funds was established. O'Connor had joined the Free State Army at the establishment of the Irish State. Before the age of 20 he had killed about a dozen men in his service of the new State, as the Civil War raged. But it was an incident in January 1923, in Athlone, that haunted him and he recounted it more than 50 years later in a thinly fictionalised book called *He's Somewhere In There*. He told the story of his neighbour and childhood friend, Johnny, who had joined the Irish Republican Army (IRA). He and Johnny had joined the Free State Army but when it split, Johnny went with the republican side. Seven months later Johnny was captured, and Tony watched as his friend was killed by a firing squad.

O'Reilly was also influenced from an early age by his interaction with northern Protestants and British people through rugby. O'Reilly's mind was always open to other people and other experiences, and even if his Irish national identity was important to him, he was sympathetic to others who regarded themselves as British. He abhorred the use of violence from an early age; his interest in war, military campaigns and military leaders did not blind him to the consequences of war, both in human misery and economic destruction. Instead, O'Reilly marked himself out early on as a fervent advocate of 'constitutional nationalism' – the belief that Ireland, North and South, should be a single nation and that the goal must be achieved through non-violent means – and held consistently to that point.

Some businessmen in O'Reilly's position may have had little or no interest in the North other than how it might impact on their profits, but the reality was that in his generation many people would have had strong private views that they kept that way. Other than politicians, most kept their heads low during this period from 1969 onwards instead of becoming involved in public discourse about the conflict in Northern Ireland, its causes and its possible resolution. There were good reasons for this: commercial organisations ran the danger of boycott, officially or not, of their products and services if they were seen to be taking sides; worse, their premises could be targeted for the destructive bomb blasts that were so common in the Six Counties and that were detonated by both republican and loyalist terrorists. O'Reilly, through Fitzwilton and IN, had plenty of business interests on the island that could be targeted.

There were also issues of personal security, both for him and family members: businessmen were targets of threats of kidnap or murder – and indeed some less well-known business figures in the North were killed. Kidnap was a major issue in the early 1980s – Quinnsworth boss Don Tidey was one victim, Dunnes Stores' director Ben Dunne was another, and the Dutch industrialist Tiede Herrema had been subjected to a lengthy ordeal in 1974. Threats were made against O'Reilly – such as bullets in the post – and whenever he was in the country he was the subject of a degree of protective Garda surveillance, limited in effectiveness as it was in the era before mobile communications. He was concerned about the security of his children also, especially when he sent the boys back to Ireland for their secondary school education. Cameron recalled one incident at his secondary school, Clongowes Wood College, when an intruder on the school grounds sparked an alert among the priests. He was rushed upstairs to the attic to be hidden while the man – who had no intentions of harming anyone and had no idea who O'Reilly was – was apprehended. Cameron was delighted by all the drama, but O'Reilly would not allow fear to dictate his decisions.

Yet he was enormously concerned by the potential for the Provisional IRA (PIRA, Provos) to raise funds in the USA that would be used to buy guns and bomb-making materials. The Provos were supported by an organisation in the USA called Noraid, which masqueraded as a humanitarian relief organisation but which in truth had more violent ambitions. There was a long tradition, going back to the 1916 Easter Rising, of Republicans raising money in the USA, a forerunner of the crowd-funding of the Internet era. Generations later there were fewer Irish-born to tap but still plenty with an interest in Ireland, even if they were not necessarily very well informed.

In 1976 O'Reilly and Dan Rooney, later to be appointed by President Barack Obama as American ambassador to Ireland, decided to create the Ireland Fund of the United States, which later became the Ireland Funds. O'Reilly couldn't remember who had told him, but he had heard there were 44 million Americans of Irish extraction, far more than there were Jews. Yet, even back in the 1970s, the American United

Jewish Appeal (AUJA) was raising over $400 million each year for Israel while Congress, after lobbying, was supplying another $2 billion. O'Reilly felt that Ireland could get something similar.

The idea was that the Ireland Funds would hold dinners, balls and other fund-raising events in cities all over the USA and deliberately target the wealthy. O'Reilly and Rooney decided that the fund should be non-sectarian and that it should tap those of Protestant or Northern extraction as much as Catholics and those with affinity to separate Irish nationhood. While the likes of Rooney and Donald Keough of Coca-Cola clearly came from Catholic stock, he also targeted the Westons, Eatons and Mellons, who were from Presbyterian backgrounds. The wealthy not only had money to give, they could also use their influence in political and investment circles. O'Reilly personally wrote or telephoned many leading Irish Americans, inviting them to functions that he promised he would attend personally – and he did.

He set down the principles of reconciliation and integration – 'a peaceful and fruitful co-existence in which both nationalist and unionist identities are mutually respected' for the organisation. He promised the money would go to community-level, self-help projects: 'It behoves those of us who know the reality of modern Ireland, who know the aspirations of young people, both North and South, Catholic and Protestant, to try to urgently communicate to them there is a new Ireland, and not the one their grandfathers talked about.'

O'Reilly liked to joke that the first Ireland Funds dinner, in New York in 1976, cost so much beyond budget that they had to run another a year later just to cover the losses on the first. Soon there were dinners in Boston, Chicago, Miami, Los Angeles and San Francisco, at which O'Reilly developed his considerable skills as a public speaker.

'Elite New York social life revolves around events for non-profits, be it museums or other cultural institutions, charities, diaspora organisations or whatever,' explained Kingsley Aikins, who became the trusted CEO of the expanding Ireland Funds for nearly 20 years. 'Tony spotted how people embraced it for networking. He did it himself. If somebody came for your event, you returned the favour for theirs. There were layers within events. $5,000 bought you a seat at the table but if you, or your company, would pay more there was the private "chairman's reception" for those who could afford it.' Aikins also said that O'Reilly understood the power of celebrity quickly. 'He would always have stars along, it was part of the brand positioning. The last thing any of these celebs wanted was anyone saying "you're buying guns".

The Jewish example gave rise to O'Reilly's favourite exhortation to his guests at the various dinners that would become the mainstay of fund-raising, at least until such time as a system of philanthropic donations was established. He famously urged fund-raisers to 'dress British, look Irish and think Yiddish'. It worked, because in a short time the charity became the second largest US philanthropic organisation, after the AUJA.

An added personal benefit was that, as much as anything else, it would give O'Reilly an opportunity to perform in front of crowds, as he used to do on Lions tours. His performances, and that was what they were, were a draw in themselves for many attendees. He would crack jokes, make relevant quotations, tell funny stories about prominent Irish personalities, introduce important points, thank whoever was required, and put the pressure on people to donate. He recycled material – he would walk to the podium and make a big show of not finding a ledge on which to place his glass, then say, 'this clearly wasn't made by an Irishman, there's nowhere to put a drink' – and stories, such as one about the co-op chairman who addressed his farmers by telling them, 'Ladies and gentlemen, when I addressed you here last year I told you we were on the edge of a precipice. Well, I'm pleased to report that since then we've taken a great leap forward.' And he did it all with pitch perfect accents from all across Ireland, with various British, American and New World voices thrown in too, the Belvedere acting training put to good use.

But he had important messages to convey, too. O'Reilly wanted to educate and inform the American public about what he saw as the complexities of Irish identity and how that inflamed passions dangerously. He felt that many Irish-Americans had 'dangerously romantic' views of the Irish situation, finding them 'simplistic, antiquated and with a medieval directness to them'. O'Reilly enjoyed taking his audience through Irish history lessons. He would take them on a form of time travel from the Norman invasion of 1170, through to the Battle of Kinsale of 1601 and the evils of Oliver Cromwell. 'The savage character and subsequent plantation of Cromwell poisoned irreversibly the relationship between the old Catholic Irish and the new ascendant

Protestant Anglo-Irish,' he declared during one speech. 'Simply put, in the period from 1601 to 1700, the Catholic Irish were dispossessed of all their possessions – their land, their citizenship, their capacity to worship publicly, their ability to secure education and their participative role in politics and the professions. No Catholic could own a horse, seek an education or practice his religion. By 1714 land ownership by the Catholic was reduced to a paltry 7%. The die was cast. Catholic Ireland was vanquished.'

One such speech was delivered on St Patrick's Day in 1985 at Boston College, at the request of Fr Monan and his board of trustees, and in which he described the USA as 'the land of my adoption'. It set out all of O'Reilly's political ideas as they applied to Ireland. He described Daniel O'Connell as the 'first great constitutional nationalist'. He spoke of the people of Ireland being denied an independent nation after they had voted for it in 1918. He told of Michael Collins 'waging a form of guerrilla warfare which was noble, courageous and ultimately victorious' against the hated British forces of the Black and Tans. He remembered that the establishment of Northern Ireland had been a unilateral act by Lloyd George. He accused the people of the new Republic in the south of being so inward-looking that they ignored 'the reality of Catholic deprivation on matters of voting, housing and employment' in the north, until violence exploded in 1969.

'I want you to know the complexity of Irish history,' he told his audience. 'I want you to know why there is such a durable struggle punctuated by a firm sense of righteousness on both sides of the tribal divide. I want you to know that there are no simple answers to the Irish question. I want you to understand that Ireland was a cul-de-sac and did not have space like America to absorb its discontent. This great nation of America was the first place on the face of the Earth where the Irish had an opportunity to cross over the tracks and to be free. America with its opportunity, its endlessly expanding economy, its space, its liberalism and its egalitarianism was the perfect place for the long-oppressed Irish Catholic and, I want to add, importantly, the Presbyterian dissenter from Ulster.'

The Ireland Funds grew quickly. In 1981 he wrote to the organisation committee and complained that 'while a great deal has been achieved in four years, we appear to have come organisationally to a grinding halt. In effect, we have become a rather sophisticated annual dinner committee with a few peripheral fund-raising activities and a coherent philosophy from a directional point of view in regard to our triple aims of peace, culture and charity.' He wanted to become an endowed organisation, with a balanced income stream independent of the annual fund-raising activities. In time it was to become that, and more.

CHAPTER TEN

THE HEINZ MODEL OF MANAGEMENT

Tony O'Reilly had a Brendan Behan story he liked to tell as part of his after-dinner speaking routine. He would break into a Dublin working-class accent and tell of a trip that the playwright had made to the USA at which he received plenty of liquid hospitality from various Irish-American emigrants. 'Well, I'm going home to Dublin,' he would quote Behan as saying on the last evening of his trip, 'and I'm going to tell them how well yiz are all doing over here, and how far up the social ladder yiz have all climbed. That'll put them in right bad form for Christmas.'

It was a well-chosen story, not just for the punchline or because it made the audience feel good about themselves but because it also insulated him, to an extent, from grudging comments. O'Reilly seemed to be doing just fine at Heinz during the 1980s, now that he was CEO. He gave plenty of interviews on both sides of the Atlantic that served to buff the glowing image of one of Ireland's great success stories. He was now signing himself as Dr AJF O'Reilly, an affectation that most of his newspapers subscribed to when requested to do so, although in the more egalitarian USA most people still called him Tony. The moniker had come about because he had submitted a 500-page thesis entitled *The Marketing of Agricultural Produce* to, of all places, the University of Bradford in England. It awarded him a Ph.D. in 1980 and he decided to use it, just as Tony Ryan and Michael Smurfit were to demand that they be called 'Doctor' after they had received honorary degrees from universities.

While some wanted to know about the material benefits deriving from his rise at Heinz, others wanted to know just how he managed the organisation, which was presumably the real secret of his success. It couldn't all be down to his charm and charisma, no matter how important they were in distinguishing him from other perhaps as talented but less obviously so executives.

Fortunately, his loquaciousness during interviews and investor presentations revealed much about O'Reilly's claimed way of doing things. Those interviews told a lot about his conservatism when it came to managing Heinz, especially when compared to the madcap expansion that had marked his approach in Ireland in trying to develop Fitzwilton. This was a man who, in 1978, told Wall Street reporters that 'the best way to get into new product development is to steal the other guy's ideas. You buy the company.' Heinz's new products under O'Reilly had come mainly through such acquisitions – of small companies with few, although highly successful, products – rather than through internal development. 'The track record of large companies in new product development is chilling,' noted O'Reilly. 'We've experimented, and find that we're not as good at it as the entrepreneur.'

And yet, with the exception of WeightWatchers, and given the weight of money that the Heinz balance sheet carried, his efforts to expand by way of acquisition were not notable, either in cost, size or number. In 1981 O'Reilly detailed his strategy in an interview with *The New York Times*. He contrasted what was going on at Mobil Oil, where he was a director and which had just announced a multi-billion-dollar bid to buy Conoco, with his approach at Heinz. 'We will not use the merger route to climb to the top of the volume mountain,' he said. 'We plan to stay in the food industry, and the field is well picked over. There are no great bargains around.' He intended to pay for any future acquisitions with cash, which was limiting as to the ambitions that could be chased. The company had kept its share base virtually unchanged for 10 years, issuing a minimal amount of new stock. 'I'm very reluctant to give away paper,' he said. The critics noted that this did not apply to the generous share options awarded to senior management … and to O'Reilly.

One of his ex-employees at Heinz once described O'Reilly as a 'commercial coward', but added that he meant that as a compliment. He said Heinz had deliberately avoided fights with bigger players, at O'Reilly's insistence. 'He likes to be in markets where Heinz has either a proprietary brand, or a dominant position, so that we are in control, as opposed to being the number three, picking the battle with the monolithic giant,' this ex-manager said. 'Or being in a less competitive market, so the profit margins are more reliable. That's one reason why in the United States we have not attacked Campbell's by introducing a major brand of soup, even though we're the brand leader in many countries around the world. Campbell's has 80% of the American soup market, and although it's a battle we'd dearly love to win, it's a battle which would be too bloody to fight. So that's commercial cowardice, but it's also good commercial sense.'

Instead, his emphasis had been on improving margins and profitability by way of cost-cutting. He had gained a reputation for chiseling out costs long before he went to the USA. Heinz UK had employed just over 12,000 when he first joined the operation, but in just over a decade that had fallen to 3,600. He saved costs by removing the back label from Heinz ketchup bottles, saving anywhere between $1.5 million and $4 million per year depending on who tells the story.

O'Reilly kept telling his subordinates that they had to grab market share, have new products for 'niche markets' and cut costs, but it was the third piece of advice that caught his attention the most. The main trend in business, as O'Reilly identified it in 1981, was that inflation had been brought under control by Central Banks. 'If inflation is no longer the underwriter, you can't price your way to profits anymore,' he said. 'If you can't get growth out of price and volume, you've got to get it out of cost.'

O'Reilly started what he called his Low Cost Operator (LCO) programme, although the wags renamed it quickly as Let's Compensate O'Reilly when it became clear the additional profits would generate greater wealth for the boss personally. 'LCO 1' began in 1982 when O'Reilly set cost-cutting goals for each subsidiary. It was up to management to decide how they wanted to reach their targets: they could shut plants, close product lines, make people redundant or invest in new technology or whatever else they wanted, as long as they cut the dollars that were demanded of them.

O'Reilly was happy with the results, but decided to extend the programme even further. The decentralised nature of Heinz, with lots of autonomous subsidiaries, meant that people didn't share ideas as to how to reduce costs across all divisions. Accordingly, 'LCO 2' started in

1985 with a so-called 'congeniality' phase. Subsidiary presidents were asked to meet frequently during the year to make forecasts, map strategies, discuss allocation of resources and exchange tips and technologies. This might be considered normal at many companies, but it hadn't been done at Heinz before.

As chairman it was Jack Heinz's job to call upon his president and CEO to speak at the AGM. At the September 1985 event he did so in a way that greatly flattered the Irishman: 'I can think of nothing more complimentary to say of him than to compare his energy, vitality and genius for worldwide salesmanship and statesmanship most favourably with the man who founded this company 116 years ago,' said Heinz.

O'Reilly had enjoyed some luck in the timing of taking over from Gookin. His predecessor introduced many changes to put things right after Heinz's flawed stewardship as CEO, but he had not gone far enough. Gookin had ducked out of the closures of some factories and product lines, often for heritage reasons. O'Reilly was far more ruthless about closing or selling things, putting the capital back into more profitable or faster growing areas of the business. When inflation slowed under O'Reilly's watch, Heinz had been able to increase its prices at a faster rate for a few years still before such opportunities evaporated.

O'Reilly's charisma brought about another benefit: he was able to persuade stock market investors, particularly the bigger institutions, that shares in the bigger, better Heinz deserved to be priced at a higher multiple to its earnings. A company's share price is a multiple of its historic or expected earnings per share, depending on what rating an investor places greater store by. Heinz, regarded as somewhat dull and unexciting, had traded prior to O'Reilly's time on a single-digit multiple of its earnings. Now the multiple was more commonly in the mid-teens, which meant the overall value of Heinz was climbing strongly too, as profits continued to grow. When O'Reilly moved to Pittsburgh, the value of the company was just $600 million; by September 1985 it was $4.3 billion. It wasn't all down to him, but he wasn't shy about claiming credit for a sizeable chunk of the improved fortunes.

So it was that at the 1985 AGM, where Heinz had introduced him in such glowing terms, he was able to list impressive achievements since his rise to the position of CEO. Money invested at the end of 1980, along with dividends reinvested in new shares, had provided a 433% increase, as against 78% of the average of American shares in general.

Fortune magazine put him on the cover in June 1986 as a symbol of the theme 'the new economy', describing O'Reilly as 'a leading apostle of cost cutting' and as 'a marketing visionary who was managing for the new economy before there was the new economy'. The magazine said his latest strategy for cost-cutting was 'about as radical as an industrial company can pursue: he threatens to quit manufacturing'. In reality, O'Reilly was examining the idea of outsourcing production, looking to see if someone else could make products cheaper for Heinz than they could make them. It was partly a way to incentivise management to do better with their own assets.

One of his big initiatives was the introduction of the squeezable plastic ketchup container. It may seem a reasonably simple thing, but such are the moves that can boost a company's profits. Heinz had discovered that customers, especially the occasional ones, were unhappy with how hard it was to get the ketchup out of the glass bottle. The problem was finding a plastic that would keep moisture out and the ketchup, which has a shelf-life of a couple of years when stored properly, fresh. It took three years to develop a suitable product, but Heinz was 18 months ahead of competitors to market with it. There were then developments with the size of the bottle; whereas once it had all been 28 ounce bottles, now there was 20, 44 and even 64 ounce bottles. O'Reilly authorised the introduction of new lines, such as Salsa-style ketchup. The growth of fast-food outlets was a godsend, as long as they were prepared to take branded product instead of looking for generic. Heinz increased market share dramatically, just as the market was expanding.

In his role as CEO, O'Reilly was prepared to be ruthless, even with friends, in a way that was not necessarily noticeable in Ireland. He faced a dilemma when the tuna business Star-Kist, run by his great friend Joe Bogdanovitch, ran into difficulties, for example. The western Pacific region had opened up its fishing waters, and competition from operators in Thailand and the Philippines meant that tuna dropped dramatically in price. Bogdanovitch, now in his seventies, was emotionally wedded to the business. O'Reilly was not; he sent in Dick Beattie, a troubleshooter, to fix it. Beattie decided the only hope for the Star-Kist business was to apply the LCO methods and that Californian wage rates were too high for that to succeed. Instead, Heinz invested heavily in new equipment and systems for processing and canning in

Puerto Rico and in Western Samoa, where wage rates were a third of the American operation. In 1985 O'Reilly closed Terminal Island and the long-standing tuna operation in San Pedro, despite massive local opposition and Bogdanovitch's personal heritage, and got rid of the fishing fleet.

O'Reilly was a dictator, claimed to be so and made no apology for it. 'I write to each of the area vice-presidents each year categorising their virtues and what I perceive to be their shortcomings,' he told *Business* magazine, 'saying things like, "You'll never be president of Heinz" or "Your style is professorial: I want you more action oriented". The notion of collegiality has triumphed and, with it, the need for me to behave like a shit has substantially diminished, though the process is not as emollient as it sounds. There are some very acerbic exchanges. What comes out of them though is absolute clarity of objective.'

O'Reilly said that Simon & Schuster had interviewed people at Heinz as to what made him different from other people as a leader. 'Extraordinary patience' was the answer, he said. 'Tremendous capacity to listen to people, and to extend the conversation, analyse and debate, and review and reanalyse before a decision is taken. All that surprised me because I don't think of myself as patient; I think of myself as urgent. Extraordinary patience to me sounded like a synonym for a prevaricator.'

A non-executive director of Heinz, Dr Richard Cyert, noted O'Reilly had a trait 'which is one of the most difficult characteristics to culti-vate, his ability to get rid of people who are doing a marginally satisfactory job. In other words, an executive you might give a 'C' to, who's not failing but you can see a better job could be done with another person. Those are very difficult people to fire. And Tony has the guts to get rid of very good people, and he does it in a very humane way – people go away pretty rich from Heinz – but they are still 'C' executives. And that's real leadership, the things to me that make him an outstanding CEO.'

'You cannot have too much information coming into your desk about your business,' O'Reilly told an Irish academic, Dr Ivor Kenny, who he had appointed to the board of IN. 'I am also devoted as a manager to the principle of rapid response. Every Friday night, from every Heinz affiliate in the world, I get the sales figures for the week with commentaries and comparisons with budget and the previous year. You might consider that to be a kind of antique notion – in management today it is not fashionable to talk about sales, one talks about being the low-cost operator, one talks about market share or geo-political strategy or financial architecture or defeasance or whatever the latest buzz words are – but it all starts with sales … The flurry of telex machines on Friday from all over the world tells me, just reading them as they come in, how my businesses are doing. If you are making the sales, then with our tight budgetary systems, everything else falls into place. If sales waver, you're going to have to do something pretty quickly.'

'I'd say that one of the best things about Heinz is that our response times to danger are remarkably quick. We can see pretty clearly what is happening and we immediately call our troops together and take action quickly and decisively. If you are fighting Heinz in the marketplace, and you gain one point of market share, that will be followed swiftly by retaliation from us and we are generally able to deliver because we have a lot of reserves. In the business of running Heinz, the secrets of its performance are clear objectives, low-cost operator status, big brand shares, niche markets and, again, rapid response times.'

'My entire career at Heinz was very devoted to the whole issue of managing,' he said. 'My management style is very collegial, very open-door. I have a view that facts are friendly. It doesn't matter if they're good facts or bad facts – all facts are friendly. I keep saying to my people: "Tell me what the situation is. Don't tell me the good news, don't tell me the bad news, tell me all the news".'

His critics were to wonder if that was really true and if it was, how much longer it would remain the case.

CHAPTER ELEVEN

THE SEARCH FOR LIQUID GOLD

Ireland has never owned its own oil supply and is not a producer. A discovery of oil has been sought for decades in the belief that, if found and brought to the surface, it would transform our economy and our society. After all, the discovery of oil has brought the Middle East from abject poverty to ostentatious wealth in a couple of generations. It has created huge wealth for Norway, Great Britain and the USA. It has long been a dream for Irish economic policy-makers to discover a supply to use for ourselves and to sell to others, and to remove our energy dependency on external sources (who can increase the price of supply dramatically in the event of shortages). That dream has existed for decades, but particularly from the late 1970s after the Irish economy had suffered serious shocks as a result of its dependency on overseas oil.

Exploring for oil is a very expensive business, particularly if the drilling has to take place underwater. The chances of a successful strike may be low and even if oil is found, it may be very expensive to extract. There may not be sufficient quantities to extract or even if there is, the price per barrel of oil sold may not be attractive enough to support the capital investment required. But that doesn't stop some men from trying – and it is a very male-dominated industry – because to these explorers, oil is liquid gold.

Many searches took place in Irish sea-waters during the 1970s. Hopes were raised many times, only to be dashed each time. There was an oft-told joke that God could not have been so cruel as to put the two islands of Britain and Ireland alongside each other but deposit the oil only in the area controlled by the British. O'Reilly, already intrigued by the possibilities in the mineral resources mining industry, loved the thought of being known as the man who struck oil in Irish waters and who brought it ashore, for the common good. 'Margaret Thatcher,' he said at one stage, 'had used the revenues from North Sea oil to "purchase the silence of the non-working classes", and he followed that with the observation that an Irish oil strike would 'enable us to pay the bill, as it has enabled Mrs Thatcher to pay the bill while she put into effect the structural changes that are going on in Britain'. That it would make him filthy rich in the process was another attraction.

The idea for an Irish company to get involved in what was usually a game for big companies with deep pockets came from his IN colleague Gerry McGuinness. He had been introduced to Jim Stafford, a reclusive but wealthy Wexford businessman who had inherited the family shipping firm. Stafford was friendly with an American oilman called Emmet O'Connell, who had come to Ireland to set up Eglington Oil. Stafford suggested to McGuinness the creation of a new oil exploration investment vehicle. McGuiness approached O'Reilly, because O'Reilly had some experience upon which to draw. He had become fascinated by the oil industry because of conversations with senior business figures in Pittsburgh, where Gulf Oil had its HQ before it was taken over by Chevron, and then by his membership of the board of Mobil Oil, one of the so-called 'seven sisters' that largely controlled the industry.

O'Reilly believed that prices would continue to rise – they had risen fourteen-fold since before the 1973 oil crisis – and that great riches would be available to those who found exploitable new fields. Fitzwilton had some spare cash to invest and O'Reilly knew the Getty Oil-led consortium, which planned to drill in Irish waters in the spring of 1981, wanted to spread its risk by selling part of its 37.5% share to a new partner in a process known as 'farming out'.

O'Reilly decided he would lead the start-up of Atlantic Resources, raising capital of £1.25 million. The company was formed in February 1981. Half of the money was provided by Fitzwilton, at a price of 50p per share. O'Reilly took a 15% shareholding on a personal basis, as did Stafford. O'Reilly's friends and business associates pitched in for smaller amounts: McCarthy, Ferguson, Leonard and McGuinness were among the number. Even Sir Basil Goulding invested, along with the solicitor James Cawley, a director of ICC Bank from 1980 to 1983. This State-owned institution would be very supportive to Atlantic Resources in providing finance and underwriting share issues at important times. Within weeks there would be a further fund-raising of £2.5 million, this time at £1 per share, a so-called second tier of investors who, because they were not connected to the original promoters, had to pay more for their shares but still got a better price than those coming after them. It was small-scale stuff in this business, but it was enough to buy a 10% stake from Getty in Philips Maroon Group and pay its share of the estimated £16 million cost of drilling a well.

O'Reilly brought in an oil veteran, geologist Don Sheridan, to run Atlantic. Sheridan had overseen Marathon Petroleum's extensive drilling programme in Ireland for the previous 13 years and established production at the lucrative commercial gas field at Kinsale in County Cork. He was originally introduced to Atlantic by Stafford – who, in turn, apparently had Sheridan recommended to him by O'Connell – but it took a personal intervention by O'Reilly to secure the deal and then only on the basis that Atlantic would apply for licences in the Celtic Sea that Marathon had abandoned but that Sheridan was convinced still had potential. O'Reilly blocked a suggestion from Stafford that O'Connell be included as a director, although he was allowed to become one of the early investors.

Shares were made available to the general public on the stock market in April 1981, a month after drilling had started in the Porcupine Basin off the coast of County Clare. The shares, for which the original promoters had paid just 50p, and the next group just £1, were now priced at 290p, less than three months after the company's formation. They went to 335p in early trading, and then 395p by lunchtime. RTÉ had sent a camera crew to cover it for the news, but somebody had forgotten to put film in the camera and the brokers were asked over lunch to 're-enact' what had happened that morning. Dealings also had to be halted briefly because things were so hectic. The shares closed the day at 340p, which meant Fitzwilton had made a 'paper profit' of £3 million and Stafford of £1 million. Some people, including those who had been introduced at £1, sold their shares and made handsome first day profits. Surprisingly, the State-owned bank

ICC was among those who quickly decided to cash in some of its shares.

Newspaper coverage referred to 'unprecedented scenes of mayhem', but *The Irish Times* cautioned about how remarkable it was that a company that had no oil, and only a 10% stake in an American company that was due to begin drilling off the west coast, could be so attractive to investors. The unspoken assumption was that an O'Reilly factor was at play that, notwithstanding the lack of success of his previous Irish investments, following him would be a good investment strategy, even for those who had never before bought shares.

The speculation put the titles under O'Reilly's control in a difficult position. Towards the end of June, Colm O'Briain, the new president of the Irish Stock Exchange, was interviewed for the *Sunday Independent* by its business correspondent Martin FitzPatrick, and he commented adversely on what had happened at around the time of the Atlantic Resources flotation. The quotes were included in the interview provided by Fitzpatrick for publication in the *Sunday Independent*.

The editor, Michael Hand, immediately asked Fitzpatrick to remove the reference to Atlantic Resources, and he always insisted that he did so without any intervention by or reference to O'Reilly. When Fitzpatrick refused, the editor made the changes anyway, as was his right. The reporter contacted the NUJ, which, mindful of promises about editorial independence made nearly a decade earlier, immediately called a mandatory meeting of all the paper's journalists. Management entered into negotiations with the union and agreement was reached, above 12 hours after the union's mandatory meeting had started. The NUJ stated that it had received 'assurances from management that they had the freedom to write about companies in which the newspaper's directors had interests on the same basis as any other company.'

Subsequently, an investigation of the share register carried out by *Business & Finance* in September 1981 discovered that some of the most prominent names in Irish business, many of them bankers, had held shares in Atlantic and some had sold all or part of their holdings for large profits.

None of this halted O'Reilly's gallop. Sheridan was a big fan of Celtic Sea exploration, believing that a find there would be far cheaper to extract because the waters were not as deep. Two months after Sheridan joined Atlantic, the company applied for and was awarded six application licences in the Celtic Sea off the Waterford and Cork coasts. O'Reilly began negotiating with Gulf Oil in Pittsburgh to come on board these new licences. Gulf Oil brought in Union Oil and the two agreed to pay $7.5 million for two-thirds ownership of the blocks, giving Atlantic a third for free and a sizeable cash contribution towards development.

Such developments meant there was an enormous amount of speculation about the company's prospects and the price of the shares see-sawed wildly. O'Reilly did not trade them, but there was always the suspicion that friends and followers did, and that belief made subsequent share issues more difficult to complete. In the 1982 chairman's statement O'Reilly wrote that 'given that revenue from Irish offshore operations must be some years away, we must accept that investors will seek the possibility of capital gains in the absence of immediate dividend income'. His newspapers were watched to see if they were promoting or reporting, but the *Irish Independent* insisted that it warned its readers against speculative gambling in Atlantic shares. There were suspicions that some writers across the titles might have been gambling in the shares, too, without declaring the conflict, which would not have been surprising given that there were 18,500 separate shareholders on the register at its peak.

O'Reilly decided that Atlantic needed to raise money, both for further exploration in the Celtic Sea beyond the initial Atlantic drill in which it was involved and also for new ventures in the USA that he thought would provide regular cash-flow while exploration in Ireland went on. The shares fell to 245p as the initial hype calmed, but O'Reilly decided to raise another £5 million in capital, at a price of 210p per share. Fitzwilton and O'Reilly took their full entitlements but Stafford, who did not agree with the American strategy, did not participate and neither did McCarthy or Ferguson, apparently because they did not have the spare cash to gamble. The shares fell to 175p, but started to rise again on rumours, the most prominent appearing in the *Sunday Times*, that the consortium had 'struck it rich' in the Atlantic. The shares went as high as 375p, and then the results came in. Oil had been found at Block 35/8, but the flow rates were poor and not commercial.

Meanwhile, Atlantic went hunting for gas in Oklahoma and West Virginia, hoping that a find would give it cash-flow. Atlantic borrowed $4 million from the Republic Bank of Dallas and McGuinness said 'we are sufficiently encouraged to want to borrow more money than to sell more shares'. O'Reilly had found these American assets after an introduction by one of his Mobil Oil board colleagues. He appointed Harold Prunner as manager of Atlantic's US interests and John McEnroe senior, father of the world's most famous tennis player of the era, was brought in as a legal adviser, charging what Stafford thought were very high fees. Stafford was furious at the whole adventure, believing Atlantic was vulnerable as 'out-of-towners' to being ripped off. Even a trip to Pittsburgh and on to Anadarko for the directors did not persuade Stafford to change his mind and his vocal opposition began to irritate O'Reilly greatly. Indeed, things were made worse by an allegation from Stafford that he had been told there was not enough room for him on the Heinz corporate jet that was used to fly his board colleagues on to Anadarko. He wanted more non-executive directors to counter the O'Reilly dominance on the board. Stafford questioned what he called 'the high costs' of running the company in 1982, arguing that, at £813,000, they were about £500,000 higher than they should have been. He questioned the necessity of first-class trans-Atlantic seats on Concorde and the use of a penthouse at the Hatch Street premises. He also alleged a loss of confidence in the company on the part of the London stockbrokers Greig Middleton, which subsequently departed its brokerage to the company in unclear circumstances as to who was responsible for the parting of ways. Their final fall-out came in May 1983, with the shares back at 120p. There was a row over his expenses and, according to Ferguson and O'Reilly, that became the issue on which he resigned. Stafford claimed to have quit over the imposition of a new share option scheme for executives that was agreed at a board meeting he had not attended.

That was embarrassing, but perhaps not nearly as important as the news that the first well on Block 49/9 had been completed and plugged. Yet O'Reilly decided to go again, raising another £4.7 million at 80p per share. This meant Atlantic had now raised £26 million in 26 months, more than half in equity, the rest in borrowings. O'Reilly took up his full entitlement of shares, but Fitzwilton only purchased a quarter of its available rights and passed the balance to the Saudi Arabian multi-millionaire Sulaiman Olayan, who served with O'Reilly on the Mobil board. His company, Competrol, paid £900,000 to take what would turn out to be an 8% stake in Atlantic. Ferguson, Leonard and McCarthy all passed on the opportunity to buy more shares.

Not surprisingly in those circumstances, the fund-raising was a near failure. It was true that oil shares were now out of fashion, but the failure of the directors to show confidence in the company by taking up their rights, even in speculative circumstances, was telling. Put simply, however, some of these men did not have the money to speculate. Even the presence of a major new international figure on the share register did not provide sufficient reassurance to many existing or potential investors. The 800 other ordinary shareholders did not even offer enough money to cover the £270,000 cost of the share issue.

The underwriter, ICC Bank, was left with two-thirds of the shares and their price crashed to 42p. O'Reilly's Saudi Arabian friend saw the value of his investment fall by almost £400,000 immediately. *The Irish Times* predicted that it would be now much harder for the company to raise further funds.

Mysteriously, with no new official information forthcoming, the share price started to rise again, reaching 85p by 4 July. On 9 July the *Irish Independent* reported 'no oil yet but the Celtic Sea hunt is on' and *The Irish Times* reported, 'Oil fever grips stock market as Atlantic Resources price soars to 105p'. On 23 July the *Irish Independent* reported that 'Gulf encounters oil/gas shows in the Celtic Sea' and the share price went up to 216p within a week. *The Irish Times* then reported that, according to unnamed industry sources, Gulf had estimated recoverable reserves in Block 49/9 of between 30 million and 70 million barrels of oil. By 6 August the share price was up to 425p. The one headline that O'Reilly and McCarthy enjoyed the most featured in the *Cork Examiner*: 'Workers dance on rig.' The *Sunday Times* reported that 'Ireland's long search for offshore oil may have paid off at last'. It said there were rumours from the rig of a find that could contain 400 million barrels of oil.

Atlantic kept quiet, even though O'Reilly had received big news on a Sunday in July, just after he had entertained Henry Kissinger at Castlemartin, having brought him to lunch with Taoiseach Garret FitzGerald in Dublin the previous day. Sheridan phoned to tell him that Gulf had made the big test of blowing the charges in the hole. Oil started coming up the pipe with increasing momentum. 'It's running at three hundred barrels a day now, and it's still building,' said Sheridan, his voice apparently cracking with excitement. By the end of the day the oil was running at a rate of nearly 100,000 barrels per day, which suggested the field contained a minimum of 100 million barrels of oil.

In the absence of any official statements the shares continued to soar as some investors plunged in, anticipating further capital gains, while others were happy to take theirs by selling. Gulf's exploration manager, Bob Kirkbride, said he didn't seem to know as much about his own operation as other people allegedly did. Gulf sent a test ship to the location in the hope that this would dampen down premature speculation about the commercial potential of the well. But the excitement continued when Eddie Collins, junior minister at the Department of Industry and Commerce and a Waterford TD, put out a statement to say that the results he had seen 'are very encouraging indeed'.

In August 1983 Gulf finally confirmed that oil had been tested at 9,901 barrels a day from the well, and that there was a gas flow too, totalling 2.1 million cubic feet per day. The shares now surged to 610p. London stockbrokers Hoare Govett said the Atlantic shares could be worth £12. Even, reported the *Irish Independent*, if the field would only supply 250 million barrels, it would supply half of Ireland's oil needs and add £50 million a year in petroleum taxes. *The Irish Times* reported that some people took out second mortgages on their homes to raise the money to buy the shares.

Canny investors, however, looked beyond the headline announcements to the highly relevant small print. While Gulf said its find was an 'oil discovery', it also said that the well would be closed temporarily and that further appraisal drilling and study would be required 'before the commerciality of the discovery is determined'. The shares yo-yoed between 300p and 600p as rumours began to circulate that things were not as good as the optimists said. The operators said nothing.

At Fitzwilton's AGM in October, O'Reilly boasted that the company's £2 million investment in Atlantic was now worth £13.7 million, at a price of 685p. 'With hindsight it may be said that we should have taken up our rights,' he crowed, excusing the 'mistake' by saying, 'we felt at the time that it would be imprudent to invest more funds when no discoveries had been made'. Atlantic was now worth more than £140 million, the fifth largest company on the stock market, five times bigger than Independent Newspapers, bigger than the Smurfit Group or Waterford Crystal or Bank of Ireland. O'Reilly celebrated that the find had put Ireland 'one step away from self-sufficiency' and said, 'it is not exaggeration to say that the oil find is a major event in the economic history of this country'.

Sheridan wanted to drill another appraisal well to prove, relatively cheaply, much of what they had seen. Gulf, as the operator, wanted to see how wide the field might be and its geologists decided to drill at a slant, using a new technique called deviation, to delineate the field. This well, 49/9-3, was to be fateful. The shares shot up to over £9 as speculation mounted, and nearly touched £10 before everything went wrong.

The drill was having many problems, as O'Reilly came to understand a little better after a helicopter visit to talk to the workmen. More money was needed and Atlantic raised another £15 million, this time placing shares with financial institutions at a price of £6 each, a massive discount on the £8.90 price on the market. Again, the directors did not participate in the new fund-raising. Some of the money was used to service mounting debts in the USA, as revenues from its gas fields were not sufficient to cover the interest costs on the debts.

O'Reilly did his best to calm the speculation. 'I believe it is important to re-emphasise to all shareholders and interested outsiders that the economic worth of any oil accumulation in an off-shore situation cannot be assessed by a single well … It is totally immature, in fact it is improper, for any individual or body to claim expertise with which to make prognostications at the present time.' At a Christmas Eve EGM of Atlantic shareholders in the Shelbourne Hotel, O'Reilly said 'only the government and Gulf know what the real situation is. Newspaper reports were built on nothing but speculation'. He said shareholders should 'be very wary of newspapers and the reports which they published as factual'. He said media reports that 'suggest a provenance of "industry sources", a "company spokesman" or a "department official" cannot be authoritative, but must be taken at their face value, that of outright rumour or speculation'. Meanwhile it was believed that Stafford had sold his shares, as had others.

In January 1984 the *Irish Press* ran a report saying the well was dry. The story was contradicted within hours by an *Evening Echo* story that declared: 'Rig workers elated: Another major oil find.' The day following his initial report, the *Irish Press* reporter Lloyd Smythe alleged that 'the Irish energy company's share price had plunged on Monday, only to recover as dramatically yesterday, as it became clear to stockbrokers that it was a manipulative operation'.

The Irish Times reported that up to 5% of the company's shares had changed hands in two days and that the value of the trade might have been as high as £30 million. In this era, prior to computer registration of shareholdings, it was possible to buy and sell within a so-called 'account period' of two weeks and not be identified. It was also possible to sell ahead of rumours of bad news and buy back again at the lower prices. It was a system wide open to manipulation.

Smythe's reports were attacked in IN titles – where one columnist, without any apparent sense of irony, renamed him 'Flawed Snide' – but within a month it would turn out that his prediction was accurate, although that may have been just luck rather than a report based on inside information. Smythe quit journalism soon afterwards, disillusioned by his experience.

O'Reilly insisted afterwards that everything that had been published had been speculation. 'Nobody knew until the very end, and even then there was a debate as to whether it was dry or not. If there had been any knowledge earlier, two things would have happened: the government would have been forced to announce it on the spot, and secondly, there was no way Gulf, at $100,000 per day, would have gone on drilling for another 30 days.' Stafford concurred: he didn't believe that O'Reilly or anyone knew the well was dry in advance of the final official announcement.

That took time in coming. By the end of February the shares had halved and in April 1984 it was announced, finally, that Gulf had found flows only of salt water in the first two zones. While testing remained ongoing in the third, it too was dry. The shares fell back to 350p and continued falling, even after each share was split into five.

O'Reilly was to receive public criticism of the type he hated. He blamed Gulf for not following Sheridan's instructions as to where to drill. He tried to explain that what had happened was not unusual in the industry. *Business & Finance* ran a story asking if Atlantic Resources was 'a vehicle which makes a lot of money for a select group of people, or is it a means whereby the amateur investor can end up losing his home and wrecking his family?' It also claimed that 'the O'Reilly spell has made its way into the marketplace and that is where it counts. If the man's magical powers cannot be turned into money, then a lot of people have been wasting their time.' He had taken a risk with his reputation – and it would be the same with other companies in the future. It was the inevitable outcome of leading a public limited company (PLC) and treating it as if it were a private company.

There was a shareholders' meeting in April 1984, but O'Reilly cited other commitments in Pittsburgh. Cawley chaired it, as Leonard and Ferguson were also missing. The shares fell to 83p on rumours that Gulf had encountered serious technical problems in its flow tests at Block 49/10. This was confirmed a few days later and Gulf said it was not likely to resume Celtic Sea drilling until 1985. The shares fell to 60p, and then it was revealed that Cawley had sold 90,000 shares a month earlier, reducing his holding to 560,000 shares. It was estimated that Cawley raised about £125,000 in selling those shares. Subsequently it emerged that other directors had sold about 200,000 shares between them over the previous seven months, but that no disclosures had been made publicly.

It wasn't illegal, but it was not considered good practice either. What would other investors have done had they known? Would they have sold, too? The sensitivities surrounding it all were enormous. *Success* magazine was threatened with litigation for libel after an article that implied share-rigging. In October 1984, Des Nicholson, now president of the Irish Stock Exchange, told *The Irish Times* that he was 'concerned about information coming out in recent weeks from what is supposed to be a tight hole'. He said that he had no evidence of share-rigging, however. Dick Spring, Tánaiste and Minister for Energy, said the government would take immediate action if allegations of insider dealing or share-rigging on the stock market could be substantiated. He said there was no hard evidence, 'but it looks as if there was unnecessary shifting of the market'.

In early 1985 Atlantic was under financial pressure, with a commitment to spend £5 million on two wells and with big repayments due on its American loans. The debts there were £11.9 million and the interest bill was £1.25 million per annum. It began talks with the Australian company Broken Hill Proprietary (BHP) about it buying half of Atlantic's interests in the six-block oil licence that contained the Waterford discovery. The transaction was discussed at a price of £14 million, but it did not go ahead and Atlantic ended up beginning legal proceedings against BHP for failing to proceed with the deal.

O'Reilly would not give up. He believed that the second well had shown an encouraging flow. Gulf believed that it showed too little to have more interest in it. O'Reilly obtained government permission to drill again on Atlantic's own licence, then persuaded Gulf to come back. Atlantic raised another £10.5 million in October 1985 and O'Reilly put in another £1 million of his own money. He issued a November 1985 statement that the results were 'both positive and encouraging' and that the Atlantic board awaited 'the outcome of future exploration and appraisal wells with enthusiasm'. He declared the Celtic Sea to be a 'new hydrocarbon province, fulfilling every hope and expectation held by the company at its formation'.

More drilling took place in 1985 and 1986 and into 1987. By this stage Atlantic's share of all the costs had been £40 million. The shares had dropped to 11p (55p before the five-for-one share split). Stafford had been proven correct on the American investments, which ended up costing $10 million in losses when they were sold or closed down. Everything was hanging on the final drill in Block 49. The initial flow found oil, but it flowed slowly and the drill soon hit sand.

O'Reilly refused to concede defeat or that he had been wrong. 'We have established a record second to none on our exploration activities,' he said. 'There can be no question but that our exploratory effort to date in these blocks has been highly successful.' It was only years later that he admitted that 'we may have hit the only puddle of oil ever found'. That, however, would not stop him trying again in the twenty-first century.

Fintan O'Toole was among those who blamed the media for pouring fuel on the fire during the hysteria of this decade. 'Throughout the mid-1980s, there were bouts of hysterical exultation and suicidal depression as the price of shares in Atlantic Resources fluctuated wildly,' he argued. 'The prices of the shares depended on speculation in the newspapers, and O'Reilly owned many of them.' While that is true, much of the speculation appeared in the papers he didn't own, such as the *Cork Examiner*, as it was called then, *The Irish Times* or the *Sunday Times*.

Garret FitzGerald felt that his Fine Gael/Labour coalition government of 1982–87 was punished for its position on oil exploration and Atlantic Resources: 'When we were in government, he [O'Reilly] remained supportive to a degree, but towards the end there's no doubt that the *Independent* swung somewhat, and I think the oil thing was the major factor. He felt that the terms we were imposing for oil were too tough and he wanted them changed. The pressure was expressed rationally enough in terms of the need to modify the terms. I didn't feel there was improper pressure. But I felt as time went on he was getting more and more frustrated and he was allowing this to influence his overall judgement. He became irritable and angry. And I didn't think he was very helpful to us afterwards as a result.' Academic Kevin Rafter noted drily that 'the fact that [FitzGerald] led a deeply unpopular government at a time of national economic crisis may also have been a contributing factor in the newspaper coverage.'

O'Reilly told *Forbes* magazine in the 1980s that he had 'influence' among Irish politicians by virtue of his wealth and his ownership of leading newspapers. 'Since I own 35 per cent of the newspapers in Ireland I have close contact with the politicians. I got the blocks he [the geologist] wanted,' he said.

However, Spring gave O'Reilly little of what he wanted; he refused to deliver all of the terms and conditions for oil exploration that O'Reilly demanded, especially in relation to tax on any exploration costs and a stake in any possible finds.

O'Reilly was of the belief that the oil exploration industry was like a poker game and Ireland simply didn't know how to play it. He believed 1983 had provided an opportunity for the country to show that it understood the business, but that 'the politicians failed the test'. His criticism of government went back to the mid-1970s, when it introduced a series of measures, including the abandonment of export tax relief and a combination of royalties, State ownership rights and corporation tax, which added up to an effective tax rate of 85% on profits. He said it had killed exploration for a decade and while it hadn't stopped O'Reilly exploring, it may have limited the interest of others who didn't share his patriotic intent.

In spite of the absence of any significant recoverable oil resources, the issue of how to tax any potential discoveries was a somewhat meaningless controversy, even though it raged across the media and among politicians right up to 1987. One of the *Irish Independent*'s financial journalists, Colm Rapple, was broadly in favour of a substantial public say in – and take from – any oil resources, and wrote articles to this effect. It contributed to an ever-widening distance between him and O'Reilly, one that was completed when Rapple took a redundancy deal and decamped to the *Irish Press*. In his absence the

Irish Independent generally took an editorial line in favour of minimising the restrictions and the tax regime in order to encourage the highly expensive business of exploration.

Oil exploration up until this point had cost O'Reilly substantially more than anyone else. He personally repaid huge bank debts incurred for exploration, even though he could have legally avoided responsibility because the debts had been incurred by a PLC. Several directors of Atlantic were burned as well – although it was not until many years later that it was revealed that O'Reilly's close friends, Ferguson, McCarthy and Collins, had been secret buyers of the shares and used secret off-shore bank accounts to do so, and that O'Reilly had moved to help McCarthy and Ferguson when it resulted in them amassing debts they could not clear.

The issue of doing business with old friends was one that caused O'Reilly trouble over the years. In particular, dealing with McCarthy's financial problems was to be an Achilles' heel for O'Reilly for many years. If McCarthy's dealings in Atlantic shares were to be a problem for him personally – and by extension for O'Reilly – then the pair's contortions around McCarthy's involvement with Fitzwilton were even more difficult to untangle.

The most controversial transaction was the sale of Dockrell's from Fitzwilton to McCarthy, at a time when McCarthy was still Fitzwilton's CEO, for the sum of £5.7 million, a 27% discount on its net asset value. The deal was described as 'unorthodox' by *Business & Finance*: 'Eyebrows have been quite naturally raised at the prospect of the chief executive of a major public company bidding for a major division of the same company,' it said, suggesting he should have resigned first. *The Irish Times* reported on an acrimonious EGM to approve the sale; angry shareholders eventually agreed on the basis that a delay of the sale, and the search for an alternative buyer, would result in increased CGT being paid, if a new buyer could be found.

Selling Dockrell's would not end Fitzwilton's financial involvement with it. The company continued in serious financial trouble under McCarthy's ownership and couldn't make bank repayments or pay Fitzwilton debenture interest payments of £95,000 that had fallen due on 30 June 1981. O'Reilly's solution was for Fitzwilton to lend Dockrell's another £750,000. At end 1980 Dockrell's had borrowings of £5.8 million, but shareholders' funds of only £4.1 million. Another EGM was held, at which one shareholder asked O'Reilly, 'why don't you bail him [McCarthy] out yourself?'

Business & Finance reported that 'the incestuous relationships that exist in Irish business life are explained largely by the smallness of the country. It is not surprising that everybody knows everybody else and that from time to time friends will do one another a good turn. They should do so however in ways that will not harm third parties who happen not to belong to the charmed circle. We are not satisfied that the Dockrell's deal was in the interests of the Fitzwilton shareholders.'

Dockrell's limped on, hobbling Fitzwilton with it. At the 1982 AGM, solicitor Eugene Collins told O'Reilly about Dockrell's that 'this is a public company, not Foir Teo [a special government rescue agency], we should not help lame ducks'. O'Reilly cited Dockrell's reaching break-even for a couple of months and said, 'everyone is waiting for it to come around'. Another shareholder said, 'you are the axe-man at Heinz, so would you deal with Dockrell's in the same way if it was a Heinz company?'

It was only one of a whole set of controversies as Fitzwilton continued the difficult business of tidying itself up, and as its share price continued to languish. More assets, such as Crampton's and the Goulding's building, were sold, and the value of the remaining holding in Goulding's was written off in 1980.

O'Reilly engaged in some revisionism. He argued, for example, that Goulding's in Cork had been saved. He said that 'those without confidence in the company's management should sell their shares', prompting one investor to condemn 'the chairman's contemptible attitude towards the shareholders'. O'Reilly bought more shares, but Leonard and Ferguson sold more. The company's main hopes resided in the investments in IN and Atlantic, a case of putting all of its eggs into O'Reilly's other baskets.

In May 1986 Fitzwilton sold £4 million of shares in IN, leaving it with a 6.64% shareholding, and then sold the rest in August for another £5 million. Its total profit on an original investment of £1.7 million was £8 million. O'Reilly said that Fitzwilton now planned to spend between £10 million and £20 million on a British acquisition that would have expansion potential and 'minimum downside risk'.

O'Reilly told Fitzwilton shareholders at the AGM on 30 December 1986 that 'there are a number of interesting investment opportunities that are being examined at this juncture. I think I can say that if events favour us in the area of natural resources, that Fitzwilton, freed from the constraints placed on it by its underwriting of Goulding's Chemicals for over seven years in its long fight back to its present prosperity, could be an exciting vehicle again in the area of acquisition of both public and private companies, particularly those with export potential and we intend to make appropriate management appointments to achieve these ends.'

In other words, it all depended on Atlantic striking oil. Shareholder Donald Pratt told O'Reilly that, 'it is clear to me that Fitzwilton is being run to effect control of Independent [Newspapers], to effect control of Atlantic Resources and to indulge themselves'. O'Reilly responded: 'We are falling on the sword of our own excellence.' It was hardly a phrase that any other similarly embattled chairman might have used.

CHAPTER TWELVE

MAKING THE NEWS

The controversies surrounding press coverage of O'Reilly's activities at Atlantic Resources had been anticipated, to some degree, at the time of his taking control of the company, even if that was nearly eight years before the oil explorer came into existence; it was considered bound to happen with something he owned or controlled. In the meantime, however, the political parties watched carefully to see if and how O'Reilly would swing the support of his newspapers for particular parties or individuals; these were times in which it was felt press coverage held some sway over voter intentions.

O'Reilly was a long-standing friend of Jack Lynch, but he also knew and liked Garret FitzGerald, who had become Fine Gael's leader in succession to Liam Cosgrave in 1977. O'Reilly's loyalties were to be tested near the end of the decade, however, when Irish politics were convulsed by major personality battles, especially when Lynch, under enormous pressure, stood down as Fianna Fáil leader and Taoiseach in late 1979 to be replaced, to his shock, by Charles Haughey.

For reasons that were never clarified, FitzGerald apparently authorised a fresh approach to O'Reilly in 1980, to see if he would be interested in standing as a candidate for Fine Gael in the next general election. He 'quite possibly' would have appointed him to the Cabinet. 'At that stage he would have had a reasonable expectation of office, if he was going to divert his whole career from where he was. And he would have been very dynamic I'm sure,' FitzGerald said.

Not surprisingly, O'Reilly said no. Why anyone would have thought that he would give up his enormously well-paid job at Heinz and all of his other commercial interests is somewhat mysterious, particularly if there was not the guarantee of a powerful office. He was the boss there, secure in his contract, whereas he would have to start working his way up again in politics, albeit from near the top, and on a dramatically reduced income. There would have been uproar had he kept his newspaper empire at the same time. However, FitzGerald knew of O'Reilly's deep interest in politics and in that era the idea of the brightest and the best dedicating themselves to public service instead of private riches was stronger, perhaps, than it is now. FitzGerald subsequently said that 'he has perhaps come to feel that Tony O'Reilly's interest is Ireland's interest, is the world's interest, the way people do when they get to his stage'.

Senior politicians believed, however, that he was worth contacting over serious issues, such was the state of flux in which the country found itself in the 1980s. FitzGerald told of how, during his period as leader of the opposition in 1982 before returning to power late in that year, he 'was in touch with' O'Reilly over allegations that the Haughey-led government was interfering with the independence of An Garda Síochána. 'In talking to him over that period it was kind of on the assumption that he had some degree of influence over the newspapers, I suppose. I certainly would have been seeking his assistance in terms of the papers at that time. If I was ringing him, it wasn't just for the general chat.'

If O'Reilly sat on the fence in the ongoing battle between Fianna Fáil and Fine Gael – which resulted in three general elections in 18 months in 1981 and 1982 – he was firm in insisting his papers give no comfort to the IRA hunger strikers of the time in the H-Block wing of the Maze prison, and to the IRA subsequently. In a 1988 interview with *The New York Times*, O'Reilly stated that he made sure that IN titles reflected his views on Northern Ireland. 'Anybody who advocates violence is totally unacceptable in our newspapers,' he said. 'We believe in constitutional solutions. All the editors know that and they faithfully follow that policy.'

He had addressed the issue two years earlier in his very detailed interview with Ivor Kenny for the book, *In Good Company*. 'For example, the reasons I bought the Independent Newspapers could be interpreted as a straightforward Citizen Kane notion of political power,' he said. 'That would be totally wrong. As you, Ivor, well know, I have never sought to exercise any political power in the newspapers. All the board of the company has said is that the paper will continue to be a paper of constitutional nationalism, it will proceed on the basis that violence and bloodshed can do nothing to bring community to the island of Ireland, and after that editors and writers can write what they want about whom they want, subject to the normal constraints of good taste and commerciality.'

Vinnie Doyle, who became editor of the *Irish Independent* in 1981 after a very successful period revamping and revitalising the *Evening Herald*, said that he'd only had one major 'disagreement with Tony' and that was over the coverage of terrorism. 'There was an exceptionally violent spate of tit-for-tat murders in the north and I decided we would publish two lengthy interviews with the then head of the UVF and of the IRA, stating their views and motives as they saw them. And we attracted quite a lot of criticism for what we had done, because people are understandably concerned when a newspaper gives a platform to terrorists in this way. And when we next met O'Reilly was fairly concerned – in fact very concerned – about the effect it would have. I explained the position to him, how it looked to us in Dublin, and how I thought the articles had been in the public interest. I'm not sure I entirely convinced him, though he saw the point of view. Normally, O'Reilly and I are like-minded because we both detest the IRA. They have sent me a bullet through the post with my name scratched on the side of it, the IRA calling card. I don't know whether Tony has ever received one. Some things are not asked in Ireland.'

Doyle was not O'Reilly's biggest fan, however, and while the relationship was one of mutual respect, it was not close. He appreciated that O'Reilly had approved his appointment as editor of the *Evening Herald* in 1979 and then promoted him to the *Irish Independent* position in 1981, but Doyle's great affection was for Kerryman Joe Hayes, who he found infuriating at times but greatly supportive and inspirational. Doyle loved his job and was extremely good at it, but often felt that O'Reilly did not give him sufficient resources to do it as well as he could have. Indeed, Doyle's love for the job could be used against him: he was so dedicated to it that he did not want to lose O'Reilly's favour and so, no matter what happened, Doyle would be loyal to O'Reilly. This would be important in various controversies over the years and Doyle was retained in his position until 2005, well past retirement age, as his reward.

Loyalty was something that could also be attributed to Aengus Fanning at the *Sunday Independent*. Indeed, Fanning might not have survived some of the many controversies that peppered his reign as editor had it not been for O'Reilly's confidence in Fanning's ability to always cover his back. Fanning had not been the first choice to become editor of the *Sunday Independent* in succession to Michael Hand. He got the job, starting in January 1984, only after the former *Sunday Tribune* editor Conor Brady turned it down, fearing that he and O'Reilly would not want the same type of *Sunday Independent* and that editorial considerations would take second place to commercial priorities. In their negotiations, Brady raised the important issue of why editors were not appointed to the boards of the various IN companies or the Group itself. 'By definition,' he argued, 'they stand behind the commercial executives in the organisation's pecking order.' O'Reilly was adamant in his response: 'I can't put you on the board. That's not how we do things.' Brady subsequently became a very successful editor of *The Irish Times*.

Hayes moved Fanning from his position as news analysis editor at the *Irish Independent*. He joined a newspaper with a very small staff and few resources, but Fanning had ideas that appealed to Hayes to carve out a distinctive position for the *Sunday Independent*. Fanning examined the market research that Hayes provided him and came to the conclusion that people were bored on Sundays and that if they were going to read a Sunday newspaper, they would want something that was far from boring. Fanning believed that the reason newspaper sales in general were in decline was because journalists and editors were making newspapers to suit themselves and perceptions as to what they were supposed to be doing, not for their readers. Hayes decided that Fanning needed additional personnel as well as resources and hired Anne Harris, wife of O'Reilly's 1970s critic Eoghan, from *Image* magazine to be his deputy. Fanning had an ambition to make the *Sunday Independent* a magazine wrapped inside a newspaper and she would be crucial in that regard, bringing what Fanning saw as a woman's intuition to an overwhelmingly male environment. The main drawback was that printing restrictions meant he was confined to a dull, poorly printed newspaper product. That meant the writing had to resonate and sparkle, although the concentration on colour and opinion rankled with competitors, just as they had condemned the rise of the *Sunday World*. O'Reilly watched approvingly as circulation and revenues improved, although there were to be many times when he would be attacked for not reining in what were seen as the excesses of the paper.

Fanning was not afraid to flatter his boss either and to dismiss those who complained about it. In the late 1980s Hayes had an idea to bring in lucrative advertising revenue. It was difficult, and expensive, to print colour advertising in the Middle Abbey Street titles. Colour advertisements had to be printed on the giant rolls of newsprint by the Smurfit Group and then those would be brought back to the Middle Abbey Street presses, where that day's news would be printed around the pre-printed colour advertisements. It was a precise and expensive process. Hayes decided to print colour newsprint supplements that would then be added to the *Sunday Independent* as an extra section. The advertising space would normally be sold to cigarette manufacturers, who were banned from appearing on television screens. Fanning decided on a series of eight-page profiles of some of Ireland's most famous people. Most famously, all copies of an eight-page special on Tony Ryan had to be pulped after the aviation boss objected to the inclusion of a photograph of a woman with whom he was enjoying a private relationship. There would be no such problems with the O'Reilly edition, once Fanning had picked him as one of the subjects.

O'Reilly faced ridicule when the special supplement appeared. It included 17 pictures of him, alongside the likes of Henry Kissinger, Margaret Thatcher, Valery Giscard D'Estaing and Robert Mugabe. It had a portrait shot of him, his wife Susan (from whom he would very soon separate) and their six college-age children, and another of him stepping off his corporate jet. It was accompanied by a series of interviews, giving him the opportunity to hold forth on Irish business and international management practices and on the government's economic policies – he approved of the hardline fiscal approach to balancing the government's finances being taken by Haughey, now restored to power. A headline read: 'A Man for All Continents'. It was something that even *The New York Times* commented upon, quoting an unnamed *Irish Independent* reporter who said: 'It was tasteless for O'Reilly to let that run in a newspaper he owns. It isn't as though nobody knows who he is here. Everybody knows who Tony O'Reilly is.'

O'Reilly's explanation for agreeing to involvement with the project was that other celebrities were given similar treatment each week, so why should he censure a valid journalistic idea just because he was the controlling shareholder? 'That's reverse nepotism,' he said. 'The editor said, "Tony, you're an interesting person. It doesn't matter that you have an interest in this paper. You are somewhat larger than life. Why are we going to be barred from writing about you?"'

There were mixed feelings about O'Reilly among his journalists, although naturally criticisms were voiced more in private than in public. His appearances in Dublin were rare and he tended to meet with financial journalists, rugby reporters and social diarists as well as editors. He went out of his way to flatter many of them.

'The legendary charm is all true,' said Brendan Keenan – who was personally headhunted from the *Financial Times* to work as business editor at the *Irish Independent*, before later being promoted to take responsibility for economic coverage at all the Irish titles – in an interview for the book *Paper Tigers* in 1990. 'When you have a meeting with him he makes it seem like you are the only person he is seeing all day. He is not like other tycoons: he never appears as if he's itching to go, never looks fretful, never looks at his watch, is always calm and relaxed. The charm is authentic, and the reason he can achieve it is superb organisation. His diary is meticulously planned. People are given 20 minutes, 25 minutes, an hour, but they don't realise this because Dr O'Reilly handles his time so expertly.'

'The charm is his genuine nature,' said Liam Healy, now the group CEO. 'At the same time I don't think anyone would feel that there isn't a genuine toughness there too. However in his dealings with people on the newspapers he is genuinely appreciative of their contribution, he remembers them, remembers what it is they do, rarely forgets a name, even out of context. If he's only met someone once before and then runs into them at Shannon Airport, he'll know exactly what they're called. People of course find great charm in that.'

It may have been a subtle way to get people to write about him and his friends in the way he wanted. Rival newspapers, politicians and businesspeople were always making allegations that O'Reilly was interfering with the editorial content of the papers, although as often the complaint was that he didn't, that he allowed individual editors and journalists too much freedom to do as they wanted without suffering consequences. The *Sunday Independent*, for almost the entire duration of Fanning's editorship, was as unpopular with many people as it was successful in becoming the dominant paper in the Irish market, often because it was accused of following O'Reilly's agendas against people or organisations. The evidence was often circumstantial and did not do justice to the genuinely maverick nature of Fanning or the personal prejudices of Harris (and her ex-husband, Eoghan Harris, who was later to become increasingly influential on an *ex officio* basis), but there were occasions when many suspected that the *Sunday Independent* was anticipating what O'Reilly likely wanted.

'He's not an intrusive owner by the standards of others,' said Keenan in the *Paper Tigers* interview, and it was a position to which he still subscribed in 2015. 'He makes his editorial point through the board, which is the proper way to go about things. But he has certainly had the effect of upgrading the standards and status of Dublin journalists, and upgrading their pay too I might add … I would say that in general he is liked and admired by his journalists. This is Ireland of course, so nobody who has made a great fortune like Dr O'Reilly has can altogether escape the usual badmouthing. But on his newspapers it is rare for people to have any particular gripe against O'Reilly; against his emissaries, yes sometimes, but O'Reilly is just a little too removed from the day-to-day scene for the average journalist to badmouth him.'

O'Reilly said that editors worked autonomously and did not phone him in connection with contentious stories. 'I don't think it would be fair on me and it certainly isn't fair on them to feel there's that level of expectation. Secondly, it's not possible for me in the job that I have, running a world corporation like Heinz, to give them the measured judgement they require. You'd become capricious and there's enough of these around.'

'I only really have contact with my Irish editors at our annual international conference, which takes place for three days at Castlemartin. All the editors are there into the long reaches of the night, which is when I really talk to these guys.'

He described his statement in the annual report as 'a kind of internal memo to all our editors: this is what we stand for'. He said they 'can read it and take what they want from it and reject what they don't like. But at the end of the day if we find an editor constantly chafes at the sort of policy we've laid down, then we obviously don't want him in the group.'

Healy said he did not prevent his other business interests being criticised in his own newspapers. 'Sometimes we'll cringe when we see it but Dr O'Reilly stands by his non-interventionist policy,' said Healy. O'Reilly's critics said it rarely happened for it to become an issue and that in the cases where it did, the journalists responsible tended to move on or be moved on.

The *Paper Tigers* profile did contain one interesting criticism of O'Reilly that, unsurprisingly, was not attributed. 'It is rare for Dr O'Reilly to say no to anything,' said an unnamed editor. 'He seems not to understand the meaning of the word, and certainly doesn't see it as a useful one in his vocabulary. By the same token he doesn't expect anyone who works for him to say no either. Occasionally in newspapers you need the word no too, saying it is part of the discipline of editorship. So it sometimes concerns me when he sees his newspaper editors and his brand managers at Heinz in the same light: people who lack the imagination to make the papers prosper without his own vision being sold to them on a regular basis. Having said that, when he summons you for a ride in the back of his Bentley, which generally means a meeting on the way to the airport because he's flying off somewhere, it never quite seems like that because he gathers you up in his charm.'

This unnamed editor also said: 'One of Dr O'Reilly's great skills – possibly his greatest skill, is that despite all the dollar-crimping that goes on, his businesses retain a kudos and swank. You never feel, on the inside, that his enterprises are tacky. And a lot of this feeling stems from Dr O'Reilly himself. He's such a charismatic, big fellow, with so much personal style, that when he jets in to wherever you happen to be, with a broad smile across his face and all the appearance of being so pleased to see you, you forget while he's there that he's made you sweat for the sake of those few extra dollars.'

Fintan O'Toole was another who was wary of O'Reilly's seductive abilities. He argued that 'because he seems to take his own air of authority for granted, he can afford to be charming, even gossipy, knowing that nobody will take advantage of the sense of intimacy he creates'. It was an astute observation. I know from experience that O'Reilly told people things, sometimes scurrilous, made acerbic or funny comments about people, even friends, confident that he could trust the recipient not to repeat them or, if he did, not to attribute it to him.

For all of those claims to great style, O'Reilly was also a tabloid proprietor and a so-called downmarket newspaper was important to the financial health of the overall business in the early years of his stewardship of IN. It may not have sat well with his image of himself, or with how others saw him, but completing the purchase of the *Sunday World*, and the Newspread distribution unit that Gerry McGuinness had developed with it, helped IN's cash-flow and profits throughout the 1980s, and persuaded him to go further into tabloid markets.

While the *Sunday World* was to be the Irish alternative to the pernicious British tabloids, in fact it ended up aping some of their worst characteristics, so much so that one particular story caused considerable embarrassment to O'Reilly at the 1984 AGM. One Sunday in February 1984 the front-page lead headline was 'Sexy High Jinks in CIE'. It quoted the allegations from two unnamed busmen that female bus conductors were enhancing their promotional prospects by having sexual relations with their superiors. Not surprisingly this caused uproar, not least because there were so few female bus conductors at the time. One shareholder at the AGM described it as 'a cheap and scurrilous attack on the sexual morality of an easily identified small group of women in this city'. He asked how much of the profits were due to 'the sexy presentation of the *Sunday World*', further implying that IN was living off immoral earnings. O'Reilly admitted that elements of the *Sunday World* were 'prurient', but maintained that the newspaper operated within the law and catered 'in a generally responsible way for a very substantial market in this country'. Before anyone could argue, he added: 'It is not acceptable to the board nor to the economic vitality of this group that the *Sunday World* should not be a part and a very important part of this group.' Then he summed up the guiding philosophy: 'In many cases we try to lead public opinion, not follow it.'

CHAPTER THIRTEEN

LOSS AND CHANGE

US President Ronald Reagan sent O'Reilly a special videotaped message to mark O'Reilly's fiftieth birthday on 7 May 1986. The Heinz chairman was a 'mere child', joked Reagan, who added, 'In another couple of decades he will be old enough to think about running for public office.' There was more: 'Whether on a rugby team, running an Irish newspaper chain or an international business, Tony O'Reilly has established throughout his life a remarkable record of achievement and accomplishment.'

The recipient was not just the CEO of Heinz but the chairman of Independent Newspapers, of Fitzwilton and of Atlantic Resources. He was a director of Harvard Business School, Mobil Oil, Bankers Trust Company, Georgetown University, *The Washington Post*, the Executive Council on Foreign Diplomats, the University of Pittsburgh and the Pittsburgh Opera. His chairmanships included the Grocery Manufacturers of America and the Food Industries International Trade Council. He was a council member of New York's Rockerfeller University, a member of the Congressional Award Board and a member of the National Committee of the Whitney Museum of Modern Art. He was a partner in Cawley Sheerin Wynne solicitors and chairman of the Ireland Funds. He had a plethora of honorary degrees: he was Doctor of Laws from Allegheny College, Doctor of Business Administration at Boston College, Doctor of Civil Law at Indiana State University, Doctor of Business Studies at Rollings College and Doctor of Laws at Wheeling College. He was a Life Fellow of the Irish Management Institute and a Fellow of the International Academy of Management.

Such accomplishments and distinctions required a party to mark the occasion of his landmark half-century birthday. Almost unbelievably, his friends and family tried to pretend they had nothing organised, other than a small family get-together at Castlemartin. O'Reilly was somewhat thrown when he didn't see any marquee erected in the grounds beside the house, as was the normal procedure when the big summer parties were held. Unsportingly, *The Irish Times* announced the day before his birthday that he would be having a secret party, but he pretended not to see the report.

The family hired the local community centre in Kilcullen and had the gymnasium walls painted with life-size murals depicting O'Reilly's life. There was one of him in his rugby kit, one dressed as James Bond, another kitted out as a pirate holding a Heinz baked beans sign. The most striking, perhaps, was him dressed as Superman, in what one female reporter described as 'a pair of very fetching red panties over seamless tights'.

On the night itself the rain lashed down, but it did not dampen the spirits of those attending. O'Reilly was late, as he was for almost everything, and he was brought in to a crowd of over 500 people who had waited dutifully since the appointed time of 7.30pm. They cheered his arrival wildly, while he laughed and expressed astonishment at the sight of various people who, in truth, he must have been expecting to see that weekend, but he was still delighted they had come. The village band mistakenly played 'Land of Hope and Glory' in tribute on his entrance, as if they were in Britain. Susan, who had escorted her husband into the hall, was suitably embarrassed and apologised loudly, telling him, 'Darling, I wanted them to play 'Hail to the Chief'.'

Cameron, a confident speaker like his father and who had honed his speaking skills as auditor of the Oxford Union, acted as master of ceremonies. There were plenty of speeches, paying proper homage to the 'golden boy' now that he had reached fifty. The most notable and remembered line probably came from Andy Mulligan: 'Now, I'm not gay, but if I were, Tony would be my man,' he declared to wild laughter.

After the meal and the speeches, O'Reilly was given a guided tour of his own life. A room off the hall had been turned into a museum of his greatest moments so far, full of photographs from his past, magazine cover stories and many other pieces of memorabilia.

The invited media were corralled on a balcony at the end of the room where, to the obvious disgust of some, they were handed airline food, complete with tinfoil on top to keep it warm, and plastic cutlery with which to eat it, but no tables to put it on. They were also told to observe, rather than mingle. They were given a copy of the guest list, with all of those on it grouped under category headings: there was a group identified as his rugby friends, another as people from Heinz USA, those from Fitzwilton, more from IN and so on. It seemed that everybody had their place, and was in it.

Writing about it in *The Sunday Business Post* many years later, Emily O'Reilly (no relation) recalled how at one point in the evening O'Reilly came to speak to the media 'and was sufficiently self-depre-cating to acknowledge the awfulness of the murals and indeed the sheer naked vulgarity of much of the affair'.

The reporter probably underestimated her namesake's ability to make such comments while not being entirely sincere; he was basking in all of the attention and taking it as his due. Susan and Olive had spent nearly a year organising the event, hiring and decorating the hall, working through the lists of the people who had been important in Tony's life, sending invites and swearing everyone to secrecy. Many people had travelled very long distances to take part, including the likes of Jack Kyle, who had come from Zambia. This was not just a gathering of the rich and famous with whom O'Reilly liked to associ-ate. His wheelchair-bound mother Aileen, now 74 years old, took pride of place. Many of his childhood and school friends were present and even his old mentor, Peadar O'Donnell. There were old Suttons, Bord Bainne and Irish Sugar colleagues, old university lecturers and even his former fiancée, Dorothy Connolly, was there. The only relation present from his father's side of the family was Fr John Geary. The more cynical members of the assorted media may not have enjoyed the evening, but almost everyone else did, and into the small hours of the following morning.

It was not surprising that the media was invited to observe the festivities. 'He is a man for whom there is no clear distinction between the private and public self, a man whose acquaintances all remark on the fact that almost every meal in one of his houses in Pittsburgh or in Ireland seems to be a public event, shared with friends, contacts, associates: people who are, for one reason or another, being wooed,' Fintan O'Toole of *The Irish Times* subsequently remarked.

His fiftieth birthday wasn't going to be a cause of celebration for all in Ireland. While his wealth and achievements might be acknowledged, they would not necessarily always be admired. 'The Irish are absolutely tops at begrudging and no slouches at envy,' said John Meagher. It led to the realisation that a political career in Ireland was now probably beyond him and that instead he would be somebody to whom politicians and governments would go for advice and help, as if he had almost risen above them all. O'Reilly had identified a new role for himself anyway: 'I suppose the thing that I like the best in those other interests is being chairman of the Independent, because that is about what John Healy, the writer, calls "nation shaping".'

Later that year, at Christmas, he sat down with Ivor Kenny, an academic at UCD, and conducted a lengthy interview for Kenny's book, *In Good Company*. The book was written entirely in the first person, with Kenny's questions excised. O'Reilly had given, and would continue to give, many interviews but this was arguably the most revealing.

He was looking to the future. 'Now that I have a certain degree of financial independence, where should I be allocating my time and energies? What time have I left? I have reached that part of my life where two major phases are gone and there's only one phase left. The real question is, should I do anything different and, if so, what?'

He spoke of a 'craving for some sort of sabbatical ... At another level, I would like to perfect my French, to spend a year living in France. I would like to write a biography of someone like John Redmond or Bianconi ... I would like to have time to – it's a terrible verb – service a lot of friendships which, with the pace of business, get brutalised: the "see you next year" syndrome.'

Alongside the professional, he also noted the personal costs of his wide-ranging achievements. 'It will, I suppose, be clear to each one of my six children that I have paid a very heavy penalty to achieve what I have achieved, which is a kind of bi-cultural life in Europe and in the United States,' he said, yet again ignoring Susan, who did not get a single mention in the interview. 'I have tried to do two things, one to build up an economic entity in this country and, at the same time, to climb the perilous, under-water rope-ladder that is the way to the top in America.'

It was a revealing interview, but he seemed far more confident in himself than he had been in a 1974 interview he'd conducted with *People* magazine, in which he'd complained: 'I'm often depicted as some super-confident guy. I'm not at all that certain. I envy others who are. I'm where I am now because of a lot of luck and a certain amount of hard work. I'm rather tired of the image of myself as the man in the big black cloak, some sort of mystical mastermind of intrigue-filled corporate corridors of power.'

O'Reilly didn't slow up – if anything, he kept accelerating. His way of living was like his way of doing business, at full throttle, and age wasn't going to alter that. His schedule left its observers in awe, and many struggling to keep up. When he travelled O'Reilly typically started his day at 6.00am, gathering every local paper possible and reading not just the business pages but the political news, too, both international and that of whatever country he was in. He would have a stack of faxes to go through as well, often of material that had appeared in the newspapers that would be relevant to his interests and that had been faxed to him either by Ted Smyth, his head of corporate affairs at Heinz, or by Jim Milton, his external PR man in Dublin. He would invite executives to a breakfast meeting in his room at 7.30am, before checking his diary and packing everything into a single suitcase for the next move. He began the day with a list, written out on 5 in. x 3 in. correspondence cards with a blue border and a legend, 'A.J.F. O'Reilly', embossed on the side. He would write down on it the people he wanted to talk to during the day, beside the meetings that had been arranged. He updated the list throughout the day.

'He always has a way of getting hold of people who will help him,' said David Sculley, a Heinz executive, of O'Reilly's incredible net-working and directness. 'He has absolutely no hesitation whatsoever in breaking the traditional chain of command and going right down in the organisation to talk to whomsoever he feels an issue may be more relevant to – if he's not able to get a particular managing director, or a senior vice-president, he will simply call the general manager in charge of sales just to talk to them, and no-one minds, because that person usually brings his superior up to date with the conversation.'

O'Reilly wrote his own timetable and his own reports, sending them back to Olive Deasy to be typed. Despite his skill and eloquence as a letter writer, he preferred the speed and directness of a telephone call instead. He was rarely off the phone, but executives noted to their amazement and horror that he could break a conversation to take a phone call and return then to the previous chat exactly where he had left it.

He was believed to have a photographic memory. If he was given a document to read, he would read the whole thing and the exhibits and appendices as well, not just the executive summary. 'It'll probably be well past midnight, then it's back to the hotel, where there's another hundred pages of faxes waiting for him,' said Sculley. What's interesting to me is that if I'm meeting him at 7am the next morning, somehow in between that and his next hundred pages of faxes and his morning newspapers, he's read a couple of hundred pages of a book that has nothing to do with business, but is the latest biography or history or book on Greek art.'

'I occasionally flap internally, but I make every effort to conceal it,' O'Reilly told Kenny. 'Sometimes, anger and irritation will show but I have analysed my irritation as a management instrument and found that I am less effective when I am angry and irritated. I am not as eloquent, not as thoughtful, and I'm often wrong. Therefore, I see anger and irritation as counterproductive managerially for me ... My best allies in any business circumstance are thorough preparation, good analysis and a receptive ear. Patience is the thing you need for good judgment. It cannot be instinctive – it cannot be hunch. Even when it appears visceral, it is probably the result of long reflection, or a substantial amount of reading, or a good deal of analysis.'

It was a schedule that would have killed off a lesser man. 'I let off steam in a physical way – by jogging or playing tennis. They're something I don't get enough of. I resent the constant dinners, the wear and tear and turmoil of big business,' he claimed, yet he did nothing to curtail his schedule. 'It's easier to manage a business like Heinz with the enormous momentum it has, brand names which have been established over 70 years, substantial cash-flows, confident managers and highly predictable growth patterns.' It was an interesting point, because he undoubtedly was having more success with it at this stage of his life than he was having with his Irish assets.

A few months after the Kenny interview, O'Reilly did something in Britain that required chutzpah. He organised for Heinz to buy Cape Cornwall, a mile of English coastline, and then he presented it to the British Prime Minister Margaret Thatcher at a public ceremony, to be placed in the care of the British National Trust. He remarked that it was 'especially piquant that an Irishman should be presenting the title deeds to a piece of English land to a British prime minister', and that he did so with a special sense of privilege. Fintan O'Toole later described it as an 'act of historic cheek, but also an act of great confidence, a public sign that here was an Irishman who didn't have to watch out for himself in England'.

O'Reilly once told *Irish Business* magazine that 'there are two of me'. Some said the number was much bigger. 'He can be one thousand different people,' said one former Heinz executive. 'He could have been a politician, he could have been an actor, he could have been Johnny Carson. He can still be a lot of those things.'

'You know, there is one tragedy in Tony's being foreign born,' Sculley said. 'He would have made a great Presidential candidate.'

While his professional star remained firmly in the ascendant, success in his personal life lagged far behind. Not long after his fiftieth birthday party, O'Reilly's marriage came to an end. Susan had become tired of many things in her husband's life, not least the hectic work schedule that meant he was almost never at home and that, when he was, he was always with someone else in their house. Nobody asked if she was aware of the time O'Reilly managed to spend with other women – in particular one woman in Ireland whom he saw regularly for over a decade, to the deep embarrassment of many who knew, including that woman's family – and nobody knew if anyone had seen fit to inform her. Whether or not it informed her final decision is not known, but the other factors were probably enough to cause a major rift anyway, if not a total one.

The separation was a distressing time for everyone involved, particularly the children who, even if now adults, were still angry, and mainly on Susan's behalf. And yet, they did not want to compromise whatever closeness to their father they enjoyed, even if they blamed him for neglecting his marriage. For her part, Susan, with a generosity and maturity that impressed everybody, was determined that her children's relationship with their father would not flounder. She would not let them take sides. She went out of her way to ensure that she and Tony would attend all of their children's family occasions, such as graduations, weddings and christenings.

In *The Player*, Fallon was exceptionally generous to O'Reilly in his interpretation of events leading to the ending of the marriage: 'The reasons for any marriage breakdown are inevitably and intensely personal, and both Tony and Susan have tried to keep it so. Outsiders could speculate, but they knew only a fraction of the overall picture, and the family closed ranks around their parents. All that can usefully be said is that the breakdown was due to a combination of factors, not least of which was the pace and pressure of O'Reilly's multi-faceted business career which had taken a severe toll on his life with Susan.' While nobody wanted to pry into their personal space, the idea that Tony should not take the vast bulk of the blame for what happened was offensive to those who were closer to Susan than to Tony. If Susan had been guilty of anything, it had been of allowing herself to be treated in the manner he treated her for so long.

'The contradictions between family life and business life raise the question as to whether, in this modern world, it is possible to have an orderly married life and a successful business career,' O'Reilly said later. It was an incredibly self-serving comment, given that many others have managed to do so successfully; they simply did not add layer upon layer of new business interests on top of those that already existed.

If O'Reilly was lauded for his many achievements and great personal qualities, such as generosity, he could also be criticised for his narcissism, for a failure to attend closely enough to those he loved, to make his own needs and desires the centre of everything. He could phone Jim McCarthy for a chat every day of his life – to gossip and talk business – but he couldn't make sufficient time to be at home in the company of just his family other than occasionally.

No formal announcement of the O'Reilly separation, and then divorce, was ever made. Indeed, something of an illusion was maintained – such as the picture of Susan with the family in the infamous *Sunday Independent* colour supplement of 1988. But at that stage the marriage was over, as many had guessed when Susan did not appear in Australia in 1988, as all their children did, to witness Tony receiving the award of an Honorary Officer of the Order of Australia. By this time Susan had in fact left Pittsburgh. Tony had purchased a house for her in London as part of the terms of their separation, and she lived there for the rest of her life.

She did come to Ireland in 1989, however, to be at Tony's side for another seminal moment in his life: the funeral of his mother, Aileen. Her final years were difficult, her mobility entirely compromised by a progressive series of strokes, her speech increasingly damaged too. She lived in some material comfort, in an apartment on Anglesea Road in

Ballsbridge, in a block that had been built by O'Reilly's old friend Sean McKone, where soon-to-be-Taoiseach Albert Reynolds was a neighbour. She had 24-hour care and a driver, but she was lonely and missed her only child, although he rang often, visited her when in Dublin and had her brought to Castlemartin whenever the family was in Dublin. She was somewhat moody, understandably given her poor health, and occasionally, if angry at Tony for perceived neglect, would have all his photographs taken down off the walls. She would then require her driver to deliver them to Castlemartin, before they would be later returned and restored to their former prominence.

She died in the Blackrock Clinic just before Christmas 1989. Her son was with her, saying later that they shared their old memory of how the priest had said at his first rugby match, 'the little red fellow's the best'. The funeral mass took place at the Church of the Sacred Heart in Donnybrook and two former Taoisigh, Garret FitzGerald and Jack Lynch, were among the gathering, as were many of those who had been at O'Reilly's fiftieth birthday party just three and a half years previously.

The mid-1980s had been marked by celebration and congratulation, but O'Reilly ended that decade minus two of his most stalwart supporters: Aileen and Susan. Both women had suffered loneliness because of his unavailability to his family, because business life took precedence over personal life. Only O'Reilly himself could give a final reckoning on the true costs of how he chose to live his life, but it did seem a high price to pay for material success.

SECTION 2

1987–1999: Legend and branding

CHAPTER ONE

EMPIRE-BUILDING: THE RISE OF INDEPENDENT NEWSPAPERS

O'Reilly could not have anticipated the significance to him of the reappointment of Ray Burke as a government minister in 1987. O'Reilly's interactions with Burke, always at a remove and often, he said, undertaken by other parties without his knowledge or approval, were to embroil him in controversy for nearly two decades.

On his re-election as Taoiseach in 1987, Charles Haughey brought Burke into his Cabinet. Burke was a divisive figure. To some in Fianna Fáil he was regarded as a tough political enforcer who maintained discipline. Others within the party, and particularly outside of it, regarded him as a political thug and bully, someone who was tainted by the whiff of corruption, albeit as yet unproven. People dealt with him because it was accepted that he had Haughey's patronage.

Most significantly, and surprisingly, Burke was given an enormous portfolio of responsibility, one that included communications (meaning newspapers and television signals distribution) and energy (including oil exploration). He was therefore the minister with the most relevance to O'Reilly's commercial interests. Although he gave up the Energy portfolio in late 1988, taking on industry and commerce instead, and was made Minister for Justice after the 1989 general election, he continued to hold the Communications portfolio until Haughey exited office in 1992.

In one of his earliest actions, Burke significantly improved the terms for oil companies prospecting off the Irish coast. Royalties were abolished and the State relinquished any stake in an eventual oil or gas find. 'I am realistic enough to appreciate that we cannot have our cake and eat it,' Burke said in September 1987, when announcing new licensing terms for the offshore sector. 'Perhaps when we are a recognized oil province, we will be able to afford the luxury of more stringent terms, but for now it is clear that concessions of a radical nature are necessary to offset to the greatest possible extent the effects of low oil prices on exploration in Ireland and the recent disappointing results.' Burke said the terms were similar to those in Britain and Spain, but it subsequently turned out that, not for the first or last time, Burke's decision was something of a solo run, contrary to the advice of a senior adviser in his department.

The next two years were marked by further failed exploration efforts and Atlantic's share price fell back to 3p. It seemed that O'Reilly's dreams of striking oil in Irish waters had evaporated, notwithstanding Burke's intervention. O'Reilly tried to brush off the disappointment with humour. In 1988 he told *The New York Times* how, as boss of Heinz, he still made time to talk to the managers of his Irish interests on a regular basis. 'I don't talk to the oil explorers, though,' he said. 'It's bad for your blood pressure.'

Outside of Heinz, IN continued to offer O'Reilly the best chance of further riches. The process of managerial change had begun in earnest in 1985 when he picked John Meagher to succeed the aging Bartle Pitcher as Group CEO. Meagher's background was in market research, not newspapers. He became involved with IN in 1982 as a non-executive director and was appointed executive deputy chairman and then CEO three years later. He largely left Joe Hayes to look after local operations while he searched for international opportunities because O'Reilly deemed the options in the newspaper business in Ireland to be limited.

His executives did not necessarily agree. The use of capital outside of Ireland caused some resentment. While much would be made of successes like American and Mexican radio interests, far less was said, other than excuses, about the performances of outdoor advertising investments in France and Germany. Hayes believed that there was potential for the Irish newspapers, but only if greater investment was made in printing and market repositioning. He also saw opportunities outside of newspapers.

Hayes and Vinnie Doyle had ambitions for the *Irish Independent*, but felt they were being curtailed in their abilities not just to expand but to defend it against encroaching competition, especially from imported tabloids, as the *Sunday World* did in its Sunday market. By 1980/81, imported daily tabloid titles had reached a high of 139,000 sales a day. By 1988 they were still selling 130,000 a day, but the *Irish Independent* had lost more than 30,000 daily sales, down to 153,000. This was a source of massive frustration to Hayes and Doyle, who felt that they were operating with at least one hand, and often two, tied behind their backs.

Their biggest issue was printing, and closely aligned to that were the work practices of the print unions. The presses at Middle Abbey Street had been antiquated when O'Reilly inherited them in 1973, but now they may as well have been held together by Sellotape. O'Reilly refused to replace them, preferring instead to drain the profits of the Irish operations for payment of dividends or to invest in overseas acquisitions. The quality of the reproduction on the presses was poor; the print could be illegible in places because it went out of register. Newsprint often smudged on the reader's hands. This was bad for advertisers too, but in time the lack of colour availability became even more significant.

A measure of reassurance was provided only by the improvement in relative market shares. The *Irish Press* titles were in what was going to prove to be terminal decline and the competitive instincts of Hayes and his editors meant that the Middle Abbey Street titles consistently won the battle for readers, using clever competitions with big prizes to drive circulation. The best editorial talent at the *Press* titles was regularly hired to the *Independent* on better terms; even if the paper often looked terrible, it had the better stories. But opportunities were being missed, particularly as *The Irish Times* used its colour presses in the latter half of the 1980s to corner the rapidly growing advertising revenues available in property and recruitment, plus the greater quality in its presentation also contributed to its increase in circulation.

Hayes had a left-field idea: he wanted to explore a possible joint venture for the Irish market with the *Daily Mirror* in London. That approach could win the so-called lower end of the market and then it would be commercially safer to move the *Irish Independent* further up-market. The *Daily Mirror* had been adding Irish sales under the aggressive proprietorship of an eastern European immigrant former Labour MP called Robert Maxwell, a man who aroused some suspicion because of his erratic, bullying behaviour – and who was saddled with the nickname 'the bouncing Czech' – but who was not revealed until after his death to have been a monstrous fraud and thief. O'Reilly put Gerry McGuinness in charge of the project, partly because of his proven success in the tabloid market and partly because of the work he had undertaken in the previous few years in partnership with a UK company called EMAP, where they had considered a joint venture of a new tabloid for the British market, a venture from which they had withdrawn sharply once the risk–reward analysis had been completed.

McGuinness and O'Reilly went to London to see Maxwell, who was childlike in the kind of psychological warfare he employed at the meeting, pretending not to know who O'Reilly was and then acting as if he worked for Campbell Soups. The Irishmen remained calm, having been warned about his likely behaviour, although it immediately made them more wary about what might be coming. They suggested to Maxwell that the *Independent* would publish an *Irish Daily Mirror*, which would benefit from the editorial synergies provided by the London end of the operation and by the management, marketing, sales and distribution abilities of Abbey Street. Maxwell responded enthusiastically. 'You scored a goal there,' he boomed.

He decided that heads of agreement should be drawn up immediately. Meeting concluded, O'Reilly and McGuinness left, hoping that a deal could be done but increasingly doubtful about the wisdom of getting involved with a clearly volatile figure. A fax arrived from Maxwell a day later, setting out terms for the publication of a joint venture; it read well until McGuinness spotted a paragraph near the end of its 36 pages which declared that the agreement between the parties would have no legal standing and would be an agreement in honour only. McGuinness rang O'Reilly in Pittsburgh to get approval for his planned next step, which was throwing the document in the bin.

The idea for a new tabloid in conjunction with a British publisher was now firmly embedded in O'Reilly's thinking. Independent Newspapers next approached David Stevens of United Newspapers, owners of the *Daily Express* group, about a joint venture for *The Star*. It was not as strong a paper editorially or commercially and had a circulation in the Republic, they were told, of about 40,000 daily. A business plan was drawn up that assumed the new title would double this circulation in a relatively short period. Staff were hired, a premises in Terenure rented to house them, and a nightly slot on the *Sunday World* printing presses secured.

The paper was nearly aborted before its first edition. McGuinness apparently discovered, by accident, that the Irish circulation of *The Star* was in fact less than 20,000. The 40,000 figure had been reached only briefly during the previous year, during a particularly intensive marketing campaign. Independent Newspapers could have abandoned and sued on the basis of misrepresentation. O'Reilly was consulted and once his anger had dissipated – this was the type of surprise he was not supposed to get, and just how they had entered a contract without first getting guarantees on fundamental information such as circulation appalled him – he decided that they were too close to launch, with too many people in place not to go ahead. The terms of the deal were renegotiated in IN's favour.

That didn't make it a success. The original plan was that not just individual articles, but entire pages, already laid out and made up, could be imported in a matter of seconds from the English paper. Irish readers wanted an Irish newspaper with the foreign bits added in, rather than the other way around. The *Irish Daily Star* launched on 29 February 1988 and in its first full circulation year it achieved average daily sales of 46,000, nowhere near enough. It only prospered after Hayes sent Michael Brophy in as editor, with Paddy Murray as his deputy, from the Middle Abbey Street papers and together they gave it far more original Irish content, and eventually it became profitable after it more than doubled sales.

For O'Reilly, the best financial contribution from an acquisition throughout the 1980s and into the 1990s came in Australia. It was a combination of chance meeting and O'Reilly's social skills that brought about IN's initial purchase of a 49% shareholding in the Australian outdoor advertising firm Buspak, before it was eventually taken over in full in 1988. On a flight to Dublin, O'Reilly sat beside Tina O'Flaherty, mother of Peter Cosgrove, her son by her first marriage, and heard how Cosgrove had moved to Australia and created Buspak, which sold advertising on buses as well as controlling outdoor advertising sites and which had offices in Adelaide, Melbourne and Sydney. Cosgrove had a Canadian partner who wanted to sell the business; O'Flaherty suggested to O'Reilly that he might be interested, which he was, although it took a year to complete a deal. The IN stake was built in stages, through a combination of shares and cash to Cosgrove totalling £6.8 million. Cosgrove joined the IN board and was a valued executive for decades to come.

By March 1988 IN was ninth in the list of the top 10 Irish PLCs, with a market capitalisation of £110.8 million. O'Reilly decided it was time to gamble again, making an acquisition in Australia as big in itself as IN.

Rupert Murdoch had been so active in purchasing more media assets that the Australian regulators told him he had to sell some to avoid monopoly issues: by 1988 he controlled 60% of the entire newspaper market. He chose to sell Provincial Newspapers Queensland (PNQ), a chain of small local papers situated north and south of Brisbane, the capital of Queensland.

Meagher assembled a team that spent nearly five months assessing the value of the potential purchase and how it could be financed. The team included Healy but also, for the first time, O'Reilly's son, Cameron. While PNQ was too big for a small purchaser to chase, it was too small for a big one to consider buying. It was making profits of A$11.5 million, but recession was looming and the extent to which the purchase price could be paid for out of future earnings was debatable. The Australian government was also concerned about foreign ownership.

First, O'Reilly had to do a deal with Murdoch. The pair met in New York, over dinner at Murdoch's Fifth Avenue apartment. The Australian wanted A$8 a share, and apparently had another bidder in place who was prepared to come close to it; O'Reilly told him he could afford only A$6.25. Twenty-four hours later, O'Reilly agreed to match Murdoch's other offer of A$7.75 a share, and Murdoch accepted.

The Foreign Investment Review Board ruled that IN could not purchase more than 15% of PNQ. However, as Susan was Australian, O'Reilly's six children qualified for citizenship. A family trust was constructed with some speed, which would have to fund the remaining 85% of the A$150 million purchase price. Independent Newspapers put in just A$1.5 million of equity. O'Reilly personally invested A$8.5 million and guaranteed a bank loan of A$25 million. Much of the money came from Bankers Trust, where O'Reilly just happened to be a director. 'I left the board room when the subject came up,' he said.

Some of the debts of A$140 million were at interest rates of up to 14%. Remarkably, part of the money came from the vendor himself. In an act of rare generosity, Murdoch agreed to forego immediate payment of A$24.3 million of the purchase price by leaving that amount in the company as a five-year loan, at a 14% rate. 'He wasn't falling over backward for us,' O'Reilly said subsequently, 'but it was helpful at the time. What I liked about Rupert Murdoch in this deal was that a) he got a good price, b) he facilitated the financing of our acquisition and c) he kept his word absolutely to the letter. Rupert doesn't chisel.'

The pressure to reform PNQ was immediate and went far beyond the immediate name change to Australian Provincial Newspapers (APN). The interest bill on the deal was A$16.8 million, more than A$5 million higher than the last profits. Cutting costs was not easy. The distance between the two farthest-flung newspapers in the group – Mackay in Northern Queensland and Coff's Harbour in northern New South Wales – was not much less than that between Dublin and Moscow. Savings were made and the monopolies the papers enjoyed meant that cover prices and advertising rates were increased: O'Reilly's favourite technique. Within a couple of years, despite the recession, management increased profits nearly threefold, comfortably dealing with the interest bill.

The ambition for APN was to float it on the stock market and to recover, in cash, a profit from the original investment. Although the flotation in 1992 reduced IN's stake to 8.5%, O'Reilly sold it another 12.5% for A$20 million, as opposition to foreign ownership by the Australian government had softened.

That was the IN branch of the portfolio, growing in a way that interested and pleased O'Reilly. Back in Dublin, O'Reilly needed to put Fitzwilton's cash to use. He asked his old school friend and tennis rival Kevin McGoran – an accountant who had spent time as a senior manager at the Smurfit Group – to become deputy CEO first and then, a year later in 1988, to replace Vincent Ferguson as CEO; Ferguson and McCarthy remained as directors. Len O'Hagan, another senior Smurfit executive, was headhunted to join the executive team. O'Reilly knew he could depend on McGoran to do as he wanted, relying on his fax each week of the minutes of the executive meetings. 'Tony brings vision and ideas – he's the overriding strategist,' McGoran said. 'He can make a great contribution to a business without spending a lot of time on it.'

O'Reilly seemed confused as to what he wanted for Fitzwilton. In the mid-1980s he told shareholders that 'we view ourselves for the long-term as an investment and not an operating company and our medium-term strategy orientation will direct itself to this end.' Two years later he said Fitzwilton 'has decided to remain a trading company and has forsaken the option of becoming a purely investment company'. One thing was certain: he was determined to change the entirely negative public perception of the company, even if his critics charged that he was attempting to rewrite its corporate history. He described Fitzwilton as 'one of the most remarkable defensive actions I have ever been through ... we had massive retrenchment and losses – that's what separates the men from the boys – and it has survived and prospered.'

While that was highly debatable, at the very least, what mattered now was what Fitzwilton would do next. The plan seemed to some to be grandiose. O'Reilly was taken with the trend in the USA to make financially huge acquisitions by way of what was called leveraged buyout (LBO). Typically, an acquiring company would borrow enormous amounts of money, with the loans only partly secured on its assets or on those of the company being purchased. The remainder of the loans – bonds held by wealthy investors or specialist funds as often as banks – were unsecured, but required the payment of enhanced levels of interest. They were known as 'junk bonds'. Any acquisition required a major increase in profits at the acquired company to raise the money to repay the bonds, or else the sale of parts of the business to release cash. It was very much how the APN transaction in Australia had been conducted. O'Reilly began talking of Fitzwilton becoming a European version of the giant US fund Kohlberg, Kravis, Roberts & Co., doing 'billion-dollar' deals.

First, though, he had to build the investor base of Fitzwilton. He had some success in early 1988. John Kluge, a 75-year-old media billionaire, put in £3 million for a 10% share. The Swedish multi-millionaire Leonard Bylock, a friend of O'Reilly's old oil backer Sulaiman Olayan, came in for 10%. Paul Demarais, a French-Canadian controller of Power Corporation, invested, as did Ann Getty, wife of the billionaire oil magnate Gordon Getty. 'We will be the front office for the guys who will revolutionise Europe,' O'Reilly said. 'You can cut through three years of business building with Fitzwilton's contacts.'

Instead, Fitzwilton's initial purchases were disappointingly unexciting by comparison with the expectations. The first investment was in a British motor dealership called Keep Trust, in which it took a 30% shareholding for £13.3 million. The *Lex* column in the *Financial Times* noted acidly that 'for those investors who like to ride on the coat tails of the 'smart money' this was not the sort of mega-deal they had been hoping for'. O'Reilly said Keep Trust met the priority 'that our investments be in profitable undertakings with expansion potential and minimum risk'. He said that 'this is my opportunity to establish a presence in a vibrant economy'.

In September 1988 the company raised £25 million from shareholders and bought 85% of the Roy Hall Cash & Carry business in Manchester. Within months Fitzwilton decided to buy out the remainder of Keep Trust for £49 million, financed with a combination of new shares and cash. Fitzwilton then bought the M6 Cash and Carry group in the UK, to put together with Roy Hall, which it now bought out in full. Since September 1988 Fitzwilton had spent about £105 million and transformed itself into a broadly based industrial and commercial holding group. Its annual turnover now exceeded £250 million, when purchases in Ireland were also included.

There was one significant subsidiary company in Ireland, a relatively small but growing engineering business called Rennicks. Fitzwilton had bought a 51% share for £800,000 in 1988 and Robin Rennicks, who stayed on as CEO, retained a minority holding. The company made road-signs and this business had potential as the government accelerated investment in the roads and nascent motorway networks. In late May 1989 Fitzwilton bought 80% of a cold storage firm called Novum, run by Paul Power, who retained the other 20%.

On 7 June 1989, with another general election campaign in full flight, Rennicks and Power went to Ray Burke's house in Swords, not far beyond Dublin Airport. The two men handed over a £30,000 cheque, made out to cash, on behalf of Fitzwilton, but drawn on the Rennicks account. The money was subsequently reimbursed to Rennicks by both its parent and by Novum.

Fitzwilton was a regular donor to political parties, but normally gave its money to Fianna Fáil HQ. This payment stood out when it was subsequently revealed publicly nearly a decade later because it was the first time the cheque was made out to cash, was not given to the party's election fund and was paid via a minister. Fianna Fáil HQ was informed of the donation, however. Burke passed on £10,000 of this money by way of a bank draft, but kept the rest, telling HQ officials who sought the full amount: 'That's as much as you're getting. Good luck.'

It was in keeping with Burke's behaviour during this period as he took advantage of the willingness of some businessmen to devote funds to keeping Fianna Fáil in power. Two building firms, JMSE and Bovale, testified subsequently about money given to him; it was reckoned that in all he pocketed about £80,000 during that campaign.

The transaction would have been significant enough a move by the Fitzwilton people to cause comment in its own right had it become known at the time – given that Rennicks was pitching to the government for contracts – but O'Reilly's other business interests were also interacting with Burke at the time.

Independent Newspapers had decided that the new liberalisation of the radio market in Ireland – for which Burke was responsible – with the very first issuing of national and regional licences in the late 1980s, was not for it. O'Reilly had been warned, unofficially, by the Fianna Fáil government that he would not be allowed to own radio licences, that it would give him too much concentration of ownership and power in media. The same applied to the awarding of a licence for a new national television service in competition to RTÉ, even though O'Reilly had expressed an interest previously in buying RTÉ's second television channel were it to be privatised, which it never was. When the first radio licences were advertised in 1988, IN did not apply. Instead, the national licence went to Century Radio, with Jim Stafford a key investor. A loser for that licence, but successful in a subsequent bid for one of the two Dublin local licences, was a thrusting young businessman called Denis O'Brien.

Instead, IN invested in the distribution of television signals. In the pre-digital and pre-satellite era, many parts of the country were unable to receive any channels other than RTÉ. A new system called Multichannel Multipoint Distribution Service (MMDS) was available, subject to licences that the government was just about to issue. Burke suggested to Hayes that this might be something in which IN might invest as an alternative to being a broadcaster. The country was littered with illegal deflector masts, however, erected on hill- and mountain-tops, which captured the British TV signals and re-routed them to those who had roof-top aerials, all for little or no cost to the recipients. Hayes worried, correctly, that IN would invest heavily but that the take-up of paying customers would be poor. Burke told him not to worry, that illegal deflectors would not be allowed continue once MMDS came into existence. Independent Newspapers invested in a subsidiary, Princes Holdings, and applications for the MMDS licences were in process at the time of the visit to Burke's home by the cheque-bearing Rennicks and Power.

Fianna Fáil was returned to power, albeit this time in a coalition government with the Progressive Democrats (PDS). Four months later Burke issued 29 MMDS licences, seven of which went to IN directly, with another 11 going to companies in which IN was a minority shareholder. The new licence-holders were given exclusive rights in the areas they covered; it should have been a licence to print money.

While success in Australia was sweet, it did not ease O'Reilly's impatience about growing IN still further. His crucial role in deal-making with Murdoch encouraged him to believe that he needed to be more visible in running the company, even as its chairman. Meagher had cut quite a dash as CEO, perhaps too much so for O'Reilly's liking. O'Reilly's critics said that he was somewhat jealous of the impact the gregarious Meagher had as an after-dinner speaker and dining-table raconteur. O'Reilly was well aware of Meagher's great charm and affability when he hired him, so such an assessment surprised some, but O'Reilly had reached a stage in his life when he did not like to share the limelight. As was becoming increasingly the case, there could only be one bull in O'Reilly's field.

In 1990 Meagher stepped down as CEO, to widespread surprise. Independent Newspapers had not been performing as profitably as investors, and O'Reilly, had wanted, and there were embarrassing write-offs on new ventures. One such was an ill-fated lottery game in the UK called Golden Grid, an idea brought to it by Rehab boss Frank Flannery and in which IN took a 15% stake; that cost £3.4 million when Golden Grid was quickly shut down after a disastrous few opening weeks. Another was an investment in the UK outdoor advertising company More O'Farrell: its share price slumped in value as the British recession hit hard, not long after IN had taken a 5% shareholding amid rumours that it was the prelude to a full bid. There was also considerable controversy about the accounting treatment of the windfall profit from the sale of a final tranche of Reuter shares and how it boosted the overall profits. But to lump all of the responsibility

on Meagher for decisions taken at board level seemed more than a bit
ungenerous and misleading. Meagher had said once about O'Reilly,
'He's a very, very valuable consultant. I don't defer to him but I almost
always refer to him before making key decisions.' Meagher was very
annoyed by his proposed removal and agreed to go only if he was
given the role of deputy chairman, a position he held for 10 years
before retiring from it in 2000, due to terminal illness.

The promotion of Liam Healy to Group CEO was a very conservative
action, but it highlighted a trend in O'Reilly's thinking: financial
management was taking precedence over marketing. While O'Reilly
had made his name initially in the latter – and continued to hold forth
on the subject regularly – he was not as keen on investing in marketing
as his posturing would suggest. Indeed, a new image of him was now
being promoted. 'When Dr O'Reilly studies a set of accounts he is like
a surgeon, having no knowledge of the personality of the patient, but
who can nevertheless find a host of inert organs waiting to be tightened
or extracted,' said one unnamed fan in the profile of O'Reilly in *Paper
Tigers*. 'He has a gift for operating on many apparently conflicting
levels at once.'

Healy was a measured, careful accountant who would tend the
numbers as O'Reilly wanted and needed. Healy did not display a detailed
understanding and care for the editorial content or the marketing of
newspapers. 'I would say that I talk to Liam Healy on the telephone
every day,' said O'Reilly. 'He's extremely crisp. And he knows detailed
things about newspapers that I'll never know, about cut-off lengths
and pagination and why we will or will not put colour on page six – all
those things that make money. He's very bottom-line orientated.'

In response, Healy said that O'Reilly was not 'a minute details man.
He's more the type that likes to be fully informed in a general way. We
talk a lot in this organisation, which is how Dr O'Reilly likes it. He has
this great business capacity for getting to the bottom of things
through discussion. He doesn't like surprises. Not at any level.
Everything has to be foreseen and discussed.'

Meagher's resignation was announced at the same time as IN
announced it had bought a 29.9% shareholding in Tribune Newspapers,
publisher of *The Sunday Tribune*, in November 1990 for over £800,000.
There was no connection between this move and Meagher's
resignation, however; indeed, Meagher was to join the Tribune board

in mid-1991, along with Healy, and serve on it for a decade until his premature death from cancer. The investment gave rise to enormous controversy, with many decrying O'Reilly's seeming desire to control as much of the Irish media as possible. O'Reilly presented it as a defensive move against the rise of *The Sunday Times* as a threat to the circulation of the *Sunday Independent*; he was wary, too, of the possibility that the relatively new but struggling *The Sunday Business Post* might broaden its appeal if it received significant foreign investment, or that *The Irish Times* might buy it or the *Tribune* or start its own Sunday title. The *Sunday Press* was a declining force. Together the *Sunday Independent* and *The Sunday Tribune* had nearly half of the Sunday market.

Some feared that O'Reilly would move to close either *The Sunday Tribune* – or change its editorial stance – or the struggling free-sheet the *Dublin Tribune*, the launch of which, in 1990, was so costly that it had ruined the Group's finances. Indeed, IN was sensitive to the suggestion that it was seeking to close this heavy loss-maker as a protection for the classified revenues of the *Evening Herald* and therefore delayed what would have been a legitimate business decision. O'Reilly provided the necessary assurances to the editor Vincent Browne and chairman Gordon Colleary on both editorial and commercial issues. Although O'Reilly and Browne were deeply suspicious of each other, they coalesced well initially.

Des O'Malley, the Minister for Industry and Commerce, moved quickly to block any further purchase of shares in the *Tribune* by IN, and received support when the Competition Authority completed an investigation into a proposal that IN would become the majority shareholder in return for injecting £1.9 million in new capital.

O'Reilly made much of his membership of the board of *The Washington Post* in citing its editorial charter: 'In a world where the ownership of newspapers is increasingly concentrated amongst a smaller group of names, the newspaper's duty is to its readers and to the public at large and not to the private interests of its owners.' He said this would be the template for a similar written undertaking for *The Sunday Tribune*. The Competition Authority was unimpressed and rejected the purchase as being likely to prevent or restrict competition, 'and would be likely to operate against the common good'. That phrase, in particular, angered O'Reilly, especially when O'Malley seized upon it.

O'Reilly had never been close to O'Malley, despite their shared revulsion of the IRA and similar economic beliefs; they had both been close to Lynch, but separately, and there had been differences of opinion between the two during the 1970s over mining issues. O'Reilly was furious with O'Malley but felt, correctly, that IN could take control by providing loan finance, as subsequently proved to be the case. Little consideration was given to the promotion of the obvious candidate to replace Meagher, if Meagher had to be replaced. Joe Hayes was held by others within the Group to have the vision and the ability to run the Group, although Peter Cosgrove in Australia had his supporters too because of his success with Buspak. Hayes would have insisted on having full powers if promoted, and it was most unlikely that O'Reilly would have handed autonomy to such a dynamic figure. Instead of admitting that, word went out that Hayes was not considered suitable because he was somewhat uncouth in his language, which was a poor excuse for not promoting the most obviously able person. It was not certain, in any case, that Hayes would have wanted the job had he been offered it, such was his mounting dissatisfaction with the way that O'Reilly did business. Nonetheless, it was still a shock when Hayes quit in 1993 – the first in a number of personnel losses IN could ill-afford.

CHAPTER TWO

LOVE, AGAIN

There was considerable surprise among O'Reilly's friends when, only a few years after his divorce from Susan, he married for a second time – with Jim McCarthy again serving as best man and Fr John Geary again in attendance. There was considerable comment as to how O'Reilly had found a woman 14 years his junior who was possibly richer than he was, even though the extent of her wealth remained private and therefore a matter of speculation.

Chryss Goulandris came from the marriage of two Greek ship-owning families. Her father, John, from the Greek island of Andros, was in the fourth generation of a family of ship-owners and had moved to London in 1941 when the German occupation of Greece began. There he married Maria Lemos, a member of another, even more prominent Greek ship-owning family. The couple then moved to New York. Chryss was born there on 27 June 1950, and her American birthplace meant that she held both American and Greek citizenship. Her brother, Peter, to whom she remained exceptionally close as an adult, was born three years later, but tragedy hit the family soon after when her father died suddenly, aged just 42. Maria never remarried. The business thrived, however: having specialised in shipping wheat and other food, the fleet expanded in the post-war era to over 200 vessels, including some of the earliest oil tankers.

Chryss grew up in considerable luxury: her family lived for a time at the Savoy Plaza Hotel in New York before purchasing a mansion on Fifth Avenue. The family also had homes in Greece, Connecticut, Switzerland and the Bahamas. Chryss went to boarding school in Switzerland and then studied French civilisation and art history at the Sorbonne in Paris, before returning to New York. One of her closest friends growing up was Christina Onassis, who was involved in a relationship with Peter for a time.

Once her studies had been completed, Chryss worked in the family business, which now included property, stocks and commodities, and she developed a personal interest in trading silver futures at one point, but that ended unsuccessfully. Her main interest was in horse breeding, both in the USA and in France, a business she had entered in 1976 and expanded in 1978 on the death of her uncle. She had some success in breeding some Group One winners, the top level in the sport, making her one of the top five breeders in France for the entire 1980s.

O'Reilly was a regular visitor to New York, often using a suite in the St Regis Hotel when he was in the city. In 1989 he was in the city, talking to Wall Street banks about possible funding for a bid for Waterford Wedgwood. He met with Peter as part of his campaign to find new investors for Fitzwilton, as a vehicle to invest in Waterford Wedgwood. Peter brought his sister to the meeting. O'Reilly was very taken with this petite, sophisticated and wealthy woman, a low-key individual who did not feature in the social or gossip pages of the media and who, although now just about to reach her forties, had never been married. Although not a classical beauty – and very much the antithesis of the blonde, Grace Kelly lookalike Susan – this extremely slim woman with deep brown eyes was intelligent, articulate, witty and multilingual and always impeccably turned out, in classical attire, with her dark hair pulled back sharply on her head. She had the type of style and class that increasingly appealed to O'Reilly. It also helped that she knew of and was very interested in Wedgwood's heritage. It didn't mean that immediate investment was forthcoming, however.

They met again in New York the following year and hearing of her keen interest in horses, O'Reilly invited her to be his guest at The Heinz 57 race meeting in Ireland in August 1990. She accepted as she had already considered the purchase of a stud farm in Tipperary and was keen to attend the races and see what other properties might be available. They kept in contact and the following Easter, Chryss met with O'Reilly at Lyford Cay, in the Bahamas, when he was there with some of his children in a rented house, and their relationship deepened quickly. They decided to marry, despite her mother expressing some scepticism about the smooth-talking, divorced Irishman with six children – not unreasonably, Maria asked if O'Reilly was interested primarily in his intended new wife's wealth. Chryss made up her own mind on the Irishman, and they were married in the Bahamas on 14 September 1991. Newspaper reports at the time said O'Reilly was worth around $520 million and Goulandris $450 million; while most of O'Reilly's assets were a matter of public knowledge, although not his borrowings, there was limited information available upon which to base speculation of her wealth. She may well have been much richer and far less encumbered by debts.

Chryss placed one condition upon the marriage: she would not be a stay-at-home wife while O'Reilly criss-crossed the world. She would travel with him, everywhere. The sceptics believed that as much as she wanted to be with him, this was also because she wanted to keep a close eye on him and ensure that he behaved. It was rumoured that Chryss's mother had insisted on this. This may have seemed like an imposition, but O'Reilly was very comfortable with the arrangement. He enjoyed greatly introducing this exceptionally stylish and wealthy woman to his social circle at the many events he attended or hosted, and for years she always sat at his side, even if most couples sat at opposite sides of the table at any events O'Reilly hosted. It was actually a big change in lifestyle for her, because she was surrendering her independence, moving around the world largely to follow his schedule. She was clearly delighted with the attention she received as the wife of a powerful man, particularly in Ireland. Castlemartin was also a great attraction to her, and she set about expanding both its size and impact as a stud. She decided to build a new house on his land at Glandore, separate to the guesthouse where he had stayed for many years and now owned. She worked hard to establish cordial relationships with his adult children and this was reciprocated and appreciated on both sides.

O'Reilly's interest in buying Waterford Crystal dated back as far as 1983. The Waterford Crystal company had been established two centuries earlier, in 1783, in the port town of Waterford, in the southeast of Ireland, by two brothers, William and George Penrose, who were developers and among the city's main exporters. Their vision was to 'create the finest quality crystal for drinking vessels and objects of beauty for the home'. But the company failed in 1851 due to a lack of capital and excessive taxation.

The business was revived in 1947 when a small glass factory was set up in Waterford by Charles Bacik, a Czech immigrant glass-maker, not far from the site of the original. Irish industrialist Joe McGrath invested in 1950 and helped scale the business quickly, making it one of Ireland's few indigenous manufacturing and exporting success stories. O'Reilly was taken by the craft of the products, their attractiveness and their appeal to consumers with money, who regarded the display of the crystal as a symbol of material prosperity. 'Tony had a massive belief in the power of successful brands,' said Redmond O'Donoghue, who was to be one of his key executives at Waterford Wedgwood. 'We often reflected that there were only five significant Irish global ones: Guinness, Kerrygold, which he created, Baileys, Jameson and Waterford Crystal.'

O'Reilly pitched the idea of buying the business to John Magnier, owner of the famous Coolmore Stud, and to Magnier's father-in-law Vincent O'Brien, the world's most famous racehorse trainer; they weren't interested. John Meagher's Irish Marketing Surveys (IMS) carried out detailed market research on his behalf – at a hefty cost of £44,000 – and it found, to O'Reilly's shock, that only 30% of Americans who bought the product knew that it came from Ireland. This didn't deter his interest, but his problem was getting others, with sufficient money, interested in working with him.

He was delighted when he saw his old friend from UCC, Paddy Hayes, accept the job of MD at Waterford Crystal in 1985, and that he was joined there by O'Donoghue, another of Hayes's colleagues from the Ford business in Cork. O'Reilly sent Hayes a copy of the IMS market research report as a gift.

Waterford Crystal was already in trouble, however. While the market for fine lead crystal in the USA tripled from 1979 to 1983, Waterford's sales grew by merely 20%, and its market share decreased to 25%. This poor performance was masked by big profits arising mainly from a strong US dollar. Hayes's solution, however, was to be a catastrophically expensive one: in 1986 he spent £250 million on buying the acclaimed British potter Josiah Wedgwood & Sons, in the hope of finding retail and distribution synergies. When Waterford Crystal bought Wedgwood, one of the potential benefits cited was the Irish company's strength in the US market, and its British counterpart's experience in the Japanese market. Waterford Crystal could now sell in Japan, while Wedgwood could now sell in the USA. It was a neat idea in theory, but in practice it worked nowhere near as well as people hoped or anticipated.

In 1988 – just as he had assembled his new shareholders in Fitzwilton – O'Reilly began talking to the Waterford Crystal deputy chairman Howard Kilroy about a possible investment by Fitzwilton. Kilroy, the CFO at the Jefferson Smurfit Group, was a tough operator. Kilroy was not going to be seduced easily by O'Reilly's apparent charm or be intimidated by his reputation, not when he worked for Michael Smurfit. No deal could be reached between O'Reilly and Kilroy, and the group's condition continued to deteriorate.

Operation Gemini was the codename given to the takeover bid for Waterford Wedgwood by O'Reilly, and it began in earnest the following year. In April 1989 Hayes resigned as chairman after it emerged that the profits of the crystal operation had been overstated by £15 million due to 'accounting errors'. Kilroy replaced him, in what was seen as a firefighting job, but he now had no choice but to engage with O'Reilly in order to source new investment. The talks would take a long time while the extent of the problems was uncovered and O'Reilly attempted to find investors who would take on such uncertainty.

Paddy Galvin was brought in to reduce Waterford's costs. He had overseen a massive cost reduction programme at Guinness in Dublin, reducing the numbers employed there by thousands. His first move was to agree a three-year pay freeze in mid-1989, but that was only the starting-point. In January 1990, Galvin demanded longer working hours, reduced bonuses and a reduction in contract staff. The unions were outraged, but something had to be done: sales of all expensive crystal products in the USA were falling, but those of lower priced units made by competitors were increasing quickly. The currency exchange rate had also gone against the Irish company: from 1987 to 1990, Waterford Crystal alone lost more than £60 million, and total corporate debt had increased to £150 million. Wedgwood was keeping the Irish business from collapse.

On 3 March 1990 an announcement was made that O'Reilly's consortium would pay £80 million for a 29.9% stake. The deal valued Waterford Wedgwood at not much more than the £230 million Waterford Crystal had paid for Wedgwood three years earlier. Fitzwilton raised £36 million by issuing more shares and borrowed the rest of its half share of the deal. The remainder came from Morgan Stanley, an

American bank; its investment bank was run by a tough American called Don Brennan, who was to be Waterford Wedgwood's new chairman, with O'Reilly as his deputy. Fitzwilton had an option to buy the American bank's 14.45% stake at a later date.

Morgan Stanley imposed enormous disciplines, O'Donoghue said, but perhaps were a touch more considerate than any other such investors might have been because of an emotional connection on Brennan's part. 'Brennan might deny it, but his family background was a factor in making the investment: his father had left Passage East, seven miles from Waterford, as a young man without an arse in his trousers,' said O'Donoghue. 'There were times when, thankfully, [Brennan] let his heart rule his head.'

O'Reilly said the combined group of Waterford Wedgwood had not fully exploited the potential of its brand names, which he called two of the 'quintessential brands in the world'. He wanted to build a 'great brands of the world' corporation and pitched the idea to his South African friends Anton and Johann Rupert, who owned Cartier, Dunhill and Rothman's. They demurred and, in any case, there was plenty of work to be done first in sorting out the financial shambles that had been purchased. Not that O'Reilly had much time to involve himself, other than at a strategic level. 'Management is a curious thing,' he said in 1990, soon after the investment had been completed. 'I won't be managing Waterford in the sense that I manage Heinz, which is the daily perusal of costs, margins, pricing strategy, advertising strategy plus the whole logistics and financial architecture of the company. But I will be interrogating, rather than managing, the marketing strategy and how we can make the concept of great brands of the world grow. You could well argue that basically the way great brands of the world will grow is by tapping into the social insecurity of the newly rich. That's a bit pejorative but it's really why some things have been so highly successful in Asia.'

Developing a luxury brands company was in many ways the antithesis of the Heinz franchise he managed. The Amalgamated Transport and General Workers Union (ATGWU), the main union at the plant at the time, initially welcomed his investment, even though he demanded 800 job losses in return, pay-cuts and radical changes in work practices. He took the main union leaders to New York in 1990 so they could eavesdrop on US shoppers. He was keen to demonstrate to them that US consumers were buying a brand, not an Irish-made product. He wanted to plant the seeds of doubt as to the importance of the company's Irish heritage with buyers. He would soon announce that Waterford Crystal stemware could be made anywhere in the world without affecting its consumer appeal. The concept of 'outsourcing' as a production option was introduced to the Irish industrial relations lexicon. There was talk of launching new brands that would carry the Waterford Crystal label but not be made in Ireland.

The 'Marquis by Waterford' crystal brand was to be machine-made in Germany and Slovenia. It would be far cheaper to make and would sell at a far lower price – about 30% below the traditional lines. The announcement came at a time when Waterford workers were on short-time hours. The unions initially fought the idea of moving away from the traditional hand-cut methods, but then offered to use the same machines in Ireland. The company said no. The workers went on strike.

The plants would shut for 14 weeks, and many feared that they would not re-open. The share price fell to 14p; the consortium was sitting on major losses on its investment. O'Donoghue and other managers who lived in Waterford had a difficult time dealing with a dispute that divided the city. 'Tony and Don backed the management and never put us under undue pressure,' said O'Donoghue. 'Tony was what I'd call a hawk on out-sourcing. He wanted to maintain Irish production but not at all costs. He was determined to have a successful outsourcing programme to lower cost, high quality locations, while balancing capacity utilisation in the manufacturing operations we owned.'

O'Donoghue winced as he recalled the emotions that accompanied the strike. 'The thing with a strike is that in week one, the board says "to hell with them, we'll stick it out", in the third week it gets into "we're in the right" mode, in the sixth week it's "we've got to sort this",' he said. 'It took an awful lot longer.' Waterford was fortunate that it had Galvin, with his vast experience, to guide it through. The settlement with the unions didn't mean that recovery was immediate and the share price fell further, to just 12p, in 1992. However, that year the company recorded its first operating profit since 1987, even if it was just £500,000. Sales picked up sharply, however, and in 1993 profits reached £10 million and the share price soared to 60p.

Galvin left the company in 1995. 'When I took over, I thought it was a matter of living in hope,' he said. 'I never expected such a transformation to a situation where we now have record sales and record profits.'

O'Reilly marked Galvin's departure by boasting that 'under his leadership, the management team at Waterford Crystal has successfully managed the transition from a production-driven entity to a profitable market-led, consumer-focused company ... To take a company that was bankrupt with almost £300m of tax loss carry forward, was overstaffed and overpaid, and make it the company it is today after taking a strike, proving that outsourcing works, and at the end giving permanent employment to the workers that remain ... is an example that should be copied by all our state and semi-state companies.'

Some of the same techniques that worked at Waterford Crystal would be applied at Wedgwood, too. For example, in 1995 it introduced a new porcelain line called 'Embassy', which was positioned in the mid-priced segment, and a new bestselling line called 'Cornucopia', a fine bone china pattern. In the year to end March 1995, profits doubled to £22.6 million and the group paid a dividend for the first time since 1988. This appeared to be good news for Fitzwilton shareholders, too, although its spate of purchases that marked the end of the 1980s had not delivered as much as had been promised and nor had the scale of expansion been anything like anticipated.

In May 1990 Fitzwilton declared pre-tax profits of £12.1 million for 1989. Yet the share price started on a long, slow decline. 'I think it is on the threshold of doing important things,' O'Reilly said. The British recession ruined the car sales business, in which Fitzwilton had invested heavily, and losses mounted. Fitzwilton sold Keep Trust in 1993 and had to take a £29 million write-off. The cash-and-carry businesses provided marginal profits. There was a retreat from Britain and instead another new dawn was heralded when, in October 1992, Fitzwilton paid £122 million for Wellworths, a chain of Northern Ireland supermarkets owned by the departing UK firm Gateway. Fitzwilton was capitalised at £45 million and was barely profitable. O'Reilly had to put in £14 million of his own money for a 50% share in the purchasing joint venture vehicle, with the majority of the money borrowed. Again, there were great plans: AIB, adviser to Fitzwilton, produced a map of all the locations south of the border where Wellworths could open stores, to create a new retailing powerhouse. Few held their breath in anticipation, however. Was it possible that Fitzwilton would do what its predecessor incarnations hadn't managed to achieve?

O'Reilly said that he began to give Fitzwilton serious attention again in the 1990s. 'The scale of my priorities was always Heinz, number one – and I never missed a board meeting or an executive meeting in all my time there – then Independent Newspapers, number two, and very much Fitzwilton, number three,' he said. 'I was interested in Fitzwilton, excited by it, sheet-anchored by it, but never really gave it any detailed attention other than in that extraordinary period 1975 to 1977 when I felt that my own career might be imperilled by the collapse of Fitzwilton. Then I went at it in a big way.' That may have encouraged existing co-investors, but it might not have been what previous shareholders in his ventures wanted to hear.

CHAPTER THREE

'BUY, BORROW AND BUY'

In late 1990 an opportunity to buy some of the world's major newspapers emerged in Australia. Fairfax was the second largest newspaper business in Australia, second only to the Murdoch empire. Its assets included the *Sydney Morning Herald* and the *Melbourne Age*, which O'Reilly ranked among the 20 premier titles in the world. It owned the *Canberra Times*, about a quarter of the country's national magazine market and also Macquarie Broadcasting, Australia's largest radio network.

Despite enormous revenues, Fairfax was in deep – and deepening – financial trouble. Ownership had changed when 26-year-old Warwick Fairfax took control in October 1987 by buying the shares of all the other family members, costing A$2.1 billion. He had borrowed the money and was struggling to repay it. He had issued so-called junk bonds – some A$450 million worth – on the advice of the highly controversial American financier Michael Milken, a man who later spent time in jail in the USA for securities fraud, and with advice too from an American publisher called Ralph Ingersoll II. Economic recession and the accompanying slump in advertising revenue caused Fairfax's turnover to fall from A$815 million in 1989/90 to about A$700 million for 1990/91, and earnings before interest and tax halved to just over A$110 million. Fairfax was having serious trouble paying the very high returns demanded by bondholders.

O'Reilly first approached Fairfax in 1989 about acquiring some of its assets or setting up joint ventures with APN. Quickly, he realised that a tie-up would not be advisable and that his ambitions should be raised. He was encouraged by contacts with ousted members of the Fairfax family. At a party given by Lady Mary Fairfax at a Sydney restaurant called Darcy's, O'Reilly was overheard saying loudly as the main course was served, 'I want Fairfax, I want Fairfax'. He received encouragement from John Fairfax, over A$300 million richer as a result of his nephew Warwick's endeavours but itching to get back into the ownership of the business, even if as a minority partner.

O'Reilly commenced a detailed analysis of the Fairfax situation, and when the company went into receivership in December 1990 he was well on the way to assembling a consortium to bid for it. This acquisition would catapult him into the big league of newspaper proprietors, with all of the attendant status. He could see plenty of scope for cost-cutting yet the newspapers still had enormous revenues, despite their decline: its classified advertising was known in the trade as the 'river of gold', and his APN boss John Reynolds believed these were still managed in a 'top-notch' manner.

It was going to be a complicated process, however. Others wanted to buy Fairfax, for the same reasons O'Reilly had identified. Fairfax would be expensive to purchase, far too much for IN to attempt on its own. There were also the foreign ownership rules, which would limit IN to 15% of the shares. O'Reilly could not use his family trust to make up the balance of the price as he had at APN; this deal was far, far too big.

There was to be a three-way fight for the Fairfax prize, conducted by the receiver Mark Burrows and complicated by the government's interest in the outcome and its own internal battle for leadership of the Labour party, which was ongoing at the same time. Bob Hawke was just about hanging on as prime minister, with the ambitious Paul Keating snapping at his heels. Hawke wanted Fairfax to stay in Australian hands. O'Reilly emphasised that he already had Australian interests and that the balance of the shares in his consortium would be owned by Australian investment institutions. Another of the bidders, confusingly named Australian Independent Newspapers (AIN), was entirely made up of such institutions and some had irrevocably committed to AIN, putting them out of O'Reilly's reach as financial supporters. The third consortium, called Tourang, had *Daily Telegraph* owner Conrad Black as its overseas investor and included the Australian billionaire mogul Kerry Packer, apparently giving it the biggest financial resources. However, Packer's ownership of major

Australian broadcasting assets caused difficulties with media cross-ownership regulations, which had a similar limiting effect to the foreign ownership rules, and the politicians simply didn't trust him and therefore didn't want him to get a foothold in newspapers. Packer would be restricted to a 15% share, at best.

Hawke's government was lobbied to allow a larger overseas investment element in any winning consortium. The most he would concede was 20%, which suited O'Reilly as IN could not afford more. O'Reilly provided journalists with the type of assurances he had made upon buying IN in 1973. 'The products are perfect for their markets,' he said. 'There is no need to interfere editorially.' He also warned them against Black. 'If you like strong-minded interventionist proprietors with Thatcherite views, he's your man,' he said.

In late August, O'Reilly visited Hawke for a private dinner at The Lodge, the Prime Minister's official residence in Canberra, following the example of Black, who had visited a month earlier. O'Reilly was accompanied by a friend, Ted Harris, the chairman of Australian Airlines who would later become deputy chairman of APN. An Australian cricket super-star from a previous generation, Harris was a business powerhouse and had been nominated by O'Reilly as chairman-in-waiting for Fairfax, should the bid be successful. Harris and O'Reilly offered Hawke a guarantee of editorial fairness in political matters should they win control. Fairfax had been traditionally anti-Labour, so this undertaking was about as good as Hawke could have expected. O'Reilly was now Hawke's 'favoured candidate', but that wouldn't turn out to mean much. Keating moved against Hawke again in October, and replaced him as prime minister in December.

O'Reilly's other problem was guaranteeing the involvement of local investment institutions as his supporters. He met with Burrows, who was supposed to get as much money as possible for creditors. O'Reilly came with an idea: he would pay a major Australian stockbroking firm to underwrite a portion of his consortium's bid. In return for a hefty fee, the stockbroker would guarantee to buy any unsold shares in the consortium in the event of it taking over Fairfax. Nobody would have to commit cash in advance of a bid and O'Reilly reckoned that if his bid was successful, he and the stockbrokers would have no problems in finding investors to buy the shares. It was a clever and reasonable proposal, but it was to eventually prove an albatross: his competitors would lobby Burrows that it meant O'Reilly's consortium was short of the required cash.

O'Reilly's group won the first round of bidding, offering A$1.429 billion, but Burrows decided to run a second round in the hope of increasing the price. On 28 November, Packer announced his withdrawal from Tourang, which suddenly made that consortium more palatable to the public and politicians, if seemingly less well funded. Before Packer could be replaced, the treasury minister John Kerin, knowing that the Foreign Investment Review Board was split as to whether to allow either O'Reilly or Black as contenders, prepared to approve the IN group as a foreign bidder and rule out Tourang on the grounds of too much foreign investment in its bid. Hawke was under such pressure from Keating that he announced a government reshuffle in a vain attempt to consolidate power, and he moved Kerin out of the Department of the Treasury before he could announce his decision.

Tourang submitted a revised offer as bids closed on 11 December that reduced the element of foreign investment, mainly from Black, to a more acceptable level. On 13 December the new Treasurer, Ralph Willis, confirmed the acceptability of the restructured Tourang bid and O'Reilly's advantage had disappeared.

Three days later Burrows decided in favour of Tourang, even though it was the lowest of the bidders. He deemed it could provide the money faster than the other two and that O'Reilly's financial guarantees were not good enough, even though his group was the highest bidder. O'Reilly had bid A$1.56 billion and guaranteed that IN would pay A$120 million in cash for its projected 20% shareholding. However, this could not be delivered until after an EGM of shareholders back in Dublin, which would take 21 days to convene. Burrows was worried that O'Reilly's deal with his underwriters gave the stockbroking firm the right to withdraw in the event of any unexpected and dramatic fall in the stock market. Such an event, even if unlikely, would create chaos for himself as receiver, for the buyer and for any potential investors. With the banks owed A$1.25 million by Fairfax, Burrows was not prepared to take chances. Tourang also had a deal in place with the bondholders over repayments. Tourang threatened to withdraw if its bid was not accepted immediately and Burrows, fearful of losing its bid and then seeing either O'Reilly or AIN falter, succumbed.

'What actually happened at the end,' said O'Reilly, 'was that the terms under which the final offers were made were dealt with, in my view, in a partisan fashion by the parties who were accepting the bidding. In other words, we were encouraged to believe that an underwritten offer, which we had for A$1.56 billion, would be an acceptable offer. And then we were told at the very end, "Sorry, but this deal is done with Tourang and you have to be good for your money on next Saturday week", which gave us the phrase "to be good for your money". This at a time when we had been led to believe that an underwritten public flotation would be an acceptable route for the receiver and for the banks. So quite simply, we felt that we were misled, led down a fool's path ... We went at it in a straightforward, honourable and honest way and we feel that we were not treated fairly and we have brought that feeling to the courts.'

O'Reilly pursued a claim for A$80 million in the Australian federal court system. Black was scathing, describing O'Reilly's efforts as an 'undignified and unseemly act of sour grapes and he's making an ass of himself'. He described him as a relentless adversary and bad loser involved in litigation that was 'frivolous and vexatious', after making a bid that had 'an endearing element of charlatanism. But we're not talking about snake oil but the future of Australia's leading news-papers'. He accused O'Reilly of defaming him. 'He's got all those Irish politician friends of his, reeking of peat and potatoes. But he never had a hope.' Black was not finished there:

> As you know he's a very charming and persuasive man and he'd gotten away with bloody murder in Australia. He'd got the whole press in the country believing: one, that he was an Australian, and two, he was a newspaper man. And I felt called upon to point out a few basic facts: I said he did not develop that splendid brogue at the Billabong, that he was no more Australian than I am and that he was a very talented man and a friend of mine. But he wasn't a newspaper man, his job is manufacturing ketchup in Pittsburgh, even though, as I pointed out, for his own tax reasons he can only spend 90 days a year in the United States. But there's nothing wrong with that, it doesn't disqualify him as the owner of Fairfax, it just gives lie to this mystique he was endeavouring to propagate as a lifelong, committed newspaper man. He was swaddling himself in the raiment of this non-interfering owner and bandying about the well-respected names of Kay Graham [proprietor of *The Washington*

Post] and Punch Sulzberger [proprietor of *The New York Times*].

I'm rather an admirer of his in a way, but frankly I don't believe he has what it takes from an economic standpoint to buy significant newspapers. He can schmooze his way with the bankers, but there's an element of horse feathers.

Fairfax may have ended in disappointment, but it gave O'Reilly a taste for the big newspaper league. Author Nicholas Coleridge asked him what sort of satisfaction he got from owning a collection of minority township tabloids in 'Florida without the kitsch', as Ted Smyth had described Queensland. 'A local provincial newspaper should be both highly provincial and investigative,' replied O'Reilly, 'without being destructive within the wider community. But also inform people that there is a "world outside", so break down the barriers of provincialism. I enjoy that mission.' Coleridge believed that 'his ownership satisfies only one proprietorial criteria – making money'.

O'Reilly made a lot of money out of APN when the ownership of the company was restructured via a stock market flotation in 1992, both personally (or at least for the family trust) and at IN, which was to become a 20% shareholder upon flotation. 'Essentially, we put 10 million dollars into a highly geared bid when I bought it from Rupert and that 10 million is today worth 138 million dollars,' he said after the flotation. 'Absolutely outstanding. We took a big risk and we got an unreasonable reward.'

His interaction with Murdoch greatly influenced his strategic thinking for expanding the newspapers. Murdoch's philosophy was 'buy, borrow and buy'. Murdoch believed paying interest on debt was better value than paying dividends to minority shareholders because the former was a tax-deductible expense. This was complicated somewhat by O'Reilly's personal need for dividends, to meet his own interest costs and to fund his lifestyle. Money generated tended to be spent on dividends rather than on reinvestment in existing products, to the frustration of managers.

O'Reilly expressed his admiration for Murdoch many times in the coming years, even though the Australian-turned-American was reviled by many for his attitude towards journalism and getting stories of doubtful value by almost any means (although he also loved and protected the existence of newspapers when his minority shareholders would have preferred investment in other media). Murdoch had come close to losing everything because of enormous debts taken on in expanding his television and film business in the late 1980s.

'I think Rupert's one of the most outstanding businessmen I've met in my life,' said O'Reilly. 'Just in the general ranks of businessmen who have courage, you couldn't possibly meet someone who has the courage and vision to withstand the last five years in the way Rupert has. He has continued to innovate in the face of enormous pressure from the banking world. It's been an act of genius.' The respect was mutual. At one stage O'Reilly, apparently not knowing that Murdoch was still in the audience at a media investor conference, joked that he wanted his media interests to have a turnover that matched Murdoch's debts. Murdoch laughed, but might not have done so if someone else had said it.

Now that he had a desire to join the big league, it wouldn't be too long before O'Reilly considered another major acquisition, this time in Britain. On 5 November 1991, Robert Maxwell either fell or was pushed from his yacht when it was moored off the coast of Tenerife. O'Reilly believed it was 'suicide from despair', such was the unfolding financial disaster that was about to be disclosed. Maxwell had stolen £440 million from the Mirror Group Newspapers' (MGN) pension fund, and the net was closing fast.

Independent Newspapers built a small stake in MGN throughout 1992, just 3%, as O'Reilly pondered a much more serious, and expensive, effort to buy a larger amount of shares. A dour Ulsterman called David Montgomery, a former editor of *Today* newspaper, had been made MD of MGN by administrators after Maxwell's death, but he had no interest in inviting IN on board – as the Irish company had planned – should it manage to buy a bigger shareholding, possibly of the order of about a quarter of the company. O'Reilly and Brendan Hopkins, who had been made head of the British operations, tried to interest Montgomery in their ideas as to how to manage MGN, but he had no sympathy for their collegiate style.

Worries about doing business with Montgomery influenced O'Reilly, but the real issue was the price IN would have to pay for a sizeable stake in MGN. The shares were sold, for a relatively small profit of £3 million. It was a disappointment, but nonetheless a sign that O'Reilly wanted IN to become a serious player in Britain. It would not be the last he would see of David Montgomery.

CHAPTER FOUR

ABSOLUTE POWER AT HEINZ

Jack Heinz died on 25 February 1987, at the age of 78. O'Reilly had worked well with him, developing a good relationship with his chairman, keeping an appropriate distance from him, but not moving as far from him as, perhaps, Gookin had. O'Reilly's affability and genuine interest in people allowed for that, but it was also part of his political DNA. He managed to achieve a balance that worked for him. He consulted with Heinz occasionally but not too often, not letting Heinz think he had more power over O'Reilly than he had over Gookin. On Heinz's death O'Reilly added the post of chairman to his responsibilities, meaning that he held the three most senior posts in the company, even though he was not a family member, had not worked his way through from the bottom of the ranks and was not American.

'There were a lot of people along the way who hurled sharp implements at me or tried to stand on my knuckles as I came up,' he once said of his rise at Heinz. That wasn't the case anymore. The chairmanship gave him total power. It meant there was no one to query his frequent and often sudden absences from Pittsburgh. He had developed the happy knack of seeming to be always there, using streams of detailed faxes, demanding answers to questions that he sent back from hotel rooms wherever in the world he happened to be.

It didn't mean that people didn't talk about his travels and commitment, even within the company, with one anonymous employee complaining once that 'he is in and out of here like a ping-pong ball'. O'Reilly had to continuously emphasise that whatever else he did, he was always in control of what was going on at Heinz. To achieve that he picked senior managers who would not complain, who were loyal to him.

He could never escape questions about whether his expanding Irish investments would demand his return home permanently. 'I have no interest in going back,' he said. 'The corporate game is here in America. So if I want to stay in business, I'll stay in the United States.'

'I don't divide my time in any strategic way, I respond to it,' he told one interviewer. 'You get to a certain level in a corporation where you've been around for such a long time that the rhythms of the company are pretty clear. Firstly, it has a staccato quality to it: that is, if they need me, that's my first responsibility. Secondly, there are periods in the year of high intensity and low intensity. An American corporation like Heinz bases itself very much on business planning. The whole process of trying to lend a spurious illusion of precision fascinates Americans and amazes Europeans, but I'm prepared to play the game. So we go through this planning cycle that takes about three months and during that period I'm incommunicado to all but the most extreme and urgent requests from Greece.'

This reference to his new wife was his usual way of ending a serious point with humour, to deflect the logical follow-on question as to how his Irish interests continued without his involvement. But he had to emphasise his commitment to Heinz. He had 10 board meetings a year that he never missed. Once a year, in either October or November, the senior executives flew to Pittsburgh or another location to present their business plans. This is where the analytic, demanding O'Reilly patiently dissected every line of what he was given, listening patiently and then examining rigorously every assumption or claim about capital expenditure, products, market share, advertising plans, cash-flows and margins, wanting to know all of the risks as much as the potential rewards. It was done with a three-year and a five-year horizon. These sessions could be brutal, with constant requests to squeeze yet another cent of each unit's costs. Executives had to compete with each other for the available capital, causing friction. Everyone knew that their personal rewards depended on meeting these targets.

The 1980s were the golden era for Heinz, its profits tripling in 10 years under O'Reilly's watch. O'Reilly had delivered spectacular profits from products – cat food, canned tuna, private-label soups, and ketchup – that were considered by many to be mundane and mature. Return on shareholders' equity had reached 25% by 1987, well ahead of the industry averages. 'O'Reilly just knows how to get things done, and year after year, Heinz ekes more growth out of the same old businesses,' said William Leach, a food industry analyst at Donaldson, Lufkin & Jenrette Securities. 'In fact, Heinz is so consistently successful that it has become an incredible bore to follow.'

O'Reilly had followed what he called 'the McDonaldization of the world' – the introduction of American tastes to overseas consumers – and often made Heinz the first company to produce condiments, French fries and other fast-food items in the developing world. He kept cutting costs and refused to ever pay more than 12 times earnings for an acquisition. It was noted, however, that the company's successes tended to be more overseas than in the USA. The one domestic purchase, at this point at least, that O'Reilly could boast of was WeightWatchers, which brought in about 11% of revenues and 15% of profits. It was second in profitability only to ketchup in the group. O'Reilly hoped to prosper further with diversification into the fitness business, which he hoped to align to WeightWatchers. 'The centers give us a beachhead on which to build,' he said. 'They will lead us into some acquisition in the wellness field that will help us respond to the graying of America.' He came to the conclusion that at WeightWatchers, pricing wasn't as important as satisfaction, that people would pay a little bit more if they believed they were losing weight.

He was relentless and he did not become complacent, at least not then. He was not wedded to the idea that what had worked in the past would continue to work. He entered the 1990s with a decision that the cost-cutting exercises that had increased margins in the 1980s weren't going to work in the 1990s. He admitted that in the past, to save money, some factories had sped up production to the detriment of product quality. He wanted to slow things down again and emphasise quality, and to this end he introduced a concept he called 'total quality management' (TQM). The production line was made the centre of attention. Product reject rates were to be brought down, staff numbers were actually increased if it meant the achievement of better production ratios and a greater emphasis was placed on the training of factory workers. 'The thing I like about TQM is that it's more Socratic than surgical,' he said.

He kept the corporate jet, even though many companies cut such costs when engaged in reviews that impact on the livelihoods of lower-level employees. He excused it on the basis that it allowed him to follow agendas that could not be facilitated on regularly scheduled flights. That was a partial truth. He also enjoyed the comforts afforded by this mode of transport, such as the ability to dispense with queues at airports. It also enabled him to attend to his personal, non-Heinz interests: once there was also something to do with Heinz on the agenda, he would not personally be handed the expensive bill for use of the company's Gulfstream aircraft.

O'Reilly's own position became even more secure when it was announced, in August 1990, that he had been signed to a new five-year contract that included options to buy four million Heinz shares. O'Reilly had been in the job for just over 10 years and James McDonald, the board member who headed the compensation committee, remembered a conversation O'Reilly had with the board upon accepting the job. Asked what he intended to do 10 years hence, McDonald recalled, 'He said, "When I reach my mid-fifties, I would probably leave business work and get into something else".'

Whether or not the rumours that O'Reilly was being wooed by any number of unnamed competitors were true, Heinz decided that it needed to incentivise its key man to stay. 'We see it as a way to put a handcuff on Tony O'Reilly and keep him at Heinz,' said McDonald. O'Reilly could not exercise the option to buy the stock until 1995 and would earn a profit only if the price exceeded the option's exercise price of $29.87. 'This does not pay off unless the stock does,' McDonald said. 'Unless the company continues to perform, it can't be a good deal for him.' O'Reilly's salary was to remain at $708,117, although there was about $2.6 million in bonuses available to him that would be relatively simply achieved.

The major focus on O'Reilly's pay deal came in 1991, when options he had been granted over the previous decade vested. This brought O'Reilly full square and centre to the public's attention: his $75.1 million in salary, bonus and stock options was a new record in executive pay.

'I'm not a hero worshipper normally, but I tell you this guy really is unusual,' said McDonald, defending this payout. O'Reilly defended stock options as 'the ultimate performance incentive'. He said: 'I probably have one of the lowest base salaries in Pittsburgh for someone who runs a company of Heinz's size.'

Criticism emerged. 'I don't think there's any question that O'Reilly is tremendous merchandise, but at some point, somebody ought to say enough is enough,' argued pay critic Graef Crystal, an adjunct professor of business at the University of California, Berkeley. 'The reward that he will now receive is far in excess of the risk that he's taking.' His argument was that CEOs should not be earning more than five times the average pay in a company; the average for top 500 company CEOs in the USA in the early 1990s was 160 times. O'Reilly did even better than that.

It was noted that Heinz's performance – impressive though it was, as shareholders gained an annual return of 27.5% for the 10 years ended 31 December 1991, far outstripping the 15.5% for the Standard & Poor's 500-stock index – was behind that of other food industry comparables, all of whom had managed over 30% returns.

O'Reilly responded to the demand for increased profits in an unusual fashion for someone whose initial reputation was based on marketing – and whose own newspapers depended on companies such as Heinz advertising to customers. He switched a lot of budget into trade promotion – the paying of retailers to buy, stock and display food products – to the horror of the advertising industry, which naturally wanted Heinz to continue promoting its brand through advertising.

Trade promotions were self-destructive, chided Robert James, chairman and CEO of McCann-Erickson, one of the world's biggest advertising agencies, because 'if you don't spend money to advertise brands, over time you are going to weaken those brands'. If O'Reilly had heeded that prescient advice, the problems that were to emerge at his other businesses many years into the future might not have happened. As ever, he took his own counsel and went his own way.

CHAPTER FIVE

PLAYING THE LONG GAME

O'Reilly's first recorded comments about *The Independent* were made in 1990, four years before he bought shares in its owner, Newspaper Publishing. In an interview he remarked that 'It has been the great encouragement to everybody who wants a fresh voice in society. The folklore was that unless you had a great amount of money, you couldn't start a newspaper. [Andreas] Whittam Smith has proved that, at least temporarily, to be incorrect. *The Independent* is in one respect like *The New York Times* – a dissonant voice. Newspapers are about dissonance. I'm suspicious of proprietors who want to push their personal prejudices, especially since most of the newspaper proprietors I've met are of limited education. Successful commercially, but limited educationally.'

The Independent was the creation of Whittam Smith, once financial editor of the *Daily Telegraph*, and Stephen Glover and Matthew Symonds, two fellow journalists who had been attracted by the prospects offered by new technology and the new lower cost printing opportunities provided by Murdoch's destruction of the powerful print unions in the UK. The three set about raising money for a new kind of paper, to be independent both by name and in nature, in which no shareholder would be allowed to own more than 10%, and they recruited journalists who didn't want to work for Murdoch. They launched on 7 October 1986 with the brilliant advertising line: 'The Independent. It is. Are you?'

It innovated editorially and circulation rose to 415,000 by November 1990. Whittam Smith became overly ambitious, however. He wanted to launch a Sunday newspaper, into a far more competitive market. In January 1990 the *Independent on Sunday*, with its own separate staff of 86 people, began publication. Quickly, it became a financial burden to the main paper; recession meant that advertising income slumped and in November 1990, Smith sold 25% of the company jointly to *El Pais* of Spain and *La Repubblica* of Italy, breaching the 10% rule. He made a £10 million bid to buy *The Observer*, probably to close it, but was comfortably outbid by *The Guardian*. Then, in September 1993, Murdoch cut the price of the *London Times* to 10p a copy: as it soared, the circulation of *The Independent* slid because it did not have the resources to cut its own price to match.

O'Reilly had also passed on buying *The Observer*. 'It's losing £10 million a year; it would have been an act of insanity for us to buy it,' he said. Towards the end of 1993, however, IN began building a shareholding in Newspaper Publishing, which at the time was still making modest profits of about £1 million each year. O'Reilly was enticed by a private approach by Sir Victor Blank, the chairman of Charterhouse Bank, who had been involved with Whittam Smith in raising the money for the original launch in 1986, and who had now decided that radical new management and investment was required if the titles were to be saved. His interest in O'Reilly's IN as a 'white knight' was prompted by the arrival on the Newspaper Publishing share register of MGN and Montgomery. The latter was making his presence felt, and Blank did not like it. O'Reilly thought he could make more money out of the business than it was achieving, even though the daily circulation had fallen below 300,000.

What O'Reilly needed was for the Italian and Spanish shareholders to sell to him. For once his famous persuasiveness did not succeed; they wanted to hold their shares and support Montgomery as manager. In January 1994, the Irish company put a £32 million offer to all shareholders; MGN responded with its own offer at £2.50 per share. Independent Newspapers responded with a stock market dawn raid, buying from anyone who would sell at a price of £3.50 per share. Doing this, IN increased its shareholding to 29.9%, the maximum permitted without requiring a full bid, and by 22 February was the company's biggest shareholder, with a holding bigger than MGN's. It was an uncharacteristically bold move by O'Reilly. He suggested to all shareholders that there should be an issue of new shares to provide new capital; the Irish company would buy those shares, giving it effective control and giving the newspapers the money they needed.

Instead, Whittam Smith made the fateful and perhaps naïve decision to align with Montgomery. Personalities played their part: Whittam Smith was the son of a clergyman and was more drawn to the Ulsterman. Whittam Smith agreed a deal for MGN to offer loans and take over the printing of the two titles. Montgomery told him that no journalists would be among the 120 redundancies. Smith was to remain as editor-in-chief and would become board chairman for three years: the sale of his shares to MGN also paid him £3.9 million.

O'Reilly and IN were now in a bind. There were to be no seats on the board, no say in the running of the business and MGN was behaving in Montgomery's abrasive manner. 'We were engaged in a focused bid to save the *Independent* titles and O'Reilly cocked it up on us twice,' said a spokesman. 'We won't invite anyone to dinner if they kick down the front door.' When board membership was eventually achieved in late 1994, O'Reilly's nominees discovered that it only met once every two months and had no real hands-on role in relation to management, or access to any detailed information. Independent Newspapers watched both circulation and revenues fall as Murdoch's predatory price-cutting at *The Times* radically changed the UK broadsheet newspaper market.

O'Reilly snapped at the suggestion that he had paid too much for a minority shareholding in a company that was now losing money, and readership, and was in need of a huge capital injection. Newspaper Publishing, with a turnover of some £80 million, was 'not a major economic enterprise' compared to that of IN, he argued, but would be 'a major visiting card for Independent Newspapers on the world stage'. It was a line he was going to use often in the years to come. The acquisition cost of £18 million was 'not a lot of money' for a company with a market capitalisation of £400 million, he claimed. Equally, his interest was essentially in the bottom line, and he was not concerned with editorial policy. He deeply disliked, he said, the appellation 'media magnate' or 'media baron' being applied to him, he told British reporters.

O'Reilly, networking as usual, had Montgomery as his guest at the Wexford Opera Festival in November. Montgomery's hostility to journalists was having its own effect on morale at the newspapers, and everyone was blaming everyone else for the continually disimproving editorial and commercial results. By March 1995 – at which stage Montgomery was also under pressure from other shareholders – the MGN side eventually accepted that IN would be a source of fresh capital if allowed to increase its shareholding. A new share issue was organised, which left MGN and IN with just under 43.5% of the shares each, and Prisa (the holding company for *El Pais*) with just over 13%. Whittam Smith left the paper and Andrew Marr and Rosie Boycott were made editors of the daily and Sunday titles, respectively. In April 1995 there was another refinancing, which increased IN's holding to 46.4%.

O'Reilly announced confidently in his chairman's statement in the 1995 IN Annual Report that he expected the two papers 'to return to profitability by next year'. It was the first in a long litany of such claims.

———

On 31 March 1995 O'Reilly received a nasty shock. Suddenly, most un-expectedly, Fitzwilton had a new shareholder, one who had not been invited, who had bought nearly 10% of the company's shares in a morning's frantic activity, and who at first concealed its identity and its purpose.

The identity was revealed, as was required by stock exchange rules: it was Ireland's biggest indigenous retailer, Dunnes Stores, a company with the financial firepower to buy Fitzwilton. Its purpose was not revealed; Dunnes Stores didn't explain to anyone why it did anything. A family-owned company, it had been riven in recent years by director Ben Dunne's exploits, including his arrest in 1992 in Florida, where he was found high on cocaine in the company of a prostitute as he threat-ened to throw himself off the seventeenth-floor balcony of a hotel. Dunne went to war with other members of his family over ownership of the family trust, and was bought out by his siblings for £125 million. There was speculation Dunnes Stores, led now by Ben's brother Frank and their sister Margaret Heffernan, might want to recover some money by joining the stock market through reversing its assets into Fitzwilton. It was realised quickly, however, that Dunnes would never sell shares to outsiders nor let its business be subjected to public scrutiny.

Fitzwilton's most valuable asset was Wellworths, its Northern retail chain, which commanded about 21% of supermarket sales, compared to about 39% for the Associated British Foods-owned Stewarts and Crazy Prices. Dunnes Stores had a market share of only about 7%: maybe it wanted to take over Wellworths, to expand in Northern Ireland as a defensive measure against the encroaching UK multiples? All were sizing up the market as potentially more profitable now that the political peace was holding, especially with the threat of bombings waning. Another theory was that Dunnes was concerned or annoyed by Wellworths' plans to open stores south of the border. It could block O'Reilly's plans by seizing control of Fitzwilton. There was also brief consideration given to whether the move was a form of revenge for the embarrassment caused to the Dunnes by the extensive coverage of the family rows in the IN titles. Dunnes Stores wasn't just refusing to comment to the media, it wouldn't even talk to O'Reilly or his Fitzwilton people.

O'Reilly was angry but he reacted quickly, deciding over the weekend that he would mop up whatever loose shares he could before anyone else bought more. There was more than Wellworths to protect; part of his ownership of Waterford Wedgwood was by way of Fitzwilton, which owned a 9.4% stake in the luxury goods group and had the option to buy Morgan Stanley's 14.9% stake. This made it vital to act, and act decisively. O'Reilly had gone into 1995 with just over 15% of the Fitzwilton shares, while his brother-in-law, Peter Goulandris, owned 6.77%. The holdings of other directors brought the total up to 23.28%. Quickly, O'Reilly and friends – particularly Peter – bought enough shares to give the board and associates what was assumed to be majority control of the company. Dunnes Stores simply hadn't bought enough shares in the first place to allow it mount a real bid to take control. Dunnes was not offered a seat on the board. It would buy a relatively small number of extra shares in the coming months, bringing its holding to nearly 10%, but it was little more than a gesture. While O'Reilly remained vigilant, he quickly became confident that he had successfully seen off Dunnes.

Dealing with the excitement at Fitzwilton and the increasing challenges at Heinz might explain why IN did not work hard enough at its 1995 bid to win the second mobile phone licence being sold by the State by way of competition. Six consortia met the August 1995 dead-line to apply for Ireland's second mobile phone licence, which would be awarded by year end by the Department of Transport, Energy and

Communications. A who's who of global telecoms heavyweights were players in consortia that also included significant Irish interests. The foreign contenders included Comcast, Motorola, Tele-Communications and Telenor, whereas Irish semi-state operations, including RTÉ, Bord na Móna and ESB, took minority shareholdings in various consortia. Several wealthy individuals, such as Martin Naughton and Lochlann Quinn of Glen Dimplex, were involved too.

O'Reilly was part of Irish Cellular Telephones (ICT), a disparate group led by Princes Holdings, an AT&T division, TCI, United, Philips Communications, Irish semi-state Shannon Development and Riordan Communications, the latter a small Irish firm owned by Limerick man John Riordan. The absence of Hayes was a major blow: it was he who had the long-term vision for IN getting into the mobile phone business and nobody else in the consortium appeared to prosecute its case with the vigour he undoubtedly would have brought. O'Reilly was some-what complacent about the quality of the work his consortium was doing, trusting too much in the status of AT&T to win the day. There was no expectation among observers that AT&T would have any par-ticular advantage over other contestants. O'Reilly was interested, but not obsessively so – certainly not in the way that Denis O'Brien, the local radio licence owner who had branched into telecoms, clearly was: he kept his Esat Digifone consortium clearly in the public eye as a serious contender and did his necessary background work as well. O'Brien got a couple of lucky breaks along the way. Michael Lowry TD imposed a £15 million cap on the annual charge the winning bidder would pay, levelling the playing field against competitors with deeper pockets. Lowry also extended the closing date for applications, allowing O'Brien time to reconstitute his consortium after losing a major investor. Somewhat surprisingly, Dermot Desmond would be revealed as the new investor, albeit exceptionally late in the process.

The business media covering the contest – despite it being held behind closed doors and therefore affording them no real insight into what has happening – did not consider O'Reilly's ICT to be a leading contender. The gossip was that the Persona consortium, led by two Irish entrepreneurs, Tony Boyle and Mick McGinley (father of golf's 2014 Ryder Cup-winning European captain Paul), would win, boosted by the presence of Motorola in its group. No pressure was put on the editorial of the *Irish Independent* business pages over its extensive coverage of the bidding process, nor was any bias shown towards any contender. There was considerable shock when, in November, O'Brien's Esat Digifone was revealed as the winner, but not that O'Reilly's consortium had lost out.

O'Reilly seemed to take the defeat in his stride, writing to O'Brien to congratulate him on his win. 'My dear Denis,' his letter began, 'many years ago at Blackrock Baths I watched your father in the national championships, I think against a certain Eddie Heron. The multitude of the Kavanagh brothers were there flexing their pectoral muscles and I was sure your father would win an Olympic Gold. In fact, he didn't and you did, and I think your achievement in securing the second digital network is your equivalent.'

O'Reilly's equanimity may have been explained by his concentration that year on completing yet another foreign newspaper acquisition, this time in New Zealand, to add to his recent South African and English acquisitions. This latest deal stretched IN so far that plans to build a major new colour printing press in Dublin were delayed yet again; putting money into a new mobile phone network, even as a minority partner, would have been very lucrative eventually, but it would have been a drain on capital at a time when it was in scarce enough supply.

The move into New Zealand led to comments about O'Reilly launching himself into another country where he had played rugby, something he dismissed as lazy analysis. The purchase of Wilson & Horton, publisher of the *New Zealand Herald*, came about entirely for commercial reasons, although his status as a former player of renown did no harm when it came to the personal relationships that played their part in negotiations.

The *New Zealand Herald* was a paper with daily paid-for sales of over 250,000; it had an image of something of a 'paper-of-record', somewhat like *The Irish Times*, which was both a strength, for authority, and a weakness, for dullness. Profit after tax had risen from just under NZ$27 million in the 1991 financial year to almost NZ$44.5 million in 1995, and there had been expensive investment that had revamped the newspaper to boost circulation and readership.

Following on from the Fairfax debacle, IN looked at Wilson & Horton as a potential acquisition, but decided that the strong family involvement in the business would make it resistant to any potential offer. A hostile take-over bid would be both potentially very expensive and it was not the way O'Reilly liked to do his business. As it happened, his opportunity came because of the brazenness of others.

Brierley Investments was a family-owned New Zealand investor that ruthlessly specialised in identifying companies that were under-valued, or mismanaged, or both, and took control of them. It tended to buy in and reform a business before selling, or asset-strip it. On 9 November 1994 Brierley moved suddenly to buy shares in Wilson & Horton – a "dawn raid" – picking up more than 20% in a morning. It demonstrated its cunning and ruthlessness in the execution of the purchase. It was tipped off that CEO Michael Horton was flying to a newspaper conference in the USA. It sent a man to watch Horton board his plane at Auckland airport and as soon as it had taken off, the share purchases began. The captain of Horton's flight received an urgent message for Horton once his executives on the ground finally realised what was happening to their share price, which soared as the buying went on. Horton had to wait until the flight landed before he could get in touch with his staff, but all he could do was get the return flight home to Auckland. Eventually Brierley, cognisant of its reputation, decided to offer Horton a deal: it would give him six months to find a third party who could buy its shares, but only at a $2 premium per share to the price it had paid. Horton had the full support of his board, which determined unanimously to replace Brierley with 'a new cornerstone shareholder experienced in newspapers'.

Independent Newspapers was identified as an option because of its experience in Australia, South Africa and Britain as a minority shareholder, even if that tended to be a stepping-stone to taking outright control. Healy and Hopkins were invited to visit New Zealand, and they liked the state of the market, the finances of the business and its management. Murdoch, the main newspaper owner on the South Island, got wind of the negotiations and, knowing that New Zealand's foreign ownership laws were almost non-existent, made a pitch to Wilson & Horton to talk to him instead. He was too late, as the personal relationships had already been formed.

In June 1995 a deal was struck between Healy and Horton over dinner. They were quiet men, neither of whom spoke much, and afterwards O'Reilly joked that their long silences were eventually broken by the wine waiter, who suggested a price that could be agreed for the shares. The initial acquisition of the 28% Brierley shareholding for

NZ$293.7 million was carried out as a joint venture by IN and the O'Reilly family trust, split 50/50. Brierley Investments collected a NZ$50 million profit. O'Reilly and Healy joined the Wilson & Horton board, the latter becoming chairman as Cameron O'Reilly and Vincent Crowley were added from APN. Horton, in turn, joined the IN main board and fully approved of the Irish company's desire to take full control of his old family company. Wilson Whineray, one of the most famous former All Black opponents of O'Reilly's, was appointed to head an independent editorial board.

In late 1996 IN moved to buy all the remaining shares, offering NZ$10.50 each. This, as Meagher noted, was a multiple of 20.5 times earnings, a 'big' price. An independent report judged the offer to be satisfactory, but the Wilson & Horton independent directors advised shareholders not to sell as the bid was too low. The offer was increased to NZ$11 a share and was accepted, but the New Zealand shareholders were offered IN preference shares in lieu of cash and nearly three-quarters of them took those, earning greater profits later as those shares increased in value. There was a controversial aspect of the offer: it included the purchase by IN of the O'Reilly family trust shares, which resulted in a sizeable windfall profit for the trust.

The deal offered great possibilities in radio, too. The New Zealand government decided to put a large chunk of its radio interests – effectively the commercial arm of public radio – out to tender. Wilson & Horton hadn't considered the purchase, but APN's radio experiences encouraged IN, with Cameron to the forefront. In September 1994 he had started the purchase by APN of a group of regional radio stations, Australian Radio Network (ARN), and had spent over A$60 million in a year buying more. Clear Channel was the under-bidder for ARN but was invited now to become a partner by APN, and a 50/50 deal was done in 1995. Clear Channel was now to be involved in the radio stations purchased in New Zealand. Something of a buying blitz ensued, with more newspapers added too, costing nearly NZ$100 million. The group ended up with 56 New Zealand radio stations, amounting to 60% of the total New Zealand radio market. In time, ARN would become the second largest broadcaster in Australia and the largest in Australia and New Zealand combined, growing to have 94 stations. It seemed a very sweet deal all round, and O'Reilly was very pleased with his latest acquisitions.

CHAPTER SIX

INTO AFRICA

The value of networking is often not repaid immediately – it is a slow investment, sometimes maturing when least expected. And so it was that IN's expansion plans in the 1990s were helped along by a meeting that had occurred a decade earlier.

In 1982 O'Reilly, and Heinz, took an enormous gamble. The civil war in Rhodesia had come to an end and a new majority-ruled state, Zimbabwe, was in existence, under the leadership of President Robert Mugabe. This was not a country in which foreign multinationals sought to invest. But Zimbabwe had a company that interested O'Reilly: Olivine Fruit Company. It made edible oils, margarine and soap, using tallow, a colourless, tasteless solid fat, caustic soda and chemicals imported from the ports of Durban in South Africa and Beira in Mozambique. Africa was a location in which O'Reilly believed Heinz could grow sales and profits more readily than in the so-called 'mature' markets where Heinz was already a major presence.

Mugabe was prepared to sell only a minority shareholding in Olivine, wanting Zimbabwe to maintain a controlling interest in what he regarded as a major strategic resource. Foreign investors were reluctant to deal with Mugabe on this basis because of his quasi-Marxist declarations on development and economic issues; this was even long before he began his greatly destructive land redistribution policy and gained a reputation as a kleptocrat. Zimbabwe would not sign any agreement with the Overseas Private Investment Corporation (OPIC), a US agency that insured American investments overseas against seizure of assets or interference with profits getting to the parent company.

O'Reilly, confident of his ability to persuade anyone, decided to meet Mugabe personally. During the preliminary small-talk they discovered something remarkable: both of them had been educated by the same Jesuit priest, Fr O'Hea, who had gone from Dublin to Africa as a missionary for a spell. Common ground established – 'I regarded him then as a strong and competent figure,' O'Reilly later said of Mugabe – the deal was done. More importantly, it stuck. This gave O'Reilly a track record and reputation for fair dealing he could bring elsewhere in Africa. It had financial benefit, too: Heinz invested about $13 million initially, but by the end of the decade sales had doubled and Heinz was making about that much each year in profit.

O'Reilly's good relationship with Mugabe meant the Irishman secured a favourable introduction to Nelson Mandela after South Africa's iconic anti-apartheid activist was released from prison on Robben Island in 1990. O'Reilly had been the non-partisan chairman of the South Africa Free Election Fund in the USA, which had generated substantial amounts of money during the transitional period. O'Reilly learnt Mandela was to visit America in late 1993 and invited him to deliver the second HJ Heinz Fellowship Lecture, at Pittsburgh University. Mandela accepted. O'Reilly later described it as a 'salutary experience, and by no means for me alone. Among the guests was Henry Kissinger, a considerable personality wryly described as the only Secretary of State under whom three American Presidents have served. Kissinger is famously unimpressionable yet, confronted by Nelson Mandela, he was hugely impressed, as everyone was, by the courage of the man, and the sheer charisma he brought to bear on us all. In so far as you can overawe Henry Kissinger, it was the only time I ever saw him slightly overawed. He actually genuflected to the ANC leader.'

Mandela, who was accompanied by Thabo Mbeki, stayed at O'Reilly's house in Pittsburgh rather than at a hotel. His lecture was a deliberate first signal to the world financial community that post-apartheid South Africa would not be hostile to foreign investment – indeed, that it needed it – and that it would play the game, insofar as it could, by generally accepted international rules. This was a dramatic shift in emphasis as previous African National Congress (ANC) policy had strongly favoured nationalisation; it was to lead Mandela into conflict with the trade union movement and the Communist party.

O'Reilly thought that during the visit Mandela looked tired, so he suggested that Mandela could use his house in the Bahamas for a two-week period at Christmas and into the New Year, with support from

O'Reilly's butler John Cartwright and the rest of the staff, and that he
and Chryss would join him at the end of the stay for a couple of days.
Mandela knew O'Reilly was close to the incumbent President FW De
Klerk, who would be replaced by Mandela in the 1994 election, and to
the former Springbok captain turned minister Dawie de Villiers. But
this did not worry him, and indeed was an added attraction. He was well
advanced in developing his own political relationships with such men as
part of his process of reconciliation. He headed for the Bahamas where,
as arranged, O'Reilly and Chryss joined him for the end of the vacation.

Those days together were the start of a firm friendship. O'Reilly
described to Mandela his first visit to South Africa as a touring rugby
player in 1955 and subsequent tours with the Barbarians touring side in
1958 and Ireland in 1961, before returning on a business trip for Heinz
in the mid-1970s. Mandela amazed O'Reilly by stating that he had been
in the crowd on the day of O'Reilly's first test for the Lions in
Johannesburg at Eden Park, one of about 2,000 black people corralled
into one section of the ground, all cheering for the visiting team.
Mandela's biographer, John Carlin, who worked for the *Independent* as
its South Africa correspondent, later expressed some amazement at the
claim, but said he would not challenge Mandela about its accuracy.
O'Reilly told Mandela that he had a deep affection for the country and
that his awareness of the 'immense moral and political challenge South
Africans were perilously deferring' did not arise until his later visits in
the 1970s. He told his guest that he had feared a peaceful transition was
implausible and that the chances of finding a leader 'strong enough
and forgiving enough to subdue the fears and the anger of centuries
was remote, to say the least'. He complimented Mandela for succeeding
in doing just that.

Fintan O'Toole described O'Reilly's ability to strike up relationships
with both Mugabe and Mandela as 'a sign of how far he had succeeded
in creating a persona that transcended history, seemed finally to lay off
the ghosts of the past. In his bright, charming, efficient persona lay the
promise of an end to history, of a politics that would be about management, not ideology. O'Reilly said that in his dealings with Mugabe, "we
discussed the notion, the model of economic nationalism ... I was
trying to teach him about the limits of economic nationalism".

That O'Reilly and Mandela developed a genuine bond was not
surprising, according to Carlin: 'They were two alpha males, paying

each other due respects. Mandela liked powerful, wealthy people, felt very comfortable in their presence. He was not averse to favours from the rich and mighty. Mandela was the consummate political animal, who seduced to win hearts and minds. He had a political purpose in winning over and flattering O'Reilly who was, after all, susceptible to flattery. Mandela valued pragmatism over ideology.'

If O'Reilly saw the Bahamas encounter as an opportunity to impress further upon Mandela the imperatives of capital inflows to South Africa to assist in economic advancement, it was clear that Mandela had arrived at that conclusion already and was seeking allies. It is not known if they discussed the future of the newspaper business in South Africa at this stage, if O'Reilly told him that he was looking at buying in the country or if Mandela knew anyway. If they had, and it would have been most surprising if they hadn't, it would be better for them not to subsequently say so publicly.

O'Reilly knew Argus, South Africa's biggest English language newspaper group, was for sale, even if a formal announcement had not yet been made, and that he was among the preferred bidders. Argus was owned by the giant mining company Anglo-American, and it produced 750,000 papers each day and had a turnover of Stg£140 million, making it one of the biggest newspaper companies in a country of 40 million people. The ANC wanted big corporations, and most notably Anglo-American, to sell some of their interests and to bring the black community into the business sector, a process called 'unbundling'. The problem was, who would have the money to buy these assets? Anglo-American knew a buyer would not be found in South Africa; instead it had to find an overseas buyer of whom Mandela would approve. Finding such a buyer in advance of the 1994 Presidential election, when there was such uncertainty as to the safety of investments from potential nationalisation, was even more difficult. Anglo-American did its best to interest a number of international media multinationals, but most of the conversations were fairly short; this was simply too dangerous a country in which to invest.

Conrad Black was the first potential purchaser to take a serious interest. Believing that he was taking part in a fire sale, he offered Anglo-American a price it regarded as ridiculously low, notwithstanding the prevailing political and economic climate. He offered little cash and demanded that he could claw-back part of the purchase

price if the investment failed to live up to expectations. He also under-
estimated the role that Mandela would continue to play in South
African politics and instead mistakenly supported Zulu leader Chief
Mangosuthu Buthulezi. Murdoch showed interest as did James
Goldsmith, the British entrepreneur, but neither felt like taking on the
risks involved. Argus decided that O'Reilly and IN might suit better
because they were Irish and because of a feeling that O'Reilly would
be accommodating and flexible in ownership rather than behaving
either as a prescriptive capitalist or as a political ideologue in editorial
coverage. Mandela, separately, reached the same conclusion.

Before Mandela ever visited the Bahamas, three Argus executives –
John Featherstone, Doug Band and Peter McLean – flew to Dublin.
They were shocked when they saw the antiquated Middle Abbey Street
printing plant. At Castlemartin they found O'Reilly unusually reticent
and, like Black, talking about a rather low price and the possibility of a
rebate if, after a sale, the economy of South Africa went into a tailspin.
The conversations petered out and while O'Reilly maintained an
interest he did not actively chase it, other than hedging his bets by
inviting Mandela to the Heinz event.

But in a happy coincidence of events in late 1993 Argus came back to
O'Reilly, suggesting IN could become the preferred owner if he paid a
fair price, did so quickly and maintained absolute secrecy prior to any
announcement. A meeting was arranged for early 1994, and was to take
place not long after Mandela had been O'Reilly's guest in the Bahamas.
The journey to South Africa included possibly the most terrifying
plane journey O'Reilly ever experienced. On its way across the Indian
Ocean, the Heinz private aircraft developed a crack in the cockpit
windscreen and had to descend almost to sea level to continue its
journey. They arrived safely, and a greatly relieved O'Reilly met with
Argus for top secret talks. On the first day, an agreement in principle was
reached. By the end of the second day, the deal was effectively on, subject
to overcoming potential political hurdles. Argus needed to know how
the ANC would regard the suitability of the prospective new owners.

O'Reilly needed to make a phone-call. He went to another room to
call Barbara Masekele, Mandela's chief-of-staff, who put him on the line
with her boss. He invited O'Reilly to visit his house in Johannesburg
immediately. 'I've been to your home, you must come to mine,' he
said. A smiling O'Reilly strolled back into the meeting room and said

that he was heading over to Mandela's house and that he would see them later on his return. He may as well have signed the contracts there and then, so gobsmacked were the Anglo-American executives by his ready access.

The minority shareholding held by IN in the London *Independent* was also a help. *The Independent* had already established an extraordinarily high reputation among black African political figures, and with the ANC in particular, because of the excellent investigative work done by Carlin. He had played a major part in uncovering various illegal stratagems, particularly the undercover financing of armed groups, engaged in by some elements of the Nationalist Party in a frantic attempt to avert the inevitable. He became very close to Mandela and authored the book *Playing with the Enemy*, upon which the movie *Invictus* was based. It was to be an early lesson to O'Reilly as to the value of *The Independent* as a calling card, something for which he personally thanked Carlin later.

The fine details of the deal remained to be worked out, even as the transition to a democratic South Africa took place. At one point, O'Reilly phoned Anglo-American executives in their HQ overlooking Library Gardens in Johannesburg, just as a march by members of Buthulezi's Inkatha Freedom Party, on its way to protest outside the nearby ANC building, passed through the square and degenerated into a riot. The gun-shots and general mayhem from the square were clearly heard by O'Reilly, but he ignored them: it was the action of an optimist and a gambler and of a man so in control of IN that the decision to buy, even if it needed subsequent ratification by shareholders, was made by him alone.

The deal was done at the end of January 1994, but the 31% of shares were not finally transferred until August since part of the deal was that Argus Newspapers had to be listed on the Johannesburg Stock Exchange. It was the largest single inward investment into South Africa at a time when mobile funds were, whenever they could, moving in the opposite direction. It must have looked like one of the greatest single risks that O'Reilly and his board had taken in 20 years of business. Before, during and after the election in April there was a widespread belief that the country's infrastructure would collapse; thousands were murdered as anarchy loomed. O'Reilly used his contacts to reassure foreign investors. He persuaded US President Bill Clinton to agree to an interview with two leading editors, which helped to provide much needed reassurance about the American commitment to the new republic. Later in 1994 O'Reilly spoke at a conference in Atlanta, organised by Vice-President Al Gore, on the theme of American investment in South Africa. His commitment to the country involved his own capital, which meant he was working for his own self-interest, but it went beyond that and was genuine – as would be proven over the years as he got others involved in the country's economic development and in the fight against the spread of AIDS. Mandela had seduced him, gaining a powerful international ally for South Africa.

Somewhat surprisingly O'Reilly missed the inauguration, although Mandela had organised tickets for him and Chryss and two others: John Cartwright, his butler in the Bahamas, and Cartwright's plus one. 'On the day itself I was sitting in a pub in the United States, watching the event on television and the TV commentator in typically stentorian American tones was saying, "We are watching one of the great scenes of political history, the presidential inauguration of Nelson Mandela, South Africa's first ever black leader, and 400 of the world's leaders are here and the American delegation is led by First Lady Hillary Rodham Clinton, with her is Vice-President Al Gore and next to them is ... is ..." and the voice tailed off and I'm thinking, "No, Jesus Christ, it's John." Right there, tucked in with the American delegation, what a moment!'

O'Reilly got back to South Africa later in the year and he and Chryss were invited for dinner at Mandela's presidential compound. 'It was just our group, no aides, nobody but the wine steward. And this man, the steward, turned out to have been Mandela's former prison warder. The meaning of his life had become clear: it was to look after Madiba. It struck me forcibly that that's an unusual event to see in one's life, to see a man in a filial attraction and affection for another he had formerly been the captor of.'

O'Reilly also commanded such loyalty from friends and staff, albeit not arising from the same circumstances. However, Carlin identified one subtle difference between the two men: 'The definition of charisma is vast self-confidence, a conviction beyond arrogance that everybody in the room will like you. Mandela had that without trying, there was no conscious effort required, he had the nobility of naturalness. O'Reilly had that but, I suspect, it was not as naturally inbuilt.'

South Africa provided enormous business challenges. Although a country of 40 million people, only an estimated 36% read newspapers, with the vast majority opting for radio and television. Independent Newspapers took an aggressive management stance once it got control. It bought the Times Media's interest in the rival *Cape Times*, which had been shared, and set about transforming it. In March 1995 it launched *Business Report*, which became an integral part of all the major Argus morning papers. Some 5,000 people, including the future President, Thabo Mbeki, attended a fireworks party for the launch. O'Reilly was not a man for starting original products at IN, but in June 1995 he launched South Africa's *Sunday Independent*, a very different animal from the Irish version, to coincide with the final of the rugby World Cup in South Africa, won by the host nation when it beat New Zealand in extra time in a tense final. O'Reilly was there, and was among those moved to tears by one of the most magical and symbolic moments in sporting history: when Mandela strode onto the pitch wearing a South African Springbok jersey – so long a symbol of oppression – to present the trophy to Francois Pienaar as the predominantly white crowd chanted his name.

Capitalising on the added value in terms of editorial content, the group increased all cover prices: even though circulation slipped as a result, overall circulation revenue improved by 29%. An investment of some R50 million on technology was concentrated on new editorial systems, which would facilitate copy- and file-sharing across titles.

O'Reilly's 1994 biographer Ivan Fallon was rewarded with the position of editorial director of the newspapers. He was to act as O'Reilly's political analyst, too, with a view to spotting an opportunity to increase the Argus shareholding to more than 50%. By early 1995, some small acquisitions of shares on the market had brought the IN shareholding to about 38%. O'Reilly suggested that IN go for an offer to gain control. He flew to Johannesburg for a meeting with Mbeki. O'Reilly's plan included an idea that if IN made an offer to buy the company, then acceptances above 60% of the shares would be transferred to black empowerment groups at the price IN had paid for them. This would be a further vote of confidence in black Africa; Mbeki was enthusiastic.

It didn't work out as planned. Many minority shareholders didn't want to sell and despite an offer of R13 per share, compared to a market price of R10, IN managed to secure just short of 60% of the shares, which meant the offer to transfer acceptances to black empowerment groups lapsed. Those who hung onto the shares made a good decision as the shares continued moving upwards in value. With Mbeki's agreement, IN's shareholding reached 70% and then it made another offer, this time at R26.5 per share, to buy all the remaining shares. Argus now became a wholly-owned subsidiary of what was now called Independent News & Media (INM).

Independent News & Media had control of the majority of English-language newspapers published in the state, selling three out of every four English-language papers in the country. However, the decade since the first non-apartheid election saw a weakening of newspaper circulations generally in the new state. Part of this was down to a fall-off in reader interest; 1994, as the year of the first free South African elections, was naturally an exceptional year for circulation, and provided somewhat of a false benchmark against which to measure. As the political situation stabilised, newspaper readership suffered. The deliberate strategy to increase profit margins by raising cover prices and not worrying about a resultant loss of circulation also had its impact. Increased prices – on average by a quarter – would bring in more revenue than would be lost through falling sales, a strategy that had also been employed in Ireland. It worked even better in South Africa as the monopoly protected market share and therefore advertising.

Significant time and effort had to be devoted to promoting black empowerment internally: hiring and promoting people who did not come from the white workforce that had traditionally staffed the white-owned media. It also meant changing the editorial content to be more inclusive and representative. The difficulty was that while new readers were gained in previously disadvantaged communities, old ones in the wealthy white sector were lost. A happy medium had to be found. O'Reilly's pragmatism was well suited to that. 'We are not right wing and not left wing – we are for the people and for the country,' he said. In other words, he would take whatever course was required to maximise and safeguard profits, while simultaneously promoting what he saw as the country's best interests. For a long time he did just that.

CHAPTER SEVEN

AN INTIMATION OF MORTALITY

I n the course of his business life O'Reilly negotiated and completed many remarkable deals, but one of the most remarkable was the purchase, in December 1994, of a near quarter shareholding in the companies that controlled the *Irish Press* titles. That its three titles – the daily, evening and Sunday papers that had for so long provided the main challenge to INM in the Irish market – subsequently closed in 1995, within six months of that investment, gave grist to the mill of those who said O'Reilly's success was based on monopolism, that he paid lip service to the notion of editorial diversity and that government was powerless or unwilling to confront him adequately.

The *Irish Press* management had only itself to blame for getting into a position where it walked willingly into the embrace of the 'praying mantis'. The three titles continually lost market share over a decade running up to 1989; they were traditional papers that failed to modernise the editorial content to suit the changing market. Management adopted a belligerent attitude towards its remaining staff, many of the best of whom had defected to the *Independent*, resulting in serious strikes in which income and circulation was lost permanently, while IN assiduously avoided such disruption. A relaunch of the *Irish Press* as a tabloid in 1988 was a disaster.

Then in 1989, seeking salvation, the company's extraordinarily arrogant CEO Vincent Jennings and its eccentric chairman Eamon de Valera, who had inherited his position, made a monumental mistake: they invited publisher Ralph Ingersoll II to become their joint venture partner, believing he had the financial ammunition to take the fight to O'Reilly and INM. They had not done their research as well as most financial journalists in Dublin quickly did. In fact, Ingersoll was in the closing stages of an acquisition binge funded with money supplied by junk-bond king Michael Milken and the US bank Warburg Pincus. He was disastrously over-borrowed, and a crazy plan to start a newspaper in St Louis was to tip him over the edge. A pompous and patrician individual, he was just as arrogant as Jennings. It didn't take long for the partners to be at each other's throats, resulting in a long-running and bitter legal battle – first in the High Court, then in the Supreme Court – that distracted management from the mounting operational crisis at the Burgh Quay operations and cost everyone a fortune in legal fees they couldn't afford.

By 1994 the *Irish Press* was in a desperate state, so bad that Jennings looked to O'Reilly – against whom he had played rugby as a schoolboy – for help. O'Reilly had just the man for the job and Jennings agreed that he could send Bernard Somers, fresh from a job at Middle Abbey Street, to examine the books at IN's greatest rival. Ominously, O'Reilly said publicly, 'rationalisation of the Irish newspaper industry is now inevitable. We need amalgamation of production: there are too many idle presses. Employees and unions have a stark choice. They can have a brutal rationalisation by a British publisher à la Wapping. Or they can have an equitable resolution involving all the parties in our industry – an Irish solution to an Irish problem.' He spoke publicly of a co-operative venture between the country's main indigenous newspaper companies – *Independent*, *The Irish Times* and *Cork Examiner* – to invest in and protect the *Press* titles from foreign competition, but none of his competitors showed the slightest interest and he made no overtures about negotiations apart from his public comments.

O'Reilly complained publicly and privately to government about the likely damage to the native Irish newspaper sector by the arrival of foreign publishers and persuaded Richard Bruton, Minister for Enterprise and Employment, to order the Competition Authority to address issues arising from 'transfrontier' competition. O'Reilly believed that, for example, *The Sunday Times* enjoyed an unfair advantage by inserting some Irish content, at marginal cost, into an edition that was largely produced out of London. He feared this would happen with more titles.

If there had been some bemusement when Somers' arrival into Burgh Quay was revealed, it was little compared to the shock caused in December 1994 by the news that INM had bought a 24.9% share-holding in the two companies that owned and published the three titles. INM paid a bargain basement £1.1 million for the shares and provided a £2 million loan secured on the group's three newspaper titles. The sum was so small that it was barely enough to sustain the companies for the next six months. It also put the future of the company in the hands of an individual whose political ideals were in direct opposition to the republican beliefs of the founders of the *Irish Press*, and of which de Valera was supposed to be the caretaker. The NUJ, not unreasonably, described the investment as being 'designed to drip feed the only real source of competition' to INM. Bruton, shocked by the development, extended the Competition Authority study to include the issue of possible dominance and its implications for competition. He did not ask about cultural significance as that was beyond its remit.

O'Reilly was ready for the political response. An INM spokesman announced that 'this is not a proposal. It is a done deal. The shares have been bought and the loan has been extended'. It pointed out that it had responded to an 'invitation to invest' from the *Irish Press*, made through its advisers. Everything had been structured cleverly. Holding an equity interest below 25% meant there was no need for a company merger notification or to seek a special resolution from shareholders to approve the deal. INM said it would have no managerial or board control and no input into editorial content. It said *Irish Press* would have closed if it had not invested the money, which may well have been true. It claimed that it would have no say in whoever the *Irish Press* chose as its new investors and that there was no desire to go above 24.9%. But outsiders saw the presence on the share register as a massive disincentive to others to invest. The loans, and the security attached, bound the *Irish Press* particularly.

It wasn't as if the *Irish Press* didn't have other options. *The Sunday Business Post* editor and co-founder Damien Kiberd – a former financial editor of the *Irish Press*, who was somewhat disdainful of O'Reilly as a businessman and who, as a republican, opposed O'Reilly's political views – had formed his own consortium. Remarkably, it included Conrad Black's *Daily Telegraph* as a partner. It undoubtedly had the resources, but Jennings and de Valera would not let them in the door, knowing that their own personal futures with the papers would likely be curtailed by new investors, and sooner rather than later. That O'Reilly persuaded them not to do so was an enormous commercial achievement: a recapitalised *Irish Press*, with proper management, could potentially have competed strongly with INM titles, having an adverse impact on the latter group's revenue and profitability. O'Reilly flattered their egos by pretending Jennings and de Valera could remain in charge of their own destiny, just by taking his magnanimous support.

The Competition Authority moved with speed, delivering its report by April 1995. It found, not surprisingly, the deal to be an abuse of a dominant position in both advertising and circulation and to be anti-competitive, designed to prevent a rival gaining control of the *Press* titles. It recommended that Bruton seek a High Court order to void the purchase of the shares as it said INM had bought them to prevent anyone else doing so 'and it represents a strong deterrent to other investors acquiring outright or substantial control of these newspapers in order to compete head-on with Independent Newspapers'.

The authority worried that O'Reilly, who it pointedly named personally rather than saying INM, would have an equity stake in three out of five daily newspapers (increasing the market share from 53% to 64%), two out of three evening newspapers (increasing share from 52% to 85%) and four out of five Sunday newspapers (increasing share from 73% to 96%). The authority said that 'This would place the few remaining competitors in an intolerable position. The acquisition of a 24.9% shareholding in Irish Press further strengthens Independent's dominance in the various relevant markets. At the very least, Independent will exert some influence, direct or indirect, over the commercial conduct of the Irish Press. The latter group's ongoing need for additional funding leaves it further dependent on Independent.'

For its part, INM's submission claimed that it was protecting the pluralism of the media on cultural diversity, that the newspapers existed not just to meet consumer demand, but also to inform, to educate and to foster debate. The authority was unimpressed by this line of argument: 'The concentration of ownership and control of newspapers and other forms of news media is particularly undesirable in a democratic society. Guarantees that editorial independence will be maintained are of limited usefulness where an individual or a single entity exercises some degree of commercial control over a number of competing newspapers. Indeed such guarantees are virtually worthless and the only way in which independence can effectively be maintained is through diversity of newspaper ownership.'

The authority also noted the potential to maintain control by way of loans, but to do so at such a small level that would just keep the *Irish Press* titles alive, but not so active as to be a challenge to the INM titles – much as happened subsequently at *The Sunday Tribune*. It noted that 'the possibility cannot be ruled out that in a relatively short period of time, the only remaining newspapers will be those owned in whole or in part by Independent Newspapers plc'.

That wasn't all. The authority recommended no action be taken in respect of the pricing behaviour of UK newspapers within the State. O'Reilly focused on this in public statements, not just because it was a deflection from the *Irish Press* story but because the encroachment of British titles was a major challenge to the Irish industry and he felt genuinely that the authority misunderstood the situation and made an incorrect finding.

Bruton dithered and circumstances overtook him. The *Irish Press* was depending on the receipt of High Court damages of £6.5 million following a victory over Ingersoll, but the American had appealed the award to the Supreme Court. In May, it held that no money should be paid. The end was nigh but the dénouement was farcical. Jennings petulantly reacted to an article written by his financial editor, Colm Rapple, for *The Irish Times* in which he criticised the *Irish Press* management. Technically, Jennings may have been correct to sack Rapple, but doing so enraged staff already shocked by the mismanagement and the threat to their livelihoods it had caused. The journalists walked out and Jennings took the opportunity to close the companies, which quickly went into liquidation. The subsequent sale of remaining assets, such as the Burgh Quay HQ, and the terms of the investment by INM meant that most of its money was repaid, making the outcome even sweeter for O'Reilly. Jennings spoke for years about restarting the *Sunday Press* and INM continued to talk about supporting this with investment, despite warnings by Bruton that he would act to stop it if it did. By the time INM said it was no longer interested in new investment, the chance for anyone else to do so with some expectation of success was deemed long gone.

O'Reilly must have enjoyed taking advantage of Ingersoll's implosion. The American had once said of O'Reilly: 'I don't think Tony knows very much at all about newspaper publishing. Tony O'Reilly knows a lot about packaged goods marketing which is what he's paid to know about. He's a very competitive individual but Tony's one handicap is that his newspaper company doesn't have any money. Independent isn't much of a company. I don't think Tony thinks a lot about newspaper publishing. I like him as a competitor.' Now Ingersoll was a busted flush, and O'Reilly was going from strength to strength.

The *Evening Herald* now had its market all to itself. Sales of the *Irish Press* had been low anyway and the *Irish Independent*, while benefiting little in circulation, picked up market share, which appealed to advertisers. The main beneficiary was the *Sunday Independent*, with its resolutely populist appeal and shrewd, if controversial, editing by Aengus Fanning. It did much better than *The Sunday Tribune* in picking up *Sunday Press* readers, even though some of the best *Sunday Press* journalists were employed there instead of at the *Sunday Independent*.

That paper appalled the chattering classes, who demanded that O'Reilly rein in its perceived excesses. Particularly controversial were the writings of gossip columnist Terry Keane, the wife of High Court judge Ronan Keane, who in her diary, 'The Keane Edge', wrote non-too-coyly about her affair with Charles Haughey, who she called 'Sweetie'. In 1993 the paper caused consternation when it published what it claimed to be an 'exclusive interview' with Bishop Eamon Casey, who fled Ireland after the revelation that he had broken his vow of chastity and fathered a child while a serving cleric. Casey denied he had ever given an interview and a major controversy broke out as to whether the bishop had been represented correctly. O'Reilly replied that he had been 'out of the country' when the story ran and that he had not read it or been briefed by his executives in advance of publication.

Probably the most controversial of the journalists employed by the *Sunday Independent* was Eamon Dunphy, a former journeyman lower league and international footballer who became a top rate football writer and broadcaster on retiring from the game. He expanded his interests and applied his pugilistic and highly opinionated writing, as a self-styled champion of the people, to a range of topics, providing outrage, mirth and celebration. Dunphy summed it up many years later as follows: 'Seamus Heaney's poems were mediocre – this two days after he won the Nobel Prize. Pat Kenny was a plank, Mary Robinson a fraud, Dick Spring a treacherous gobshite'. Heaney was a close friend of O'Reilly's, someone he liked to quote often. Kenny became a regular at Castlemartin bashes. And then there was John Hume, a constitutional nationalist as head of the SDLP and a frequent guest at O'Reilly's Pittsburgh home.

'Worse was to come when I attacked John Hume for conspiring with the Provisional IRA,' wrote Dunphy. 'The Hume/Adams talks began in 1988 and were conducted parallel to the IRA's vicious terror campaign. Official Ireland was shocked by the frequent and vicious attacks on Hume, then and now regarded (rightly) as a saint. So was John Hume. He regularly rang the editor to complain, and made it clear that he would prefer if I were not writing for the newspaper. In a Republic that was, to say the least, ambivalent about IRA terrorism, the *Sunday Independent*'s savage onslaught on the embryonic peace process caused great offence.'

And what of his paymaster's view on all this? 'For Tony O'Reilly, there were heavy consequences at home and, in particular, among his influential peers in the wealthy Irish-American community. One of the popular Irish-American publications carried a bitter attack on the *Sunday Independent* for its 'McCarthyite' campaign against the push for peace. The Clinton White House let its displeasure be known. O'Reilly was answerable for our crimes. Fortunately, O'Reilly's resolve never wavered either. Old-style is the right style when you're placing your own interests second, your journalists first. Owing me nothing, O'Reilly defended my right to express an opinion.'

O'Reilly was not as detached as that might suggest, and as Dunphy later admitted. 'During this fraught period, I met Tony O'Reilly in west Cork, where I was living,' he wrote. 'We discussed the North, he established where I was coming from and told me to keep going.'

The *Sunday Independent*'s position on Northern Ireland softened in 1994, however. O'Reilly had ignored the pressure put on him by both the Irish government and the Clinton administration to rein in the newspaper's hard editorial line, which was apparently unhelpful to the behind-the-scenes work going on. That changed when O'Reilly discovered the seating arrangements at a White House function: he had been placed at a table near the kitchen door. Phone calls were made and a meeting was arranged between Hume and Fanning and other INM executives. For a couple of weeks the *Sunday Independent* went quiet on the Northern question. It then resumed its coverage, which was far more considered and understanding than it had been previously, if not still sufficiently positive to be welcomed by the hardline nationalist constituency. O'Reilly was restored to a more prominent position at subsequent White House events.

————

Late in 1995, O'Reilly fell seriously ill. It was close to Christmas 1995 when he was admitted to the Blackrock Clinic in Dublin, under the care of a leading cardiologist. The illness was described subsequently to all those who asked as an inner-ear infection, a condition that leads to loss of balance and falls. Few believed the story and there was considerable speculation about a stroke – a condition that had afflicted both of his parents.

It was readily understood within his circle as to why the inner-ear infection line had to be told and held. It wasn't just a matter of personal privacy relating to health issues, or the protection of O'Reilly's pride: it was a financial necessity for him and for many others. His position at Heinz could be undermined if there was public knowledge of a serious and potentially long-term debilitating ailment. The stock market value of his other personal investments could be badly affected, too, if the market perceived that O'Reilly would not be in a position to provide his usual leadership. Stock market investors do not like this type of news, particularly for the prices of shares at organisations that are regarded as highly dependent on the leadership skills of dominant individuals. Heinz had a product portfolio and a management structure that provided some protection against such reverses to its top man – and there would be an expectation that others, if required, could step into the breach. However, the share prices of his Irish interests were particularly dependent on him remaining in the full of his health.

In some respects it was remarkable that his health had not suffered previously, and more often, from the constant punishment his body endured, the lack of sleep being the most obvious, but also the continual moving between time-zones as he flew around the world. Colleagues had remarked how, in the air between meetings, he could be slumped in his seat, exhausted, but then an hour later, before addressing an audience or going into a meeting, it would be as if he had received some sort of infusion of energy because he was pepped up again, full of attention and vigour.

It helped that he did not drink alcohol in anything other than small quantities. 'I felt almost unpatriotic not being able to enjoy a pint of Guinness,' he joked once. 'I just don't like the stuff. When I'd go out with my rugby teammates they'd order a round of stout and "a pint of Beaujolais for my friend here". I fit the definition of an Irish queer: a fellow who prefers women to drink.'

He had fallen ill despite claims that he was taking things at a relatively more sedate pace, at Chryss's insistence. He had started taking holidays, especially a week in the Bahamas in January. They had found a house to buy at Lyford Cay, being sold by a German at a price apparently 50% higher than any other house in the area had ever cost. O'Reilly bought it on condition that everything, other than clothes and personal belongings, was left exactly in place for the couple to enjoy. He played tennis and swam there, but there were still plenty of late dinners, with up to 20 guests at a time being served by his staff.

At the Blackrock Clinic he recovered relatively quickly, but had to be seen to be up and about. The journalist Brendan Keenan was invited to the USA to meet with O'Reilly and after waiting a few days to be given a slot for interview, he met with his boss in Miami. The interview appeared on the front page of the *Weekender* section of the *Irish Independent* on 19 January 1996, under the headline, 'O'Reilly takes stock'. Keenan wrote that reports of O'Reilly's recent illness were 'greatly exaggerated', but that 'even the intimation of mortality for a man who is not used to thinking of it has forced him to take stock'. O'Reilly admitted that 'it has just been too much of too much' and that it was 'probably a signal from the Almighty that it is time to review the lifestyle'.

'I have done the building of the Irish companies and others can do the building now,' he said. 'I've got good kids. If they can continue it, well and good. If not, others can do it.' They had much to mind: Keenan noted that the value of O'Reilly's known assets had increased from £470 million to £600 million over the previous 12 months.

His management of time was a skill that he had developed during his years as a student. 'I learned in those five years the vital lesson of how to manage blocks of time, even if I am not always punctual – or more accurately, always not punctual,' he said. That was true: he had a tendency to be very late arriving at meetings, but that was because he gave his full attention to whatever he was doing and it took a lot for him to break away from something in which he was interested. He gave people his attention. But it mystified people how he had time to party, to read, to travel and to attend not just to the work of a major multi-national in Heinz but also to a succession of Irish companies that always had many conflicting issues to be resolved. It was said that he was a Superman, but if he was, then maybe someone had introduced him to Kryptonite.

He recovered to resume his exhausting schedule, spending nearly another two years in a full-time position with Heinz before moving to the role of part-time chairman. He had looked after himself somewhat better after that scare, eating more carefully to combat the weight gain to which he was prone and exercising more sensibly, usually through vigorous games of tennis, although it was not as if he had not been following that approach before. He noticeably chewed gum incessantly during public appearances; the speculation was that he did this to produce sufficient saliva to avoid dry-mouth during speaking engage-ments or meetings. He took to drinking can after can of diet cola. He employed the services of a nurse, Sabina Vidunas, previously a masseuse at Heinz, who travelled with him to monitor his health, administer medications and make arrangements for necessary healthcare supplies during his travels. Her role soon expanded to assisting in the planning and scheduling of his calendar and making arrangements for his frequent business and pleasure travel, on which she often accompanied him and Chryss.

Late in 1995 he completed the £1 million purchase of a four-storey-over-basement Georgian townhouse in Dublin's Fitzwilliam Square, converted from offices into luxury living accommodation. It was owned once by William Dargan, the founder of the National Gallery of Ireland and Irish Railways. He and Chryss invested in a money management business called Lockwood Financial, after an investment banker friend introduced him to Leonard A. Reinhart. The couple took a 47.5% stake. Lockwood grew rapidly to manage more than $6 billion for high-net-worth clients such as actors and athletes.

But it was a gift he purchased for Chryss that caused the biggest stir. In April 1996 he paid $2,587,500 (£1.66 million) for the 40.42 carat Lesotho III diamond engagement ring that shipping magnate Aristotle Onassis gave to the former First Lady, Jacqueline Kennedy, in 1968. It was nearly three times the asking price Sotheby's had set for Lot 453 at the four-day auction of much of her personal property, a treasure trove from the so-called 'Camelot era', raising $35 million in total. It was the biggest diamond ring Kennedy Onassis ever owned.

The bidding for O'Reilly was done by Lippert, who bid for the trophy by phone against an unnamed competitor, simultaneously keeping in touch with O'Reilly at Castlemartin. It was in the early hours of the morning in Ireland when the lot came up. Lippert later described the contest as 'complete bedlam' and as 'very intense'. Hushed silences were punctuated by wild cheers as the price of the Marquise-cut stone, valued by Sotheby's at $600,000, soared above $2 million. When the gavel fell, said Lippert, O'Reilly calmly told him, 'I think I'll go take a walk.'

O'Reilly described the ring as being of 'symbolic significance ... The ring symbolised a lot of elegance and history and the Irish American connection'. First given by a Greek shipping owner to the wife of an Irish American President, it now went to a Greek shipping heiress from an Irishman. While it was a present for her, it was also a sign of how he had moved up in the world. 'Tony's done a lot of extraordinary things in his life,' said John Meagher, 'but I don't think he's done anything quite as dramatic as this.' It was a statement of wealth, of taste and of status, and everybody heard it loud and clear.

SLINGS AND ARROWS

The *Sunday Independent* was to suffer a disaster in 1996 when Veronica Guerin, one of its leading journalists, was murdered. Guerin was an outstanding investigative reporter, with an uncanny ability to persuade people to give her information, often confidential written documents. She had broken a number of business exclusives for *The Sunday Business Post* before moving to *The Sunday Tribune,* where she embarrassed the *Sunday Independent* by delivering a comprehensive on-the-record interview with Bishop Eamon Casey. She was persuaded to move to the *Sunday Independent,* where she developed an interest in writing about the criminal underworld. In 1994 she was shot in the leg, allegedly by a member of a criminal drugs gang, but the injury was minor. She continued to work as a crime reporter, even though her confidence was badly damaged by a more serious incident in September 1995 when she was savagely beaten by a drug-dealer called John Gilligan. A prosecution for assault against him was in process when she was murdered on 26 June 1996. The country was outraged and those close to Veronica were deeply shocked as well as appalled and angry.

O'Reilly happened to be in Ireland at the time of the funeral because INM was sponsoring a race meeting at the Curragh which, notably, it did not cancel as a mark of respect. The corporate hospitality continued as normal, with O'Reilly having a meeting with Minister for Transport, Energy and Communications Michael Lowry in his private box – a meeting that subsequently proved controversial.

O'Reilly visited Bernie Guerin, Veronica's mother, at her house and Graham Turley, her husband, and their son to offer his condolences. He attended the removal on Friday evening and the funeral mass the following morning, as did Taoiseach John Bruton.

Many questions were asked subsequently of Fanning and of Harris as to whether or not they had 'controlled' Guerin's work sufficiently, whether they should have refused to publish her material that arose from situations where she put herself into danger, instead of looking to boost circulation. Some of the questions were legitimate, although Guerin believed strongly in the need to cover the stories and that she should not be intimidated into stopping. Some of the criticism was aired by those who had their own agendas against O'Reilly, the *Sunday Independent* and INM and who cynically used Guerin's murder as a convenient way to get at their foes. It also somewhat distracted attention from those who were really responsible for her death – the man who shot the gun and those who ordered and organised it. O'Reilly subsequently attended a number of commemorations and INM funded scholarships in her memory.

John Bruton had succeeded Albert Reynolds as Taoiseach in 1994 and he rewarded Lowry, a Tipperary North TD, with an appointment to the Department of Transport, Energy and Communications. Lowry's ability to persuade rich people to part with money to finance Fine Gael had led to his quick rise up the ranks. He was to prove a worthy successor to Ray Burke, with his similar liking for tax evasion, personal relationships with wealthy businessmen and eager denunciations of the media for allegedly harassing him. In his new role he would become central to O'Reilly's ambitions for zinc mining at Galmoy, County Kilkenny, through Arcon, the family-controlled public company that had grown out of Atlantic Resources. Lowry would also be the central figure in the mobile phone licence award and it would fall to him to solve the problems created by the State's haphazard issue of MMDS licences.

The State had failed to crack down on the illegal competition from television signal community activists. Ray Burke had given Joe Hayes a 'letter of comfort' in early 1991, in which he promised that action would be taken to protect the licences that Princes Holdings had been awarded. In it, Burke stated: 'Immediately MMDS service is available in any of your franchise regions, my department will apply the full rigours of the law to illegal operations affecting that franchise region. My department will use its best endeavours to ensure that there are no illegal broadcasting systems affecting that region within six months after the commencement of MMDS transmissions.' Significantly, notation on the letter included a coding rarely used by civil servants, to indicate that the content came from the Minister and not from the Department.

This implied that Burke was departing from official advice, but INM did not know that. Encouraged by this assurance, Princes Holdings began to roll out the service from 1992. It got little traction and the losses mounted, making O'Reilly very angry, especially as his American co-investors complained bitterly.

'Accumulated losses since 1992 have reached £18.5 million by the end of 1995 with further losses expected in 1996 and bear no resemblance to the original business plan,' O'Reilly wrote in the 1996 INM annual report, in a rare admission of failure. 'The principal difference relates to the non-achievement of anticipated subscriber growth which is directly related to on-going pirate activity … The failure to police exclusive licences granted by the government and issued by Minister Ray Burke in 1991, has led to significant pirate activity.'

Lowry, however, did nothing. He relied upon the advice of Attorney General Dermot Gleeson that Burke had acted unlawfully and *ultra vires* of his authority. The reality was that Lowry was acting politically, fearing the loss of Fine Gael votes in constituencies where the deflectors were popular and where there would be a backlash if they closed down. O'Reilly went over Lowry's head to Taoiseach John Bruton and there was a private meeting between the two, followed by correspondence and meetings between their underlings that remained private at the time but caused great controversy when revealed publicly years later.

Lowry was forced to resign as minister in December 1996, when some of his dodgy dealings caught up with him. Sam Smyth revealed in the *Irish Independent* that Lowry had secretly accepted Ben Dunne's largesse: a £300,000-plus gift of an extension to his mansion in Tipperary. That this revelation appeared in one of O'Reilly's papers served to feed Lowry's paranoia, although in truth O'Reilly had no inkling of the story until after it had appeared. The resignation led to a chain of events, which included Haughey's unmasking as another beneficiary of Dunne's millions, and the establishment of the McCracken Tribunal and, subsequently, the Moriarty Tribunal. If O'Reilly was to take pleasure in Lowry's fall, Haughey's subsequent unmasking was to give him pause for thought, given the Des Traynor connection, and in time he would find himself caught up in the climate of scandal and the web of various tribunals.

In May 1997, at the INM AGM, O'Reilly said that Princes Holdings had now accumulated losses of £26 million as 'various governments did not police the enforcement of their licences in an effective way'.

Alan Dukes, who had replaced Lowry as minister, was more sympathetic to O'Reilly's complaints, but he wasn't going to do anything either in advance of the general election.

The election in June resulted in the Rainbow government being ousted from power by Bertie Ahern's Fianna Fáil, although the bigger party again had to rely on the Progressive Democrats to form a coalition government, just as in 1989. On the day before the election the *Irish Independent* ran a surprising front-page editorial that declared: 'for years we have been bled white – now it's payback time'. The appropriateness and impact of this editorial would be debated for years to come, with much attention focusing on whether O'Reilly had ordered it, something that editor Vinnie Doyle denied adamantly. Dick Spring, who saw the Labour party suffer a dramatic loss of seats, leading to his resignation as party leader some months later, called the editorial 'disgraceful and despicable, a new low in Irish journalism'.

Ahern shocked many when he appointed Burke as his new Minister for Foreign Affairs. Rumours had been swirling for months that Burke had been the recipient of corrupt payments from builders prior to the 1989 general election. Ahern responded that he had been 'up and down every tree in North County Dublin' seeking evidence, but there was none. However, in July 1997 *The Sunday Tribune* revealed details of a £30,000 payment from a firm called Bovale, run by Mick and Tom Bailey, and *The Sunday Business Post* published allegations from an elderly retired executive called James Gogarty, which implicated JMSE, another big developer, in making payments. Burke tried to hold to power, but by October he was gone not just from the government but from the Dáil. He later faced investigation at the Planning Tribunal and also court charges relating to tax evasion – arising from money he had received from Oliver Barry of Century Radio – which eventually led to his conviction and imprisonment.

It was not until 1998, however, that details were revealed of the pre-1989 general election visit to Burke's house by Rennicks and Power of Fitzwilton. Immediately after the publication of this revelation in *Magill* magazine, O'Reilly hired the services of one of the country's toughest and best-connected barristers to represent him, former attorney general Dermot Gleeson.

That anyone might even consider that he had corrupted the political process was anathema to O'Reilly. Even though he was chairman of

Fitzwilton, he didn't want anybody to suggest that he had any know-ledge of the actions of his subordinates – and nobody had evidence to suggest otherwise. Shortly after the *Magill* report on the Fitzwilton payment appeared in 1998, a front-page news report in *The Sunday Tribune* referred to the possibility of investigation into the payment to Burke by Fitzwilton, 'a company in which Tony O'Reilly is the controlling shareholder'. It may have been a plain statement of fact, but that and the offending paragraph's positioning down near the bottom of the report did not spare me, as editor, the wrath of O'Reilly's proxy. Late that Sunday afternoon I received a phone call from the INM CEO Liam Healy, who was also a director of *The Sunday Tribune*. He was furious that the reference to O'Reilly had been included in the article. He told me that Gleeson had advised O'Reilly that he had grounds for a libel action, even though it would be against his own newspaper. He wanted to hold the reporter who had written the story responsible, but I told him that I'd been fully aware of the text before publication and had approved it and that I was responsible. I was forced to assure him that 'greater care' would be taken before any further references would be made in the future. Nothing more was said about it.

When Fitzwilton was subsequently called upon to explain the payment to Burke, it said he had been 'well aware' that the money was not for him but was to assist Fianna Fáil in its election campaign. It insisted that it did not become aware until 1998 that the politician had retained £20,000. Fianna Fáil said it had issued a receipt to Rennicks for the £10,000 it had received, which would have alerted Rennicks to a potential problem over the other £20,000; Fitzwilton insisted that it never got a receipt.

Not surprisingly, there was rampant speculation as to what Burke might have been asked to give, if anything, in return for the money, and Princes Holdings was dragged into the debate too.

'At no time during the meeting was the subject of IDA grants discussed,' Fitzwilton insisted. 'No favours were either sought or received for the political contribution. Fitzwilton does not have, and never had, any trading or business connections with Princes Holdings, nor has it made any payments to any individuals or organisation with MMDS licences.'

Not surprisingly, the issue became the subject of major debate in Dáil Éireann, with members of the deposed Rainbow government, led by Labour's Pat Rabbitte, arguing heatedly on the subject and asking hard questions. 'When huge donations like this are transferred to politicians most people ask *cui bono?* Who benefits and who profits from it? Does it support democracy or are there other reasons for it?' Rabbitte asked, not unreasonably. 'We are assured that Tony O'Reilly knew nothing of this £30,000 donation. However, as Minister for Communications, Mr Burke would have been well aware through Dr O'Reilly of the connection of the Rennicks' subsidiary to Princes Holdings, to whom he granted 19 of the 29 licences awarded from the MMDS system.'

The *Irish Independent* responded with another front-page editorial, claiming that its parent company had been 'the subject of a vicious, calculated and damaging smear campaign which has sought to suggest that the company was linked in some way with improper payments to a politician.' It was a campaign of 'malicious denigration' and the company had 'been attacked on the flimsiest of evidence'. Rabbitte returned to the Dáil on 3 June 1998 to criticise what he called 'a frenetic four day campaign by Independent Newspapers to defend the economic interest of their [sic] proprietor'.

The Irish Times got in on the act then: '"Lying letters, phantom meetings and calculated smears" screamed yet another front-page editorial in the *Irish Independent*. As the tirade continued, one conclusion is inescapable: if ever there was a doubt about the undesirability of a dominant position in such a sensitive industry, then the conduct of Independent Newspapers over the weekend removed that doubt. Journalists and columnists were used in such an overkill to defend the economic interests of their proprietor that the public was given a glimpse of what abuse of dominant position means in practice.'

The Irish Times was clearly enjoying itself, and the former Taoiseach wasn't going to miss the opportunity to put the boot in either. 'It is an abuse of press power for a major newspaper group to use their columns and editorials over four days running to concoct replies on behalf of their owner to one speech in the Dáil,' said Bruton. He accused the newspaper group of being in a 'state of denial' about the matter, citing an editorial in which it accused him of abusing Dáil privilege to link INM and its chairman with payments to a politician. Bruton said: 'The statement I made on that matter is factual in that Dr O'Reilly is chairman of the company that made the payment, so there is a link between him and the payment, whether or not he con-sented to or was aware of the payment ... So that is a statement that could be made anywhere without benefit of privilege.'

A spokesman for INM merely responded that 'Mr Bruton was wrong to attempt to create a link between Independent Newspapers and Fitzwilton'. While this argument would disappear from the front pages, the issue would not, as various tribunals and courts would hear in the coming years.

Other things were going better for O'Reilly however, particularly his investment in Waterford Wedgwood. The company had started 1996 with a change of management and emphasis. Out went Paddy Galvin, who had done so much to restructure the manufacturing business, reducing costs by as much as possible – assisted for a period by Leslie Buckley, a cost-cutting specialist who later became Denis O'Brien's most trusted lieutenant and who was critical, subsequently, of the lack of time and attention he felt O'Reilly paid to manufacturing issues.

Galvin's replacement by Redmond O'Donoghue underlined the intention to switch emphasis from manufacturing, survival and restructuring to branding and growth. Galvin had a strategy of extending the Waterford brand to non-crystal products, such as linen, which were often associated with Ireland but not actually made here. In the case of linen, it was being produced for the company in the Philippines, China and Belgium. O'Reilly decided this strategy was more suited to the skills of O'Donoghue.

Whereas Galvin was a measured and cautious interviewee, O'Donoghue was a far more ebullient and accessible character. He decided that the major concentration would be on expanding in existing markets because 'it takes years to build substantial sales in new markets'. Operating under O'Reilly's imprimatur, he said that Waterford Wedgwood would become a giftware group with strong brand names. 'The total premium crystal market in the US is $325 million. Even if we got all of it, it is limiting,' he said. 'If we see ourselves in the giftware market – a $7.5 billion market – only a small proportion would make us very significant.'

O'Donoghue was put under pressure from the moment he took up his new position. O'Reilly had come up with a concept called 'the chairman's challenge'. This aimed to double sales by the end of the century, to a level of US$1 billion, both by organic growth and by acquisition. O'Reilly admitted the targets were 'ambitious', but said they were 'designed to challenge the very best in management skills'. For his part, O'Donoghue reaffirmed his commitment to the plant in Waterford, even though the level of outsourced production was now nearly a quarter of sales. He said that it made sense to use the Waterford plant, where possible, because of the fixed overhead costs already in place there. What he wanted was 'multiple competing sources' of production.

Before the brand could be expanded into other products, however, the existing crystal products had to be updated. Research had confirmed the suspicion that the Group's products were losing favour, regarded as too fussy and cumbersome by younger potential buyers. Couples getting married no longer wanted wedding guests to chip in to buy the big set that would only gather dust on display shelves. They wanted something they could use and not fear breaking because of the cost of replacement. It was an irony, but the rise in the popularity of the home dinner party coincided with the increased popularity of more casual tableware. The new generation didn't want status symbols, they wanted lightweight and practical glassware that could be put in a dishwasher, not heirlooms. Those in the branding business call this problem the 'evergreen challenge'. Waterford Wedgwood had to retain the loyalty of existing devotees while simultaneously changing those products sufficiently to attract new buyers. It had to anticipate and, in some ways, dictate what buyer tastes would become.

The answer, for the crystal division at least, was to come from an Irish fashion designer called John Rocha. He designed sets of heavy but clear wine glasses that became extremely popular for a time, even at relatively high prices. The Rocha wine glasses first became available in late 1997, and Waterford Crystal introduced 90 new products in the first few years of O'Donoghue's stewardship, while the cheaper outsourced Marquis brand brought 47 new products to the market. Sales improved strongly. 'In Slovenia we've got low labour costs, although a lot of manual labour,' said O'Donoghue. 'In Germany they had perfected the technology. We had the best of all worlds.'

Waterford Crystal introduced a super product in the closing years of the twentieth century, in anticipation of the Millennium. It intro-duced 'toasting flutes' – solid, long stem, long body crystal glasses to fill with champagne to toast big occasions, such as the turn of the century. The Millennium Collection products became enormously successful: differently designed sets evoking concepts such as love, peace, hope, health and happiness were released over four years and were so successful that the prices kept rising, from $70 per pair on the first release to over $120 a pair on the last. They remain, even now, collector's items that sell for those prices, second-hand, on the Internet.

Ironically, given that its profits had kept Waterford Crystal afloat in the years before the O'Reilly investment, Wedgwood was now becoming a drag on the group. Brian Patterson became CEO of Wedgwood in June 1995. He said the chairman's challenge was 'a target that forces you to lift your eyes up and see what can be done'. Not only were his managers told to double sales but to treble profits; the margins being earned on sales were way too low and a poor return on capital. O'Reilly warned Patterson and his subordinates to be sure of their figures because failure to adhere to the numbers could be 'career threatening'.

Patterson also planned to 'freshen the brand to make it more relevant to a younger market without losing core values'. He revealed underinvestment in marketing, at just 5% of the annual cost of sales and concentrated on 'pattern advertising'. He aimed to increase sales on brand advertising to 9% of revenues, with the Wedgwood name appearing on 'home enhancement items', such as vases, bowls, statues and personal accessories, including jewellery and fragrances, alongside the traditional dinner service and table-top sets. His strategy was to create an accessible, everyday brand that still spoke of good taste and self-indulgent luxury. This way, Waterford Wedgwood could appeal to a wider variety of consumers.

Wedgwood had already been targeting younger consumers and developing less formal tableware, both to complement its formal ranges and to satisfy increased demand for informal tableware. Patterson continued to struggle to improve margins, though. Every penny earned on manufacturing improvement was lost elsewhere, usually on currency fluctuations. The Asian crisis of 1998 also depressed demand in some of the most important export areas for Wedgwood.

During the 1990s it did seem as if Waterford Wedgwood was getting on top of its financial situation. By 1996 net debt had increased slightly to £56.9 million, but gearing – the measure of borrowing to share-holders' funds upon which lenders depend – continued to improve, dropping to just 37%. O'Reilly took it as his cue to go buying again.

His first purchase, in 1997, was of the German porcelain products company Rosenthal. It had a fascinating heritage, not least that it had retained its Jewish name even during the Nazi era. No less a figure than the notorious Nazi propagandist Joseph Goebbels had recognised the value of its well-known brand name and said: 'If we change the name, we will no longer be in the position to exploit their porcelain.'

Rosenthal was a loss-maker when purchased and the modest purchase price reflected this. Its sales were about one-third of the level of Waterford Wedgwood's, but O'Reilly felt that it would benefit from being part of a bigger luxury brands group. It signed a six-year licensing agreement with Bvlgari, the contemporary Italian jeweller, to manufacture a range of products under the Bvlgari name.

Versace was the next partner, for a range of bathroom products. O'Reilly said working with a 'co-partner' like Versace was how Waterford Wedgwood would grow. There was excess capacity in the ceramics and crystal markets, but by being 'a low-cost operator, the company would flourish'. He said there were a number of ways to do this, including greater levels of outsourcing. The problem for Rosenthal was that even when it returned to profit, it failed to make enough money to finance the costs of the acquisition, even after plants were closed down.

There was to be another purchase, this time in the USA. All-Clad was a cookery pots manufacturer whose products were endorsed by the likes of celebrity chef Martha Stewart. In announcing the acquisition, O'Donoghue said Waterford Wedgwood was responding to changes in lifestyle trends, where younger consumers had come to regard cooking as 'almost a participative activity ... Each saucepan has to cook well, but also look well – it has to be aesthetically pleasing.'

O'Reilly said the acquisition moved the group closer to 'luxury living' status. 'I firmly believe the luxury cookware market is largely untapped and that consumers will be looking to enhance their homes with a premium product – that is what we have acquired.' Waterford Crystal was having a tremendous time, increasing sales in the booming US economy, where its market share in crystal had now reached 50% as the decade ended, compared to just 25% at the start of it. The group needed sustained sales growth in the US market for glassware and a turnaround at Wedgwood and Rosenthal.

'I am trying to build companies that will exist long after I'm gone,' O'Reilly said. 'Waterford Wedgwood, I hope, will be a real monument.

We were savagely attacked by everyone when we went in, but look at it now – and it will be there for generations to come. If we hadn't put in that $100 million injection it was gone, and that would have been the end of Ireland's greatest exporter.' To his eyes, it was a brand new beginning of a long-term success story. The truth for Waterford Wedgwood – and for O'Reilly – was to fall short of these heady expectations, but it would take years for this to be realised.

CHAPTER NINE

TAKING FULL CONTROL

Since 1995, when INM had increased its shareholding in *The Independent*, there had been efforts to forge a productive partner-ship with Montgomery and the MGN, but these simply had not worked. Andrew Marr, then editor of *The Independent*, put it down to a clash of personalities:

> No writer of exuberant fiction could have dreamed up the confron-tation between Montgomery and O'Reilly. One was a lean, dry, sarcastic Ulster Protestant; the other was a large, extrovert, passion-ate Catholic Irish tycoon. Their mutual dislike was instant and apparently absolute.
>
> O'Reilly was everything that Montgomery was not: charismatic, boomingly self-confident and a vigorous proponent of the enjoy-ment of life. He wanted *The Independent* because to be a national newspaper owner in London would put him into the big league. If he didn't have an empire on the Murdoch scale, it was a pretty fair-sized kingdom. And O'Reilly was a pretty fair-sized king, even in old age – a broad, large, fresh-faced man with piercing eyes, a billow of white hair and a generous grin – though, as with many powerful men, his eyes always seemed just a little colder than his smile. We knew that he was careful with money, an excellent marketing man with a huge business reputation, and broadly liberal in his politics – pro-European, as the Irish tend to be, and at one remove from the British Establishment. As tycoons went, he seemed made to measure for *The Independent*.

Montgomery, by comparison, was a philistine. He wanted to constantly cut the editorial budget and take the paper into the middle market dominated by the tabloid *Daily Mail*. Marr believed that Montgomery wanted to prove that his original vision for *Today* – a tabloid that Murdoch had seized control of and then closed – could still work. Montgomery, according to Marr, saw *The Independent* as a Yuppie paper full of stories for and about expensive, ambitious people, preferably being mugged for their Rolex watches in Mayfair. 'We wanted young, aspirational readers. They might have a social conscience, Monty conceded, but they enjoyed the good things in life. They wanted to get on. They would be driving Porsches. We didn't want dreary scenes of poverty in the paper, or "dead black babies". That would just put people off.'

There may have been some sense in leaving the congested upper end of the market, where Murdoch's price-cutting initiative at *The Times* was permanent, but O'Reilly was not alone in seeing this as the wrong editorial and marketing strategy. It made Marr's task of trying to serve two competing masters an almost impossible one. He described his job as 'less a poisoned chalice than a pint glass of lukewarm ricin'.

Marr said that O'Reilly 'valued good journalism enormously and, like me, considered people like [Robert] Fisk to be the whole point of the paper'. However, Marr identified a major flaw in O'Reilly's ability to deal with difficult situations: he wasn't there to do it. 'He was rarely in town to express his views. Instead, he had a man in London – a former toiletries marketing executive called Brendan Hopkins, who had a fine glossy head of hair, a good collection of expensive suits and a lovely wife ... A ritual developed. I would call O'Reilly to complain about the latest Mirror Group depredations. A "breakfast with Brendan" would be prescribed. We would meet at an expensive hotel, where Hopkins would order an omelette, with two grilled tomatoes on the side, before assuring me that "Tony is watching things carefully".'

O'Reilly seemed well aware that the investment in *The Independent* was a major gamble. 'About the first thing he told me, in a self-mocking way, when I arrived to see him at Castlemartin, was that he had been to see Vere Rothermere in Paris to ask his advice about how to turn around *The Independent*. "Well, Tony," he had said, his languid drawl mimicked by the Irishman, "the first thing is that you have to have a lot of money. Then you have to spend a lot of money – for year upon year upon year. And then ... (long weary pause) very occasionally, sometimes, it works"'

O'Reilly was supportive, but he remained essentially conservative. Marr created a radical redesign of the paper, one that would have required major investment, especially in marketing, with no guarantee that it would increase sales. Indeed, it had the potential to lose them. 'He summoned me to his study,' wrote Marr. 'He was wearing a white towelling dressing gown ... I unveiled the papers. He looked long and closely at them, then sat back. "Well, Andrew," he said. "I like them. I think they are very bold and daring. Personally I like them very much." I sagged with relief and began to smile. "On the other hand," said the great man very slowly, "I thought exactly the same about New Coke." That, of course, had been the most infamous marketing catastrophe in US corporate history. It was a gentle way to let me know that I had boobed. My radical redesign never saw the light of day. A far less extreme redesign did. It proved to be my undoing.'

By 1998 both sides realised they could not continue with such fundamental disagreements as to what type of paper they should own. Independent News & Media made an agreed cash offer for the 54% of Newspaper Publishing it didn't already own, valuing the whole of the company at Stg£6.4 million. For its part, MGN got £3 million for its shares and £26 million through the repayment of loans and guarantees. Montgomery also tied the INM titles into a considerable number of service contracts, covering key areas like information technology, office space and circulation management. It would cost the Irish group a small fortune over the next four years. There was the usual nonsense about having the highest regard for MGN and the 'operation efficiencies will continue to be available and look forward to a long-term warm relationship between our respective companies', but the reality was that a bad deal was done.

Buying complete ownership of *The Independent* meant that O'Reilly had taken over losses of up to Stg£20 million per annum in a market blighted by Murdoch's deliberate underpricing. 'A total market of over IR£800 million produces no profit whatsoever,' he complained subsequently in the 1998 INM annual report, and yet he had bought into it. An excuse that would be used in other situations was offered, to the effect that the losses could be used to offset against profits in the rest of the UK operations in order to reduce the tax bill.

O'Reilly disputed suggestions that it had been his 'dream' to become a publisher in Britain. 'This is not a trophy purchase,' he said. 'The London market is the centerpiece of a great deal of both political and newspaper activity as far as printed words in English are concerned, and to own a major broadsheet, a quality paper at the top end of one of the most visible markets in the world has a halo effect on Independent Newspapers and its claim to be a truly independent newspaper group,' O'Reilly said. Years later, Marr said O'Reilly had told him that he bought the paper 'because it was simply nice to be able to go through the door of 10 Downing Street and be accepted there'. For public consumption O'Reilly said that he felt Britain lacked and needed 'an independent voice, neither right nor left, a voice for inquiring, skeptical Britons'. It was a valid position to take, but it also fed the criticism of O'Reilly that he was a man without real convictions.

Asked why he should be considered different from other wealthy newspaper owners who meddle in their newsrooms, O'Reilly said: 'Get a telephone and ring any of the 200 papers we have around the world, *The New Zealand Herald,* the *Cape Times,* the *Johannesburg Star, Diario* in Portugal and ask, "Has he ever interfered, has he ever phoned and talked to you?" and you will get a 100 percent response. Not that I don't have the right to do it; it's an entirely valid thing for a proprietor to do, but it simply is not applicable to me. I don't do it.' Again, it was true, but there were occasions when his subordinates in management did the job instead, ringing editors to let it be known that they were unhappy with something and that, by extension or implication, O'Reilly was unhappy. More than a decade later Marr told the Levenson Inquiry into press behaviour in the UK that during his time as editor he 'certainly knew what O'Reilly thought'.

O'Reilly reset the targets for the two London titles: these were to achieve circulations of 250,000 for the daily and 300,000 for the Sunday within a three- to five-year timeframe. Do that and they would be profitable, 'particularly if the current predatory pricing in Great Britain is intercepted by a free market pricing environment'. Even these targets were well below the 1994 circulation figures.

On his way out the door Montgomery had removed Marr as editor, to replace him with Charlie Wilson, a foul-mouthed Scottish former Murdoch executive. O'Reilly reinstated Marr as comment and analysis editor and gave Rosie Boycott, a famous feminist writer, the editorship of the daily paper. This was another first for O'Reilly, who did not have a track record of senior appointments for women in any of his organisations. Marr told readers: 'Rosie Boycott and I have been told in simple terms to make the paper steadily more intelligent and serious. During an era when most papers are dumbing down, it came as an unusual and exhilarating instruction. Further, we have been given some money to spend on journalists – another happy surprise.'

However, Boycott did not last long and Marr departed to the BBC. O'Reilly appointed Simon Kelner, a *Daily Mail* sports and features specialist, as the new editor. It was an inspired choice. Kelner was dynamic and different, but not so much as to do damage. Kelner stabilised circulation and the papers got a disproportionate share of the broadsheet advertising market. But losses continued at £15 million and more annually, and the debts climbed to over £100 million.

There was some relief when MGN was itself the subject of a merger, which produced the Trinity Mirror Group. There was a provision in the service contracts that they would be ended if there was a substantial management change at MGN, which there clearly now was. As a result, INM was able to get new deals on newsprint costs, printing and distribution, which cut the losses by over £10 million.

To O'Reilly's satisfaction, his indulgence of *The Independent* received praise among the chattering classes. Stephen Glover, one of the paper's founders, who became a media columnist with *The Spectator*, praised O'Reilly's efforts and investment nine months after the takeover occurred. 'It feels like a proper newspaper again, with proper news and some good stories. All in all, it's a considerable achievement. *The Independent*'s new editor, Simon Kelner, has much to be proud of,' he said. However, he also noted that new readers had not materialised, unfair though that was, and that it would be near impossible to recover fully after so many botched relaunches and abortive redesigns since the early 1990s. It seemed that praise and damnation could exist side-by-side in the cut-throat world of newspaper creation and printing.

———

O'Reilly was to discover that the Northern peace dividend delivered in a way from which he would struggle to benefit. Fitzwilton failed to get the finance to further its ambitious plans to bring Wellworths south of the border. Sites for stores were identified, such as a lucrative venue on Dublin's northside at Clare Hall that later became a mammoth Tesco superstore, but the company did not have the internal resources, or the confidence of bankers, to develop these properties. It also struggled somewhat north of the border. Sainsbury's announced its expansion into the Six Counties in 1995 and opened its first store in December 1996, while Tesco opened its first store in October 1996 and purchased the Stewart's/Crazy Prices group in 1997. Fitzwilton tried to delay things by objecting to Sainsbury's planning applications, but this worked for only a short time. The new competition had names that excited consumers, stores that were more inviting and had greater product ranges and far more purchasing power and resources.

In June 1997 Fitzwilton signed a joint venture deal with Safeway, a British supermarket retailer, which led to 15 of its Wellworths stores changing name to Safeway. The remaining Wellworths stores, which were smaller, convenience-sized outfits, were sold to the Cork-based Musgrave Group, which ran Centra and Supervalu and other retailers on a franchise and supply basis and which was also aggressively expanding into the North.

Things were going wrong at Fitzwilton again. It seemed as if the company had finally turned the corner when, in April 1996, it reported profits of £15 million for 1995, representing a 79% increase on the previous year. There were issues with debts, amounting to £106 million, but the company said profits covered the interest bill by a 'comfortable' 2.6 times. It was to be the latest in a series of false dawns. By 1997 the group was losing money, £7.6 million for the year, and was unable to pay shareholders a dividend. The only positive was that its debts had fallen to a more manageable £49 million from the previous level of £83 million because of further asset disposals.

It was time to take long-suffering, non-O'Reilly-connected share-holders out of their misery. O'Reilly, Goulandris and their friend, the billionaire Lewis Glucksman, a philanthropist who subsequently paid for a major art gallery at University College Cork and whose wife, Loretta Brennan Glucksman, succeeded O'Reilly as President of the Ireland Funds, combined in a company called Stoneworth to offer to buy the shares of all other investors for 50p each. This valued Fitzwilton at £136.8 million. O'Reilly stepped back and allowed the 'independent' directors of Fitzwilton to assess the value of the offer, which compared favourably to the 37p price at which the shares had been languishing prior to the announcement. As board members, Kevin McGoran and Patrick Dowling were not part of Stoneworth and therefore they were deemed, despite a challenge to the Takeover Panel, to be sufficiently distant from their friend and mentor to make a positive recommendation to other shareholders that they should accept the offer. They warned shareholders that if they didn't sell, they wouldn't get a dividend in the future.

What they said was 'reasonable', business columnists in *The Irish Times* described as 'paltry', bemoaning that it only gave value for the shareholding in Waterford Wedgwood and more or less threw in Fitzwilton's other assets for free. The shares had traded at over three times that price only a decade earlier, but had fallen in value in the strongest rising market in the history of the Irish Stock Exchange. Over five years they had underperformed the ISEQ index of all shares on the Dublin market by 62%. Investors took their money and the company left the stock market to pass into private ownership. They got lucky. Four years later, Fitzwilton sold its remaining half of Wellworths to Safeway for just £45 million.

CHAPTER TEN

STEPPING DOWN AND MOVING ON

The life of a public figure is often characterised by high highs and low lows, and this had always been the case for O'Reilly, too. For every award, there was a stinging criticism; for every word of praise, there was a word of censure. So while he was the recipient of many awards and much recognition for his work in various fields throughout the 1990s, at the same time questions were raised again and again about his salary, the amount of time he devoted to Heinz and his packing of the Heinz board with so-called cronies. Major American publications, such as *The New York Times*, *Forbes* and *Businessweek*, persistently drew attention to, and created, controversies on many occasions – especially when shareholder activists took up the cudgels – painting O'Reilly as poster boy for excess.

'You get the feeling that he is only spending 25 percent of his time at Heinz,' William Leach, an analyst with Donaldson, Lufkin & Jenrette Securities on Wall Street, told *The New York Times* in 1994. It was a charge to which O'Reilly was particularly sensitive. 'My commitment managerially speaking is 102 percent to H.J. Heinz,' O'Reilly responded, insisting that being Heinz's largest individual shareholder placed his own interests solidly in line with those of the company.

Performance was also an issue. Leach charged that 'he kept expectations too high. He kept pretending that Heinz was doing better than it was.' Prudential Securities analyst John McMillin said: 'I think he is not as good as everyone said he was in the 1980s and not as bad as everyone says he is in the 1990s.'

O'Reilly was criticised for boosting earnings – which he needed to do to qualify for the exercise of stock options – by selling assets and engaging in questionable accounting tactics. 'He has used more tax credits than I knew even existed,' McMillin said. O'Reilly responded that it was the responsibility of any good CEO to take tax credits 'where you can get them'. He said only 'financial illiterates' could not see Heinz's actual operating experience was good in difficult markets.

In March 1996 *Forbes* declared O'Reilly the fourth highest paid boss in the USA, but added that his 'ego and paycheck are bigger than his accomplishments'. The *Forbes* survey of 800 CEOs, taken over five years, put 'the flamboyant' O'Reilly's earnings at $119 million. The average pay for the 800 bosses over the period was $6.9 million. 'Heinz's results have been disappointing over the last several years,' it said. 'Earnings per share have risen an average of 6.5 per cent over the past five years. And during this period Heinz stock has failed to keep pace with the Standard and Poor 500.'

Ted Smyth, O'Reilly's Irish corporate affairs director at Heinz, said that his boss's pay was linked to performance, and most of his earnings related to Heinz profits in the 1980s, which outperformed most competitors. He cited a piece in the *Wall Street Journal*, which had reported that O'Reilly had delivered a promise made two years earlier to revive Heinz's fortunes.

Now, O'Reilly had to act. In September 1996, Heinz announced that it would sell underperforming businesses and reduce debt. Everything was under review, although O'Reilly determined they would continue to concentrate on the six core businesses that earned about 75% of the profits, namely food services, baby food, condiments, pet food, tuna and WeightWatchers foods. O'Reilly agreed the sales proceeds would not be included in the earnings figures. As importantly, however, he was forced into dealing with succession issues, effectively nominating Bill Johnson as his heir apparent by naming him as president and Chief Operating Officer (COO) in 1996. There were also issues about modernising the products. Ketchup now trailed salsa in sales, something O'Reilly described as 'an adult phenomenon'. He admitted that 'Ketchup has receded to being a kids' food'.

For the first time in 56 years, Heinz decided to put a different-looking label on some of its ketchup bottles. It was as big a move as introducing the plastic bottle in the 1980s, which had been a success.

Heinz replaced the basic black lettering with colourful, curving characters, to suit the late twentieth century. 'We're not really changing the icon,' O'Reilly said. 'We're adjusting it for our main audience, which is children.' A survey for Heinz had discovered that 67% of those questioned misidentified ketchup as a vegetable, 16% said it was a fruit and 5% said they didn't know what it was. Only 12% gave the answer the pollsters were looking for: a condiment. More importantly, O'Reilly realised that 'kids determine, in a supermarket context, more and more of the behaviour of adults. They tell the parents what to buy, and the parents do it.'

It was a big decision, approved by O'Reilly personally. He said the 200 Heinz subsidiaries around the world could change the ingredients for other Heinz products as necessary. 'But if they change anything on the ketchup, they have to come to me,' he said. 'In our organisation manual we say, "You change it, you've got to go to the very top".'

By March, Heinz announced it would sell or close at least 25 plants around the world and dismiss 2,500 employees, or 5.8% of its work-force of 43,300. The company would spend $650 million in what was called Project Millennia. It sold most of its Ore-Ida Foods frozen-foods business for $500 million. But O'Reilly wouldn't sell WeightWatchers, despite Johnson's urgings, instead spending $55 million to revamp it; he was wedded emotionally to it. Critics said Heinz was the slowest of the major food companies to restructure, and many on Wall Street believed it did not go far enough.

Businessweek devoted the cover of its 4 September 1997 issue to O'Reilly and Heinz under the title, 'The CEO and the Board'. It was prob-ably the most damning critique of O'Reilly that had ever appeared in print, and it may well have hastened the end of his reign as Heinz CEO.

It started with a description of that year's Heinz 57 race in Dublin and said the 500 guests 'gathered under chandeliers in a mammoth white pavilion set up at the swanky Leopardstown horse-racing track outside Dublin. More than half were flown in from around the world, put up at Ireland's finest hotels, and feted at a lavish three-day bash … From a gala ball at O'Reilly's own Georgian mansion to the main event, the Heinz 57 Phoenix Stakes, no expense was spared. And with Heinz picking up the tab, O'Reilly was clearly the star of the show. Arriving last to the pre-race luncheon, he and his wife, Chryss, stepped gingerly from a blue Bentley. As they made their entrance,

O'Reilly began working the room, offering handshakes, jokes, and whispered asides with a politician's natural ease. "When he walks into the marquee, the whole place comes alive," recalls a recent guest. "Short of a u.s. President's arrival, I've never seen anything like it".

The magazine noted that O'Reilly's 'lavish bash' was the fifteenth in a row, even though Heinz was removing 2,500 employees. Heinz said the event, which also included meetings with analysts and big customers, was 'an effective corporate marketing tool that is no more expensive than sponsoring a golf tournament'.

The article moved from the entertainment expenditure to the charge that the Heinz board included 'many insiders, business associates, and even personal friends of the charismatic CEO', raising questions as to whether it achieved what it should. It followed the agenda of so-called 'activist investors', who were using corporate governance issues to increase their influence, saying those shareholders believed Heinz to be a 'textbook example of what a board should not be: a cozy club of loyalists headed by a powerful and charismatic chieftain'.

'The board is way too large, way too dominated by very old men, and it has not had enough turnover,' said Kayla Gillan, a lawyer acting for one of the big pension fund investors, CalPERS. *Businessweek* had ranked corporate boards and put Heinz as the third worst. Heinz responded that these were just 'philosophical differences' as to how companies should perform and that there was 'no empirical evidence out there to show this stuff matters'.

The statistics were working against O'Reilly, however. Total shareholder returns averaged 31% a year in the 1980s, nearly double the Standard & Poor's 500 stock index's 16.8%. Since the start of the 1990s, operating earnings had grown by 43%; by contrast, rival Campbell Soup Company increased its income by 140%, to a projected $1.5 billion for fiscal 1997. In the five years to 1997, Heinz's annual shareholder returns of 13.9% consistently underperformed the Standard & Poor's, as well as the Standard & Poor's food index. It took Johnson's appointment as president – and heir apparent – to bring the share price back towards an acceptable level.

'Nevertheless, the Heinz board continues to pay O'Reilly like a superstar,' argued *Businessweek*. 'His total compensation of $182.9 million in the past six years ranks him among a handful of the best-paid CEOs. In five of those six years, he has won the dubious distinction of being among the five CEOs cited by *Businessweek* as giving shareholders the least for their money.' Yet the rewards kept coming. In 1996 O'Reilly got a new options grant on 750,000 shares. That was more than the 646,800 shares Campbell chairman David W. Johnson got in the previous seven years combined.

O'Reilly's critics complained that he had 'captured' the board by loading it with 'insiders' and that it was incestuous, with O'Reilly selecting friends from other boards on which he had served.

'If you have only one insider,' O'Reilly said, 'the only person who talks to that board is the CEO, and every view is filtered through one mind to the board.' Johnson insisted the insiders said what they thought. 'I'm sure there were times when Tony or a couple of other senior guys were rolling their eyes when someone said something he wished he hadn't heard,' said Johnson. Ten of the 19 board members were current or former Heinz employees. 'Why would an insider challenge the boss?' asked Charles Elson, a law professor and corporate governance expert. 'That's a nice way to lose your job very quickly.'

Three outsiders were also directors of Mobil Oil, where O'Reilly had been a board member. He also brought in Coca-Cola's Don Keough, with whom he had served as a director at *The Washington Post* as well as on the board of trustees at Notre Dame University. When Tom Foley retired as Speaker of the House of Representatives in 1996, O'Reilly organised an extravagant tribute to him in the Capital Hilton ballroom and then put him on the Heinz board. 'This is not a cronies' board,' said O'Reilly, insisting every member was chosen for the best interests of the company.

'Tony is larger than life, and he knows it,' said Keough. 'This isn't a show-and-tell board.' Richard Cyert, another part-time director, said, 'he frequently goes around the room to see how people feel about an issue. They'll argue back and forth. It's not necessarily tough on Tony, but it shows the independence of the board'. But he also said, 'he has a million stories and tells all of them well. When you sit down to lunch with him, it's like going to a movie theater for entertainment.' Nicholas Brady said: 'Three-quarters of O'Reilly is better than 100% of most people. He's that talented.' Smyth said the directors were chosen for 'their independence, business understanding and for their willingness to be professional in the execution of their legal responsibilities and to act in the best interests of all shareholders'.

O'Reilly not only hiked the pay of all outsiders but added lifelong director pensions. Later, O'Reilly added other raises and perks, including a $1 million donation to charity after a director's death. Along with annual retainers of $30,000 and yearly grants of 300 shares of stock, directors received $1,500 for each meeting they attended. Critics said they were bought and kept bought.

The average age of the Heinz board was more than 66 years; only one of the nine outside members was below the age of 65. The 85-year-old Bogdanovich had been a director for 34 years. CalPERS argued that board members who stayed for a decade or more should no longer be considered independent.

'Most of us are rather aged, but we are quite viable,' said 77-year-old Eleanor Sheldon, a Heinz director of 18 years' standing. She had been forced to retire because of age from the boards of Citibank, Equitable and Mobil.

O'Reilly also had an executive committee, which had the authority to act when the board was not in session. It met the day before the full board and sometimes even when the full board was not meeting. 'O'Reilly has created two classes of directors: those that make the decisions and those that bless them,' claimed John Nash, president of the National Association of Corporate Directors.

Businessweek gave O'Reilly the chance to dispute the charges laid before him. On the award of share options he responded that 'there could be no more honourable or fairer way in American capitalism'. He defended his directors. 'Outsiders are outsiders. They simply are not committed to the board in the same way as people who have their careers at stake here. Boards that listen to one man will be the prisoners of that man,' he said. *Businessweek* argued that Heinz's inside and outside directors alike were already prisoners to O'Reilly.

The campaign undermined O'Reilly. He announced on 2 December 1997 that he would be retiring as CEO, but staying as chairman. He did not get the headlines he wanted. *Businessweek* magazine online declared: 'Tony O'Reilly steps down at Heinz – and investors cheer'. Indeed, on that news alone, investors drove Heinz's stock price to a 52-week high. 'Heinz is a merge, purge or scourge story,' US Trust analyst Herb Achey said.

It was time for the hindsight assessment of what O'Reilly had achieved – and what he had not achieved. During his 18-year reign as

CEO, he presided over major growth. Sales leapt from $2.15 billion to $9.3 billion. Average annual return to shareholders was 21%; during the 1980s, it was closer to 31%.

'If there is one image that would say it all about Tony,' said McMillin, 'it would be the picture of the pool at the back of his castle in Ireland. There is a telephone next to the pool. Now a lot of people have phones near the pool. But this is different. It looks like an office. Even when Tony is relaxing he is working. Business is his life.'

McMillin argued that, during the second half of his tenure at Heinz, O'Reilly simply had 'too many balls in the air. In the 1980s he was hailed. In the 1990s the industry environment became more difficult. They undernourished brands. They cut advertising'. The comments about brands and advertising were damning about a man who had made his reputation as a marketing genius, and they were to be highly relevant to other of his interests in the twenty-first century.

Businessweek was somewhat kinder to O'Reilly when it returned to him in late 1999 for an article entitled, 'Tony O'Reilly: "I Want More of Everything"'.

This article outlined the dilemmas of his life, wondering 'whether his wife's new Jackson Pollock is hung right side up'. It described how it found him 'padding around the presidential suite of the St. Regis Hotel' in New York, which is where he was just before heading to Pittsburgh for the gala 9 December opening of the $20 million O'Reilly Theater. It was the interview in which he made his 'maximalist' comment.

'If Tony was 40 years younger, you get the sense he would be working for an Internet company,' said McMillin to *Businessweek*. 'He can smell action.'

'He has always been more interested in newspapers than ketchup or baked beans,' said son Gavin, in a comment that might not have impressed Heinz shareholders. 'I would like the papers to be a major force in world media over the next decade,' O'Reilly added. He was not going to wind down. The goalposts had moved, but he still had tries to score.

CHAPTER ELEVEN

'FOR SERVICES TO NORTHERN IRELAND'

In late 1999, O'Reilly received another award, on primetime Irish television, on RTÉ. He was named at the ESB/Rehab People of the Year Awards as the overall Irish Person of the Year for his 'economic, charitable and cultural contributions to Ireland'. He received the presentation in New York, by way of a satellite TV link, with Chryss sitting by his side. His words did not receive as much attention in some quarters as his chewing of gum during the interview; it was seen by some as rude, by those who knew him as another example of his need to deal with dry-mouth since his illness in late 1995.

There was some limited debate – not in the publications he owned – as to the appropriateness of giving an award to someone so rich and powerful, when these awards were more usually given to 'ordinary' people who were recognised for doing something outstanding in their community. Questions were raised as to who had suggested to the awarding committee that O'Reilly should be its choice, whether any lobbying on his behalf had taken place. O'Reilly's friends argued that his wealth should not disqualify him from such an accolade, that the work of the Ireland Funds, his other charitable donations and his efforts to persuade others to invest in Ireland were appropriate achievements.

O'Reilly saw himself as a salesman for Ireland. He was, and he didn't shy away from seeking credit either. 'I am highly involved with the IDA in America,' he told *Irish Business* magazine during the mid-1980s. 'I do an awful lot of work for them over there. I've been very much behind

Westinghouse coming in over here and I've been encouraging Al Rockwell to put a plant in. I've spoken to Alcoa at great length. US Steel I've encouraged to come in and Emerson Electric. Every time I get a chance I'm selling and I'm very close to [Jim] Cashman [the IDA American director] and his people over there.'

O'Reilly championed what he saw as a shift in attitudes that was making Ireland more entrepreneurial, market-oriented and outward-looking and that, as he saw it, would eventually make the country more prosperous. He championed his contemporaries, Smurfit and Ryan, but also the names of Neil McCann of Fyffes, the banana distributors, and Alastair McGuckian, whose Masstock company pioneered intensive farming in non-traditional locations.

'These are the new Elizabethans of Ireland,' O'Reilly said regularly, 'people who go out and plant the flag internationally.' He said:

> ... every time one of them plants the Irish flag in a foreign country, it acts both as a reproach and as a stimulant to other Irish businessmen to dream the same dreams and share larger risks and, more importantly, rewards.
>
> We Irish are small in number, well-educated, imaginative and innovative. We are not any better than anyone else, but we have, I suspect, some special characteristics for this world that is evolving. It's not a contemplative world, it's a world of action.
>
> I'm comfortable with my Irishness and very proud of it. I see myself as a manager in the world of Heinz. But in Ireland I see myself as an innovator, a creator and a pacifier.

He was asked by author Jeffrey Robinson in 1990 about the responsibilities of being a hero in Ireland. He did not demur from the description.

> I think there is responsibility that goes along with that, but I also don't think any of us should take ourselves too seriously. There's a lovely line of Sydney Smith, a great nineteenth-century wit, who said: "The Irish and the English defied the laws of physics. The English who are a dull lot have risen by their gravity and the Irish, a humorous crew, have sunk by their levity." My view is that there's an important responsibility to show that you're hard-working and

ambitious and compete on the world stage. That then widens the opportunities for other Irish men and women to perform in a similar situation. But beyond that, I think, one would take oneself a little too seriously if one thought one had a kind of national obligation to be a daily talisman to everybody. You should live your life in your own individual way and enjoy it. There's a great wit called Hal Roach and he has this final line at the end of his show that goes: "Lads, live every day as though it's going to be your last and one day you're going to be right".

For all of the myth-building interviews, there were occasional critical articles – which enraged O'Reilly, or enraged others on his behalf. Fintan O'Toole of *The Irish Times* wrote a piece entitled 'Brand Leader' for *Granta* magazine in 1996 and it led to attacks on his bona fides in O'Reilly titles. It was the type of piece, even if rare, that brought about the standard O'Reilly response of 'small countries don't like tall poppies'.

'Tony O'Reilly seemed the perfect citizen of Ireland that had escaped from itself,' wrote O'Toole. He argued that O'Reilly had made his own story 'a parable of globalisation, of a man rising from a specific time and place into a great network of global power'.

O'Toole's essay contended that O'Reilly 'wants to be a new Irish brand name, a standard held aloft under which the masses of Irish around the world can congregate; to be, in his own words, 'a representative of the hopes and dreams and aspirations of the Irish around the globe', the man who 'planted the flag of the New Ireland abroad in various forms – Independent Newspapers, capitalism, entrepreneurial spirit, managerial competence … The New Ireland which sees we have a right not just to be colonised but to go to other countries and to harvest and prosper there.'

He returned to O'Reilly's domestic business past, his greatest achievement, to make his point: 'The golden wrapping, the sonorous name, turned slabs of butter into desirable objects. The allure of the image, the magic of the brands, had been released into an emerging Ireland, and O'Reilly was the conjurer.'

O'Toole based much of his analysis on a presentation that O'Reilly had given at a conference in Belfast in December 1995. 'He seemed to suggest that he really believes that history is over, that the business of the world, now and for ever more, is business,' O'Toole wrote, quoting

O'Reilly on how history had 'emerged from the permafrost of communism. Theological nationalism is re-emerging'.

O'Reilly had described the opening of the first McDonald's fast-food restaurant in Moscow as not just a product launch but 'a social and cultural event of international proportions'. O'Toole argued that while others were thinking about the peace dividend at the end of the cold war or about the triumph of democracy, O'Reilly 'was thinking about the beginning of global marketing and the arrival of the new, placeless consumer, belonging to a world where allegiances to brand names have replaced the more dangerous and visceral loyalties of history and geography'. O'Reilly predicted that while the twentieth century was dominated by ideological competition, the twenty-first century would belong to commercial competition. He believed that the most powerful force would be that of 'capital ruthlessly seeking the best rate of return', of 'the emergence of the global consumer'.

O'Reilly had started his address to the audience with a bold statement that his theme would be about 'the island of Ireland – united'. The pause that followed drew half gasps, and not just among the unionist contingent, but then he smiled and added '… to a global economic system'.

No reference was made in O'Toole's article to the Ireland Funds, its role in combatting IRA fund-raising and the functions it facilitated to aid the peace process, and this omission, as much as what was in the piece, upset O'Reilly too. He believed that the money raised by the Funds, the events it organised and the meetings it conducted with unionists who were invited to feel comfortable with those who were unambiguously Irish deserved some acknowledgement – and praise.

O'Reilly's claim that by the end of the 1980s his commitment to the Ireland Funds was about 30 days a year was an exaggeration. But the work did involve considerable time, an application of intellectual energy when he was stretched greatly across a range of jobs and investments and the donation of large amounts of his money. He was proud not just to be Irish but to be seen to be Irish. 'We believe that the Ireland Fund is a fund which lights a candle and does not curse the darkness,' said O'Reilly.

It also provided an opportunity to spend time in the company of Judith Hayes – a Northern protestant, married to a senior businessman in Dublin – who had by this stage become a close friend of O'Reilly's.

Hayes ran the Ireland Funds operation in Ireland. She was an effective figure in her own right, but she also introduced O'Reilly to Maurice Hayes (not a relation), a Northern civil servant who had been described as the Ken Whitaker of Northern politics. 'Hayes had everything. He was erudite, sophisticated, educated, humorous and pragmatic,' said one associate. 'He was also a genuinely nice, modest man.' He would not only guide the Ireland Funds in making a valuable contribution to the peace process but would join the boards of INM and Fitzwilton, and write columns for the *Irish Independent* until he was in his mid-80s.

O'Reilly had not limited the work of the Ireland Funds to America. While so many Irish had emigrated to Britain, and were doing so again in huge numbers during the 1980s, there was still an enormous amount of ignorance about the Irish and openly expressed prejudice. O'Reilly had long been appalled by what he saw as the ignorance of Irish history, even among the well-educated British with whom he played rugby and did business. He argued that there could be no political solution achieved until far more people understood the complexity of Irish history.

'The attitude of other nations to Ireland – particularly Great Britain, for which parenthetically I have a great admiration and affection – has often somewhat irked me. "Typically Irish, deah boy": the paddy-bashing that goes on, the categorisation of the Irish as somehow amusing but incompetent. I believe we are hard-working, hard-driving, imaginative and competent.'

In 1988 the Irish took over the ballroom of the famous Claridge's Hotel, beloved of the Royal Family and Winston Churchill, for the first official function of the Ireland Fund of Great Britain. There were no flags or anthems on display, the determined policy of the Ireland Funds. However, there were 300 or so of the most successful of Britain's Irish-born men and women who hitherto were satisfied to blend more generally into the business, academic and artistic sur-roundings of their adopted home across the Irish Sea. 'Until now, the Irish in Britain, no matter how successful, have not wished to put their heads above the trenches,' said O'Reilly.

The Ireland Fund of Great Britain committee included as its chair-woman Josephine Hart, the novelist and wife of Maurice Saatchi, the advertising guru regarded as responsible for helping Margaret Thatcher to power; committee members included the famous BBC radio and television broadcaster Terry Wogan, publisher Kevin Kelly, and Lord Gowrie from the family that once owned Castlemartin. Participants at the dinner hailed it as an important measure of Irish pride, marking both individual success and general progress beyond the dark stereotype of Irish immigrants as rebel 'gun-runners' and simple 'Paddy' labourers.

The ball took place as the Anglo-Irish Agreement gave the Dublin government a legitimate voice in Northern Ireland's affairs. While terrorist atrocities continued, the flickering hope of the beginning of peace talks was emerging. O'Reilly responded that many of the participants voiced considerable criticism of Britain's Irish policy, which he often shared.

The ball had its critics, too, people who didn't like the ostentatiousness and snobbery of women preening in expensive dresses and men strutting to be seen by their peers, acting in a way that to some seemed as if they were trying to be British. It was a business occasion for some, as much as a patriotic act, and a valuable networking opportunity. O'Reilly knew that and actively sought to make that accommodation, unworried by class-based objections. He wanted to make sure that the 'heavy-hitter' emigrants, now that they had succeeded, had not forgotten where they had come from, but also wanted to celebrate those who had succeeded and broken free of Irish ghettos like Kilburn.

The important political visits to the White House during the nascent Northern peace process, and beyond, owed much to the Ireland Funds, even if O'Reilly was not always physically present. The Ireland Funds, because they were controlled by O'Reilly, were denigrated by Sinn Féin but eventually they too came to the events, especially those at the White House. It was an opportunity to meet their political opponents on neutral ground.

'The unionists came out assuming Irish America was green,' said Kingsley Aikins. 'I remember a St Patrick's Day dinner that Mo Mowlam called the dinner of the potted plants. David Trimble was there, and Jeffrey Donaldson, in kilts. No one wanted to be seen. They were all hiding behind the foliage. Now they have such a good time we have to shoo them out. The relationship fundamentally changed. Unionists were embraced and engaged by Irish America and that made a huge difference. Irish America reached out and said, "we'll give you a fair hearing".'

In 1997, the Ireland Funds provided a grant to bring the leaders of the Northern political parties to South Africa. 'We did it quietly,' said Aikins. 'They wouldn't fly together, they wouldn't stay together and they wouldn't listen to Nelson Mandela together. Jeffrey Donaldson said to me that it was the best $25,000 the Ireland Funds ever spent.'

O'Reilly paid for much of this. In December 1997 he exercised share options to buy Heinz shares that gave him a profit of almost $35 million. He gave $5 million to the American Ireland Fund charity, the largest single donation the charity had ever received, on top of previous donations that totalled 'several millions', according to Kieran McLoughlin, who succeeded Aikins as CEO. He described it as a 'leadership gift'. O'Reilly challenged other millionaires to match his donations.

All of this work was cited for his knighthood nomination in 2000, awarded for his 'long and distinguished service to Northern Ireland'. He said of the award: 'I think it is also signal recognition of the thousands of people in the Ireland Funds all around the world, who have worked for peace and reconciliation in Ireland – North and South.' In initial interviews he said he would sometimes make use of the title of Sir Anthony O'Reilly, 'although generally I'll still be known as Tony O'Reilly'.

His acceptance of the knighthood shocked many close to him, even more so when he did adopt the title. For all of his Irish heroes that O'Reilly cited in his speeches, he also regularly quoted one Englishman above all others, his 'great hero' from the Second World War. 'His life to me was and continues to be an inspiration,' he said of Winston Churchill. 'I think he was a very selfish man. He believed he was the epicentre of all that was happening. He was … a truly conceited man. He felt that he was very important, and I suppose that is one of the principal criteria of success – to believe in yourself so strongly that you are the epicentre of everything that is happening.'

His last Heinz annual report as chairman was to come in 2000 and he was as much the theme as the company he had served. In the report he reflected that 'Life, it is observed, is a random walk. Yet of the many surprises that have advanced my life, none has been so rewarding as my long association with Heinz.'

He dispensed his benediction to his successor. 'I am supremely confident in the leadership of Bill Johnson and his management team. Bill Johnson is only the sixth CEO in the 131-year history of your company, and his troops have readied Heinz for the opportunities of a new century and set it on a course for accelerated growth and profit. I bid them fair voyage and, as a fellow shareholder, look forward to their success as they continue to make Heinz the best international food company in the world. Our founder, Henry John Heinz, proclaimed that "to do the common thing uncommonly well brings success". It is a pithy summary and it will be our motif for the future years.' Even in his note of departure he was trying to set out the template for the company's future.

He recalled what he regarded as a breakthrough moment in his management of Heinz. 'Some 20 years ago, we held a seminal manage-ment meeting at which we determined that 85% of the world's population had not been exposed to a Heinz brand. Therein lay a limitless opportunity. The world's fastest-growing countries were then beyond our pale, housing billions of consumers whose increasing affluence and exposure to Western media would generate an enormous appetite for Heinz products. That revelation set us on a course of geographic expansion that continues to this day.'

O'Reilly would not stay in Pittsburgh once his chairmanship of Heinz came to an end. The house at 835 Fox Chapel Road, near the Fox Chapel Golf Club, was put on the market for $2.4 million, after 30 years in O'Reilly family ownership. The now 34-room Tudor-style house, on its seven acres, had been extended to 8,000 sq ft but it had been a family home nonetheless and, in reality, Susan's home, so now there weren't enough people to justify its use. The six children were adults, living all over the world, and Susan was in London, so a new owner would get to enjoy its advertised eight bedroom suites, all with attached bathrooms, the 20 x 28 ft kitchen, the seven-car garage, the solarium, guesthouse, greenhouse and Japanese-style garden.

O'Reilly had not emotionally committed to Pittsburgh fully as a home; it remained a stepping-stone to other things. As he told *The New York Times* in 1988, though he had lived in America since 1971, 'I never really felt I left Ireland, certainly not emotionally. I feel a sense of loyalty, commitment and, indeed, debt to Ireland.' He would not return to live in Ireland, however, for tax reasons, flitting in and out of the country, making the Bahamas his domicile.

At the turn of the century, O'Reilly faced a level of freedom he had not enjoyed in years. He still had his many different business interests, of course, but without the need to prioritise Heinz, the way was now open for new ventures to engage his still considerable energy. What would he do next?

One possible avenue that some expected him previously to pursue was politics. O'Reilly had always encouraged the notion of wanting to serve. Some years earlier, he had mentioned ambassadorship to Japan, for example, but on behalf of the USA, not Ireland. 'I'd be ruthless with the Japanese. They can be subtle and devious and self-serving, but they do understand power.'

He had spoken once, many years earlier, of wanting to be Ireland's European Commissioner. There were rumours of him serving the first George Bush as US secretary of commerce, but in reality it suited his ego to be mentioned for jobs he had no real interest in filling. There was no chance of him putting himself up for election to public office, to risk the possibility of losing. 'O'Reilly has a sharp sense that the global business tycoon and the global media mogul have more power than politicians do,' said one friend. Henry Kissinger once called him 'the consummate business-statesman,' and O'Reilly appeared to see himself in that role. He saw the twenty-first century as an opportunity to advance his business interests but also to have his say, from outside of the political process, as to what would be best for Ireland and, indeed, the world.

SECTION 3

2001–2006:
A man for a new century

CHAPTER ONE

BEST FOOT FORWARD

In the first year of the new century sales of Waterford Wedgwood products climbed and O'Reilly watched proudly as the group was set to exceed the €1 billion sales mark for the first time, seemingly building on the publicity garnered from the Times Square exposure. Under O'Reilly's direction, the company was now more focused on marketing, using the cachet of celebrities and well-known designers to push the brands and expand the range, and thereby increase consumer spending in its major markets.

To this end, in 2000, O'Reilly unveiled Sarah Ferguson, Duchess of York, as the new face of Wedgwood. She was paid €800,000 per year for two years to be a brand ambassador, which entailed appearing at up to 50 stores each year, where she would show customers how to lay tables with Wedgwood products. She also appeared at O'Reilly's side at a number of functions. She was, as O'Reilly claimed, a useful marketing tool in the USA, where the British Royal Family held a fascination for many people; O'Reilly also greatly enjoyed her vivacious company. She was already a well-paid advocate for WeightWatchers, although her income from this latest endorsement was apparently less than half what she was paid by the American firm. Personal appreciation for the personal help she had received from O'Reilly persuaded her to take the still very well-paid gig. She said she had been 'racked with fears, doubts, inadequacies,' when O'Reilly offered her the original WeightWatchers role. 'His outstretched hand of friendship came at a pivotal point in my life; he returned me to the land of the living and thus gave my children their Mummy back ... without that job and that friendship I dare not think what might have become of me,' she wrote in her autobiography.

Alongside its brand ambassador, the company also continued to select top designers from other fields to lend their skills to Waterford Wedgwood products. Jasper Conran, Paul Costelloe and Nick Munro were among the star names they attracted. An expanded range of luxury branded products was launched in 2000: now there were Waterford Crystal writing instruments and holiday heirlooms, and Wedgwood gourmet foods, linens and cutlery. There were even Wedgwood ceramic dog-bowls at $90 each. The singer Elton John was so impressed that he bought a dozen of them, specially inscribed, for his pets.

Better still, given that sales growth was not always matched by profitability, the company was heading towards record profits of €85 million for 2000. The share price rose accordingly and shareholders received generous dividends. The All-Clad acquisition was pulling its weight and proving highly profitable. O'Reilly claimed that 'the company's strategy of new product innovation and design would continue to keep it relevant to twenty-first-century tastes'. He boasted that 'our momentum continues to build' and that 'we have exceeded our original expectations'. What he didn't highlight was the extremely small profit margins being earned by the Wedgwood division: profits of just €15 million on sales of nearly €400 million, even after the closure of six manufacturing plants and 2,000 job redundancies. The previous big acquisition, the German glassware manufacturer Rosenthal, was not living up to expectations either, but O'Reilly argued that the key to acquisitions was patience. He promised that Rosenthal would deliver significant profits within three years.

O'Reilly wanted Waterford Wedgwood to get much bigger, much more quickly and felt that organic, or internal, growth would not deliver sufficiently. O'Reilly's executives spoke about paying €100–€200 million for acquisitions, but O'Reilly mused publicly about going as high as €500 million. He chased expansion into leather goods and high-end watches as against what he described as the more 'ephemeral' fashion-driven areas of the luxury goods market. His ambitions were big: he had in his sights Coach, the leather goods company that made handbags, gloves, outerwear and scarves, and the watchmaker Jaeger-LeCoultre. Both companies could cost over $900 million each to acquire, but he seemed relatively unconcerned by the figures involved.

Sporting young boy: While rugby and cricket were his first sporting loves, O'Reilly also spent much of his summer months playing tennis. On the right is Kevin McGoran, who remained one of O'Reilly's closest friends throughout his life, and who was on the board at Waterford Wedgwood with him when O'Reilly lost control of it. O'Reilly, who had not yet grown to be bigger than his counterparts, is third on the left. (*Courtesy of Belvedere College*)

The prefects: O'Reilly was a sizeable, commanding figure even as a teenager. While much of his time at Belvedere College was devoted to sport, particularly rugby, he was also regarded as suitable to be a school prefect and he dressed accordingly. (*Courtesy of Belvedere College*)

The philosophers: O'Reilly used the year he repeated his Leaving Certificate to hone his debating skills. His subsequent command of language and ability to make an argument was central to his success in business. (*Courtesy of Belvedere College*)

Youthful international: a boyish looking O'Reilly before an Ireland game against England, just 21 years old but in his fourth year as an international. (© S&G/S&G and Barratts/EMPICS Sport/Press Association Images)

Returning hero: the 1955 tour had made him a teenage hero, but the 1959 British & Irish Lions tour confirmed his status as one of the icons of the game. (© *PA/PA Archive/Press Association Images*)

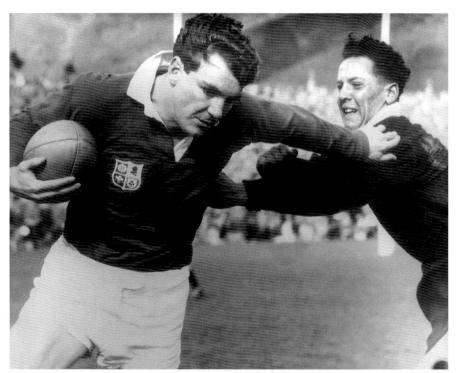

Record try-scorer: in action during his second Lions tour, this in New Zealand in 1959. His exploits with the British & Irish Lions brought him international sporting fame, his running power and ability to hand off opponents being particularly notable aids to scoring so many tries. (© *Central Press/Getty Images*)

The comeback: in 1970 a somewhat out-of-condition O'Reilly added to the legend when, as a 33-year-old, he was plucked from seven years of international exile to play for Ireland against England at Twickenham. At training the day before, his weight and jowls caused much comment among the players and press. (© *s&g/s&g and Barratts/*empics *Sport/Press Association Images*)

The proud parents: Aileen and Jack supported him in everything. One of their rewards was to see him qualify as a solicitor, having taken a law degree at University College Dublin. (© *Irish Photo Archive*)

The first fiancée: Dorothy Connolly was O'Reilly's first serious girlfriend, although he was known as a young man to enjoy the company of other young women. He became engaged to Connolly before the 1959 Lions tour, but broke it off after his return. They remained friends. (© *Independent Newspapers Ireland/NLI*)

The first marriage: O'Reilly met Susan Cameron in Australia in 1959, on the first leg of the Lions rugby tour. She came to England in 1960 and they were married in Dublin in 1961, before divorcing in the late 1980s. (© *Irish Photo Archive*)

The best man: Jim McCarthy (on the left, beside an unknown garda) became and remained O'Reilly's best friend. He was best man at both of O'Reilly's weddings and also to O'Reilly's father Jack when he eventually married Aileen in the 1970s. Also in the photo are Andy Mulligan, another of O'Reilly's closest rugby friends, June Finlayson and Helen Hayes. Macca's son, James McCarthy, is the page boy. (© *Irish Photo Archive*)

The rapid rise: O'Reilly got his big break at Bord Bainne, developing the Kerrygold brand, but it was his achievements in dealing with a crisis at the Irish Sugar Company that got the attention of Heinz and was the starting point for his international business career and accumulation of vast wealth. (© *Irish Photo Archive*)

The first near disaster: O'Reilly's first major Irish investment, Fitzwilton, almost ruined him financially before the age of 40. He stuck with it and by his friends, Lord Killanin, Sir Basil Goulding, Vincent Ferguson and Nicholas Leonard, but it didn't change his attitude towards taking risks. (© *Irish Photo Archive*)

The grown family: five of O'Reilly's six children (Cameron, Tony jnr, Susie, Justine and Gavin; Caroline is absent), with their mother Susan, are present for an event in Dublin. (© *Independent Newspapers Ireland/*NLI)

Holding onto Heinz's most famous product: O'Reilly was the first non-member of the Heinz family to become the food company's chairman. He was also chief executive of the board and chief operating officer. (© *Alan Levenson/ The* LIFE *Images Collection/Getty Images*)

Uplit at the podium: O'Reilly had an enormous reputation as a public speaker, both at annual general meetings of his corporations and at charitable functions, using his skills as a mimic and storyteller to enthral audiences. (© *The Irish Times*)

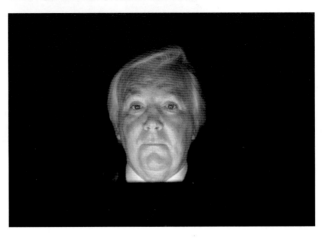

Passing on the deeds: O'Reilly, in his role as chairman of Heinz, bought Cape Cornwell in Britain and enjoyed, as an Irishman, passing the deeds to British Prime Minister Margaret Thatcher at 10 Downing Street, for transfer to the British National Trust. (© PA/PA *Archive/Press Association Images*)

Balls in the air: O'Reilly's globetrotting became a topic of conversation in American corporate circles as he continued to invest outside of Heinz, despite being one of the most highly paid executives in the USA. (© *Gene J. Puskar/ AP/Press Association Images*)

Connecting with Taoisigh: O'Reilly enjoyed close relationships with many political figures in Ireland, particularly with Fianna Fáil leaders from Jack Lynch to Bertie Ahern. (© *The Irish Times*)

Dealing with Sinn Féin: O'Reilly's antipathy to the violence of the IRA was one of the driving forces of his life and his direction of Independent News & Media (INM). Standing alongside former IRA terrorist Martin McGuinness, Deputy First Minister of Sinn Féin, was a major development for both men. Also in the photo are (from left) Michael Bloomberg, Mayor of New York, Ian Paisley, First Minister in the Northern Executive, Gordon Brown, British Prime Minister, and Brian Cowen, Taoiseach. (© *John Harrison/ PA Archive/Press Association Images*)

Second wife: O'Reilly married Chryss Goulandris in 1991. Her love of horse racing meant they were a regular presence at tracks throughout the world, and often at events sponsored by O'Reilly's companies. Her brother Peter lost hundreds of millions of euro in supporting O'Reilly's ill-fated investments in Waterford Wedgwood. (© *Damien Eagers/PA Archive/Press Association Images*)

Proud memories: O'Reilly collected awards and trophies throughout his life, but one of his most cherished was his introduction to the International Rugby Board Hall of Fame, alongside his great friend the former Welsh out-half Cliff Morgan. (© *Getty Images*)

Under pressure: O'Reilly thought his family's name would always be over the door at Independent News & Media, but his last annual general meetings of the company were torrid affairs as he came under pressure from rival shareholder Denis O'Brien. (© *The Irish Times*)

Nemesis: younger businessman Denis O'Brien usurped O'Reilly not just as the largest individual shareholder at INM but in his position as the wealthiest Irish-born individual. (© *Ramin Talaie/Bloomberg/Getty Images*)

Green tie: O'Reilly's Ireland Funds made a significant contribution to the peace process in Northern Ireland and encouraged the likes of President Bill Clinton to throw the White House open to the Irish on St Patrick's Day and to commit to engagement with ending terrorism in Northern Ireland. (© *Reuters*)

Genuine friend: O'Reilly's friendship with Nelson Mandela was long standing and deep. They visited each other's homes and spoke regularly. It enabled O'Reilly to make one of his most valuable investments, in newspapers in South Africa. (*Courtesy of Queen's University Belfast*)

When he had hosted the Waterford Wedgwood AGM in May 2000 at the crystal manufacturing facility in Kilbarry – and hired the 'Tralee Dome' used for the Rose of Tralee festival to accommodate over 1,000 shareholders and workers – he had dismissed concerns raised about the level of borrowing. Debt:equity ratios, as a measure of risk and control, 'went out the window five years ago,' he said dismissively.

'My long-term ambition for Waterford Wedgwood is to make it a luxury goods company that represents the best of the best in the world. It has just got to make two or three really important takeovers,' he said, during our interview in Deauville. He was in something of a corporate *Catch-22* situation, however. Waterford Wedgwood was already highly borrowed – at around €311 million at the end of 1999 and rising – and to make a sizeable acquisition would need money raised by selling shares. The company's share price was still on a multiple of about half to a third of other stock market quoted luxury goods companies. This would mean selling more shares than might otherwise be the case to raise money, thereby diluting O'Reilly's shareholding unless he stumped up a big portion of the new cash.

'My job with Waterford Wedgwood is to build up a lifestyle company that originates in Ireland but does not necessarily produce in Ireland,' he said. 'That makes a profit for shareholders and conveys to the world at large a notion of excellence. I feel the same sense of pride in my newspapers.'

His departure from Heinz meant he could now focus more intently on Waterford Wedgwood and on his newspapers. Independent News & Media was designated as his new full-time occupation, with the full salary and benefits to match, even if he would not be devoting all of his time to it because of other commitments. His trusted lieutenant, Liam Healy, CEO for the previous 10 years, had stepped down to a part-time role. His son Cameron, long regarded as heir apparent at INM, had surprised many the previous year by quitting as boss of the Australian newspaper operations. His brother Gavin became COO, reporting to his father as executive chairman. Neither O'Reilly nor his departing son would publicly admit to tension between them, especially as Cameron was staying on the INM board in a part-time capacity, but there was plenty of angst involved, hidden from public view despite much speculation within the company and in media commentaries.

Cameron's departure added another layer to what was already an often difficult relationship between father and son. As the eldest child, he had not been afraid to confront his father about family issues, often taking his mother's side, or to strike out to do his own thing. Although brought up in Pittsburgh from the age of five, he finished his schooling in Ireland, at Clongowes Wood boarding school in County Kildare, and then progressed to Oxford University to undertake a degree, finishing in 1986. He had travelled extensively, including a motor-cycle trip across China, and quit a job in Goldman Sachs in 1987 after the stock market crash in order to set up his own trading business in Brussels. His father persuaded him to visit Australia in 1988 and, to his surprise, he had enjoyed both working in the newly acquired Australian Provincial Newspapers (APN) and living in the country. He stayed, and after a couple of enjoyable bachelor years he met Isla, who he quickly married and with whom he would have four children. Cameron was not without ambition in business or the smarts to achieve. He won the respect of those with whom he worked at APN: while he may have received his initial leg-up by reason of lineage, he more than did the work required and in a way that greatly impressed his colleagues.

He spent more than a decade with the APN subsidiary and as CEO gained the experience required in running a publicly quoted company with the disciplines required. He knew that Healy, who was 71 years old, wanted to retire, and he saw few other obvious contenders within INM. He did not feel entitled to the job but considered himself to have the experience of being the CEO of a PLC and success at doing it, something that, for example, his younger brother Gavin didn't have at that stage. That experience and success would be a useful retaliation to charges of nepotism.

Cameron was at an age when he felt he could take responsibility, the same age his father had been when he brought the family to the USA and the new life at Heinz. His children were young and he felt it was a good time for them to move for education, before they hit their teenage years. He and Isla wanted to go to Europe and Cameron decided that it would as be CEO of INM in succession to Healy. If that didn't happen, he would leave the group.

O'Reilly demurred, but not until after a lengthy to-and-froing, much of it via e-mail and hand-written letters. O'Reilly argued that the elevation had come too soon for Cameron but, in reality, the move had come too soon for the father. Cameron was far less deferential and would, as CEO, expect to be given his head, without having to refer constantly to his father for approval. O'Reilly was not ready to cede control. Cameron, along with everybody else, had missed the possibility of O'Reilly, after over 25 years as part-time chairman, assuming the position on a full-time basis while doing away with the role of CEO entirely. While Cameron was disappointed by this outcome he was not bitter and, importantly, did not fall out with his brothers, even though they tried to talk him out of leaving, shocked by his decision. His father described it as 'the worst decision in the history of capitalism', but it was not going to bring about a break in their relationship as long as the fracture was presented to the public in a way suitable to O'Reilly.

Many executives at INM were disappointed; while they liked Gavin and knew that they would get on with him, he had not shown the leadership qualities that Cameron had already displayed, something that would become a recurring topic of private conversations in the years to come.

The stock market reacted positively to the announcement in January 2000, jumping the share price by just shy of €1 to €7.30. Investors speculated that a more engaged O'Reilly would be more demanding of managers to deliver bigger profits and eager to buy more assets to build a business that already published 15 million newspapers and magazines each week. The expectation was that his focus would be commercial rather than editorial. His emphasis on building brands was clear from that year's annual report, in which he stated that 'we are attempting – and I hope succeeding – in focusing world-class resources on making our products more appealing and relevant everywhere'. More contentious was his claim regarding the maintenance of editorial standards. He wrote that 'we attempt to underline the impartial, to entertain and to inform, to expose corruption and praise achievement. Mostly we get it right; occasionally we get it wrong; but at all times we endeavour to be fair, reasonable and independent'. Some disagreed bitterly, both in political and business circles, and most especially in Ireland. Within his own stable of publications, mutterings were heard as to its success in that regard.

O'Reilly had relented finally, in 1999, to the long-standing complaints by his managers in Ireland about the poor printing facilities, and the advertising revenue that was being lost as a result. He authorised investment in a colour press at a green-field location in Dublin. In late 2000 the first copies of the *Irish Independent* rolled off the presses at the new €65 million printing plant at City West, on the road south out of Dublin that led towards Castlemartin. In his new role as COO, Gavin was charged with the task of extracting cost-savings to pay for the investment.

It hadn't gone unnoticed within the group, or elsewhere, that O'Reilly had spent far more on an acquisition north of the border. He spoke with pride about the acquisition of the *Belfast Telegraph*, although even then many described the €478 million purchase price as jaw-dropping and it brought INM's debts to well over €1 billion. 'It is our best deal yet,' O'Reilly said.

The *Belfast Telegraph* was owned by Trinity, which had merged with MGN, which in turn owned the *Belfast Newsletter*. The British mono-polies and competition authorities had demanded that the newly merged entity sell some assets to avoid an excessive concentration of titles within the one entity. O'Reilly prevailed in a competition to buy the *Belfast Telegraph*, but in doing so had to assure the authorities on both sides of the border that the *Belfast Telegraph* would be part of INM's UK-managed operations. He emphasised the importance of maintaining editorial independence, given the newspaper's tradition of largely serving the unionist majority. The cost of the deal horrified many of his executives and although it was not disclosed publicly at the time, his three sons felt it was necessary to argue with him about it, to lobby that he not proceed with it. They were ignored. 'It was his company and he saw ownership of the *Belfast Telegraph* at that time of the peace process as his contribution to nation-building,' said Tony jnr in 2015.

O'Reilly was aware of the potential threat posed by ever greater Internet usage to newspapers, even though circulation figures in general were increasing in an apparently booming global economy. 'Papers will have to market themselves much more vigorously,' he told me. 'Papers today, compared to 10 and 15 years ago, are fantastically vivid things. Papers offer great value. The cost of a mobile phone call is the cost of a newspaper. I believe newspapers have a great future. In Dublin we have moved seriously to protect our market share and we are investing heavily in a new printing press to do that.'

His belief was that other forms of media were more vulnerable than newspapers and that 'television will suffer because of fragmentation and because the Internet is made of an audio-visual medium. If you have been staring at a screen all day at work, you're not going to want to go home and stare at the Internet when it is part of a television experience. I think we have covered virtually all of the possible avenues in which the Internet will come at us, given that you have only two eyeballs, two ears and 24 hours.'

'We are in Internet defensively,' he said, giving the example of I-touch, a company that provided a limited amount of real-time information to mobile phone subscribers, and in which INM was a majority shareholder. 'I-touch is a chance to get a brand on the mobile phone. I believe in the future of mobile phones, but I don't know how their future will evolve. I can't believe it will be attractive for using the Internet apart from the provision of a few repetitive functions because of the size of the screen.'

He distrusted the high market valuation of an unproven company such as I-touch, particularly by comparison with an 'old' established company such as Heinz, suggesting that the latter was of the kind that would get an upward re-rating on the stock market when what he saw as an 'Internet bubble' burst. Investors, he felt, would return to focusing on traditional valuation measures, such as sales, pre-tax profits and earnings per share instead of others that justified enormous share prices based on a multiple of hope.

The irony was that one of the big criticisms of O'Reilly prior to this had been of his similar promotion of Atlantic Resources, a stock that had traded on hope and hype. He described Providence and Arcon, the two exploration and resources companies that he had brought into the twenty-first century, as 'the butt ends of Atlantic Resources', but was keen to talk them up. 'I think we deserve the most incredible praise for what we have done with those companies. I am not embarrassed to blow my own trumpet on this because of all the things we stuck with, we stuck with Atlantic Resources. I must have invested $60 million in them.'

Later that year O'Reilly was to make appointments at Waterford Wedgwood that would copper-fasten family control of the business. Peter Goulandris had become executive chairman of the entire Wedgwood subsidiary in February 2000. If that was something of a surprise to CEO Brian Patterson, who now reported to Goulandris before he got to O'Reilly, he had another coming in November. Tony jnr left his full-time position at Arcon to become deputy CEO at the Wedgwood division.

Redmond O'Donoghue confronted suggestions of nepotism head-on. 'You always get those allegations, but these guys are bright too and he's got a lot of achievement behind him. I very much welcome this ... Tony O'Reilly jnr knows our business. I think he's the right age with a lot of achievements and a can-do attitude. We have to appeal to people under the age of 25 and 30 and I think he'll play a large role there.' Tony jnr would continue as part-time chairman of Arcon. Whatever about the extra work the son would take on, yet more would be added to his father's agenda at the end of the year.

CHAPTER TWO

DIALLING UP THE NUMBERS FOR EIRCOM

A lthough he had INM, Waterford Wedgwood, Arcon, Fitzwilton and other businesses demanding his attention, O'Reilly was still keen for something else to engage him. He chose Eircom, Ireland's largest telecommunications company, which had joined the stock market in mid-1999 but was by now, as a result of the bursting of the dotcom bubble, in big trouble with angry shareholders because they had already lost sizeable chunks of their initial investments.

Rumours of O'Reilly's supposed interest in buying Eircom first emerged in November 2000. Denis O'Brien had gone public that month with an initial offer of €2.25 billion to buy what would remain of Eircom once it had completed the sale of its mobile phone division to Vodafone. O'Brien was flush with cash after the sale of his phone business, both mobile and fixed, to BT nearly two years earlier, a sale that had made him more than €250 million richer and, thanks to his legal tax planning, those funds were fully available to him to make further investments. At this stage, few took too seriously the idea of an O'Reilly involvement in the bidding, not least the O'Brien camp. O'Reilly seemed stretched by his other investments and his knowledge of and interest in telecommunications was not considered to match O'Brien's. The field seemed clear for O'Brien to make a major acquisition.

That Eircom was vulnerable to takeover was shocking. The government had sold Telecom Éireann, renamed Eircom, out of public ownership via a stock market flotation in 1999. It had raised €5.5 billion from investors, which was used to start the National Pension Reserve

Fund. Initially, the sale was held out as an enormous success – an example of shareholder democracy that involved about 500,000 citizen investors. Some of those who bought shares at €3.90 each in the flotation sold them quickly at a sizeable profit. About 90% of the buyers held on; the share price slumped in late 2000 and early 2001, creating large losses for those who still held the shares.

Although Eircom had been caught up in an international trend, the so-called bursting of the 'dot-com bubble', the board panicked in the face of considerable media criticism. Eircom decided to sell Eircell, its mobile phone business, to Vodafone for a combination of cash and shares, at a price that was subsequently shown to be far too generous to the buyer. This left it as a traditional fixed-line telecoms business, with good assets that produced a sizeable cash-flow, but with nothing 'sexy' for the future, as the market wanted. Two of the foreign shareholders, telecoms groups KPN and Telia, which between them owned 35% of the Eircom shares, decided to bail. The share price slumped, making it vulnerable to takeover by a third party.

Eircom swiftly rebuffed O'Brien's November 2000 approach, which was priced at a lowball €1 per share. O'Brien said it was a friendly offer and that he had no intention of making a bid that did not have the backing of the board. That would change.

He continued his preparations for a bid, but these were disrupted somewhat by the unexpected emergence of an unwanted news story. In early March 2001, as editor of *The Sunday Tribune*, I published a story on the front page that told of a payment made to Fine Gael in 1995, just six weeks after the announcement by the government that O'Brien's Esat Digifone consortium had won the contest for the mobile phone licence. The report outlined how the £50,000 payment had been made by O'Brien's consortium partner Telenor, but the Norwegian company claimed it had been made at O'Brien's request and that Telenor was repaid subsequently by Esat Digifone; how the late David Austin, a close associate of Michael Smurfit and an unofficial Fine Gael fund-raiser, had been the conduit for the payment; how the money got 'stuck' within Fine Gael, which didn't know what to do with it; and how the party tried to return it to the donors, who didn't want it back. O'Brien denied that he had ordered the payment, saying it was a Telenor initiative that it was now trying to blame on him. He was furious because, correctly, he anticipated that it would lead to an investigation by the Moriarty Tribunal into how the licence had been won (an investigation that eventually went on until a final report was delivered in 2011). He wrote to O'Reilly, complaining bitterly about the content of the newspaper report and others in *The Sunday Tribune* and other INM titles, especially referring to his tax residence, that he felt were deliberately targeted to damage him.

O'Reilly finally confirmed his interest in Eircom publicly in April 2001, as chairman of a consortium named Valentia. O'Reilly was brought in by the giant US investment bank Goldman Sachs if not quite as a figurehead, then as a required Irish investor to alleviate possible complaints about Eircom falling into the hands of solely foreign owners. Goldman Sachs was represented in Ireland by former Irish rugby international Hugo McNeill, who approached O'Reilly. O'Reilly and McNeill had a good relationship, despite a 30-year age gap. Both had played for the British & Irish Lions test teams and were also similarly gifted intellectually. The eye-catching member of Valentia was the billionaire Hungarian-born financier George Soros, who had gained some notoriety in 1992 when his Quantum Fund had made profits of over £1 billion on betting that sterling would have to exit the EU's exchange rate mechanism. He became known as 'the man who broke the Bank of England'. Soros's involvement this time was by way of Soros Private Equity Partners, a fund that put $3.5 billion (€3.9 billion) into private equity transactions. An American investment bank, Warburg Pincus, was also included initially, although it was to drop out before the eventual conclusion of the purchase.

Most important, perhaps, was the involvement of a venture capital firm called Providence Equity Partners, an entity that managed about $2 billion in funds. An American called John Hahn was about to become a very influential figure in O'Reilly's life. A veteran of many profitable telecoms deals in recent years, Hahn had been recruited by Providence Equity Partners in 2000 and put in charge of European private equity investment activities.

O'Reilly did not run the Eircom bid, although he was actively and deeply involved. 'He was the chairman but the chief executive was very much John Hahn,' said one adviser to the consortium. Hahn shared physical similarities with O'Reilly: he was an imposing 6 ft 3 in. tall and had ginger hair (although O'Reilly's had gone grey by this stage). 'He was very bright, very sarcastic,' said one adviser, 'but he was respected by everyone and he got things done. O'Reilly developed a very strong relationship with him, even though Hahn was by no means deferential to him, while others in the group were. Hahn was one of those who was never going to call him 'Sir'.

Various advisers were hired in Ireland as PR consultants, including former broadcasters Fintan Drury and Conail O'Morain. Drury, who had just sold the successful PR company that bore his name, was selected after Jim Milton was deemed conflicted by his work for INM, although Milton did continue to maintain a presence on the periphery on O'Reilly's behalf. Drury found O'Reilly to be very conscious of his image in Ireland and the required PR. He was not the first or last in that regard.

The media, and the public, were not too impressed by the idea of Eircom becoming a play-thing for the rich. The media – including *The Sunday Tribune*, which advised small investors not to sell their shares – was alert to the potential economic dangers of a sale to a group led by either man. An *Irish Times* editorial in May 2001 stated that 'from the point of view of public policy, the danger now is that a successful bidder may focus on turning a quick profit by seeking savings at Eircom and selling it on in a couple of years. This is far from the development strategy envisaged at flotation and raises questions about the spread of advanced telecommunications services. However these issues are unlikely to feature highly in the Eircom boardroom, where the pressure is on to secure the most favourable short-term deal for shareholders.'

In late May, the Moriarty Tribunal reported that it had come into possession of additional information connecting O'Brien to Lowry. Vast sums that went to the ex-minister allegedly originated in O'Brien's bank accounts and travelled via circuitous routes to the politician. O'Brien angrily denounced any suggestion of knowledge or wrong-doing – a position he has never changed – but he was aware the whole episode would cast a shadow over the takeover battle as he would now have to give evidence at public hearings of the tribunal.

O'Brien wanted public attention focused on Eircom instead of on his personal issues and he went on the offensive. He accused O'Reilly of planning to asset-strip Eircom, complaining that his consortium would break up and sell off the company within three years. He said that allowing the national phone company to fall into the hands of a group of 'trigger happy venture capital companies' was 'South American'.

This contrasted with his consortium, which was 'Irish-controlled and took a 10-year view ... We have a 10- or 20-year horizon because I am only 43 and we like what we are doing and we want to go back into business,' he said. 'I think the management of Eircom will want to make sure that the new custodian of this business will look after the business and not break it up and sell it and put everyone out on the street.' It was regarded in some quarters as hyperbole, while others suspected that O'Brien would take many of those very actions himself were he to win control of Eircom. As it happened, the prediction turned out to be a relatively accurate assessment of what would happen, irrespective of its motivation.

Among these comments was one that O'Reilly's advisers said insulted the older man deeply. While O'Brien's description of the O'Reilly consortium as 'already having one foot in the departure lounge' may have been intended to convey that O'Reilly's team would be in and out of Eircom quickly with a big profit, O'Reilly took it that O'Brien was suggesting he was, if not near death, near irrelevance, which was almost as bad. 'The departure lounge comment made his head spin,' said Drury. 'It really troubled him, the way O'Brien referred to him. He genuinely could not understand it. O'Reilly in some respects is old-fashioned, very much a product of his generation. He could be cut-throat to get what he wanted, but there was a way of behaving, a certain decorum that he believed should be applied, even with his enemies. He was iconic, wealthy, powerful and yet these comments hurt him, did not flow off like water off a duck's back. His reaction was emotional, he was hurt by it.'

June was marked by offer and counter-offer and it was then that O'Reilly's group made what seemed like a winning move. O'Reilly and his advisers had realised quickly that winning control of Eircom came down, ultimately, to who could offer a better deal to the Employee Share Ownership Trust (ESOT). O'Reilly's hopes were raised by an expectation that the ESOT was largely hostile to O'Brien. A host of negative comments O'Brien had made about the old Telecom Éireann when he had been in competition with it at Esat Telecom and his reluctance to deal with trade unions, which many regarded as outright hostility, would now work against him.

The unions were not necessarily much more enthused by O'Reilly, even though he had a track record of engagement with unions at INM and at Waterford Crystal and of striking deals. His involvement with the unions during negotiations was limited, for strategic reasons. 'He was not the right person to engage with the unions,' explained Drury. 'Put it this way: we had a cast who we put into each scene as appropriate. O'Reilly was most definitely one of the leading players, but you don't need the star in every act. We didn't want the unions focusing on him rather than the deal.'

If the ESOT's members were suspicious of both consortia – and of the intentions of their leading men – the main issue remained as to who would give them the best financial deal. The ESOT wanted to remain as an investor in the company – it had 15% of shares as things stood – and to increase its involvement, if it could. The key negotiator for the ESOT was Con Scanlon, the boss of the Communications Workers Union (CWU), who was more interested in dealing with O'Brien than most of his colleagues. O'Brien had what he thought were fruitful negotiations with Scanlon. In a 2015 interview for this book, O'Brien said: 'Con Scanlon shook my hand and walked me out of the CWU headquarters to my car and said to me, "we have a deal to go into partnership to buy Eircom". Within a week he reneged on the deal.' Scanlon denied that to this author. 'I am well aware of the significance of a handshake and I didn't do that because I didn't have the authority to make that commitment. A trust is a very different animal to a company.'

The ESOT sought to structure a deal in a way that didn't trigger a large tax bill for its members. O'Brien asked the unions to take it on trust that he would allow the ESOT to use its money to buy a substantial shareholding six months after completion of the original sale. Valentia instead offered to include the ESOT not just as a member of its consortium but to allow it buy its way to a near 30% shareholding. The ESOT would sell its existing shares to Valentia for €450 million and then reinvest €200 million of the proceeds in buying 30% of the new Eircom. The balance would be distributed to ESOT members.

The other Valentia members were not entirely happy with giving the unions the level of control that a 30% shareholding would confer. They didn't want the size of the union shareholding to act as a brake on the actions that would have to be taken to turn some quick profits. The solution was the creation of preference shares for the ESOT, which would provide a guaranteed annual return on the investment but not voting rights. That created a new problem, however: the existing tax rules did not permit such an arrangement; cash would have had to be distributed among members of the ESOT and that would have triggered an immediate tax bill for the workers.

Finance minister and Fianna Fáil TD Charlie McCreevy received a request from the tax advisers to the unions, not from Valentia, asking for a change in the tax laws. McCreevy agreed to introduce legislation to allow the ESOT to hold preference shares under the same tax terms as would apply for holding ordinary shares. The ESOT trustees could not have opted for Valentia without this undertaking, which was kept under the radar, being available to it.

The tax angle was not revealed until 2003, after a series of questions by Green Party TDs Dan Boyle and Eamon Ryan in the Dáil. As McCreevy subsequently admitted, O'Reilly's consortium could not have beaten O'Brien without the necessary tax change. He excused it on the basis that it had been done to benefit the workers. McCreevy told the Dáil: 'If this change had not been made, it would have favoured the Denis O'Brien consortium and the deputy can imagine the hullabaloo that would have caused. The legislative changes simply provided the membership of the Eircom ESOT with a level playing-field to choose to support whichever bid they wished to support … both Valentia and e-Island had the same chance to strike a deal with the Eircom workers and I understand the ESOT was more inclined to vote for the Valentia consortium.'

That was true, to a point. O'Brien's idea to involve the unions as part of his e-Island structure had been more complicated. It entailed the ESOT supplying loans that were exchangeable for preference shares but that could not be called part of the capital investment in the acquisition. The members would have been entitled to cash immediately because of this mechanism, and this would have triggered a tax bill. E-Island calculated that the members could receive a €15,000 tax-free takeover bonus, although the exact size of the figure was disputed. Had the e-Island consortium known what McCreevy was doing, it might have changed the structure of its own bid to make it more attractive. Both offers were put to ESOT members, the CWU plumped for Valentia and the O'Reilly consortium won more than 90% support.

Winning the support of the ESOT was only one part of the equation, however. There were other large shareholders and all the small shareholders to be won over, too. The ESOT was in a difficult position. It couldn't attempt to improve its position at the expense of other shareholders, but the lower the offer price accepted by Eircom, the cheaper it would be for the employees to build up their stake in the new entity. Every additional cent per share on the eventual sale price would cost the ESOT an additional €22 million in building its stake in Valentia. Other shareholders, on the other hand, wanted the Eircom board to extract the highest possible price, especially as they had suffered heavy losses on their initial investment.

An added complication was the decision of the Moriarty Tribunal to call O'Brien to give his initial public evidence in mid-June. O'Brien's father, Denis senior, went on the RTÉ Radio 1 programme *Liveline* and accused the tribunal of engaging in a McCarthy-style 'witch-hunt' against his son: 'Let's be absolutely frank about it. Denis was the underbidder in Eircom. He was bidding against the O'Reilly consortium. It's a heck of a coincidence that the main [O'Reilly] papers, the *Independent* during the week and the *Tribune* on Sunday, are the most critical of them. If you look at it [the coverage], I mean, it's incredibly biased without anything said in Denis's defence.'

O'Brien's father also took aim at O'Reilly, whom he had known since his youth. He described him as 'not that bad a fellow. He is very bright, very talented. He was a very good rugby player, a beautiful player. It is unfortunate he took on Denis, particularly when he knew me so well. I don't know why he did it. Maybe it's just to make news.'

O'Brien consistently increased his offer, going 5 cent per share, or €110 million, higher than Valentia at the end of June, valuing Eircom at €3 billion, or €1.32 per share. Remarkably, however, KPN and Telia had given irrevocable undertakings to accept the Valentia offer for their combined 35% shareholding, undertakings that could only be broken if somebody else offered €1.355 per share or more. By mid-July O'Brien lifted his bid to €1.36 per share, putting him 9 cent ahead of Valentia. The formal e-Island offer was submitted on 25 July and shareholders were given until 13 August to accept it.

Crucially, however, the ESOT indicated that it wanted to stick with Valentia. Its advisers worried about the structure of O'Brien's offer because of the element of trust required. It would have to rely on the word of O'Brien and his advisers, Investment Bank of Ireland and JP Morgan, that the ESOT would be allowed buy 29.9% of the company for €180 million. That O'Brien had put the commitment into his offer document would have been enough for most people, but not for those running the ESOT. Scanlon said that 'there is not a hope in hell' that the workers could back a deal on a promise, rather than on the certainty of a contract. Hahn described it as a 'trust me deal' that 'could not be done by a prudent businessman'. O'Brien countered that he and his colleagues were 'people of their word'. He charged that a takeover by O'Reilly would be 'bad for the country', a statement that the Takeover Panel forced him to withdraw but with which many people later came to agree.

In early August, Valentia raised its offer to €1.365 per share, made up of €1.33 per share in cash and a 3.5 cent dividend. As a clincher it tied in KPN and Telia, which agreed to that price as long as they didn't get an offer of over €1.50 per share, something that was never going to happen. O'Brien's bid was potentially marginally higher, but with KPN, Telia and the ESOT onside, O'Reilly was clearly going to win.

The financing of the deal, when it became public, amazed many. The five main shareholders in Valentia – O'Reilly, the ESOT, Goldman Sachs, Providence Equity Partners and Soros – put up €676 million in November 2001 and borrowed the remainder of the €3.2 billion purchase price from banks and from the ESOT, which put in €247 million in preference shares. That was to prove a lucrative investment.

In December, Eircom left the stock market, crystallising losses from about 450,000 of the half a million or so citizens who had been lured into buying the shares just 27 months earlier. Those who had held on to the end lost 30% of their money.

Now that the deal was done, fears were expressed about the extent of O'Reilly's influence, even as just a 4% shareholder in Valentia. Dick Walsh, an acerbic political commentator in *The Irish Times*, claimed that O'Reilly's involvement in Eircom would give him almost as much control over communications as Prime Minister Silvio Berlusconi enjoyed in Italy. O'Reilly brushed off the criticism: he had won. However, his initial comment on winning – 'we believe that a strong, developed and efficient telecoms infrastructure is critical to Ireland's competitive position and attraction as a business location' – became one that would be thrown back at him many times in the future. O'Reilly was genuine in his belief, but he also meant it in tandem with making a lot of money for himself.

Members of the Eircom consortium didn't see O'Reilly's motivation as wanting to best O'Brien for personal reasons. 'I suspect he was something of a deal junkie at that stage,' said one adviser. 'The motivation wasn't necessarily the money. Winning was the prize itself.' Another said: 'He regarded himself as something of a national treasure. He could see that the financial architecture of the deal held out the promise of a massive financial return, but that was not necessarily the only motivation, or even the primary one.'

It was no surprise that O'Brien's team was angry, and remained so. Speaking in 2015, O'Brien still described the outcome as a 'stitch-up'. The €15 million paid in compensation by Eircom to e-Island to help cover its costs did little to assuage the pain.

Once the cards had fallen, O'Brien affected not to care, later saying there was far more money to be made in developing a mobile phone network in the Caribbean than in owning a small bit of Eircom, which subsequently turned out to be true. Nonetheless, the experience of defeat clearly rankled, and in March 2004 he made a formal complaint to the Office of the Director of Corporate Enforcement (ODCE) and the Stock Exchange Takeover Panel (SETP) about the special tax deal. It made no difference, but it was significant nonetheless: it showed that he did care, and that he would not forget.

CHAPTER THREE

WIN SOME, LOSE SOME

In the midst of the wrangling over Eircom, O'Reilly celebrated his sixty-fifth birthday in May 2001 with a spectacular party for his inner circle of friends and family. He hired two luxury yachts to cruise along Italy's beautiful Amalfi coast. Every second evening the guests disembarked at a chosen port and dined together in a local restaurant. On the other evenings the guests on the second yacht joined him on his yacht for dinner, tables set with Waterford and Wedgwood products, of course. No expense was spared, not surprisingly.

Ceremony and occasion were becoming more and more important to O'Reilly. In the same month former US president Bill Clinton was his guest speaker at the eighth annual Independent lecture in Dublin, at a fee estimated at more than €100,000 plus expenses. Clinton flew into Shannon Airport and stayed first at O'Reilly's Dromoland Castle, a five-star luxury hotel, where he enjoyed a very late night in the company of Gavin and Bono, the lead singer of U2. Clinton arrived into Dublin the following day, late for a lunch appointment with O'Reilly and his INM editors at the Fitzwilliam Square residence, somewhat to O'Reilly's annoyance, but to the amusement of those O'Reilly had kept waiting on many occasions over the years.

That evening Clinton delivered his lecture at Trinity College and afterwards the 400 or so guests moved to a marquee in the grounds for a dinner. Clinton was escorted by the O'Reilly family into the event, in a procession led by bag-pipers. It was quite the sign that while INM may have been denoted as a public company, it was run by and for the O'Reillys, with benefits to those who played along.

On 5 June O'Reilly collected his knighthood from the British monarch, Queen Elizabeth II. The ceremony involved him kneeling in front of the Queen and bowing his head while she tapped each shoulder with a ceremonial sword. Somewhat surprisingly, the O'Reilly investiture did not feature in the *Irish Independent* the following day. 'He has finally tumbled to the fact that going down on his knees before the English monarch doesn't play very well in Ireland,' said *Irish Times* business reporter Jim Dunne in his contribution to a major feature published in the *Pittsburgh Post-Gazette,* which described what the city's old Heinz boss was doing now. O'Reilly said that he had publicly commented on the knighthood when it was first announced, but that the ceremony at Buckingham Palace was private, and he chose to maintain his privacy on this occasion.

The same article quoted one of his advisers, Robbie Vorhaus, instructing its author, Cristina Rouvalis, to address O'Reilly and Chryss as Sir Anthony and Lady Chryss before adding, 'the people in Ireland think he should be sainted, not knighted'. O'Reilly said that he had received only good feedback about his knighthood, saying the Irish were proud and excited about the honour bestowed on him in recognition of his peace efforts. He also announced that in light of his new exalted status, 'I have throttled back a lot and am trying to act my age'.

He was conscious of emphasising his Irish identity in the many international press interviews he conducted that year. In January 2001 there had been a major feature in *The New York Times* by Greg Winter under the title, 'A quest for Irish business glory'. Much was made of the contribution of the Ireland Funds and of his ambitions for the future. 'I've never seen him so on fire,' said Kingsley Aikins, CEO of the American Ireland Fund. 'I don't think there was any doubt what the theme in his life is. He sees the Irish as one of the great tribes of the world and he's a leader of it.' His old associate from Heinz, Ted Smyth, offered that 'his heart was always in Ireland'.

O'Reilly informed his interviewer that he saw himself as an 'ambassador of democracy' via his newspapers. Asked why he avoided direct involvement in politics, he said it was not because of a fear of the limelight but because of an aversion to compromise. 'Everyone owns a piece of politicians, and that's what I object to,' he said, as he sat in the presidential suite he kept at the St Regis Hotel in New York. 'Business is autocratic. It is not democratic.'

Among his business empire, O'Reilly was most proud of the growing international footprint of INM. It employed more than 12,000 people, had a turnover of €1.5 billion and gross assets of €3.5 billion. But it also had debt, plenty of it, about €1.5 billion. It was time for another bit of financial engineering, a restructuring of the Antipodean assets. A decision was taken to transfer the New Zealand newspaper and radio business Wilson & Horton from INM to APN in return for €690 million in cash and the transfer of near to €400 million in debt from Ireland to Australia. Independent News & Media used part of the cash it received in this deal to buy new shares in APN, which increased its shareholding to 45%, with the balance used to reduce its existing debts. The deal doubled the size of APN.

That wasn't enough to sort out the INM balance sheet. This was emphasised by the surprise issue of new shares by INM in September 2001, even though the shares were trading at a two-and-a-half-year low. INM raised €100 million by placing shares with new investors. The move was interpreted in some quarters as meaning that INM was forced to act because of concerns that it was about to breach banking covenants, something the company denied angrily. However, the money raised would only make a small dent in the €1.5 billion debt and it meant that any aspirations to use further borrowings to make more acquisitions were most unlikely to be fulfilled.

Independent News & Media was not the only O'Reilly company forced to scale back its ambitions for growth. The plans for Waterford Wedgwood to acquire other companies had not come to fruition and he had to deal with important internal issues too. The company ended the twentieth century with a pressing problem: what product would replace the Millennium flutes as a cash cow? The final sale of the glasses amounted to over 70 million units. There was no new product with a fraction of its cachet. To make things worse, the US economy had slowed slightly throughout 2000 and 2001 and the sellers of luxury goods were, as they usually are, among the first to suffer. The company, so dependent on US sales, was also vulnerable to a decline in the value of the US dollar. The shares continued to improve during 2000, however, reaching a high of €1.46 at the end of November, before beginning a gradual and permanent decline.

Thanks to the Millennium flutes, in March 2001 Waterford Wedgwood was able to boast that 2000 had been its best ever year and that trading in the first couple of months of the New Year had picked up even further. The company had crashed through the €1 billion sales barrier for the first time, rising by nearly a quarter in a year. Of this, crystal sales had gone up by 10% to €435.7 million, and ceramics sales grew by 21% to €481.4 million.

'We are now widely recognised as one of the world's major luxury lifestyle brand companies, with strong market share and number one brand status in each of the world's key trading blocs,' O'Reilly said. 'We will continue further to develop and contemporise our brands while growing the group through selective acquisition.' He found that the stock market did not share his beliefs, however.

The problem was that while sales were up, profit margins remained thin. While O'Reilly continued to demand 15% profit margins, industry experts said he would do well to beat 8% on average. The feeling was that crystal and cookware products, with All-Clad now looking an excellent acquisition, could more readily achieve that 15% threshold, but that it would be far more difficult for the ceramics divisions to achieve that goal.

Chief executive Redmond O'Donoghue stated that O'Reilly did not expect Waterford Wedgwood to be severely affected by a downturn in the US economy. 'If there is a downturn, I don't think it will be sustained. America is the biggest consumer market and will remain so. To be big in the US is something everybody aspires to,' said O'Donoghue. His only worry was the outbreak of foot-and-mouth disease in cattle in Ireland early in 2001, which resulted in travel restrictions that damaged incoming tourist numbers. In fact, that was to prove the least of the company's worries.

The terrorist attack on New York and Washington of 9 September 2001 obviously had a very high human cost, but it had economic implications too, just as those responsible seemingly intended, copper-fastening the US recession, hitting the value of the dollar and contributing to something of a hiatus in Irish and European economic growth. The repercussions hit O'Reilly's companies hard.

The attack coincided with the realisation that Waterford Wedgwood was already enormously vulnerable to a downturn in the US economy – from which it derived about 45% of its revenues – and this was now greatly exacerbated. On 12 September 2001 the company revealed that profits in the first half of the year had fallen by 6.6%, after years of uninterrupted growth. But the shares fell in response by 18% in one day as investors anticipated a sudden retrenchment in consumer spending, particularly at the luxury end, and in travel. It was estimated that some 60% of sales depended on tourists deciding to buy high-end mementos. O'Reilly was reduced to claiming that the group had performed 'admirably' against the backdrop of difficult trading.

The group moved relatively quickly in response to the changed environment. By November it had unveiled a new advertising campaign, with images 'of warmth and comfort' for 'a focus on family and friendship', what the Americans call 'cocooning'. O'Donoghue predicted that 'in spite of all of these events, gift giving will go on. People want to celebrate births, anniversaries, graduations, and we have the brands to help them do that.' But would they be coming to Ireland to buy them? In Ireland, which was the second biggest market for Waterford crystal, the number of tourists from the USA was expected to fall from a million in 2001 to half that number in 2002.

In response, the group moved to reduce costs by cutting 1,400 staff. This time, €20 million was spent on cuts at Wedgwood. The closure of the Stuart Crystal subsidiary, a smaller British competitor to Waterford which had been purchased as recently as 1995, saw Waterford Wedgwood's shareholders hit for €24 million, while the end-of-the-century party left an unexpected hangover that saw a €13 million write-off from unsold stock in the Millennium product line. In the same year, refurbishing the firm's retail outlets cost another €5 million.

The global effects of 9/11 were apparent in the INM annual report for 2001, published in the spring of 2002. Here, O'Reilly was in unusually reflective mood:

It would be hard to experience a more surprising and, at times for all of us, a more alarming year than 2001. It culminated in the extraordinary and horrific events of September 11th, but before that there was a general spirit of decline and malaise evident in most economies. September 11th was a dramatic coda to all this and caused almost all people everywhere to examine their lifestyles, ambitions and goals, to see if, in fact, they were pushing the right ends in an uncertain world. Most of us felt that we had perhaps neglected some of the more obvious well-springs of a balanced life. The resource of family, the affection of our friends, the joy of nature, the capacity to be satisfied with what you have and, sadly for the travel industry, the ability to stay at home. It has all, I think, subsided a little since that date, but we still have a pervasive feeling of heightened uncertainty. Somehow the verities, which seemed so certain three years ago, have been challenged – and challenged in many cases by feelings which are unaffected by modern technology.

September 2001 also brought further bad news from O'Reilly for Arcon shareholders. Zinc prices hit their lowest level in 15 years and production had to be curtailed. Losses climbed to €10.8 million for the first half of the year as sales slumped by nearly 20%. Things only got worse. By 2002 the price of a tonne of zinc had fallen to $800, a 60-year low made worse by the US dollar/euro exchange rate. The company's debts were mounting, now standing at over $100 million. One of O'Reilly's companies, Indexia Holdings, had advanced nearly 60% of the working capital needs in the previous two years, costing O'Reilly nearly $10 million. O'Reilly had to act or else it was almost certain that the banks would withdraw their working capital support and demand repayment of debts, resulting in closure of the mine.

O'Reilly had to do deals. One of his companies, Fairfield Holdings, purchased most of Arcon's bank debts of $85 million. He paid only $20 million, causing the banks to take a large write-off. Fairfield in turn required Arcon to repay just $20 million, and agreed new terms for the timing of the repayment of this money, reducing the annual interest repayments for Arcon to far more manageable levels.

In addition, O'Reilly handed the banks a 10% shareholding in Arcon. He also organised a new issue of shares to raise €28.75 million. Most of the existing shareholders did not follow their money and O'Reilly had to purchase their rights instead, bringing his control of Arcon to 71% of the shares. However, he clawed back some of the money as it was used to repay Indexia's previous investment. Arcon gambled that zinc prices would recover. It increased the capacity of its processing plant to bring down the unit cost of production, and to increase exploration in adjacent areas of the mine to try and extend its life-span. Tony jnr denied it had been a 'rescue job' and promised that the new-look Arcon would be 'a totally and fundamentally changed business proposition'. There were 220 jobs saved.

O'Reilly was becoming somewhat stretched financially, but coverage in the Irish media of this was in short supply. The greater focus came from outside. A *Forbes* article in early 2002, for example, critically examined how he managed his money – and those who followed him by investing in his companies. Entitled 'Dethroning Tony', the article said that the 'legend' of O'Reilly had been built on his leadership of Heinz, leading it into 17 new counties and almost quintupling overseas sales to $4.6 billion. It reported, however, that a 'tally of just his public holdings shows losses of nearly $924 million on their $1.7 billion market value since 1998, a 54% decline. That compares with a 16% drop for the s&p 500 during the same period. When asked about his battered portfolio, O'Reilly responds with mock incredulity. "Excuse me!" he exclaims. "Tough times make good companies even better".'

The article was savage in its appraisal of INM, pointing out that its shares had fallen by nearly three-quarters from their price of two years earlier, that in 2001 it had made a tiny profit on revenues of nearly €1.5 billion, and that its debt of €1.5 billion was 1.7 times the market value of the company. It criticised the purchase of the *Belfast Telegraph*, made reference to O'Reilly's residency in the Bahamas, 'presumably to avoid paying taxes to Dublin', and pointed out that the shares traded on a multiple of 12 times projected earnings, compared to 21 times for *The New York Times* and up to 16 times for Australian chains. It also raised serious questions about the performance of Waterford Wedgwood.

'As for criticism of his own investment results, O'Reilly folds his arms. "Begrudgery," he mutters, the oft-used word in Ireland for those whose envy is the same shade as the shamrock.'

His spin-doctors dropped one bit of good news to financial reporters in August 2002, when they reported that O'Reilly, wife Chryss and brother-in-law Peter made a claimed profit of just over €100 million when they sold their stake in financial group Lockwood – a us-based provider of individually managed account services to independent financial advisers – to the Bank of New York. They had founded the business in 1995 and developed it away from the public eye. It offered investment research, managed money services and portfolio performance, reporting to investors through independent advisers. It certainly had all the hallmarks of a major success.

There was more good news for O'Reilly in June 2002. The eventual publication of what had become known as the Ansbacher Report, conducted by a specially appointed inspector called Gerard Ryan, was most notable for what it did not include: O'Reilly's name was not listed as one of the depositors in Ansbacher Cayman, an off-shore bank that had gained infamy in Ireland. Being named as a depositor with this bank was one of the great disgraces of Irish public life at the turn of the century. Ansbacher, once known as Guinness & Mahon, was used by many of its clients to hide undeclared income from the tax authorities. In effect, Ansbacher Cayman was a bank operating illegally in Ireland for the benefit of an elite, who had full use of the money deposited with it even though the money was held, in theory, in Cayman, and who did all of this to evade tax.

O'Reilly had been rumoured to be one of the clients of Guinness & Mahon, although this confused many observers. Why would he have need of such accounts when he had not been tax resident in Ireland since the early 1970s? He had no need to hide income from the Revenue Commissioners in this fashion. He endured a long battle with *The Irish Times*, in particular, over this, issuing legal proceedings against the paper in 1999 after it claimed he would be named in the Ansbacher Report as a depositor. His spokesman had made a public statement that 'he does not have, nor did he ever have, directly or indirectly, an Ansbacher deposit account'. His relationship with the bank was as a borrower, the spokesman insisted, and there was nothing improper in that. Yet *The Irish Times*, just two weeks before the report was published, had written how the report would 'name depositors, many of whom used the bank for tax evasion purposes' and described O'Reilly as someone 'we should be looking out for'.

The Irish Times apologised within weeks for this claim, saying that it was wrong to have implied this and that it accepted O'Reilly's assurances. As it happened, O'Reilly's name did feature in the report, but in another context. Two of O'Reilly's closest associates, Ferguson and McCarthy, both directors of Atlantic Resources, had secretly bought shares in the company in the 1980s using large loans from Guinness Mahon Cayman Trust, as Ansbacher Cayman was then known. The two men lost large sums of money on their speculation in Atlantic shares and didn't have enough funds available to clear their bank debts. O'Reilly had stepped in with his own money to help clear their debts: in Ferguson's case, the sale of his house and part of his famous art collection had not been enough to cover his debts and, in a remarkable act of generosity, O'Reilly and Chryss stumped up over €1 million to make up the shortfall.

CHAPTER FOUR

EXTRACTING THE MAXIMUM FROM EIRCOM

Anyone involved in Eircom who had presumed that O'Reilly would be an occasional presence as chairman, given his other commitments, was soon forced to readjust their thinking. 'He was available any hour of day or night, you could call him and his ability to be "always on" was remarkable,' said his commercial director David McRedmond, who came to admire him enormously. 'He kept business simple. He set out a series of things he wanted to achieve at Eircom: to keep prices down for customers; to improve service; to get back into mobile; to get government to do a deal on rolling out broadband. He did that, irrespective of what his critics said.'

There were many critics. Some disagreed with the scale of the achievements claimed by O'Reilly and his colleagues, and some were disgusted by the scale of the riches that Valentia extracted from Eircom in double-quick time.

One of the first things that O'Reilly did at Eircom was to appoint a new CEO to replace Alfie Kane, who received a €3.8 million pay-off. He was replaced by Phil Nolan, also from Northern Ireland, a man who was polished in the way that O'Reilly liked. With somewhat typical hyperbole, O'Reilly claimed that Nolan's appointment as CEO 'marks an important first step towards meeting the objectives I have consistently set in relation to our pursuit of excellence in the Irish telecommunications industry'. In reality, Nolan acted much as one would expect of a venture capitalist in trying to recoup and enhance the Valentia investment with as much speed as possible, while smoothly insisting much the opposite in his public utterances. He was hiding in plain sight. In press interviews he decried 'the short-term horizon' of private equity owners while effectively acting like one.

'In a private equity-led ownership the drive is to grow profits, not to grow top-line revenues or market share,' said McRedmond. 'Eircom was turned into a modern professional company during Valentia's ownership. There was a criticism that we needed more investment, that the State made a mistake in not holding onto the network which was a wonderful, world-class asset that we exploited. It was such nonsense. The network was in rag order and was improved by our investment.'

Other Eircom executives at the time said the venture capitalists were always in the background, demanding changes, seeking to extract money as quickly as possible. Several found John Hahn, in particular, to be 'hard work, quite aggressive in his demands, always looking to see who was getting in his way, always treating those who were not totally supportive almost as enemies, never satisfied, nothing ever good enough'. This was put down to his own personal financial involvement. 'I suppose he had so much at stake personally,' said one. 'He was always in the background behind O'Reilly, pushing the agenda, never satisfied … nothing was ever good enough.' The Soros representatives were regarded by the executives as more accommodating and pleasant. Con Scanlon remained positive about O'Reilly's contribution during the Valentia years. He was a 'modifying influence' on the intentions of the private equity investors, Scanlon said. 'He was a very fair-minded man and I think he always tried to do what was best for Eircom.'

O'Reilly demanded that Eircom find a way to maintain its revenues. The company worked hard to keep its dominant market share of the fixed-line market, then worth over €2 billion in annual revenues, and maintained an 80% share despite active competition.

Nolan began an immediate programme of price hikes for Eircom customers, at a time when mobile phone usage was still far from ubiquitous. The company insisted that it lost money on line rental because of the spread of the population and the cost of providing to rural areas, as required by law. The price of landline rental was increased three times in just 18 months, by about 15%, which was way above inflation. However, the company would not have got away with it had there not been a reduction in prices for actual usage. It maintained that the balance between the two meant average bills were up by just 3%, which was the level of inflation at the time. It gained some confirmation from ComReg when it agreed that telephone bills had fallen by 40% in real terms since 1999. Rivals argued, however, that the three price rises added €100 million in revenue as the company prepared to return to the stock market. Its competitors also claimed that reducing its price was anti-competitive behaviour, designed to stop them attracting new customers. Eircom continued to insist it was championing the consumer.

Nolan, clearly acting with O'Reilly's imprimatur, demanded changes to the State's regulatory regime as a 'prerequisite' for Eircom to make investment in the network. Eircom said it could not invest if it could not be confident of the return it would get on its money, especially as the regulator was demanding that Eircom gave even greater access on its network to its competitors, who would then be saved the need to invest as much themselves. The argument was that when the State had agreed the sale of Eircom to the private sector in 1999, it had had implicitly accepted that it was abandoning its role in providing finance and that future investment in telecommunications infrastructure would come from the private sector. That meant, automatically, that new investors would have to be allowed to earn a commercial return.

O'Reilly's proxy argued that at that time there had been plenty of competition in the sector and easy access to capital, and that regulation was set accordingly. Limits had been put on the size of the return any company could earn on its investment in infrastructure. This served as an indirect price cap, but now Valentia argued that the rates of return allowed were too low to justify further investment. It also argued that retail prices had been capped at a level where no operator could make enough money. Whatever intellectual merits such arguments had, they were also entirely self-serving. Critics immediately pointed out that the regulatory relaxation being sought by Nolan had more to do with enabling Eircom pay down its debt – and thus enriching its shareholders – than with securing the investment needed for Ireland's telecommunications infrastructure.

One person O'Reilly didn't get to put his case to was the Minister for Communications, Dermot Ahern TD, despite various efforts to do so. O'Reilly never met Ahern during the latter's term of office in this department but formed an opinion about him, based partly on

Ahern's decision to reject an invitation to dinner at Castlemartin shortly after he took over as minister. It was pointed out to Ahern's officials that all of his predecessors had accepted such invitations, including Mary O'Rourke only the previous year, and that it would be appreciated if the new minister was made aware of this. The reply came back that Ahern was more than happy to meet with O'Reilly if he wanted to make an appointment to come to the minister's office. O'Reilly did not take him up on the invitation.

Ahern was not entirely convinced by Eircom's promises of investing in the provision of widespread broadband. Ahern was of the view that the one thing worse than a public monopoly was a private one, and he was not slow to say it.

It quickly turned out that the €3.2 billion price paid by O'Reilly's group for Eircom was relatively cheap, and that the selling shareholders had not been told the true value of what they were selling. This was not O'Reilly's fault; it was a fairly damning indictment of the awareness or confidence of the previous board in dealing with the offers in front of them. Nonetheless, it afforded Valentia the opportunity to start repaying itself the cost of the acquisition as quickly as possible. Its first act was to use Eircom's available cash to refund its €40 million 'costs' incurred during the takeover battle. The feared asset-stripping began quickly: the *Golden Pages* subsidiary was sold to a Dutch company, raising €185 million, which was 10 times the valuation that had been on the books; and the retail stores network was closed. Then Valentia decided on an accounting exercise: the revaluation of Eircom's remaining assets. It declared a surplus on the Eircom pension fund of €208 million and, with the Irish property bubble inflating, put a new value on property assets and the network itself that further increased the strength of the balance sheet by €715 million. This was not just academic frippery. The move allowed Valentia fresh leverage with its bankers. It needed it, because it had an annual interest bill of €106 million arising from the costs of buying Eircom. These were all moves that the old board could have made in advance of any bid to change ownership of Eircom.

By mid-2003 Valentia had net debts of about €1.8 billion. It decided that Eircom would issue a new €1 billion bond to investors, to replace some of the bank debt it owed. The banks had been charging 5% for loans, but new holders in the bond would be paid interest of just

2.5%, producing an enormous immediate interest saving to Eircom and improving its future cash-flow. However, Eircom also decided to borrow an additional €1.4 billion from the banks at this reduced and fixed rate of interest. This increased Eircom's entire debt to €2.4 billion, an increase of €600 million.

It was the use of the extra money that caused consternation when revealed publicly. Valentia announced that €512 million of this money would be paid to its shareholders to redeem €66 million worth of preference shares, the rest by way of a special dividend. O'Reilly got about €21 million of this money. Eircom's riches had been extracted not because of any spectacular revolution in the management of Eircom but rather through the juggling of figures, an increase in prices to its customers, the sale of assets and a rearrangement of the company's considerable debt. However, Valentia found that the political and public reaction to the super-dividend was nowhere near as loud, hostile or prolonged as had been feared in advance of its disclosure.

Critics quickly pointed out that the money could have been used for investment in infrastructure or expansion of the business. It was noted that capital expenditure on repairing and improving Eircom's fixed-line infrastructure had fallen from €504 million in the year to March 2001 to just €197 million in the first year of Valentia's control. This newly raised money was not going to be invested in upgrading the infrastructure to allow for the quicker roll-out of broadband, for example, something that was still not widely available in the country despite the wider economic benefits that it would bring. The plan was to restrict such investment to just €200 million each year, which was less than the amount at which Eircom's capital assets were depreciating.

It wasn't the only behaviour that caused adverse political and media comment. Valentia arranged to transfer the ownership of Eircom out of the State to a shelf company in Britain purchased for just £2. It did this to avail of what was called 'less stringent company law' requirements in the UK and to allow 'a more flexible distribution of dividend payments'. That was regarded as a euphemism for avoiding or diminishing some of the tax that would otherwise be payable in Ireland. It copper-fastened the widespread view that the owners of Eircom were only in it for the money, and as much of that as possible, and that the national interest was not being best served, no matter what O'Reilly and others claimed to the contrary.

CHAPTER FIVE

FAVOURING OLD MEDIA

Y ears later, when his continued involvement with INM was under assault, O'Reilly would be attacked for not knowing or caring about new media and for being somewhat romantic and unrealistic about the future for newspapers. That was a somewhat unfair assessment; it might have been more accurate to say that he had started the process of modernisation at INM but pulled back on it because he was unconvinced by the financial returns available. A clear strategy was laid out in the 2001 annual report, which was put before shareholders in the spring of 2002:

> In regard to our foray into other media, we indicated to share-holders two years ago that we would be prudent and cautious in our investments, but equally, that we would make the necessary investment in the broader (but still unproven) media matrix to protect and enhance our core newspaper offerings. That strategy has delivered an impressive 51 sites, registering 95 million page impressions per month through our worldwide network of papers, all of which are now able to accept on-line classified advertising on property, cars, jobs and other related areas, similar to our printed offering. This dual strategy of providing advertising within both of those media outlets encourages participation in our newspapers, protects our margins and makes us more competitive to the consumer. Despite our growing on-line presence it has arguably been a case of 'profitless prosperity', which ironically should be of great comfort to each of us. Far from redirecting both consumers and advertisers away from our newspapers, this new media has become complementary, and that required judicious investment ...

The results are, we think, as good as, if not better, than any company has achieved in this area.

By September 2002, INM's group debts remained at €1.3 billion, its share price had fallen by 33% in the first nine months of the year and while it said that it could cut debt by €150 million through lower capital expenditure, interest costs and better management of working capital, much more had to be done if investor confidence in the company was to be restored. Yet O'Reilly's ambitions were not sated. He wanted to buy more assets, even if outsiders were suggesting measures such as selling the Australian radio stations at APN should he continue to refuse to offload newspaper titles.

'The size of the borrowings was not a concern internally,' said one executive senior in the company at the time, 'because much of the money was owed by APN and was consolidated into our balance sheet so we could take the top-line revenues into our profit and loss accounts to make the profits look bigger. The debt did not stop with us. Tony always believed that it was the job of a publicly quoted company to use debt to increase returns to shareholders. You had to use debt to add to your equity to make yourself bigger. We were a little constrained in financing our own acquisitions, but Tony kept coming back with ideas for involvements with others, where we go into a consortium, get management fees, a share of the equity and the possibility of increasing our stake.'

The biggest fish that O'Reilly tried to land for INM was his partner in Eircom, George Soros. By late 2002 there was newspaper speculation about Soros taking his own large shareholding in INM, something that would undoubtedly have lifted the share price and provided the opportunity for INM to leverage in making acquisitions.

Shares in INM were standing at near five-year lows, which suggested that it was a good time for Soros to buy if he shared O'Reilly's confidence. In 2000, its stock had traded as high as €5.59, but now was as low as €1.35.

It might have seemed odd that O'Reilly would seek to involve someone who might have looked for a degree of control in return for investment. O'Reilly, however, turned to history to justify his interest. He quoted from a book about Napoleon that had persuaded him that the key to success was making the right alliances at the right time.

However, even Soros seemed perturbed by the level of debt INM carried. He never invested, or if he did it was at a level so small it did not require disclosure, either in INM or in any of the purchase vehicles O'Reilly wanted to set up.

O'Reilly's unwillingness to cede control of the share register may have inhibited the growth of INM, according to some insiders. 'He was told that if he allowed his shareholding to be diluted, he could grow at three times the rate,' said one of his most senior executives. 'But he refused to dilute. He preferred to borrow instead because he reckoned that would allow him to keep control. Once he was over 25% he would have both a blocking share and management rights and he reckoned the market had seen what he had done with the company and would continue to be pleased by it. The family never envisaged going below a 25% holding for that reason.'

By March 2003 O'Reilly had to use his own money again, for the second equity fund-raising in two years. The net debt remained stubbornly high at €1.35 billion and INM's corporate bonds had been trading at a discount of 30%, meaning that they were described in the terminology of the trade as 'junk bonds'. One stockbroker suggested that €270 million of debt would fall due for repayment that year. Associated Newspapers, owner of the *Daily Mail*, was making a concerted attack on the circulation and advertising revenues of INM titles in Ireland through its purchase and heavy marketing of a relatively new title called *Ireland on Sunday*. It developed a large circulation through an aggressive promotional campaign involving free CDs, magazines and an attractive cover price. Associated Newspapers had deep pockets and could cause plenty of trouble for O'Reilly in his highly profitable home base.

Independent News & Media announced a rights issue – a sale of shares to existing investors – to raise €103 million and the sale of its British regional newspaper business for €88 million. It said it would raise a further €59 million through the sale of some of its non-core assets and the replacement of existing preference shares with new ones paying a lower rate of interest. O'Reilly indicated that he would take up his full entitlement of new shares at a personal cost of around €28.7 million. Independent News & Media could have raised a lot more money, and done a lot more debt reduction and/or expansion, if O'Reilly had been willing to raise even more equity from other sources. As it was, the recapitalisation programme allowed the company's gearing to fall from 150% to 100%. O'Reilly expected the restoration of the company's debt rating at investment grade, which would allow INM to raise money for investment on better terms. O'Reilly was talking about more acquisitions again.

First, though, he had to deal with the continuing debacle of the investment in television signal distribution through Princes Holdings, later renamed Chorus when in partnership with American billionaire John Malone's Liberty.

The business, in which INM maintained a 50% share, had 200,000 subscribers but it couldn't make a profit. In 2001 it lost €36 million and INM's half share of that would have had disastrous consequences for the overall INM profit and loss account had it been included in its overall group results. But INM used an accounting device – and a pledge that O'Reilly had given to the regulator on becoming involved with Eircom – to ensure that it didn't have to recognise those losses in its accounts, or its share of the mounting debts: its share in Chorus was declared as being for sale and therefore not relevant to a proper reading of the performance of the ongoing business.

That may have been correct technically, but what was even truer was that INM kept failing to complete a sale. There had been talk of an American firm called Telewest paying €500 million for the business but that deal was not completed, ironically on the basis that INM and Liberty wanted even more. Then it seemed that INM would get in a still very substantial €100 million by selling the half share in Chorus to Liberty itself. An outline of a deal was agreed, but each time INM went to complete it market conditions changed and Liberty dropped the price it was willing to pay. Soon the deal could not be done at all.

If INM couldn't find any other buyer, the Chorus investment would have to be written off. It was to be a sizeable hit on the INM balance sheet, involving a write-off of €82 million in previous investment and an injection of a further €10 million in the company during 2003 while the search for a buyer went on. O'Reilly said the Chorus write-down 'reflects the difficult economic conditions faced by the cable television industry in Ireland and globally'. The whole fiasco made O'Reilly even angrier about the failure of the State to protect the investment in televisions signal distribution.

O'Reilly was happy to boast about a stock market valuation of INM of €1.9 billion, which he compared favourably to longer established giants such as the New York Times Company (€3.6 billion) and Trinity Mirror (€2.8 billion). In the 2002 INM report he emphasised that 'our major capital investments of the last four years costing €1 billion are now completed. We do not see any major fixed capital investments for at least the next five years'. He also wrote about editorial independence: 'We believe in it strongly and all our editors both enjoy it and speak enthusiastically about it. This is not a freedom necessarily enjoyed by certain other groups but let me hastily say that that is their entitlement. Newspapers represent to me the true democracy. If you don't agree with them you don't have to buy them … They, and not the Internet, are the perfect browsers, and this estimable congruence confirms that our papers will be around 25 years from now in ever new and improved and exciting forms.'

However, his dual role as chairman and CEO, and the continued board membership of many directors who had been there for well over 20 years, was becoming an ever bigger issue with some shareholders. Independent News & Media claimed it was 'fully compliant with all corporate governance requirements', but it also had to arrange a meeting with the Irish Association of Investment Managers (IAIM), which represented shareholders, that would, eventually, have repercussions.

Later in 2003, O'Reilly plotted a bid to buy the *Daily Telegraph*, one of Britain's most popular broadsheet titles. The problem, as always, was raising enough money. A year earlier INM had looked at a €285 million bid for Scottish Media Group – publishers of the *Herald* in Glasgow – a year earlier and had made an indicative bid of €57.5 million in September to buy Trinity Mirror's Northern Ireland-based titles. In both cases O'Reilly had drawn on his Eircom contacts, with both bids to be financed by Hahn's Providence Equity Partners and INM taking fees mainly from a management role, as well as a small equity involvement. The same structure was envisaged for a bid for the *Daily Telegraph*. As figurehead of a takeover consortium, O'Reilly would move into the first division of international media moguls. It wasn't to be.

O'Reilly would rationalise the decision not to proceed on the basis that he had one crisis newspaper to attend to in *The Independent* without taking on a second as well. 'Isn't that enough for any man?' he joked. Returning his focus to crisis management at INM, O'Reilly ended 2003 determined to reduce costs at all his INM businesses, but in particular at his Irish operations. He wanted to be 'the low cost operator in all our markets'. He announced that INM would spend €54 million on a restructuring plan that would reduce staff numbers worldwide by 5% and produce annual savings of €18.4 million by the end of 2006. Gavin, as group COO, said 2004 would be about stripping the 'fat' out of INM.

A decade earlier O'Reilly's Irish newspapers made up about two-thirds of INM's total turnover and profits. The international expansion meant that its contribution had now fallen to a third, but it remained the strongest performer of all the divisions, at least as measured by profit margins. The strong growth of the Irish economy encouraged INM that its operations could become even more valuable, especially with advertisers seeking more space to show their wares in a booming consumer economy. But the share also had to be defended from other publishers, who now saw the Irish newspaper market as more attractive than they ever had previously.

Incorrectly, O'Reilly thought that Associated Newspapers would pull back on its major investment into Ireland, but he decided nonetheless that additional investment in his publications had to be endorsed if INM's market position in its domestic market – where its titles were the only indigenous ones showing strong profits – was to be protected. It was one thing to boast that the *Sunday Independent* outsold all competitors combined – as long as one didn't regard the *Sunday World* as a competitor – but not to assume that its 'cocktail' of features and analysis and a smidgeon of hard news would always remain popular. O'Reilly believed that people were reading more, but that they had greater choice, and not just among newspapers. The *Sunday Independent* needed a magazine, for example, just as the *Irish Independent* had been given for its Saturday edition, and that would require expensive investment. To provide the money to expand the products and market them he wanted to reduce costs, indeed to apply the level of costs that were available to publishers in Northern Ireland to the Republic.

He believed newspaper managers were often slow to recognise the inherent strength of their franchise, and that they continued to do what they had always done. This was somewhat unfair to many of his editors, who had long complained of underinvestment in the INM products, in pagination and editorial budgets in particular, but also in budgets for marketing executives. Following intense lobbying by eager editors, supported by Barry Brennan, the ambitious but often frustrated marketing director at INM, O'Reilly was coming around to the idea of greater marketing for his titles. It may have seemed odd that the great marketer had to be persuaded of the merits of an increased spend, but INM's spend of 6% of turnover on marketing compared unfavourably to the likes of Proctor & Gamble, for example, which spent up to 20% of turnover on the marketing of household goods. They may not have been directly comparable products, but still the gap was too wide. It was hard to go to agencies promoting the importance of marketing if the newspaper titles in which such advertising was carried weren't themselves advertised elsewhere.

O'Reilly was also lobbied hard by management on the question of salaries. Many were outraged by the reality of some people working just 27-/28-hour weeks and earning €48,000–€49,000 each year for turning in. They felt that this had engendered a sense of entitlement and that this now had to be challenged. Management saw the O'Reilly strategy up to that time as one of conceding to union demands, then increasing margins on sales to increase profits. This time, however, was different.

It was a huge surprise not just for staff but for management too when O'Reilly endorsed a major redundancy programme for the Dublin operations and whole new ways of working, including the outsourcing of telesales, copy-taking, wages and even security, and the putting in place of a structure of editorial syndicating and archiving across the group; INM set aside €23 million to shed 205 people. The company was prepared for criticism that it was doing so while making operating profits in the Irish market of €75 million annually. Irrelevant, argued O'Reilly, when costs were out of line with international competitors who were increasing their footprint in Ireland. O'Reilly took to talking about being 'location indifferent' when it came to producing his products, which meant that within years copy for Irish papers was being sub-edited and laid on finished pages in France. He planned to print a lot more north of the border, but was delayed by the cost of redundancies in Ireland. 'Down south redundancy costs €125,000 per person whereas in the UK it's €20,000,' he told one friend. He was all talk of 'cost anomalies' and of addressing 'historical legacy issues'.

Independent News & Media's management was delighted by the support it received from him. 'He was highly attuned to the detail of operations and how to restructure,' said Michael Roche, one of the senior executives in Ireland who was charged with implementing the strategic plan. He asked all the right questions, had the greatest sense of the risks involved.' Management's big fear was that the NUJ would strike in support of those who were being made redundant or outsourced. The NUJ walked away from any confrontation, however, as many of its members were jealous of the superior working conditions available to clerical and printing staff and felt they should not be continued or supported. It was understandable, but a mistake: in time, many of the journalists would find themselves made redundant, too, enticed to join a third-party sub-editing company on inferior terms and then, in time, with no work at all.

As the cost-cutting took centre-stage, the need to become a 'low-cost operator' was emphasised across all parts of the business. It gave INM a new story to sell to potential investors: a low-cost, high-growth company ready to reap the maximum benefit from the recovery underway in the advertising market. It was a big change from less than two years earlier when the size of the company's debt was a drag on its share price and the Chorus debacle rankled with shareholders. Investors liked the new tougher talking – and acting – O'Reilly and pre-tax profits for 2003 rose almost 20%, to €154.6 million. Meanwhile, APN's market capitalisation had touched A$2 billion for the first time, something O'Reilly liked to compare to *The New York Times*, in existence for 150 years and worth US$5.5 billion. O'Reilly wanted to be that big.

So it was that in the 2003 INM annual report he was able to boast that after the two share issues, in September 2001 and May 2003, 'we have produced a balance sheet which is now, happily, approximately investment grade status, and leaves us open to future opportunity either on our own, or with partners who are more than willing to join us if the right media property is identified'. Perhaps it was due to his age as much as his ego, but he wanted to grow the business quickly and regarded the taking on of debt as the best way to pay for things, especially as media properties became available on the market so rarely.

O'Reilly began to let it be known that he was interested in media acquisitions in eastern Europe and Russia. This was somewhat surprising, given his previous adherence to investing in countries that carried out their legal and commercial affairs in a way that derived from previous British rule. But despite the scepticism of others, he saw potential for increased newspaper circulations in these markets as capitalism and consumerism continued to develop. He was reasonably happy to be situated in what he called the 'second rank of world newspapers' and hoped to rise to the top of that by judicious investment in rising small markets.

O'Reilly was also willing to speculate in new media, buying a 20% stake in British online gaming company Cashcade, which owned getminted.com, for just under €10 million. Independent News & Media now owned PropertyNews.com, a property portal in Ireland, and the Irish classified offering Loadza.com, and jobs sites like Search4 and Worksearch in New Zealand and Australia, respectively. But it had cashed out of I-touch, making a €62.7 million profit, but giving up on a seemingly exciting new way of getting news to customers.

Unsurprisingly, O'Reilly's love continued to be newspapers, which in 2005 brought him in an unexpected direction. India was one of the biggest markets in the world and in *Dainik Jagran* it had a newspaper that sold over 2 million copies daily, each copy read by at least eight people, which made it the biggest paid-for and most read newspaper in the world. The Hindi-language *Dainik Jagran* published 25 separate editions from 25 printing centres across the country. Its owner, Jagran Prakashan Private Limited (JPPL), was a company owned by the wealthy Gupta family.

Independent News & Media acquired a minority stake of 26% in JPPL, at a cost of just over €27.3 million. The entry to India was preceded by many years of relationship-building and a change to the local laws regarding foreign investment in the national media. O'Reilly was fascinated by India, from a distance, for personal reasons as much as anything else: his aunt, his father's sister, who he had never met, had served in India as a nun for her entire adult life.

He saw the vast population and rising living standards, but believed the cost of much new media would be prohibitive for years to come. People could afford to buy newspapers, however, and would desire them for reasons perhaps some in the Western world had forgotten, while advertisers would see them as essential for marketing the products desired by this newly consumerist society. O'Reilly was therefore entitled to boast that INM had bought into the world's 'fastest growing newspaper market'. Pearson, publisher of the *Financial Times*, and the New York-based Dow Jones had already entered the market, but INM may have bagged the best deal of all. 'We are investing in the world's biggest democracy,' said O'Reilly. 'We see this as a real opportunity to grow. We are investing in an economy that is growing at 8 per cent per year and which has a stock exchange that is on fire.'

It was to be one of the few ex-British colonial countries in which INM would invest that did not have a rugby union tradition, but it did have a rule of law based on the British common law tradition it had maintained after achieving independence. It had a law of contract that clarified what INM would buy and what the transaction meant, something that wasn't available in all markets, such as Portugal, where O'Reilly regarded INM's investment as a poor one.

Mahatma Gandhi had established a law in 1955 preventing foreign ownership of media, but this had been repealed in 2003. The Gupta family saw this as an opportunity not just to bring in new investment but also expertise. Independent News & Media had a good reputation internationally in the newspaper industry for how it had done things to date in South Africa, not just increasing profitability but doing so in a way sensitive to local political interests. Two members of the Gupta family spent two years working with INM in Dublin prior to the investment, seeing how the Irish did things and developing trust. O'Reilly was determined to demonstrate that the Irish were the best people with whom the Indians could partner – and to emphasise that INM was content to be a minority partner, although that could increase in time. It was to get three seats on the local company's board, which was much the same basis on which it had originally entered Australia, South Africa and New Zealand.

Independent News & Media saw plenty of areas where it believed it could bring its expertise to bear and increase profits. The most significant cost that *Dainik Jagran* faced was newsprint, the blank rolls of paper on which the newspapers are printed. It represented 60% of *Dainik Jagran*'s costs, as against an average of just 12% across the rest of the group. Part of that could be explained by the exceptionally low labour costs in India, but INM believed it had the ability to reduce the cost of newsprint by at least 10% and improve profit margins that, at 8%, would not have been accepted at INM (other than at *The Independent*).

Many investors and analysts anticipated that INM in India would seek to replicate much of what it had done in South Africa. Low disposable incomes in both countries meant that the opportunities to push up cover-prices, a regular occurrence in Ireland, were more limited, although it had happened in the early years in South Africa. The key would be to gain more advertising revenue, befitting the circulation numbers.

One of the most interesting on-the-record insights into how INM ran its southern hemisphere businesses was given in a book called *Independent Newspapers, A History*, published in 2012. In it, former *New Zealand Herald* editor-in-chief Gavin Ellis, who retired in 2005, wrote about the management approach enforced by the Irish owners – and it was one that Irish editors, in particular, would recognise. Job cuts in South Africa were described by Ellis as:

> … typical of the reaction to economic downturns: any shortfall in budgeted revenue growth was redressed by cost reductions. Editors learned not to rely on budgets set at the end of the previous year and while there was short-term investment in new sections or products aimed at attracting advertisers, there was little new investment in core journalism in the group's antipodean newspapers.
>
> A pattern emerged in the way the South African and Australasian businesses operated. Three words came to dominate the way they were expected to do business. They were the 3Bs: brand, budget and bottom line. The southern hemisphere came to understand the meaning of a series of phrases that emphasised the 3Bs: 'the brand leader', 'the weekly forecast' and 'the low cost operator'.

Australia and New Zealand showed consistent, year-on-year increases in operating profit from 1992 to 2005. South Africa was less consistent, but there was a six-fold increase in annual operating profits over the same period. Ellis said that editors were given editorial control and that there was no evidence that O'Reilly or Liam Healy interfered in the content of their newspapers in the southern hemisphere. He said that O'Reilly subscribed to the principles of editorial independence, but at the same time he saw his newspapers as products and his abiding interest was in their bottom-lines.

It was therefore in O'Reilly's own interests to encourage economic growth in South Africa, although he did have a genuine interest in improving things for citizens of the country. O'Reilly's deep and long-standing relationship with Nelson Mandela meant that he parsed his words carefully when speaking about South Africa, even after Mandela retired. He saw South Africa as being quite like Ireland in that the State regarded itself as having guardianship of the written and spoken word. 'You're not making cement or ketchup,' he said.

Mandela referred to this himself in 2002 when he said that 'none of our irritations with the perceived inadequacies of the media should ever allow us to suggest even faintly that the independence of the press could be compromised or coerced. A bad free press is preferable to a technically good, subservient press.' He said he'd had his own experience of these 'irritations'. Mandela was known to complain to any newspaper editor – or proprietor – when journalists had, in his opinion, strayed off-side, either by phone or by summoning the offending person. O'Reilly might have been busy with other matters, and often unwary of the so-called offending item, but he would receive angry phone calls and sometimes be told a face-to-face was required to resolve a particular issue.

Ivan Fallon, in his time running the South African operations, and his editors would have annual meetings with government ministers in Mandela's office and he said they often degenerated into shouting matches. After one report in the *Sowetan* (a paper in which INM held a minority shareholding), to which Mandela had taken exception, O'Reilly and an aide were summoned to meet Mandela while the South African leader was on a stopover in Geneva, in order to sort out the problem. Fallon noted wryly that while no politician likes criticism, South African politicians might be more vocal than most in telling the media that.

O'Reilly was openly critical, however, of South Africa's ability to attract foreign direct investment and said publicly that, compared with Brazil, India and China, its efforts were 'paltry' and 'embarrassing'. The encouragement of the mobility of capital, and rewarding it, was his overarching political and economic belief, but it was not uncommon. President Thabo Mbeki set up an International Investment Council and included O'Reilly in its membership. Two issues dominated the Council's discussions: black empowerment and Zimbabwe. O'Reilly heard a lot of aspirations for greater black share ownership of companies, but he doubted the promises that these would be paid for with hard cash. From where, he wondered, would the money come?

CHAPTER SIX

FALLING OUT OF FASHION

Vulgarity isn't something that might be associated with the sophistication of Waterford Wedgwood products, but CEO Tony O'Reilly jnr and his colleagues at Wedgwood made an exception when it came to naming the ceramics manufacturer's production strategy. Their *modus operandi* was summed up as 'the 3Fs': fill the fucking factories.

This approach stemmed from the near impossibility of making decent profit margins at Wedgwood unless the factories worked at full production. The idea behind the 3Fs was that as many of the costs at Waterford Wedgwood were fixed, increasing the volume of goods produced would reduce the unit price per piece produced. There was only one catch: any extra manufactured goods would have to sell. If they didn't sell, Waterford Wedgwood would have to liquidate stock, leading to a significant waste of cash.

The decline of Waterford Wedgwood was to be slow and painful, not just for O'Reilly and his brother-in-law, but for 26,000 shareholders, thousands of pensioners and over 8,000 employees. In truth, Waterford Wedgwood was the walking dead from as early as 2003 and many people said as much, but O'Reilly refused to believe them. As a charismatic salesman, he was able to persuade some managers, investors and creditors that the company was not just viable but could have a glittering future. 'It was a problem he had, that he could be too persuasive,' said a family member.

Waterford Wedgwood went through the first decade of the twenty-first century undercapitalised and over-borrowed. It manufactured and supplied products that were going out of favour. It had some good marketing ideas to sell new lines, but never spent enough money on promotion because it had to use whatever cash was available to sort out over-capacity in its plants. It had an owner who simply wasn't ruthless enough when it came to making the necessary decisions, especially the reduction of manufacturing output in Ireland, when more of it could have been delivered from far cheaper locations in Asia, or even Europe. O'Reilly was reviled by many in Ireland as the embodiment of capricious capitalism, especially because of his behaviour at Eircom, but the reality was that when it came to Waterford Crystal, he was far too soft-hearted. Love of Waterford Crystal and of its Irish heritage, in particular, and his wife's similar infatuation with Wedgwood's beauty and history, made him blind to commercial realities.

By March 2003 Waterford Wedgwood's net debt of €354 million was about 80% greater than the value placed on the business by stock market investors. O'Donoghue spoke of 'times of great uncertainty, particularly for luxury branded products' but claimed that creative marketing, manufacturing and sourcing strategies were in place to provide a strong financial performance for the years ahead, despite a weakening dollar and a poor sales outlook, which was attributed to a likely drop in tourist travel caused by both the second Gulf War and the outbreak of a 'flu-like illness called SARS that raised fears of an epidemic. A falling share price indicated what investors thought of O'Donoghue's optimism.

By June hard action was being taken, with more than 1,000 workers at the company's Johnson Brothers plant in Stoke-on-Trent losing their jobs; that line was to be produced in China instead. However, there were major immediate costs involved in getting long-term savings. The restructuring cost to Waterford Wedgwood would be €35.7 million in 2003 and €28.7 million in 2004. There was local political objection to what the Irish were doing to a British icon, but O'Donoghue responded that if he hadn't acted, Johnson Brothers 'could bring the whole Wedgwood business down'. He also revealed that the switch to outsourcing would cut costs by 70%, raising questions as to why this decision had not been taken earlier.

O'Reilly took action that was out of character: he authorised cutting the dividend to shareholders by half. He was under pressure from the banks because of fears that the situation had deteriorated so badly it might trigger legal clauses in loan agreements, which could allow the banks to demand immediate repayment of all outstanding money. Financial director Richard Barnes stressed that the talks with the banks were about 'renegotiating' repayments rather than 'restructuring' the debts and expressed shock at the notion that Waterford Wedgwood might miss an interest payment. It was then announced that the banks had agreed to the suspension of the loan covenants, which was an ominous sign as to the company's true financial health. Barnes denied that the banks had told the company to cut its dividend, but documents released that October to support a planned bond issue revealed that the consent of the majority of banks would be required if the board wanted to declare any dividend for the full year. The banks also demanded that stock levels be reduced and that all capital-expenditure activity be suspended. The company even had to provide monthly management accounts and fortnightly cash-flow forecasts to its lenders. O'Reilly had not been treated like this since the Fitzwilton days of the 1970s. The company needed to raise €190 million by issuing bonds late in 2003 but, in a sign of future trends, would not be able to raise all of the money or as quickly as needed.

O'Reilly ordered his managers to put their best foot forward in public comments and show they were in touch with changing consumer trends. He highlighted an increasing emphasis on lifestyle, rather than luxury, in the product range. He claimed that these lifestyle products could be sold at a lower price than the traditional, classical products, but that doing this would not impact on the prices already charged on the traditional products.

The revised sales strategy made All-Clad all the more important, and there were angry responses from the company to any media speculation that it might be sold. It was conceded that a sale would reduce debts dramatically, but such a move would also remove the profits it provided in a group where most other businesses were losing money.

The 29 October deadline for the bond issue passed. In mid-November the company announced that it was going to combine the bond issue with a share issue instead. The bond issue would raise a lower amount of €165 million, while the rights issue to existing shareholders would raise another €38.5 million. However, the professional fees charged by various stockbrokers, lawyers and financial advisers almost wiped out the entire rights issue proceeds. The bond was priced at an interest rate of an expensive 10%.

Much of the money raised would be spent on redundancies, but O'Donoghue insisted the company would not transfer its Irish manufacturing to China. 'We wouldn't have spent €16 million on a new tank furnace in Waterford if we were going to contract out the operation,' O'Donoghue reassured Irish workers.

In early 2004 Waterford Wedgwood said it had received a 'significant, unsolicited third-party approach' from an unnamed third party that wanted to buy All-Clad. That this development was announced, and was not immediately rejected as unwanted, was telling. Despite all of the previous protestations that All-Clad was too valuable a part of the business to be sold, the debts had become so serious that a sale had to be considered.

A deal was done quickly. A French buyer paid $250 million, which was worth about €205 million to Waterford Wedgwood, once various expenses were subtracted. It seemed like a very good deal given that All-Clad had cost $110 million to buy in May 1999 and the price was $39 million ahead of the valuation on net assets.

The deal would seemingly make a sizeable dent in Waterford Wedgwood's debts, not just in reducing the core debt but saving about €10 million in annual interest repayments as well. While net debt would remain high after the transaction, at €180 million, the sale would also reduce the debt:equity ratio from 190% to less than 80%. What wasn't acknowledged, however, was that the interest rate on the bonds was so expensive that Waterford Wedgwood would still have problems meeting its interest payments on remaining debt.

The overwhelming stockbroking and media assessment was that Waterford Wedgwood had surrendered its best asset in selling All-Clad, but that the debt reduction opportunity was too good to refuse. The initial assessment that All-Clad was too valuable to sell was correct. It accounted for some 12% of group sales but about 45% of its trading profits, making it by far the best-performing part of the group. The sale meant a significant contraction in Waterford Wedgwood's overall business, reducing its trading platform. Sales were already lower than in 1999 and this would only make things worse. It also diluted the idea of repositioning the company closer to the so-called 'luxury living' status and heightened dependence on the low-growth tableware market.

O'Reilly spoke about All-Clad having been 'a marvellous investment', but most investors had seen it as an integral part of the group, not as something to be traded for a profit. Yet O'Reilly said that 'this transaction transforms our balance sheet. The proceeds will put us in a position to take control of the future direction of the company, to reduce debt dramatically and to post substantial capital gain while simultaneously investing to support the sales of Waterford, Wedgwood and Rosenthal without sacrificing margin'.

It was the usual optimism put out for public consumption, but 11 years later O'Donoghue admitted that the sale of All-Clad was deeply distressing to all concerned at the time. 'But it was the most saleable asset, even though selling it nearly broke Tony's heart,' he confirmed.

Waterford Wedgwood pitched the sale as part of a new strategy dubbed the 'Plan for Growth', with O'Donoghue saying that Waterford Wedgwood would now be able to place more 'oxygen' behind its other brands.

O'Donoghue further claimed that the company's period of restructuring, which has seen 3,000 workers leave the group since the turn of the century, was now complete, with the firm much more focused on marketing and branding. He signalled 'better prospects for the year to come'. But soon the company reported a pre-tax loss of €45 million in the year to end-March 2004, compared to a profit of €7.2 million the previous year. Revenues dropped by nearly €120 million, to €832 million, with crystal sales down 16.3% and ceramics sales off nearly 12% – and that was before the sale of All-Clad would impact on the following year's figures. An exchange rate hit of €30 million on the weak dollar was partly to blame, but there were even lower sales volumes and a rise in costs. O'Donoghue admitted it was a 'poor performance'.

There was a rare statement of public support from O'Reilly's co-investor in the main fund-raisings. 'I believe strongly in the Waterford Wedgwood brands and, with the chairman and my sister, I am committed to their development in the coming years. Indeed, Waterford Wedgwood is the only public company in which I am directly involved. That is a measure of my commitment,' Peter Goulandris said after the All-Clad sale.

The All-Clad boss, Peter Cameron, stayed with Waterford Wedgwood after it was sold, having pocketed a €2.6 million bonus for the successful conclusion of the sale, now becoming coo for the entire group. His expertise in selling high-end homeware products in American shops and malls was anticipated to be very useful in taking advantage of an end to the recession.

The problem for Waterford Wedgwood was that tastes had changed significantly, or rather that the pre-recession trends of changed behaviour were now accelerating. Consumers didn't want to spend large sums on top-end luxury goods, no matter how beautiful they were or how expertly produced. They wanted more practical crockery and mass-produced glassware instead of fine china and delicate crystal. There was a flourishing home dinner-party culture in Waterford Wedgwood's main markets, but such dining was far less formal than the type O'Reilly engaged in and to which he assumed everyone else aspired.

Wine consumption soared, which should have been good news, but people were as happy to put a bottle on the coffee table in front of the television, as sitting to drink it with a meal in a more formal setting. They didn't want to be afraid of knocking over and breaking expensive glasses, which was more likely with Waterford's preferred long-stem designs, and they didn't want something that would chip easily when they went to wash it, often after a bottle or two of wine had been drunk. When people began drinking more expensive wines they liked to be able to see it, which made thick or heavily-cut glass impractical. Many Waterford glasses were made for old-fashioned aesthetics rather than modern tastes.

Cameron wanted to put greater emphasis on casual ranges rather than on the more established brands and he was correct in that assessment, but late coming to it. Consumer tastes had long-since changed radically and the well-off wanted expensive brands they could wear, such as clothes and accessories. In tackling this issue, though, he faced another problem: his chairman seemed as much in love with the style of traditional products as with the brand itself, even if he was forced to reduce product lines, mainly at the insistence of the banks.

Regardless of personal preferences, O'Reilly and Waterford Wedgwood had to face up to the fact that there was no point producing volumes of goods that nobody wanted to buy and that took up space in a warehouse. If crystal was a problem sector – and the likes of Baccarat was having it as bad as Waterford – the entire ceramics industry was in crisis. Massive over-capacity led to severe price competition and discounting of prices at a time when logic suggested production had to be pulled back until such time as the existing stocks were shifted.

If anything was to symbolise the way in which Waterford Wedgwood could turn every triumph into disaster, it came in 2004 courtesy of a horse and its rider.

On 27 August 2004, Cian O'Connor, a 24-year-old showjumper previously unheralded outside of the sport, won gold in showjumping for Ireland at the Olympic Games in Athens, riding a horse named *Waterford Crystal*, in recognition of its sponsor's role in its purchase. It was a major achievement, the first time an Irish rider and horse had won gold in equestrian sports and only the sixth Irish winner of any Olympic gold since the establishment of the State in 1922. It was also the highlight of what was otherwise a very disappointing Olympic Games for Ireland – O'Connor's winning round was shown in full on RTÉ television nine times on the day of his victory. The pictures of O'Connor receiving his gold medal, with tears of joy streaming down his face while he sang the Irish national anthem, made him famous.

Within seven weeks O'Connor suffered the infamy of being told that his medal would have to be returned and his achievement deleted from the record books because the horse failed a drugs test – assuming, of course, that the second test of samples confirmed the original finding. As if that wasn't bad enough, things were made worse when the required 'B' samples of the horse's urine and blood went missing during the appeals process, in a most extraordinary fashion, creating an enormous controversy and frenzied speculation as to what had happened and why.

O'Connor's success – and the consequent scandal – meant that many people wanted to know who he was and how he did it, at such a young age. The general public soon learnt what had been well-known in equestrian circles – and what had been the subject of much envy as the young man set up his own stables and bought some good horses: Tony O'Reilly was his godfather.

O'Reilly had taken a remarkably detailed interest in his godson's activities, providing finance for the establishment of his Karlswood stables near Ashbourne, in County Meath, as soon as the boy had completed his Leaving Certificate (final second-level exams). This was a considerable boost to O'Connor's ambitions, but it left him open to many envious comments from rivals in the sport who could only dream of such patronage.

It was noted that O'Connor's grandfather was the former Irish rugby captain Karl Mullen – a good friend of O'Reilly's since the latter was a student at UCD – and that O'Connor's mother, Louise, was a regular guest at many of the functions that O'Reilly hosted. 'When he was young, Tony would do anything for Cian, so it's quite natural that they would develop a relationship,' explained Mullen, in the days after the medal was won. 'Tony would be just as thrilled as I would be at Cian's success.' After the win, O'Reilly said: 'All I can say is that it is a great day for Cian, for Ireland and everyone involved.'

O'Connor first became interested in horses after going on hunts with his father, Tadhg. He separated from Louise in the late 1980s and O'Connor increasingly looked to O'Reilly for mentoring. O'Connor, at 14 years of age, decided that he wanted to be a showjumper, even though it was an expensive sport. He wrote a business plan for his godfather and O'Reilly increased his investment as O'Connor became more successful, but only after he had completed his school exams. O'Connor's ambition, even at a young age, was notable: his first horse transporter bore the inscription 'working towards the summer Olympics 2004'. But O'Connor would get irritated by the suggestion that his rise was all down to the patronage of O'Reilly.

His self-confidence was regarded as arrogance by many and his swift rise to the top was not greeted with the same acclaim as accompanied his godfather's rise in rugby. He also found that there was not universal appreciation within his sport for his Olympic achievement and a considerable amount of schadenfreude expressed when the International Equestrian Federation (FEI) announced that a sample taken from *Waterford Crystal* had 'proved positive for prohibited substances'. O'Connor insisted he had won fairly, and that his horse had 'not been given anything that would make him jump better'.

In order to retain his medal, the so-called B samples of urine and blood would have to be clear of the banned substances – although the likelihood that they wouldn't, based on experiences across a range of sports, was exceptionally slim. The A samples had been analysed in Paris and the FEI's plan now was to send the B samples from Paris to a laboratory in Hong Kong. O'Connor requested that they be sent instead, 'for financial and geographical reasons', to be tested in Newmarket, England.

On 20 October an order was made to DHL Couriers to send the B sample in a sealed package to Newmarket. Then there came a second call, by someone with knowledge of the 10-digit confidential customer code, to request it be rerouted. There was nobody to collect it at the new, rerouted address, so the DHL courier went to the originally nominated testing lab at Newmarket. Somebody met the courier at the security barrier and signed for the package, which was never seen again.

The disappearance of the B sample meant that O'Connor's guilt or innocence could not be proven conclusively. Some people might have thought this would help him to retain his medal, but it wouldn't; while nobody could now conclusively call him a cheat, by the same token he would never be able to shake off the stigma of what remained unproved either way.

To further complicate things, there seemed to have been a break-in at the Kildare HQ of the Irish equestrian organisation and a FEI file – this time concerning a separate doping conviction for a horse ridden in competition by O'Connor at an event in May – was stolen and pages from it faxed to the RTÉ newsroom. That earlier incident involved the same banned substances – including one to treat schizophrenia in humans but not to be used on horses. There were serious questions as to who would have done that, given that it seemed designed to further damage O'Connor's credibility.

The matter ended almost as seriously for O'Connor as it could have. In April 2005 the FEI came to a final decision: he was to be disqualified from competition for six months, as the substances found in *Waterford Crystal* constituted 'serious attempts to influence the performance of the horse by medication'. O'Connor had not tried to deny the presence of prohibited substances in the samples taken from *Waterford Crystal*, but the FEI's judicial committee decided that it was 'satisfied that the PR [person responsible] has established that he was not involved in 'a deliberate attempt to affect the performance of the horse'. Remarkably, it had rejected the convictions of its own veterinary department and accepted the arguments made on O'Connor's behalf by Professor Tom Tobin from the University of Kentucky, USA.

O'Reilly stayed steadfastly by O'Connor's side throughout this episode.

As all of this controversy was unfolding, O'Reilly had to arrange new bankers for Waterford Wedgwood. In October 2004 the company disclosed that it had arranged new borrowing facilities with the British subsidiary of the US group Wachovia. The interest terms seemed expensive, reflecting downgrades by credit rating agencies Standard & Poor's and Moody's. Waterford Wedgwood announced that the money would be used to provide new working facilities and to repay existing debt. But, incredibly, the company also revealed that it was in negotiations to buy the remainder of Royal Doulton, of which it already owned 21.6% of the shares, for cash. This was done despite having to make a €16.2 million accounting write-off against the shareholding in the 2002 accounts, to acknowledge that it had overpaid for the assets.

It is not hindsight to say that Royal Doulton seemed an odd acquisition; many critics said it at the time. It specialised in tableware and 'collectables', the type of ceramic figures that featured prominently in weekend newspaper supplement advertisements, and which appealed mainly to an older, more conservative audience. There was no question of O'Reilly being anything other than sincere when he announced that 'the possible acquisition of Royal Doulton would transform Wedgwood. The benefits of such a deal are immediately apparent. With Royal Doulton's restructuring largely completed, we could add Royal Doulton's revenues to our top-line sales without greatly increasing our costs. This would increase the profitability of the combined businesses.' He said that he expected to integrate Royal Doulton with 'minimal disruption' and that its introduction to the mix would lay down the foundation for improved profitability.

Given that Royal Doulton had already moved the bulk of its manufacturing to Asia, the idea of synergies seemed a bit stretched. Waterford Wedgwood thought it could close Royal Doulton plants and move remaining production to under-utilised Wedgwood plants, bringing the acquired company's revenues to its own bottom-line. 'Royal Doulton was purchased for the fine bone china manufacturing facility it had in Indonesia,' explained O'Donoghue later. 'It was impossible to find something else as good as it to which to outsource production.' Waterford Wedgwood's many critics saw the purchase as merely increasing the company's exposure to a contracting industry.

Having used the All-Clad proceeds to repay debt, Waterford Wedgwood had to find money elsewhere to pay for this latest initiative, which would cost €47 million in payments to Royal Doulton share-holders and another €20 million in restructuring costs, with yet more needed for working capital. There was to be another issue of shares. Every shareholder would be given the right to purchase five shares for every three already held, at 6 cent per share, which was less than half the existing share price. The intention was to raise €100 million and O'Reilly and Goulandris promised, or underwrote, to buy any shares existing investors passed on buying. Cuttingly, *The Sunday Times* remarked that the 'strategy is being driven by personal pride as much as business logic'.

It wasn't as if the company had good news about its ongoing performance with which to entice investors. Sales were down another 5% despite improving consumer spending, and the small profit of €8.9 million was due only to a once-off gain of €103 million on the sale of All-Clad. 'While trading performance in the six months to September 30th was behind last year, we are confident that planned marketing initiatives and the previously announced cost-saving measures will lead to a reversal of this trend,' O'Donoghue said.

There was another distracting issue hanging over the company too, although compared to the company's financial woes it appeared minor to O'Reilly. Just at it had at Heinz, and as it would at INM, O'Reilly's habit of stuffing his board of directors with family and friends became an issue. Institutional Shareholder Services (ISS), a company that acted as a shareholder activist, conducted a survey of 1,785 non-American companies for *Businessweek* magazine and it was published in early 2004. Waterford Wedgwood scored the worst among the companies surveyed in Ireland.

In its commentary, ISS had a very long list of criticisms. It condemned the incestuous nature of its board and compensation committee; non-disclosure of term limits for directors; non-disclosure of the mandatory retirement age for directors; lack of public disclosure of board meetings to review its own performance; non-disclosure of a policy whereby the board regularly approved a succession plan for the appointment of a CEO; the non-disclosure of each director's attendance at board meetings; a dual-class capital structure with unequal voting rights; and the non-disclosure of a policy that limited the number of other boards directors could serve on. 'The board is controlled by a majority of insiders and affiliated outsiders,' ISS stated baldly.

At the time there were 21 members of the board, including O'Reilly, his wife, his brother-in-law and his son, Tony jnr. Although his son – by nature a diplomat – was raising more and more issues of concern, O'Reilly was not hearing from enough independent voices. With no one to challenge or question him, no one to rein him in, Waterford Wedgwood blundered on, towards its inevitable demise.

CHAPTER SEVEN

THE CASE FOR
THE INDEPENDENT

Just as O'Reilly loved all his children, he loved all his newspapers. And just as Susie was his favourite child – as he admitted once, somewhat unwisely, in a magazine interview and then cheerfully repeated regularly – *The Independent*, his British title, was favoured within his newspaper portfolio even if, like a naughty child, it sometimes tested his patience and cost him a lot of money.

O'Reilly did not have a significant commercial or investment presence in Britain other than *The Independent*, which was of doubtful value, and Wedgwood. He didn't have much reason to push a particular commercial and political agenda beyond the obvious that most proprietors shared. He wasn't like Murdoch, for example, with his vast television empire that his newspapers sought to promote, or an agenda to be a king-maker in the political process through the reach of his press titles.

The Independent did matter, however, small as it was. It had perceived prominence among the political classes and voters. Also, it served not just as his international 'calling card' but as the source of much copy in other INM titles throughout the world; the independent reputation of *The Independent* in London was paramount. In the 2001 INM annual report O'Reilly boasted that *The Independent* was 'the most editorially independent of any, I repeat any, broadsheet paper in the UK. *The Independent* is a paper for the young, affluent and upwardly mobile and the profile of our readers reflects this very clearly'.

All of that may have been true, but the problem was that it continued to lose money – lots of it – although the amounts were carefully masked, most especially once it was put into the same division of INM as the *Belfast Telegraph*. Critics kept telling him to close or sell, that he didn't have the financial resources to invest the amount needed to give it a bigger market share, not when INM was so highly indebted. It suffered by comparison with the resources of *The Times, The Daily Telegraph* and *The Guardian*, which could invest much more in editorial content and marketing. Murdoch had continued with the price war that continued to drain everybody's resources. But O'Reilly loved his paper. He loved its cachet and much of its content. He loved being known, not just in Britain but internationally, as the man who facilitated the paper's continued existence. It gave him profile and credibility in British society. If his work for Northern Ireland had been the reason for his knighthood, then his ownership of this paper was the factor that brought him to the attention of the Tony Blair-led Labour government. While *The Independent* was not perceived as soft on the Blair government, it was seen as fair. O'Reilly enjoyed the respect that earned him, particularly as his friendships with Peter Mandelson and Gordon Brown deepened. That was not to survive *The Independent*'s coverage of the British involvement in the invasion of Iraq in 2003, however.

There were two attention-grabbing initiatives at *The Independent* during the first decade of the twenty-first century that will go down in newspaper history – and for which O'Reilly deserves great credit for authorising. One was editorial: against his own prejudices, O'Reilly supported his editor in using the newspaper for a principled, if partial, stance against the British involvement in the Iraq war. The other was commercial: O'Reilly approved an initiative that was to limit the dramatic fall in the sale of quality newspapers, at least for a time.

The latter was a groundbreaking commercial decision made in 2003: he allowed *The Independent* to move to a tabloid format – or 'compact' as he and his lieutenants liked to emphasise – for commercial reasons, but it was nonetheless a brave step to take. There was snobbishness at the time about the format in which a newspaper was produced. Broadsheets bespoke quality, informed and excellent writing and notions of accuracy. Tabloids were grubby, a lesser thing, aimed at the lowest common denominator. The perception was that a newspaper audience would reject a quality newspaper produced in a smaller format. There might also be an issue with advertising revenue.

Some advertisers wouldn't want to pay the same full rate for a full-page ad, rejecting The Independent's argument that a full page was a full page to the reader and of the same value. But O'Reilly authorised taking the chance because full-page advertisements in the broadsheet made up only 6% of the total ad revenue. O'Reilly was also terrified that if the concept was a success, then Murdoch would try to kill The Independent by halving the price of The Times.

Bets were still hedged at the start, at O'Reilly's insistence: the first compact edition of The Independent was produced on 30 September 2003 and for a spell the newspaper was prepared and sold each day in two versions, both broadsheet and compact, for fear that a tabloid-only version would alienate existing readers and cause a loss in sales. It was distributed mainly within the M25 ring-round around London; readers outside London were only offered the broadsheet. There were substantial costs involved in this approach. Initially, the broadsheet was prepared as normal, then a separate lay-out team came in to fit the same content into the tabloid format, under instructions not to cut copy to a shorter size. It was a challenge to make the tabloid attractive while working under that constraint.

It soon became clear that the compact version, with its attractive design, was the preferred choice for more readers and it was felt, correctly, that broadsheet readers would transfer if the compact was their only choice. Fallon described the initial £5 million outlay in producing the compact as 'the best money we've ever spent ... The perception of The Indy has altered completely. We have gone from being the ailing Indy to being described as innovative, pioneering and bold'.

The paper was rewarded with an initial surge in sales, by about 20% or 30,000 a day, which lasted for a couple of years and gave it its highest market share in a decade. The gain was unheard of in the UK broadsheet market, where circulations had generally – with the exception of The Guardian – been eroding slowly but steadily. There were days when it sold almost as much as The Guardian did and the take-up in the advertising-friendly 15–44 age group soared and among women, too. But older people also liked it and research showed that commuters, in particular, found the smaller size more manageable. Within seven weeks the new look paper had reversed a market decline of seven years' duration.

It was only a matter of time before the broadsheet would be abandoned. Kelner and Fallon knew they were doing something right when Vinnie Doyle at the *Irish Independent*, who would have loved to have done something similar years earlier, copied them and, crucially, *The Times* did too. *The Guardian* invested heavily in new presses to produce a hybrid paper in Berliner format. Over 50 major broadsheet papers converted in the following years. Within two years *The Independent* had lifted its six-monthly average circulation to 257,721 in the first half of 2005, its highest figure since 1997, and its highest market share (11.7%) since April 1996.

The newspaper not only hit upon a format that captured the imagination of readers but also a way of doing things – and a cause – that captured the zeitgeist of the time. *The Independent* became the most outspoken and highly regarded, by those against the war at least, media opponent of the British involvement in the invasion of Iraq. As other papers became cheerleaders for the onslaught, *The Independent*, driven by the ferocious insights of Robert Fisk, in particular, and Patrick Cockburn – the former a part-time Dublin resident and regular guest at Castlemartin; the latter who had grown up in Cork as the son of legendary journalist Claude Cockburn – became a small but important counterbalance. As Rupert Murdoch's biographer, the acerbic media commentator Michael Wolff, put it: '*The Indy* fought a good anti-war as the most forthright opponent of the invasion of Iraq. It became a necessary paper for readers who wanted to read the case against Bush and Blair.'

It was to O'Reilly's enormous credit that he allowed Kelner his head as editor, much as it was to the frustration of the Blair government. Kelner liked to tell a story of a lunch in London, before the war in Iraq began, which was attended by his management, board members and Alastair Campbell, the British government's director of communications. 'At the time we were pretty well a lone voice in opposing the war, we had gone out on a limb about that. We had a big discussion with Alastair which was quite robust. At the end of the discussion he said: "Right, we have all had our say, who is against this war?" I put my hand up and I am proud to say that all the senior editorial people put their hands up. Then he said, "Who's for the war?" Tony O'Reilly, Lady O'Reilly, the chief executive and the managing director all put their hands up. I saw Alastair Campbell about a week later and he said if ever the independence of *The Independent* is under question you should relate that story because the only people who were against the editorial mind were the proprietor, the proprietor's wife and the senior management.'

As Michael Wolff noted in a 2005 feature for *Vanity Fair*, 'going tabloid—with big, bold, lacerating, crowd-pleasing, anti-war, anti-American, anti-Blair front pages—does for *The Independent* exactly what every worrywart (especially the ones at *The Guardian*) has said that the tabloid format would do: it makes everything louder, more simplistic, and appealing. What *The Independent* does by going tabloid, at least in *The Guardian* sense of things, is to depart from quality-newspaper ranks. What it becomes is something other than a newspaper (a "viewspaper" is Kelner's happy term; a "viewspaper" is Alan Rusbridger's disparaging term). But while *The Guardian* can see what's louche about the new *Independent*, what is not-of-our-journalism-class, it can't see what's irresistible. *The Independent* has become an alternative weekly gone daily—amusing, magaziny, purged of newspaper repetitiveness and earnestness (indeed with less news).'

One of the stand-out early front pages of the new look *Independent* came early in 2004 when the British government was in the throes of a major crisis provoked by the suicide of scientist Dr David Kelly. Dr Kelly's death came about in circumstances connected to mounting controversy about the reasons for Britain's decision to enter the war as an ally of the USA, the so-called availability of weapons of mass destruction to Iraq and the construction of a dossier that was 'sexed-up' to convince wavering British MPs of Saddam Hussein's threat to security. The bold editorial line at *The Independent* found its most dramatic expression on the morning of publication of the Hutton Report into these events. The top half of the front page, beneath the masthead, carried nothing except the single word: 'Whitewash?' Beneath, taking up the rest of the front page, was an editorial in bold type that lacerated Hutton's findings.

By coincidence, INM's International Advisory Board (IAB) was meeting in Cape Town under the chairmanship of Ben Bradlee, the legendary former *Washington Post* editor. He and others, former Canadian prime minister Brian Mulroney especially, and former British chancellor of the exchequer Kenneth Clarke, were not happy at this trenchant editorial line, believing it to be too firmly anti-Blair and too critical of Hutton.

Ironically, Blair's great confidant, the controversial former Northern Ireland secretary Peter Mandelson, who had been a house guest of O'Reilly's at Castlemartin, declined an invitation to attend, even before this particular front page had been published, writing that *The Independent* had in recent times 'sunk to a new intellectual low', a letter that was read in part to the meeting.

Yet O'Reilly went public with his support of that day's paper. '"Whitewash?" was a great cover,' he said. 'Nobody [on the IAB] agreed at that stage with the conclusion of "Whitewash?". Nevertheless, we decided that the editor has the absolute right to make that statement and we were not going to interfere.' It helped when the sales figures arrived from London. The IAB was to learn that 'Whitewash?' had provided the best-selling edition in the history of the newspaper.

In an interview with *The Daily Telegraph* in 2004, O'Reilly was asked if he ever interfered in the running of *The Independent*. 'OK, it's Kelner's paper in the sense that he represents the editorial side. But if he gets it consistently wrong, and circulation started to go down consistently, I mean every editor …' O'Reilly was acknowledging the reality that an editor's role was as much commercial as editorial. Kelner said that 'the days when an editor would come in to do the morning conference, dictate the editorial line, go to have lunch at the Garrick until half-past three and then come back, sign off the leaders and head off for dinner with a High Court judge are over. Editors these days are very commercially minded and marketing minded. I would regard part of what I do as a marketing function. The front page of our newspaper is a form of marketing, it is where marketing and journalism collide. My discussions with Tony O'Reilly would be about more commercial things.'

If Kelner and O'Reilly disagreed on politics, they were united in their goal of selling more newspapers. 'If we were making £50 million a year, we would still be under pressure to keep our costs down,' Kelner said. 'People who run huge businesses like Tony O'Reilly are not known for their wastefulness, that is why they are very successful. Costs are kept under very tight control and I would always argue for more money and he would always try to argue me out of it. That is the nature of the relationship. He would never say: "If you took this line you would sell more copies of the newspaper" or "If you supported the war you would sell more copies of the newspaper". I could not imagine a set of circumstances where that would take place. I wake up every morning and regard myself extremely fortunate that I do not have to work in that environment.'

Kelner testified subsequently to a House of Commons committee that 'I could tell you a hundred stories about the independence of *The Independent* and the fortunate position I am in *vis-à-vis* our ownership structure. All I need to say is that we are owned by a company whose chief executive owns 27% of that company and is effectively the proprietor. We are owned by someone who is broadly Euro-sceptic, supported the war in Iraq, and is a sort of reserved admirer of George Bush. For anyone who reads *The Independent* you will be able to understand that is not our editorial direction. He is fiercely proud of that fact.'

On a different day at the same Commons hearings, one of Kelner's predecessors, Andrew Marr, now the BBC's political editor, noted that 'proprietors are going to choose editors whose opinions are likely to chime with their own. Very few proprietors, who are losing, many of them, a great deal of money, in addition to the loss of money are going to want to see a paper coming out with issues they disagree with day by day. I had in my brief and inglorious time as an editor an enormously forgiving, relaxed and arm's length proprietor in Tony O'Reilly, but even then I was afraid of what he thought.'

Kelner survived for 13 years – with one brief interlude when he became managing director – because he enjoyed his job so much and believed in his paper so strongly, as much as the fact that he was damn good at what he did. He was also a larger-than-life character whose company O'Reilly greatly enjoyed and the feeling was mutual. He was not running a profitable newspaper – as O'Reilly would have preferred – but it had a reputation that reflected well on O'Reilly as the proprietor, one that satisfied his ego. But Kelner had to work with the same frustrations felt by nearly all editors in the O'Reilly empire. If there was to be a criticism of O'Reilly's stewardship of *The Independent*, and of all the other newspapers under his control, it was of under-investment, something to which he was sensitive but which was nonetheless accurate.

The problem for *The Independent*, however, was that once others copied it, the paper lost its edge of distinctiveness. The loss of public interest in the war against Iraq was another blow: it was hard to find other issues that suited the front page as readily to hold the public's attention. In 2006 the media columnist Roy Greenslade, who was well disposed towards O'Reilly and *The Independent,* wrote in *The Daily Telegraph* that *The Independent* and its Sunday sister had lost a further £10 million in 2005. 'With the exception of *The Daily Telegraph,* no serious morning paper makes money,' he wrote. He described the *Belfast Telegraph* operation as underwriting the losses at *The Independent* titles, having returned a £20 million profit, but that didn't take into account the cost to INM of the finance for buying the northern paper, which had to be paid out of profits. The initial fears about advertising transfer – that advertisers would not pay the same rates for a compact page as a broadsheet – had proven true: the ad rate for the compact had settled at about 70% of the broadsheet.

Greenslade reasoned correctly that 'The initial upward circulation surge has hit a brick wall. The audience for a leftish, liberal "viewspaper", as its editor, Simon Kelner, likes to call it, appears limited to fewer than 250,000.' If only it had stayed that high. O'Reilly continued to justify the mounting losses on the basis that it was building the brand for the entire group. Its editorial talents could be shared among many of the group's other titles worldwide, even if some editors didn't necessarily want to publish Fisk's copy on the Middle East, for example.

The history of newspapers showed that proprietors liked having a prestigious title in the portfolio, one that burnished their reputations by association, even if it lost large sums of money. It was what distinguished them from being widget-makers or, dare it be said, ketchup manufacturers.

Stephen Glover, one of *The Independent's* founders, was to write years later: 'I am still not starry-eyed about any proprietor, but Sir Tony has honoured the traditions of *The Independent,* and never interfered in its editorial line'. He also argued that it was not unusual for a newspaper group to have one prestigious, loss-making title, a loss leader so to speak. Murdoch had *The Times,* Associated paid for the consistently loss-making *Evening Standard* in London, *The Guardian* and *Observer* were heavy loss-makers for Guardian Media Group, paid for by other commercial ventures in the group. Glover said that 'owning *The Independent* is not primarily an affair of the heart. No doubt Sir Tony feels proud of it, but he would not keep supporting it without sound commercial reasons. That is why anyone who admires

The Independent, for all its imperfections, should be rooting for Sir Anthony O'Reilly. If *The Independent* had to have a proprietor – and history suggests that it did – it could have scarcely found a better one.'

ALL THE GOVERNMENT'S FAULT?

In February 2004 O'Reilly had to acknowledge one of the biggest failings in his commercial life in Ireland up until that date, one that made him very angry as he felt he most certainly was not to blame.

That month INM sold its shareholdings in Chorus (once Princes Holdings) to its joint venture partner, Liberty, for a nominal sum, just to escape from its mounting obligations. Liberty immediately headed for the High Court to seek protection under the examinership laws while it tried to find a way to deal with historic debts and be in a position to continue trading. It was a financial disaster: the second largest examinership in the history of the State, topped only by the original rescue of the Goodman Group of beef companies back in 1990. Mr Justice Peter Kelly was told that the company would be liquidated if an examiner was not appointed and that the estimated shortfall between assets and liabilities would be about €490 million.

Chorus owed about €220 million to 18 banks and further debts, including shareholder loans, brought the total up to €385 million. The company was unable to pay interest to its bankers or its liabilities to the Revenue Commissioners. It blamed the burden of making payments on businesses bought during the dotcom bubble that were now worth just a fraction of what it had paid for them. But Liberty, now 100% owner, was prepared to invest another €100 million in improving and extending digital TV and Internet services to the 200,000 customers and make payments in settlement to creditors. The deal got done. Later that year, Liberty abandoned the claim for damages against the State that had been lodged at O'Reilly's insistence many years earlier.

'I doubt if any business experience in Ireland made him more angry,' said one associate. His chairman's statement in the 2003 INM annual report, published in 2004 shortly after the examinership, pulled few punches. O'Reilly argued that Chorus:

… represents a case study in broken promises, over-regulation and a consistent inability to reflect that, if the government was serious in its attempt to ensure that broadband had universal application in Ireland then cable was going to be one of the major vehicles in achieving that end. That it has not and that it will not ever is a stinging indictment of the regulator and of the inaction of the government of the day in policing the law of the land. Their tolerance of pirate deflectors, which cut off vital revenue to Princes Holdings/Chorus and Cablelink/NTL may have bought temporary political popularity but the price was the long-term erosion of the economic viability of all cable companies. I might add that the principal competitor to the cable companies, BSkyB, was not price controlled at any time during this period.

Your company and its shareholders have written off its entire investment in this sorry episode.

This is a particular issue for State owned industry which still provides the bulk of essential economic services, such as energy and public transport. Too often, government objective has been to keep prices down for the public, while refusing to endorse the changes in costs and efficiency which would permit long-term improved services on a commercial basis. The result is inadequate investment which hides – but only for a time – the poor financial performance of the incumbent. The pursuit of temporary political popularity in this fashion will make Ireland, as a location for inward investment for use in Ireland, a hazardous place to be.

Analysts reckoned that the whole adventure had cost INM about €100 million. 'He would regularly say that "the worst place to be in Ireland was as an Irish private business because the government is against you. It's different if you are a multi-national or a state owned company". That is what he believed and told us regularly,' said one of his executives at Eircom who watched this unfold at the rival company. 'He warned regularly to "never fall into the trap of giving something to government in the expectation that it will give something back".'

Gavin returned to the entire saga in 2015, in an interview he gave to *The Sunday Business Post*. 'I know all the talk now is digital, but we were one of the first ISPs [Internet service providers] in Ireland, back in 1999. We had a really super cable business, which is now UPC. The capital appetite for that business was perhaps more aggressive than we would have liked. We should have stuck with it. There are certain things that if you could play them over again, you would. But hindsight is a luxury.'

It was a reasonable assessment about the loss of potential. However, INM was highly indebted at the time and originally O'Reilly had sought to sell the half share of Chorus to fund the *Belfast Telegraph* acquisition. That was the primary issue: O'Reilly's continued preference for print. He was reluctant to spend more money on Chorus, but he could have sold more equity in INM to provide funds had he seen the opportunity. The problem was that this would have diluted his own interests substantially, and that was not something he was prepared to do to fund any acquisition or investment.

O'Reilly's experience at Chorus was central to his appearance at the Moriarty Tribunal that year, which was investigating the circumstances of the award of the second mobile phone licence, in 1996, to Denis O'Brien. While Chorus itself was not linked to that, O'Reilly's interactions with the government during that time, which included the licence award, were coloured greatly by the Chorus debacle.

On 24 March former Taoiseach John Bruton gave evidence to the tribunal. He told it that he had met with O'Reilly at a social reception at a private house in West Cork in July 1996 and that, after a brief conversation, Bruton agreed to visit O'Reilly at his Glandore home the following day. Bruton gave evidence that O'Reilly listed four matters for discussion at that meeting and agreed with the suggestion that O'Reilly had come forward with 'gripes'. He reported that O'Reilly was 'very dissatisfied' with the failure of the Rainbow government to take action against the TV deflector operators, who continued to operate without a licence. Bruton said O'Reilly also expressed 'some unhappiness' at the manner in which the 1995 mobile phone licence competition had been run, but said that he wasn't looking for anything to be done about it. He said that O'Reilly brought up the issue of grant assistance for a Heinz manufacturing unit in County Louth and access difficulties for the Arcon mine at Galmoy in County Kilkenny.

Bruton said one of the reasons why he had been happy to meet O'Reilly was that he had hoped to persuade him to come to some arrangement with the deflector interests. O'Reilly, he said, was not interested in the proposal. He said that O'Reilly felt there had been a 'general under-appreciation of the contribution he would be able to make', referring to his investments in the country. In order to end the meeting on as amicable a note as possible, Bruton said he would have his special adviser, Sean Donlon, meet O'Reilly's nominees and he quickly asked Donlon to see if he could do anything for O'Reilly 'in the areas in which proper discretion could be exercised'. Bruton revealed he had received a letter from O'Reilly two days after the meeting. In it, references were made to Heinz, INM, Fitzwilton, Waterford Wedgwood, Arcon and a number of luxury hotels and their investments in Ireland.

The meeting between Donlon and O'Reilly's nominees did not take place until September 1996, at the INM offices at Hatch Street. The tribunal lawyers brought Bruton through what was described as the intended evidence of Donlon and Michael Lowry. Bruton was told that Donlon would say that his meeting with INM had been 'most difficult', that some 'very harsh' comments had been made about the government and individual ministers and that 'in spite of the relaxed mood I was left in no doubt about the newspapers' hostility to the government parties if outstanding issues were not resolved to their satisfaction'. Bruton's memory of what Donlon told him on return from that meeting was limited. He said he couldn't remember if he'd been told by Donlon that Lowry was a 'persona non-grata' with INM, or even if Donlon had reported back to him in this manner, but said he was 'well aware that these newspapers didn't love us particularly'. Bruton was told that Lowry would say that he had been told by Donlon that the INM executives had said the government would lose INM as friends if its 'demands' were not met. Bruton replied that he thought INM's view would be 'conveyed in a more subtle way' but that such a message being conveyed to the government by INM would not surprise him. When Bruton was told that Lowry would say that Donlon had told ministers that he was concerned that the government was being 'held over a political barrel', Bruton said he had no recollection of that being said.

He did say, however, that it could be taken that INM had threatened him and his government and that subsequent to these events the newspapers it controlled did punish him and his government with negative coverage because it had failed to satisfy O'Reilly's commercial demands. He said the infamous *Irish Independent* front-page editorial at the subsequent general election urged 'people not to vote for a government that had succeeded in getting a 9 per cent annual growth rate during its term of office'. It indicated a 'certain perversity of political opinion,' he said.

Bruton was followed in his evidence by Donlon, the former senior civil servant turned GPA executive who had returned to politics as a special adviser to Bruton. Donlon had not been present at O'Reilly's meeting with Bruton in Glandore, yet he said O'Reilly's complaint in relation to the licence competition was that he hadn't won. 'Complaint may be putting it too strongly,' Donlon conceded during his evidence. 'Disappointment might be more appropriate. He knows he didn't have any right to win the competition.' Donlon said O'Reilly's career had its origins in State companies, and he was very aware of how processes here worked. It wasn't as if O'Reilly was 'a US tycoon coming into Ireland who doesn't know how it operates'. He conceded that while O'Reilly was unhappy with how he was treated, it wasn't a case of 'I scored that try back in whatever and I should have got the licence'.

This all meant that the stakes were very high for O'Reilly when he followed Bruton into the witness box a week later. It was 31 March 2004, and O'Reilly's became the latest name to be added to the extensive cast of prominent politicians, bountiful businessmen and cagey civil servants who had been required to present evidence and face cross-examination at an Oireachtas-appointed tribunal of inquiry investigating alleged corruption. O'Reilly had considerable reason to be anxious: he was going into direct conflict with evidence given by a former Taoiseach of the country about a major issue of significant public interest. Even if O'Reilly knew that he was not facing any allegations of financial wrong-doing and was to be examined on a previously submitted written statement, there remained the potential to be embarrassed by hard or unexpected questions. Serious questions about his use and abuse of his commercial power had been asked, and allegations about improperly pressurising a government had been made. As a result, there was bound to be detailed analysis of his answers in the media, some of which was not loyal to him, some even potentially hostile.

For some, appearing at either the Moriarty or Flood (later known as Mahon) tribunals had been a relatively innocuous experience: they simply recounted facts about events in which they were involved or told what they knew about other people's activities. They performed, were offered thanks for their time and effort, and left. For others, the experience was far more difficult: they had done things that were not easily explained, or that were quite clearly wrong, even if they dutifully denied this; or they were probed at length for flaws in their carefully constructed stories, sometimes unravelling with catastrophic con-sequences. It was a minefield, and it had the potential to ruin reputations.

This was not the type of attention or stage O'Reilly sought or enjoyed. For all of the well-wishers who offered encouragement, there were others who wanted to see him beaten down, just as there had been during his rugby career 50 years ago. It had the potential to be a highly noted and public corporate 'walk of shame'. O'Reilly's previous criticisms about the prurience of the tribunal system, uttered before it had ensnared O'Brien, came to mind.

O'Reilly prepared carefully, just as he did for all of the shareholder general meetings he had chaired, for all of those speeches he had delivered during his glittering career. In those instances, however, he was in control: nobody ever heckled a speech and it was rare that a disgruntled shareholder questioned him. On those rare occasions when he was confronted by publicly spoken investor opposition, he had the wit to deliver the politely or humorously chosen retort or, alternatively, the power to deliver a devastating put-down. Here at the tribunal, however, he had to follow a procedure that somebody else had set down and show deference to the tribunal chair. He consulted with his solicitors and barristers and accepted their advice that this was not the venue for jokes or haughtiness or overt confrontation. He had to be respectful and answer questions directly, without deviating into lectures or speeches. He had to stick to his previously submitted statement and resist from expanding upon it. He had none of the protection normally afforded by the presence of PR advisers and other handlers – Jim Milton's role being restricted to dealing with press queries afterwards and shepherding O'Reilly to his car in the Dublin Castle courtyard, past the press. He did have the protection afforded to him by his lawyers – in particular Paul Gallagher, possibly the most highly regarded senior counsel working in the courts at the time – and also, as he saw it, by the facts.

O'Reilly had always said that facts were friendly. His personal finances were not in question and, crucially, the Moriarty Tribunal was not raising accusations of giving money to any politician in circumstances that required explanation. There would be a conflict with Lowry's evidence, but he was confident of winning that exchange. Whatever some people felt about O'Reilly, there had been greater condemnation of Lowry's behaviour. There had been a roll-call of revelations about Lowry that meant many had made up their minds about him in advance of any tribunal report.

O'Reilly spent just two hours in the witness box that day. He was taken through his interactions with Lowry, with Fine Gael and his editorial control of INM by the tribunal's senior counsel, John Coughlan. Much attention was paid to the date of his first meeting with Lowry. Coughlan referred to Lowry's statement of intended evidence and his claim about meeting O'Reilly at a horse-racing event at the Curragh in June 2005. O'Reilly denied this, believing that meeting to have taken place in June 2006 and said that their first encounter was at the opening of the Arcon Galmoy mine in County Kilkenny in September 1995.

O'Reilly gave evidence that on walking with Lowry to the tent where they and hundreds of invited guests were to have lunch, Lowry remarked to him, 'Your fellas didn't do too well yesterday'. O'Reilly said he didn't understand what Lowry meant. 'It was such a strange turn of speech to me because I wasn't aware of who these "fellas" were.' He said that Lowry explained that he was referring to the oral presentation made to his department by representatives of O'Reilly's bidding consortium for available mobile phone licences. The significance of this, and what interested Coughlan, was the suggestion that Lowry had an unauthorised and improper access to the ongoing competition.

O'Reilly gave evidence that he was not aware at that time of the rules of the competition. Coughlan then asked O'Reilly if he was 'motivated by malice towards Mr Lowry' and if he had 'made up' the alleged Galmoy conversation to cause difficulty for Lowry in his dealings with the tribunal. O'Reilly replied that he had 'no malice towards Mr Lowry and certainly not in relation to this matter. The question of malice would not come into it.'*

O'Reilly also denied that he had met with Lowry in his corporate box at the Curragh Races on Derby Day July 1995 and that he had told Lowry that he had 'expected' to win the mobile phone licence; he believed the meeting occurred the following year, on 30 June 1996. 'In any event, Mr Lowry had seriously misrepresented what took place,' O'Reilly told the tribunal. He said he never informed Lowry that he expected his consortium would be successful in its application for the licence. He said he was 'taken aback' when he was informed that Lowry was making these 'unfounded allegations' against him and could only conclude that he was doing so with a view to causing him as much damage as possible.

O'Reilly was also asked about the meeting at his Glandore home in 1996 with then Taoiseach John Bruton and what had flowed from that. He said his recollection was that he had not mentioned the mobile phone licence competition and that Bruton had sounded 'tentative' in his evidence on the meeting while his own recollection was 'very clear'. He said he considered the matter of the licence closed once the result was announced on 25 October 1995 and he disclosed how a few days later he had written his note to O'Brien, congratulating him on winning the competition. He had not discussed the result with the then US ambassador Jean Kennedy Smith, as had been implied. This was believable to those who knew that his relationship with her

---

Author's note:

I met with both Lowry and O'Reilly at Galmoy that day in September 1995. I spoke to Lowry first and listened while he complained bitterly about the attention another Irish Independent *reporter Sam Smyth and I had been paying to various controversies in which he had become involved. I later spoke with O'Reilly, who was clearly furious despite the excitement of the official Arcon opening. He told me during an off-the-record conversation that Lowry had made the comment to him about the AT&T presentation not having gone well. O'Reilly elaborated that he had no idea how the meeting had gone but that the idea that his partners AT&T, as one of the biggest telecoms companies in the world, had made a poor presentation was unbelievable to him. Lowry continued to deny making the comment.*

brother, Ted Kennedy, had suffered after a friend the American had brought with him unexpectedly to Castlemartin had left a tap running and caused extensive flood damage to one of the rooms.

Coughlan brought O'Reilly through Donlon's evidence about the meeting with INM executives when he had been left in 'no doubt' as to the 'hostility' of INM towards the government. O'Reilly said that use of the word 'hostility' might have been slightly 'pejorative'. Much was made of the statement at that meeting that the government would lose INM as friends, which was taken by the government to be a threat. 'I think it is absolutely, unequivocally clear, that this particular use of the word *friends* related specifically to losing us as friends in this debate internally within our consortium [PHL], to stop them [the US shareholders] from taking the State to law, and allowing us to exhaust all the various means that we could to remedy the deflector crisis,' responded O'Reilly. He explained that the US shareholders had been 'seething with us as well as with the government, at the amount of money they were losing in Ireland'. He was 'absolutely unequivocal' that the reference to the government losing INM as friends was a reference to potential litigation as against editorial content.

When Coughlan said the infamous front-page editorial in the 1997 general election could be described as 'interventionist', O'Reilly said such a description could only be assigned to it by 'enemies'. 'The general view, I would say, about Independent News & Media, is that governments always feel they are being maligned by it, whatever government, and opposition feel that they are being ignored,' he said. He agreed that the editorial was 'unusual', but said he had no input into it. 'Absolutely none, nor do I interfere in the editorial process whatsoever in the INM group throughout the world.' He said he did not cause the editorial to come into being and 'nor did I know that it was going on the front page'. He insisted the board of INM did not interfere in the editorial policy of INM titles. 'That can be ascertained by direct contact with any of the editors in the group,' he told the tribunal barrister. He insisted the Rainbow coalition was not given hostile coverage in INM titles as a result of commercial disputes. Indeed, he pointed out that Fine Gael actually increased its vote in the 1997 election. 'It could be that the front-page editorial helped them,' he claimed.

One person who was not slow to voice his displeasure at O'Reilly's evidence was the former chairman of the Competition Authority,

Patrick Lyons, the man who had overseen the interim report of the study into the newspaper industry back in 1995. He wrote to *The Irish Times*, and had his letter published, condemning O'Reilly's comments to the tribunal about that report and seeking to 'set the record straight'. He denied that his Authority had been 'rude' to representatives of INM, as O'Reilly had alleged, or that its conduct had been 'frankly disgraceful', as again claimed by O'Reilly. 'If the Authority had not behaved with total courtesy and fairness during several days of meetings with Independent Newspapers, there would have been objections from the representatives and from their solicitor and counsel, who were present at all times. There were no such objections,' complained Lyons. 'I strongly object to the claim that the Authority "gave the clear impression that they had made up their minds before the arguments had even been heard". The Authority had come to no prior conclusions in this matter. It questioned and carefully listened to the points made by many representatives of organisations, and it held many lengthy internal discussions before reaching its conclusions.' Lyons concluded his letter by noting that 'nine years after the Authority's report, the "long-term efforts of Rupert Murdoch and his lieutenants in Ireland from simply taking over the Irish media scene …", the doomsday scenario forecast by Dr O'Reilly in 1996, has not taken place'.

If O'Reilly still had to wait for a finding from Moriarty – and it would not come until 2011 – he had to wait for the Planning Tribunal to even hold a public hearing about issues pertaining to him – if, indeed, it was to have one. That was the last thing O'Reilly wanted. The issues mentioned briefly at the Moriarty hearing – O'Reilly's alleged antipathy to the Rainbow coalition government because of its failure to regulate television signal distribution according to the law – would have been expanded upon, but going back further into the origins of the original securing of the licence and that controversial and not easily explained Rennicks' payment to Ray Burke. This was the material the Planning Tribunal wanted to cover, and it could have been catastrophic.

Not surprisingly, O'Reilly's strong preference was for this issue, with its potential for great embarrassment and perhaps even more, to go away. He wasn't interested in a hearing to clear any lingering suspicion. He just wanted it out of sight and out of mind.

Fitzwilton heard nothing from the Planning Tribunal between April 2000 and January 2003. O'Reilly presumed from that silence that all of the previously supplied written explanations had passed muster, that the tribunal accepted that the £30,000 payment was meant for Fianna Fáil and that it had been unaware that Burke had pocketed a chunk of it.

Then, to his horror, the tribunal wrote to Fitzwilton in February 2003, informing it that it was considering making further orders of discovery on the matter. Cue further written legal submissions from Fitzwilton, in which it contended a public inquiry into the political contribution was not warranted. Meanwhile, the Criminal Assets Bureau (CAB) began asking questions, not because of an investigation into O'Reilly or Fitzwilton but because of charges on other tax matters that had been proffered against Burke in the courts.

Meanwhile, the government had become frustrated with the slow pace at which the tribunal's work was apparently being done. In 2004 the tribunal reported to the Oireachtas that it might take up to 2015 for it to complete its investigations into all the matters it had put on its to-do list. The government prompted an Oireachtas response that this was too long and that it should limit its workload. It didn't define what the tribunal should prioritise, but officials were given a 1 May 2005 deadline for identifying what would be brought to public hearing. It said that the tribunal must list the specific matters that were to proceed to a conclusion. The tribunal was told to record these decisions formally and 'duly notify' the parties concerned.

The tribunal waited until almost the last moment to make its decision. The list of what it would investigate was not finalised until 28 April 2005, just two days ahead of the deadline, and the 'Fitzwilton-MMDS-Payment to Ray Burke by Rennicks' was included, although the list was not made public. The way the intended investigation was titled, with the clear linkages it implied, angered O'Reilly when he subsequently became aware of it.

The tribunal was a little too clever in the official wording of its decision, however. It declared that it 'may decide to continue its inquiries and/or to proceed to public hearing in respect of one or more issues which are currently part of a matter designated and listed herein'. It was intended as a get-out clause for the tribunal if it didn't gather enough evidence to proceed with a particular module; inadvertently, it would blow up the future of the tribunal – although this was not to become clear for a while yet.

In mid-July 2005, Fitzwilton received a letter informing it that the tribunal was to hold a public hearing into the Rennicks payment. This was later described in court as 'a bombshell'. Although lawyers can be given to hyperbole, this was not an inaccurate description of the effect of the letter upon O'Reilly.

The time had come for Fitzwilton to fight by way of the legal process. O'Reilly's lawyers sought a copy of the record of the tribunal's decision that public hearings would start in September. The copy furnished revealed that the previous April, the tribunal had not recorded in writing a formal decision that the Fitzwilton matter 'shall be proceeding to a public hearing'. As far as O'Reilly's lawyers were concerned, this did not comply with the mandatory requirements of the amended terms of reference, and that provided the grounds for legal challenge.

Fitzwilton got to the High Court in September 2005, with barrister John Gordon representing the company and, by implication, O'Reilly. First, it sought an injunction preventing the public hearing going ahead in advance of adjudication on the point of law it was raising. Gordon complained that Fitzwilton had been deeply frustrated for seven years by the tribunal, which he said had investigated the matter twice and then dropped it. Then, he alleged, 'out of the blue', in July, it had decided to pick it up again 'for its own purposes'. He said that the 28 April document effectively subverted that resolution by drawing up a list that apparently contained an enormous amount of material – 47 separate matters – in which Fitzwilton had featured as one line, but not as a definite subject for inquiry.

Fitzwilton was granted its injunction, but the High Court reserved judgment as to whether it would allow the Planning Tribunal continue with its full hearing. For this most significant decision, O'Reilly would have to wait.

CHAPTER NINE

RINGING MORE CHANGES AT EIRCOM

E ircom's return to the stock market, confirmed in February 2004 by way of an initial public offering (IPO), was met with some scepticism, indeed even cynicism. The shares were not offered to the general public but to pension funds, insurance companies and other sizeable professional investors; it was not anticipated that there would be much demand among the general public, given the losses so many investors had incurred in the 1999 IPO. Things were made worse by the revelation of how much money exiting investors would make from Eircom rejoining the stock market, on top of the super-dividend they had pulled out of the company already.

The plan was that the company would raise money for its own use by way of a 'primary issue' of new shares, raising about €300 million – of which €85 million came from the ESOT as part of its way of increasing its shareholding in Eircom. Of this 'new money', about €200 million would be used to reduce borrowings, with the balance being used to pay the enormous fees demanded by the banks, advisers and stockbrokers involved in the endeavour.

However, Valentia announced that it would simultaneously hold a 'secondary offering': the sale by existing investors, other than the ESOT, of their shares. O'Reilly sold his entire 5.6% stake in the company, bringing his estimated total potential profit from his two-year involvement in Eircom to more than €58 million, once the previous year's dividend had been included. Providence Equity Partners brought its entire profit to an estimated €405 million. The rumour mill suggested that John Hahn made €50 million personally from his share. Soros Private Equity made about €170 million.

The Valentia shareholders, despite their massive profits, were a little disappointed that the new market value of the company, at around €1.15 billion, was at the lower end of initial expectations. Eircom had made a net loss of €72 million in the nine months to the end of 2003. Valentia went to potential new shareholders with a story that it had strong and steady cash-flows, had not taken one of the 3G licences that had saddled many other telcos with overbearing liabilities, and continued to have a dominant position in Ireland's fixed-line market. Potential investors were told that the company would pay dividends each year worth half of the cash left in its coffers after paying its tax bill, the interest and repayments on its debts, and also after spending around €200 million on capital investment. It projected the dividend yield to be about 6% annually. Eircom was to remain highly indebted, at €2.2 billion, after the exercise but this was a period when everyone had fooled themselves that this didn't matter because interest rates were so low.

Valentia was no more: it changed its name to Eircom Group plc. Somewhat surprisingly to some, given that he had no further economic interest in Eircom's shares, O'Reilly decided to stay as part-time chairman on an annual fee of €130,000. He had fallen in love with the company. His emphasis as chairman from 2004 onwards was on broadband deployment, regulatory reform and re-entry to mobile, all of which became running themes over the three annual reports issued to the public during his term as chairman.

Eircom management was surprised by how much importance he attached to the annual report and to his chairman's statement as a document for historical purpose and by how much care he put into its preparation. 'He always wanted things on the record, keeping detailed notes of conversations and decisions,' said David McRedmond, the company's commercial director. 'He had an enormous interest in history and spent a lot of time on deciding the precise wording of his chairman's statement, providing what he saw as an accurate record that could be referred to in the future as telling it as it was.'

O'Reilly's Eircom statements contained the usual mix that shareholders in his other companies had become used to reading: personal stories were interspersed with praise for management, self-justification that verged on boasting, the constant optimism, statements that verged on hyperbole, exhortations about the future and carefully modulated slap-downs of his critics.

He was not in the least bit embarrassed by the massive profits he had made from Eircom. Indeed, his friends suggest he revelled in it. 'At the time I was the chairman of and investor in Valentia, I was constantly reminded that, in the words of one analyst, we had paid too much for Eircom after an "overheated bidding process". I was confident that we had recognised Eircom's underlying value,' O'Reilly said.

He had an ideological point to make, too, alongside a rebuke for those who criticised the company's behaviour: 'As someone who worked for State enterprises for most of the 1960s, I have felt especially privileged over the last three years to witness the transformation of Eircom from former state monopoly into a vibrant commercial business at the centre of the Irish economy. I particularly want to celebrate that transformation because Eircom's public image, tarnished by its previous experience as a public company, has not yet caught up with its performance.'

He defended the company for allegations of price gouging and insisted it was doing all it could to increase broadband take-up. 'The price of the average telephone bill has continued to reduce in real terms each year. The average Irish phone bill is below the European average. Our market is among the most liberalised in Europe. We have led the drive to connect the country to the digital world so that broadband is now being rolled-out nationally, and the take-up rate is impressive.' He claimed that 'Eircom has built 'Broadband Ireland' because connecting people is our business and is a key platform for national growth.' He boasted that Internet usage was higher than in the UK and above the European average.

He complained bitterly that Eircom was fully regulated while competitors, both fixed and mobile, 'unbelievably' were not, despite the Commission for Communications Regulation (Comreg) describing the main mobile operators as having significant market power. 'Eircom is forced to sell access to its networks to other operators below cost. Imagine if brewers or builders or bakers were forced to sell at less than the cost of production to encourage other companies "to develop competition", he complained. He said that the restricted rate of return allowed to Eircom 'does not recognise the reality of the investment required to improve a core telecoms network. And the regulator assumes a valuation of the network that bears no relations to its replacement cost ... one-sided regulation does not work and does not encourage investment.'

His overall message for Eircom employees and shareholders was that 'costs must continue to be reduced. Regulation must be reformed to encourage investment in the networks; broadband take-up accelerated to strengthen our customer franchise; and a viable route negotiated back into mobile.' There was the line familiar to those involved in other companies: he exhorted workers and management 'to do the common things uncommonly well'.

McRedmond believes that more was achieved to the benefit of Eircom during the Valentia period, in the private equity days, than subsequently. Fintan O'Toole, writing in *The Irish Times* in November 2004, remembered how, as a State company in 1997, Eircom had recorded profits of £197 million. 'As a private company owned by Wall Street venture capitalists, it reported losses of €233 million in 2002, €40 million in 2003 and €103 million in the year to last March. If it were still a State company and these kinds of figures were being published, the chorus of demands for the privatisation of Eircom would be deafening. We would be told that private-sector initiative, efficiency and vigour were the solution. Since it is already private, however, there is a curious silence,' proclaimed O'Toole.

Eircom lost €71 million during the 2005 financial year, its first full year back in public ownership, but that did not stop O'Reilly describing the company as 'this great national enterprise'. Eircom was not just a company as far as O'Reilly was concerned. He identified its stock market return as putting it 'back to the heart of Ireland's economic life as the builder of the key infrastructure for the 21st century'. He boasted that Eircom had delivered for investors, but admitted it needed to do more for customers:

Now here is something that you have not heard often enough from Eircom: the customer is always right. When I discussed this theme recently with the eircom board I was reminded of the American business adage: rule #1 'the customer is always right'; rule #2 'if the customer is ever wrong, please refer back to rule #1'.

You can never do enough for customers. I have learnt that in a lifetime in business in which I have had the privilege of being associated with great brands, both in good times and bad. And what makes great brands and keeps them great is relentless concern for the customer and an intimate understanding of what they want.

He said management often pointed to a gap between the perception of the company and what it was actually delivering. 'I never tire of pointing out that our prices have fallen by 50% in real terms since 1997, an outstanding achievement in one of Europe's most high cost economies; our universal service obligation is delivered enthusi- astically in every corner and parish of the country; look, for instance, at Eircom's delivery of broadband, delivered despite the scepticism of our critics ... Broadband is now an imperative and in Ireland only Eircom is a ubiquitous provider.'

He said that those who had it were delighted with the service, but that those who didn't blamed Eircom:

Quoting the impressive speed of rollout and take-up is of little consolation to the customer who desperately wants this service. Eircom's task is clear, if difficult and costly to achieve. We believe everyone should have broadband and we are constantly striving to overcome barriers to near-100% availability.

It remains beyond comprehension why a cable into a house is unregulated, a mobile signal is unregulated, a satellite service is unregulated, but a copper wire is regulated to within an inch of its life. As competition increases and technology platforms converge, this situation is clearly a nonsense.

Our investors are rational and will go to wherever they can get the best rate of return. It is ironic that the main barrier to investment is the risk created not by the market but by the regulator ... The physician's motto "*primum non nocere*" (first, do no harm) should be carved above the regulator's door.

The irony of this subsequently, of course, is that much of the economic disaster that befell the country was blamed on light-touch regulation, albeit in the financial sector, during that same era. Most businesses want lighter regulation, it's just people like O'Reilly who are confident enough to loudly and regularly demand it.

It took O'Reilly longer to get Eircom back into the mobile market than he had hoped. A non-compete deal with Vodafone, signed at the time of the disastrous sale of the mobile phone arm Eircell, expired in March 2004. There was talk of Eircom buying the mobile phone company Meteor from the American group Western Wireless for as little as €150 million, but nothing happened. Eircom demurred, blaming poor coverage, a market share of less than 5% and significant network problems. Instead, it waited to see if the company would get sorted out.

Things moved quickly in 2005 when Western Wireless decided to sell. Eircom had competition if it wanted to buy. Smart Telecom was an aggressive competitor at the time, and had wealthy backers in O'Reilly's friend Lochlann Quinn and his Glen Dimplex partner Martin Naughton, and Brendan Murtagh, director of construction group Kingspan, as well as Richard Branson's Virgin Mobile. Pertinently, Denis O'Brien also showed a keen interest and had got US private equity firm Permira in as a partner. Western Wireless set up a sealed-bid auction.

Those hoping for another public battle between O'Reilly and O'Brien were to be disappointed. The nature of the sale process by a private entity meant there was no point in courting public opinion. There was no public denigration of each other. The existence of three bidders pushed up the price, however, and as the July deadline for offers neared, O'Brien decided that any price he would put in would be too expensive. If his objective had been to push up the price for Eircom, as some suspected, then he had succeeded. Eircom's need was probably greater than Smart's and it had the ability to return to shareholders for new money to finance any purchase. In July, Eircom won out and secured a deal for €420 million.

The price astonished many, even if they could see the logic in Eircom, with a declining fixed-line income, returning to mobile. Davy Stockbrokers called the deal 'expensive, absolutely and relatively' and other analysts concurred. The share price fell 11% on the day the deal was announced.

O'Reilly was shaken enough by the criticism to give an interview to *The Sunday Times* defending the price paid. 'I am amazed at that,' said O'Reilly. 'It is like an autonomic response, tap the knee of an analyst and they will say "overpaid".' He argued that the price was 'sensible' when compared to other Irish mobile phone acquisitions, although the critics had issues with how quickly Eircom would be able to grow the business to generate the profits that would recoup the investment. It would have been far worse, however, O'Reilly said, if Eircom had 'jumped in' blindly 18 months earlier. He boasted that 'we have the Ryanair of the pre-paid market, Meteor is the low-cost network', and promised aggressive pricing to win a bigger share of the post-paid contract market at the expense of O$_2$ and Vodafone, something that the analysts again would claim was easier said than done.

O'Reilly described Eircom as like a 'child reborn' with the Meteor acquisition. He maintained that 'without this deal, Eircom would be in that stockade called declining fixed-line market'. He emphasised his commitment to the company by buying shares in it again, although his €140,000 purchase of 75,000 shares was small beer by his standards. Had O'Reilly seen what was coming down the track, he might have been tempted to make an even bigger investment.

The Meteor acquisition, despite its apparently high price, made Eircom a more complete company and therefore a more attractive option for ownership. Now it was back in mobile, it could bid for one of the 3G mobile phone licences that was being sold by the State.

One of Europe's largest telcos emerged as a serious suitor: Swisscom. For those who bemoaned the Irish State's exit from telecoms provision, there was a strange irony at work here. Switzerland may have been regarded as a bastion of capitalism, but the State owned a majority stake in the company. Swisscom entered into negotiations and asked for permission to examine Eircom's books, based on it indicating its willingness to offer €2.40 per share. O'Reilly, his directors and Eircom's management were all highly impressed by the Swiss visitors and saw enormous potential for the Irish company under this new owner and its deep pockets.

And then things went wrong.

Eircom failed to win a 3G mobile phone licence. Instead, it went to Smart, a company that would go into examinership three years later because of the costs involved in trying to expand its business. Swisscom was spooked by this: the purchase of Meteor was what had attracted it to Eircom, but how much would that benefit be limited by the inability to compete with other operators on 3G? The Swiss government expressed misgivings, and suddenly the Swiss were gone – to O'Reilly's great disappointment and probably Ireland's great loss.

CHAPTER TEN

THE SOUND OF BREAKING GLASS: THE TRUTH ABOUT WATERFORD WEDGWOOD

Tony O'Reilly had no reason to think he would ever come into the line of sight, and fire, of Elliot Spitzer, the high-profile and combative New York attorney general who made a name for himself as the scourge of Wall Street, fearlessly targeting business corruption. Spitzer started 2005 by making a claim of perjury against one of O'Reilly's old friends and Heinz board colleagues James Zimmermann, and specifically Spitzer alleged that Zimmermann had lied about discussions he had held with O'Reilly. Importantly, he made no such accusation against O'Reilly.

Zimmermann had retired only a year previously as chairman of Federated Department Stores (FDS), a company that owned the famed Macy's and Bloomingdale's. Both stores were in bitter competition with the ever more popular, and downmarket, discounters that tried to undercut prices. One such discount outfit was Bed Bath & Beyond. In 2001 it decided to try to force its way into the bridal registry business – the process by which an engaged couple provides a list in a store and asks their wedding guests to select a gift from it. Its problem was getting the right kind of stock, including sets from the likes of Waterford Wedgwood and Lenox, providers of fine china and giftware.

Spitzer's claim was that FDS persuaded companies such as Waterford Wedgwood not to supply Bed Bath & Beyond. 'Companies are not allowed to enter agreements that prevent competitors from offering choices to consumers,' said Spitzer. He was alleging collusion.

Spitzer did not bring the case to trial. Instead, in 2004 he persuaded FDS, Waterford Wedgwood and Lenox to contribute to the costs of a $2.9 million settlement, without admitting liability, with the Irish company's share the smallest at $500,000. Waterford Wedgwood also agreed to supply Bed Bath & Beyond with its products.

The only outstanding problem was Zimmermann's evidence. In April 2004 an assistant attorney general travelled to Cincinatti and interviewed Zimmermann under oath. This interview included the question: 'So I gather you never said to him in words or substance that Waterford [Wedgwood] opening Bed Bath & Beyond would not be a good thing for the brand, fair?' Zimmermann's reported reply: 'That is correct.' Later in the same testimony, the assistant attorney general again pressed: 'You say you've never discussed Bed Bath & Beyond with Sir Anthony O'Reilly, right?' Zimmermann: 'That is correct.'

Zimmermann had joined the Heinz board only in 1998, when O'Reilly was still chairman but had stepped down as CEO. It would have been surprising if they had never discussed Waterford Wedgwood products and their sale in Zimmermann's stores, but that didn't mean there had been collusion in keeping product out of Bed Bath & Beyond. Waterford Wedgwood was genuinely worried about under-cutting its own margins if its premium products appeared on the shelves at discount stores.

When Zimmermann was arraigned, Spitzer's staff alleged they had evidence that a 'deal went down' between FDS and Waterford Wedgwood and that Zimmermann wasn't telling the truth about it – something he denied forcefully. Somehow, O'Reilly was spared having to attend, but O'Donoghue ended up giving seven minutes of evidence to the Grand Jury.

As ever, O'Donoghue tried to make a positive out of the situation in his public comments. He said the resolution of the Spitzer action and the decision to supply Bed Bath & Beyond was 'unconnected' and that 'I don't think we've gone down-market. This is simply a new channel for us. Well-heeled people shop in these stores.' He boasted that Waterford Wedgwood was now on 6,500 wedding lists in 35 Bed Bath

& Beyond stores. 'Macy's and Bloomingdale's are hugely important, but the consumer is king,' said O'Donoghue. 'We will go where our consumers want us.' He must have been concerned, given his boss's previously expressed fear that concentrating on Internet sales might alienate those outlets, but he began looking at the supply of Crate and Barrel, another well-known American superstore. The hope was that these outlets might attract a new, younger following, particularly for the company's more contemporary designs.

There were more concerns to field in the production end of Waterford Wedgwood, too. Early March 2005 brought the fifth warning in two years that profits would not meet investor expectations and also the shock departure of Paul D'Alton, the finance director, less than 12 months after he had taken the job and with the task of integrating Royal Doulton still incomplete. The share price fell to a new low of 3 cent, which meant that the new shares that investors had received in January were now worth one-third less than they had paid for them.

Sales for November and December 2004 were up a little on the previous year, but fell by 11% in the first two months of 2005. A gamble that consumers would accept a 5% increase in the price of Lismore crystal goblets, up to $68, did not appear to be working, which was not a surprise in a market in which all crystal sales were suffering; Lenox, its main competitor in the US market, had also suffered a fall in sales and had been put up for sale by its owner, the drinks company Jack Daniel's.

Standard & Poor's downgraded Waterford's junk-rated debt a further notch, citing 'liquidity concerns' and fears of a further deterioration in sales. O'Donoghue admitted that the sales fall 'was hard to explain', other than suggesting consumer sentiment was 'weak' about homeware purchases.

Waterford Wedgwood said it continued to have the support of its principal shareholders 'as it seeks to reduce the company's fixed cost base'. It admitted, though, that it was considering a third rights issue in a little more than 18 months, again to be underwritten by O'Reilly and Peter Goulandris. Despite the sale of All-Clad, borrowing had climbed again, to €320 million, and the company was not generating enough cash to meet a €25 million-plus annual interest bill. Working capital management remained a major issue, despite a reduction in product lines by two-thirds. The €100 million pension fund deficit was now attracting attention.

Details of the latest €100 million rights issue came in May, at a time when Waterford Wedgwood was valued at just €120 million on the stock market. The plan was to achieve cost savings of €90 million a year, reduce the headcount by 1,800 and close the plant at Dungarvan, County Waterford. Many thought it was merely a delay of the company's inevitable demise, despite spending on new technology in Irish and British factories that was now put at €325 million.

'Absolutely there is hope,' O'Donoghue said. 'We have the best brands in this sector in the world. If we can do no worse than hold sales at current levels and the dollar doesn't weaken, then there's a very good chance that we'll return this business to financial strength. It will be another dawn. We're not selling as much as we'd like to or as much as we used to, but we've still got sales of €800 million.'

This time investors who had bought rights at 20 cent per share in early 2004, followed by more at 6 cent in early 2005, were being asked to go again, at 6 cent per share. The shares were trading at less than 5 cent, however, the supposed minimum or face value of the shares. They were being asked to pay a premium for near junk. But if they didn't, they faced a 64% dilution in their existing holdings.

O'Donoghue said the latest fund-raising 'gives us the ammunition to get the business back to profit'. O'Reilly described this latest contraction as a 'bold but necessary restructuring programme'. While he regretted the job losses, he said that 'these changes are vital to ensure the long-term prosperity of this historic company and its key heritage plans in Ireland, England, and Germany as we face increasing competition from low-cost economies in Asia and elsewhere'.

The losses at Waterford Wedgwood were reaching levels far beyond anybody's expectations. At the pre-tax level, losses increased to €149.2 million in the 12 months to end March 2005, compared to €44.9 million in the previous 12 months. Investors were annoyed that stockbrokers, acting on guidance from the company, had not predicted such large losses. Product sales were continuing to fall, but O'Donoghue said they would grow in the second half of the year on the back of a couple of 'substantial contracts' that had recently been won. 'If sales were to be flat for the year, it would be a good outcome,' he said, and added that he would be 'sad' if the company was still making a loss the following year.

O'Reilly remained committed to the belief that the brand remained strong and got support for this contention from the results of market research carried out in the USA. The brand was indeed strong; it was the products that people didn't like, they didn't want crystal golf figurines and corporate paperweights. While the John Rocha designs were going out of favour in Europe, they had no impact whatsoever in the USA.

A decision was taken to find a well-known US designer to do for Waterford Crystal in the USA as Rocha had originally done for it in Europe. But the company was warned not to pin all of its hopes on a relationship with a fashion designer for fear that the resulting products would be seen as his/hers, rather than Waterford's. The brand value could be subsumed under the bigger brand of the designer, making Waterford Wedgwood look little more than an outsourced manufacturer for the more visible and important other brand. Wedgwood was enjoying some success with a tie-up with wedding dress designer Vera Wang, for example, but the Wedgwood branding on products was subsidiary to hers.

There were signs of divisions in the public comments from executives. Cameron said the company would outsource to eastern Europe and elsewhere an increasing amount of the 'more elaborate, labour-intensive pieces' of Waterford Crystal and Rosenthal products.

'I don't see further outsourcing as a huge answer to this,' said O'Donoghue. 'The challenge is filling our state-of-the-art factories. When the factories are full, we can make handsome profits.' A plan was put in place to return the manufacture of 2 million pieces of Royal Doulton china from Indonesia to a Wedgwood plant in Stoke-on-Trent.

In August 2005, O'Donoghue announced that he was to retire. O'Donoghue had been with the company since 1986 and had seen it all, but had been particularly unlucky to have overseen the business at the time of a collapse in value of the dollar as against the euro. Between 2002 and 2004 the dollar had deteriorated against the euro by 50%. He had overseen a business whose profit margins could be destroyed or inflated by currency fluctuations. While those things were outside of his control he, along with O'Reilly, had to take responsibility for other serious errors of judgement. The shares had fallen by 89% in his four years in the top job. In most companies he would have been told to shut the door after himself on the way out.

Instead, the 62-year-old was rewarded for his loyalty and continued optimism not just with a seat on the board as a non-executive director but with a contract as a special consultant to O'Reilly and Goulandris. O'Reilly described him as 'an outstanding servant' to the company. 'In the face of great adversity, especially the unprecedented fall in the US dollar, he has led our business with style, dignity and an unshakeable belief in the potential of our market-leading brands,' O'Reilly said. Whatever flaws O'Reilly had, a lack of loyalty to those who had served him with loyalty was not one of them – although others would have said that was in itself one of his big problems.

Peter Cameron was promoted to replace O'Donoghue. The big question was how much change the American would be able to persuade O'Reilly to undertake – along with how much money would be there to carry it out. Cameron pushed the issue of the lifestyle changes of the target customer base and finding a suitable distribution channel for the right type of customer service. He wanted to realign Waterford Wedgwood as a low-cost manufacturer of a product range that would appeal to younger customers with more modern tastes.

'The company has to find structures that allow it to be profitable at existing or even lower sales levels,' said Cameron in an interview with *The Irish Times*. 'But we also have to get the margins that are associated with premium products. It is those margins that allow you to do the marketing, advertising and brand-enhancing activities that are required for a successful, profitable consumer product company. Obviously that gets into being a low-cost manufacturer, but it also entails fully pricing your products in a way that people still aspire to attain them and are willing to pay the premium for the cachet.'

Cameron promised up to a dozen initiatives 'that you would describe as elegant casual products that will be breaking into the market, some by the end of the current financial year … The critical thing for Waterford Wedgwood, given the importance of the US market, is catering to US tastes. That means catering to a younger American customer who is not currently participating in the Waterford Wedgwood franchise because we don't have the products that are compatible with their tastes.'

Peter Cameron resembled O'Donoghue in his bullishness, a trait O'Reilly admired. 'I couldn't be more confident about our ability to accomplish this stuff,' he said. 'It's eminently doable. My expectation is that we will leave fiscal 2006 with a structure and a velocity that creates a profitable entity in 2007 and that includes a fully-integrated Royal Doulton.'

But he had a job of work to do in deconstructing the management layers at Waterford Wedgwood, which was a contributing reason to the decision of Tony jnr to leave the company in 2005. 'It would take months for decisions to work their way down,' one former executive said regretfully. It wasn't just an issue of dealing with excessive costs, but with unnecessary complexity in the organisation as well. Waterford Wedgwood was simply dysfunctional.

Apart from the new CEO, confidence that things could be saved was low. From late 2004 to early 2005 remaining production staff at Waterford Crystal in Ireland had taken seven weeks of involuntary, unpaid leave. There had been so many restructuring programmes – over half a dozen in the past 10 years – involving plant closures, redundancies and short-time work, that many employees and investors could hardly keep track, other than knowing that it was costing them dearly.

There was no doubting the personal commitment that O'Reilly was making to the attempted restoration of Waterford Wedgwood's fortunes. He was putting plenty of his own hard cash into the company and had provided personal guarantees for the repayment by the company of its bonds. Had that not been forthcoming, then it is likely that Waterford Wedgwood would either have shut down or, more likely, that its entire production would have been moved to Asia, if not under O'Reilly's control then under new owners who would have purchased the brands and shut everything else. However misplaced his optimism, O'Reilly was clearly committed to keeping Waterford Irish and keeping Wedgwood British.

That it was O'Reilly who was doing this gave some people confidence. Somebody as smart and successful as he was would not throw good money after bad, would he? But all of the evidence suggested that O'Reilly, Chryss and Peter Goulandris were getting it wrong, that their aesthetic appreciation of the beauty of Waterford and Wedgwood products had obscured the hard business realities: the company was unable to produce and sell the goods for a profit.

CHAPTER ELEVEN

A QUESTION OF TRUST

I n 2005 O'Reilly decided to show off his wealth, his sophistication and his artistic knowledge by commissioning the publication of what was to him a very special book. There were to be only 500 copies produced, at a cost of €125,000. It would be sent as a gift to the then President of Ireland, Mary McAleese, to Queen Elizabeth II and to a select collection of family and friends. The book, 15 cm thick and edited by Suzanne MacDougald of the Solomon Art Gallery in Dublin, was a bound catalogue of the combined collections he and Chryss owned. Leading experts were commissioned to write accompanying articles and catalogue entries: Hilary Pyle on Jack B. Yeats, S.B. Kennedy on Paul Henry, Bruce Arnold on William Orpen, Roy Johnston on Roderic O'Connor – just some of the artists whose work featured on the walls of Castlemartin and at other O'Reilly properties. A picture of his famous Monet purchase, *Le Portail*, featured prominently, of course, as did a Picasso that hung for years in the vestibule at Castlemartin, along with a Derek Hill portrait of O'Reilly. His ownership of works by JMW Turner and Jackson Pollock was also highlighted.

'Our collection is made up of a variety of Irish and international artists but it all started on that dark night so long ago in the west of Ireland with a delightful man and a charming little painting,' he said. He delighted in telling the story of his first purchase: a small oil painting by an artist called Michael O'Gara from Ballaghaderreen, who did an interpretation of Paul Henry's *The Potato Diggers*, a work he had admired as a child. 'O'Gara was so poor, and yet so locally famous, that on the evening of the purchase I had to drive my car on the footpath to shine its lights into his studio shop on the main street. I paid £10 for it,' he said.

O'Reilly was one of the first of the modern generation of successful businessmen to appreciate the beauty and potential monetary value of paintings by Jack B. Yeats. In 1972, when he moved to Pittsburgh, he decided he wanted something Irish to hang in his new Heinz office. He purchased *By Streedagh Strand* for £9,500. In his book *Sold*, an early twenty-first-century look at the then burgeoning market in Irish art, journalist John Burns described O'Reilly's taste as 'overwhelmingly conservative', showing a liking for 'pretty, safe pictures that would almost certainly hold their value', although he conceded others were guilty of this tendency, too.

Burns described the highlight of the collection as being *My Beautiful, My Beautiful*, a large-scale Yeats oil of a man bidding farewell to his horse, which some critics believe is the artist's very best work and which had been bought directly from Yeats by Sir Basil Goulding in 1955. His widow, Valerie Goulding, sold it to O'Reilly in the 1980s based on a Sotheby's valuation.

O'Reilly and Chryss also boasted ownership of a Fabergé egg and there was a collection of sculpture works, too. He was known to have paid $3.31 million for *Diego au chandail*, by Alberto Giacometti, in May 2002 at Christie's in New York, and the Goulandris family was known to have even more expensive pieces of Giacometti's work. 'Our collections are assembled without any particular objective other than giving satisfaction and enjoyment to the beholder,' he boasted.

Notwithstanding the dreadful tribulations at Waterford Wedgwood, O'Reilly seemed to have money with which to play. The refinancing of Arcon back in 2002 was proved to be an inspired decision when the pay-off came in 2005. Newly discovered deposits of zinc, lead and silver both extended the life of the Galmoy mine and, with lower operating costs now in place, made it more profitable and attractive to others. Zinc prices began recovering from shortly after the deal was done and the company made a small profit in 2004, after losses of €40 million in the previous three years.

The sale of Arcon in 2005 was negotiated by Tony jnr in his role as chairman of the company after he had received an approach from Macquarie Bank, a large Australian outfit, representing a Canadian/ Swedish competitor called Lundin Mining. The Australians organised a meeting for Tony jnr with Vas Lundin, a Swedish son of Lundin Mining boss, Adolf. The two struck up a good relationship and Tony was persuaded that a deal was a good idea as rising commodity prices were finally in sight. It was agreed that the two fathers should meet, and the four men convened in Geneva.

'It was a great lunch, one that went on for hours,' recalled Tony jnr. 'Adolf had been involved in mining in South Africa and knew people AJ did and they spend hours swopping stories. At the end of it all AJ said he was so sorry that they hadn't met years earlier. "All the lies we could have told together," he joked. Adolf died just three weeks later.'

O'Reilly was persuaded of the merits of a sale. 'It was easier when he wasn't involved in the management of the company and was somewhat more detached,' said Tony jnr.

The proposal was for Lundin Mining to pay €93 million to buy Arcon, with a mixture of cash and shares in Lundin as the proposed consideration. The deal seemed like a sweet one for long-suffering Arcon shareholders, and for O'Reilly in particular. He was offered over €30.5 million in cash and an 8.9% holding in Lundin. It would have been worth another €27 million to him if he had received cash instead of shares at that time, but within 18 months, as Lundin's value soared, his shareholding there trebled in value to about €90 million and he sold the shares then, turning a massive profit.

As an additional bonus, the Lundin deal meant that he was released from his position as personal guarantor of a €6.6 million mine-closure bond. Debts of €18.5 million, outstanding as a result of the 2002 refinancing, were repaid as part of the takeover. This was important as the mine had only a five-year life span remaining. Tony jnr joined the Lundin board – representing Arcon shareholders in the world's twelfth largest zinc producer – and the O'Reillys still had Providence Resources for speculation.

It was almost impossible to work out how much money O'Reilly had spent on Arcon over the years, if the investments in Atlantic were taken into account too, but his spin-doctors estimated it at €60 million when exchange rates and other factors were taken into account. That implied that his mining adventure, over the long term, had been profitable.

But not everybody was happy, especially other shareholders in Arcon, many of whom had followed O'Reilly since the Atlantic days and who didn't feel they were getting the full benefits of this deal. They complained that Davy Stockbrokers had forecast 'bumper' pre-tax profits of €16.5 million for 2005 on the back of high zinc prices and a better-than-expected performance of the dollar versus the euro. They pointed out how Tony jnr had boasted about the quality of the ore body being 'the second richest in the western world'. While the price being offered of €0.522 per share was better than the average stock market over the previous three years, it was still below the €0.60 price per share being quoted on the market.

Indeed, rising zinc prices quickly allowed Galmoy to make profits of €8.7 million in 2005 and €42.7 million in 2006. Zinc prices hit about $4,500 per tonne – fuelled by demand from China and India to galvanise steel products for construction and car manufacture – a long way above the $800 of earlier in the decade. It wasn't to last. Prices halved again and then fell again, just as energy prices soared and the dollar weakened against the euro. Profits fell to €22.2 million in 2007 and early in 2008 Lundin announced that the mine was to close, ahead of the original schedule. The timing of O'Reilly's depart-ure had been fortuitous, to say the least.

O'Reilly remained very sensitive to any criticism of him or any of his companies, as he had been throughout his career. It did not ease with age. One adviser said too much time was spent in advising how to deal with negative press. 'He would ask, "is this journalist for or against us?" I'd say neither, that there was no agenda, but he wouldn't see that. He would go through an article that might be utterly factually correct, but he'd skip the 95% that he liked and focus on the 5% he disliked. It was surprising because he loved news, loved journalists and had a unique ability to see the whole business from start to finish.'

He was very sensitive, too, to allegations about not paying enough tax. 'It was his Achilles' heel,' said one friend. It created problems because he wanted to be seen and acknowledged as very rich, as if that conferred status, but at the same time he did not want to be seen as someone who had short-changed the State. Nonetheless, even after he had left Heinz, he did not return to Ireland to become resident for tax purposes, even if the country clearly was the centre of his economic empire. He continued to limit his days in Ireland to ensure he did not become liable for Irish tax on foreign-earned income. Indeed, his shareholdings in all of his Irish companies were registered to foreign companies, particularly in places like Cyprus.

In spite of his worries about the slant taken by the press on him and his affairs, this was a smooth time in his working life: if Waterford

Wedgwood was the blot on his current day copybook, as well as the drain on his finances, everything else seemed to be going well. INM provided him with the entrée to the echelons of society in which he liked to move. He had no reason to believe that this would come to an end, other than by illness or death, and he continued to believe himself, at almost 70 years old, to be fit and active, if not capable of working at the same extraordinary pace as before. He was enjoying his new role as CEO of INM. He had succumbed to pressure from institutional investors about holding the dual role of chairman and CEO, but had reacted in a way that surprised – and did not necessarily please – everybody. Instead of becoming part-time chairman, as had been expected, and giving Gavin or Ivan Fallon or Brendan Hopkins the role of CEO, he had taken that job, and its major salary, for himself. He moved the little-known and little-heralded Brian Hillery in as chairman. Hillery was a Fianna Fáil senator who few would have regarded as a strong, dominant figure; it was to Hillery that O'Reilly would 'report'.

The idea of O'Reilly not chairing meetings at INM, as he had since 1973, surprised many. 'He's not happy if he's not top of the table, chairing activities,' said one of his former executives at another company. 'That's where he is best suited. He has a wonderful ability to see things as they are and to articulate them that does not come easily to most people. That works best when he's in the chair, in a large group. He's not as good in one-to-ones or very small groups, where he can become perhaps too intense, perhaps even a little moody.'

Presciently, one of his non-executive directors at APN warned him at the time that it would be a bad idea, arguing that he would have as much influence as he wanted as a non-executive chairman, but without being in the firing line as CEO if things went wrong. O'Reilly listened politely and carried on regardless.

O'Reilly and his seven-man – no women – executive team were happy that they were on the right track and working well together. There were lots of conference and individual calls each day, tracking information and suggesting solutions to problems. A big emphasis was placed on relative informality, frequent communication and collegiate decision-making. Independent News & Media benefited from a greater degree of simplicity than applied at Waterford Wedgwood. It didn't have inventory issues. The product had a day to sell, or it didn't sell.

O'Reilly felt his job was, in the main, commercial, not editorial. He was the driving force, setting down the culture of the organisation. He brought a lot of that from his experience at Heinz. He regarded media as exciting. He liked to mix business with pleasure. He enjoyed driving people, and then rewarding them handsomely for financial performance. It helped maintain loyalty. He always had new targets, never being satisfied with what had been achieved, always wanting more. He continued to love the travel, moving from one luxury suite to another, meeting people new and old, dining out in fine restaurants, being feted as important. He was not ready for retirement, certainly not ready to pass on any mantles.

Whatever about the debt and banking issues he faced at Waterford Wedgwood, he felt he had no such problems at INM. His finance director, Donal Buggy, whom he trusted greatly, had managed to change the structure and terms of INM's debt, taking advantage of the willingness of banks to practically throw money at companies. The banks didn't even look for the newspaper titles as security for loans any more. Independent News & Media didn't even have a formal credit rating, not believing that one would improve the terms of its borrowing.

O'Reilly believed that INM would not have achieved what it had without him at the helm and there were few within INM to disabuse him of that notion. He was aware of his own business acumen and achievements and of how to use his personal magnetism. But just as he packed his boards with people he enjoyed and with whom he was in agreement, he was falling victim to the tendency of many long-term leaders to surround themselves with acolytes and believers. Scoffing at the requirements of corporate governance was not just arrogant, it was unwise. It was incorrect to believe that the requirements of all shareholders were in alignment with his own, or indeed that all shareholders would agree with decisions he would make on share buybacks, dividends or acquisitions.

He was constantly thinking about the future for the newspaper industry, convincing himself that it had a glorious future, that the Internet would be a complement rather than a replacement, that his industry would challenge the rise of the Internet as an advertising medium. He dismissed the notion that the print industry was a 'sunset industry'. 'It is a sunrise industry,' said O'Reilly. 'Newspapers are tactile, hugely cheap, reliable, go with a cup of coffee. You can trust newspaper writers. Can you trust a blogger?'

O'Reilly said that the newspaper industry would also challenge the 'rise of the Internet as an advertising medium. A whole range of goods would not be congenial to be advertised "on a PC", he said, believing personal computer penetration to be levelling off, but failing to anticipate the rise of mobile devices.

He believed that newspapers were increasingly becoming the mass medium of the future, not of the past. The issue, though, was going to be how long he got to share in that future – although that was not something that he had even remotely considered.

SECTION 4

2004–2009: A threat to all he'd built

CHAPTER ONE

EXITS AND NEW STRATEGIES

Tony O'Reilly was a voracious reader, seeking to learn from the successes and failures of the lives of others and to apply these lessons to his own work. He concentrated on books about nineteenth- and twentieth-century military campaigns, and biographies of army commanders and their political masters. 'I'm fascinated with warfare,' he said. 'It's the ultimate management test, because if you get it wrong, you're dead.'

He had a dictum that one should 'fight on the ground of one's own choosing'. He applied this phrase to the passing up of opportunities for business expansion, citing the failed Napoleonic and Nazi pushes against Russia as examples of militaristic hubris. In common with other major business leaders, however, he failed to appreciate both his vulnerability to assault by others and his capacity to make errors of judgement, no matter how much thought and analysis had gone into a decision.

There was one battle he considered fought and decisively won: O'Reilly assumed that he would remain in control of INM until his death – and his family in control of it beyond. He was proud of the fact that there was no other public company of its size in Ireland where the controlling family held onto a 28% share. He compared it to Smurfit, where the family holding had fallen into low single figures, or Kingspan, where the Murtagh family owned a similar share but the company was less than half the size of INM.

He had organised that, upon his death, his shares would be bequeathed to a trust for the benefit of his six children, but no assets were placed in the trust in advance of that outcome – he did not want to reduce his flexibility at this juncture by having assets tied up in the legal requirements of a trust instead of being readily available. He did not want a situation arising as had occurred at News International, where Rupert Murdoch's adult and juvenile children were involved in rows about future ownership and control and current roles. He maintained that Gavin would not automatically succeed him, saying that he was in competition with Ivan Fallon and Brendan Hopkins for the CEO's role when he retired, although he was very careful not to make any suggestions as to when he might step down. While both of Gavin's brothers were part-time directors of INM, neither now featured as possible replacements at that business: Cameron had removed himself from that process and Tony jnr had never been part of it, concentrating instead on his father's other interests. The three daughters had never even been considered for management or other business roles.

Although he regarded INM as 'his' company, he realised that the potential existed for somebody else to buy shares in INM and to accumulate a shareholding similar to or bigger in size than his, allowing that person or entity to mount a challenge for its control. He knew that control of a public company did not convey the same advantages of ownership as did a privately owned institution, but he never seriously considered that anybody would dare to try to take INM from him or would have the resources to do so.

In early 2006, Denis O'Brien announced that he had purchased just over 3% of the shares in INM, at a cost estimated by others at about €57 million. O'Brien had parked his tanks on O'Reilly's lawn. The question was whether the guns were primed to fire and, if fired, what sort of damage would be inflicted on O'Reilly. Would O'Brien be able to storm O'Reilly's citadel and wrest control and ownership of it from him? Was that his intention, indeed, or was there another agenda at play that remained unknown as of yet?

The move came as a complete shock to almost everyone, including those in O'Brien's camp, and most certainly to all in O'Reilly's. There had been no hint that this might happen and immediately there was rampant speculation as to what O'Brien was doing. His announcement was not necessary under stock exchange rules – he could have built a 5% stake before saying anything – yet he wanted O'Reilly to know about his presence, as if he were taunting him.

But what were O'Brien's intentions? Would he be a passive investor or seek to become an active shareholder? Was he looking to make a quick profit on these shares or would he look to buy more? If it was the latter, how many would he want? Would he actually be so bold as to want to take control or try to buy the company? Having looked at, and walked away from, buying telecoms companies NTL and Meteor in recent times, was O'Brien somebody who would dare follow through on buying something as big as INM given that it would be far more expensive? Did he have sufficient funds available to buy more shares or access to backing if he needed it? This was O'Reilly's prized asset: did O'Brien want to take it from him and, if so, was it for financial reasons or to take vengeance for perceived slights and hurts? Or was O'Reilly worrying too much, that this foray by O'Brien would ultimately be no more damaging to him than the time in the 1990s when Dunnes Stores bought a shareholding in Fitzwilton but ultimately did nothing with it?

There was no official comment on the acquisition by INM other than to 'welcome new shareholders'. Quickly, O'Reilly was reminded by Gavin of two letters of complaint O'Brien had written about coverage in INM titles: one in 2001, as the Eircom takeover battle was kicking off and *The Sunday Tribune* had published details of the Telenor payment to Fine Gael at the conclusion of the mobile phone licence award; and the second in 2003, when the Special Olympic World Games . had been completed. In the second letter, O'Brien had promised that he would 'rectify the damage' to his reputation, for which he held INM responsible. 'I happened to be one of a number of people who was singled out for unreasonably biased and critical coverage,' said O'Brien in 2015 in an interview for this book. O'Reilly and Gavin, and assorted lieutenants, reviewed the public comments that O'Brien had made in interviews about him specifically and about his attitude to competitors in general. One statement leapt out: 'I spend my time thinking of ways to create a downfall for my competitor, particularly if they are big.' Surely that wouldn't apply to O'Reilly? Surely he was too big, too rich, too powerful for O'Brien to take him on?

O'Reilly and his people did their sums quickly. A buyer of the company would need to pay about €2 billion to buy all the shares. O'Brien didn't need to buy all of the shares to control INM, however. He would only have to bid for the company if he passed a 29.9% threshold, according to stock exchange rules. He could make an offer that O'Reilly would refuse, but still end up owning over 50% of the shares if enough other investors sold to him, with O'Reilly and others reduced to the role of minority observers. A shareholding of even 29.9% would greatly strengthen any O'Brien claim for representation on the board of directors. There he could cause considerable mischief. But surely he wasn't spoiling for a fight that badly?

There were rumours that O'Brien was motivated by a desire for revenge after losing out in the Eircom takeover battle of 2001. 'The commentary by financial journalists was clueless,' said O'Brien, in his comments for this book. 'I invested in INM because I viewed it as a good long-term investment opportunity. It also was in an industry that I had a good understanding of and it was also a hedge against telecommunications. I sought professional advice and our view was INM had some very strong assets capable of further growth and expansion. The company's own forecasts were always positive, along with all the broker research reports, particularly Davy's. The INM annual reports were all blue skies, in reality it was a company being operated for one shareholder.' He said that if he had been interested in taking control of one of O'Reilly's companies, then Providence would have been an easier capture.

From his point of view, O'Reilly could see that he was vulnerable to an accumulation of shares by O'Brien. However, there was nothing he could do to stop anyone buying shares in *his* company, given that it was quoted on the stock market for anyone to buy or sell its shares. Independent News & Media paid a handsome annual dividend to shareholders, one that gave a 4.5% yield on shares purchased at the market price of the time. This meant that O'Brien could cover the cost of any borrowings incurred to buy the shares with the dividend income. O'Brien had other sources of wealth anyway: he was taking so much money out of his mobile phone businesses in the Caribbean that almost any bank would provide the loans to finance his foray.

Regardless of all the speculation and suspicion, O'Brien would spend the whole of 2006 sitting tight and waiting before signalling his next steps, and there was little O'Reilly could do other than brood: he had no way of removing those tanks from his lawn.

O'Reilly wasn't going to allow the presence of O'Brien on his share register to upset a little junket he had organised for that February. He celebrated the Indian acquisition of the previous summer by bringing the members of the International Advisory Board and their spouses, as well as some key board directors, on a trip to enjoy the sites and culture of India. The travelling party was over 40 strong and the bills mounted until the final cost passed €1 million. There was all the usual sight-seeing and a ride on elephants and meetings with Mrs Sonia Ghandi and Prime Minister Dr Manmohan Singh. There was even a trip to the Taj Mahal, but that did not turn out as expected or desired. The party arrived in two mini-buses, but a massive and excited crowd gathered as soon as people saw Sean Connery get off one of the buses. 'It is Mister James Bond,' they shouted. They surrounded Connery and the remainder of the INM entourage, and anxious police officers immediately demanded that the group return to their buses in case the crush should lead to injuries. It was the only disappointment on an otherwise enjoyable trip.

O'Reilly was very excited about the potential for INM in India. *Dainik Jagran* joined the stock market in February, raising €55 million to invest in upgrading the printing facilities and to finance new business plans in outdoor media advertising and event management. The profits were small, at just €4 million in the first quarter of 2006, but the potential was enormous and there was also the possibility of expanding into radio. They also looked at the launch of a lower priced paper than the flagship *Dainik*. These were exciting plans and O'Reilly loved the idea of being an investor in India. It also gave him a new audience to impress, to show that his interests ran further than merely making money.

In December 2005 he spoke at the Jagran Foundation Forum in India on the theme of 'Democracy: not the best, but the best we have'. He quoted five of the great heroes of his life: Abraham Lincoln, Franklin D. Roosevelt, Mahatma Gandhi, Pandit Nehru and Nelson Mandela. 'You will note that all these men share a common and passionate belief in democracy,' he said.

'If you ask anyone in this room what was the greatest discovery of the twentieth century, they would say, possibly, the internal combustion engine, or perhaps electric power or penicillin or flight or the computer or the telephone. And yet, all of them would be wrong, because the greatest discovery of the twentieth century was democracy. In the year 1900, not one single country in the world enjoyed universal democracy, defined as universal suffrage. No woman in the world had voted, and so in 1900, with the commencement of this century, not one single country in the world practiced true democracy,' he said, expanding on his theme. 'And so the notion of democracy with its twin attendants, accountability and transparency, is central to the notion of free speech, freedom of association and the separation of powers.'

He spoke of the investment in *Dainik Jagran* with utter and complete confidence in the probity of the Indian system of government, the future growth of the Indian economy and, as ever his belief, the exciting opportunities for foreign investment in what he called 'this hugely turbulent subcontinent'. He said: 'Democracy can and will be improved by a vigilant press – indeed, a vigilant press is a condition precedent to a thriving democracy. We are concerned, we are committed, and we articulate value systems that try to impart on a daily basis the give and take of democracy. The fact that all democracies are based on compromise, the fact that you cannot have it always your own way, the fact that the give and take of debate and analysis and concession, produce a system in which measured progress yields progress for all. These are the central beliefs of *Dainik Jagran*, and of *The Independent*, and we will sustain and expand them in India in the years ahead.'

Like all good storytellers, he had the personal story, one that allowed him to make a connection with his audience: 'My aunt, Sister Mary Joseph of the Loreto nuns, joined the Order in the town of Drogheda, in Ireland, where my father was born. On that very day, the future Mother Teresa of Calcutta joined the Order with her. She is buried at Lucknow, having gone to India in 1936 and died there in 1981 … Mr Prime Minister, I feel great pride in sharing this platform with you, both because of my own personal family connection with India and because of the standards of democracy that have been developed in this country where freedom of assembly, freedom of speech and the doctrine of the separation of powers are so clearly a part of your concept of government … We are proud and expectant participants in the great future that beckons your country.'

While he was very much focused on the future at INM, O'Reilly's time at Eircom was coming to an end. A new Australian investor, Babcock & Brown, began buying shares, taking just over 11% of the company by February 2006. It entered into the seduction of the ESOT – much to the ESOT's subsequent regret – separately to the company's board, and offered a plan for a joint bid with the employees to buy out all the other Eircom shareholders. It offered the ESOT a deal that would allow it to increase its shareholding to 35%, with the Australians holding the remaining 65%. Agreement reached, an offer to all shareholders was made, valuing Eircom at €2.4 billion.

O'Reilly was nowhere near as impressed by the Australians or their financing as he had been by the Swisscom option of the previous year. However, given the links the Australians had forged with the workers – and the profits that would be available to the shareholders – he felt he had no option but to agree a deal. 'The independent directors believe that the cash offer … is fair and reasonable and is in the best interests of Eircom ordinary shareholders, who will receive a sub-stantial return on their investment since the Eircom IPO in March 2004,' O'Reilly said. That return would be 62%, a profit of €6,200 on every €10,000 invested.

The Babcock & Brown offer came at a time when the public was largely weary of the constant stories about who would own Eircom. It was nearing the end of the Celtic Tiger boom but few had realised that, and the national party was still in full flight. Although sections of the financial media highlighted the increasingly fragile state of Eircom's balance sheet as a result of this second leveraged buyout, and the doubtfulness of Eircom's ability to make the profits that would cover the costs of Babcock & Brown's purchase of shares, few complained too loudly. Those who did noted that it wasn't just going to cost Babcock & Brown €2.4 billion to buy Eircom; it would, of course, also be taking on nearly the same amount in debts within the company. Eircom's revenues in the last financial year, at €1.6 billion, were €200 million lower than they had been when the company had first joined the stock market in 1999. Back then the company had net assets of €1.35 billion, whereas now that figure had slumped to €550 million. It was a very small base upon which to support such massive debts in a very expensive purchase. If the Australians were going to be obsessed with recouping their investment, then it would have even greater implications than previously for Eircom's ability to invest sufficient capital in the network and to provide a good service for the country's citizens.

O'Reilly's final chairman's statement in the 2006 annual report was to be a valedictory, if a tad defensive. He claimed that the investment made by Eircom under his chairmanship had been 'judicious' and in the national interest.

Avoiding the excessive and wasteful investments of the dot-com boom-to-bust era, Eircom has nonetheless invested in its network at a rate consistently above our European peers, under Valentia ownership and through the IPO in 2002 to the present day … History will record that Eircom, despite the fiercest criticism, became the first private entity in the State to roll out a major nationwide infrastructure at no cost to the tax-payer.

When Valentia acquired Eircom in 2001, shortly after its flotation by the government, the company had no broadband, no mobile, a rapidly declining market share, an inefficient cost base and a deeply disgruntled shareholder community. In contrast today Eircom has enabled Broadband Ireland, re-entered mobile with a flourish, stabilised its market share through good products and services, delivered prices cheaper than the EU average reflecting its efficiency and satisfied shareholders with exceptional returns.

'I can't over-emphasise how good a chairman he was,' McRedmond said. 'He didn't try to be the dominant figure. He would sit there without saying too much unless he had to, the Diet Cokes dropped in on a regular basis. He had a very American style, introducing levity and humour at intervals, but he timed it all very well. But he kept everyone working well together. As a chairman he turned on a show, but it was not all about him. He was democratic, respectful and unprejudiced, his great strength.'

This was to become a more pertinent point in retrospect. O'Reilly is blamed in many quarters for setting up Eircom for its subsequent fall, for overseeing the erosion of the asset base of the company while loading it with too much debt. Such sentiment is coloured by resentment in some quarters at the personal financial bonanza he harvested at the company. Those are valid criticisms, but they can be applied with equal force to the consistently applied self-interest of the ESOT, which matched venture capitalist investors in its avarice. From a narrower corporate or investor viewpoint, Eircom may have been O'Reilly's finest achievement of the twenty-first century. He got in and out at the right time and made enormous profits from doing so. He had notable successes in building the business from where he had found it, making it valuable to suitors, even if the Australians eventually overpaid disastrously.

That final board that O'Reilly praised in his last annual report, containing people such as Irial Finan, Maurice Pratt, Kevin Melia and John Conroy, as well as the Eircom executives, and the board that preceded it, before Providence and Soros exited in 2004, were both full of people far more independent of him than the often deferential cronies who populated the boards of INM and Waterford Wedgwood. At the PLC – once the initial buy-out consortium had returned the company to the stock market – O'Reilly had not been focused on maximising his own personal wealth and there was a more defined focus on running the business for the benefit of all shareholders. It was not *his* company and maybe because of that it was his best corporate performance of the twenty-first century.

Exiting Eircom at least gave him more time to deal with the continuing crisis at Waterford Wedgwood. In early January 2006, O'Reilly and Peter Goulandris used their New York contacts and announced they had arranged loans amounting to €250 million, with Bank of America as the new Waterford Wedgwood main banker.

Cost containment remained the priority for Waterford Wedgwood, but by mid-2006 it was clear that restoring sales growth would be essential to regain the confidence of investors and bankers. This meant targeting new markets. Every new relationship was milked for whatever positive publicity it could bring. Waterford Wedgwood announced a tie-up with Eduardo Xol, a US home designer with a big following in the Hispanic community. The ambition was to win a portion of the $1 billion spent each year on gift-giving for Quinceineras, the Latin community's coming-of-age celebration. Waterford Crystal now made up only a little more than a quarter of group sales and badly needed a lift. A deal was done with US wine brand Robert Mondavi, to produce a range of grape-specific wine glasses – for example, buyers could purchase a Bordeaux glass or a Chardonnay glass – designed by wine-makers under the Waterford brand. A new 'homewares' range was developed in association with British celebrity chef Gordon Ramsay for the Royal Doulton brand, Jasper Conran designed a new range for Wedgwood and there was also a garden range and other, less formal products created in the hope of drawing in younger consumers. The idea was to boost sales by more than €120 million annually.

The losses continued to mount, however, totalling €189.4 million in the year ended March 2006, even if that wasn't as bad as in the previous year. Chief executive Peter Cameron admitted the figures were 'underwhelming', 'unacceptable' and 'plainly disappointing'. Borrowings increased to €371.8 million, from €305.2 million a year earlier. There was also an enormous pension deficit of €293 million that had to be accounted for on the balance sheet.

More money was needed, but as the banks would not provide it, it would have to come from shareholders yet again. Other businessmen might have considered the terms for surrender, but O'Reilly was determined to fight on doggedly. In June 2006, O'Reilly invited shareholders to participate in the third rights issue in under two years, in an attempt to raise another €58.3 million. Just 2,700 out of the 25,000 eligible shareholders subscribed. They had lost faith in O'Reilly. He and Goulandris, as owners of just over half of the shares, purchased their entitlement – at a cost of over €30 million – but it didn't end there. Davy Stockbrokers was left with an enormous number of shares to sell to other investors and wasn't confident it would be able to do so. It told O'Reilly that if it didn't sell those shares within 12 months, it would require O'Reilly and Goulandris to buy them at the issue price, which would bring the O'Reilly/Goulandris shareholding to 60.5%. The money was to be used to provide working capital while 'the turnaround continues and the restructuring is completed'. A decision was taken to close the Dungarvan plant in Waterford, costing 300 jobs. To pay the €33 million closure costs, the company sold 20 acres of land in Waterford for housing development.

May 2006 marked O'Reilly's seventieth birthday but he delayed his birthday celebrations by two weeks, to a date when a group of his closest friends were able to travel with him to Rome. There was a crisis when the men realised that their expensive hotel did not have a Sky Sports service and that they would not be able to enjoy rugby's Heineken Cup final between Munster and Biarritz, which was taking place in Cardiff on 20 May. A pub in Rome with the requisite satellite service was found and O'Reilly celebrated with friends such as Jim McCarthy, Kevin McGoran and Redmond O'Donoghue when Munster won by 23 points to 19.

The weekend's festivities over, O'Reilly returned to Dublin, where the Australian Prime Minister John Howard was on an official four-day State visit to Ireland. Howard visited O'Reilly at his Fitzwilliam Square residence for a private meeting. O'Reilly used the opportunity to continue lobbying for a change in Australia's 20-year-old restrictions on foreign media ownership of newspapers, radio and television. INM was confined to a 41% shareholding in APN, but also was limited in how APN could expand its interests. Even though it owned 123 newspaper titles and operated 132 radio stations in Australia and New Zealand – as well as outdoor advertising interests in those markets and in Hong Kong, Malaysia and Indonesia – it could only have either one type of business or the other in many parts of Australia and in the big cities, in particular. The apparently good news for O'Reilly would come within months: the rules were to be relaxed from 2007 onwards. He intended to make the most of the opportunity.

O'Reilly wanted to engage in some financial engineering, to either help reduce INM's debts dramatically or to produce new cash it could use for share buy-backs or acquisitions. O'Reilly made his first run at APN in October 2006, making an A$3.8 billion (€2.29 billion) approach with private equity group Providence, led by his old friend from Eircom days John Hahn, to buy the company out of public ownership.

The idea was that the new buying company – in which INM would hold about a 40% share, similar to its existing investment in APN – would borrow the money to buy APN. But this is where accounting jiggery-pokery, all perfectly legal, came into play. Whereas APN was known presently as a subsidiary company of INM's, so that all of its profits and turnover could be taken into the INM group accounts, under the new arrangement it would be described as an associate. That meant that INM's turnover and profits would no longer be as impressive, but the APN debts would not have to appear on the INM balance sheet, removing up to €800 million at one stroke of a pen. Management of APN would be totally in the Irish company's hands. Even better, the money borrowed by the new company to pay APN's shareholders would provide a cash boost to INM of anywhere up to €420 million. It would be transformative of INM's balance sheet and would arm O'Reilly with far more power to fight off O'Brien. Additionally, INM would also have the option to buy Providence's APN shares at a future date; should that happen it would require fresh INM borrowing and full accounting for it on the balance sheet, but it still appeared to be a valuable option for the future.

The initial approach failed, however, although this didn't seem to discomfort anybody too much. APN's directors, or at least those unconnected to INM, did not offer encouragement at the mooted price of A$6.02 per share and the bidding consortium was not prepared to offer more. The expectation was that INM would come back at a higher price, but with a different consortium.

While management at INM was supportive of the APN concept, many were still concerned about O'Reilly's continued loyalty to *The Independent* in London and the cash drain that it remained. *The Independent* remained one of the smallest players in the British media scene and its influence and reach within the country was debatable, even if the name retained some international cachet. What was the point in maintaining it, especially when it cost so much money and the circulation was now down to 170,000, not far removed from what the *Irish Independent* was achieving in the far smaller Irish market? The promise of just a couple of years earlier, when the move to tabloid format was groundbreaking in the industry, had now dissipated. The criticism was whispered, but many regarded it as a vanity project and wanted rid of it. Fallon, as the UK CEO, and Kelner, as editor, continued to flatter O'Reilly about both *The Independent*'s importance and its potential to return to profit.

O'Reilly and his associates were used to backbiting about *The Independent*'s prospects from competitors in the UK media, but many took note when Peter Wilby, a former editor of the *Independent on Sunday* and a continued supporter of the paper, described it as 'peripheral' in a column for the *New Statesman* in October 2006 to mark the paper's twentieth birthday. He said the paper did not 'make many waves these days. The reporting and analysis of news from the Middle East, particularly Iraq, has been relentless and magnificent; no other daily paper comes close. Its specialist correspondents on education, the environment and science, for instance, are still among the most reliable and authoritative. But *The Independent* is not much talked about in Westminster, Whitehall or any other power centre. It does not set the agenda; it is not, in the jargon, "a player".'

It would be unfair to say Kelner had been putting lipstick on a pig, given the quality of much of what the newspaper did, but it was true that it had lost its way. He did a better job than most would have been likely to do in working with such limited resources, but he simply didn't have enough money to maintain a coherent and consistent product. O'Reilly gave him thin rations, but was wise enough to realise that other editors might not be able to perform as well as Kelner was managing: he flattered him sufficiently to keep him going in the job. Their mutually appreciative relationship was summed up by an anecdote from O'Reilly at the paper's twentieth anniversary celebrations: 'When I was first introduced to Simon Kelner, I thought I was interviewing him as my editor, whereas he thought he was interviewing me as his proprietor. Simon's view of me was that I should put up, pay up and stay [put out of the way] in Ireland, which I've done.'

In his efforts to rescue Waterford Wedgwood, O'Reilly decided to go even further afield with the outsourcing of production. The Royal Doulton acquisition had been predicated upon gaining control of its fine bone china manufacturing facility in Indonesia and now O'Reilly was prepared to invest us$125 million in its operations in Western Java, near Jakarta. O'Reilly travelled there in early October 2006 and was greeted at the presidential palace by President Susilo Bambang Yudhoyono for the usual mutually flattering speeches and photo-opportunities.

By November, Waterford Wedgwood was claiming the sales decline had been largely 'arrested'. Its pre-tax loss narrowed to €20.7 million in the six months to the end of September, from €94.5 million in the year-earlier period. O'Reilly hoped the company was finally on the road to recovery, notwithstanding the continued high debts.

There was good news across O'Reilly's investments, in fact. Things were improving at Fitzwilton, thanks more to success at low-profile life assurance businesses in which it had invested than at the Rennicks engineering company, even if the latter was benefiting from continued strong construction activities in Ireland. In October the company, now profitable, repaid €115 million to bondholders and had no bank or other borrowings on its balance sheet at the end of the year, thus eliminating annual interest charges of €11 million.

Trading was looking good at INM, too. Just before Christmas, the company announced that it expected to be able to report that earnings for 2006 had risen by 10%, prompted by a rise in advertising and circulation revenues. Its operating margins would be reported at 20%

when the full year results were confirmed in March 2007. It boasted that the online assets were performing better than the newspapers in getting additional advertising and details of a range of Internet ventures, albeit without the accompanying figures, were given. 'The group is extremely well-positioned for continuing strong growth for the future, in line with current market expectations,' O'Reilly said. His enthusiasm and belief in the prospects of his companies was genuine, much in keeping with the buoyant national mood in Ireland at the time. Of course, now we all know that the country was, in fact, herded to the edge of a steep precipice and about to take a nasty tumble.

CHAPTER TWO

THE POLITICS OF BIG BUSINESS, THE BUSINESS OF POLITICS

O'Reilly may have been as busy as ever, confident that he was indestructible, but his advancing age could not be ignored: even more had to be done to build his legacy, to ensure that his place in the history books as one of the great Irishmen was assured. He wanted to be remembered for his achievements, he wanted to leave behind him successful companies that would grow further after he had gone, he wanted his family's future to be secure – now was the time to achieve those things.

In June 2006 he made a €2 million personal gift to the Ireland Funds, offered after the organisation had secured a €10 million donation from the Irish government. Furthermore, he announced a campaign to raise €20 million in charitable donations. That would reinforce his reputation for giving but he also needed more publicity, to emphasise his continued standing and relevance.

O'Reilly rarely shied from giving interviews during his career, using them to market himself and build his personal brand. With the uncertainty created by the presence of O'Brien on the INM share register, O'Reilly decided to re-emphasise his standing in Ireland with an international audience. He went to New York to record an interview with the veteran American journalist Charlie Rose, which was scheduled to be web-cast near the end of 2006. He was so happy with

the outcome that a DVD copy was subsequently circulated to journalists in Dublin by PR firm Murray Consultants.

O'Reilly used the Rose interview to copper-fasten the image of
himself as a disciplined, self-made man, to describe his work and
achievements and to portray himself as a patriotic Irishman who
thought deeply about what was best for his country.

'It is the ambition of every boy in Ireland and Europe to come to
America, as I did in 1971, to ascend to the high altar of being CEO of an
American Fortune 500 company,' he said, seemingly oblivious to the
fact that most boys would never have even considered or desired his
chosen career path. 'America is seen in the business sense as the most
level playing pitch – tough, highly competitive, tremendously mobile
but very fair. If you are good, you get to the top. You get to the top not
by any old school tie, not by who you know, not by where you went to
college, but because you were lucky enough to perform well in your
given theatre.'

He spent much of the interview speaking of Ireland. When it was
pointed out to him by Rose that Ireland, the poorest country in Europe
eight years earlier, was now regarded as its richest, O'Reilly said: 'How
has the miracle of Ireland occurred? Ireland has failed a great deal of
the way, since 1921 when it became a country. But failure is as
interesting as success and Ireland learnt from its failures. What you
know as Sinn Féin, and I will translate for your viewers as Ourselves
Alone, is an economic doctrine, not a bomb throwers' doctrine. Sinn
Féin meant Ourselves Alone, it meant quotas, it meant permanent
tariffs, it meant protection and we did away with that and we invited in
American capital in a big way and we lowered the corporation tax rate
to 12.5% and that was an act of genius by a finance minister called
Charlie McCreevy, and that operates across every business in Ireland
… Ireland is a magical country for foreign investment.' O'Reilly had
given credit for the lower tax rate to the wrong man: it had been
introduced by Ruairi Quinn, Labour party Minister for Finance in the
Rainbow government of 1994–7 that O'Reilly so despised.

O'Reilly wanted to promote this economic 'miracle' for Northern
Ireland, too. 'If you look at Ireland, the south, foreign investment was
€27 billion two years ago, highest per capita income in Europe, and
you look at Northern Ireland it is as plain as a pike-staff that if you
give Northern Ireland the same tax rate as the south, you will have a

location indifferent island where any international businessman will look to locate his factory and in a sense you will communify Ireland in its prosperity by making Northern Ireland as prosperous as the south.' He said that affluence made people realise that 'true freedom, true sovereignty was the ability to feed, clothe and educate our people of our own volition'.

Rose asked if he dreamt of one Ireland? 'No,' he replied. 'I dream of a communified Ireland. I don't dream of a United Ireland. I think the political map of Ireland [means] we are Europeans now, the old flames of nationalism that flickered and then burst into light very strongly 30 years ago have now been quenched by prosperity and by partnership in Europe. As a result, Northern Ireland is sort of an anomaly. Politically it will want to be different. But I see the two economies becoming ever closer united. It will quell the violence for all time in Northern Ireland. It will not make the two communities there, Catholic and Protestant, love each other. These are strong tribal instincts.'

Rose asked him, 'what is it to be Irish, what does it mean?' Rose starting answering his own question, prompting O'Reilly with a list: 'we think language, green, drinking, fellowship, larger than life character, literature, big poetry'. O'Reilly stopped him there. 'Big poetry,' he repeated. 'We think Heaney. We think the English language, how beautiful it is, how we have taken the language of the oppressor, turned it on them. Heaney speaks beautifully to it. Heaney talking about Belfast. How is this for a line of poetry?' He broke into a Belfast accent and quoted from Heaney's poem, *Whatever you say, say nothing*. 'O land of password, handgrip, wink and nod, Of open minds as open as a trap.'

Rose enquired, 'why have you never gone into Irish politics in a big way?' O'Reilly replied: 'I think I have in the sense that newspapers are very much a part of the political life of a country.'

Rose: 'That makes you part of the conversation, but does that not mean you are standing for election?'

O'Reilly: 'You have interviewed thousands of politicians and you know the enormous sacrifice all politicians make, because everyone owns a piece of them. It is an extremely difficult profession. There is no privacy and I cherish my privacy.'

Rose: 'Did you want to avoid risking defeat?'

O'Reilly: 'You play for Ireland, you are used to defeat. We very rarely win.'

It was said smugly, but as a side-step it worked nicely and Rose diverted to other topics.

In fact, it had been a year in which O'Reilly, with a mind to the 2007 general election, had been very active in making personal assessments of the calibre of Ireland's leading politicians, their views on the economy and the continuing Northern peace process. O'Reilly had maintained a regular interaction with Irish politicians during the late twentieth century, but he now had more time to do so than at any previous stage since he took control of INM in 1973. Many of the prominent Irish politicians of the first decade of the twenty-first century followed in the footsteps of their predecessors by making regular visits to Castlemartin. PJ Mara, who had been Haughey's government spokesman and who had become a public affairs consultant to O'Reilly before going to work for O'Brien, now became one of Bertie Ahern's most trusted advisers too, and he insisted that Ahern, even as Taoiseach, accept O'Reilly's invitations whenever they arrived, according to his availability. One of Ahern's key associates said that Ahern clearly enjoyed his trips to Castlemartin, particularly as his partner of the time, Celia Larkin, did even more so. 'He affected to be a bit put-out by the need to go there, another imposition on his time, but he was far more put-out anytime he didn't get the nod, worrying about why he wasn't being included,' said one of his key advisers between 1997 and 2007, speaking on condition of anonymity. Celia, meanwhile, never needed persuading; this adviser described her as 'social ambition on steroids'. But the relationship also had some warmth to it. On O'Reilly's desk at his office in Citywest stood one lone framed photograph, not of his family but of O'Reilly and Chryss enjoying the company of Bertie and Celia in what had all the appearances of a holiday snap.

There were other, more formal meetings throughout the decade, both at O'Reilly's Fitzwilliam Square residence and, when it was with Fianna Fáil, in Government Buildings on two occasions, although more often these almost always involved Gavin and executives and editors of the INM group meeting for discussions with the politicians and their advisers, rather than O'Reilly himself. More time was devoted to Fianna Fáil and Progressive Democrat politicians, and not just because they were in power. The contact was actively encouraged and sought by the government parties, who believed in proactive management of the government's relationship with the media. 'We would meet with anyone in the media who would talk to us if we thought it would help get our message across,' one of Ahern's closest advisers revealed.

However, this adviser also confirmed that there were at least three meetings that he knew of at Fitzwilliam Square between O'Reilly and Ahern in the life of the 2002–7 government, and not just the one prior to the 2007 general election that subsequently caused such controversy when it was revealed to the public. The calculation was that RTÉ had to be seen to remain neutral and that *The Irish Times* would never be seen to support Fianna Fáil; INM's Irish titles had to be kept onside. 'But don't forget that the Bert [an affectionate nickname for Bertie Ahern] was meeting with News International people as regularly,' said the adviser. 'There was no exclusivity. It was not a monogamous relationship.'

In the run-up to the 2007 general election, O'Reilly decided to get to know Ahern's opponents a bit better. Despite his rows with Fine Gael during the Rainbow government, and with John Bruton subsequently, Michael Noonan, his successor as leader, was a new century guest of O'Reilly's at Castlemartin. Fine Gael had a disastrous 2002 general election and Noonan resigned on the night of the count. The relationship with Labour improved after Dick Spring stepped down in 1997 to be replaced by Ruairi Quinn, whose brother, Lochlann, of Glen Dimplex and formerly of AIB, was a friend of O'Reilly's. Quinn was replaced in turn by Pat Rabbitte in 2002, the former student union leader who had first witnessed the O'Reilly charm at first-hand during a student debate in Galway in the late 1960s and gaped at how O'Reilly had worked the audience of adoring students. Rabbitte, the former radical and Workers Party TD, was also invited to Castlemartin. He remembered how he and his wife were given a tour of the house. 'It was straight out of *The Great Gatsby*. We got to see the Turners, the Yeats, the Monet. He was playing the part of the tycoon to perfection,' he said.

Rabbitte met with O'Reilly for dinner at a neutral venue in late 2006, preferring not to go to O'Reilly's, and meeting at the house of a businessman whom he preferred not to name for this book. Rabbitte formed the impression he was being sized up as to what type of government he would influence as Tánaiste – the likely position he would almost certainly hold in a coalition with Fine Gael, should they win enough seats. He didn't form the impression that he was being lined up to do anything specific for O'Reilly if he came to power. The talk was of the economy, media, offshore exploration and, particularly, Northern Ireland. Rabbitte was very taken by the fact that O'Reilly wanted to know his opinions about Martin McGuinness, while offering none himself. Rabbitte took it that O'Reilly was sufficiently clued in to conclude that McGuinness was the real power and intellectual force in Sinn Féin, not Gerry Adams. 'I remember thinking, why would O'Reilly pursue me on that? He knew exactly what was going on,' Rabbitte said. The former Labour leader did not regard O'Reilly's political contacts as inappropriate. 'A businessman like O'Reilly was entitled to make his case to politicians or government and we must have regard for his opinion, but a government must reserve the right to make its own judgements,' said Rabbitte.

There were meetings with Enda Kenny too, one in London, another at O'Reilly's house in Fitzwilliam Square, according to the Fine Gael leader's advisers. Kenny was preparing for his first general election as leader of Fine Gael. He entertained hopes of unseating Ahern and Fianna Fáil in the 2007 contest, notwithstanding the party's trouncing in the 2002 election under Noonan's leadership. Fine Gael had enjoyed a successful 2004 local and European elections and in September 2006 sensational allegations about Ahern's management of his personal finances emerged at the Planning Tribunal, seemingly undermining his credibility very badly. Fine Gael had begun its work of attempting to repair relations with O'Reilly and INM a year earlier, at the urging of its key election strategist Frank Flannery. He was able to act as a conduit to INM as he was personally friendly with several INM directors and had in the past attended a couple of O'Reilly's Castlemartin functions.

Kenny wanted to know where Fine Gael, under his leadership, stood with O'Reilly and whether O'Reilly's complaints about Kenny's predecessors, Bruton and Noonan, would extend to him, if he would be held liable for their supposed transgressions. Kenny had not enjoyed a previous relationship with O'Reilly, not having been one of the chosen guests to attend Castlemartin soirées. He understood that his membership of the Rainbow Cabinet that O'Reilly so despised would not help him either, that O'Reilly blamed Fine Gael more than he did Labour for that period. That Kenny was perceived as still friendly with Lowry, despite his departure from Fine Gael, was not in his favour either.

Kenny had not sought invitations, being somewhat careful to not be seen as in thrall to O'Reilly, and was somewhat suspicious of his motivations too. Nonetheless, he was persuaded that he had to cultivate a relationship with O'Reilly, not least because Fine Gael feared that the 2007 election would turn into a repeat of 1997 and the infamous 'payback' editorial that endorsed Ahern. It regarded that incident as not just important in itself but as the initiation of a long relationship between Ahern and INM that had endured in the decade since. Fine Gael didn't entertain many hopes that it could woo O'Reilly from his support of Fianna Fáil, and Ahern in particular, but the leadership decided that it had to try to ensure that it got something approaching fair, if not equal, treatment in INM titles for the 2007 general election campaign. Indeed, Kenny's adviser, Ciaran Conlon, had some success with the *Irish Independent* in that regard, developing relationships with various political reporters and getting fair coverage for the various issues that Fine Gael wanted to highlight, albeit not with the *Sunday Independent* to anything like the same extent.

O'Reilly and Kenny did not connect strongly at a personal level. 'They did not become warm buddies,' said an intermediary. They were simply too different. Kenny was a former school-teacher who took over his father's seat when he died: amiable and subsequently some-what more capable than his critics had suggested he would be if he ever got into power, he was not an intellectual heavy-hitter of the kind O'Reilly liked and was somewhat provincial by O'Reilly's standards. Ahern may not have been an intellectual giant, but he was exceptionally clever and O'Reilly admired his tactical abilities, as well as his commitment to a peaceful political settlement in Northern Ireland. They were both northside Dubliners with all of the commonalities that entailed. This mattered, despite O'Reilly's rise in the world, as did mutual friend PJ Mara's honeyed words. Ahern had become something of an international statesman of the kind O'Reilly liked. He was a player, firmly liked and respected by international leaders like Clinton and Blair. Most importantly to O'Reilly, Ahern had also achieved strongly in the politics of Northern Ireland, whereas Kenny, while appreciating their importance, did not seem quite as interested or engaged by the need to deal with those ongoing issues.

Support for Ahern in INM titles during the 2007 election campaign did not come automatically, however, and the circumstances in which it did emerge were highly controversial. Ahern had been left to fight for his political life from September 2006 onwards, when the same Planning Tribunal that O'Reilly so detested for its Fitzwilton investigation found details of Ahern's mysterious accumulation of cash from sources outside of politics and of his refusal to use bank accounts in a way that most people would consider normal or acceptable. Even the *Sunday Independent* could not resist piling in with criticism of Ahern's outrageous and unbelievable explanations, delivered on one occasion during a tearful television interview in which he referred to marital difficulties of more than a decade earlier, as if that could excuse his secret accumulation of cash.

Ahern wasn't the only one having problems with that Planning Tribunal. Justice Kevin Feeney ruined O'Reilly's Christmas in December 2006 when he declared in the High Court that he was satisfied that all of the tribunal's paperwork was in order when it had recorded, in writing, its decision to proceed to a public hearing of the Fitzwilton module of investigation. O'Reilly's lawyers moved swiftly, demanding and getting an extension to the injunction preventing public sittings in advance of an appeal being heard at the Supreme Court in early 2007.

O'Reilly's own issues with the Planning Tribunal only heightened his interest in what was happening to Ahern. The *Sunday Independent*, its populist nose sensing the way the wind appeared to be blowing, added to Ahern's woes in early 2007 by mounting a ferocious campaign against his government's refusal to reduce stamp duty on residential property transactions, apparently believing such a move would provide a safety net to prevent property prices falling, as many correctly feared was about to happen. Hopes rose among the opposition parties that the media would continue tearing into Ahern and undermine him further, with the influential *Sunday Independent* in the vanguard, despite O'Reilly's perceived closeness to Fianna Fáil over the past decade.

Few in Fianna Fáil were confident, though, that O'Reilly had detailed or effective control over the *Sunday Independent*, which was regarded by them as the most influential of his titles because of its million-person readership. The newspaper's hostility spooked them badly as Fianna Fáil's opinion poll ratings slumped, especially as it ran counter to most of what they had experienced over the previous decade. 'The

Sunday Independent relationship with Ahern had a life quite independent of Ahern's relationship with O'Reilly,' said one of Ahern's advisers. 'It was ghastly, all of this tittle-tattle that would be supplied by us about the Bert and his lifestyle, but it worked. It always felt very volatile though. We were feeding a beast, but you never knew when it would turn on you. Aengus was very mercurial. You were nervous when he wasn't onside, but even more so when he was.'

Yet, when push came to shove, the *Sunday Independent* returned to supporting Ahern in the month before the 2007 general election, and even turned hostile against Kenny.

On Sunday, 22 April 2007, a week before Ahern formally announced the election, the *Observer* newspaper carried a report, by its Ireland correspondent Henry McDonald, stating definitively that 'Sir Tony O'Reilly is to swing his Independent Newspapers group behind Bertie Ahern in the Irish general election next month. The *Observer* has learnt that all three of O'Reilly's main national titles – the *Irish Independent*, the *Sunday Independent* and the *Evening Herald* – will back Ahern to get re-elected. Support from the newspaper group that controls the overwhelming majority of the press in the Republic is a major boost for the Taoiseach. Fianna Fáil sources said the party was "cracking open the champagne this weekend" over the news … As well as editorials supporting the current Fianna Fáil/Progressive Democrats coalition, high-profile Independent Group columnists, such as Eoghan Harris in the *Sunday Independent*, are also expected to call for the coalition's re-election.'

More details of how that agreement might have come about emerged on the Sunday before the election. Brian Cowen, then Minister for Finance, was questioned at a press conference by the journalist Vincent Browne about a meeting that he and Ahern had held with O'Reilly at the latter's Fitzwilliam Square home, at a date unspecified but seemingly in the previous month, just before the *Observer* article appeared. Browne argued that O'Reilly's extensive corporate and media investments made whatever was discussed a matter of public interest. Cowen said that the meeting was private, but that it was only about Fianna Fáil putting its position formally to 'proprietors of newspapers to try and see what way we can make sure that we get our message across'. He said there was 'no question' of O'Reilly's corporate interests being discussed, that it had been about 'the future and the election and all the rest of it and preparation for the election in the normal course of events'. He confirmed he had not met any other newspaper owners. Other senior Fianna Fáil ministers said it was the first they had heard of Ahern and Cowen meeting with O'Reilly to discuss the election.

This was grist to the mill of those who believed in a conspiracy theory. But the behaviour of the INM newspapers during the 2007 election campaign was far too complicated to prove that all editors and journalists acted to a set of instructions sent down from on high. The *Irish Independent*, in particular, carried a long list of opinion polls and reports, at least until a week before the election, which suggested that the government would not win enough votes to be returned to power.

Ironically, it was Fanning's notorious unpredictability that may have turned the *Sunday Independent* against Kenny rather than the outcome of any meeting involving Fanning's boss. On 15 April, two Sundays before the election was called, the *Sunday Independent* carried a sensational front-page story claiming that many years earlier a named former Garda had transported cash in a briefcase to Britain on Ahern's behalf, money that had not been declared to the relevant authorities. The day before the story broke, Fanning had been sitting outside a coffee shop in Ballsbridge in Dublin, near to where Kenny just happened to be campaigning. Fanning said that when Kenny, apparently alerted to the presence of the editor, arrived to say hello, Fanning asked him about the story and to provide a comment. Kenny allegedly declined to make an on-the-record comment but said privately, 'this is going to be big'. But after the story appeared Fine Gael not only refused to make an issue of the revelation but ran a mile from it, insisting it was not a political issue but one personal to Ahern. Fanning was furious at the absence of endorsement for the story when Ahern denied its accuracy and, as if in retribution, the following week, on 22 April, the guns of the *Sunday Independent* were turned on Kenny and the suitability of his candidacy for Taoiseach.

Fine Gael was sufficiently outraged by the hammering Kenny got that one key adviser tracked O'Reilly down to Indonesia – where he was finalising a subsequently announced investment by Waterford Wedgwood – to complain over the phone and to request editorial balance, knowing that support would not be forthcoming. 'We wanted to take the vicious edge off it,' he explained. O'Reilly repeated the usual mantra of not interfering in editorial matters, but Fine Gael felt that subsequent coverage, for the duration of the campaign, was toned down from its original hostility, even if it still skewed towards support for Fianna Fáil. Eoghan Harris continued to write in strong support of Ahern, however, even if the likes of Gene Kerrigan and Alan Ruddock did not, and other journalists in the newspaper backed off in their pursuit of the story of Ahern's finances.

As it happened, the same day's newspaper published an interview with Ahern in which he promised the property stamp duty reform the *Sunday Independent* had sought if he was returned to power. It was the start of a rebuilding of relations with Ahern that led to a stunning scoop for the newspaper a week later.

The following Sunday, 29 April, later editions of the *Sunday Independent* – printed and distributed too late for other papers to 'lift' the news to publish as their own – had one of the most remarkable scoops reporters could remember. It revealed that Ahern was going to Áras an Uachtaráin at the crack of dawn to request President Mary McAleese to dissolve the Dáil and set the election date. There was a lengthy interview with Ahern, by Fanning, about stamp duty reform again, inflation, health and Sinn Féin, but nothing about his bizarre personal finances. Instead the one question about the Planning Tribunal was: 'Do you think the tribunal is worth the money?' To this Ahern replied: 'As I'm involved, I'd better say nothing.'

There was a front-page story on 6 May 2007 that went under the headline: 'Most voters want Bertie as Taoiseach despite money issues'. On 13 May there was another interview with Ahern in which he did speak about his personal finances but now under the headline: 'It's all related to my judicial separation'. On 20 May, the Sunday before the election, the headline was: 'Bertie boosted in poll – blow for Fine Gael' and another headline on the front page stated: 'Media tried to scupper Bertie, claims loyal Miriam' (a reference to Ahern's former wife) and inside: 'Ahern personal finances not an election issue'.

Just how much of this helped Ahern is a moot point, but Micheál Martin recalled that the opinion polls just a week before the election had Fianna Fáil 10 percentage points lower than its eventual vote tally. However, the most significant intervention by Eoghan Harris during the 2007 campaign may have been during an RTÉ *Late Late Show* debate rather than in his *Sunday Independent* column. He defended Ahern eloquently during an exchange with John Waters and Eamon Dunphy and the perception was that he succeeded in bringing wavering voters back to Fianna Fáil. Ahern denied that his subsequent choice of Harris as one of the Taoiseach's 11 nominees to Seanad Éireann was a reward for services delivered. Kenny, meanwhile, did himself no favours in a television debate with Ahern on the Monday prior to the election: mistakenly he steered clear of attacking Ahern on his personal finances and when the issue was raised by the moderator, Miriam O'Callaghan, it seemed to stir Ahern into action and cause Kenny to flounder. Fianna Fáil won enough seats to be able to form a coalition with the Green Party.

Fanning died in 2012 and O'Reilly will not talk about these events, but it is not unreasonable to assume that the late editor knew of his proprietor's bias towards Ahern. Eoghan Harris bluntly said that the *Sunday Independent* shifted sides when it got what it wanted on stamp duty. Anne Harris, deputy editor before her promotion to editor after the death of her husband, Aengus Fanning, later said they went with Ahern because he was giving them the stories they wanted to boost sales. O'Reilly's demeanour was such that he might not have been inclined to intervene, but the coincidence of his meeting with Ahern and Cowen – details of which were never disclosed publicly – added some substance to the belief that orders, or at least suggestions, were handed down to support Fianna Fáil.

If this was the case, it may not have been to promote his personal or corporate business interests. As relevant seems to have been his belief that Ahern's continued presence as Taoiseach was essential to sealing the still fragile peace in Northern Ireland and to providing the economic stimulus O'Reilly believed the province needed.

'I think O'Reilly came to the conclusion that Bertie was good for us as a country, particularly on the north, and in fairness I can think of nobody who could have done a better job at that juncture in dealing with the northern situation,' said Rabbitte.

O'Reilly continued to insist that he did not interfere with editorial decision-making. Richard Siklos of the *New York Times* interviewed him not long after the Irish election, but his printed interview made no mention of it. Instead, Siklos referenced Rupert Murdoch's pursuit of ownership of *The Wall Street Journal* and editorial interference.

'Rupert interferes in his papers because he has the time, inclination and the talent to,' commented O'Reilly. 'But people forget how clever Rupert is. I bought my first newspaper in 1973, the same year I was made president of Heinz. I made an election not to interfere in my newspapers. I had no time – I was selling ketchup in Pittsburgh and soup in London. I decided not to interfere, and because of that, my own views in regard to the war in Iraq would be more akin to Tony Blair's. I think he's been a fantastic prime minister of Great Britain.'

Blair did not reciprocate the praise, at least when it came to *The Independent* as a paper, as he made clear in comments on his departure from office as Prime Minister in the summer of 2007. In criticising media coverage in general, he singled out *The Independent* in particular as a 'metaphor' for what happened to news coverage during his tenure, saying that it was 'well-edited and lively' but 'is avowedly a viewspaper, not merely a newspaper'. Questioned subsequently about that by *The New York Times*, O'Reilly was unperturbed: 'I think the fundamental point was that we were the first and most persistent critic of the Iraq war. I took it to be a compliment, because we are a "viewspaper". We've had to mutate: we're not doing news any more. News is so instantly available that the analysis of the world is much more important for the nourishment of the mind. You can't be nourished really by TV or by the Internet.'

Blair may have seemed as important to the peace process as Ahern, but O'Reilly was confident that his successor, Gordon Brown, could be trusted to continue on the same path. Indeed, he hoped that as the former Chancellor of the Exchequer, Brown might be more persuadable when it came to O'Reilly's big idea for Northern Ireland: the adoption of a corporation tax rate to match the Republic's.

There was some very good news for O'Reilly that June, the month after Ireland's general election. Fitzwilton's legal campaign against the Planning Tribunal proved successful, with the Supreme Court making a decision that would effectively curtail the life of the entire tribunal, although not in time for Bertie Ahern, as well as ending O'Reilly's problems with it. The court decided that the tribunal had no legal jurisdiction to investigate Fitzwilton.

The decision hinged on the manner in which the tribunal had informed Fitzwilton of its decision to investigate it. Chief Justice Susan Denham declared that the tribunal had 'reserved' its decision at the relevant time when it had been instructed by the Oireachtas to 'make' the decision: 'I am satisfied the tribunal did not make a decision – it deferred its decision on April 28th, 2005. The document of April 28th clearly indicates a postponement of the decision. This is not a record of a decision to proceed to public hearings. It is a document plainly indicating a contrary decision, a postponement of the decision … Consequently the tribunal has no jurisdiction to proceed with the £30,000 Fitzwilton module.'

Denham added pointedly that 'the tribunal was established in 1997. The concept behind the establishment of a tribunal is that there be an inquiry into definite matters as a matter of urgent public importance. The fact that the tribunal is still inquiring 10 years later is the antithesis of an urgent public inquiry.' It was the first time that the Supreme Court had stopped a tribunal module from going ahead.

A spokesman for Fitzwilton said it was pleased with the Supreme Court's decision, in what was something of an understatement: 'We had always believed that the tribunal had failed to comply with its terms of reference. This was a critical issue of law that required clarification. [Fitzwilton] is pleased that the position it has taken before the courts is entirely vindicated.'

O'Reilly took advantage of the Supreme Court decision to emphasise his personal position, too. His solicitors, LK Shields, issued a statement on his behalf that he had not been aware of the payment to Ray Burke until 10 years after it had been made. For accuracy, it should have read nine years. But the point had been made. To have been caught up in a public tribunal hearing would have been a disaster, especially at a time when he hoped that the outcome of Denis O'Brien's own tribunal encounters might somehow act as a constraint to his ambitions for INM. Time would tell a different story.

CHAPTER THREE

CORPORATE PROVOCATION

.

E arly 2007 had seen the dashing of any hopes O'Reilly may have held that O'Brien's interest in INM was going to be limited to the 3% shareholding he'd bought a year earlier. Between 16 January and 6 February there was unusually heavy trading in the INM shares. A number of stockbrokers were buying, but O'Reilly immediately feared that it was O'Brien in action, although there was always the possibility that a third party was looking to take advantage of any looming corporate battle by accumulating its own stake for subsequent sale at a profit. In early February, O'Brien confirmed that he had increased his shareholding in the company to just over 5%. It was calculated that he'd spent about €50 million in doing so.

It was to become a regular pattern during 2007 as O'Brien regularly returned to the market to buy more shares. In April he made a big and public move: he placed an order with brokers to buy another 5% of INM's shares, something that would cost €130 million if achieved. He would not be able to get all of the shares immediately – although by May he would be up to 7% – but it created an unwelcome distraction for O'Reilly as he sought to complete a resurrected APN refinancing deal and was forced to deal with yet another funding crisis at Waterford Wedgwood.

O'Reilly had faced corporate provocation before, but rarely with this intensity. His initial reaction was to be patient, that in time this irritation would pass. But O'Brien was unpredictable and, to O'Reilly's mind, seemingly irrational. 'When O'Brien arrived on the share register the seriousness of the situation dawned on Tony quickly,' said one of his key executives. 'It was a case of all hands to the pump, how do we deal with this? It was all dressed up about protecting the company, but in reality we all knew that it was all about what this meant for him. It became all-consuming and the effort some people put into it was extraordinary. It dominated meetings. He was obsessed with finding what ammunition O'Brien had, how real his wealth was.'

Some information was in the public domain. After losing in his attempt to buy Eircom, O'Brien headed for the Caribbean, where he was to enjoy enormous entrepreneurial success. O'Brien built a large and highly profitable mobile phone business very quickly, focusing on supplying low-priced services to countries and customers that richer companies had ignored or dismissed. Digicel – as the new company was named – went into 30 countries and impressed investors so much that when O'Brien decided to restructure the business in 2006, he was able to construct a complicated but remarkable deal that gave him an enormous cash windfall. While Digicel was to be left with billions in debt and would require enormous cash-flow to service it and a high level of risk, O'Brien was able to take out more than $800 million in cash for himself. This was now available for him to fund other investments and it provided the basis for additional borrowing on top of that.

It was the type of financial engineering that O'Reilly so admired and in which he used to specialise. He wasn't in the mood to give O'Brien credit, however, and as a result, by focusing too much on the attendant risks he perceived O'Brien to be taking, he badly under-estimated O'Brien's financial resources. 'He refused to believe that O'Brien had seemingly limitless access to capital,' said one insider, on condition of anonymity. 'He took the view that he didn't have what it took to go a lot further than owning a few percent of the shares. Cameron was far more wary. He tried to persuade his father that they shouldn't underestimate O'Brien's resources or make any assumption that he couldn't do it, that he must have had some plan beyond wanting a few percent to make an irritation of himself.'

O'Reilly was being stretched in different directions. There had been some rare good news for Waterford Wedgwood at the start of the year: 2006 had produced the best Christmas in five years as demand for its products increased, in particular for Waterford Crystal. But it was to prove a chimera. By April 2007 the company had to announce its fifth issue of new shares since 2003. It had to sell another €100 million in preference shares, bringing the amount of new equity raised in less than five years to €400 million. On top of that there had been a €165 million bond issue and the sale of All-Clad in the USA for €250 million. And even that might not be enough: the company announced that it might raise a further €100 million in even more preference shares later in the year, if necessary. O'Reilly had a long-standing reputation for always following his money, but this was bringing that tendency to new heights. This particular outlay would cost him and his brother-in-law a minimum of €51.35 million, with a good chance they'd be left to fund much of the balance of the €100 million themselves if other shareholders declined the opportunity to subscribe. Preference shares are supposed to provide a guaranteed dividend each year, a bit like an interest repayment on a loan. However, in an acknowledgement that Waterford Wedgwood would be unable to generate the cash to make such payments, shareholders were told of these repayment terms: each year over the next five years, subscribers would be given eight new preference shares for every 100 instead of a cash dividend. Only after that period would an 8% cash dividend or additional shares be paid. It was hardly an attractive investment proposition for anyone without almost blind belief in the company's future.

Waterford Wedgwood explained its latest fund-raising by saying that 'a range of opportunities for further rationalisation' had been identified during the last redundancy programme in May 2005 and that it wanted to take these now. That plan 'is on track to achieve annual savings of €90 million at a cost of €90 million,' it said. Waterford Wedgwood told potential investors that it had shifted some ceramic production to Indonesia, where labour costs were one-fifteenth what they were in the UK. It closed two more British factories and cut its workforce by 2,200. It stopped selling products at discount outlets and lifted its prices, an action that implied that the volume of sales was actually down.

That was only part of the story. The company was unable to access further bank borrowings. Its debts had climbed to €412 million by end March 2007 and while the pension deficit had fallen from €283.7 million to €147.8 million, thanks to the strong performance of equity market investments, this did not provide any cash benefit to the company. The bankers, increasingly nervous in an unpredictable economic climate, were taking a much tougher approach to the provision of new loans. Ominously, O'Reilly and Goulandris had to provide additional personal security over borrowings of €30 million.

At the subsequent EGM to approve the issue of the new preference shares, Peter Cameron told a shareholder who wanted to know if the company was bankrupt that 'we have made the products more relevant, we have arrested the sales decline and we have achieved a significant improvement in gross margin'. Waterford Wedgwood wasn't bankrupt, but investors had reason to worry that it was heading that way very quickly. O'Reilly headed off to Indonesia to declare another US$25 million investment, an increase of employment at the local plant from 1,350 people to 2,000 and a doubling of the production capacity for ceramics from six million pieces a year to 12 million.

He travelled not long after the sudden death of one of his closest friends and business allies, Vincent Ferguson. O'Reilly spoke warmly of Ferguson at his funeral, saying there had been few moments in his life, when faced with various choices, that he had not sought Ferguson's advice. Advice was something he needed now, as his problems mounted again on many fronts.

The first effort to restructure the ownership of APN Media had ended in failure, but a new consortium was formed to make a second run at buying it. Venture capitalist Providence remained on board and was joined by another major international private equity investor, the Carlyle Group, which was closely connected to the first Bush White House Administration and many of O'Reilly's friends within it. Independent News & Media was to have 35% of the new consortium, Providence 37.5% and Carlyle 27.5%. The intention of this deal was much the same as the last: to give INM a sizeable cash injection, around €375 million, and to remove the APN debts from the INM balance sheet. This initial approach put a value on APN of A$6.05 per share, just 3 cent higher than the original approach the previous October.

Immediately, though, it ran into opposition from independent shareholders. The company's biggest institutional shareholder was a fund called Perpetual and its head of Australian equity investments, John Sevior, took a high-profile position against the offer. 'Compared to the recent multiples paid for television assets, it looks fair or in line, but compared to multiples paid for newspaper business, it looks low,' he said. The INM-led bid went in at A$6.10. It wasn't going to be enough:

even though the APN board accepted it on the basis that nobody else was likely to come in, Sevior, and other institutions who were taking encouragement from the hardline position he was adopting, held out.

A higher bid had to be made, but there were rows within the consortium as to how far to go. The consortium was willing to go to A$6.18, but was aware that Sevior wanted another 2 cent again. Goldman Sachs, as advisers to the consortium, urged it to add the extra 2 cent per share, but the consortium investors only did so eventually when the American merchant bank was persuaded to forego a portion of its eventual mooted fees, worth 1 cent per share. A formal and final offer of A$6.20 was made and the consortium was confident this would win over dissident shareholders as it was offering A$50 million more than it had originally intended. The delay proved to be fatal. Over the next four weeks the Australian stock market went up by another 15% and Providence wanted the price increased to reflect that. That was never going to happen after all of the arguing about the original 2 cent increase.

It all meant that the May 2007 EGM of INM, held with the aim of getting shareholders to ratify the deal, was somewhat surreal. It was noted that O'Brien, by now a 7% shareholder, did not attend or send a proxy. Independent News & Media behaved as if it was certain that the APN transaction would be completed, allowing it to 'maintain a significant interest in APN, which is considered by the board to be both a valuable and strategic asset'. While O'Reilly, in the 2006 annual report, wrote of the potential of INM using the money 'to consider acquisitions of up to €1 billion, without in any way straining the balance sheet of the group', the meeting itself was somewhat woolly on how the money arising from the deal would be used. 'While these proceeds are intended to be applied with the objective of accelerating the group's expansion in its global markets, maximising shareholder returns, reducing debt and for general corporate purposes, neither the precise application of the proceeds nor the amounts available for these purposes has been determined by the board at this time,' the EGM was told.

The board wouldn't have to, in any case. Gavin and his executives flew to Australia for the APN EGM, within days of the INM EGM, for a vote they knew they were going to lose. Independent News & Media could not vote its shares, and three-quarters of those investors representing the other 60% of the shares had to vote in favour of the deal for it to pass. In the end it just about got a simple majority in support, which was not enough.

Independent News & Media managed to convince the stock market that the non-completion of the deal was not a disaster – and it was notable that nobody focused on the deal as an important way to pay down debt but instead as a missed opportunity to provide finance for new purchases. Goodbody Stockbrokers analyst Philip O'Sullivan said: 'The glass half-full argument would be that the rejection of the A$6.20 a share offer highlights the value of the firm's investment in that market. While this is true, the failure to unlock resources to fund continued global expansion is a disappointment, but we note that INM still has ample firepower to fund deals in attractive emerging economies such as India.'

In retrospect the deal might have been transformative of INM's finances in the amount of debt it would have reduced. But not everyone is so sure. One senior INM executive noted that: 'The APN deal was so highly leveraged that it was probable that it would have gotten into trouble and that we would have been asked to put more cash back in to maintain our 35% share. But I admit we could have opted not to do so and we would have had the money from the deal to pay down group debts. Our responsibility for debts at APN would have been on a non-recourse basis,' meaning INM would not have been liable legally to pay them. The debts at APN were substantial in themselves – peaking in 2007 at A$850 million – and would act as a drag on the APN share price and the value of INM's investment in the years to come.

O'Reilly's reaction to losing out on the APN deal was for INM to start buying its own shares and cancel them. The reasoning behind this move was two-fold: it would reduce the number of shares available for O'Brien to buy in the market if he was being outbid by the company for them; and it would help to effectively give O'Reilly an increased shareholding in INM without having to spend any more of his personal wealth. The company spent about €38 million in a week buying about 10 million shares, with borrowed money. 'In hindsight, lots of people have given out about it as a bad use of money, but few people said so at the time,' said one of the INM executives responsible for the transactions. 'The banks lent us the money readily and Denis O'Brien was in the market buying shares at the prevailing price at the same time.' But it didn't stop O'Brien adding to his shareholding, and on 6 June he announced that he now owned 8.35% of the company.

O'Brien also decided to put O'Reilly under pressure over the steward-ship of his company, asking awkward questions. To O'Reilly, it was an uncomfortable reminder of the situation that had blighted his final years at Heinz, when activist shareholders and *Businessweek* magazine had focused on his Achilles' heel – his generosity to himself with the shareholder wealth he minded. It was reminiscent, too, of the tactic employed by JP McManus and John Magnier as shareholders at Manchester United when in dispute with the football club's manager, Alex Ferguson: questions would be asked that were sure to cause considerable embarrassment once they were made public, almost no matter how they were answered.

In the build-up to that year's AGM, O'Brien tabled 42 questions to INM in seven letters to directors. His questions dealt with general governance issues, pensions, corporate and social responsibility and, most sensitively of all, O'Reilly's remuneration and expenses. O'Brien said O'Reilly's remuneration details 'should include salary, bonuses, share options, pensions, insurance, transport, expenses, entertain-ment; any and all payments under whatever heading, made to him or on his behalf'. He wanted to know if 'INM or any of its subsidiary or associated companies pays any staff or other costs, expenses or allowances in respect of private residences owned or occupied by the chief executive, in particular at Fitzwilliam Square, Dublin; Castlemartin, Co Kildare; Lyford Cay, Bahamas; and any other private residence owned by the chief executive?' He focused on the use of a yacht, the funding of parties and the need for a corporate jet, asking if the directors of INM ever used the corporate jet for private use and, if they did, at what rate they provided reimbursement. He looked for details on INM's charitable donations over the previous five years, including those made to buildings named after O'Reilly or his parents in University College Dublin, Queen's University Belfast, Trinity College Dublin and Dublin City University.

The company could not ignore letters from a shareholder. Gavin dealt with each piece of correspondence personally, drafting each letter of reply. Independent News & Media responded that it was 'at a loss as to the provenance and nature' of the questions being asked by O'Brien and was fully satisfied that all requisite and relevant information was fully and appropriately disclosed in its accounts. It said that all payments it made were properly approved and disclosed. On the question of the legendary parties, INM said that where it 'uses the private residence of any executive for a company function, the costs relating to that function or event, having been appropriately approved, are paid for by the company'. It said that the use of a Gulfstream IV by executives for their duties had been deemed 'appropriate and of commercial benefit' by the board. 'For security reasons, the group insists that the group chief executive flies on this aircraft at all times. The annual running cost of this aircraft is fully consistent with the operation of an aircraft of this type … On occasions where the aircraft is used by any executive for non-INM business-related purposes, a commercial rate is applied and paid to the group.' It revealed that INM had made average charitable donations globally over the previous five years of approximately €700,000 per annum, with the Wexford Opera Festival one of the main beneficiaries, something it justified on the basis of 'publicity and goodwill'. It had promised to give Stg£1 million annually to Queen's University Belfast from 2007 until 2010 to fund the O'Reilly Library and added, pointedly, that O'Reilly had personally given more than €50 million to various universities and institutes during his career.

All of this letter-writing had taken place in private. However, a public ambush was launched at the AGM on 16 June at the Culloden Hotel, Cultra, near Bangor in County Down. O'Brien sent a stockbroker with a prepared speech to read out, in which he described INM as 'more representative of a wholly controlled family company than a major internationally traded entity'. He asked if the 'independent' directors were really that and alleged cronyism, using research he had commissioned from Davis Global Advisors, a corporate governance consultancy set up by an academic from Yale School of Management. He described the board's composition as the company's 'Achilles' heel', and alleged 'a dated style of corporate governance' that appeared out of step with the company's 'changing 21st century business ambitions'.

It was left to Brian Mulroney, the former Canadian prime minister and head of the nominations and corporate governance committee, to respond that the company was 'unsurpassed in the integrity with which it conducted its affairs'. Gavin added that 'Mr O'Brien seems to be positioning himself rather strangely as the poster boy of good corporate governance'.

O'Reilly had been particularly enraged to learn that James Morrissey, O'Brien's PR adviser and a former friend of O'Reilly's, had distributed the Davis Global Advisors corporate governance report to journalists in advance of the AGM. O'Reilly decided that he wanted to sue Morrissey personally for defamation, despite warnings that this might not be a good tactical move. Even if O'Reilly didn't like it, Morrissey had been entitled to act as he had and was unlikely to back down. O'Reilly was not looking for financial damages. He insisted that INM's libel lawyers issue a demand for a retraction and an apology from Morrissey and a demand to be given a list of all those people to whom he had given the report. Failure to do so would result in court proceedings for defamation. Predictably, Morrissey called his bluff – saying that he was just doing his job on behalf of his client, that the analysis was accurate and fair and that it had been intended for public consumption. The failure by O'Reilly to carry through with his threat was perceived as a sign of weakness by the O'Brien camp.

It wasn't his only weakness. The warning signs started to emerge that O'Reilly's wealth was not as large as had been widely assumed. At the end of June 2007 solicitors Matheson Ormsby Prentice (MOP), where O'Reilly was part-time chairman, made an announcement to the stock market on behalf of Waterford Wedgwood. It said that Bank of Nova Scotia now held a mortgage over shares in the company held by O'Reilly and Goulandris, to the value of €53 million at the time.

If that was significant, what was to follow was more so. The stock exchange received another letter from MOP the following day, in which it said it acted for Cartson Holdings, a vehicle that held some of O'Reilly's shares in INM. This letter indicated that the Bank of Nova Scotia was a mortgagee of a security interest in three million INM stock units held by Cartson, valued at just under €11 million at the time. The revelation was disastrous for O'Reilly; it indicated financial weakness to O'Brien. O'Reilly was livid and the following day INM issued a statement to say that the notification had been released in error. 'This announcement is incorrect and must be disregarded.' As the denial was official and so definitive, the incident was forgotten by most people. However, the issue of using his shares as collateral for loans was going to become a most serious one for O'Reilly within a couple of years.

O'Reilly was not behaving as if worried by financial constraints, however. In October 2007 he organised for those surviving and able members of the 1955 and 1959 British & Irish Lions touring parties to join him in Paris for the Rugby World Cup final between South Africa and England. He secured and paid for the tickets and, according to former Lion Hugh McLeod, 'we stayed in the Le Bristol Hotel, which was about £600 per night' – a sum far beyond the means of many of the ex-players. It was deeply appreciated by his former colleagues. 'There are not too many of us left, and we have not had a reunion for some while,' said Phil Davies, who also recalled that O'Reilly had organised the previous reunion for the team, too. 'We last met in Ireland, staying with Tony O'Reilly, watching his wife's racehorses and his pedigree herd of Belted Galloway, which, as we sipped wine on the terrace in the evening, slowly meandered across the lime-tree avenue down to the River Liffey for a drink. As it got dark we withdrew to the two drawing rooms to admire the Picasso and the Monet of Rouen Cathedral. Wonderfully civilised.'

That month, too, O'Reilly bought more property in Ireland, paying €7.4 million at auction for the 60-acre Hollyhill Stud in Carnalway, near Brannockstown in County Kildare, just a few kilometres from Castlemartin. It was a 10-room property, with an adjacent cottage, also on the banks of the Liffey, but what was most notable was the €125,000 per acre he paid – a record price at a time when many people thought the property boom was coming to an end. He had a plan, however, but one that was coming too late in the Irish economic cycle. The house was for his daughter, Justine, and her husband, Peter, who were going to return to Ireland from Australia. Their big idea was to redevelop about 200 acres of the Castlemartin estate for housing, well away from the big house but close to Kilcullen. O'Reilly had toyed with the idea of a straight sale of the land to a developer, but didn't think the €25 million or so he'd get would be an adequate return. While he had no experience of house-building himself, his son-in-law was convinced that he could do the job and that the potential return could be anything around €100 million. They began to draw up plans, but they had left it too late. The housing boom in Ireland was drawing to an end.

That O'Reilly had even considered getting into the property game, albeit through his daughter and son-in-law, surprised some of his friends. He had never been a fan of property investment, let alone speculative land investment. Indeed, almost as soon as he committed to this idea at Kilcullen, he began to realise that the market had gone out of kilter and friends said he started to talk of looming problems for Ireland. From late 2007 commentators had been predicting a major slump in the property sector, a sharp rise in unemployment and a return of large-scale emigration. Indeed, O'Reilly had probably spotted it earlier, but like so many others had not taken the potential for collapse seriously enough. *The Washington Post* business columnist Steven Pearlstein had written a piece in 2006 in which he had expressed scepticism about the building boom-led expansion in Ireland being sustainable, and a story related to him by O'Reilly featured prominently: 'Last week, he regaled me with the story of his butler, Martin, who, after pouring him a cup of tea one recent afternoon, asked his famous boss for his view on "Bulgarian property". Turns out Martin had invested in not one, but three condominium apartments with a view of the Black Sea, after taking a holiday at a new Bulgarian resort.'

If there was to be a downturn, then it was bound to adversely affect the profitability of INM. This raised the question: if he had seen all of this coming, why did he initiate such a large-scale purchase of expensive INM shares? 'He had to try to protect his position,' said one friend. 'He had always felt that he has born under a lucky star, that he would always be able to ride things out.'

O'Brien also remained confident enough about the prospects for the Irish economy and media sector to continue buying shares in INM towards the end of 2007, notwithstanding that he had already added to his radio interests in Ireland by buying Today FM in the summer at a net cost of €140 million. Gavin lobbied Micheál Martin at the time about the growing level of O'Brien's ownership in the Irish media. As the Competition Authority and the Broadcasting Authority of Ireland had forced O'Brien to sell the Dublin local radio station FM104, which his Communicorp group had purchased from EMAP as part of the Today FM deal to get over problems with market dominance, then why would the State allow O'Brien to simultaneously build a shareholding in the country's largest newspaper group? Nobody in authority saw it as an issue: O'Brien did not have control of INM, and it would only become an issue in the unlikely event that he did gain control.

O'Brien was again active in the stock market in November, buying another 2.35 million INM shares, raising his stake from 11% to 12.2%. The shares were now cheaper to buy, INM's share price having fallen

15% in a month, and 26% in a year, in an ominous sign of what was to follow. The group was still valued at €1.6 billion on the stock market. O'Brien did not say what price he had paid for these latest shares, but it was somewhere in the region of another €5 million.

As significant, however, was O'Brien's decision to escalate his campaign of public denigration of O'Reilly and INM and, pertinently, he did not deliver his criticism merely to the media in Ireland. In a series of print and television interviews, mainly in London and New York, he described O'Reilly as an 'old-style media mogul', implying that because of his age he was out of touch, particularly with the potential and importance of developing an Internet strategy. 'It's time for Tony to step aside, let somebody else lead the board,' O'Brien said in one interview. O'Brien called for the sale of the loss-making London *Independent*, calling it a 'vanity' investment, and also at various times for the sale of the group's highly profitable Australian radio interests and South African newspapers, although at no stage – seemingly mindful of how it would be perceived in Ireland – did he call for the closure or sale of the perennial loss-maker, *The Sunday Tribune*.

O'Reilly was furious – and insulted – but left others to make his responses for him. 'What a bizarre comment,' said a spokesman for the company. 'Independent News & Media plc is one of the top performing media stocks worldwide, as Mr O'Brien is well aware.' He said the call for the sale of overseas assets displayed an 'ignorance' of the 'dynamic nature' of the group's activities worldwide. Losses at the London *Independent* could be offset in a tax-efficient manner against the profits earned by the *Belfast Telegraph* in Northern Ireland, it was claimed. 'It is also an extra source of editorial material for all of our titles worldwide and is a very good calling card for the company,' he said. Little was said publicly at this stage by anybody about INM's large borrowings.

There was some sympathy, however, within INM's management to the idea of dramatically downsizing the board and disbanding the International Advisory Board, as O'Brien now loudly demanded. The latter was regarded internally as an expensive affection, a chance for O'Reilly to travel and posture with his friends. Executives were being told constantly to be rigorous about cutting costs, about being the ultimate low cost operator in the sector, but meanwhile, as they saw it, their savings were used for O'Reilly's self-indulgence. The board itself was full of O'Reilly's old friends, many of whom had long become overly comfortable, enjoying their fees and trips but offering little of real commercial value. It was not a challenging board in the way that the Eircom board had been to O'Reilly, and as a result it allowed O'Reilly to be autocratic and not get the best out of himself.

His refusal to at least give the appearance of caring about social governance requirements was motivated partly by pride, partly by wanting to continue to provide for his friends. 'He didn't want to be seen to be responding to Denis,' said one of his executive directors at the time. 'And in many ways that's an understandable human reaction, even if it wasn't the best one. But some of his own people agreed with the O'Brien analysis on the London *Independent* and knew that the level of corporate expenses, which were his personal expenses, could not be justified, but nobody was going to say that. Trouble is that some of them had been sharing in it too.'

He couldn't find investors to share in the expense of trying to rescue Waterford Wedgwood either – the mid-year issue of the new preference shares was not a success. O'Reilly and Goulandris had to purchase €83.4 million worth of the €100 million in shares available. The delay in raising the money was to have serious consequences for the company's ability to finance the manufacturing of sufficient stock to fill orders that Christmas. The money only arrived in August, and Peter Cameron said that it was 'frustrating' and 'tedious' that it would not be able to supply the market with its goods ordered.

Sales for the first half of the financial year were 7.1% lower, at €317.4 million. 'There was genuine consumer enthusiasm for our products, especially in the US, but sales were affected by product shortages over the six months to September, and adverse currency fluctuations,' Peter Cameron said. The company posted an operating loss in the six months to end-September of €28.6 million before exceptional items, compared with a loss of €12 million in the same period in 2006. There was an admission that attempts to turn around Waterford Wedgwood's fortunes had 'stalled'. The interest bill over six months was €44 million alone, as net debts now climbed to €418 million. Standard & Poor's, the rating agency, listed the group among the companies in Europe it viewed as most likely to default on debt.

More cuts were promised in response. Peter Cameron pledged a 'final root and branch restructuring' by March 2008. It was clearly needed, but for all the cutting some selling had to be done too. He announced plans to improve its marketing efforts, saying that the group intended to increase its spending on marketing to 6% of sales from the current 3%. Business analysts were amazed that it had been so little and doubted that even 6% was going to be remotely near enough, when other luxury goods companies put between 20% and 30% of revenues back into marketing, but it was a clear consequence of having so little money available.

It meant that by October 2007, Waterford Wedgwood needed to issue another €100 million in preference shares. O'Reilly and Goulandris wanted to take only €17 million worth of shares, with €50 million coming from a new investor, which later turned out to be American venture fund Lazard, and the balance from other investors.

O'Reilly's public comments about Waterford Wedgwood were becoming rarer, although he told *Time* magazine that 'this is the biggest tabletop company in the world ... We've got fantastic brands.' He left it to others to announce and explain bad news, but in October 2007 he chaired the company's AGM. He said the declining dollar had 'hurt this company more than almost any other company, certainly in Ireland and possibly in the British Isles. For the company to get back to where it was five years ago, the dollar needs to appreciate by 60 per cent. We must, where possible, and cognisant of our heritage and brands, significantly reduce our manufacturing costs.'

O'Reilly had always been a fan of outsourcing to foreign locations, but he was now becoming more and more convinced of the merits of moving even more of the production away from Ireland and Britain. The outsourcing by Waterford Wedgwood of some 40% of its products to lower cost areas had kept the group in existence. O'Reilly said the firm's two best investments had been the €90 million restructuring of operations of which Peter Cameron had boasted, and the purchase of a factory outside Jakarta, in Indonesia, where the currency of choice was the US dollar, eliminating the company's heavy exposure to currency fluctuations.

In November 2007, O'Reilly announced that Waterford Crystal was to cut production at its Irish plant with the loss of 490 jobs, as part of a further loss of 1,400 jobs worldwide, with production to be outsourced to cheaper locations, such as Slovenia and, notably, Germany. 'Seventy per cent of our sales are in dollars, and this is a major problem with the euro at $1.48,' he said. It raised questions as to whether production in Waterford was really necessary for the brand at all. What damage would be caused to the brand if none of the manufacturing took place in the country? Would any loss of custom that resulted from people being upset at Waterford no longer being Irish be more than compensated for by far bigger profit margins on the remaining sales that took place?

Management began talking about producing little more than the Lismore brand of heavy, crafted traditional cut glassware in Waterford. As compensation to the local area, details of a plan to expand the visitor centre were announced, with the aim of doubling tourist numbers to 600,000 per annum. But even that would take money and where would O'Reilly be able to get it?

Waterford Wedgwood first met with officials in Micheál Martin's Department of Enterprise, Trade and Employment just before Christmas 2007, to make a pitch for financial support. Martin was to see more of O'Reilly's emissaries that month. Martin had to make a final approval on the sale of Today FM to O'Brien's Communicorp. Independent News & Media decided to object to the deal to both the Competition Authority and to Martin's department on the grounds of cross-media ownership. Gavin and Vincent Crowley went to Martin, arguing for changes to the Competition Act that would prevent any single person or firm from controlling large parts of the print and broadcast media. Martin listened politely, then approved the Communicorp deal.

CHAPTER FOUR

WATERSHED

Once Waterford Wedgwood had a foot in the door of Government Buildings, the lobbying for help would become intensive. There were to be five subsequent meetings between Waterford Wedgwood executives and government officials in the coming months, a series of written communications and numerous phone calls. In February 2008, O'Reilly went to Government Buildings himself and met with Micheál Martin and Minister for Finance Brian Cowen. It was a difficult sales pitch, to put it mildly. O'Reilly had just announced 490 job losses at the crystal manufacturing plant in Waterford, but wanted support to protect the remaining 550 jobs. He brought with him a business plan that envisaged how things could be turned around in about two years if the company was given another chance, notwithstanding how all of its promises over the past six years had proven to be hopelessly optimistic.

O'Reilly was insistent that he was not looking for grants or equity, knowing that these would take more time and that any objections could lead to fatal delay. His idea was that the government should act as guarantor on new loans from the USA that he would source for the company, totalling €39 million, although it was possible that amount would have to be increased. In reality, everyone knew it would be difficult to get that money from the USA, even with the State guarantee, and that the loan would probably have to come from the Irish State. If the money was provided by an American bank, the chances of it being repaid were slim, meaning that the guarantee on repayment would almost certainly be exercised. It was an extraordinary request for Ireland's apparently richest man to make, based on an implicit admission that he could not provide the guarantee himself, let alone new equity.

In going directly to government, Waterford Wedgwood had by-passed Enterprise Ireland and IDA Ireland as the usual conduits for State support to private business, although both were called in by the government to become involved. It was hard to see how Waterford Crystal fit the usual criteria for aid. For indigenous industry, support normally went to start-up and research-heavy organisations. For international industry, the emphasis was on profitable companies that would provide employment. The EU had strict conditions laid down as to the circumstances under which loss-making indigenous companies could receive support.

'You couldn't dismiss it, he was not some sort of fly-by-night, he had tried to save the company and put tens of millions into trying,' said Martin. 'But there was something almost naïve and desperate about what he was suggesting. He had left it too late.'

That didn't mean that the rejection came immediately. As a minister who served the Waterford constituency, Fianna Fáil's Martin Cullen was worried about the political implications in his native county. It was a view shared by other ministers. Cullen argued strongly that something had to be done. 'We looked at every way possible of saving Waterford Crystal,' said Martin. 'The previous closure of the plant in Dungarvan had been ameliorated somewhat by the provision of new jobs in the county, but that was at a time when the economy was moving well. We feared that losing Waterford Crystal would do to that city what closing Ford and Dunlop had done to Cork in the 1980s. We got consultants in to look at everything, cash-flow, production, marketing, the lot. But Enterprise Ireland had no confidence in the management. And there was a problem with him looking for us to guarantee the repayment of loans. Normally you talk about equity, research and development grants, soft supports, but this was different, new ground.'

There were many practical issues. In this particular case, there was a fear of opening a Pandora's box: that once one commitment was made to Waterford Wedgwood, further commitments would be required to protect that original promise. Propping up an ailing, privately owned company, especially when it had already shed about three-quarters of its workforce, might only postpone the eventual closure of the Irish manufacturing operations. Then, not only would this money be lost but there would be even bigger political hell to pay for giving money to a lost cause. There were also concerns that the money might be applied to the group's non-Irish operations, particularly in the even worse performing ceramics businesses. The government could see that only a quarter of the group's total turnover was coming from the crystal division – and while that was the only profitable part of the group, it wasn't clear how much of that profit was due to the outsourced manufacturing rather than the Irish operations.

The group had admitted that it employed 1,300 staff in Indonesia for the same wage cost as 90 staff in Britain, itself a cheaper labour market than Ireland. How, in those circumstances, could it commit itself to continued manufacturing in Ireland?

O'Reilly's personal status was also an issue. He was still perceived as filthy rich, even if that was not the reality. In the annual *Sunday Times Rich List*, published in April 2008, O'Reilly was ranked as the fifth richest Irishman, with assets worth €1.853 billion, an increase of €180 million on the previous year. The total pleased O'Reilly, who was always somewhat obsessed by his place on the list, but the ranking did not as he dropped from third, behind Sean Quinn, Galen Weston, John Dorrance and O'Brien. In any event, the built-in shortcoming of the *Sunday Times* rankings was highlighted by the absence of any estimate of borrowing, to provide a net assets rather than a gross assets estimate. And an assumption had been made, almost certainly incorrectly, that he remained a major shareholder in Heinz. O'Reilly was in something of a *Catch-22* situation once again. If he boasted to government of his wealth, then he was giving it the opportunity to respond that he had his own resources at hand to save a private company. If he admitted his finances were stretched, then word would get out and it would undermine his campaign to keep control of INM.

Martin said O'Reilly was insistent that Waterford Crystal was 'the original iconic Irish brand' and 'he couldn't comprehend how the government would allow a brand like this to go down, that when you don't have many Irish world-class brands, when it takes so much to create one, that you would leave it go'. O'Donoghue confirmed that this was the argument O'Reilly offered. It was an emotionally appealing argument, but the government wondered what real benefit would accrue to the country in trying to protect the brand. In any case, if any of that was true, then why wouldn't the shareholders and banks do what was necessary to save it?

'I think he had an old-style view of how business and politics inter-
acted, going back to his experiences of the 1960s,' said Martin. 'You
met and you got it sorted. He had too much confidence in the process
and in the ability of the ministers to deliver, but this was not the way
things were done in a modern government. He was never threatening
in his personal behaviour. It was as an old teacher of mine in Cork
used to tell me, "you can catch more flies with honey than vinegar".
He was charming and entertaining, but that didn't count for anything.'

The belief was that the European Commission might block any
guarantee as anti-competitive – citing unfair State aid that would
disadvantage glassware-makers in other Member States – although
Waterford quickly claimed that its sources said that the Commission
was not raising this as a significant issue and would not veto State aid.
This wasn't exactly what the government needed to hear: if such
support was allowed, it might create an expensive and possibly dangerous precedent, with other Irish and multinational companies in
trouble looking for similar financial support.

Ahern was torn. He had his own political reasons for saving jobs in
Waterford and he also wanted to remain on-side with the country's
largest media owner. But at the same time he couldn't be seen to be
financially supporting O'Reilly by providing special support for an
unsuccessful investment. Ahern was already under considerable
pressure about his own behaviour; while he might want to keep INM's
newspapers on his side, there would be enormous kickback from
everywhere if he was perceived to be using State money to do that. In
typical Ahern fashion, he held out hope while doing nothing: he
indicated to O'Reilly and Waterford Wedgwood executives that he was
sympathetic to their plight and willing to do everything he could … if
only he could, that he'd be back to them later, once his people had
looked at a few more things. But Waterford Wedgwood needed a
decision now.

––––––

Independent News & Media was still acquiring assets as late as
February 2008, using its equity to do so, with the elevated share price
making it a seemingly sensible alternative to more borrowing if

acquisitions really were a good idea. The US firm Clear Channel, with which O'Reilly had a long and good association, took a 4.7% stake in INM in return for INM buying the 50% stake in African outdoor advertiser Clear Channel Independent that it did not already own. The deal was valued at €87 million. Furthmore, INM also bought *The Sligo Champion*, a small provincial newspaper, at a jaw-dropping price of over €20 million, this time borrowed, to add to its portfolio of Irish regional titles.

There were also more share buybacks, with INM spending €28 million buying 1% of its own shares. O'Reilly was also in the market to buy shares personally. He bought €20 million worth in March 2008, another €8 million worth in April and another €10 million worth in June, at an average price of over €2 per share, in an effort to copper-fasten his position. He borrowed much of the money. It increased his shareholding to 27.2% of the overall total. But by this stage O'Brien was now up to 22.15% of INM. While O'Reilly did not anticipate the fall in the INM share price that was to come later in the year, he knew that he was already in deep trouble at Waterford Wedgwood. He was also sufficiently clued in to global economic events to discern the significance of the Bear Stearns collapse in March 2008 for the further provision of bank finance and for the valuation of assets. Yet he still borrowed and bought.

He had decided to take the fight to O'Brien publicly. Private investigators were hired to get ammunition and – in a move that was to prove grist to the mill of O'Brien's theory that journalists in INM were acting as pawns for their masters – some journalists were encouraged to dig for information about O'Brien's finances, something that had not been asked of them before. Somewhat to the surprise of some INM executives, it was *The Irish Times* and other publications that were more successful in raising questions about O'Brien. The INM management suspected some of their own journalists were reluctant to dig in case O'Brien eventually ended up winning control, and they would then suffer the consequences.

The first metaphorical punch to be thrown publicly was swung in late March 2008, when O'Reilly decided to label O'Brien as a 'dissident shareholder'. He instructed Gavin to make a statement to that effect to the stock market and to hold a press conference at the Shelbourne Hotel in Dublin. Gavin put himself in the firing line when he accused O'Brien of trying to damage the company's reputation with a campaign of 'lies and innuendo' and of not acting in the best interests of shareholders. At the press conference, Gavin let fly:

Having taken appropriate advice, the board of INM believes that Mr O'Brien's comments and actions regarding INM, its board, its management, strategy and its governance, are designed to destabilise the company and run counter to the principles of a fair and orderly market for INM shareholders. This company has nothing to back down from. We've just delivered record results. We have a very, very clear vision for the future. We have supported shareholders. This is a battle, this is a war of Mr O'Brien's choosing, not of ours. As far as we're concerned we're going to continue to run our business to the best of our ability, evidenced by the results that we've just produced … O'Brien has sat there, he's run around the place throwing hand grenades, and hid behind his PR people. And the press has been uncritical in its questioning of Mr O'Brien … He is free to buy shares, as indeed is any institution or individual. What he is not free to do is to continue to issue misleading, defamatory information.

Gavin also accused O'Brien of having a 'persecution complex' over coverage in INM titles. 'In the light of this, we believe it is reasonable to question Mr O'Brien's emotive reaction to the legitimate news coverage.'

As Gavin took questions from the floor, a page titled 'Some Questions for Denis O'Brien' was circulated to journalists. It included 18 questions in all, some of which questioned his management credentials and the losses incurred by Communicorp, his radio group. Another asked whether O'Brien's Caribbean mobile phone company, Digicel, was worth about US$1 billion less than its outstanding debt.

O'Reilly's adviser, Rory Godson, recalled the decision to label O'Brien as a 'dissident shareholder' as 'catastrophic', and several directors who spoke for this book on condition of anonymity agreed. 'It gave O'Brien the status, to some, as the necessary anti-O'Reilly person. The term had no legal standing here. I was told that this was the way things were done in the United States and maybe it was, but it wasn't going to fly here.'

O'Reilly affected a degree of indifference to O'Brien's assaults, at least publicly. 'You have to realise that I was for twenty-five years the president of the HJ Heinz company and in America the whole issue of dissident shareholders is a constant theme in almost every board that I've ever been on. And I've been on the board of Mobil Oil and Banker's Trust and *The Washington Post* and the HJ Heinz company, so I am somewhat a veteran of the wars in terms of dissident shareholders.'

The reality was that he was shocked. 'The O'Brien assault was staggering to him. He just couldn't understand it. He was utterly perplexed,' said one of his advisers.

Gavin was determined to defend his father's reputation – and his own. 'It's an easy target to look at myself and my two brothers,' he said. 'I find it slightly outrageous that this shareholder would seek to impugn my father, who has essentially created this company. He took a small company back in 1973 and turned it into one of the first-class media companies in the world. There isn't anything, as far as I'm concerned, in Mr O'Brien's history of running media that makes me feel he's well qualified to make these comments.'

O'Brien countered that INM's statement was a 'highly personal and unwarranted attack. I have always been, and remain, committed to investing for long-term value for all shareholders and look forward to seeing signs of a similar approach from the board of directors.'

O'Reilly continued to leave interaction with the government on media issues to Gavin and Crowley. He was pleased when, in April, Martin, having previously approved the Today FM acquisition by Communicorp, established an inquiry into media ownership rules. The Government said this followed a call from the Competition Authority, which encountered difficulty when examining the Today FM deal because it did not have 'the expertise' to decide plurality in the media. O'Reilly hoped for an outcome that would block O'Brien from buying any further shares in INM, or even demand that he sell some if he was going to leave his radio empire untouched. At the very least he felt it bought him time.

——

Time was not something Waterford Wedgwood had, at this stage. By April 2008, with the government still procrastinating, John Foley, CEO at Waterford Crystal, was given the job of applying the pressure publicly to get a decision. He claimed that any government assistance would be akin to the public bailouts of Northern Rock in Britain, Bear Stearns in the USA and the rescue in the 1980s of Insurance Corporation of Ireland. It was put to Foley by *The Irish Times* that all of his examples involved systemic risk in the financial markets and were not remotely similar to Waterford Wedgwood's experience. He responded: 'I argue that this is such an iconic brand and company and so part of the Irish psyche, not only in Ireland but internationally, that it is every bit as important to us as those other situations in other countries.' Some of his colleagues worried that he had gone down the wrong track in the examples he had selected.

Redmond O'Donoghue felt that the public servants were 'very timid' in their response to the request from Waterford Wedgwood for aid: 'The politicians were better at seeing the bigger picture. The public servants kept banging on about State aid and "national champions" not being allowed by the EU. But at the time we were reading about the German government protecting Opel by putting in €6 billion in loans and underwriting guarantees. In France, PSA Renault got €8.5 billion in supports. In the United States, General Motors and Chrysler got US$62.5 billion and US$13.5 billion respectively, and look at General Motors today.'

The pressure didn't work. In May, soon after Ahern had been replaced as Taoiseach by Cowen and Brian Lenihan had been promoted to become Minister for Finance, the government formally rejected the loan guarantee proposal. Martin's replacement as Minister for Enterprise, Trade and Employment, Mary Coughlan, said that it was 'not possible to devise an approach' that would be acceptable to both the Government and the company. 'It would have allowed us to buy time,' said O'Donoghue. 'It wasn't just the money, it was also about the signal that it would have sent to the market, the message that the Irish government was four-square behind us.'

In both the O'Reilly and the O'Brien camps the belief was that, notwithstanding the controversy surrounding his resignation, O'Reilly was interested in appointing Ahern to the board of INM once a suitable period of time had elapsed after his stepping down as Taoiseach. Former taoisigh, such as Jack Lynch and Garret FitzGerald, and former Minister for Finance Ray MacSharry had taken corporate directorships on leaving politics and while INM did not have a track record of appointing former Irish ministers or taoisigh, O'Reilly had appointed many prominent foreign former politicians, including prime ministers, in recent years. Given their relationship, Ahern was an obvious choice, notwithstanding the inevitable controversy it would have caused. In the summer of 2008 that might have been possible, in spite of O'Reilly's need to reduce the bloated size of his board to fend off criticism from O'Brien. However, the swift collapse of the INM share price and O'Reilly's loss of control were to put paid to the idea.

Ahern's departure from politics threatened to derail O'Reilly's key plan for Northern Ireland. Tax was an issue that greatly occupied O'Reilly's time and intellect, although his critics claimed it was always with a view to minimising his own payments. For states and their governments he was a big believer in the 'less creates more' principle, and even with his own personal financial problems increasing he didn't lose sight of his political ambition for Northern Ireland. In May 2008, O'Reilly spoke at a special international investment conference in Belfast, at the Northern Assembly parliament buildings at Stormont, which was attended by British Prime Minister Gordon Brown and the new Taoiseach Brian Cowen. He used the occasion to promote his economic idea for Northern Ireland, which he had floated previously but to no avail: that it receive a special deal within the UK and the provision of a low corporation tax rate similar to that which applied in the Republic of Ireland, as part of the transfer of some fiscal auto-nomy. It was a notion to which Brown was strongly opposed. O'Reilly argued that Northern Ireland had to be 'allowed to open wide the economic throttle' if it was to make up the lost ground and missed opportunities of the Troubles: 'We must achieve quickly a situation where new investors are delighted not only with their pre-tax profits but with their after-tax profits as well.'

The event was accompanied by the publication of photographs in various media. The photographs were remarkable in one respect: alongside a smiling O'Reilly was a beaming Martin McGuinness, Sinn Féin's Deputy First Minister, along with the Democratic Unionist Party's Ian Paisley and the Mayor of New York Michael Bloomberg. Given the antipathy between O'Reilly/INM and Sinn Féin/IRA, it was a landmark occasion and photograph. Clearly others beyond Rabbitte had convinced O'Reilly that McGuinness was somebody worth doing business with; by the same token, Sinn Féin, north of the border at least, had long become convinced of the merits of working with the Ireland Funds, and therefore McGuinness was prepared to be seen in O'Reilly's company.

There was an implicit endorsement, too, of Sinn Féin and McGuinness in O'Reilly's speech to the conference, when he described the executive as a 'very strong ministerial team'. He claimed that 'investors will be impressed by that and by the way they are so sharply focused on creating an increasingly vibrant economy'. In keeping with the themes he had promoted throughout his career, he described Northern Ireland as a 'very competitive location where companies can make good profits'.

It had escaped the attention of few of his newspaper employees in the south that the north was becoming home to more INM investment, as part of the cost reduction drive. In 2007 INM had opened a new Stg£20 million, 60,000 sq ft printing press plant in Newry, just on the northern side of the border. At the 2008 conference O'Reilly announced an expansion of that plant, involving another Stg£7 million in capital expenditure.

Also in May, INM released its annual report for 2007, in preparation for an AGM in London in June 2008 that was likely to see O'Brien fire another salvo across the bows. O'Reilly used his CEO's statement to make claims that were designed to burnish and bolster his personal stewardship of INM. 'We make no apologies for saying we are the right company with the right products and we intend to work these products for the benefit of each and every one of our shareholders,' he declared. In growing earnings per share, 'we have comfortably out-performed our global media peer group'. He cited the 2007 Daily Mail and General Trust (DMGT) annual report, which described INM as the best performing media organisation as measured by total shareholder return in the period 2002–7. 'I think all of this will suffice to convince you that you are investors in one of the best-directed and most successful media companies in the world.'

He boasted of consistent growth in revenue, earnings and control of operating expense. 'Over the last five years the group's core pub-lishing division has been refocused and re-engineered as part of a transition to become the industry's leading low cost operator.' Independent News & Media increased both advertising and circulation revenues during 2007 and 'there is almost no media company in the world – certainly not one that operates on such a broad scale as INM – that can make a claim of that nature.' He cited geographic spread as a protection against economic downturn. 'It is the view of the board and management that significant opportunity still exists outside of the developed markets of Europe, North America and Asia and INM is uniquely equipped to exploit these. I believe truly innovative companies are those that intelligently identify new markets around the world, develop new workflows and processes to cut inefficiencies, leverage strong brands and assets for both global and local expansion, and that identify market segments poised for substantial growth.'

Everything in the report seemed to be written with O'Brien in mind, but without mentioning him. 'We have a frugal management structure which combines both independence and collegiality in equal measure,' he wrote. He emphasised his own work ethic. 'During the past three months I visited almost every single operation of our company, ranging from Yandina in Queensland to India, Indonesia, South Africa, Germany, Britain, Northern Ireland and the Republic of Ireland.' He defended the non-executive directors from criticism. 'Representing a very broad church … they are individuals of intellect, insight and experience. Their sound judgement and direction to the executive directors is immense and is of significant benefit to the company and its shareholders.'

There were some little digs seemingly aimed at O'Brien. 'As a board we share important objectives and understandings about the nature of and structure of society and the responsibility, particularly of the press, in regard to objectivity and non-interference in the editorial process,' he declared. He also tried to emphasise that INM was a giant and, by implication, that O'Brien's Communicorp was a minnow by making a rare reference to INM's broadcasting assets: 'Our radio stations, with almost 6 million listeners, exceed the entire audience of RTÉ and all private stations in Ireland.'

None of this got the attention that O'Reilly craved. While O'Reilly placed enormous emphasis on his statements in annual reports, believing that investors would devour and believe whatever he wrote, the media rarely reported such material, believing it to be merely propaganda and not newsworthy.

There was news in the weeks running up to the AGM that gave him both hope and fear. At the end of May the Broadcasting Commission of Ireland (BCI), the regulator for the radio sector, announced that it would review the extent of O'Brien's radio assets. The BCI's legal remit was to promote the plurality of media ownership and to guard against any person having 'control of, or substantial interests in, an undue amount of the communications media'. However, just because the BCI had the power to block media mergers on the basis of cross-media ownership did not mean that it would take any action. And the BCI action was not motivated by any feeling that it needed to do something in the public interest: the review was triggered automatically by O'Brien stepping over the 25% ownership threshold in INM. There was a further bit of bad news in that, by having more than 25%, O'Brien could now block any proposals from the INM board to change its internal rules or the number of shares in issue. That share ownership issue was significant because O'Reilly and son Gavin made their last additional purchase of shares just before the AGM. Together with other directors, they now owned 29.49% of the group.

O'Reilly and his board waited for the inevitable O'Brien assault at the AGM at the Park Lane Hotel in London in June. O'Brien had a new report to support him, from Glass Lewis, a voting advisory service for American investment funds. It argued that the board was too large, at 20 people, had too few independent directors and an audit committee too closely affiliated with management, especially as Stg£333,000 had been paid to directors for consultancy services over and above standard non-executive fees. Another voting adviser, ISS, recommended opposing the re-election of three non-executive directors.

'This should be a matter of grave concern,' O'Brien said in a statement. 'It is in the interests of all shareholders that our board carries out its duties and responsibilities in a totally objective and impartial manner.' He called for the resignation of O'Reilly as CEO, for the board to be slimmed down and demanded the sale of the London *Independent* titles. He also condemned what he saw as the lack of a digital strategy.

Independent News & Media described his report as a 'malicious and wholly inaccurate assessment'. It commissioned its own governance report, carried out by Harvard Business School professor Jay Lorsch, which gave it a clean bill of health. 'The dissident shareholder can't beat something with nothing and, frankly, that's exactly what he's offered shareholders,' Gavin said. 'He has offered no alternative vision, strategic or otherwise – no directors, no bid, nothing. All he's done is pursue a Don Quixote-like campaign in an area where he has no experience and, to judge from his less-than-stellar Communicorp results, no expertise either ... The Internet is a wonderful place if you know what you are looking for, but we run the risk that running headlong into digital will turn our dollars into pennies.'

O'Reilly was unhappy that O'Brien's criticisms got such an airing in the rest of the British media, which turned up in force to witness a rival's discomfort, but having been forewarned, he and his colleagues had at least turned up forearmed. He was somewhat fortunate, too, that he would get some publicity from a function at the Cannes Lions international festival later than month, which he would attend to pick up a 'Media Person of the Year' award. He was happy to see the advertising industry bible *Campaign* write in glowing terms about him, describing his most prodigious quality as being 'charm. This alone marks him out among media barons, so many of whom reveal themselves, despite their best intentions, as masters of all that is cantankerous and misanthropic. Those who have come under his spell say O'Reilly is easily the world's most charismatic media mogul.' He might have been less impressed that the headline compared his longevity to that of Silvio Berlusconi and his Italian media interests.

O'Reilly was into whatever good press he could find. He invited Martha Stewart, still immensely popular despite her conviction for tax fraud, to his Castlemartin home and she wrote about it on themarthablog.com in July 2008. She wrote gushingly about the house, gardens and the hospitality, enjoying 'spring lamb chops and fresh garden peas' before a dessert of 'sour lemon meringue tart' in the company of Brian Mulroney and his wife, Mila, as well as the O'Reillys. There were photographs of the grounds but none of Waterford or Wedgwood products, which was presumably the point of bringing her there other than just flattering his ego.

All the good press in the world couldn't change facts, though, and the fact was that the value of INM shares slid dramatically from August 2008. It was like watching a car crash in slow motion. Down they sailed towards €2 and then, once through that, to €1 each. Then, when that floor was breached, they continued all the way down to as low as 9 cent each – giving one of the giants of Irish corporate life a value of just €80 million. The consequences for the wealth of both O'Reilly and O'Brien were catastrophic. Both owned shares worth as little as €20 million at that low point – had they been able to find someone to buy them. It was more expensive in cash terms for O'Brien, as he had bought the shares recently and at much higher prices than O'Reilly would have paid for the bulk of his many years earlier. Although never confirmed, O'Brien may have spent up to €500 million on his accumulation of INM stock, implying huge losses, and much of the money had been borrowed from Barclays Bank in the UK. But O'Reilly had spent tens of millions of his own money too, much of it borrowed, and the company's decision to spend €130 million, also borrowed, buying its own shares now looked even worse than it had at the time.

What caused this slump in the share price – and enabled the bankers to force radical change upon the company? The impact of a quickly enveloping recession in Ireland was obvious for both advert-ising and circulation revenues, and the other economies in which INM was active also suffered badly, and quickly. The banking world was changing quickly, too, as liquidity issues meant that banks were suddenly reluctant to provide or refresh the loans as they had so readily done in previous years. This was even before the crisis for the banks that brought about the Irish government's introduction of a guarantee in late September 2008 to save some of the Irish banks from collapse. It also predated the realisation that many of the property loans given by the banks would not be repaid and that, without the injection of tens of billions in fresh capital by the State, insolvency would result.

The banks were far quicker to move against INM than against any of their property-reliant clients. The first indication of the new powers of lenders to INM came in August 2008, when the group announced that it had 'succeeded' in securing a new €105 million bank facility to replace a bond that had matured in December of that year. But success was relative because the group of lending banks, led by AIB, demanded security by way of a charge over INM's main Irish newspaper titles, specifically the *Irish Independent, Sunday Independent* and *Evening Herald*. It provoked memories of what had happened to the *Irish Press* titles more than a decade earlier, when a profitable business with established and successful titles was dragged into the mire by rows between shareholders and mounting debts. As lead banker in pro-viding the loan facility, AIB was also granted a charge over *The Independent* newspaper title in London and the controlling stake in

The Sunday Tribune. This requirement to potentially give effective control over the central assets showed the fear the banks now harboured about INM's ability to repay its debts. Suddenly, INM needed to raise money, and fast.

There was little fat to be cut from the business (although Irish employees did take pay cuts late in 2008) because INM had been ruthless previously in slashing the costs of producing its titles, out-sourcing advertising sales and sub-editing of its Irish titles to cheaper service providers. While the Irish newspapers operated at profit margins that were the envy of the global industry, the company had not used its profits to pay down debt sufficiently: too much of the money went towards feeding the voracious appetite of the share-holders for cash through dividends. The company looked quietly to sell assets overseas, but could find no buyers.

There were about to be two dramatic developments at INM that would emphasise just how weakened O'Reilly's position had become. In November, O'Reilly took the extraordinary decision to consider the sale of the INM shareholding in APN, 20 years after the family and Irish company had taken effective control of it. Independent News & Media claimed that it had been in receipt of 'a number of expressions of interest' in buying its shares, although not giving any details as to the identity of likely buyers. It suggested that a sale would reduce net debt on its books from €1.4 billion to less than €600 million and that the transaction would be 'earnings neutral' in 2009 as the consequent reduction in its interest bill, which had exceeded €93 million in 2007, would offset the loss of profits from APN.

At the time APN was valued at €1.18 billion, meaning that INM's interest was worth €241.62 million, but INM said that was not reflected·adequately in its own share price. Many were confused as to who the likely buyers would be, especially when Fairfax – for so long touted as a possible candidate for O'Reilly's expansion plans – publicly denied any interest in buying into APN or any assets, such as the *New Zealand Herald,* that it might offer for sale. Fairfax highlighted a problem any potential buyer would have: low share prices meant an equity-funded purchase would be expensive, and banks were not looking to lend money for acquisitions either. Realising that his own investment might not survive if he didn't act to protect it, O'Brien decided to initiate peace talks with the O'Reilly camp.

In early November 2008 O'Brien wrote to INM's chairman, Brian Hillery. In return, the one-time so-called dissident shareholder was quickly offered a meeting at Citywest not with his foe but with his one-time social friend Gavin O'Reilly. O'Brien, his adviser Paul Connolly and stock market strategist David Sykes met with Gavin, COO Donal Buggy and Vincent Crowley. It was such a cordial meeting that, significantly, the visitors were given a tour of the plant, news of which quickly found its way into non-INM-owned newspapers. The INM executives outlined to O'Brien and his people what the company would do to stave off ruin. 'Gavin was the subject of a charm offensive by Denis and he became convinced that he could work with him. He told his father that too, but convincing him was a far more difficult task. His father was very sceptical,' said one INM executive on condition of anonymity.

Gavin's interaction with O'Brien followed a very difficult meeting he and his brothers had with their father. Gavin had become acutely aware of the financial dangers being faced by INM: 'Welcome to Waterford Wedgwood Mark 2,' he drawled ruefully to one adviser as the financial noose on the company tightened. The realisation was dawning that rolling over INM's debts – the repayment of loans as they fell due with new loans of the same size – would now be much harder than had been anticipated. Gavin spoke with his brothers – both directors of INM, albeit in part-time capacities – and the three sons came to a difficult decision: they would confront their father over the dramatic deterioration in his wealth and his approach to dealing with it. They were worried that he would waste what he had left on a further folly at Waterford Wedgwood and would be forced to bow at INM to O'Brien's greater financial resources. They wanted him to com-promise. This meant a trip to Deauville in November 2008, where they presented a united front in one of the most difficult meetings imaginable with their father.

O'Reilly had always had the attitude of 'I made the money, it's mine and I'll decide what to do with it', but although he was slow to realise it, that didn't apply anymore. Cameron had never been afraid to chal-lenge his father, but Gavin and Tony jnr had always been somewhat more reluctant. Their father might listen, but he was autocratic and had never been shy about saying that. He was always tougher with his sons than he was with other management. That the three travelled together was hugely significant. But the fact was that the sons' inheritance was at stake and, in Gavin and Tony jnr's cases, their continued livelihoods too. Both men had broken first marriages and the costs that arose from that, as well as being in new relationships. Their message to their father was clear: there should be no more money for Waterford Wedgwood, and a compromise with O'Brien at INM was the only way to save the company. O'Reilly listened, but he made no promises to his sons.

As a 25% shareholder, O'Brien had enormous legal and effective power. The banks, in particular, understood this and sought to make O'Reilly aware that O'Brien could not be ignored. The fall in the stock market value of INM to below €200 million meant that, under company law, any attempt to sell assets for more than a combined amount of €100 million would require approval at an EGM. The banks could not afford O'Brien using his shares to block any initiative O'Reilly might have sought to undertake without him, such as the APN sale.

The revelations that APN was for sale and that the O'Reilly and O'Brien camps were talking to each other was seen as a sign that they had realised they had to work together to save INM. This gave the share price a temporary boost. The company also conceded publicly that it would have to cut operating costs at its loss-making *Independent* and *Independent on Sunday* titles in London. In addition to a previous cost-saving deal it had done with Associated Newspapers, the publishers of the *Daily Mail*, it said it would look to introduce so-called 'shared-services operations' with rival British national newspaper groups that would 'create more efficient editorial work flows' while somehow preserving the titles' editorial ethos. Few people in the newspaper business could see how that would work, but it was a sign of O'Reilly's emotional attachment to these particular titles that he would look to do all of these things, if he could, just to keep ownership of the papers. However, Gavin, with O'Brien encouraging him, was sounding out potential buyers.

O'Reilly found it hard to deal not just with his growing financial misfortunes but with his inability to control events. 'He always had to win everything, always had to be right and he simply wasn't used to things not going his way,' said his adviser, Rory Godson. He was now into his seventies and while his remarkable intellect was still razor sharp and he retained much of the high level of energy that had made him so formidable, he had become somewhat set in his ways, certain of his interpretations, even when others disagreed. As a keen military historian O'Reilly was well aware of the dangers of having to fight battles on too many fronts with limited resources. As events at INM overwhelmed him, he had to face an equally serious situation at Waterford Wedgwood.

O'Reilly made one last effort to raise new equity for Waterford Wedgwood in September 2008. He sought to raise €153.7 million, but found it almost impossible to get potential investors interested, even though the planned share issue was backed by 'irrevocable under-takings' from O'Reilly and Goulandris to stump up €60 million. Another €15 million was coming from Lazard, the fund that had invested €50 million the previous December. Other directors were told they too had to contribute, painful though it was for them with their more limited resources, because failure of a director to get involved would be interpreted as a loss of confidence in the company from within.

It didn't work. The company got just short of €80 million in new funds and had to admit that it would not be able to raise the remainder of the money required at the price suggested. It would try to raise the balance on different terms 'and which, significantly, may encompass a comprehensive financial restructuring'. All of its com-ments to the stock exchange were carefully worded because of legal concerns. The directors had 'reason to believe that their senior lenders will continue to support the company whilst discussions with potential new investors continue'.

Waterford Wedgwood said the money would be used to implement the business plan that David Sculley, O'Reilly's old Heinz colleague, had been working on since the previous April when he had taken over from Peter Cameron as CEO. The promise was that the plan 'will remove complexity from the business, targeting substantial annualised cost savings as well as a significant reduction in monies tied up in working capital'. It promised that debts would be reduced and that, crucially, it 'should ensure we have the requisite working capital in place well ahead of the vital Christmas trading period'.

All sorts of promises were made in the latest effort to entice new investment. 'The three-year cost reduction programme will go further than any plan before it with proposals to streamline all areas of the business … We must align our cost base to a position where we are not reliant on significant sales growth to achieve our goals.'

In retrospect, there may have been an opportunity at this stage to opt for the process known in the Irish legal system as examinership, as had happened at Chorus in 2003 without INM. An application to the High Court could have been made and, if secured, would have given the company between 60 and 90 days' protection from having to repay its creditors. A 'scheme of arrangement' could then have been formulated, in which O'Reilly and Peter Goulandris would have used the money that was going into the futile rights issue as a new investment instead. The process would have allowed Waterford Wedgwood to write off a large chunk of its debts, albeit with the support of the creditors. O'Reilly could have organised all of this in advance – a so-called 'pre-pack' – which would have locked out the chances of somebody else coming in instead to own the business, subject to the agreement of the courts.

O'Reilly wouldn't do it.

'He always refused to countenance that,' said O'Donoghue. 'He believed it would be terribly wrong to see employees, pensioners and thousands of creditors going unpaid so that the business could be started again. He wouldn't screw people. His honour demanded that he wouldn't do that.' Kevin McGoran, a director of Waterford Wedgwood since O'Reilly's first investment in 1990, concurred that if the idea was mentioned, it was most certainly never discussed; it was simply not the right way to do things.

But if O'Reilly wouldn't do it, then the pension fund trustees most certainly could have, and indeed should have taken action to appoint a receiver to the company much earlier, on the grounds that the deficit in the pension fund had become too large and was not being adequately funded by Waterford Wedgwood.

In October 2008 the company confirmed that its manufacturing at Waterford was to be further reduced, by another 280 people on top of the 490 announced the previous November, to concentrate on 'a range of prestige hand-crafted products, its tourist trail and its gallery operations'. It said that 'it remains committed to the retention of its intellectual property in Ireland'. Foley spoke of the company being 'proud of its heritage' and said that 'the city of Waterford remains its home' and that the retention of a high-value, hand-crafted crystal manufacturing presence in Waterford was 'critical to the DNA of our brand'. It accompanied an admission, however, that 'maintaining manufacturing operations in Ireland at their current level is not feasible'.

Waterford Wedgwood's market value was now less than €50 million, but it had debts of more than €470 million. The dollar was weakening and an international recession that would certainly impact further on the purchase of luxury items was taking hold. The pension fund deficit had been reduced, but it still was just a couple of million euro short of €150 million. As O'Reilly had not ever considered the possibility that Waterford Wedgwood could go under, the realisation of the impact this would have on the company's pensioners – particularly those in Ireland, where the same State-backed legal protections did not exist as in Britain – came late to him and horrified him. 'He seriously considered gifting his shareholding in Waterford Wedgwood to the pension fund in an effort to put some value back into it,' Godson said. It was too late, however, given that the shares were largely worthless.

Waterford Wedgwood's bankers were becoming even more anxious. The existing covenants – or legal agreements relating to them – had been breached. The representatives from Bank of America and other banks had extended a number of deadlines and would do so again one more time, in November, for another 30 days on interest repayments. It warned that after the fourth such deferment, and in the absence of new equity, the full terms of the loans would be exercised and full repayment would become due from 2 January 2009. The amount of additional equity required, beyond a further €33 million that O'Reilly and Goulandris had scraped together and were prepared to invest, was a further €78 million. There was nobody who would put that in. Peter – the self-declared 'very good brother-in-law' – had regularly invested further money on the basis that it was the only chance he had of getting back some of his original money. Now he too was reaching the point of no more.

Within the Waterford Wedgwood board there was a feeling that they were deeply unfortunate with the timing of the company's needs, as a global financial crisis took hold. 'I truly believe that if you wanted to buy something for €10 million, say, and you had €9 million and wanted to borrow the other €1 million in late 2008, you just wouldn't have been able to raise it, so paralysed was the banking system at that time,' claimed O'Donoghue. While that was true, it was also the case that everybody outside of Waterford Wedgwood had run out of confidence in its ability to trade its way out of its crisis.

There were no assets that could be sold quickly enough by the company, O'Reilly had no more money left to give and his brother-in-law had decided that he had given enough. They could not even guarantee repayments on loans. O'Reilly would have to return to the Irish government, but even this legendary salesman had little he could offer to get what he wanted and needed. He met with Minister for Finance Brian Lenihan in his Fitzwilliam Square home, where much of the conversation was about the crisis in which the country found itself. They had a connection as Belvedere College alumni and O'Reilly was readily engaged by Lenihan's intellect and somewhat eccentric manner, as well as by his willingness to listen and debate ideas. Lenihan was as interested in O'Reilly's views in the banking and economic crisis he was facing as Minister as he was in hearing about O'Reilly's troubles at Waterford Wedgwood. 'I quite like meeting rich men,' Lenihan told a friend with a smile when he returned to the Department of Finance, 'they are very interesting to listen to, but that doesn't mean you have to do anything about what they say.'

On 17 November the company issued a statement that it would be discontinuing its listing on the London Stock Exchange, keeping one only in Dublin. It admitted a further slowdown in sales, by 19%, in October compared to the same month a year earlier, blaming the world economic environment, an acceleration of the trend of recent months. In a clear example of straw-clutching, the statement claimed that Waterford Wedgwood was 'generally outperforming its competition' and was retaining or increasing share in its key markets. More prose about the standing of the brands was included in the statement.

The company made a prediction for 2008 sales of €615 million, down from €672 million in 2007. It said the new management was giving 'stringent' priority to cash generation over earnings, making a big effort to reduce inventory levels. It admitted, however, that the group was heading for another €200 million loss for the year, when €80 million of costs involved in the latest restructuring plan were included, to add to the previous year's €241.6 million loss. David Sculley's promises – to improve gross margins, reduce indirect costs and restrict the product range – were all designed to boost cash-flow.

It was not the last trading statement from the company as a PLC. That came in early December, when figures for the six months to end October 2008 revealed an operating loss of €29 million. Sculley said that 'despite immense challenges, there are a lot of things that are right about this business and the group has a future that is worth fighting for. We are currently in negotiations with a number of interested institutional investors about a possible investment in the company on terms which, if consummated, would be different to those described in the prospectus and which, more significantly, are likely to require as a pre-condition a comprehensive financial restructuring.' In other words, the delay in getting money meant that Waterford Wedgwood now needed more than it had originally sought, more than it had been unable to raise previously.

It was true, however, that a potential partner was in serious negotiations. 'We continue to make good progress with potential investors and currently enjoy the support of our senior lenders,' Sculley claimed. He made it known publicly that Waterford Wedgwood had managed to secure a further 30-day deferment on interest repayment on loans. But 2 January 2009 was the deadline for the provision of new funds and if that was not met, then the banks would demand immediate repayment of all loans. Failure to meet the repayments would result in the appointment of a receiver.

O'Reilly went back to government in a last throw of the dice, but the then Minister for Energy and Communications, Eamon Ryan, does not recall any new formal or specific proposals for Waterford Wedgwood being brought forward for consideration at Cabinet, even if there was plenty of discussion about what could and should be done. One idea being suggested, but which didn't reach Cabinet, was that the government would buy the property hosting the visitor centre and lease it back to Waterford Crystal.

'There was no sense of Fianna Fáil feeling that it owed anything to O'Reilly,' Ryan said. 'The government didn't fear negative media comment much either. By that stage it [the government] knew it was in so much trouble that what the papers wrote hardly counted.'

Ryan noted that 'the timing of what O'Reilly wanted was all wrong … Martin Cullen pushed hard, but the government had just guaranteed the banks and had introduced an emergency Budget. It couldn't be seen to be bailing out a business that had little chance of success, especially when it had such wealthy backers. Brian Lenihan, in particular, was strong on not providing anything.' Lenihan's position was never disclosed to O'Reilly and his allies, who had hoped that the old

Belvedere school connection would stand to them. Years later, the Waterford directors still believed that Lenihan was the minister most favourably disposed towards helping the company, second only to Cullen and matched by Martin; they had misjudged Lenihan's friendly, can-do attitude for a real willingness to deliver.

'Ultimately, we wanted to save Waterford Crystal,' said Micheál Martin. 'It would have suited us. We had put enormous investment into Waterford as a city and county in previous years and got no benefit out of it. All of the goodwill was lost because we were in power when Waterford Crystal closed. But we couldn't do it.'

The government assisted O'Reilly in one last effort. The Sunday after Christmas Day 2008, O'Reilly visited Taoiseach Brian Cowen at Government Buildings to enlist his help with one last appeal to Bank of America to continue rolling over its loans to Waterford Wedgwood. Cowen was reluctant, given his own negative assessment of the situation, but was persuaded by O'Reilly's desperation and got on the phone to the USA. He was met with a polite response. Put it in writing, he was told. It was a brush-off, and Cowen suspected as much even if O'Reilly, displaying almost naïve optimism, told him that this was a breakthrough. Cowen made the written request anyway, one that would be put to the consortium of banks when they met on 3 January. As Cowen suspected, it would be ignored.

CHAPTER FIVE

COLLAPSE

On 3 January 2009 representatives of nine banks met at the Bank of America offices in midtown Manhattan to discuss Waterford Wedgwood. The letter from Taoiseach Brian Cowen requesting a further extension of forebearance on loan repayments and another refinancing proposal tabled by O'Reilly were not enough. The loans of over €400 million were technically and legally in default because of the failure to make interest payments, triggering the right of the banks to demand repayment of principal as well as the outstanding interest. The creditor banks, knowing that Waterford Wedgwood could not make the repayments, decided to appoint receivers in Ireland and Britain to recover as much as they could by selling the business as a going-concern, if possible, or its assets. Deloitte, the accountancy firm, got the job as receiver. Waterford Wedgwood's accumulated losses stood at more than €1 billion.

On 5 January 2009 the receivership was confirmed and immediately O'Reilly, Chryss, O'Donoghue and Patrick Molloy, the former Bank of Ireland CEO and recently returned chairman, resigned as directors, as required under company law. O'Reilly issued a statement in which he thanked the company's suppliers, employees and customers for their support. 'We are consoled only by the fact that everything that could have been done, by management and by the board, to preserve the group, was done,' he said.

Their shares were worthless and there was no chance of a surplus to be distributed among shareholders by the receivers. The personal losses incurred by O'Reilly and Goulandris may have been larger than anyone had calculated. When everything was added in, it appeared that the two had invested €579 million of their own money since 1990 and taken out only €35 million in dividends over that 18-year period, giving a net loss to the pair of €544 million. Of that investment, €400 million had been made between 2005 and 2009 alone, in a desperate and futile effort to stave off the company's collapse. The pair had also guaranteed a €40 million loan from Anglo Irish Bank and put €25 million on deposit with other banks to cover possible defaults, on top of that investment in ordinary and preference shares.

'He has invested not only his personal wealth but also a huge amount of emotional capital and effort; in fact, he is devastated,' said Fallon. David Palmer, the Englishman who had run INM's Irish operations for a spell, believed a form of economic patriotism contributed to O'Reilly's mistakes. 'If you cut him open, his blood runs green. He's an Irishman before anything. And perhaps that goes some way to explain his commitment to Waterford Wedgwood,' he said.

'He is an extremely forceful personality, who is used not just to carrying the day but to carrying everyone else over the line with him too,' said Godson. 'Nearly all of the big chances he'd taken during his life had paid off for him. It was so hard for him when this one didn't.'

Six years on and O'Donoghue was still baffled by the failure of the government to intervene: 'In my view, it is a tragedy of almost biblical proportions that the Irish government did not offer us the support we sought. Unquestionably, the request for help was an unusual one, but these were unusual times. Someone, at the time [Mary Coughlan, Tánaiste and Martin's successor as Minister for Trade and Enterprise], likened the collapse of Waterford Wedgwood to the failure of the Fruit of the Loom clothes manufacturing business in County Donegal [her political constituency]. That failure too was tragic for the people involved, but the comment shows clearly that there was absolutely no understanding of the role that a successful iconic Irish brand plays in the Irish psyche. If that had been properly understood, the Waterford brand and the Waterford business could still be under Irish control today. Instead, an ancient, unique and highly skilled Irish craft tradition has probably been lost forever.'

There was to be a nasty additional twist to the whole sorry story. In the last months of his control of Waterford Wedgwood, O'Reilly had pinned significant hopes on an American venture capital house, KPS, becoming a major shareholder. Indeed, KPS had worked with Waterford Wedgwood's management on its new plans and, having gone through the books, appeared to be supportive. It liked the business and discussed injecting capital. Had it invested, O'Reilly and Goulandris would have been diluted dramatically in their percentage shareholdings, but at least they would have remained as investors and directors. They had worked together on a plan that would have given KPS a very sizeable return on its investment had it all gone ahead. However, KPS decided that the company was radically under-capitalised and had far too much debt to service. It was also terrified of becoming responsible for the pension fund deficit. It decided that there was an even bigger return available to it in buying the company out of receivership, taking full ownership for itself and taking control of the management. The new deal that was now available to it would remove the legal or financial obligations to creditors and pensioners, giving it a far greater chance of profit and success. It ditched O'Reilly and Goulandris, to their distress but not to the surprise of other advisers. It was simply business, ruthless as the approach to the pensioners – and the outgoing owners – was.

O'Donoghue's admiration for O'Reilly increased during the collapse. 'Tony was extraordinarily calm in a crisis. He was angry, yes, but he was always plotting a way out. It was amazing to watch his brain in action.' McGoran concurred: 'Tony always thinks that he can solve a problem, he never thinks that things are beyond him. He was always very calm, very measured. He never shouted on the phone, he was always mannerly.'

'Tony felt that our world-beating brands would see us through, particularly the Waterford brand. We used to refer to it as the brand that would not die, and actually events have proved that to be the case,' said O'Donoghue.

The announcement of the receivership allowed all sorts of uncon-nected people the opportunity to weigh in on where it had all gone wrong. One of the most interesting post-closure analyses was offered by Judith Flanders, author of *Inside the Victorian Home*:

While high manufacturing costs, declining demand for luxury goods and a weak dollar may have precipitated matters, this is not a credit-crunch story — it is a history lesson. The company is in trouble because it has long forgotten the lessons of one of its founders: Josiah Wedgwood, among the greatest and most innovative retailers the world has ever seen. If the modern operators of Wedgwood had shown a tenth of Josiah's intuitive grasp, his flair, his zest for selling, it would not now be dying.

Today, in the Waterford Wedgwood showroom here on Piccadilly, the various lines of china are piled up bargain-basement style. While the product is still good, the marketing is dreadful. The company has been both profligate and miserly — it has hired hot designers, but then has scrimped by not spending money to change the moulds; as a result, contemporary design is crudely imposed on 100-year-old shapes. Indeed, the company has returned to Josiah's 'diffusion' principle — offering cheaper lines for different segments of the population — but has failed to advertise this fact.

As the news of the company's travails broke, it was clear from Web chatter that most people think Wedgwood is a 'luxury' and a 'traditional' brand, with no inexpensive lines or innovative designers. Neither is true, but perception, as Josiah knew, is the ultimate truth. Twenty-first-century Wedgwood has been more old-fashioned than 18th-century Wedgwood, and that has been its undoing.

Keith Farrell, CEO of the British Ceramic Confederation for the previous 15 years, argued that it was too simple to blame the crisis on a flawed marketing strategy. 'It is all about changing lifestyle. People don't eat together like they used to. There's no formality. Wedgwood used to be so exclusive that it could justify its cost. But now it is expensive and not exclusive,' he said.

Tom Wedgwood, a descendant of the founding family, said 'there is so much interest in food today, with all those programmes on television. How can you serve wonderful food on rubbish plates?' He said the company didn't market the brand enough in Japan and China, where European tableware is regarded as prestigious. 'All of the [investment] was going to the US,' Wedgwood said. 'There was a huge disconnect with the customers.'

The criticism that the company had failed because of marketing shortcomings must have been humiliating to O'Reilly. But it comes back to the point that had often been made about him, especially by his managers in INM, albeit *sotto voce*: for all of his talk about brands, he often preferred to pay lip-service to them and rarely invested enough in their maintenance or development. The use of celebrities to promote branded products was the correct marketing strategy for Waterford Wedgwood, but he was parsimonious in funding their proper use and the point about attaching their names to inappropriately designed products was an important one. Instead, the money produced by his companies was spent on redundancies or further acquisitions or on paying large dividends so that O'Reilly could service the cost of his other investments.

Waterford Wedgwood was not just his greatest failure as an investor but as a manager, too. He showed himself to be a relatively poor manager of available resources, no matter how well intentioned he was or how willing his friends were to champion him. He was unduly sentimental when it came to shutting uneconomic Irish or British production and over-compensated by producing too much product to try to reduce manufacturing unit costs at those plants, instead creating expensive stock build-ups. Cash was managed badly, meaning that it was not available when required urgently; often the money coming from fund-raisings was delivered later than was required. The idea that people would not accept fine china or crystal made in Indonesia may not have been the relevant point: the issue may have been whether they wanted fine bone china or heavy cut crystal at all, because such products were not in keeping with modern tastes or price points. If such products retained their cachet, then maybe it was in aspiring Asian markets that O'Reilly approached only cautiously, while his obsession remained the USA.

If he had been guilty of sentimentality in continuing to believe in the style of brands with which he had grown up, he also stood accused of complacency. 'There was a degree of wish-fulfilment involved,' said one source. 'When it came to Waterford Wedgwood, it was almost as if, if he said something often enough and with enough conviction, it would all happen because he believed it should happen, as much as wanting it to happen.'

O'Reilly never complained publicly about the government's performance, although Gavin, in 2011, argued that the government 'could have been a little bit more inspired and proactive' and, echoing something his father had said many years earlier, claimed there was 'a kind of reverse nepotism when it comes to domestic companies'.

'Most people recognise the extraordinary lengths my father went to that Christmas of 2008. Whether it was Christmas Day or St Stephen's

Day or the days afterwards, my father, as a non-executive chairman and as a shareholder, was doing everything he possibly could,' he told journalist Justine McCarthy. 'I don't think my father was looking for hand-outs that any other would-be investor wasn't getting. God knows, he put hundreds of millions of euros of his own money into it ... It was a great loss for the southeast, a great loss for Ireland and a real financial and emotional disappointment to my father, who laboured so long with Waterford Wedgwood.'

O'Reilly had been the delusion-maker-in-chief, constructing an edifice that was so unbalanced it was bound to fall. When it did, it was like a crystal glass falling from a great height and shattering into thousands of pieces, no matter how carefully or lovingly it had been constructed, no matter how attractive it had looked. His saving grace was that he did not mug other people to feather his own nest; he suffered the consequences of his own ill-judgement harder than almost anyone else, although the pensioners were to suffer greatly, too.

In spite of its immensity, O'Reilly did not have time to wallow in self-pity about the Waterford Wedgwood collapse. He was still full-time CEO at INM and its crisis was deepening. At the end of January he admitted that the efforts to sell APN were being abandoned and instead other 'non-strategic' assets were to be sold, although this would produce only a fraction of the money the sale of APN would have raised; belatedly, offically for sale was his cherished London *Independent.* Efforts were to be made to sell a new bond to replace a €200 million bond that was due for repayment later that year. There would be no final dividend paid to shareholders from the 2008 profits, saving INM the €60 million it had been projected to cost.

That was a seminal moment. As recently as November 2008, despite the shortage of funds, O'Reilly and other shareholders had benefited from the payment of an interim dividend, which in his case amounted to more than €10 million. 'You invested in INM for the dividend,' said one key executive. 'It was viewed as the safest in town because O'Reilly needed it so he'd always pay it. Nobody ever thought the money wouldn't be there to pay it.'

The loss of dividend income would be devastating to O'Reilly. In the decade up to 2006, O'Reilly had pulled an average of €14 million per year in dividends out of INM and in 2007 he had taken a record €30 million. He needed that money to pay his sizeable bills.

In its statement INM forecast pre-exceptional operating profits of some €275 million for 2008, down from €349.2 million in 2007. It was the first time since 2004 that operating profits would not exceed €300 million. It said the fall in the share price, down now by 88% in less than a year, was 'unwarranted'. It said its stock market valuation 'did not fairly reflect the true value of its underlying assets, its trading performance' or the 'inherent profitability' and cash generative nature of its operations. More than 33% of its revenues did not depend on advertising, the company said. It was straw-clutching time, just as it had been at Waterford Wedgwood.

O'Reilly always believed that things would come right for him if he waited because they always had. But he had left it too late this time. 'Too often he spoke about how he'd done things 20 years ago and 30 years ago and we'd have to say "but that was then and this is now and things have changed", said one of his loyal executives.

The end was imminent. Gavin, who felt he was working well with O'Brien and particularly with his adviser, Paul Connolly, didn't want to continue simply as a go-between flanked by his two major share-holders. An arrangement was made for O'Reilly and O'Brien to meet for the first time since the latter had become an investor in INM.

The meeting took place in late February 2009, the day of an Ireland vs England rugby international in Croke Park that both men were attend-ing. O'Brien refused to go to Castlemartin for talks and a suggestion that they use the house of mutual friend, Ray McLoughlin, was nixed when he said he had decorators in and that it was unavailable. Instead, they met at O'Reilly's Fitzwilliam Square townhouse. O'Reilly had been involved in many confrontational meetings throughout his career, and usually had come out on the winning side. This one threatened to be different, however. A younger, more determined, more unpredictable and seemingly ruthless enemy threatened him and had the money to carry out that threat. O'Reilly was determined not to concede ground.

The meeting did not start well: O'Brien felt that the chair offered to him was at a lower level than the one O'Reilly intended sitting in, and deliberately so. New seats, at equal height, had to be brought in. O'Reilly had a table set for lunch, full of Waterford and Wedgwood products, but O'Brien was not for eating. Nonetheless, O'Brien told this author that the meeting was 'cordial. Tony kept on asking me why I bought the shares in the first place.' That was hardly the point given the situation in which the company found itself. 'I suppose he felt we were aggressive in our demands, but the business was on the brink of receivership.'

No agreement about INM was reached as they debated its financial condition and management, other than that they would meet again after the match, this time in the company of Gavin, Connolly and McLoughlin. This was when the most serious blow was delivered. O'Brien indicated that if O'Reilly did not retire, he would requisition an EGM to remove him. O'Reilly could not be certain that he would win such a vote, given the strength of O'Brien's voting power and the possibility that other shareholders would come to the same con- clusions as O'Brien and the lenders as to O'Reilly's responsibility for the perilous state of INM's finances. Resigning now would offer some cover against indignity, but losing a vote publicly would be humiliating. In addition, the campaign before an EGM vote would result in even greater scrutiny of the company's finances and likely an even greater fall in the share price, further eroding what was left of O'Reilly's assets. It might even have tipped INM into either examinership or receivership, things were that precarious. O'Brien made it clear that he had the resources to withstand such an eventuality and that he considered that O'Reilly did not. It was a game of poker and while both held poor hands, O'Brien's was the better.

O'Reilly was bewildered by what he saw as O'Brien's aggressiveness. While he was willing to concede on certain points, he did not want to capitulate. One thing that he most certainly did not want to give up was his seat on the board; if he had to relinquish the role of CEO, he wanted to remain as chairman. Nor did he want to give O'Brien's representatives seats on the board. As he saw it, that would be surrender. He suspected the offer of their involvement on the board as partners was something of a Trojan horse.

The meeting broke up without agreement but O'Reilly now knew, if he hadn't before, that his very existence in 'his' company was nearing its end. 'He had such a grip on the business as CEO and a weak chairman in Brian Hillery and he controlled every aspect of the decision-making process [that he had to go],' said O'Brien in his interview for this book, explaining why he was so determined to remove O'Reilly. 'They thought it was News Corporation they were running.'

———

The blows kept coming. O'Reilly was particularly upset by an article that appeared in *The Wall Street Journal* a few days later. Its main claim was that he had asked Murdoch's News Corporation to buy a 3% or 4% stake in INM the previous autumn, but that Murdoch had 'nixed' the idea. An O'Reilly spokesman denied any such engagement, but the claim was still published and in a paper that Murdoch owned. That was not O'Reilly's main concern, however. He felt humiliated that the newspaper, read by all of his old peers in American business, had devoted such extensive analysis to his crisis, focusing both on Waterford Wedgwood and INM and predicting, correctly, a fire sale of remaining assets. 'His big bets on newspapers, luxury goods and the remaking of Ireland itself made him the richest man in the country,' said the article. 'Now each of those areas has boomeranged on him.' It described how O'Brien had become his 'business nemesis'. O'Reilly was upset by the tone and content of the article. 'My friends in America are all going to see that and know what has happened to me,' he said angrily to one adviser.

Within two weeks O'Reilly was put under further pressure by his sons and by the board to step down, not just as CEO of INM but from the board entirely. There was speculation that the banks had made his departure a condition of refinancing the business, but that wasn't the case. The pressure had come from within, as those around him realised that further resistance was futile and that they were at risk of losing everything. One of O'Brien's criticisms was that, 'unfortunately, Tony O'Reilly did not listen to his board, his advisers or his friends.' O'Reilly still had to be persuaded, but those were the people who were belatedly exerting the necessary pressure.

O'Reilly spent 12 March at Citywest, INM's corporate HQ as well as its main printing facility, discussing plans with Gavin and Tony jnr, board members and executives, demanding they not surrender. He did not receive encouragement. It was an emotional and difficult day for all concerned. He went home to Castlemartin to think and later rang the boardroom, where all of his executives and available directors had assembled. He was put on speakerphone. He asked each person in turn if they agreed that he should step down and allow O'Brien's nominees onto the board. The outcome was stunning to him. 'It had always been his show and if you didn't like it, you got off the board. This day was totally different,' said one participant in the meeting.

Reluctantly, each replied that he, and they, had no choice but to say that he should go. In one of the most difficult moments of his life, O'Reilly gave in – albeit arguing that they would all regret this – and hung up the phone to be left in his study at Castlemartin with his thoughts. The bitterness he felt would never really leave him, even if it ebbed in time.

He could not admit to this disquiet publicly, however, not when he was still a major shareholder dependent on a recovery in the share price, not when Gavin was now the CEO and had to work with O'Brien's people, and not when to do so would be a public admission of failure. Gavin communicated the news of the impending resignation to Connolly and once agreement on Gavin's own elevation to CEO as part of the deal was confirmed, they went to work on writing the statements for release to the stock market. This had to be handled gracefully. The fiction had to be maintained that O'Reilly had chosen his own time of leaving, that he had not been forced. Part of this involved giving him the title of 'president emeritus' and allowing him to step down the following 7 May, his seventy-third birthday, rather than immediately.

'I welcome the changes to the board and the appointment of Gavin O'Reilly as group CEO,' O'Brien said. 'I would like to thank Tony O'Reilly for his long-standing contribution to the company. I welcome Tony as president emeritus and also take this opportunity to wish him well on his retirement.'

Gavin also put his best foot forward, dismissing talk of ongoing tension with the O'Brien faction. Gavin conceded that both sides had 'thrown grenades at each other' and that this had been foolish. 'I'm very happy to say that it's water under the bridge. We've been working with and talking to Denis and Denis's colleagues for quite some time now. This is a triumph for common sense and in the interests of all shareholders.' And as for himself: 'It's a fairly humbling position I find myself in, with very big shoes to fill. I have the endorsement of both Tony O'Reilly and Denis O'Brien, which is pretty good, especially when they represent 55 [sic] per cent of the company.'

Gavin went further in an interview with the *Financial Times*, in which he declared that differences with O'Brien were 'a thing of the past … We wanted to articulate a unified front today in this announcement, but the real work of disposals and refinancing and other capital market alternatives has been going on and, well, we are right in the middle of it.' Gavin said it was a 'win-win' for all shareholders and that there were 'no losers' in the shake-up.

I spoke to Gavin in a live radio interview on 13 March and once he had repeated many of those sentiments, I asked him how confident he was about INM's ability to repay its loans. 'You have to presume that I know a little more about this than you do,' Gavin replied acidly. 'I think I could say that I'm very confident.'

I moved to finish the interview by asking about his father's legacy. He spoke of his pride in the scale and reach of the business empire that his father had developed. 'I think creating Ireland's first media multinational, flying the flag very, very high for Ireland in markets as far-flung as New Zealand, India, Indonesia, South Africa, I think that's probably his greatest achievement. He set out back in 1973 with a very clear vision of how he wanted the company to expand and largely that has been achieved.'

I had expected that he might express some pride in the quality of some of the newspapers that INM owned and sponsored, and his father's role in ensuring that the editors and journalists had sufficient freedom to do as they felt necessary in the honourable pursuit. When I asked him about his father's editorial legacy, O'Reilly paused and coughed and then spoke briefly of his pride in his father's 'non-interventionist policy', which had been enshrined since he had first invested in the company back in 1973.

The power shift within INM was enormous, with Gavin's own promotion the only concession by O'Brien to O'Reilly family interests. O'Reilly did not share his son's optimism about developing a relation-ship with O'Brien, but saw it as his best shot of retaining power by proxy, no matter what Gavin might say about his own independence in the role. O'Reilly had a line he often liked to use in interviews and speeches. Whenever two great rivals in business ended up helping each other, he would joke that it was the most unlikely alliance since the Stalin–Hitler pact. Now he was part of such an arrangement.

Gavin was put in a near impossible situation, notwithstanding his efforts to put a brave face on things and newspaper profiles that argued that his time had come by right. Despite the relationship he had established with Connolly and all of the nice words agreed for press releases and public statements during the transition of power, Gavin knew that he would remain answerable to his father as one major shareholder and to O'Brien as another, while simultaneously having to fulfil his legal and ethical obligations to all shareholders, the staff and creditors, including the banks.

Brian Hillery said O'Reilly's retirement marked one of the most remarkable executive careers in Irish history. 'Tony has been a significant business leader for more than 45 years and has been a key figure in the making of modern Ireland. Tony can be immensely proud that, from modest beginnings 36 years ago, he has helped to build a truly global communications business … When Tony first invested in a local Irish newspaper operation back in 1973, it had a turnover of €12 million. From that starting point, he immediately applied – with his colleagues – his flair, vision and enormous energy to create a €1.5 billion worldwide communications group.'

O'Reilly added a comment to the statement that said it had been his pleasure to have worked with a range of highly talented and hugely committed directors and colleagues at INM. 'My appreciation of them is undiminished by time. Together, we have expanded this Irish newspaper group and enshrined a fiercely independent editorial policy that is widely respected across the world.'

The company's shares, down more than 94% in the 12 months before the accord, went up upon release of the news, but the market capitalisation was still just €142.67 million and the business had debts nearly 10 times that amount. But what many overlooked at the time was the significance to O'Reilly of losing his income as CEO at INM – €1.4 million the previous year and as high as €4 million in 2006 and 2007 – on top of the earlier loss of dividends.

While it was O'Reilly's departure that got the headlines, it was also significant that the board was to be reduced in number from 17 to 10 at the same time as three O'Brien directors joined the board. Two of O'Reilly's sons, Tony jnr and Cameron, would leave, as well as long-standing loyalists such as Bernard Somers, Peter Cosgrave, Charles Daly, Maurice Hayes and Ivor Kenny. The company said that the resignations and appointments were 'consistent with the board's stated policy of achieving best practice in all matters relating to corporate governance'. It was yet another vindication of O'Brien's tactics.

Much to O'Reilly's disappointment, the political establishment didn't seem to care a jot about the change of control at INM. There was barely a word publicly from anyone in the political system, despite the significance of what was happening. Everyone seemed to have more important things to worry about, because of the way the economy was collapsing. O'Brien apparently had got much of what he had wanted in INM – a degree of control, albeit not to be copper-fastened until a later date – but at an enormous financial cost. Some months earlier, the BCI investigation concluded that there were no cross-media ownership issues involved in O'Brien owning so many radio assets and a quarter share of INM. It didn't change its position immediately when O'Brien got his three seats on the board, although some months later it announced another review into his level of media ownership. When that concluded, in late 2009, it declared there was no problem in maintaining the status quo.

While O'Brien was now in the driving seat to control events at INM, this did not occur automatically. While many saw Gavin as simply a proxy for his father, and subsequent events would emphasise that for a short period at least that was close to the case, the real power, for the moment at any rate, lay with the company's bankers.

If O'Reilly had suffered a devastating blow because of the loss of income, he also suffered a psychological one from the loss of position. He felt he was performing a public service role as proprietor at INM, albeit an unelected one, and that he was well suited to it, and that it behoved him or whoever ran INM to exercise an appropriate duty of care in overseeing editorial functions. He believed that he exercised his power carefully and responsibly and that, notwithstanding what others said about the 1997 general election controversy, he had never sought to emulate Rupert Murdoch, who actively sought to change governments.

The controversies of the late twentieth century in Ireland – when O'Reilly's newspapers were accused of interference in the political process to support his commercial ambitions – meant that the editorial behaviour of influential newspapers within his media empire was scrutinised closely by politicians and rival media outlets up until the time of his departure. There was a remarkable absence of comment – either positive or negative – outside of his own newspapers upon his stepping-down from an executive role at INM. It was as if his old rivals didn't want to kick a man on the backside as he was heading out the door, a case of applying the old Irish tradition, usually more relevant in death, of saying nothing if there was nothing good to say.

Alternatively, they may have been worried that it could turn out to be a case of *be careful what you wish for*, because the man effectively replacing him was suspected, rightly or wrongly, of having even greater interventionist tendencies. This reluctance was all somewhat strange given the perceived hold O'Reilly had held, supposedly, over political coverage in his newspapers during the previous 36 years. But it may also have been that many did not really regard him as being gone, at least for as long as Gavin remained in place.

Eoghan Harris, his old critic from the 1970s during his days as a Workers Party activist, was now a senator, appointed by Bertie Ahern after the 2007 general election, as well as a *Sunday Independent* columnist. He spoke glowingly of O'Reilly, live on *The Last Word* on Today FM, on the same day as Gavin, describing him as a highly significant figure in Irish cultural and political life. 'The important thing is that he was a huge force for peace for thirty-five years at the head of Independent Newspapers,' Harris said. 'There was a dictat, an unwritten, informal one: no truck with terrorism ... he played a huge part in keeping this society stable for 30 years ... he was the biggest single presence apart from Jack Lynch, Garret FitzGerald and Bertie Ahern, he shadowed them. He was a huge force for liberal democracy and his Ireland Fund played a huge part in getting people together – Catholic and Protestant – on the ground with hard cash behind them.'

Harris insisted there had been no editorial interference, which differed from his experiences in working with the *Sunday Times* and RTÉ: 'I've never worked for anyone who has interfered less ... all that stuff you read, he meets Cowen, he meets Ahern, it's all rubbish ... I genuinely, hand on heart, have never encountered any evidence that Tony O'Reilly interferes with the political agenda of any newspaper. I know that is hard to believe, but I would know if he did and there were some times over the years I would have wished that he'd interfere with the political line. He would stand behind me or Gene Kerrigan or Alan Ruddock or Robert Fisk and I know that there were times when he would violently disagree with what we would write, but we never heard anything back.'

Harris contended that O'Reilly was 'the victim of jealousy at every level and not just commercial. He's tall, he's glamorous, he's good-looking, he's witty, a very good speaker, he has that rugby background, very handsome, incredibly successful, naturally people are going to be begrudging ... There is also a political agenda about some of the people who obsess about him, particularly his radical socialist republican enemies, because he was the single biggest media influence, a colossus, standing in the way of the Provisional IRA and any other threat to Irish democracy. He was a core figure in defending threats to Irish democracy, as I know Gavin will be too.'

In interviews for this book one of those closest to him, who spoke on condition of anonymity, insisted that O'Reilly had been 'exemplary in his performance as a press baron. He felt strongly that being the chairman of INM was a public role, albeit an unelected one, and as an unelected one it behoved him or whoever ran INM to do so while exercising an appropriate duty of care. He was never a Murdoch, never somebody who actively wanted to change governments. Yes, he loved the feeling of power, the proximity to it, the interacting with it, but he didn't seek to exercise it.'

It was a contention with which many were likely to argue, both north and south of the border. 'If you look at the treatment of, for . example, John Hume by the *Sunday Independent* during the early stages of the peace talks in Northern Ireland, it was an absolute disgrace,' said Denis O'Brien. 'Here was a man who had devoted his life to the pursuance of peace on the island and he was villified. It took a huge toll on his health. There were many others who were subjected to poisonous attacks. The coverage of Liam Lawlor's death by the *Sunday Independent* was one of the lows of Irish journalism in my lifetime. And what was done about it? Absolutely nothing. No one was fired, no one was suspended. I think it is reasonable to assume that the board and management condoned such conduct by their lack of action.'

There was also something of a lack of analysis of O'Reilly's managerial performance, although perhaps that was down to the relentless coverage of it in the preceding years, driven by O'Brien. One of the more interesting analyses came from Gavin Ellis, former editor of the *New Zealand Herald*. He argued that no single factor accounted for the turmoil and decline. 'Like Rome before it, O'Reilly's media organisation was the victim of multiple forces, some of its own making, others visited upon it. The audacity that accompanied the early expansion carried high risk, manageable while O'Reilly's luck, and the international markets, held good. But when fates turned, an empire founded on high debt and low costs lacked the strategies to stop the thread unravelling.'

Ellis described how O'Reilly brought to INM the same tactics as applied at Heinz. 'He had perfected the strategy at Heinz where executives had to account for their operating income in a challenging gathering of their peers over which he presided,' he said. But he echoed the criticisms of Joe Hayes from the 1980s when he quoted an unnamed executive who said the annual Castlemartin meetings, upon which O'Reilly placed so much emphasis, were not just about the numbers. 'I don't think you can overlook the forelock-tugging aspect of the carnival. It was at least partly about paying homage to the emperor and the emperor responded by applauding and rewarding the efforts of all, however insignificant. This was undoubtedly a highly motivating experience for some, and regarded as a depressing waste of time by others,' he said.

What Ellis wrote about South Africa was typical of the experience at any of the newspapers O'Reilly controlled. Job cuts were 'typical of the reaction to economic downturns: any shortfall in budgeted revenue growth was redressed by cost reductions. Editors learned not to rely on budgets set at the end of the previous year and while there was short-term investment in new sections or products aimed at attracting advertisers, there was little new investment in core journalism in the group's antipodean newspapers.' Ellis was supported by South African professor Anton Harber, who said that after a good start in reorganising and redeveloping the old Argus group, for a number of years O'Reilly 'has treated it like an extractive industry' [a pointed reference to the Argus group's former mining associations] by putting profit ahead of all else.

O'Reilly's performance during the crisis of 2008 and early months of 2009 was more of the kind that might have been expected from a chairman than a CEO of a besieged company. Much of the heavy lifting was left to Gavin and Donal Buggy, as finance director. 'It wasn't that he was unaware of what was going on and was not hands-on day-to-day,' said one insider. 'He was, very much so, being aware of every move and negotiation and he had all the details. But he didn't go to the meetings with the banks, other than a few. I remember him being at one with AIB and he was clearly very uncomfortable. It was a little bit humiliating for him at this stage of his life to be somewhat beholden to those banks. It was a matter of pride.'

Up until his departure in 2009, 'he always maintained his equilibrium and his sense of humour even if there were ever more regular dark moments. No matter what else was going on, at Waterford or elsewhere, he was always able, always continued to function, and with considerable good grace.'

Some of his former executives still defend him, although for various reasons they don't want to speak publicly. 'Everything is perfectly clear in hindsight. There are plenty of people who say now that the business was too highly geared, but I don't remember many people saying that before 2008. Denis O'Brien clearly didn't think so or else why would he have spent so much money buying shares in the company?' said one.

'I took the view that the board took the decision for a €140 million share buyback and to pay dividends of over €250 million over the past two years that effectively drained the company of cash,' said Paul Connolly in 2009. It was a hard point against which to argue.

Another of O'Reilly's executives said that by gearing the company heavily with debt, he had left no wriggle room for things going wrong. He had then worsened the situation for the company by failing to refinance loans early enough, by having it buy back its own shares and by continuing to pay generous dividends when the priority should have been cutting debt. 'The share buyback was so myopic and afterwards Tony blamed other people, which was so unfair,' said one executive. A number of interviewees for this book, all connected to INM, believed that money that had been wasted on Waterford Wedgwood could have been used to save his position at INM. In the end, neither could be salvaged. The 'what ifs' are purely theoretical because by now, in 2009, O'Reilly's carefully built position, wealth and reputation had been largely erased.

SECTION 5

2009–2015:
'If you can meet with Triumph and Disaster and treat those two impostors just the same ...'

CHAPTER ONE

THE BATTLE LINES ARE DRAWN

The fall, an actual, physical one, could not have come at a worse time. Chryss had insisted to her husband that he hold his head up high, despite his misfortune. She wanted him to continue to go to the events they enjoyed and be seen to be there. There were races held at Leopardstown in April 2009 and they went. As they left the racetrack after the day's racing and walked to their waiting car, O'Reilly stumbled over a kerb he hadn't noticed and fell flat on his face, unable to react quickly enough to put his arms out to break the fall, to prevent damage being caused to his face or eyes.

The physical pain was intense. He had been injured many times on the rugby pitch, of course, but that was over 50 years earlier and entirely to be expected in the context of a highly physical contact sport. Back then, nobody regarded such injuries as a sign of weakness or incapacity. Now, he was 72 years old and the fall was a shockingly unexpected incident. Although few witnessed what had happened or even heard about it afterwards, as a discreet silence was maintained, it emphasised to O'Reilly his advancing years and suggested physical frailty. It was an inelegant episode, an affront to the dignity he prized, and it dented his self-confidence.

Chryss insisted on immediate treatment for his injuries and they were driven straight to the Emergency Department at the nearby private Beacon Hospital (purchased by O'Brien in 2014, as it happens). O'Reilly was diagnosed with a detached retina in one of his eyes. The condition is reasonably common in men who spend long hours travelling in aircraft, as he had spent much of his life doing, and also happened to men far younger than him. The treatment was going to be challenging, though – a month lying motionless on the flat of his back, in a darkened room – but it would be essential to save the sight in the affected eye.

The recovery period was difficult. He could not read, the activity he probably prized the most and which of course made retaining his sight so important. He could not pour over the financial statements and letters, faxes and e-mails pertinent to his financial predicament, nor could he read for pleasure or diversion. He had the phone on the bedside locker beside him, but he had to get others to dial the numbers for him if he wanted to use it.

He was confined to, if not imprisoned in, Castlemartin by his injury. O'Reilly had long been a man of action, constantly on the move around the world, rarely satisfied to stay in one location for long, irrespective of how comfortable the surroundings. Now he was restricted physically, just as he was financially. Friends suspected that he was sometimes prone to dark moods and that he dealt with these through constant activity. Now, just as he had so much to worry about, he had been given the time and space in which to do exactly that: to ponder upon what he had lost and, worse still, on what could still be lost.

His position of power and influence had been eroded almost entirely now that he had lost control of that prized newspaper empire; he no longer had easy access to and the ear of prime ministers and presidents, willing to indulge his company or his point of view – something that may indeed have been as important to him as the vast sums of money he had taken annually from the company and the capital value of his stock there. While there would still be a welcome for him in many important places, now it would be more out of politeness and respect for his past, whereas previously it had been for what his present and future represented and promised. He would fall down the pecking order when invitations were being sent out; and he would not be hosting his own large parties because he could not afford to do so, and even if he did, how many people other than family would come? Yet even if he was fast becoming yesterday's man in those terms, he could not escape the cold fact that those previous borrowings would remain ever-present and continue to dictate his future years.

What he and his closest associates knew, even if it was not yet readily obvious to anyone else – although the request to government for help at Waterford Wedgwood was a giveaway – was that he was financially compromised, to put it mildly. His income and capital were both greatly diminished at a time when he still had large loans to both service and repay. He could not have it become known widely how serious his predicament was because he was dependent now on the attitude of his lenders. He found it hard to believe that it had come to this. He did not believe that he had been reckless in his personal borrowing, indeed he believed he had been conservative in matching his debts to his assets. It had only been in the mid-2000s that independent experts had trawled through his personal balance sheet and declared him to be a bona fide billionaire, the value of his assets exceeding his liabilities by €1 billion. But now his interest in Waterford Wedgwood was gone and the value of INM had collapsed by 90%. He didn't have the income to cover repayments of both interest and capital on debts, even though they were no bigger than they had been months previously. All around Ireland there were men and women bemoaning the loss of fortunes because of the implosion of the property and construction bubble, but here was O'Reilly, who had eschewed such speculation, in an even worse state.

He completed his medical treatment as set out by his doctors and his sight was saved. He emerged from his bedroom physically lighter, having taken the opportunity of being bed-bound to fast and reduce his weight as an aid to good health, although some put his lack of appetite down to distress about his circumstances. He appeared to others as ready for the fight, but without the necessary firepower. The challenge threatened to be, for the first time in his life, too much for him.

As part of the enforced settlement with O'Brien, O'Reilly had set his retirement date from INM for 7 May 2009, his seventy-third birthday. This deadline meant that he would not enjoy a valedictory final AGM of shareholders, as he had enjoyed at Heinz, but then, there was little to celebrate. After March's enforced abdication he attended just one final INM board meeting. At it, he had to greet the arrival of O'Brien's three nominees to the board. It was a great demonstration of grace under pressure on O'Reilly's part. He made no reference to the circumstances in which he had been removed and instead was most generous in his welcome of Leslie Buckley, Paul Connolly and Lucy Gaffney. He made favourable reference to Buckley's previous work on his behalf as a consultant at Waterford Crystal in the 1990s, and to the rugby activities of Connolly's father going back to his time at Belvedere College. He complimented Gaffney on bringing some 'glamour' to the boardroom. She was not insulted by what other women might have interpreted as sexism. 'Now if it had been Gavin who'd said it, I would have objected given how hard I've worked to get to where I am,' she said, 'but from Tony it was what somebody of his age saw as a compliment and courtesy and I took it in that way and it didn't annoy me at all.' The business of the meeting was conducted and, with great sadness, even if pride demanded that it was not displayed, O'Reilly took his leave of 'his' company.

He had a final statement to write as CEO of INM, for its 2008 annual report to be presented to shareholders. Understandably, given that it was his last opportunity to do so, he was determined to paint what he had created in a positive light: 'INM remains a magnificent organis-ation in all its iterations around the world ... Together we have expanded this Irish newspaper group and enshrined a fiercely independent editorial policy that is widely respected across the world ... As a global media group, INM has distinct advantages – geographic diversity, complementary and synergistic media platforms across publishing, radio, online and outdoor, and innovative production techniques – all of which allow us to deliver market-leading products more com-petitively than most of our peers.'

It was telling that he still didn't see, or at least would not admit, that his diversification had not coped with great change, that the company was too dependent on old or traditional media, that he didn't have the resources or scale to move into the far more profitable types of new media although, in truth, many of his rivals struggled greatly with these developments, too. But then, he still had a shareholding to protect and therefore a need to have its value restored. He had no interest in undermining the company further.

He continued to believe that people would and should pay for their news: 'Common to all of INM's media operations around the world is our distinct and uncompromising emphasis on great journalism and editorial independence. It is instructive that even in these most chal-lenging of times the substance and quality of our publishing offering underpins our robust circulation performance around the world. In 2008, circulation accounted for 20 per cent of group revenues.'

Tellingly, he made no direct reference to O'Brien in the report, instead taking the opportunity to look back at the contribution of his predecessors in the role of CEO. He paid tribute to Bartle Pitcher, John Meagher and Liam Healy, 'whose courage and tenacity, perspicacity, and frugality have produced an organisation of scale and independence that is a monument to their industry and that of their colleagues along the way'. He made it clear, however, that he was not going to be entirely removed from activities at INM, even if that was O'Brien's intention. He thanked the board for asking him to stay as 'President Emeritus' for life, 'which I do with a mixture of pride and humility'. What wasn't stated in the report was that INM would pay him a hefty honorarium of €300,000 annually for doing nothing. He promised that 'as the largest shareholder, I will continue to support their legacy and this wonderful group in the furtherance of its strategy'. This was taken as an indication that he would continue to be in Gavin's ear, that he expected his son to work to the template he had set out previously, even if it was not necessarily one that the new board might wish to continue.

He praised his chosen son as working 'unrelentingly and creatively, but most importantly, good humouredly with his colleagues. He faces the present challenge of extraordinary and unique change and a huge reduction in media expenditure with the knowledge that he has a profitable organisation, extremely impressive colleagues and a structure that throughout the world is dedicated to being the "low cost operator" producing the best products in their fields.'

However, he had to give excuses for leaving at a time when the company's share price had collapsed, even if he did not refer directly to that fact. His exit was marked by an overall loss at INM in 2008 of €164.4 million, reached after accounting provision was made for exceptional losses of €373 million, including a reduction of the value of the newspaper assets by €290.9 million. This point was important as many of INM's loans were secured by reference to the value of the assets as security. The company's debts amounted to €1.3 billion and were almost entirely unchanged from a year earlier. The interest bill for the year had been €91.5 million, an indication of the enormous drain on resources the debts were proving to be. For the first quarter of 2009 trading had been 'tougher than expected', but 'assuming advertising and credit markets do not deteriorate further', the company promised operating profits for 2009 in the range of €200–€230 million. The shares were trading at as low as 26 cent each by this stage, having reached €3.87 a little more than two years previously.

'The first half of the year is captured in our half-year accounts; the next two months continue that trend – a trend of uninterrupted progress and growth over three decades. In September, and from then on, the world changed dramatically from a banking point of view and, in particular, from an advertising and media point of view.' He blamed 'the most extraordinary change in advertising revenues and, indeed, consumer behaviour and purchasing activity that has ever been experienced in the last four decades. It is fair to say that the speed of the change was unprecedented and alarming, and allied to the banking crisis, constitutes trading conditions which no one has ever previously experienced.' He was far from the only corporate boss to cry 'not our fault', but not too many outside of the property business were in a position where they were in serious danger of breaching their banking covenants.

Independent News & Media didn't just have enormous debts, it had made commitments to repay sizeable chunks of them in the very near future. The most important immediate debt was one of €200 million, falling due on 18 May, just 11 days after his resignation. Another €50 million was due in September, as well as a further €340 million tranche and another €200 million a year later in 2010, before even bigger amounts in 2012.

That was Gavin's issue to deal with, even if it was going to be essential to his father, too. O'Reilly had his own financial issues to deal with simultaneously. As well as personal debt, he was experiencing severe cash-flow problems.

His answer to those problems was to borrow, almost as if in the hope that something would turn up. Remarkably, he was facilitated. In the summer of 2009 he borrowed €4 million from AIB, offering as mortgage security his old holiday home in Glandore, West Cork, which he valued at €4.3 million, as well as the rights over a balance of €278,000 in the account of a company he owned called Brookside. Crucially, he also gave the bank a personal guarantee, giving it the right to pursue all of his assets in the event of default on repayment.

It was a remarkable decision by both parties. That O'Reilly had decided that his situation would be resolved by further borrowing emphasised not just that he was willing to gamble but also that he had to gamble, that he had no other cash resources available to him. That alone should have alerted AIB to the dangers involved in advancing him money. Of course, the fact that AIB – existing only because of the generosity of the State's infamous 2008 guarantee to all of its creditors, and in need of a capital rescue from the Irish government amounting to an enormous €21 billion – was willing to advance such a large sum to a 73-year-old man based on a property mortgage was just as extraordinary. It was already clear that property prices were collapsing and that there might be a struggle to find any buyer for the Glandore property, let alone at that price. Clearly, AIB didn't feel that O'Reilly would be in a position where he would be unable to repay the loan and that it would have to enforce its security by selling the property from under him.

It wasn't the only personal loan that O'Reilly took out that year. Three months later, he raised the same amount again from ACCBank (owned by the Dutch Rabobank) by remortgaging his Fitzwilliam Square townhouse and Castlemartin and giving it first call over those properties. But the really big loan came from Bank of Ireland. It provided O'Reilly with €27 million in December 2009, allowing him to participate in an emergency fund-raising among shareholders at INM. This brought O'Reilly's total borrowings by the end of the decade to nearly €300 million, spread across AIB, Bank of Ireland, IBRC (formerly Anglo Irish Bank), ACCBank, Ulster Bank, Trust Bahamas, EFG, Lloyds TSB and Mellon Bank of the United States. The loan from Bank of Ireland was essential, because without it O'Reilly's share in INM would have dropped dramatically. But that it was necessary was only because of the failure of O'Reilly's biggest effort in 2009 to rid himself, and INM, of O'Brien.

Gavin had taken to his new role as CEO at INM with gusto, but the honeymoon period was extremely short. It wasn't just a case of looking over his shoulder to see when O'Brien's mood would change again, he faced an immediate crisis that was common to all share-holders: the €200 million in bonds that had to be repaid on 18 May was the most pressing issue.

When the bonds had been sold originally by INM, it had not been contemplated that replacing them at the time with new bonds would be a problem. Indeed, it had been expected that the replacement bonds or loans would be replaced at an even more favourable rate of interest. But the nature of capital markets had changed dramatically. A short-age of liquidity on the part of financiers, and greater demands for certainty on repayment of debts, meant that nobody would provide new loans that would automatically 'refinance'. As a result, INM had to make one of the most serious declarations possible for a quoted company. 'The group currently does not have sufficient financial headroom available under its existing facilities in order to meet this maturity and service its debt obligations,' it said.

Assets had to be sold instead to raise the cash to meet the debts and as quickly as possible. O'Reilly was going to have to look on as the empire he had spent 35 years building was dismantled: the only question at this stage was how much of it would have to go, although the prices to be achieved were important, too. The company had not only left it too late in talking to the bondholders but also in raising cash from asset sales: as a known distressed seller, and selling into a deep recession, the prices it would receive for assets were likely to be disappointingly low, if they could be offloaded at all.

First to be offered for sale were the South African advertising business INM Outdoor and INM's minority shareholdings in casino software firm Cashcade and price comparison firm Verivox. It targeted €150 million in proceeds from these companies, but quickly realised that it couldn't get any of the cash before the third-quarter of the year. Its 20.7% stake in the Indian newspaper interests was put up for sale, unofficially. Most importantly, however, the efforts to sell the 39% share in APN, announced in January, failed. Gavin said that there had been two offers, but that potential buyers had been unable to raise the money to complete the purchase. He said he didn't want to sell anyway and while that might have been true on an emotional level, it didn't reflect the practical realities of the situation. But APN had its own debt issues and had to raise capital itself; as a result, INM's shareholding was reduced to 31.6%.

O'Brien was spooked by all of this, sharing the belief of executives that the idea of selling APN in any case was entirely incorrect. O'Brien began to worry even more about Gavin's ability to formulate the right strategy to rescue INM from its crisis with the bondholders and, even if he did come up with one, to execute it. 'I don't believe in having media outlets just for the benefit of journalists and great writers,' he pointedly told journalists, sending a shiver through their collective spine. He described the chances of a refinancing of INM's bonds as less than 50-50 and began agitating publicly against the demands of the bondholders for full or near complete repayment. 'If they think Denis O'Brien is going to write a cheque to the bondholders, then they are smoking dope,' he said of himself.

Gavin was hard at work coming up with a refinancing plan, having first secured a 'standstill' from the bondholders: they agreed not to demand immediate repayment of the money owed, although interest on overdue money began then to be added to the existing bill, leaving INM to watch like an anxious taxi customer as the metre ticks over and the final destination is still not in sight. By June, Gavin considered going to shareholders for another €60 million in new equity. He also proposed to give bondholders 10% of the proceeds of a sale of businesses valued at a total of €150 million. In return, the bondholders would wait an additional three years for repayment of their original capital and be further compensated by increased interest payments of 5.75%. Gavin wrote to bondholders that 'this proposal is framed as a pragmatic and sensible compromise position'.

O'Brien thought the offer to bondholders too generous, wanting to offer a lower interest rate and to have the maturity date on bonds extended by five years. He recommended that all proceeds from the sale of assets be used to pay down a separate class of lender, those who held what was called 'senior debt'. O'Brien was worried that the capital fund-raising of €60 million would not be enough and that another tranche of money would be required again later in the year. 'There is no point in putting together a Band-aid solution when major surgery is required. Any further investment must be about the future and not shoring up the past,' O'Brien argued. He began putting his objections in writing to Gavin and the board. He even spoke publicly of examinership, a process whereby the company would get protection from its creditors but shareholders would temporarily lose control and potentially not get it back. O'Reilly feared this option: he would not have the money to buy the company out of examinership whereas O'Brien, if he so wished, appeared to have it.

But sorting out the bondholders was not the only issue. Further bank borrowings of €50 million fell due for repayment that September and these were what was categorised as senior debt, meaning they had to be repaid first, before the bondholders, in the event of a default. That the bondholders were willing to engage in a 'standstill' suggested that they had confidence that the other lenders would not pull the plug on INM, or not yet anyway.

At the end of August 2009, Gavin hosted a press conference at which he admitted that falling advertising revenues had led to a 22% drop in overall revenue at INM in the first half of the year, to €608.8 million. There was a pre-tax loss of €34.7 million after various accounting write-offs were made. The costs of not making the bond repayments, including professional fees and penalties to investors, came to €8.4 million to date. O'Reilly said an examinership or any other court process would not be in the interests of the company or its stakeholders. What O'Reilly did not reveal publicly at this stage – although details were to appear in two newspapers the following Sunday – was that a rollicking row with O'Brien had taken place over the telephone the evening before publication of those figures.

Gavin had been in his Citywest office when a call was patched through from O'Brien, who was holidaying in Ibiza. It was a three-way conversation, although the third participant, Connolly, said almost nothing. They started with what had transpired at a previous board meeting, on 19 August, which had endorsed, by majority vote, the sale of the South African outdoor advertising firm, raising €98 million, despite objections from O'Brien's representatives that this price was not providing sufficient value for a profitable asset and indeed should not be sold at all. The debate was described by O'Brien, who had not been present at the meeting but who had been told about it by his directors, as 'the lowest of the low he had ever seen at a plc'. He claimed that the seven 'O'Reilly directors' had 'ganged up' on his three nominees and he took particular offence at the perceived treatment of Gaffney by Margaret Jay, the board's senior independent director.

O'Brien told Gavin that in March they had 'agreed to be aligned', but that Gavin's actions constituted a 'solo run', which meant he had 'broken the agreement'. When O'Brien told him that he 'needed to start to consult with shareholders', Gavin replied that he did and that he was surprised to hear the complaint about solo runs for the first time the previous week. Gavin insisted that management was merely trying to find a solution to the crisis. It was like waving a red rag at a bull.

Gavin reported afterwards that O'Brien became more 'agitated', said that 'things needed to change' and that unless they did, he'd call an EGM of shareholders 'tomorrow'. Gavin told O'Brien that this was his right, but said that O'Brien became more aggressive in response to this reasonableness. As O'Reilly continued to protest, O'Brien told him he 'wasn't capable of delivering a deal' with the company's bondholders. Then came the most inflammatory comment of all: he told Gavin that if he wanted a fight, 'I will destroy you and your father and I will go after everything.'

It didn't finish there, even if Gavin was reeling at the directness of the invective. O'Brien's tirade turned to the continued propping up of the London *Independent* newspaper titles and his claim that in the absence of appropriate 'action', INM could become 'another Waterford Wedgwood'. Ironically, it was an expression that Gavin had himself used in other circumstances, on other occasions. Gavin was told brusquely that he needed to 'listen to people who have experience'. He was told that the company needed 'a new, proper board' and a 'sane discussion' about the choosing of a new chairman.

Although extremely shaken by the experience, Gavin had the presence of mind to immediately write down, after the call had ended, a full note of what had transpired. He had not taped the telephone conversation – to have done so without consent would have been illegal – even though he was to be accused of that later. Gavin took advice as to what to do. He was told not to make reference to any of it at the following day's results, to carry on as normally as possible. However, the story was then given to both the *Sunday Independent* and *The Sunday Times* newspapers. In response, O'Brien gave comments to *The Sunday Times* that the crisis at INM 'has been escalating for years' and the banks, bondholders, investment community and staff had seen it coming. He claimed people with responsibility 'took no action'.

In an interview for this book O'Brien said, 'I think Gavin was rather selective in his disclosures to journalists during this entire period. Mysteriously, Gavin was able to remember, word for word, conversations which he was able to transcribe after having these conversations.' He also explained how and why he had lost confidence in Gavin. 'I always said he was a spoofer and a silver spoon merchant,' said O'Brien, 'and when I got a letter from him that was four pages long I began to question his ability and direction. Confidence just evaporated. As an example, Gavin thought the Internet was for people who believed in fairies.'

O'Brien's comments to the media were mild compared to what he put into a six-page e-mail he sent to the INM company secretary Andrew Donagher the morning after his telephone conversation with Gavin, demanding an EGM to block the South African sale. He stated that Gavin was incapable of saving the situation and slammed the capacity of the other six directors too, claiming that they operated under the influence and control of O'Reilly, which compromised their independence and judgement. 'It is clear that the seven remaining O'Reilly legacy directors have been party to a whole series of bad decisions and have failed all stakeholders. The equity value of the company has collapsed from €3 billion to €200 million in less than two years and these directors have presided over this collapse.'

O'Brien claimed that at board level there was no culture of demanding action where overall business or individual business units missed their budgets, ignoring the explanations of management that they were facing unprecedented general economic conditions that affected both advertising and circulation revenues. Indeed, O'Brien mocked them. 'Shortcomings are met with a shrug of the shoulders and an acknowledgement that market conditions are indeed tough out there. These are all symptoms of a board with "no skin in the game", who have presided over a steady erosion of stakeholder value and defaulted on bond payment terms.'

Somewhat doubtfully, O'Brien claimed that it appeared it was only his board appointees who were concerned about current company performance and future trading prospects. He claimed that efforts by board members appointed by him 'have been constantly thwarted and obstructed at every turn by the existing management and other board members. Any effort to revitalise and bring about change in this company has been met with at the least, suspicion, and at the most, outright resistance.'

That wasn't all. O'Brien was determined to expose O'Reilly's soft underbelly, calling for an EGM to 'address the serious concerns relating to the company's corporate governance and to seek to avoid further destruction of stakeholder value'. He wanted shareholders to call for a 'detailed schedule' of all board member expenses since the start of 2000 and to have these applied to both executive and non-executive directors, sensing that any disclosure of the information would cause considerable embarrassment to Gavin and his father. O'Brien called for a vote to cancel the €300,000 annual payment to O'Reilly, which had been agreed only five months earlier, in respect of his titular position as president emeritus.

Publicly calling the continued ownership of the London *Independent* titles a 'vanity project', O'Brien published 'research' that claimed the losses were running at €27 million per annum. Independent News & Media had continued to claim that the papers were moving towards break-even, which would apparently be achieved by the end of 2010, and that it would cost nearly €40 million to close the titles because of contractual obligations. It claimed that the cash losses that would be incurred between then and the end of 2015 would be less than half the closure costs. O'Brien disputed this, arguing that falling circulation would reduce cover price revenues and that advertising would fall at least proportionately, increasing the losses.

O'Brien didn't believe that Gavin's profit projections could be achieved, if past experience was any guide. He pointed out that INM was now predicting operating profits for 2009 at the lower end of its previously published €180–€210 million range. He contrasted that to the €290 million operating profits of the previous year. He said that as INM had decided to 'sell off profitable divisions in an effort to appease its bondholders', the protection of loss-making titles 'does not seem to be a strategy which is in the best interests of shareholders'. It was hard to argue against.

Gavin was in a terrible position. He was in regular contact with his father, in his capacity as a major shareholder, about the financial restructuring with the banks and bondholders, because he had to be able to convince all lenders that O'Reilly and O'Brien were working together to save the company. He had legal requirements to obey as CEO that meant he could not favour, or be seen to favour, one share-holder over another, but his father's prior role in the company and O'Brien's insistence on targeting him complicated matters dramatic-ally and made such discussions with his father more difficult. The 'I will destroy you' comment did not cause any extra concern to the O'Reillys, however; they were working on that assumption anyway.

The response from INM could be described as dignified or muted, but Gavin most certainly was not going to answer the questions as set down by O'Brien and thereby allow him to dictate the terms of public engagement. The company issued a stock exchange statement, confirming that O'Brien's request for an EGM would be considered by the board. 'It is noted that Mr O'Brien has unilaterally chosen to issue a statement this morning in advance of formal consideration of his request by the board of INM, which, as he has already been advised, has already been convened. While the company is fully aware of Mr O'Brien's personal views on a number of matters … it notes that a number of the resolutions proposed by Mr O'Brien for consideration are at variance with decisions previously taken by the board of INM.' It did, however, comment on the €300,000 annual gratuity to O'Reilly, offering the somewhat bizarre and weak defence that it was not a contractual entitlement and therefore could not be voted upon.

The battle lines were now drawn publicly. 'It was no surprise,' said one of Gavin's key executives. 'We knew it would come and it was only a question of when and what excuse would be used for it.' Gavin was seeking to make a big asset sale in direct contravention of O'Brien's wishes, and O'Brien did not own enough shares to stop him if O'Reilly could get the support of other shareholders.

It was the start of a sustained public campaign by O'Brien to undermine banker, bondholder and other shareholder confidence in Gavin and, by extension, the O'Reillys. He complained that Gavin's restructuring plans would turn INM into a 'zombie publicly quoted company'. While O'Brien was arguing these points publicly, he was also working privately with the banks and bondholders, independent of the company's management. This irritated Gavin greatly: 'The matters facing INM are very serious and this is a time for serious behaviour, not what appears to be a personal vendetta that is directly impacting stakeholder value. If Mr O'Brien has a constructive proposal to put to shareholders, let's hear it before asking shareholders to abandon an agreed road map to financial stability. Conversely, if Mr O'Brien's aim is to unilaterally wrestle control of this company, then he should avoid the back door and make a transparent bid for the company.'

O'Brien made four attempts over the next couple of months to persuade INM's bondholders and banks to accept an alternative restructuring plan. The most remarkable of these was an offer to invest 65% of a new €100 million capital injection in return for a majority stake in INM of around 51.3%. This, had the bondholders gone for it, had the potential to cause a major political situation for the government: at that level of shareholding, there could not have been any Jesuitical or legal argument as to whether or not O'Brien had control of the company. This would have forced the Irish government to make a decision about the size of O'Brien's media ownership, given the scale of his existing radio interests. That O'Reilly offered a deal with more money to the bondholders and banks – and they accepted – eased that potential problem for the government.

But before Gavin secured a deal with the lenders, his father came close to a remarkable deal with a third party. He had decided that if he couldn't retain control of INM, he would at least deny O'Brien that opportunity by doing a deal with a friendly party who would save the company, keep Gavin as CEO and allow him and his family some titular and financial involvement, at the very least, in a new structure. In the late summer of 2009, O'Reilly came very close to closing a transformative deal with the German publisher Axel Springer, one that most likely would have made O'Brien's involvement in INM largely insignificant. O'Reilly proposed an arrangement whereby he would sell Axel Springer a chunk of his own shares, to give it a foothold as a major shareholder in INM. The Germans and O'Reilly would then announce that they were concert parties, something that would become very significant if their combined shareholding exceeded 29.9% of all the ordinary shares in the company. The idea that O'Reilly would deliberately sell some of his shares in the company may have seemed surprising, but he knew that the solution of the problem with the banks and bondholders would almost certainly involve a dilution of his shareholding anyway. A placing of new INM shares to bolster the balance sheet without O'Brien's approval was also impossible without it being passed at an EGM. Indeed, the issuing of new shares before the Germans had come on board ran the risk of allowing O'Brien to take control. But if other investors and creditors saw the deal between such a respected and powerful newspaper group as Axel Springer and O'Reilly, they would likely support it rather than anything O'Brien, unproven in the newspaper industry, would have to offer. A new share issue with the Germans, and O'Reilly subsequently in funds from the proceeds of the sale of some of his existing shares, might have a chance of succeeding and in doing so either dilute O'Brien to a very small amount or force him to invest heavily to maintain his stake, without the prospect of any influence. He could opt to sell, but it would be at a very low price compared to the €500 million or so he had paid for the original shares. The willingness of O'Reilly to declare publicly that he was in concert with Axel Springer implied that he saw a chance to force O'Brien out entirely by taking the company private.

But there arose a problem so significant as to derail and destroy the hoped-for deal. O'Reilly had pledged some of his shares in INM as security for loans he had taken. This had a double effect. First, any money raised by selling shares to the Germans would potentially have to be used to repay his personal debts rather than for reinvestment, unless he could persuade his lenders to let him use the money in the way he wanted. Secondly, he had not declared in the most recent annual report that his shares were pledged as security for loans. Although this was not required by the Irish Stock Exchange, it was still a material issue that would have to be declared to the London Stock Exchange under new rules that had been introduced only recently. His advisers cited the example of what had happened to David Ross, the multimillionaire co-founder of British retailer Carphone Warehouse, the previous December. Ross had been forced to resign his position at the company when it was disclosed that he had used shares worth around Stg£160 million as security against personal loans without disclosing that information to the company. Other investors in the company had assumed that Ross, rated at the time as the 87th richest person in Britain with a fortune estimated at almost Stg£900 million, was not in hock to his banks – information that, had it been available, might have coloured their view of Carphone Warehouse. If the deal with the Germans was to go ahead, O'Reilly would therefore have to disclose that he had broken the regulations in similar fashion. It would have been embarrassing, to say the very least, and would also have created an entirely different public perception of his wealth.

That wasn't the biggest issue, however. Axel Springer said, 'we have no problem in doing a deal with you and working with you, but what happens if the banks call in the security and you lose the shares? Who are we in partnership with then?' O'Reilly's associates despaired. They had worked hard on the deal and saw it as the last chance of fending off O'Brien. The information that he had pledged his shares was made available to them only at the last minute and immediately ruined the chances of a deal, one that a number of well-informed INM insiders said was nearly done, despite the lack of public knowledge about it at the time.

There were small reports in the British media, barely picked up on in Ireland, that a deal had been discussed but had fallen down on the issue of price. That was incorrect: the price at which the shares would be transferred was not the issue. Gavin tried to maintain the relationship, appointing Lothar Lanz, CFO and COO of Axel Springer, as a non-executive director of INM in November 2009, but the opportunity to do a deal had passed.

This increased the pressure on Gavin to reach an agreement with the bondholders before O'Brien could take control. Gavin won the first battle at the end of September, when the directors of INM formally rejected O'Brien's plan and supported his, albeit on the basis of a majority rather than unanimous decision. Pointedly, INM's confirmation statement said the refinancing deal agreed in principle with bondholders and banks would deliver on the objective of achieving a solution that was 'capable of implementation outside of a court-administered process'. Direct reference was made to O'Brien's alternative, which it said failed because of 'significant competition law and media plurality issues' and it was specifically stated that the O'Reilly family's existing shareholding was 'capable of blocking those special resolutions which would be required to implement Mr O'Brien's proposals'.

The eventual deal with the bondholders, while it saved the company, was still humiliating for O'Reilly. The bondholders were to get 46% of the ordinary shares in INM in return for writing off €123 million of the outstanding principal amount of the bonds. There was then to be a rights issue among existing shareholders, which raised €94 million, with this money being used to pay off the bondholders. The new shares were sold at a price of 5 cent per share, compared to the existing 27 cent share price. Both O'Reilly and O'Brien invested fully in their rights, costing O'Reilly about €27 million, which he borrowed from Bank of Ireland. It left O'Reilly with 14.7% of the shares in the newly reconfigured company and O'Brien with 13.8%.

There followed weeks of further acrimony, especially at various EGMs that were called either by the board, to approve measures Gavin wanted to implement, or by O'Brien, to try and stop them happening. The O'Reilly-dominated board received the backing of shareholders in them all. 'A lot of these EGMs have very little to do with the business of the company,' Gavin said, adding that there had been 'too many sideshows. Hopefully we can now move on, having gotten a very strong endorsement by shareholders'. He claimed that the refinancing was 'affording the company a secure and stable foundation, with a significantly reduced debt profile, from which to leverage INM businesses and key strengths across its global portfolio of assets'.

There was a degree of wishful thinking in all of this. Whatever about denying O'Brien control, the reality was that the banks were now firmly in the driving seat. New bank documents revealed that 'if one or more persons acting in concert gain control of the company (control being defined as 35 per cent of the maximum number of votes that may be cast at a general meeting of the company), a lending bank is not to be obliged to fund further utilisations and can declare outstanding borrowings immediately due and payable.' This was a poison pill against anyone launching a bid to take control of the company without the approval of the banks or without €745 million of finance available to replace still existing loans. The banks also banned the payment of dividends, put restrictions on future share buybacks and limited capital expenditure. Acquisitions, unlikely as they were, could only be made if funded by new equity from shareholders. Instead, the priority remained further debt repayments, even if €350 million had been repaid in 2009, but it was going to be almost impossible to do this without further asset sales. It was not a good time to get good prices, in the teeth of an advertising recession and with serious doubts growing about the ability of printed newspapers to survive in a new digital media environment.

Within weeks of seeing off O'Brien's challenge, Gavin admitted that INM would not meet its operating profit projections after all. At the end of October it reduced these to a range of between €170 million and €190 million, the third reduction in six months. Gavin decided to promote Vincent Crowley as the new COO across the group, with Joe Webb replacing Crowley as CEO of its Irish division. Crowley's main job would be cost-cutting in ongoing operations. Gavin had to concentrate on selling parts of the empire that his father had assembled.

Two of the sales were particularly painful for his father. The sale of shares in *Jagran Prakashan*, purchased only in 2005, had begun in June 2009 and was finished by August 2010. This turned a very healthy profit of €68 million for INM. It was an excellent return on the original €26.5 million investment – vindicating O'Reilly's shrewdness in identifying the original acquisition and Healy's capabilities in completing it – but it also indicated that there was considerable potential remaining in the business that would be left to others to exploit. This was a part of the world where old media still had considerable value.

More significantly, however, the London *Independent* newspapers were sold to the Russian businessman Alexander Lebedev, a former KGB agent who already owned the *Evening Standard* in London. He paid just Stg£1 for the titles but, more importantly, agreed to pay Stg£9.25 million (€11.7 million)· of the existing debts and assumed 'all future trading liabilities and obligations'. It would be considered a good deal in retrospect as *The Independent* made an operating loss of Stg£12.4 million in 2009 as circulation fell below 100,000; Lebedev made losses of a further €40 million in his first three years of ownership.

The sale raised legitimate questions as to whether O'Brien had been vindicated in his stance on *The Independent*. 'The issues in relation to Denis O'Brien, I'm sure he's going to claim ownership for some of these … I think the important thing is that we as a management team are doing the right things for our shareholders. Denis O'Brien is one of those shareholders,' Gavin said curtly. 'We didn't get very wealthy last year as managers and neither did our shareholders; 2010 is about rebuilding the equity story for all our shareholders.' But there were plenty of senior people within INM who felt that the sale should have taken place years earlier, and that it would have happened if ownership of the title had not been so emotionally important to O'Reilly.

As Gavin continued the process of trying to sell INM assets to reduce debt, his father's personal position got worse as he tried to deal with his own debts of nearly €300 million. The penny was dropping for many of O'Reilly's banks that all was not as they had assumed. O'Reilly's lenders were becoming anxious about his ability to repay his debts. His lack of cash-flow and sellable assets was dawning on them. Questions were being asked of him as to when repayments would be made and he was unable to provide the required answers. Interest charges were ratcheting up, continually increasing the size of his debts.

The banks started doing some calculations. He was presumed to have shares in Heinz, although nobody knew how many as, since leaving the board in 2000, he was no longer required to declare either the size of his shareholding or any sales of those shares. The extent of the INM shareholding was known but was now worth little, and the expectation was that this would be the last thing sold. He had a size-able shareholding in Providence Resources, but its saleability was doubtful. He owned a good chunk of a Swiss-based electricity metering company called Landis+Gyr, which his son Cameron had built, but the shares might not be easily tradable. He had his vast array of trophy properties, but who wanted or could afford to buy those in the down-turn, especially those in Ireland? There was plenty of art and even if Irish buyers were now few and far between, international traders might be persuaded to buy some of that at good prices. However, what the banks also feared was that some of those assets had been mortgaged and that the proceeds of any sales were therefore ear-marked.

O'Reilly turned to Bernard Somers for help, as he had done many times over the last 20 years. Somers was an insolvency specialist, among other things, and he had done a remarkable job on behalf of Larry Goodman when the beef baron got into enormous trouble in 1990 after a period of reckless stock market investments, property punts and failure to recover money owed from Iraq left him with debts of over IR£500 million. Somers had been a director of INM since 1998, having previously worked as a consultant to the group. He had also been a director of AIB for many years, although he resigned in late 2008 'to avoid conflicts of interest' for his business: he had anticipated correctly that many of his clients would require him to act as inter-mediary with their lenders. One of those he represented subsequently was the former Anglo Irish Bank (now IBRC) chairman Sean Fitzpatrick, until the latter opted for bankruptcy.

Somers visited all of O'Reilly's nine banks and issued a plea: he wanted all to consent simultaneously to a so-called 'stand-still agree-ment'. This would give O'Reilly three years in which he would try to sell as many assets as possible to cover his debts, without the fear of a bank suddenly moving to enforce a debt. Keeping the arrangement secret would not just spare O'Reilly's blushes, it would also stop the fall in the potential price he could achieve for those assets that would be caused if his financial distress became known to buyers. A pragmatic approach was taken by many of the banks: they believed that better prices might be achieved in a recovering economic climate and that a gamble on waiting was justified. There was also a belief among some that his business career and his contribution to Ireland's economic development had earned him the right to time. There was a feeling, too, that O'Reilly was serious about honouring his obligations, that he would not engage in the jiggery-pokery in which some other prominent Irish businessmen indulged when faced with straitened circumstances. As a result, Somers got his client the necessary agreement.

That agreement came at a high cost, however. Some of the banks required additional security in return for not demanding immediate repayment of debts. For example, he had two loans with Anglo Irish Bank, one for €55 million that was secured on INM shares now worth far less, and another for €10.5 million relating to Waterford Wedgwood, a company from whose ownership he was now excluded. A weakened O'Reilly gave Anglo Irish Bank full personal recourse, as well as new collateral: some of his shares in son Cameron's Landis+Gyr company.

There was considerable irony involved in having to depend on Cameron; things might not have come to this had Cameron been put in charge of INM. But the fact that the younger O'Reilly had struck out on his own, successfully, now created the potential for the raising of cash that might rescue his father.

CHAPTER TWO

A NEW ORDER EMERGES

In early 2011, O'Reilly discovered that INM had a new major shareholder and that he and Gavin had a second disgruntled heavyweight to deal with: Dermot Desmond arrived on the scene, and in improbable circumstances.

Desmond had been an unconventional character in Dublin financial circles over the previous three decades. He created NCB Stockbrokers, which in the space of less than a decade had broken the traditional monopoly on share dealings enjoyed by two long-established firms, Davy and Goodbody. Like O'Reilly, Desmond was from Dublin's northside, this time Marino. He was close to Charles Haughey, whom he had persuaded of the merits of government backing for the International Financial Services Centre (IFSC). His rise was stymied temporarily when he was identified as a key player in a major public scandal in 1991 involving the purchase by then State-owned and Michael Smurfit-chaired Telecom Éireann (later Eircom) of a valuable plot of land in upmarket Dublin 4. He was the subject of damning findings over the affair in a report compiled by a High Court-appointed inspector, in which he and JP McManus were named as the ultimate financial beneficiaries of the deal. Desmond was greatly displeased by the findings and disputed them publicly, although he never published his so-called 'alternative report' that he said would 'vindicate' him. It did not stop his rise in business, however. He went on to make large sums of money from judicious investments and became the main shareholder in Celtic Football Club in Scotland.

Most pertinently, Desmond had become involved in O'Brien's Esat Digifone mobile phone consortium at a very late stage in the 1995 bidding process. When Esat was sold in 2000, Desmond's International

Investments and Underwriting (IIU) outfit made a €100 million profit, although it was never revealed if all of the profit was his or whether IIU represented a group of undisclosed investors. He had given plenty of evidence to the Moriarty Tribunal about this and also defended large sums of money he had advanced to Charles Haughey – including 'loans' for a yacht – during Haughey's time in political office and afterwards.

Desmond had a highly confrontational approach to media coverage, often sending solicitors' letters· about newspaper articles that displeased him. In 2002 Desmond had objected to two separate articles in the *Sunday Tribune* – both of which I had written when I was editor – and started legal proceedings against both the paper and this writer. Proceedings were delayed for many years, but Desmond sought to have the first of the cases – an article relating to his investment in a company called Greencore – heard at the High Court in late 2010. No judge was available to hear a case that was being defended; all the witnesses were available at the court, only to be told they would have to come back another day.

A date for a libel trial was set down for February 2011. But just weeks before the trial was due to be heard, INM decided to withdraw its financial support for *The Sunday Tribune*, which meant the company was swiftly put into receivership. It was a decision that everyone involved in swears was motivated solely by the exceptionally serious financial position at INM. Indeed, Gavin closed the paper without first consulting his father who, as other executives noted, would not have agreed with the decision. 'He would never have closed *The Sunday Tribune*,' said one, '[he] would have said that democracy needed it, find the money from somewhere to keep it open. The accountants, however, had their say. INM was simply unable to provide the money to keep it going.' Another concurred: 'The eventual closure of *The Sunday Tribune* was caused by the group running low on cash. Executives had wanted to close it for years, but Tony refused, believing it to provide a useful voice in the Irish market. He also didn't want to be seen as a person who closed a paper.'

I was left to defend Desmond's action on my own. My lawyers recommended that we settle both cases rather than risk losing one or both, leaving me with a bill for both damages and costs that I would not be able to afford now that *The Sunday Tribune* was no longer there to indemnify me. We settled both cases for a small donation to a charity and the reading of a short, agreed apology to Desmond in court.

That was not the end of it, however. Days after the settlement was agreed Desmond rang Gavin, who was in South Africa, claiming that he would have won €500,000 in damages and costs had the case been run and that he wanted compensation for INM's decision not to back me. Other INM executives listened in with mounting disbelief as Desmond, preparing to tee-off at a major pro-am golf tournament, turned the air blue. Gavin denied that the closure of *The Sunday Tribune*, which by this stage had run up accumulated losses of more than €60 million that could not be recovered, had anything to do with avoiding the possible costs of losing a libel action with Desmond. When Gavin refused to promise to pay him any money as compensation, Desmond replied that there would be adverse consequences arising from this decision, something he later put into writing: 'Believe me this will not go away and I will not be folding my tent. I look forward to my cheque.'

Within months Desmond was a significant shareholder in INM. In May 2011 *The Irish Times* was in a position to reveal that Desmond had bought shares. His shareholding at this time was small – less than the 5% level at which public disclosure is required – but it was enough to spook O'Reilly and Gavin, especially given his known good relationship with O'Brien. Nobody in the O'Reilly camp believed that the outcome of the libel action was the motivating factor. Rightly or wrongly, they regarded the excuse as a form of insurance policy. Had Desmond bought the shares without supplying a personal reason for doing so – no matter how far-fetched – there would have been the danger that he would have been deemed as acting in concert with O'Brien, given their previous relationship. This might require the two, if at any future date they ended up owning more than 29.9% of the shares between them, to make a full offer to all shareholders to buy their shares.

Amidst these continual fluctuations, there was at least one good day for O'Reilly in 2011: the March day that the Moriarty Tribunal published the long-awaited findings of its investigation. The news was good for O'Reilly, but not so for his adversary, Denis O'Brien, against whom findings were made about which he complained bitterly and which he rejected out of hand. The findings as they applied to O'Reilly were, by and large, a vindication of his evidence, albeit largely overlooked by most of the media because of the concentration on the findings about O'Brien and Lowry.

The tribunal came down on O'Reilly's side in deciding that, on the day of the opening of the Arcon mine in Galmoy, in the middle of the 1995 mobile phone licence competition, his version of the conversation with Lowry, and not the ex-minister's, rang true. The official conclusion was that 'in all the circumstances, the tribunal finds that a remark, consistent only with knowledge on the part of Lowry of unfavourable assessment of the performance of Irish Cellular within the previous twenty-four hours, was made by him to O'Reilly, and that this in turn must have resulted from disclosure to Lowry from within the Project Group ... and clearly in breach of the intended seal of confidence.'

On the controversy as to whether O'Reilly and Lowry had met at the Derby in 1995 or 1996, the tribunal found that the 'comparative force' with which O'Reilly recounted that the Galmoy encounter was the first occasion that he had met Lowry, and the considerably more fraught relations with the government in 1996, 'seem to incline the probabilities in favour of the occasion having taken place in 1996. Whilst it is unnecessary that a specific finding be made in that regard, it is however clear that whatever passing remark was made by Mr O'Reilly in relation to the [mobile phone competition] outcome, the overwhelming weight of his grievance, as apparent from the evidence of subsequent dealings described, related to the MMDS issue.' In other words, he had not been a bad loser on the mobile phone licence competition, but had been motivated by the serious issues with that Rainbow government regarding its failure to adhere to the law on television signal transmission.

The tribunal also accepted O'Reilly's contention that he did not order the controversial 'It's payback time' editorial that so marked the 1997 general election. However, it stated that 'it would nonetheless seem surprising if so unprecedented a course was adopted without some degree of perceived assent or imprimatur on the part of a chairman and major shareholder who, however diverse his overseas commitments, had invested significantly in terms of both finance and hands-on involvement in matters in dispute with the government.'

Anyone in the O'Reilly camp who thought that the eventual publication of the final report of the Moriarty Tribunal would soften

O'Brien's cough or hamper his attempts to win control at INM was wrong. The carefully worded report found that Lowry had 'secured the winning' of the 1995 mobile phone licence competition for O'Brien's Esat Digifone and that O'Brien had made two payments to Lowry, in 1996 and 1999, totalling about IR£500,000, and supported a loan of Stg£420,000 given to Lowry in 1999. O'Brien rejected the tribunal's findings loudly and angrily, saying that they only constituted one man's opinion and had no legal standing. He said that he had not given 'one red cent' to Lowry and was unaware of what other people had done with money he had given to them for other things. Cabinet members of the new Fine Gael/Labour coalition government – many of whom had been ministers during the time of the award of the licence – largely stayed silent. It became obvious quickly that there would be no significant consequences for O'Brien arising from the report: he could continue with business as usual. The INM titles reported and analysed all of this in detail, but so did all the other media. Indeed, O'Reilly's people noted that the *Irish Independent*, perhaps with an eye to the future, was muted in its coverage about O'Brien, preferring to concentrate on Lowry, and that only the *Sunday Independent* gave it the type of full rein they might have expected.

Meanwhile, Gavin got on with running the company, refraining from personal comment on the Moriarty findings at this stage – perhaps mindful of his father's previous condemnation of tribunals as 'prurience' – but reporting on business matters to O'Brien's directors despite the breakdown in relations with O'Brien personally. Indeed, at this stage communications between Gavin and his father had become far more limited. Gavin, for example, did not ring his father to tell him of Desmond's outburst and demands.

Nonetheless, Gavin and his father both watched anxiously, for different reasons, as O'Brien continued to accumulate shares. O'Brien had noted that many bondholders who had received shares as part of the 2009 settlement did not want to have them for the long term so he bought when he could, building his shareholding back up to a level of 21.6% by early 2011. O'Reilly was financially unable to buy more and could not rebuild his position, still stuck at 14.7%.

Independent News & Media was generating cash and paying down debt, reducing it by end April 2011 to €446.3 million compared with €473.6 million at end 2010. But that wasn't fast enough for O'Brien, or for the banks. His people continued to criticise management internally at increasingly fractious board meetings. Also, they were about to resume public hostilities.

The 2011 AGM, to approve the accounts for 2010, was due to be held on 3 June. This was normally a formality at any publicly quoted company, but Buckley, Gaffney and Connolly revealed publicly that they would vote against the adoption of the director's report and financial statements. It was a fairly dramatic step for any directors to take and Gavin called it 'bizarre'. O'Reilly was asked by Bloomberg if a new fight with O'Brien's people was looming. 'Do I think we have suddenly reached the point of a commencement of hostilities? No, I don't.'

But the tipping point had been reached. The O'Brien camp realised, to its shock, that Buckley's re-election to the board was far from automatic. Two institutional investor advisory groups, ISS and Glass Lewis, recommended that shareholders vote against his reappointment at the AGM. Many saw the irony that O'Brien's ally was being hoist with the same petard O'Brien had used to undermine O'Reilly's stewardship of the board some years earlier. The ISS group said Buckley was not independent by virtue of being a nominee of O'Brien, with whom he had business connections. It also said O'Brien was over-represented on the board of INM and that the board was unbalanced, with less than a majority of its members being independent. It also cited Buckley's 'lack of directly relevant experience', but in an effort to show that it was independent and even-handed it also recommended that INM investors vote against the re-election of Brian Mulroney because of his own previous business relationship with INM and his poor attendance record at meetings over the previous two years. O'Brien's people didn't buy this stated neutrality: they suspected O'Reilly's hand in the effort to remove Buckley.

The AGM was held in the conference rooms of the Aviva Stadium at Lansdowne Road, alongside a pitch where O'Reilly had many mixed days wearing the Irish rugby jersey. It was a stormy affair, notable, among other things, for the first public statements on INM's future by Desmond. He sent a representative, John Bateson, the finance director at IIU, who expressed 'grave disappointment' at the likely removal of Buckley from the board, given that he was 'the director most qualified in digital commerce' and that it 'remains a company of very modest internet assets'. 'We're particularly pleased,' Gavin responded drily, 'that Mr Desmond has bought into the company on value grounds.' But the intervention was not sufficient to convince the majority of shareholders and almost 58% voted against Buckley's re-election.

Buckley did not take his demotion well and nor did his colleagues, Gaffney and Connolly, who declared the decision 'bizarre' and a 'sad day'. Buckley accused Gavin of 'actively canvassing company share-holders' to vote against his re-election. This charge was denied by Gavin, who pointed out that both he and Hillery had publicly voted for Buckley. Gavin suggested that Buckley 'should be careful with his language' and said his allegations suggested 'a conspiracy mentality' within a subset of the board. Buckley had not changed his point of view that Gavin was, in fact, acting on his father's instructions. 'The final vote was his father's,' he told *The Irish Times* a year later and he confirmed that he continued to hold that view in an interview for this book in late 2014. Gavin, for his part, always maintained that he didn't know how his father had voted.

In retrospect, some of Gavin's advisers came to regard the ousting of Buckley as a mistake. 'It showed O'Brien's camp that it wasn't as hard as people thought to vote somebody off the board of an Irish public company,' said one. 'We had decided to embrace all the best tenets of corporate governance, including making directors seek re-election each year. It meant that Gavin would be vulnerable the next time a vote came up. We provided them with the road-map.'

In the meantime, before he would get a further opportunity, O'Brien decided it was time to go public again with his own criticisms of INM management. His first target was Hillery, even though it was widely known that he wanted to step down as chairman and would do so as soon as a suitable replacement could be found. 'I think it is inappropri-ate that the outgoing chairman had such a strong involvement and business association with one shareholder for many years. Mr Hillery was not an independent chairman and the company has suffered gravely because of this,' O'Brien said. It was a legitimate point, given that Hillery also chaired Providence Resources, a company that O'Reilly had established and in which he was still a significant shareholder.

O'Brien said Gavin and Hillery were 'delusional in their total denial of the extremely chronic financial situation' and that the group 'repeatedly informs the market how well it is performing while the share value falls year after year'. Independent News & Media replied that 'it is not very helpful for a major shareholder to be talking down the company, especially when it is in complete contradiction of the facts.'

But O'Brien was not finished yet. He wrote to Hillery on 21 July, not only demanding his resignation once again, as he had in 2009, but also calling for Gavin to be replaced too, arguing that 'the very exist-ence of INM is now under threat'. He claimed Gavin did not have the 'confidence of the market' as CEO and 'does not understand new media and has no strategic vision for the company'. He was critical of him being based in London, away from key executives. He suggested the company should raise €100 million in new equity and address forth-coming debt repayments, and also called for a 'slim-down' of its head office to a €4–€5 million cost base.

The company responded publicly that the strategy being pursued was one that had been agreed by the board, including Connolly and Gaffney. Hillery also sent O'Brien a letter: 'Let me say that INM is not under threat … INM is a very profitable company, well-capitalised and fully compliant with all its lending covenants.'

Hillery reminded O'Brien that he had voted in favour of his re-election as chairman and that of Gavin to the board of INM at the recent AGM. In an attempt to mollify O'Brien, he agreed to a meeting on neutral ground. They met in early August at the unprepossessing venue of Moran's Red Cow Hotel, by the M50 motorway in Dublin, and O'Brien demanded that Buckley be reinstated to the board. Hillery would not budge.

The next major flashpoint came in October. The *Sunday Independent* had become increasingly critical of O'Brien since the publication of the Moriarty Tribunal report and on 21 October published two articles that infuriated O'Brien to the point that he sent a solicitor's letter alleging defamation and demanding a 'full retraction and apology' from the newspaper. One related to the government's invitation to O'Brien to attend its Global Economic Forum at Dublin Castle. The other covered Today FM's decision to drop Sam Smyth's Sunday morning radio show from its schedule, the radio station being fully owned by O'Brien's Communicorp. Smyth was the journalist who first exposed Lowry as being in receipt of money from Ben Dunne and who had written acerbically about O'Brien's relationship with the ex-minister. Gavin authorised the publication of a statement denying an agenda and claiming 'a strict policy of non-interference in editorial matters we, as a company, will always vigorously defend freedom of expression and the absolute and unequivocal right of our journalists and contributors to report and comment on matters of public interest and national importance. We believe that this is absolutely essential in order to preserve a free press in Ireland.'

O'Brien's next step was to write a piece that was published in *The Irish Times*, in which he claimed that he had been the victim of a vendetta at INM, that his 'punishment' for being a shareholder for the previous four years had been a 'prolonged, nasty, well-orchestrated campaign against me across a range of issues' by many of its papers. He alleged that 'articles are regularly published without me being given an opportunity to respond. But then the normal demarcation between board and management, on the one hand, and editorial on the other, does not exist … the hostile reaction to my shareholding in INM has been seamlessly executed through the editorial pages of all their publications. The editorial pages reflect the views of senior management faultlessly,' he alleged.

He further alleged that a previous article in *The Irish Times*, written by one of his own former employees at Newstalk radio station, Eamon Dunphy, in which O'Brien was heavily criticised for apparent short-comings as a media owner, could not be described as objective and unbiased. He recalled an admission made by Dunphy in a *Sunday Times* interview of May 2010 that he had written the piece at the request of Tony O'Reilly. O'Brien cited the exact quote from Dunphy: 'It was a favour to [Tony] O'Reilly, who asked me to write it.'

Independent News & Media denied the charges and decided upon a pointed reply. 'As a self-professed supporter of journalism and free speech he, equally, cannot expect to be rewarded, with fewer references to the Moriarty tribunal for example, simply because he happens to have acquired more than 20 per cent of our stock since the tribunal began its hearings,' a spokesman said.

Gaining little public traction with this line of criticism, O'Brien returned to the financial performance of INM and again publicly sought Gavin's removal as CEO. He seized upon the latest trading update, which he called 'its second profit warning in three months', claiming it had resulted in 'a further erosion' in shareholder value. He said INM was 'now a company in crisis' and there was 'the added risk that the company will again encounter difficulties with its bankers'. He alleged that 'it is obvious the senior management team do not have the experience or vision to put in place a strategy that will ensure the company's survival. For the sake of all shareholders, it is time for change.'

The company described O'Brien's statement as 'ludicrous' and said it was a veiled attempt by the businessman to take control of the media group without having to finance the costs of a bid. A spokesman for INM said: 'For Mr O'Brien to be claiming that a media company that has just affirmed a profit range of €74 million–€78 million in the worst trading conditions in recent memory is in crisis is clearly ludicrous. Mr O'Brien's intention here is and always has been to take control of Independent News and Media. If he wants to do this, he can make a bid for the company. Mr O'Brien has become increasingly animated about INM's editorial coverage since the publication of the Moriarty tribunal. This statement is just the latest instalment in his attempts to destabilise a highly profitable company for non-commercial reasons. It won't succeed.'

In the meantime a new chairman had entered the fray, but not one who was to O'Brien's liking. Solicitor James Osborne had become managing partner at A&L Goodbody at a very young age, in his thirties, having previously set up a New York office where he catered for Tony Ryan's aircraft leasing company GPA; he later achieved public prominence as an adviser to the controversial beef baron Larry Goodman. Osborne had served on the board of a number of leading Irish companies after leaving the legal firm and continued as chairman of the newsagents Eason's, as well as the senior independent director of Ryanair. He had no known links to Tony O'Reilly and had met him only once before he took up the INM position, during the time when the former had been chairman of Punchestown Racecourse. Osborne had legal responsibility for settling the will of the artist Derek Hill and the dispersal of his assets. He found an unfinished portrait by Hill of O'Reilly – a finished version already hung in Castlemartin – and delivered it to O'Reilly at his box at the races one day, pausing only briefly. He received a phone call a few weeks later from O'Reilly's secretary, inviting him to dinner at Castlemartin. Osborne asked how many people would be there and when he was told about 300, he replied that he didn't go to dinners with more than 10 people present. When he told O'Reilly about this many years later, O'Reilly said that this message had not been relayed to him. He offered no apologies to Osborne, however.

Connolly and Gaffney voted against his appointment as chairman, but Osborne was to prove himself properly independent in the coming months; he showed neither fear nor favour in doing what he believed to be the right thing. Osborne had never been close to O'Brien, even though they had been co-investors in some companies many years earlier. He was aware that O'Brien did not gel with Osborne's good friend Michael O'Leary, a distance that had developed when they both worked closely with Tony Ryan and that had widened over the years.

Osborne saw the job as something of an interesting puzzle. It was a control game, but even at that stage it was obvious that there could only be one winner: O'Brien had more shares and more financial resources. Osborne thought it would be interesting, to say the least.

Osborne was to meet O'Reilly on three occasions during his brief tenure as chairman – all at O'Reilly's Fitzwilliam Square home – although he was to be the recipient of regular gifts from him. O'Reilly sent Osborne books on the First and Second World Wars, and on the political environment in the intervening period. Osborne told friends that he wondered if he was being sent some subliminal message, although he enjoyed reading the books nonetheless. But it was ideas put forward by O'Reilly at one of those meetings that totally flabbergasted Osborne. Despite the still sizeable debts that had to be reduced – and the instructions from the banks as to how money had to be spent – O'Reilly suggested borrowing even more money and mortgaging the remaining South African assets to do so. Osborne wondered if O'Reilly had taken leave of his senses. It was at total variance with the approach being followed by Gavin and the management team, who quickly distanced themselves from the idea when told about it.

There was supposed to be a fourth meeting between the two men, but there was no answer when Osborne turned up at O'Reilly's Dublin townhouse at the appointed time and rang the bell. Osborne rang O'Reilly on his mobile to ask why no-one was there and was told that he was delayed and to come back at 6.30pm. Osborne replied that he was busy and wouldn't be available then, even though he lived only a fifteen-minute walk away.

Osborne also told friends that it appeared to him that O'Reilly had continued with a paternalistic approach towards the company, as if INM was still his when at this stage it was clearly lost. Osborne's greater interest, however, was in Gavin and in what he could do as CEO. At their first meeting Osborne told Gavin that he would be fair, but that he kept a stiletto in his sock and would use it if he had to. Osborne formed the impression that Gavin deliberately deported himself as his father did, that he felt that behaving in the same way would persuade people of his importance and they would treat him accordingly. He interpreted Gavin's approach as being that if he put himself up on a pedestal, he would be impossible to get off it. Osborne, on the other hand, thought others would see that as a perch from which Gavin could be knocked. Osborne was not impressed with Gavin's financial projections for INM, becoming particularly annoyed on one occasion by an assumption in a crucial budget document that circulation revenues would increase, albeit marginally, after years of circulation decline.

One of his fellow directors said: 'I think Osborne came in thinking that he could broker a resolution. Within a couple of months he realised that he couldn't. He looked at it and saw there could be only one winner. Denis [O'Brien] had the money.'

Osborne's relationship with Gavin deteriorated quickly. Partly because of his experiences at Ryanair, Osborne was somewhat parsimonious. He was appalled by the way Gavin continued to spend money at a company that had none. Osborne travelled to Australia to visit APN, but was disgusted to find on his arrival in Sydney that Gavin had procured a chauffeur-driven car and was hosting a dinner at the city's most expensive restaurant overlooking the Sydney Opera House, among myriad expenditures. He reprimanded him for comments he put into e-mails about O'Brien and finally lost his cool when Gavin revealed that he intended stopping off in Dubai for 10 days on his way home, to attend a newspaper conference. There was a crisis to be attended to and such waste could not be tolerated.

Osborne was very unhappy, too, at the manner in which Gavin announced to him that Anne Harris was to be the new editor of the *Sunday Independent*, to replace her husband Aengus Fanning when he died in January 2012. It wasn't the choice of person – Osborne suspected that nobody else could equal her credentials for the job – but rather the manner in which it was executed. Osborne was informed of the appointment at Fanning's funeral, as he and Gavin stood on the steps of the church. Osborne protested that this appointment should not have been made without board approval; Gavin replied that it was a management issue.

It all meant that Gavin lacked a key supporter when Desmond increased the pressure and one of INM's main bankers joined in, too. Desmond told Osborne in March 2012 that Gavin was 'useless' and that he would have to get rid of him. Pointedly, Desmond informed Osborne that he remained an admirer of O'Reilly senior. When Bank of Ireland began expressing similar concerns about management's capability, Osborne's mind was made up.

Osborne had actually started the process a week earlier than the conversations with Desmond and the bank's Pat Gaynor. He had sent Gavin a strongly worded three-page letter on 6 March in which he noted how INM had issued two profit warnings in the past 12 months and that the budgets for the current financial year were under pressure. He said that a number of board members had expressed 'concerns' about O'Reilly's draft paper on Project Resolute, a cost-saving plan aimed at reducing its addressable cost base of €197.6 million. He doubted Gavin's ability to raise capital to pay for the cost-cutting plan, such was the lack of regard for him among shareholders and bankers.

If those criticisms of his ability were not bad enough, Osborne also threw in matters that would embarrass Gavin once they came to light. He questioned why Gavin's remuneration was 70% paid to a company in Jersey and 30% to an Irish registered entity. He required company secretary Andrew Donagher to provide a witness statement that showed Gavin had spent only 103 and 73 working days in Ireland in 2010 and 2011 respectively, and how, when in Dublin, Gavin charged the company for stays at expensive hotels, including the Four Seasons, and for his ironing to be done. Osborne questioned how his expenses could have amounted to €120,325 in little more than four months at the end of 2011.

Gavin's reply to Osborne's criticism amounted to 14 pages and much of it was devoted to taking issue with his chairman's tone. He defended his own performance strongly, arguing that the €75.5 million operating profit achieved in 2011 was within the €74–€78 million range agreed by the board the previous November. He had also made his own effort to repair relationships with Bank of Ireland, meeting with it in early April at the bank's office in Burlington Plaza. It was a difficult meeting, with the bank bluntly informing Gavin that it regarded INM as one of its 'most challenged corporate relationships'. He also learnt from Gaynor that 'the overriding view of the bank was that substantial changes to management were required'. He was told that INM's debt level was not sustainable when compared to a 2011 operating profit of €75 million, that the digital business was not growing quickly enough and that further cost reductions were required. Tellingly, the bank also questioned whether INM appreciated the seriousness of its debt position. The only concession was that 'INM's management was seen as operationally good but needing strategic support', that what was being offered was 'informal assistance' and that there was no demand for 'regime change'. Gavin didn't take much comfort from that.

Meanwhile, the *Sunday Independent* continued to fight its now largest shareholder in public. The main section of the first issue of April 2012 seemed to concentrate on O'Brien and little else, his name featuring on more than 100 occasions. O'Brien's response was to accuse INM of abdicating all responsibility for journalistic standards and ethics in its coverage of him. O'Brien's PR adviser, James Morrissey, wrote to INM claiming that coverage in that edition ranked as 'one of the most concerted and biased campaigns ever waged against any individual in this country'. Morrissey claimed news was merged with comment in 15 contributions to produce 'a cocktail designed solely to discredit Denis O'Brien. It was as calculating as it was contrived … Not one request for a response emanated from the *Sunday Independent* to enable Mr O'Brien to give his side of the story or defend himself. What we witnessed was pernicious journalism at its worst.'

Morrissey said that he had raised the issue of bias against O'Brien previously, in 2010, but had been told that none existed. However, he claimed that the newspaper's 'agenda-driven journalism' had continued unabated and had intensified. An INM spokesman said O'Brien was one of the major news stories for that week's paper and the suggestion that the *Sunday Independent* covered him only as a result of management pressure was 'comical'.

Anne Harris felt moved to defend herself publicly. In April 2012 she wrote: 'Let me here dismiss any idea that the *Sunday Independent*, through me, is doing the work of Gavin O'Reilly. I last met him at the funeral of my late husband Aengus Fanning in January. He embraced me and uttered hardly a word. Neither did I. I have not spoken to him – or anybody on his behalf – since. In fact, it occurred to me that the strong comment in the *Sunday Independent* might be making things more difficult for him. But if so, I have not heard. And I never would. That's how it is with editorial and the board here.'

Osborne got drawn in as well, much to his displeasure. He took a call from O'Brien the following Saturday morning and agreed that the coverage in the previous Sunday's paper was extraordinary and excessive. However, he caviled when O'Brien demanded that Osborne arrange for a single article – about a number of businessmen who owed money to IBRC, including O'Brien – be pulled from the following day's paper. It wasn't. This incident, in combination with other circumstances, would hasten Osborne's departure as chairman.

Gavin's end would come first, though. He had been left in an untenable position. His colleagues admired his stoicism and continued good humour in the face of such a stressful situation, but he was too tired to keep going and, in truth, too unhappy. The battles with O'Brien and his people had been enough, without Desmond coming into the fray as well. Now he was at loggerheads with his chairman and, even if they were polite to his face, one of the main bankers had little or no confidence in him.

Worse still, his relationship with his own father had suffered very badly. Gavin's only real fault had been to reassure his father, back in late 2008 and 2009, that he could develop a working relationship with O'Brien, that with effort there could be mutual co-operation. His father was wary but had allowed himself to be persuaded, in reality because there was no other option. His father was furious when Gavin failed in that objective and again when he was not able to come up with a deal to rescue his wealth. Deep down, O'Reilly must have known it was a near impossible task for Gavin, but he was loathe to admit it.

Harris was among those who defended Gavin publicly. 'The Irish operation at INM is very profitable, but Buckley was prolific in his criticisms of it,' she wrote. 'We should be making more of the online business, taking the whole thing digital. Well, wouldn't that be ironic? Gavin O'Reilly to be ousted because he failed to do what Rupert Murdoch, Guardian Newspapers and a host of others couldn't do. Making money out of online newspapers has yet to be figured out.' But as another of the executives, who left soon after Gavin, said: 'it was the trading performance that got us. It was hard to argue with anyone when revenues were sinking and losses were mounting.'

Gavin hung on longer than most would have in the circumstances, out of a sense of duty to his father. But he realised that a formal push to oust him was likely at the forthcoming AGM in 2012, that he had two major shareholders who were determined to oust him and a chairman not minded to protect him. It was not practical to stay on. He needed to get out before the 2011 results were announced. What he wanted was a good enough financial exit deal, given that he had little independent wealth of his own and that his shares in INM were almost worthless. He did not seek his father's opinion. He stood down and that was that. O'Reilly did hear in advance of the formal squaring of a deal and, notwithstanding Gavin's reasoning, was upset and rang other directors and executives he regarded as loyal, asking that they try to talk Gavin out of his decision. They politely refused, reckoning that Gavin had done everything possible, had made up his mind and didn't need efforts to dissuade him. Gavin sought a package worth €3.33 million, but eventually agreed one worth €1.87 million, plus €97,000 in adviser fees. This package was agreed with Osborne the weekend of 14–15 April and the announcement of his departure came on 19 April 2012, ending 39 years of his family's control at INM.

'After 19 eventful years with the company, it is time for me to pursue new opportunities,' he said. 'It had become clear that recent and public shareholder tensions were proving an unnecessary distraction for both me and the company and this was not in the best interests of the company. The board and I agreed that what the company needs now is a board, management team and shareholder base that is purposefully unified and aligned for the company's immediate challenges and for the many opportunities that exist in the future.'

Osborne said Gavin 'leaves by mutual and amicable agreement'. O'Brien was silent. So was Gavin's father, the man who had handed his son a poisoned chalice. Gavin may have been a party to the debt-fuelled expansion, but there was no doubt but that the decisions to spend heavily – and the initial defence to O'Brien's raid on the fortress – were all taken by the father and implemented by the son at his bidding. He shared his father's bad luck in that the length of the Irish recession meant that recovery in newspaper advertising revenue simply didn't happen. Things were made worse by the drift in circulation as a modern generation of readers sought free news via the Internet both in the home and on mobile devices, despite the turn-of-the-century predictions by O'Reilly. The papers were still very profitable, but simply not profitable enough compared to the debt repayments they had to support: INM's net debt still stood at €426.7 million at the end of 2011, even after repaying more than €400 million in debt over the previous three years.

Osborne was voted out at the subsequent AGM. Desmond and O'Brien both voted against Osborne's re-election to the board and O'Reilly, who was not present but had sent his vote by proxy, abstained on this particular motion: his way of protesting about Osborne's role in Gavin's departure. Osborne's last words as chairman were: 'this concludes the AGM of Not Independent News & Media'. The remark was seized upon by the non-O'Brien-controlled media.

Finance director Donal Buggy was also voted off the board; regarded by the new regime as an O'Reilly loyalist, he departed the company soon afterwards. Other executives were to follow, although Vincent Crowley took over as CEO, albeit only for little more than a year before he too went. 'Everyone was in a corner and you had to pin your colours to the mast, you had to support the chief executive unless he wants to do things that are entirely off the wall,' said one executive. 'There was a sense of solidarity with and loyalty to the O'Reilly family, but it didn't really help your position once they were going.'

Osborne subsequently gave an interview to the *Sunday Independent*, where Harris had continued her stance of confronting O'Brien at every opportunity. He said: 'I don't think I was either pro-O'Reilly or pro-O'Brien, or anti-O'Reilly or anti-O'Brien. I took a view on what needed to be done in the business and I believe that was the right view. It was quite difficult to persuade some of my directors that this was the right thing to do but as to how independent they will be, we will wait and see.' O'Brien's view on Osborne, in his interview for this book was: 'To be honest, I think James was way out of his depth. He is very good at law, but has no knowledge of business whatsoever. I don't think he ever understood the enormity of the problems at INM.'

But even if O'Reilly and his family now had no managerial role in the company, they still had an investment. What followed next – now that O'Brien was in control and with a restored Buckley not just brought back onto the board but installed as the new chairman – was another effort to clean up the balance sheet, by bringing net debt down from €435 million to €118 million. 'I am very proud of what the new board and management have achieved,' O'Brien said, 'led by Leslie Buckley when he became chairman in August 2012. The new board saved the business when they ousted Gavin O'Reilly. At that point, the company had bank and pension liabilities in excess of €630 million. I don't think people generally realise that INM was as big a basket case with the banks, owed so much and the business was perilously close to collapse.'

O'Reilly watched as the group's remaining South African newspaper business was sold for €170 million and the trade unions in Ireland reluctantly agreed to a deal to close the defined benefit pension scheme for Irish employees. But there would still have to be a further deal with the banks and a call on shareholders for more equity.

Eight banks – AIB, Barclays, Lloyds, RBS, Bank of Ireland, HSBC, KBC and ANZ – were persuaded to convert debt to equity, giving them a major stake in the company, similar to the deal with bondholders three years earlier that had given them a major share in the company. However, the deal involved asking those banks to write off a total of €100 million, a so-called 'haircut', something that wasn't being given to home mortgage-holders or to individuals with debts they could not repay, or indeed to the State by foreign lenders. Opposition politicians asked why a company controlled by such rich men would get write-offs from banks that included some who were in receipt of support from the Irish taxpayer. If those individuals were not prepared to repay those loans in full, why didn't the banks simply take full control of the business, wiping out the equity held by shareholders?

There was a risk of a relatively good company, employing 1,100 people, going bust if the banks had pressed for full repayment of loans. There would, arguably, be a cultural and social issue involved if Ireland's biggest-selling newspapers disappeared overnight. There was a better chance of survival with the interested parties agreeing a deal, one that involved shareholders injecting more equity and banks agreeing to reduced repayments. Independent News & Media would have been crazy not to seek a deal, irrespective of the identity of its owners or the ownership of the banks. As Buckley put it: 'On the assumption that a financial institution would only provide debt relief to enhance the recovery prospects of outstanding loans, it follows that any decision in this regard would be based on pragmatic and operational grounds, as to do otherwise would be inimical to the commercial interests of lenders'.

It would stick in O'Reilly's craw, however. The banks would show no mercy in pursuing him for the loans they had advanced to him. Yet those who had the financial clout to outmanoeuvre him at INM, and who would then put in more money to copper-fasten their control, were benefiting from what could be called a gift from a number of banks, some of whom were in the control of the State.

As part of the deal with the banks, existing shareholders were required to participate in a €40 million capital fund-raising exercise. O'Reilly was unable to take part, not just because he didn't want to but because he could not afford to do so. 'That surprised us,' said Buckley. 'We didn't realise that he wouldn't be able to come up with the money'. O'Reilly's shareholding was now diluted to 5%, while at a cost of €11.3 million Desmond was able to increase his stake from 6.4% to 15%, making him the second largest shareholder in INM. The new order was complete, and O'Reilly's hold had been severed forever.

CHAPTER THREE

A SHOT TO NOTHING

O'Reilly needed a sizeable slice of luck if he was to escape financial oblivion. He looked to his experience in the 1970s, when a combination of patience, improving economic conditions as he waited, the sale of some, if not all, assets and, if truth be told, some luck allowed him to survive. This time, however, it looked as if he needed nothing short of a roulette win, something big to counterbalance the spectacular level of his losses in the past few years. That need for something big brought him back to oil exploration, which, especially in Ireland, has chances of success something akin to that. It was time for O'Reilly to put his remaining money on black.

O'Reilly was still in oil exploration, albeit at a far more low-key level than in the 1980s when the Atlantic Resources hype often dominated the newspaper front pages and radio headlines. Atlantic was now called Providence Resources, providence defined in one dictionary as 'foresight: prudent management and thrift: timely preparation: the foresight and benevolent care of God'. In the early years of the 2000s, Tony jnr had toyed with the idea of selling the business but, although it was no longer a priority of his, O'Reilly had wanted to keep it, if not as an insurance policy, then as a gambler's chip for a rainy day.

Tony jnr went to work full-time for the company as its CEO in 2005. He had gone to meet his father to announce that he was quitting as deputy CEO at Wedgwood because of continued disagreements with his father about the strategy that was being implemented. What Tony jnr had anticipated as a difficult meeting in the 'green room' of Castlemartin turned into something amicable and agreeable. His father suggested that he move to a full-time position in Providence instead and Tony jnr, who is the natural optimist of the O'Reilly children, leapt at the opportunity.

It took until 2010 before a strategic decision was made to begin drilling for oil again, even though that would require the expenditure of sizeable sums of money for uncertain, if any, return. What O'Reilly needed was for Providence to find proven reserves in Irish waters that he could then sell to others to exploit: if the existence of sufficiently large amounts capable of profitable recovery could be established, then O'Reilly could sell Providence and use the money to repay the remainder of his debts. In that event, he would have more than enough money to fund his final years, but none of the stresses of battling with creditor banks or the humiliation of his financial troubles becoming publicly known.

First, though, Providence needed more money and with its borrowings already high, it had to raise equity by selling shares. Instead of 'rights issues' among existing shareholders, giving them the opportunity to maintain their portion of the overall company if they put in new money, the company opted to 'place' new shares with new investors. O'Reilly's shareholding was diluted; in truth, part of the reason was that he simply didn't have the cash to buy the new shares himself.

The company raised €16.3 million in early 2010 to cover its working capital needs and to increase production. It returned to the market in early 2011 for an even larger amount, €46 million this time, reducing the O'Reilly family share of the company to 20%.

The plans for drilling in Irish waters were ambitious. The talk in 2011 was of a €500 million programme of drilling 10 wells over the coming two years, alongside the likes of Exxon Mobil and Eni, of Italy, as partners, to which Providence would contribute €75 million of the overall costs. Tony jnr told reporters that 'any one of these is a game changer'. He boasted that 'there has been no drilling programme like this before off Ireland. We are going everywhere. In the Celtic Sea, off Dublin, off Northern Ireland, off the west coast of Ireland in the deep water. The oil price and the technology to get at this oil has all come our way.' Normally sober newspapers, like *The Times*, carried pieces predicting that Providence would resuscitate the Celtic Tiger and enable Ireland to go some way to being energy-independent.

By January 2012 Tony jnr claimed that Providence's Irish acreage held about 450 million barrels of oil, as well as gas. 'We should call Ireland north-north-west Nigeria or something ending in "stan",' he said. 'There hasn't been the commercial success … [but] when you buy a financial product, past performance is not an indicator of future performance. Such is the case with us.' Two months later Tony jnr claimed Providence had a one-in-four or one-in-five chance of making a commercial oil find off the Dublin coastline. He spoke of his father: 'We talk every couple of days. I'm very happy for him. His involvement goes back to 1981 and he has put a lot of money in. He has been vindicated — though he wouldn't say that himself. He would say that he's happy and encouraged, but there's a lot more to do. And there is.' His father never said anything publicly about it all, but he cannot have been but impressed with the hoopla his son, almost as proxy, was developing, reminiscent of 30 years earlier.

Much of Tony's excitement resulted from his hopes for the Barryroe field, located 50 km off the south coast of Cork in the North Celtic Sea basin, covering an area of 300 sq km. Four wells had been drilled there in the 1970s by Esso, with a further appraisal well drilled in 1990 by Marathon Oil. The findings were small and prices at the time of US$35 for a barrel of crude oil made further exploration economically unviable. But now prices had soared and technology made discovery and extraction more feasible.

The well drilled by Providence in 2011, details of which were released in early 2012, provided encouragement. The first phase of Providence's well-testing programme in the Barryroe basin discovered flow rates of 3,514 bopd (barrels of oil per day), double the target that apparently had been considered a commercial threshold. The quality of the oil was also better than expected, defined as 'light, sweet crude', and had been discovered at a depth of about 100 m in the seabed. The initial estimate was that the find was part of a field probably containing 373 million barrels of oil, and possibly as much as 893 million.

While the Irish media was circumspect in its reporting, elements of the British media began an immediate hype. *The Times* reported that 'the discovery of Ireland's first commercial oilfield has raised the hope that the country's ailing economy might be revived. Possibly worth $110 billion at yesterday's prices, the wealth is comparable to the €85 billion emergency bailout arranged for Ireland in 2010.'

Further drilling was required, however, to further assess the potential of the field. Most sober analysts ventured that it still seemed small by international standards. This would make difficult the securing of a major partner with the money to finance production and the skills to operate the field.

By July, Providence had decided to make bigger claims for Barryroe via an official stock market announcement, in the process driving up the share price to just under €9, a 250% increase since the start of the year. It said it expected to find between 1 and 1.6 billion barrels of oil, which was up to four times initial estimates, though Tony admitted to doubts as to how much oil would actually be recovered.

But Providence, as 80% owner, and with the even smaller Lansdowne Oil and Gas holding the remaining stake, was simply not in a position to finance significant further exploration, let alone production. The planned next phase alone would cost US$1.3 billion. It would have to find partners who would pay for whatever further work was required, in return for a big shareholding or, if it came to it, would simply have to sell Barryroe or Providence itself in total to a bigger, better financed company.

Tony jnr promised that Providence would make a profit from the Barryroe field as long as oil prices stayed above US$40 a barrel. At the time oil prices were above US$90, and would climb beyond US$100; in two years' time they would fall sharply.

Tony jnr claimed Providence had received approaches from big energy companies: 'People have already tried to talk to us, but we held off up to now. We haven't been out soliciting interest. Now we know what we have, we will move to that stage. We will look to trade down our equity, to farm out, and bring in industry partners who can take the project to first production … The question now is what deal we do to hold on to the maximum value for our shareholders,' he said. 'I don't foresee lack of interest.'

Tony jnr was in a very difficult position. He was genuinely excited by the possibilities, but knew there were few or no certainties about Barryroe's ability to deliver. He wanted a partner, but didn't want to be seen to be desperate for one, and yet he also knew that getting somebody to stump up cash without demanding complete control would be difficult. He knew that his father needed money and quickly, so the option of an outright sale of Providence would have to be considered, but his own reputation, as well as his fiduciary responsibilities as CEO, meant that he had to get the best deal possible for all shareholders. O'Reilly could have looked to sell his shares at this stage, but it would have been interpreted as an admission that the prospects for the company were not as claimed.

O'Reilly needed others to believe in the potential of the find so that this would be reflected in the share price of the company. Fortunately, there were others at hand to do this. Providence got support from the stockbroking community. Davy, the company's Irish broker – working in sterling rather than euro because of the emphasis on attracting British investors – predicted the shares could be worth Stg£17.45 if it could recover 121 million barrels from Barryroe, valuing Providence at more than Stg£1.1 billion. Liberum Capital, a London broker, increased its price target from Stg£12.45 to Stg£20. Cenkos, another London house, had a price target of Stg£23.49. Barryroe alone was worth 'a conservative' Stg£15 a share, or Stg£966 million, according to the broker, which estimated Barryroe could produce 100,000 barrels a day, every day, for 15 years.

In July 2012 Providence was valued at just under €500 million, even if the stockbrokers said it might be worth many times that. The immediate priority was to raise money through the issue of new shares, although this again meant a further dilution in the O'Reilly shareholding, this time to 15.5%. Providence sold more than 13 million shares at Stg480p, raising €75.6 million, to a range of more than 30 institutional investors, suggesting that the story was gaining widespread traction.

The then Minister for Energy, Pat Rabbitte, was among those watching with great interest. 'I used to get other ministers coming to me and asking, "We're saved, are we?" and I'd ask my own officials and they'd say, "well Minister, not quite". We were all a bit wryly amused by it.' Rabbitte described much of went on as 'puffing like hell', but said his own officials told him that this was the way things were done in the industry and that Providence was not doing anything out of line and that it was a well-run company. 'Drilling was hugely expensive, you have to raise money and you don't do this by playing down expectations. You couldn't describe Barryroe as a failure. There is oil there, but it is a just a question of when it will be commercially viable and extractable.'

Providence was in a *Catch-22* bind: it wanted to talk up its chances of success, to improve its value and its chance of sale, but not so much as to attract comment that might lead to political support for increased taxes.

Shares in Providence increased in value by 223% in 2012, making it comfortably the best performing share on the Irish Stock Exchange. But that was as good as it got.

By early 2013, Providence was excitedly talking up the prospects for its Dunquin field in the South Porcupine basin, a 25,000 sq km region between 150 km and 200 km off the Kerry coast. Exxon Mobil, the us oil giant, had committed to drilling the field, where Providence had a minority 16% stake. The work started in April as a drill bit bore an area the size of a small coffee table one mile beneath the Atlantic Ocean. Providence's contribution to the potential us$200 million cost was just us$12 million, but Tony jnr called it 'the Eureka moment' – one of the largest offshore wells to be drilled in north-western Europe in a decade. Davy predicted a one-in-six chance of success and said that Providence's share of that could be potentially worth €1.4 billion.

The search was a failure. Within months Exxon Mobil announced that it would abandon the drilling after finding minimal quantities of oil or gas that could be recovered for commercial use. Worse, it said it no longer had plans for any further drilling in the area. Ever the optimist, Tony jnr said Exxon's findings were 'encouraging', that the presence of residual oil – the remains of a reservoir that has drained away – vindicated his claim that the area's geology indicates that it could contain commercial quantities of oil and gas and that Eni, the Italian producer, was the main explorer anyway. 'We thought it would be gas, but it's oil and that helps to refine what we already know,' he said. 'International oil companies will be intrigued by this.'

But it wasn't the biggest disappointment of 2013. That had come three months before the Dunquin announcement, back in April. Tony jnr had come close to completing the sale that would have ended all of his father's financial woes.

Providence had appointed Rothschild to help with the farm-out of Barryroe. The giant bank used its extensive contacts to persuade some of the world's biggest majors to attend the Providence data room. Providence changed some of its ambitions for developing Barryroe, trying to reduce the immediate capital needs while simultaneously hurrying its ambitions to begin production. The Indian State-owned energy company Oil and Natural Gas Corporation (ONGC) was so impressed by what it saw of Providence, it offered to bypass the farm-in option and looked to buy full control of the company itself.

It opened negotiations with Tony jnr and offered a deal that would have valued Providence at close to €1.3 billion, more than double its value on the stock market at the time. This would have given O'Reilly a cash windfall of nearly €200 million for his 15.5% stake, enough, in conjunction with other asset disposals, to have cleared his debts. The ONGC deal could have been the life-saver.

And yet, it didn't happen.

Tony jnr was told one Friday afternoon that the formal offer at the agreed price would be announced to the London Stock Exchange the following Monday morning. No announcement was made. Tony jnr frantically tried to find out what had gone wrong. Eventually, he was told that it wasn't happening. The Corporation was majority owned by the Indian State and government officials, told over the weekend about what was planned by the board of their company, were worried about being seen to overpay, having done so recently in a deal with another company called Imperial Energy. Tony jnr could not persuade them otherwise. To make things worse, he watched as ONGC went for a much bigger deal instead, worth US$10 billion, in Mozambique. It wasn't the last frustration that Tony jnr would have with the Indian company. He maintained good relations and months later, in October 2013, he spent weeks in Delhi, negotiating a fall-back deal: a farm-in on the Barryroe prospect that would have brought in much-needed funds. That deal fell through, too.

The stock market no longer believed the Providence story and the share price began to slide. Early in 2014 it emerged that Providence would have to spend €30 million of its own funds in drilling a new appraisal well at Barryroe, money it would struggle to raise.

By mid-2014, as O'Reilly was in the High Court because of a dispute over the repayment of loans to AIB, Providence shares were trading at just Stg£1.40 in London, valuing the whole company at €120 million – a year after it was worth €1.1 billion. O'Reilly's shareholding was now worth just €18.6 million. Tony jnr continued to put a brave face on things. Shareholders were told at the AGM in August that the process of finding a partner for Barryroe was 'nearing completion'. Hillery told them: 'Deals are taking much longer to achieve in the current environment. It's not a question of getting a deal, it's getting the right deal.'

The end of 2014 and start of 2015 were to provide nothing but bad news for Providence, as the price of a barrel of oil crashed, first through the US$100 per barrel level and then down as far as US$50, notwithstanding the geopolitical pressures caused by the Russian presence in eastern Ukraine and the threat to middle-eastern oil supplies posed by ISIS. The popularity of fracking – an environmentally controversial practice of extracting oil and gas on-shore at a fraction of the price of deep-sea exploration – changed the dynamics of the industry, temporarily at least. It was possibly just a cycle, from which the industry would recover, but at a time when the big producers were mothballing existing oil fields on the basis that continued production was uneconomical, the idea that any would invest money in speculative ventures around the Irish seas seemed foolhardy at best. The idea of selling the company disappeared; the best that could be hoped for was that some private equity speculator would help to finance further exploration at Barryroe.

But even if that was to happen, the chances of O'Reilly profiting had all but vanished. In February 2015 AccBank took possession of part of his shareholding, not selling it but holding it for itself until such time as it deemed it a profitable time to sell. O'Reilly was reduced to just 9.5% of Providence, worth a miserable €2 million or so, and with the prospect of that being taken from him by his creditors, too. Providence would not deliver salvation.

CHAPTER FOUR

A VERY PUBLIC HUMILIATION

The 'stand-still' agreement that Bernard Somers struck with the banks on O'Reilly's behalf was to run for three years, but it didn't mean that O'Reilly was eager to sell assets. It wasn't just that he wanted to wait until they would secure better prices, he was so emotionally wedded to some that he simply didn't want to let them go. Accordingly, the first chunk of significant money came from an asset over which he had no control.

Cameron's successful sale of Landis+Gyr in late 2011 was a bitter-sweet victory. Cameron had proven his capabilities outside of the family empire, had become an independently wealthy man and was now in a position to effectively provide his father with some resources to pay down part of his debts; his father may have invested the money upon which he was getting his return, but it was Cameron's shrewd management of that money that created the benefit.

Cameron had waited carefully after his departure from APN, taking time out to concentrate on his young family while working out options as to how to progress his career. He brought his family from Australia to France and there he developed the concept of what he later called 'a premium capital investment group', as distinct from a private equity firm. He would persuade investors to back one big project and to back him in this as a long-term investment rather than looking for a quick return. He set up a company called Bayard Capital. It was named after a French military hero, Pierre Terrail Bayard, who was known as 'the knight without fear and without reproach'.

Cameron used his contacts in Australia to put together the fund, with the input of some of Australia's wealthiest businessmen, such as Kerry Stokes, John B. Fairfax, Jack and Robert Smorgon and Douglas Myers. Other shareholders included Dubai International Capital and the New South Wales government, and his father stumped up enough money to take a 7% share.

Cameron's big breakthrough deal came in 2004 with the purchase of electronic smart metering company Landis+Gyr. It manufactured electricity meters that provided two-way communication between utility companies and homes and commercial premises, replacing the electro-mechanical meters in use for more than a century. This allowed utility firms to distribute energy loads more efficiently and home-owners to monitor their consumption more closely. Cameron made a further 13 acquisitions of competitor companies and built a group that, by 2011, operated in 30 countries, including China, employed more than 5,000 people and had revenues of US$1.59 billion. He then sold the business to Toshiba for a US$1.3 billion return to equity-holders, once loans of another US$1 billion had been repaid from the proceeds of the overall deal.

A 7% share of Landis+Gyr should have been worth about US$91 million to O'Reilly and given him considerable resources to pay debts. His shareholding had been diluted by a major fund-raising in 2008, however, when plans for a stock market flotation, which would have released funds to him, had to be abandoned because of the turmoil on world markets at the time. This private fund-raising raised US$260 million and O'Reilly did not have the funds then to participate, thereby causing his shareholding to fall. It was not the only fund-raising, as Bayard made 14 acquisitions over the years, some of which required money from shareholders. Having been one of four main original shareholders, O'Reilly was the ninth largest shareholder by the time the business was eventually sold. His final tally from Bayard, still sizeable, was not revealed other than to his relevant lenders, who held security over the shares.

It was the same with the sale of his remaining Heinz shares. On leaving Heinz in 2000, O'Reilly still had nearly 2% of the overall company stock. With no role on the board, he was no longer required to notify the New York Stock Exchange of any transactions involving the shares. He sold many of them over the years, never telling anybody how many, and in doing so he missed out on a major windfall when Heinz was sold out of public ownership in February 2013. The world's most famous investor, Warren Buffett of Berkshire Hathaway, combined with the Brazilian investment firm 3G Capital to buy Heinz for US$23 billion. Buffett said that one of the reasons he bought Heinz was that he had become fascinated with the company after hearing O'Reilly tell tales about it when they dined together at the home of then *Washington Post* publisher Katherine Graham in the early 1980s. He had kept a file on the company ever since. Berkshire and 3G paid a price per share for Heinz that was 19% higher than its biggest ever price as a quoted company. A 2% shareholder would have received US$460 million. Such a sum would have allowed O'Reilly to comfortably clear all of his debts and still be a millionaire many times over. That it didn't, and that he remained so highly indebted, implied that he had either sold the shares over the years to finance other transactions or had gifted at least some of them to family members. It was far more a case of the former.

In late 2013 O'Reilly's shareholding in INM fell to just under 6% when O'Brien and Desmond led yet another equity fund-raising in which O'Reilly did not participate, this time to raise €40 million. His stake fell further in April 2014. O'Reilly discovered that ACCBank was going to be very tough in dealing with his debts. He had a long-running relationship with the bank, going back to its days when it was the State-owned Agricultural Credit Corporation and he was the boss at Bord Bainne and then Irish Sugar. Now it was owned by the Dutch Rabobank, an institution that had sustained enormous losses in Ireland because of its reckless lending practices at just the wrong time; it didn't care who O'Reilly was or about his history. ACCBank told him to sell nine million INM shares at 16 cent each, raising a paltry €1.5 million. But what was more significant was that it was the first time he had ever actually had to sell shares in INM. It was a process that was going to carry on into early 2015, with ACCBank insisting on the sale of INM shares held by his Indexia Holdings company at times of its choosing, bringing his stake down to just 3.6% by February 2015 and in the process raising about €2.5 million for the bank. The remaining shares were to be sold when the opportunity arose.

By early 2014 the full scale of O'Reilly's predicament was widely known; attempts at discretion had failed. ACCBank also had the mortgage for 2 Fitzwilliam Square and it now insisted that he sell it to clear his debt. He tried to do so in as low-key a fashion as possible: no placard was placed outside the front door or ads put in the papers; it was on offer 'off market' for a price of more than €3.5 million. The agent, Paddy Jordan of Jordan Town & Country in Kildare, went quietly to a list of rich potential buyers, offering a 6,300 sq ft house 'remodelled with great flair and impeccable taste in 1997'. It was suggested that it would make 'an ideal family home, ambassador's residence or Irish headquarters for the chief executive of an international blue-chip company'. An added attraction was a 1,400 sq ft mews, 'in need of refurbishment'. No address was supplied. There was no mention of the lunches and dinners that had been hosted for the likes of Mandela, Clinton and Kissinger, or the many politicians from both sides of the border who had met O'Reilly or his newspaper executives there.

Unfortunately, it was too early to catch the wave of rising prices for domestic property in Dublin. In May 2014 a small notice on the back page of *The Irish Times* advertised a private residence for sale on Fitzwilliam Square: 'Immaculate Condition. With Mews. Email: property3046@gmail.com.' The new guide price was €2.3 million, a sign of the vendor's desperation considering that houses in the Square, many used as offices and in need of conversion, had traded at €6 million or so before the property crash. Even the attractions of three-bedroom suites on the upper floors, a drawing-room and dining-room on the ground floor – the latter 'Wedgwood style with blue and white walls' created by the artist Michael Dillon – and a further dining room and kitchen at basement level, with access to the private gardens in Fitzwilliam Square, did not provoke a clamour for an immediate sale. Yet ACC insisted on going ahead quickly.

The sale came during the summer, when three bidders gathered in a room at the Conrad Hotel on Earlsfort Terrace in Dublin 2, across the road from where O'Reilly had attended the old premises of UCD as a student. The bidding opened at €2.5 million and rose in bids of €100,000 until the property was knocked down to an unidentified purchaser, represented by an agent, at a price of €3.3 million.

Details of this particular sale were to reach the public arena, but only after it had emerged that O'Reilly had sold assets for close to €150 million since 2011 to slash his debts. But his creditors were demanding more, and at the front of the queue were State-owned banks.

O'Reilly got no special favours from the State when it came to dealing with his debts. Indeed, he and his advisers worried that he had been singled out for adverse treatment from those taking advantage of his loss of power, although there was no evidence to support that.

Somers tried to do a deal with the State-owned IBRC (Irish Bank Resolution Corporation, formerly Anglo Irish Bank) on the €50 million debt still outstanding after the Landis+Gyr sale. The discussions went on for well over a year. For its part, IBRC examined all of the details of O'Reilly's financial statements, and other loans, and quickly came to the conclusion that O'Reilly had little or no assets left that could be used to cover the debt. Although other IBRC borrowers owed more money, many of them were in a better position to pay a large proportion of their debts. Partial settlement was all that could be hoped for in O'Reilly's case, but IBRC was reluctant to do a deal that might be appropriate to O'Reilly's financial position because it might cause political difficulty if it was to be somehow disclosed publicly.

The bank's sensitivity to the political dimension was heightened by the fact that former Fine Gael leader and finance minister Alan Dukes was its chairman. Dukes had had dealings with O'Reilly in both of those positions and had also been the local TD in Kildare for many years. Dukes had taken over from Lowry as Minister for Communications in 1996 and had been sympathetic to O'Reilly's view that the State should have stopped pirate transmission of broadcasting signals, although hamstrung by the unwillingness of his political colleagues to do anything about it. He and his wife had been regular invitees to an annual Christmas service in the church on the Castlemartin grounds, so he absented himself from any direct contact with O'Reilly while keeping an eye on interactions to protect the best interests of the State.

Dukes decided that Department of Finance officials would have to be made aware that there were issues with O'Reilly, and that it was one of its most difficult cases, without giving away any details that would breach confidentiality. Indeed, IBRC warned that it might have 'to do disagreeable things' in order to recover as much of the money as possible. It didn't come to that. Initially the IBRC CEO, Mike Aynsley, an Australian who, ironically, had formed a firm friendship with Denis O'Brien since arriving in Ireland, found Somers gave very little ground during negotiations. One thing was made very clear to IBRC by Somers: Chryss was not going to make any contribution to settling

O'Reilly's debts. The IBRC people wondered if this was because O'Reilly's pride would not allow him to ask her for help, or if she had decided not to spend any more of her money to bail out his debts. They also wondered if it was simply a negotiating position on O'Reilly's part, and that eventually Chryss would step in to help, using her own vast wealth.

Their expectation that Chryss might provide funds to O'Reilly was shared by a number of his creditor bankers. There were a number of problems with that hypothesis, however. One was the scale of her wealth, which was largely unknown, despite all sorts of assumptions: she might not have had the money available, even if she had wanted to help her husband. Nobody had any idea of the value of her family shipping assets in Greece and the USA or of how much of those she owned. It was assumed that she had property interests and other assets, although again nobody knew the extent of these or how they had been affected by the economic downturn. There was also an issue as to how much of her assets were held in joint ownership with brother Peter, whose patience with O'Reilly had run out because of his losses at Waterford Wedgwood and who was not inclined to allow his sister waste any more of her money on her husband's adventures. What was known was that she had a vast international stud farm empire, which owned, bred, trained and raced horses and operated under the names Petra Bloodstock Agency and Skymarc Farm. She had inherited *Hara de la Louviere*, a 420-acre stud farm and estate in Normandy, France, from her uncle, Constantine Goulandris. She had stock bred in Sussex, in England. Her interests in the USA were at a stud called *Matagorda*. Equestrian journals estimated that she had about 100 horses in training and 128 brood mares. To finance operations she had a policy of selling mare foals. Clearly she had assets, but did she have liquidity?

Another issue was her desire to help O'Reilly, or her husband's to ask for that help. If she hadn't given personal guarantees, then she was under no obligation to fund personal debts of her husband's or of the companies in which he was an investor. And yet another problem faced O'Reilly's creditors: who owned what assets, especially the houses?

Eventually, in late 2012, Chryss indicated that she would deal with IBRC on her husband's behalf. Her advisers offered a deal in which she would buy O'Reilly's debts and a compromise was worked towards that would have involved her spending up to €22 million on settling the remaining debt for her husband. Negotiations went reasonably well, going so far as involving amiable phone conversations between Aynsley and O'Reilly.

There was a delay in finalising a deal, however. The bank was still concerned about the political dimensions – that if details leaked, it would be accused of facilitating a special arrangement for a high-profile figure who wasn't prepared to repay the full amount he owed. And then more bad luck struck O'Reilly: the government unexpectedly and suddenly decided to liquidate IBRC in early 2013, catching all but insiders on the hop. All deals that had not been completed – and some were in the days before the government announcement – were now off the table, as IBRC's management surrendered its powers to the liquidator. Instead, IBRC would sell its loans to others who would collect.

So from a position of almost completing a satisfactory deal to put things right, suddenly O'Reilly was faced with having to deal instead with Lone Star. This was an American so-called vulture fund that purchased a portfolio of IBRC loans lumped into a package, called Tranche14, which IBRC eventually sold for over €1 billion. O'Reilly's brother-in-law, Peter, took fright at the idea of dealing with Lone Star and repaid his loans to IBRC's liquidator, at par, before their sale to the Americans was completed. O'Reilly was left to deal with a whole new set of negotiations. Chryss apparently indicated that she was no longer interested in buying O'Reilly's debt from its new owner. In financial circles it was suggested that the value ascribed to the O'Reilly loans as part of IBRC's Lone Star transaction was less than Chryss had been willing to pay. The question now was how O'Reilly would raise the money to pay Lone Star without her help, along with all of his other creditors.

That proposed but not completed deal was to have further ramifications, however. In May 2014 AIB did what would once have been considered unthinkable: it went publicly to the commercial courts to seek a judgment that would require immediate repayment by O'Reilly of his debts to it. Allied Irish Banks knew full well that O'Reilly was not in a position to repay in full, that he was working through a process with a large number of banks and that he would be described in court as insolvent and would be humiliated publicly by the revelation. And yet the bank pressed ahead.

The amount AIB sought by way of summary judgment was
€22 million against O'Reilly personally, and also for €18.6 million and
€4.1 million respectively against two of his investment vehicles: Cyprus-
based Indexia Holdings and Brookside Investments. The reason cited
was O'Reilly's failure to repay the €4 million he had borrowed from AIB
in 2009, mortgaged on the Brookside-owned Shorecliffe holiday compound in Glandore, in West Cork. Clearly, a mooted €1.75 million sale of
the property would not clear the debt. This gap seemingly triggered AIB's
decision to attempt to recover the remainder of his debts by forcing him
to sell other assets on foot of the personal guarantee he had also given.

This action brought visibility of O'Reilly's real financial position
into the public domain for the first time. The commercial court heard
that O'Reilly owed €195 million to eight banks and one fund, and that
his debt to AIB represented 11.6% of his overall personal liabilities. By
seeking summary judgment, AIB hoped to jump to the top of the
queue in securing money from the sale of any unsecured assets. It said
it wanted the judgment immediately because it feared that other
banks might get money from the sale of assets in the Bahamas and the
British Virgin Islands ahead of it.

In seeking its judgment AIB had to paint O'Reilly in the worst
possible light to the court. Time after time it emphasised that O'Reilly
was insolvent. It variously described his plans to repay his debts as
'very optimistic' and 'an expression of hope' and that his chances of
doing so were as likely as 'Mr Spock from *Star Trek* coming back to
the table' in a movie. Judge Peter Kelly, who presided, asked the bank's
lawyers if its position could be summarised as: 'whatever rush occurs,
if there is a rush, you will be in front?' 'Precisely so,' a lawyer for AIB
replied. 'It is a terribly simple point.'

What O'Reilly wanted was more time. He had debts that were secured
on assets, others that weren't. Somers was engaged in a juggling act.
The position was clear on secured assets: when they were sold, the
money would go to the lender who owned the security. The issue was
timing – to get the best price possible and to leave little or nothing
outstanding. After that, O'Reilly would have to sell the assets to which
no loans were attached, to pay off the balance of money owing on
unpaid secured debts and also to cover unsecured debts. Somers had
promised that this would be done proportionately.

O'Reilly feared that if AIB secured its judgment against him, his other lenders would break their forbearance arrangements and pile in on him to secure their place in the queue for a share of the proceeds of the sale of unsecured assets. His lawyer, Michael Cush, argued that O'Reilly just wanted a six-month stay of registration and execution to allow for the orderly completion of a sale of his unsecured assets and of Castlemartin, for which he had already received 'expressions of interest' from potential buyers; AIB already had a mortgage over a portion of the land.

Cush presented to the court letters in support of O'Reilly from his other banks. He said O'Reilly was prepared to give AIB a commitment that he would inform it of any move by any rival creditor in return for a stay against registration and enforcement of any judgment. He argued that O'Reilly had tried to maintain a degree of transparency with all his lenders, so that each would be aware where it stood compared to others. Serious expressions of interest in Castlemartin had been received from international bloodstock concerns and AIB had been given the brochure for sale, proving that O'Reilly's intent was real. He outlined the likely proceeds from the sales of Fitzwilliam Square and Shorecliffe in West Cork, and said that his remaining shares in INM were available for sale whenever his banks wanted.

It turned out that O'Reilly had few enough unencumbered assets available to him. These included his 50% shareholding in Fitzwilton (which had few assets left other than its shares in the Rennicks signage company), house contents worth up to €1 million, a 'cottage' near Castlemartin that had been purchased in 2007 along with Holyhill Stud, and two €1 million pensions. The status of his art collection, once estimated to be worth €150 million, was unclear, but it was assumed that much of it had been sold.

O'Reilly's lawyers read into the record of the court a document in which O'Reilly said: 'I have spent my whole life in business. I believe that, throughout a range of different commercial interests across a host of countries in several continents, I have built a reputation for honest dealing and straight talking.'

When Mr Justice Peter Kelly delivered his judgment during a 40-minute speech, his final decision was that AIB could have what it wanted. Desperately, O'Reilly's lawyers asked for just for four days more, to allow O'Reilly and his advisers to conduct further talks with his other lenders over the fate of Castlemartin: they feared that a sale would be scuppered by AIB's victory. O'Reilly would 'be prepared to fly back in from France over the weekend' for talks with all of his banks if only he could get a short stay. But AIB argued against this, saying that it would 'create too much uncertainty'. Judge Peter Kelly decided that AIB had already waited too long, and that further delays could allow other banks to make their own bids to get their money ahead of AIB. He granted the order immediately, allowing AIB to register judgment mortgages against O'Reilly's unencumbered assets and not just those over which it held security.

The judge further noted that AIB was entitled, if it wished, to appoint receivers: 'The plaintiff has not done so to date. Indeed, it appears that it does not intend to do so at present.' Within days, AIB appointed Luke Charleton and Marcus Purcell of accounting group EY (Ernst & Young) as receivers to O'Reilly's assets.

The actions of AIB were a shock to anyone with experience of its behaviour since the introduction of the 2008 bank guarantee. It had gained a reputation in corporate circles in previous years of maintaining a degree of reasonableness when it came to collecting debts; while it was not soft, it cut realistic deals to recover as much as was possible, without causing undue hardship or going public in its efforts. Part of this was attributed to a sense of collective guilt on the part of those in management who remained when other senior members had been removed. After all, its own recklessness and rank bad judgement in lending had resulted in it needing a €21 billion rescue from the State. It wasn't in a position to assume the moral high ground with regard to the inability of its customers to meet their debts. However, such empathy was not necessarily shared by new management who had been recruited to rescue the bank. O'Reilly was subjected to a far more public and aggressive approach than almost any other significant customer.

Nobody could explain why this was so, and to this day AIB won't. In a clear case of having its cake and eating it, AIB has refused to make further comment as to the reasons for its actions, citing client confidentiality, despite having made such damaging assertions against its erstwhile client in court. Naturally, this gave rise to all sorts of speculation: was AIB trying to send a signal to other customers that it would pursue debts, no matter how high-profile or supposedly important that person or entity? Did somebody in AIB have a personal issue with

O'Reilly, either historic or rooted in the circumstances of the 2009 loan, that persuaded it to seek a form of retribution? Was it an unwillingness to be seen to do a deal with such a high-profile individual? Was it a fear of being seen to do a deal with an adviser who was a former director, as Somers was? Or was it payback time in political circles now that a Fine Gael/Labour government was in control of a 99% stake in the bank and could influence its decision-making? The matter was never discussed at a government Cabinet meeting but Minister for Finance Michael Noonan had been aware, informally, that AIB would move on O'Reilly, but he had not been asked for authorisation or even his opinion. When I asked him if he had any sympathy for O'Reilly's plight he replied simply and firmly, 'No'.

At least two ministers from that government, who subsequently stepped down in a reshuffle of personnel during the summer of 2014, said that they did not agree with the way AIB handled the matter, given its handling of other issues and O'Reilly's contribution to the country. Ruairi Quinn and Pat Rabbitte, both Labour ministers who served in the Rainbow coalition, believed that O'Reilly's contribution to seeking a peaceful political settlement in Northern Ireland should have counted for at least something more in how AIB went about recovering its money.

It was not clear that AIB had given itself any real advantage with its actions, so few were the unencumbered assets. However, it seems that AIB's actions can be attributed to misjudgement of its client's ability to repay and frustration regarding its inability to recover its money quickly. It had heard on the financial grapevine about the decision by Chryss to become involved belatedly in trying to settle her husband's debts with IBRC. It appears that some senior executives miscalculated that O'Reilly would buckle if they put enough pressure on him over Castlemartin, and that Chryss would ride to his rescue. She didn't. His insistence that Chryss would not take responsibility for his actions was real.

Few people were willing to speak publicly in opposition to AIB's actions; AIB still has considerable power and holds many people's loans. From among the super-rich, Michael Smurfit and, most surprisingly, Dermot Desmond did and also former government minister Ivan Yates, who had gone bankrupt as a result of his own high-profile dispute with AIB over its loans to him. 'It would be true to form for

AIB to take extra punitive action with someone of a high profile,' said Yates. The director of the Irish Mortgage Holders Organisation (IMHO), David Hall, who had no association with O'Reilly, said AIB's actions 'made no sense' and that the only way of rationalising the decision was to conclude AIB wanted to send a message to all its borrowers. 'My own personal impression is that they are sending the message that nobody, no matter who they are, is beyond the reach of the bank,' said Hall. 'Given the publicity this case is getting, you could not get better advertising if you wanted to keep people in line … Imagine if you were an AIB customer and you were a businessman with a €10 million debt and you see the bank taking on Tony O'Reilly. How brave would you be now?'

O'Reilly got hundreds of letters from well-wishers after AIB's action, many from people who hadn't been in contact in years, some from people who had been the beneficiaries of his generosity over the years, others from people he barely knew or didn't know at all. Kevin McGoran said that all the surviving schoolmates of O'Reilly's from Belvedere who could be found signed a letter of support that was sent to him and there was also a similar message from Old Belvedere rugby club. O'Reilly appreciated all of the messages and the effort that had been made to write but, somewhat bitterly, he noted that it didn't change his position. People were expressing sympathy and emphasising the high esteem in which they held him, which was some support to his battered ego, but, as he saw it, they were not jumping up to come and help him. Their kind words would not fundamentally change anything. One of his family said he spoke about being like 'the victim of a drive-by shooting'.

O'Reilly took hit after hit. Losing Waterford Wedgwood had been crushing. In his 1994 biography, O'Reilly told Ivan Fallon of the importance Waterford Wedgwood had for him: 'I am trying to build companies that will exist long after I'm gone. Waterford Wedgwood, I hope, will be a real monument. We were savagely attacked by everyone when we went in, but look at it now — and it will be there for generations to come.'

It may well be, but not in circumstances that are in any way pleasing to him.

What initially was a small consolation to him – to learn that his much loved Waterford Wedgwood brands had been saved by new investment in 2009 – turned bitter-sweet in 2015, when the company's new owners put the slimmed-down, reformatted, recapitalised business up for sale at a guide price of €650 million, giving them a massive return on their investment in buying the company out of receivership.

The administrator, Deloitte, had sold Waterford Wedgwood to an American firm called KPS Capital in February 2009. More accurately, it had sold assets, including the brands, giving the new owners the chance to start with a relatively clean sheet, unhindered by trying to cover the cost of excessive borrowing. Accordingly, KPS put the assets into a holding company called WWRD, but axed most of the jobs in Ireland. The main manufacturing plant at Kilbarry closed, with the loss of 480 jobs. The new owner licensed production of Waterford Crystal products to third-party contract manufacturers in eastern Germany. All that was kept in Ireland was a small sales back office and a new visitors' centre, saving 176 jobs of the 708 that had been there at the start of 2009. Investment was made in a new visitors' centre, but the manufacturing conducted there was of very small scale.

The irony of all this was that KPS had been introduced to the company by O'Reilly, that he had brought it in as a partner but found instead that it exploited its inside knowledge to profit at his expense. It restarted some Wedgwood and Royal Doulton manufacturing at the group's British operations in Staffordshire, but again most of the work was done overseas, mainly in Indonesia, as O'Reilly had organised belatedly. It also followed the O'Reilly marketing template by continuing to work with designers like Vera Wang and Jasper Conran and introducing new celebrities, such as supermodel Miranda Kerr to promote a Royal Albert tea-set. The sales emphasis, unlike in O'Reilly's time, was now in Asia and particularly China, where tea-sets became popular. About 40% of sales were in the Asia-Pacific region. The company projected annual profits of over €60 million to potential buyers. O'Reilly noted to friends that the new buyer had not made 1 cent of a contribution to sorting out the pensions of the former workers whereas he had, belatedly as part of his final rescue bid, offered to transfer his shareholding to ownership of the pension fund. In May 2015 the sale of WWRD Holdings was completed to the Finnish consumer products company Fiskars for $437 million, less than had been anticipated, but KPS had taken $66 million in dividends too. 'We've been doing professional turnarounds for 25 years, but this was certainly the most shattered business we had ever encountered,' said Michael

Parsons, the managing partner of KPS. 'No one else had wanted to buy it, so if we hadn't stepped in, it was going to be liquidated.'

All of this meant that O'Reilly's legacy would include an assessment that his management skills were not as honed or as sharp as had been claimed often. He had been something of a financial illusionist. He had been a master of finance, accounts and leverage to make something as big as it could be without needing more capital. But this provided something of a soufflé effect: he didn't put enough money into many of his products or brand redevelopment, for all of his talk of loving, nurturing and developing them. Instead he took as much of the cash-flow from them as he could, either to take out the money for himself in dividends, to put into other of his investments, or for that company itself to buy more assets. In other words, everything was geared to boosting his own financial footprint. As a result, his companies did not have enough capital to provide an effective lifeboat when a tsunami hit, and he didn't have it either.

CHAPTER FIVE

INSULTS HEAPED ON INJURIES

Tony O'Reilly had been used to commanding the room, to being the centre of attention, to holding court. The days of hosting large parties or small gatherings of the powerful and famous had come to an end. Now he didn't even want to be seen in public, afraid that people would recognise him, whisper about him, pity him. In Deauville, he no longer frequented his favourite old haunts; he went to alternative restaurants where he was unlikely to meet anyone he knew. When in Dublin for meetings, he would insist on lunch being brought to his solicitor's office instead of going out to dine. In New York, he mostly stayed in his hotel room. Friends explained, with considerable sympathy for his plight, how O'Reilly's self-confidence was shattered.

The Ireland Funds wanted to honour him. It was to the great disappointment of prominent Ireland Funds members that he absented himself from most of its functions from 2010 onwards, not allowing himself to be the subject of a major dinner, to be the recipient of an award at a ceremony to celebrate his contribution and leadership.

There was good reason to recognise the importance of both the Ireland Funds and his role in it. It had played an essential, if often underappreciated and insufficiently praised, role in facilitating the Good Friday Agreement, which brought power-sharing to Northern Ireland, ended the sectarian violence he'd always opposed and mended bridges between unionism and nationalism. The money it raised did not merely go to good causes but reduced the opportunity for the IRA to raise money outside of the country to spend on bombs, bullets and guns to use against fellow Irishmen and British people. It had facilitated contact and dialogue between nationalists and unionists, those at the fringes of the formal political process, at critical times. It had helped redefine and expand the notion of Irishness, to move it away from the simplistic, narrow nationalism that had prevailed too often on one side, and the utter rejection of it on the other by those who denied their identity by pledging allegiance only to Britain. It would have been easy for him to have done nothing, especially when the IRA was threatening kidnap and murder against the wealthy and prominent, but his belief in the potential of Ireland and his love of the country motivated him to do his bit and more.

O'Reilly's last prominent appearance at events hosted by The Worldwide Ireland Funds was in 2010. The 273 delegates at a three-day conference had been welcomed to the US embassy at the Phoenix Park by the new US ambassador to Ireland, Dan Rooney – the man who had set up the organisation with O'Reilly – and that evening enjoyed a dinner in the National Gallery. At one of the functions a comment was made by Martin McGuinness that went largely unrecognised in its significance at the time. He paid tribute to the work done by the Ireland Funds and endorsed the idea of further official collaboration by the new Northern power-sharing executive with O'Reilly's creation. 'This project and approach is another step as we build our economy and promote growth … We want to build our partnership with The Ireland Funds to further the process of peace-building and ensuring no community is left behind and we seek to create a better future for all.' McGuinness, the Sinn Féin/IRA leader who intrigued O'Reilly the most, was now using the type of language and expression that O'Reilly had been using for decades. O'Reilly's long-standing championing of tolerance, mutual respect and inclusivity, as well as rejection of violence, were now Sinn Féin's mantras. Though some less mature Sinn Féin acolytes misunderstood the motives of the newspapers he controlled, or the right of those papers to express a dissenting voice to their demanded consensus, and therefore despised him and wrongly tried to portray him as anti-peace process and a 'West Brit', O'Reilly's words had quietly won the argument and, in effect, that war. It was unfortunate that the use of the appellation of the knighthood under-mined him in some eyes – that it was a decision apparently motivated by ego that diminished his standing with some in Ireland – but it didn't diminish his achievements or contributions. O'Reilly had been a leader for Ireland, even if, perhaps because, much of his life was spent outside of the country.

Sir Anthony should have been prominent when Queen Elizabeth II came to visit in Ireland in 2011. Although it was a historic event for which O'Reilly could claim – justifiably and no matter what the begrudgers would retort – that he had helped lay the groundwork through the work of the Ireland Funds, O'Reilly loitered in the background whereas once he might have been expected to stride to the centre stage. The British Queen had decided to indulge her passion for horse racing with visits to John Magnier's Coolmore Stud, from which the public was excluded, while there was more prominent publicity for her visit to the Irish National Stud. As chairwoman, a position she had held since 1997, Chryss met with and guided the Queen around the stud and was photographed with her. O'Reilly followed in one of the mini-buses that was part of the entourage, sitting on his own at the back until other guests decided to join him and engage him in conversation that he greatly enjoyed. Uncharacteristically, he steered clear of the photo opportunities. It wasn't just a case of allowing his wife her moment of glory, although there was some graciousness in that, but of him not wanting to be seen and commented upon.

His phone calls to associates had become less frequent. Some of the recipients were relieved as they felt O'Reilly's discourse had become almost entirely negative, being particularly obsessed with the state of the world economy. In 2010 he wrote to one friend how 'the world is faced with a more testing decade. Institutions that we respected and relied upon are no more, or have changed irredeemably because of government intervention which seemed at a minimum three years ago. It is now vital for economies everywhere to achieve even moderate growth. The 'blame game' is in full swing, and nowhere is this more evident than in Ireland.'

But it wasn't that he was uncaring about others. When he learnt after Christmas 2009 that Ireland's finance minister had been diagnosed with an extremely serious form of cancer (to which he later succumbed), he told a friend that 'Brian Lenihan is a magnificent figure both in clarity of thought and commitment to his brief, and has prestige with the entire population. Tragically, he has been stricken by an illness of a frightening and unknowable kind.' He also contacted friends with knowledge of treatments of the illness and passed information on to Lenihan, in case it might be of any use.

His relatives were aware of the rumours that he suffered from depression or that he was in the early stages of Alzheimer's disease, robbing him of his prodigious memory, but both stories were disputed robustly. 'He was frustrated and he was angry, those emotions defined his mood, and he was always prone to elements of darkness, but I wouldn't say that he became depressed. He was always too much of a fighter,' said one friend, loyally. As O'Reilly had gone into near-reclusion, it was impossible for others to judge his state of health or mind but of the many people interviewed for this book who had been in regular contact with him none was aware of any signs of mental decline other than would be natural for a man of his age.

The major issue for his health was caused by his back. He had serious problems with his back throughout 2014 and in the summer of that year he underwent surgery on his spine in London. It was not the success he anticipated or wanted. He had to travel early in 2015 to New York for further rectifying surgery, nine hours in duration, this time with a doctor from Cork based there, and it was more successful. Part of the new reality of his new financial position was that he had to fly commercial, something that he had eschewed for decades when travelling by private jet. He was somewhat surprised to discover the greater number of security checks he had to endure, the delays that everyone else takes for granted.

Chryss bore the brunt of his bad humour. 'You know the way it is with some people, that often the person you love the most gets the worst of you?' suggested one relative. 'But Chryss has been magnificent. She has put up with a lot but loved him and stood by him and it will always be appreciated.' It was a view widely shared among his family. She got him to do more things, to go more places than would have been the case had he been on his own, without his businesses to occupy him. O'Reilly and Chryss developed the habit of spending Christmas and the New Year in Rome in their later years. They liked the atmosphere of the city at that time of year, loved wandering the Vatican and its museums, admiring the artworks. She insisted they go to boxing matches and football, even if he would not be seen at rugby games. Chryss was there for him when many others weren't.

He did not have many close friends among the super-rich in the way, for example, John Magnier and JP McManus hung out together and looked after each other. He had been close to Tony Ryan, who had provided a St Bernard dog for O'Reilly's children in Castlemartin as a gift, but that friendship stalled when Ryan bought *The Sunday Tribune* in the early 1980s. 'AJ couldn't understand why Tony wanted to be a competitor of his,' Tony jnr said, 'although the two did become close again in the years before Tony [Ryan] died [in 2007], which was good.' But he had never formed close relationships with younger rich men as equivalents, rather than as people who worked for him.

In his revealing interview with Ivor Kenny in 1986 he had said, perhaps to some surprise among his many friends and acquaintances, the guests at his many parties: 'I suppose I am something of a loner. Success, and the reaction to success in Ireland, forces that on you. Although I am gregarious and extrovert, I am, in the final analysis, self-reliant. I enjoy being alone. I try to make space to be alone and look forward, with some sense of anticipation, to a period of solitude.'

People wanted to see him, but he wasn't available. 'My wife said two things to me about Tony when I said I was meeting you,' Kingsley Aikins said to me. 'One is that we used to laugh so much, he made us laugh, was so much fun to be with. The other is that he was loved, people loved being with him, loved his company, loved what he was, who he was. He was a great man.'

He still had a life to live, albeit greatly constrained, physically, intellectually and financially compared to what he had enjoyed before. He would effectively end his days enjoying the charity of his wife, something that would be difficult for a man of his generation to endure, as someone who saw his role as providing for his women. There would be no great financial rewards to leave to his children, no significant endowments to leave to charity, as he had hoped.

O'Reilly has his solitude now, his time to read, to listen to music, but also to wallow now that he has relatively little to plan. He had told Kenny in 1986 that he liked 'to take out great sheets of paper and to make some order out of the chaos of life, because I get such little time to ask myself the question, "What am I doing?"' He had spoken in that interview of thinking of death, 'but purely in the sense of its inevitability ... I think about death not with dismay or foreboding but in quite an amicable way, certainly not in the adversarial sense, and it gives a certain urgency about tasks undone. It accelerates the thought processes, not simply in relation to tasks undone, but to tasks not even thought about. What might be done? Have I gone through the entire liturgy of things I could do with whatever talent I have?'

If O'Reilly had taken that great sheet of paper in early 2015 and written a list of his achievements, rather than the failures that were consuming him, and had come to the realisation that there was nothing left to achieve other than peace of mind and reconciliation with his family, then what could he have said about himself?

He could look back at a happy childhood in which he basked in the love of his parents, despite the trauma visited upon him as a teenager of finding out his parents' well-kept secret. He could thrill at memories of his rugby career, still one of the most outstanding in Irish sporting history, and the off-field friendships it brought him as well as the fame he exploited. He could remember with pride the creation of the enduring Kerrygold brand (and indeed he often described his time at Bord Bainne as the happiest of his career). He had gone to the USA and achieved what no other Irish-born business-man had done previously, rising to the top of one of its major indigenous companies. He had invested much of his wealth in Ireland and even if part of his motivation was to increase that wealth, he had sought to develop major multinational business out of Ireland, to help his country be more ambitious. He had acted as an ambassador for Ireland, using his contacts to help attract foreign investment that created jobs. He could claim, with some justification amid dispute, to have acted honourably and fairly in his business career. He had not run away from responsibility to his debts. He had contributed gen-erously to charity when he had the financial opportunity to do so and had been generous on a personal level in ways that had gone unseen, whereas other donations, such as the giving of millions in educational scholarships by his foundation, were done in the public eye.

His name will live on, or his family's will, in certain buildings, if people care to ask or find out the provenance of the construction. He paid for the construction of the state-of-the-art 600-seat O'Reilly Theatre in Belvedere College, and regularly funded other projects at his alma mater. There is an O'Reilly Institute at Trinity College, the O'Reilly Hall at UCD and The John and Aileen O'Reilly Library at DCU. But it was significant that he asked, in 2009, just before he stepped down at INM, that his name be removed from the library being built at Queen's University Belfast, at a cost of £44 million, with £2 million coming from him personally and the same again from INM and the Ireland Funds. At the start of construction the university's Vice-Chancellor, Professor Peter Gregson, said: 'The library will be the focal-point of the campus. We are honoured that this building will be named after one of our most distinguished honorary graduates, whose dedication to the advancement of society in Ireland is legendary. This is a milestone in philanthropic giving.' But it seemed that the constant public criticism from O'Brien about his spending of corporate money had sapped O'Reilly's confidence about having his name put to things, that he feared people saying that seats of learning were merely monuments to his ego. His name will not now appear over the entranceway to that library.

That money was not his main motivation was a consensus opinion among most of those interviewed for this book, even if money was a way of keeping score, of getting the respect of others, of overcoming his own insecurities. One former employee said: 'The money was important only in what he could do with it. He did things because they were fun. He loved newspapers, so he bought ownership of them, even ones like *The Independent* and *The Belfast Telegraph* that he couldn't afford at the prices they cost, but which he felt were important and had to be supported. He bought Waterford Wedgwood because he genuinely loved the look and feel of the products. He bought things in countries where he wanted to meet his friends, to relive his old rugby days. He made decisions for emotional as much as intellectual reasons. Those aren't the sort of reasons other rich men have for what they buy. He was a soft capitalist, one who didn't want to shut Irish manufacturing of crystal when that was the logic, who overpaid on redundancies in Ireland because he wanted people to think well of him.'

Some of those closest to him conceded that he tried to go on too long, that he should have stepped back earlier, when he had his wealth, and enjoyed his retirement, instead of constantly looking to prove that he was better than everyone else, always greedily seeking more. Unfortunately, the ability to 'step back' didn't seem to be one he possessed. He found it hard to conceive that what had always worked for him might not work anymore. 'He had a feeling that rules don't apply to me, I can get away with things that people won't get away with, not in the sense of breaking laws but almost as if defying gravity. He convinced himself that he was almost some sort of Superman,' said one interviewee.

'He had become distant from the world, had lost his understanding of modern trends and tastes,' said another of those closest to him ruefully. 'That happens if you are flying around the world in a Gulfstream IV jet, you are not close to what's going on in the world and it's not helped when you are staying in suites in the very best hotels, eating only in the finest restaurants. Earlier in his career he would not have missed the shifts in consumption that affected the sales at his businesses. He became too settled in his ways, didn't adapt to new ones. He never learnt how to use a computer, for example.'

O'Reilly had been obsessed not just with the accumulation and enjoyment of great wealth but with how others perceived him, both in Ireland and abroad. As one of his journalists, the former group business editor of INM's Irish operations Brendan Keenan, with whom he has remained in regular contact during this difficult period, noted wryly but somewhat sadly: 'Tony wanted to be both widely loved and very rich, but those are not necessarily compatible aspirations.'

'In his career he was naturally defensive about, or perhaps assertive of, his reputation, as that reputation was clearly intertwined with his commercial exploits,' said one source. 'He is human. He likes good press just like the next guy and having been in the media for the past 40 years, he paid attention to media coverage.'

It wasn't just the media. He was one of the biggest figures of modern Irish life, impossible not to have an opinion about if you had ever met him – whether you were caught up in his charisma or rejected it as excessive – or even if you had not met him. He provoked strong reactions, some of them irrational – what some would have called jealousy and envy, what others would say was an appropriate response of disdain or even revulsion at his excess. For all those who praised and celebrated him there was also resentment shown towards him and suspicion of his motives, a constant chorus that he misused his media power to promote his business interests and his understanding for the unionist position in Northern Ireland. His fall played to all of that, prompting sympathy and derision.

'To the new generation of people, it may be "Tony who?" But to others, he was an inspiration, and what is happening now is deeply shocking, and a great tragedy,' said Ivor Kenny. Aikins argued that the successes we now take for granted in Ireland, even after the economic meltdown – in sport, the arts, in business – were rare in previous decades, and that many of them could be attributed to O'Reilly. 'He was a superstar,' he said.

'In a way, he was the Daniel O'Connell of Irish business,' said Redmond O'Donoghue. 'He was the first Irish Catholic to become a major business success, and in that way he emancipated us. Up until then all of the big business figures had been from the Anglo-Irish ascendancy, but he did it and he did it with incredible success.'

That he did, just as he also did things that were wrong, that hurt others, that showed weakness of character and judgement on his part. But whose life does not have those failings? And his life is not going to be defined by whether he finishes it billionaire or bankrupt. The old Corinthian adage from rugby, that how you plan the game is more important than the final score, was one that he had cited earlier in his life and would do well to remember now.

As 2015 progressed, O'Reilly came ever closer to reaching a final agreement with his creditors – still owed €135 million despite a series of asset sales, with the bulk of the money owed to accBank, Lloyds Bank and Lone Star – that would allow him to settle his debts for a fraction of what he owed. He decided to seek a form of bankruptcy called a 'composition with his creditors' under the law of the Commonwealth of the Bahamas, where it turned out he was resident for tax purposes, as many had suspected all along. Once agreement was reached that a sum, kept private, would be paid to his creditors, they would then leave him alone to get on with the rest of his life.

His relationship with aib had deteriorated to the point where the Irish bank only became aware of what he was up to on 20 April, just 10 days before a crunch meeting of his creditors in London that would effectively agree a deal.

O'Reilly did not attend that meeting, at which Bernard Somers presented creditors with what was legally called an 'extraordinary resolution'. His solicitors also provided a statement of assets and liabilities, along with a medical report from his New York doctor, dated 14 April, saying he was unfit to travel for at least the following two months because of his recent back surgery.

Allied Irish Banks was furious. It feared it would not be able to recover its money and it argued strongly against the deal. It found itself outvoted by the other creditors, who felt the terms on offer were the best they were going to get. A further meeting was scheduled for 14 May in London, at which it was intended to register the resolutions agreed at the creditors' meeting and confirm the composition with creditors by trust deed.

Allied Irish Banks decided it had to return to the courts in Ireland before that date. The Irish courts could not block the deal, as it was taking place in a different jurisdiction, but the bank had a plan to throw a spanner in the works. It made an application to the Commercial Court seeking first rights over the proceeds of the sale of shares O'Reilly held in the company that owned Dromoland Castle, a luxury hotel property in County Clare that was on the market for sale. The bank complained that it was still owed €15.2 million by O'Reilly personally, and that two of his companies still owed over €22 million – even after it had received its share of the proceeds of the sale of Castlemartin when the deal was completed early in 2015. The bank got €7.4 million of that sale price, but it wanted money from other asset sales and it was afraid that this 'composition' process would put it at the back of the queue for whatever money was being distributed from the sale of remaining assets.

As a result, AIB played hardball in its desperate attempts to get something. It asked for orders from the court to allow it conduct a detailed trawl of O'Reilly's financial affairs, implying that he had been less than forthcoming with it. It demanded disclosure, on oath, of any asset transfers of over €10,000 in value made in the previous five years and fully audited accounts and records from eight named companies. It asked for charts displaying the ownership structure of any assets held indirectly and/or beneficially by intermediate companies. It threatened to move to bring O'Reilly to Ireland, despite his infirmity, to give evidence publicly.

It seemed to be a bluff to get money, a threat to derail the entire bankruptcy process in the Bahamas and to an extent it worked. Although another creditor, BNY Mellon, had the first mortgage over O'Reilly's shares in Dromoland Castle, AIB wanted first rights to the proceeds of the sale of those shares, arguing that it had only just become aware of the American bank's first claim over O'Reilly's Bahamian home, *Lissadell*. As this had a net value of €18.5 million, AIB claimed this could be used to repay a €7.4 million first mortgage to EFG Bank & Trust (Bahamas) and all of the money due to BNY Mellon. The American banks agreed to AIB's claim lest the entire deal be brought down.

O'Reilly could only wonder as to AIB's motivation; at his age and remove there was no-one there to whom he could talk, to try to sort it out. As far as he was concerned he was trying to resolve matters as best he could, with the resources available to him. Worse was to come. The bank went back to the Irish courts in early June, seeking to have more orders made against him, asking Mr Justice Brian McGovern to require O'Reilly to swear, within three weeks, an affidavit outlining all his assets and liabilities, claiming 'an extraordinary and remarkable reluct-ance' by him to do so. In particular, it wanted to know what happened to artworks that it said had been valued at around €7.6 million in 2014, but were now said to be worth around €1.5 million and which had been secured in favour of another creditor. It was simply a question of Sir Anthony 'playing the game with the cards facing up on the table', AIB's lawyer said.

Bernard Dunleavy, now O'Reilly's barrister, responded that it was a 'disreputable application' designed to 'humiliate and embarrass' his client. He said AIB had not challenged the two medical reports that stated O'Reilly was confined to bed and being medicated with painkillers. He also said it was notable that AIB had not suggested that the statement of affairs provided by O'Reilly was not complete or not genuine.

Mr Justice Brian McGovern said he would give O'Reilly three months, rather than three weeks, to swear the affidavit, setting a 9 September 2015 deadline. He said there was nothing to stop O'Reilly instructing lawyers and accountants to prepare the information, even though he 'unreservedly accepted' that O'Reilly was incapacitated and could not travel to Ireland for some time following his surgery.

O'Reilly was distraught when informed of the news. He described it to friends as a 'gross injustice', believing that he was doing everything possible to settle his affairs as honourably and as equitably as possible. He could not equate the kind wishes he was receiving from so many people in Ireland with the aggression with which he felt AIB was hounding him. It was to consume him as he stayed in his hotel room in New York, dealing with lawyers and bankers, drafting replies to demands, desperately seeking to bring this all to an end, so he could try to enjoy the rest of his life.

Whoever would have thought it would come to this?

EPILOGUE
THE LIFE OF A MAXIMALIST

It was a function of his age, as he neared his eightieth year, that O'Reilly was becoming used to infirmity and death among his closest friends and associates. Some had died many years earlier, such as John Meagher and Andy Mulligan within a month of each other in 2001, Vincent Ferguson in 2005; others had passed more recently, such as Karl Mullen in 2009 and Cliff Morgan in 2013. Two of his most important editors had died: Vinnie Doyle in 2010, five years after his retirement; and Aengus Fanning in early 2012. It was noted that O'Reilly did not appear at the latter funeral, nor at that of Billy Vincent, also in 2012, who had soldiered for so long with him at the Ireland Funds. Nelson Mandela died in 2013 and Ben Bradlee in late 2014, prompting O'Reilly to pen a beautiful tribute to the former that *The Independent* in London published, and to write to *The Irish Times* citing his admiration for the integrity of the legendary ex-*Washington Post* editor. Louise O'Connor, mother of his godson, Cian, died in late 2014. Don Keough, the ex-Coca-Cola boss who had joined him on the board of *The Washington Post*, died in early 2015, as did Jack Kyle, one of his great rugby friends.

Liam Healy endured years of serious ill-health. Jim McCarthy, his most trusted presence, was 90 years old and in declining health by the time Castlemartin was put up for sale by AIB; his family kept news of it and of O'Reilly's other financial troubles from him. McCarthy died in April 2015. O'Reilly did not attend the funeral, three of his children doing so in his stead. His inability to travel because of his health problems was noted and readily understood by McCarthy's son, James, in the oration from the altar, in which he spoke with great affection of the close friendship his father and O'Reilly had enjoyed.

Susan, his first wife, passed away in November 2014, from terminal cancer. She had entered her eighties. Her children and grand-children all spent considerable time with her during her final illness and the children became closer to each other than perhaps they had ever been as adults. All had loved her greatly but also greatly admired her stoicism, her grace, her humour and her loyalty. As they had always said, she was 'the glue that kept the family together'. Together the family enjoyed the memories provoked by an RTÉ documentary about O'Reilly's life that was screened in October, just weeks before she died, her children joking about the footage in which Tony jnr and two of his sisters were seen running around in the snow, wearing short pants in his case and short skirts in theirs. 'Did you not have better clothes to put us in, suitable for the weather?' they teased.

Susan's death brought about a thaw in O'Reilly's frosty relations with Gavin. The father had partially blamed his son for the loss of control of INM to O'Brien, for not consulting him as much as he would have liked after taking up the role of CEO, and then for stepping away from the company without telling him. When Gavin remarried in London in December 2012, at his mother's house, his father was not present. He had been invited but did not reply personally to Gavin, instead sending a note of apology to Gavin's new wife, Christina Grimm. In late 2014 he accepted an invitation to Cameron's fiftieth birthday party, a small affair that was to be held in the House of Commons; it's possible to hire rooms in the British houses of parliament for such occasions. However, hours before the party was due to start he sent a message to say that he was suffering from an extreme toothache and would not be able to attend. His family were dis-appointed because they all still love their father and want him to remain an active part of their lives, but they were not surprised.

A memorial service in Susan's honour was held in April 2015 in London, before her ashes were brought to France to be interred in the grounds of Cameron's house, a place that she had come to love dearly. O'Reilly was invited to the service but could not attend, again because of his inability to travel due to the required recovery from his back surgery. Instead, he wrote a tribute to Susan that was read to the audience. All of Susan's grandchildren read, in turn, a couple of lines from a poem. Susie had produced a display of family pictures, having gone through an archive of over 9,000 photographs. The family was appreciative of the many people who attended the service, particularly old colleagues of the O'Reillys from their time in Pittsburgh who arrived at the service unexpectedly.

Susan was not the only key figure in O'Reilly's life to die in 2014. His friend, his cousin Fr John Geary, the intermediary who had set up O'Reilly's meeting with his parents in 1973 to finally broach the subject of his illegitimacy, the bridge-builder between O'Reilly's father and his estranged family, the member of O'Reilly's father's family to whom he had been the closest by far, also succumbed to cancer, on 31 December, aged 83. As head of the Spiritan Order in Canada, Geary had been close to Susan, calling her 'one of the great women of my life', and he had driven from Toronto to Pittsburgh each Easter and Thanksgiving to spend time with the family, discussing theology, philosophy and family with O'Reilly into the small hours of each morning. He had been a regular at Castlemartin each Christmas, too. An acclaimed academic as well as teacher, Geary had returned to Canada in the years before his death and had not seen O'Reilly as regularly, removing a wise and trusted presence from his cousin's life. He was someone who almost certainly would have told O'Reilly not to distance himself from his children, not to make similar mistakes to those that Jack had made with the four children of his first union. His children did not want there to be a distance. 'I suspect he feels embarrassed, that he was up on a pedestal for us and that he had fallen from it, but that's not the way we feel about him at all. We know what happened to him and how, and that doesn't change that he is our father and that we do love him,' said one.

His family had become part of the diaspora he had once tapped to boost the Ireland Funds. Gavin moved to Los Angeles in early 2015, in his new role as chairman of a major artists' representative agency, The Agency. Susie also lived there. Tony jnr was now settled in Malta with Michelle, his second wife, and his children and hers from their respective first marriages. Cameron was in France, Justine in Australia and Caroline was considering her future in Ireland now that her children were reaching adulthood and showed an interest in utilising their rights to Australian citizenship. It looks like there will be no O'Reilly dynasty in Ireland. His three sons had reason to wonder how their business relationships with their father had impacted on their personal relationships: he had been less forgiving of their perceived weakness or failures when issues arose that displeased him than he might have been of non-family executives. The daughters were not really considered for inclusion in business matters, but may in fact have benefited from that exclusion.

O'Reilly returned to Castlemartin for the very last time shortly before Christmas 2014. He and Chryss had to arrange for the boxing and taking of their personal possessions, many of which had remained on display during the sale process: some would be taken to the small Kildare home that remained available to them, others would be transported to France. O'Reilly was in physical pain from his constant back problems, but this leave-taking was an entirely different type of pain. This was his domain, his greatest pride, a physical definition of his success, the place where he had expected to die and be buried, alongside his beloved parents. The Latin inscription over the teal blue front door, which translated as 'the forgetfulness of a busy life is very agreeable', screamed at him now that he had so little to do other than deal with banks and lawyers about his debts. The blow of losing Castlemartin was almost as bad to Chryss as it was to him: she had rarely been happier than when she was working there with her horses and their staff. It had truly become her home, too. They met with the staff that day, many of whom had served O'Reilly for decades and whose affection and respect for each other was mutual. It was, understandably, a deeply emotional occasion.

The identity of the estate's new owner was revealed early in 2015. It was to be an American of Irish descent, well known to O'Reilly, although not personally close to him: John Malone. Remarkably, the men had a business connection. Malone was the main shareholder in Liberty, the company that had been a joint venture partner with INM in the controversial television distribution venture in the late 1990s, before it took full control of the venture on INM's exit in 2002, and that now owned UPC. Malone paid close to €28 million for Castlemartin, one of the highest figures ever achieved for a private Irish estate and not far below the asking price, although the price was not important to O'Reilly at this stage, other than the help it would provide in clearing his debts.

His visits to Castlemartin had become more infrequent in recent years, but that didn't mean that the house and estate hadn't remained special to him, that he did not have plans to pass it on to his children.

It was not just a house but what he had once called his 'spiritual home'. It was where he had planned to be buried.

The old church on the estate, about a 10-minute walk from the house, the Church of St Mary, was built originally in 1490. It had been restored by O'Reilly when he found it as a roofless ruin, at the suggestion of his father. He had hired the restorative architect Percy Leclerc to do the work, at great expense. The work involved was extraordinarily complex, taking archaeologists and craftsmen three years to complete. And yet it is extremely simple, its only adornments being a plain wooden altar, an ancient effigial tomb, which was restored, that contains the remains of a Norman knight, Sir Richard Portlester, and a small version of the organ housed in the National Concert Hall, and also, in an invisible nod to modernity, underfloor heating. O'Reilly said at the rededication, 'The Christian message in this country has been used to drive people apart. The restoration of this chapel is part of my contribution towards reconciliation.'

His children had been married here, and both his parents were buried in the adjoining graveyard, as were two of his grandchildren who had predeceased him. His father's remains had been reinterred here in an emotional ceremony involving members of Jack's first family many years earlier. His parents were commemorated with bronze busts overlooking their graves. It was a condition of the sale that O'Reilly would be accommodated by the new owners in any visits he wished to undertake to the burial ground. But would he himself be buried there? 'I had a particular attachment to both my father and my mother, enjoying the shelter of their love for me, and was very close to them,' he had told Ivor Kenny in 1986. Given all that had changed and all that had been lost, including Castlemartin, would this attachment continue in death, as he had planned?

He might, of course, have many years left to enjoy; who knows what twists and turns his life might yet take. Undoubtedly, though, 2015 was a year of great frustration for him. He was confined physically by his back injury, this man who loved moving around the world, stuck in a hotel suite in New York. His time was consumed by his attempts to arrange a final solution with his creditors, made far more difficult by the aggressive approach of AIB, which sat starkly in contrast to the attitude of the other banks that had lent him money. That an Irish bank would treat him in such manner angered him greatly. And yet, friends said that he was thinking of ways to start again, once the current impasse has been overcome, thinking of ways to regain his lost wealth and rebuild his legacy.

There could be no final reckoning yet, given that the current chapter of his life was still running, the players were still reciting their lines, with the end as yet unclear. What can be seen was that this was a man who wanted to be the best and to give the best to what mattered to him, but he was spancelled by his own deepest weakness: whatever he had, whether in reduced circumstances or at the best of times and no matter at what age, it was never enough. He was dominated by a need, a drive, a greed, perhaps, that would not let him rest and be content with great achievement. The desire for more spurred him on continually, and he chased down all that was possible, every experience, every accolade, every cent. In that frenzy of seeking, he found that it was quite possible to want too much. Such were the consequences of those elements of his personality that made him the maximalist.

SELECT BIBLIOGRAPHY

Bower, Tom (2006). *Conrad and Lady Black, Dancing On The Edge.* Harper Collins: London.

Brady, Conor (2005). *Up With The Times.* Gill & Macmillan: Dublin.

Burns, John (2008). *Sold, the inside story of how Ireland got bitten by the art bug.* Red Rock Press: USA.

Carlin, John (2013). *Knowing Mandela.* Atlantic Books: London.

Coleridge, Nicholas (1992). *Paper Tigers, The Latest, Greatest Newspaper Tycoons and How They Won The World.* Heinemann: London.

Creaton, Siobhán (2010). *A Mobile Fortune, The Life and Times of Denis O'Brien.* Aurum Press: London.

Dunlop, Frank (2004). *Yes, Taoiseach.* Penguin: Ireland.

Fallon, Ivan (1994). *The Player, The Life of Tony O'Reilly.* Hodder & Stoughton: London.

Glover, Stephen (1993). *Paper Dreams.* Jonathan Cape: London.

Jones, Stephen; English, Tom; Cain, Nick; and Barnes, David (2012). *Behind the Lions, Playing Rugby for the British & Irish Lions.* Polaris: USA.

Kenny, Ivor (1987). *In Good Company, Conversations with Irish Leaders.* Gill & Macmillan: Dublin.

Kenny, Ivor (1994). *Talking to Ourselves, Conversations with Editors of the Irish News Media.* Kenny's Bookshop and Art Gallery: Galway.

Kiberd, Damien (ed.) (1997). *Media in Ireland, The Search for Diversity.* Open Air: New York.

Leahy, Pat (2009). *Showtime, The Inside Story of Fianna Fáil in Power.* Penguin: Ireland.

Marr, Andrew (2004). *My Trade, A Short History of British Journalism.* Macmillan: London.

O'Brien, Jacqueline and Guinness, Desmond (1992). *Great Irish Houses and Castles.* George Weidenfeld and Nicolson: London.

O'Brien, Mark and Rafter, Kevin (eds) (2012). *Independent Newspapers, A History*. Four Courts Press: Dublin.

O'Toole, Fintan (1996). 'Brand Leader'. In *Granta* 53: Spring 1996 (ed. Ian Jack).

Robinson, Jeffrey (1990). *The Risk Takers, Five Years On*. Mandarin Paperbacks, Reed Consumer Books Ltd: London.

Walsh, Harry C. (1992). 'Oh really O'Reilly'. Bentos.

I also drew from a vast array of interviews that O'Reilly conducted with various newspapers and magazines throughout his career. These publications included *The Sunday Tribune, Irish Independent, The Irish Times, Business & Finance, The Sunday Times, The Daily Telegraph, Forbes, The New York Times, The Wall Street Journal, The Washington Post, People, Pittsburgh Post-Gazette*, among others.

INDEX